PSYCHOLOGY

of

HUMAN

ADJUSTMENT

PSYCHOLOGY
of
HUMAN
ADJUSTMENT

BY

Lester D. Crow

BROOKLYN COLLEGE

ALFRED·A·KNOPF New York

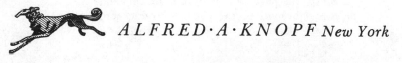

Acknowledgments

*The author and publisher gratefully acknowledge permission
from the following publishers and organizations to quote from
the works listed below.*

Howard H. Kendler, *Basic Psychology*. Copyright © 1963, Meredith
Publishing Company, Appleton-Century-Crofts.

Rudolf Ekstein, "Psychoanalysis Looks at the Origins of Values in
Children," *Educational Leadership*, May, 1964. Copyright © 1964 by
the Association for Supervision and Curriculum Development.

John N. Rosen, M.D., *Psychoanalysis Direct and Indirect*. Copyright 1964 by the Doylestown Foundation, Inc., Doylestown, Penna.

Eric Berne, *Games People Play: The Psychology of Human Relationships*. Grove Press, Inc., New York. Copyright © 1964 by Eric
Berne.

A. H. Maslow and Bela Mittlemann, *Principles of Abnormal Psychology*. Copyright 1941, 1951 by Harper & Brothers. Harper & Row,
Publishers.

T. M. Newcomb, R. H. Turner, and P. E. Converse, *Social Psychology: The Study of Human Interaction*. Copyright © 1965 by Holt,
Rinehart and Winston, Inc.

Glen A. Holland, *Fundamentals of Psychotherapy*. Copyright ©
1965, by Holt, Rinehart and Winston, Inc.

R. S. Woodworth and D. G. Marquis, *Psychology*, 5th ed. Copyright © 1947 by Holt, Rinehart and Winston, Inc.

John E. Anderson, *The Psychology of Development and Personal
Adjustment*. Copyright © 1949 by Holt, Rinehart and Winston, Inc.

Gordon W. Allport, *Pattern and Growth in Personality*. Copyright © 1961 by Holt, Rinehart and Winston, Inc.

Lester D. Crow and Alice Crow, *Understanding Our Behavior*.
© Copyright, 1956, by Lester D. Crow and Alice Crow. Alfred A. Knopf,
Inc.

John Hall, *Psychology of Motivation*. J. B. Lippincott Company.
Copyright © 1961.

Henry A. Bowman, *Marriage for Moderns*, 4th ed. Copyright
1960. McGraw-Hill Book Company.

[v]

Robert Calvert, Jr., and J. E. Steel, *Planning Your Career*. Copyright 1963. McGraw-Hill Book Company.

J. E. W. Wallin, *Personality Maladjustment and Mental Hygiene*, 2nd ed. Copyright 1949. McGraw-Hill Book Company.

A. Q. Sartain, A. J. North, J. R. Strange, and H. M. Chapman, *Psychology: Understanding Human Behavior*, 2nd ed. Copyright 1962. McGraw-Hill Book Company.

J. P. Guilford, *Personality*. Copyright 1959. McGraw-Hill Book Company.

Henry C. Smith, *Personality Adjustment*. Copyright 1961. McGraw-Hill Book Company.

Lester D. Crow and Alice Crow, *Adolescent Development and Adjustment*, 2nd ed. Copyright 1965. McGraw-Hill Book Company.

M. R. Jones, ed., *Nebraska Symposium on Motivation*. University of Nebraska Press. Copyright 1957.

David Levine, ed., *Nebraska Symposium on Motivation*. University of Nebraska Press. Copyright 1964.

William G. Cowan, "Sex Among Teen-agers," Letter to the Editor, March 27, 1966. Copyright © 1966 by The New York Times Company.

"Teen-ager's View of Sex," Letter to the Editor, April 24, 1966. Copyright © 1966 by The New York Times Company.

George F. J. Lehner and Ella Kube, *The Dynamics of Personal Adjustment*. © 1964. Prentice-Hall, Inc.

Louis P. Thorpe, Barney Katz, and Robert T. Lewis, *The Psychology of Abnormal Behavior*, 2nd ed. Copyright © 1961. The Ronald Press Company.

Robert W. White, *The Abnormal Personality*, 3rd ed. Copyright © 1964. The Ronald Press Company

B. C. Bosselman, *Neurosis and Psychosis,* 3rd ed., 1964. Courtesy of Charles C Thomas, Publisher, Springfield, Illinois.

Paul J. Stern, *The Abnormal Person and His World*. Copyright 1964, D. Van Nostrand Company, Inc., Princeton, N.J.

Ruth Benedict, "Continuities and Discontinuities in Cultural Conditions," *Psychiatry*, Vol. 1, 1938. Copyright by the William Alanson White Psychiatric Foundation, Inc.

Preface

IF AN INDIVIDUAL is to develop successful and satisfying patterns in his daily life activities and relationships, it is essential that he recognize and understand the various areas of adjustment basic to the achievement and maintenance of a full and rich life. His behavior often appears to be governed by impulse rather than reason. He does not always recognize what motivates his behavior nor how his actions affect the attitudes of those persons with whom he associates. Also, although he can observe the behavior of other people in their reactions to one another, he may be unable to explain the fundamental reasons for the displayed behavior.

Human adjustment is a complex process. The making of desirable adjustments to the various demands of life is influenced by the differing inherited characteristics and varying environmental conditions and situations to which an individual is exposed. The achievement of desirable life adjustment is dependent upon the recognition of the significance of inherited potential and environmental conditions as these affect his way of life.

In *Psychology of Human Adjustment* I attempt to present those psychological principles that underlie personal and social adjustment and maladjustment. Beginning with an interpretation of what is meant by human adjustment, I consider the basic factors of adjustment and present the effects on human behavior of motivation and the emotions. The interpretation of personality characteristics and their evaluation are explained rather fully. The effect of frustration and conflict on human behavior is treated in detail. This is followed by a description of significant mechanisms of adjustment which often are employed to develop a better pattern of adjusted living.

Many people suffer serious maladjustments. Hence, detailed discussions of anxiety and of mental illness are included in the book. The psychoneuroses and the psychoses are briefly but succinctly considered. Special attention is given to the therapeutic treatment of personality disorders. Also, since maladjustment is often rooted in sexual aberrations, considerable attention is devoted to the prevention of maladjustment in this area of life.

In the past, stress has been placed on the cure of mental illness. At present, psychologists, psychiatrists, and educators are placing increasing emphasis on the prevention of mental illness and the preservation of good mental health. Accordingly, I have included in this treatment a brief survey of the factors of mental health.

Human adjustment does not take place in a vacuum. It is closely associated with the various areas of an individual's daily activities. Positive life adjustment applies especially to the ways in which an individual attempts to satisfy his needs, wants, and interests, in relation to those of his confreres. He needs constantly to adjust to the people and conditions which surround him. Hence, suggestions are offered for meeting the problems that are likely to arise in an individual's home, occupation, and leisure-time activities.

The discussion of the various aspects of adjustment is approached from a positive point of view. The purposes of *Psychology of Human Adjustment* are threefold: (1) to help the student gain insight into the problems of human behavior, (2) to enable the student himself to make healthful and satisfying life adjustments, and (3) to serve as a guide to those who are in a position to be helpful to others.

Questions and problems are provided at the end of each chapter to stimulate class discussion or to be assigned as special study projects. Suggestions for further reading or research are also provided for each chapter. And, for those who wish to supplement the classroom study with audio-visual aids, a list of selected films is presented at the back of the book.

Brooklyn, New York   LESTER D. CROW
July, 1966

Contents

[ix]

[xi] *Contents*

Tables

Figures

PSYCHOLOGY
of
HUMAN
ADJUSTMENT

THE BASES
OF
HUMAN
ADJUSTMENT

HUMAN BEINGS, as other living organisms, struggle constantly to satisfy their needs by relating in one way or another to their physical environment. In addition, the human being needs to adjust to other factors of influence, such as the psycho-social environment in which he develops. He strives to satisfy his need for emotional security, self-acceptance, self-esteem, self-fulfillment, and the like. This is a never ending process of interaction in which there are many observable cause and effect relationships.

MEANING OF ADJUSTMENT

Adjustment is a term much used both by psychologists and lay people. The latter, however, tend to use the term improperly. They seem to assume that adjustment is desirable behavior. Actually, it is a general term that connotes either good or successful adjustment, or poor adjustment (maladjustment). As the reader follows the discussion of human adjustment in this book, he should keep in mind the general significance of the term in its application to a human being's degree of success or failure in meeting his needs.

Much of our daily activity is concerned with adjusting, fitting, or regulating. Windows, watches, carburetors, microscopes, heating devices, and innumerable other mechanical instruments are adjusted in one or another way to increase their effectiveness. Adjustment refers to the extent to which an object fits the purpose for which it is intended. A door is adjusted or fitted to the space that it is to fill; a watch is adjusted so that it will keep accurate time; the speed of a train is regulated for safe travel over its tracks; the weight of one's clothing is adjusted to the demands of weather conditions. In all these cases the purpose of the adjusting or fitting process is to satisfy the needs or interests of those persons who use them. In a similar way we attempt to adjust situations and conditions in our environment in such ways that our daily program of activities runs smoothly. The housewife organizes her daily routines to meet the needs and interests of the family. Business or industrial management is concerned with the adjustment of worker responsibilities. The student adjusts his daily schedule of activities to include adequate time to be devoted to his studies. Some adjustments are relatively simple; they result from previous experiences in similar situations. The adjustment of a delicate mechanism or of a difficult situation, however, is a job for the specialist.

We are constantly attempting to adjust or fit environmental elements to meet our needs and interests. At the same time we are engaged in the process of adjusting ourselves—our attitudes and behavior—to meet satisfactorily the demands made upon us by our personal problems and our social relationships. Both processes—adjustment of environment and adjustment of self—constitute the bases of personality development. From birth onward the individual is concerned consciously or unconsciously with making whatever positive changes are needed, within and outside himself, that will provide for him personally satisfying and socially acceptable patterns of behavior. The extent to which an individual is able to achieve successful life adjustments depends on (1) the environmental stimuli to which he is successively exposed during his life span, especially during his childhood and adolescent years, and (2) his inherited and acquired power to make whatever changes within himself that shall serve as the bases of constructive thinking, feeling, and doing. Poor environmental conditions and/or deficient potentiality are more than likely to encourage the development of maladjustments that can be harmful both to the individual himself and to those other persons whose lives are affected by his demonstrated attitudes and behavior.

THE PROCESS OF HUMAN ADJUSTMENT

There are two points of view concerning the process of human adjustment. According to one point of view, an individual is personally responsible for his attitudes and behavior in all areas of his life relationships. Emphasis is placed on the individual's ability to chart his course of action; he is "master of his fate." Proponents of the other school of thought claim that an individual's beliefs, attitudes, and general pattern of adjustment at any one time are determined to a great extent by the effects on his developing personality of his previous experiences and his present environmental influences. In either, human needs must be aroused and then satisfied.

An individual's degree of successful life adjustment probably is closely related to past experiences, environmental influences, and personal strengths. An individual possesses the power to select, and to apply to himself the environmental elements and the experiences that may seem to him to be best suited to satisfactory adjustment. At the same time, however, the operation in a person's life of scientifically evolved principles of cause and effect cannot be disregarded.

Basic Principles of Adjustment

To the lay person, adjustment often represents a relatively vague belief that to achieve a desired condition or situation will result in successful adjustment. The trained person recognizes the fact that human beings of all ages constantly are in the process of adjusting to this or that condition or situation, or to interpersonal relationships. They recognize also that the form of the adjustment may or may not be conducive to the attainment of personal success or of social welfare. An individual's adjustment is adequate, wholesome, or healthful to the extent that he has established a harmonious relationship between himself and the conditions, situations, and persons who comprise his physical and social environment. An individual who is unable to surmount obstacles in his path to achievement or who is rejected by the members of his group may become inadequately adjusted. Complete rejection or repeated failure to achieve is likely to be conducive to maladjustment.

An individual's patterns of behavior and attitudes generally represent his adjustment status. However, one or another characteristic attitude or form of behavior may constitute a significant factor of adjustment. Satisfactory adjustment includes personal and social value standards. Among the criteria that encompass the important components of adjusted behavior are the possession of (1) a wholesome outlook on life, (2) a realistic perception of life, (3) emotional and social maturity, and (4) a good balance between the inner and outer forces that activate human behavior.

Cause and Effect Relationships

Scientifically interpreted, the term *adjustment* implies a cause and effect relationship. The study of human adjustment poses a problem, in that the kind and degree of adjustment achieved by an individual usually are dependent upon a multiplicity of causes. Moreover, human nature is so complex that it is almost impossible to assert didactically that any combination of causes is certain to have a specific effect upon an individual's behavioral pattern. The same environmental factor may become the cause of stress or strain for one individual but have little or no effect upon another person.

Human beings are alike in many ways, but they differ from one another in physical constitution and health status, degree of mental alertness, and emotional status. Temperamental differences show themselves in individual likes and dislikes, compelling interests and ambitions, and attitudes and behavior toward other people. Yet, there is one thing that most individuals have in common—the desire to become contented and well-adjusted men and women.

Interaction and Adjustment

No one lives unto himself alone. As an individual engages in his daily activities he constantly is interacting with other people:

members of the family, school or work associates, friends, and acquaintances. He also responds to other environmental influences, such as climatic conditions and other physical features of the environment. Many examples could be cited to illustrate differing patterns of interaction. The "only" child's adjustment to family life is different from that of a person who has brothers and sisters. The highly intelligent student develops a different form of adjustment to schoolwork than that of the slow learner. The employer adjusts to his position of authority and the employee learns to accept the authority of his employer. An individual is likely to adjust differently to friends of the same sex than to friends of the opposite sex. Age differences among the members of a group also affect adjustment patterns. Appropriate adjustments are made to life in a cold or a warm climate. Urban living demands one type of adjustment; rural living may lead to another form of personal adjustment.

As one attempts to adjust in his interaction with environmental elements he may either attempt to adapt to them or try to change them in light of his own interests and needs. One function of schooling is to help the developing young person adjust his behavior according to community-accepted standards of behavior. The child or adolescent attempts to adjust to interpersonal relationships in such ways as to find a respected place for himself in his various groups. Hence, he is encouraged, for example, to consider the interests and needs of other persons as well as his own. Concerning the process of interaction, Lehner and Kube state:

> Some people believe that to adjust means to conform. But conformity is only one kind of adjustment, one kind of interaction; and the quality of adjustment it produces depends on circumstances. In choosing a career, for example, one young man may be content to conform to his parents' wishes because these correspond to his own desires and abilities and because he has confidence in his parents' judgment. To another, who finds himself in conflict with his parents and suppressed by their authority, conformity may mean a surrender, damaging his self-esteem and leaving him in a state of doubt about himself. Still a third may lack the abilities for the career his parents want him to enter, and conformity to their wishes might mean job failure.

Interaction between ourselves and our environment is an integral part of living. At the outset our environment involves principally the members of our families. As we interact with these people we unconsciously acquire from them certain methods of adjusting, methods which we modify to suit our needs. As we grow older we interact with larger groups of people and acquire additional methods for adjusting. During this process of interaction—and often without being aware of what we are doing—we experiment with methods we have observed in others and so evolve the behavior patterns that constitute our own individual pattern of adjustment.[1]

Continuity of the Adjustment Process

Adjustment is a continuous process that tends to bring out more or less changing attitudes throughout the individual's life. As he is stimulated by differing environmental stimuli, he is likely to respond to them with his accustomed adjustment habits. However, to the extent that the new stimulus differs markedly from past experiences, attitudes take on new patterns. For example, if a person becomes a teacher his attitude toward learning activities changes considerably from what it may have been as a student.

A person may have developed one attitude toward a racial or national group as a result of his indirect experience in reading about them or hearing others discuss them, but the attitude may change if he comes into direct relationship with one or more members of the group. A person who has spent much of his life in rural areas removed from the meeting of various types of groups usually finds his attitudes affected toward these new groups by his moving to an urban community in which they are found.

During his entire lifetime every human being is struggling toward the attainment of one or another goal—self-expression, self-realization, self-esteem, adventure, economic and social security, and the like. Overt behavior responses are the expressions of inner desires, urges, wants, interests, ambitions, and attitudes.

[1] George F. J. Lehner and Ella Kube, *The Dynamics of Personal Adjustment*, 2nd ed., Englewood Cliffs, N.J.: Prentice-Hall, 1964, pp. 4–5.

A person's compulsion toward activity and its overt manifestation are influenced by the interests, ambitions, and attitudes of other persons. When an individual and the other members of his group are motivated by similar interests and ambitions, their cooperative activities tend to be productive of individual and group satisfaction and interadjustment.

AREAS OF ADJUSTMENT

At this point only a brief reference is being made to some of the problems that are inherent in human relationships that are experienced by the developing person. Later in the book these are taken up in greater detail.

Adjustment is an active process that occurs as the individual lives in his family situation, advances educationally, pursues vocational outlets, and engages in social relationships. His adjustment is helped as he acquires new experiences, accepts ideas and behavior with which he may not agree, conforms to the ways of the members of the group or to the mores of society, and strives to attain self-realization.

Life consists of many experiences that need to be interwoven or integrated from day to day. A normal adult probably is, or at some time in his life has been, motivated by the desire to marry, rear children, experience a happy home life, and earn success in a chosen vocation. In addition, he desires to enjoy the companionship of friends and associates of his choice, and to spend his leisure time in interesting and relaxing activities. He also strives to achieve a position of respect among his associates, to enjoy democratic rights, and to establish the foundation of an economically and socially secure old age.

Children, adolescents, and adults are faced with the problem of so ordering their attitudes and behavior that they achieve maximum success and satisfaction in their home, school, work, and social activities, without interfering with or limiting the interests, ambitions, and activities of other members of the group. Adjustment to environmental conditions and human interrelationships is a gradually developing process that begins early in childhood and continues throughout life. Moreover, an understanding of what constitutes good adjustment and a willingness to become a well-adjusted person probably can be achieved best through the study and application of the psychological principles that are basic to the development of healthful living and wholesome behavior.

Family Adjustment

The family is the basic unit of society. It is generally agreed that as the home is so will be the larger social group. The intimate relations that are inherent in home and family life may build up either closely knit loyalties or disrupting discords.

Bickering, faultfinding, resentments, display of extreme individualism, disregard for the rights of others, and shirking of responsibility in the home are more than likely to be carried over into other group relationships. Through the centuries the home has changed gradually from an independent autocracy dominated by the "head" of the family into a more or less loosely organized social unit. Former rigid parental control of child behavior and more recent child self-assertion can find a meeting ground through a conscious effort to build the home upon a foundation of cooperative family interrelations that are aimed at the healthful development of every member of the family group.

Educational Adjustment

A young person's degree of successful adjustment in his learning experiences is affected by many factors: the learner's degree of mental ability; learning readiness; interests and ambitions; appropriateness of curricular offerings; teacher attitudes, and teaching techniques. Problems of adjustment arise in the school life of a young person when or if any one of these factors is inadequate to help him select and engage in the kind of educational experiences that will prepare him for successful participation in his present and future life activities.

To provide proper financial support for education is the responsibility of the nation, state, and local community. The value of education as a means of improved educational adjustment is receiving increased recognition. Better educational facilities are made available for children and adolescents; educational opportunities are being extended to meet adult needs for continued schooling. Adequate financial aid is needed to provide extensive and intensive education. Yet money alone cannot solve all the educational problems of the school community. Educational leaders are faced with the problem of supplying the kind of education that will help young and older learners achieve success in their marital, family, occupational, and social adjustments.

A well-balanced, forward-looking educational program is essential to the development of individual and group adjustment to personal and social demands. The task of organizing and administering such a program is tremendous. Will individual communities be able to meet this responsibility? How much state aid will be needed? Should the Federal government give financial assistance when or if a community cannot meet its educational obligations? Are taxpayers willing to support nursery schools and kindergartens? To what extent is the public responsible for maintaining junior colleges, colleges, universities, and special schools? What is to be the content of study? How extensive can be the equipment? What is to be the maximum of educational preparation and of remuneration for teachers? How can community facilities and resources be utilized as learning aids? These are some of the educational problems that are closely related to educational adjustment.

Occupational Adjustment

Job adjustment is dependent upon job conditions, worker attitudes, and degree of efficiency. A worker's chances to perform adequately on the job and to experience personal satisfaction in the work are conditioned by: vocational selection based upon personal interest in the work and ability to meet its demands; appropriate and adequate preparation; available job opportunities; healthful working conditions; intelligent and understanding supervision; pleasant coworker relationships, and adequate financial remuneration. Poor worker adjustment in any one of these areas may give rise to worker inefficiency, discontent, resentment, feelings of frustration, or seriously maladjusted behavior.

This is a critical period of occupational and economic adjustment. High cost of living has brought about disagreement concerning adequacy of remuneration. Technological changes are opening new occupation fields and closing others. Fear of economic insecurity interferes with the occupational adjustment of the worker; uncertainty as to the most effective ways in which human resources and occupational opportunities can be integrated constitutes a serious problem of management adjustment.

Social and Community Adjustment

Participation in organized or informal group activity is a test of an individual's power to adjust his own attitudes and interests to the interests, needs, or rights of other people. His interest in community welfare and his cooperative attitude toward community projects are as important as is the exercise of similar interest and attitudes in home and work relationships. In all these associations a person experiences many problems of adjustment that become increasingly serious as group needs and interests change with changing conditions.

Community problems that demand intelligent leadership and citizen cooperation include safety regulations, recreational facilities, health protection, adequate housing, and efficient transportation. Community well-being is dependent not only upon the provision of these environmental conditions, but also upon the displayed attitude and the behavior of community members. Good individual or group adjustment can be hindered by frequent occurrences of asocial acts committed by some of the group members. Accounts of burglaries, muggings, assaults, reckless driving, heavy drinking, fights, and illicit sex relations are featured in the daily newspapers. Apprehension of offenders and prevention of antisocial behavior constitute important areas of community concern.

THE SCIENTIFIC APPROACH TO THE STUDY OF BEHAVIOR

Many patterns of individual adjustment to people, objects, and situations are achieved more or less unconsciously. In light of his various relationships an individual becomes aware of specific needs and interests experienced by himself and others. In order to gain personal satisfaction he may unconsciously make what are to him desirable adjustments to the many various stimuli to which he is exposed. His attitudes and behavior reflect the extent to which he adapts to these stimuli or the degree to which he can alter conditions to meet his wishes.

During childhood and adolescence, the developing individual strives to achieve successful adjustment. An important area of the study of adjustment is the technique to be employed in discovering the bases of his adjustment status and an evaluation of his kind and degree of adjustment. Hence, in this discussion, the author reviews briefly the points of view of several outstanding schools of thought concerning the significance of learning situations. This is followed by a consideration of the evaluation of causative factors of adjustment and the dynamics of human adjustment.

Theories of Adjustment Through Learning

The newborn child possesses certain potentialities of growth and development. The developmental and adjustment patterns that he achieves during his life span are associated closely with the many various learning experiences in which he engages. Viewed broadly, to learn is to change. Since adjusting implies the bringing about of changes within one's self, adjustments can be considered to be the products of learning. What takes place within the individual during the learning or adjusting process is not yet completely understood. Study and research have led to the formulation of various theories of learning, however.

The theory of *connectionism*, propounded by Edward Thorndike, is an attempt to explain learning as bond connection between stimulus and response. Thorndike's well-known laws of exercise and effect apply to the adjustment process, in that an individual tends to adjust to a situation or condition to the extent that he has experience with it. Moreover, a person is likely to adjust satisfactorily to a situation or condition, or to an interpersonal relationship, if he derives pleasure from the experience. Inadequate adjustment is associated with annoying or unsatisfying experience.

Behaviorism is based on stimulus-response connections which grow more complex as they form new connections between originally unrelated stimuli and responses. According to behaviorism, man's behavior is considered to be made up of discrete, independent stimulus-response units. The advocates of behaviorism exerted a great influence on American psychology because they developed specific research methods and stressed objectivity in research. John B. Watson was a proponent of this theory.

The *Gestalt* theory advocated by Wolfgang Koehler stresses the totality of human reaction to stimulation by a whole or entire learning situation. According to the gestaltists, a person reacts to a situation in the form of a configuration or Gestalt, in terms of his valence (the positive or negative stimulus influence upon him of objects, situations, or conditions). Through insight the individual gains an understanding of his adjustment problems and learns to react to them as an integrated person.

Sigmund Freud's *psychoanalytic* approach to adjustment is diametrically opposed to the behavioristic explanation of learning. Freud emphasized the significance of emotional experiences as determiners of behavior reactions and as adjustment motivators. Psychoanalysts accept Freud's theory that the "unconscious mind" is the seat of maladjustments that are rooted in previous forgotten experiences that had damaged the individual's ego. According to Freud, there is a close relationship between the kind and degree of adjustment of an individual and the functioning of his *id, ego,* and *superego.*

The psychoanalytic approach continues today with varying emphases depending on the particular leader. Among the leaders who have strong followings are Freud, Horney, Jung, Adler, and Sullivan. Since the ideas of each are based on points of view rather than on experimental procedures, the worth of any one is not easy to demonstrate. Yet merit can be found in the application of these points of view by those trained in the use of the psychoanalytic approach.

The *functional* approach to learning places emphasis upon the value in learning and adjustment of overt activity and breadth of experience. The functionalists regard psychology as the study of man's adjustment to his environment including the evolved techniques that aid him in his adjustment as well as the means by which he can improve his adjustment through learning. They consider behavior and consciousness to be composed of elements that have mental states and stimulus-reponse acts, both of which have adjustment value to the individual. This is the basis for their application of psychology to learning.

Many psychologists utilize the *eclectic* approach. They do not adhere strictly to any one psychological theory, but rather select from each theory of learning whatever they consider to be pertinent in specific learning or adjustive situations. In their work with students and clients, guidance counselors and clinical psychologists are achieving considerable success in helping inadequately adjusted individuals think through their personal problems toward a possible solution.

Considerations in this treatment are based on a dynamic approach that deals with active human beings and the factors and forces that motivate their behavior. Of special interest are the strivings of individuals, emotional behavior, and human adjustments. Knowledge based upon experimental findings as well as that brought forth by thoughtful insight are the source material for the ideas that are contained in this discussion.

Purpose and Function of Evaluation

Regardless of the psychological approach that is utilized in the resolution of adjustment problems there is needed a recognition of the nature of a problem, its relation to the client's total personality pattern, and an evaluation of possible or probable causal factors.

The practical and common-sense approach to an evaluation of an individual's adjustment status would seem to be to observe him in action. In his daily activities and in his relationships with his associates an individual is likely to exhibit certain habitual attitudes, interests, and forms of behavior that are either self-satisfying and socially acceptable, or self-disturbing and socially disapproved. To observe or to experience, however, is not synonymous with to understand or to improve. Moreover, good adjustment tends to induce better adjustment; inadequate adjustment is likely to intensify the inadequacy. According to Anderson:

Desirable behavior also carries an overlay of social consequences. This overlay in many instances makes adaptation easier and simpler than it otherwise would be. When we say that "nothing succeeds like success," we mean that the well-adjusted person to a large extent is continually creating an environment which makes it easier for him to adjust, and that the poorly adjusted person is continually creating an environment which makes it more difficult for him to adjust.[2]

[2] John E. Anderson, *The Psychology of Development and Personal Adjustment*, New York: Holt. Rinehart and Winston, 1949, p. 12.

Through casual observation of a person's behavior may come a recognition of the fact that the individual observed is displaying what is considered to be good or inadequate adjustment. Conclusions that are based upon informal, noncontrolled observation are likely to be highly subjective. The observer's own degree of personal adjustment, prejudices, and set of values exercise a potent effect upon the objectivity, accuracy, and adequacy of his observation. Valid observation is controlled in terms of definite purpose and specific area of observation, is conducted by a trained observer, and is free from personal bias or emotional involvement. Moreover, the findings of the observation are reported immediately and accurately.

To observe and to record behavior characteristics do not constitute the whole of evaluation, since good or inadequate behavior is the overt manifestation of inner states. We need to discover, in so far as it is possible, what inner urges, interests, desires, worries, feelings of thwarting, or frustrations motivate the observed behavior. Of equal importance is the analysis of the environmental conditions or situations that are the causes of inner motivation of overt behavior. Hence scientific techniques need to be utilized to obtain pertinent data that can serve as the bases of objective and valid evaluation.

Many measuring instruments have been devised to evaluate various human attributes and their effect upon behavior. These techniques vary in *validity* (measuring what they are supposed to measure) and *reliability* (yielding consistent results). The performance of an individual on one or a few of these measuring instruments does not constitute sufficient evidence upon which to evaluate an individual's kind and degree of adjustment or the underlying causes of his adjustment status. A test, scale, or other measuring device can be regarded as *one* tool of evaluation, however. The administration of a measuring instrument may yield some insight into the nature of a client's adjustment problem.

VARIOUS METHODS OF INQUIRY

Sound knowledge in reference to human behavior is not easy to acquire. Much of what can be learned about behavior of human beings comes through casual and controlled observation. Various methods are used in learning about human behavior and its motivations. Among these are the scientific method, involving clinical research, and the experimental method. Brief consideration is given to each approach.

The Scientific Method of Inquiry

In the application of the scientific method the scientist exercises great care in observing, recording, and evaluating. There are definite recognized steps to be utilized in this procedure. The procedures include: (1) awareness and comprehension of the problem, (2) discovering, evaluating, and organizing the data, (3) discovering relationships and formulating an hypothesis based on the information available, (4) evaluating the hypothesis, and (5) verifying the conclusions. In other words, the scientist is involved in reflective thinking as he undertakes to interpret and understand the implications that are inherent in the problem situation.

Various techniques are utilized to implement scientific inquiry. Among the most common are observation, the interview, questionnaires, standardized paper and pencil tests, projective tests, and the sociogram. In an analysis of behavior all forms are often used.

Observation of displayed behavior is used to discover behavior traits of an individual. Observation may be either (1) informal and unplanned or (2) planned. The latter is based on specific purposes of study and is conducted by a trained person relatively free from personal prejudice. Either the planned or the unplanned observation can be conducted through a one-way vision screen, or motion pictures can be taken of the subject when he is not aware of the fact that his behavior is being studied.

The interview can be an effective method of gaining greater understanding of an individual's interests, beliefs, and thought patterns. For reliable results the interviewer needs to be skilled and know how to achieve responses from the interviewee. The success of the interview depends on the care taken in preparing for it, the extent to which there is an informal and relaxed atmosphere during the interview, and the degree to which provision is made for the interviewee to express himself freely.

Questionnaires, in the form of personality inventories or standardized tests which measure achievement or degree of intelligence, as well as projective tests such as the *Rorschach Ink Blot*

Test and the *Thematic Apperception Test,* serve important but different purposes in the evaluation of human behavior. Also picture and role-playing situations can be used to give basic information in the study of an individual's behavior. This is discussed further in the chapter dealing with personality evaluation.

The sociogram is a technique that often is used by the teacher to discover peer relationships among the members of his class. Children are invited to respond to a question asked by the teacher or a leader of a group. For example, the teacher invites each member of his class to list the names of three members with whom he would like to work, or to name three of his best friends. The purpose is to discover which class members are most popular and which pupils seem to be rejected or possible isolates.

The Method of Clinical Research

The clinical method is especially suitable for use in studying the total behavior of individuals. Although it cannot be reduced to objectifying all data, it does conform to the requirements of scientific inquiry. Information obtained through the use of this approach helps give insight into behavior exhibited by individuals in one or another type of situation.

In an educational clinic, for example, the social worker, the psychologist, the pediatrician, and the psychiatrist are involved in the study of the behavior of the boy or girl sent there for study. A referral has been made by the school authorities largely because of the overt behavior of the boy or girl. For example, a boy may have been rude to his teacher and his classmates. He may prefer to be alone and, when with others, tend to push, boss, and intimidate them. He may fight with children smaller than he, or he may become involved in stealing from his classmates. All the facilities of the clinic staff become involved in the study of the problem behavior, and through the inductive approach they arrive at suggestions for a possible change of behavior.

The clinical method does have defects as an approach for the gathering of data. Pertinent data may be forgotten or the data selected may adversely affect the conclusions. Hence, clinical research may be less effective for testing hypotheses than for proposing them.

The Experimental Method

The experimental method is essentially a form of directed observation of an isolated factor under carefully controlled conditions. In addition to the study of behavior that has taken place and is taking place, the experimenter can set the conditions to prompt behavior responses. In other words, he can provide essential stimuli to encourage their occurrence. Experimental investigations of human characteristics, nevertheless, are difficult to organize and conduct in any area of human behavior except those concerned with simple reaction patterns.

It is difficult to reduce human factors to well-controlled laboratory conditions. There are some instances, of course, during which a high degree of objectivity can be secured in the use of the experimental approach with human beings. Even when fear-producing stimuli are provided, the reaction of one individual is likely to differ from that of another. Sometimes effects of deliberate frustration can be observed.

In spite of the limitations of the experimental method it is superior to the clinical approach because it is likely to yield more precise results than can be gained through the use of clinical studies. A synthesis of the clinical and experimental methods may be more effective in producing worthwhile findings. According to Shaffer and Shoben, Jr.:

> Both the clinical and the experimental research methods have faults as sources of dependable information about human adjustments. Their deficiencies, however, are complementary. The clinical method is too inexact and the experimental attack is too restricted. An integration of the two gives the best-balanced approach. An experimental finding that does not hold up in clinical application probably has something the matter with it or has been misapplied. A clinically derived generalization that is contrary to pertinent and well-established experimental evidence must also be regarded with suspicion. The greatest confidence can be given only to principles that ring true both in the clinic and in the laboratory.[3]

[3] L. F. Shaffer and E. J. Shoben, Jr., *The Psychology of Adjustment*, 2nd ed., Boston: Houghton Mifflin Company, 1956, p. 19.

Throughout this book attention is directed toward a consideration of those factors of adjustment that have some validity in that they have been subjected to scientific study. Since ability to adjust changes with changing conditions, however, study and experimentation need to be continued as a process of isolating causative elements and relating them to their possible effects.

THE DYNAMICS OF HUMAN ADJUSTMENT

The term *behavior* implies inner and/or overt activity. At no time is a functioning organism completely passive. For example, a man is sitting in a chair in a relaxed position. He does not speak or change his position. Except for overt signs of breathing, he appears to be in a passive state. Yet he may be daydreaming, thinking through a problem, or creating a bit of poetry or prose which later he will transcribe on paper.

An individual is being stimulated constantly by animate and inanimate factors of this environment. Human behavior is the resultant of interaction between the individual and his environment. Human behavior is dynamic. There is continuous activity that involves the functioning of the various phases of the "self," and is affected by inner purposes and external influences.

Our understanding of the *why* and the *how* of human adjustment is far from complete. Without much more intensive study we cannot expect to obtain all or even most of the answers. One reason for this lies in the complexity of the human organism as well as in the multitudinous array of environmental factors by which the organism is affected. Moreover, existing superstitions or false beliefs concerning the causes of human behavior are deep-seated because of their emotional implications. Hence they cannot be changed or eliminated easily. Progress is being made, however, in that there is evidenced among lay persons as well as among professionals a growing interest in and application of scientifically sound psychological principles.

Wholesome, healthy adjustment can be recognized by noting that an individual displays certain definite characteristics. He recognizes himself to be an individual, both like and different from other individuals. He is self-confident, but with a practical realization of his strengths and weaknesses. At the same time he is able to appreciate the strengths and weaknesses of others and adjusts his attitudes toward them in terms of positive values.

It is not always easy to distinguish between normality and maladjusted behavior. At times, human beings display behavior that may appear to be abnormal, yet is typical of individuals during the growing-up years. In his discussion of the relativity of what is considered normal, Louis Kaplan says:

> . . . the difference between normal and abnormal adjustment is a quantitative difference—one of degree. The line between the normal and the maladjusted is a thin one, across which many people seesaw for temporary periods at various times during their lives. No person is completely adjusted; he is adjusted only to a degree. Nor are seriously disturbed people entirely maladjusted at all times and in all respects. Normal individuals carry within them the potentialities for poor adjustment which under extreme circumstances can be activated and lead to irrational behavior. The maladjusted person, except in cases where behavior is frozen into unalterable patterns of reaction dominated by unconscious processes, has the potentiality for learning another way of life and the hope of achieving a normal existence.[4]

The well-adjusted person feels secure in his understanding of his ability to bring to his interrelations those attitudes that are conducive to effective living. He is helped by his self-confidence and sense of personal security to so direct his activities that they are pointed toward a continuous consideration for the welfare of himself and others. He is able to solve adequately the more or less serious problems that he encounters from day to day. Finally, the individual who has achieved successful adjustment gradually evolves a philosophy of life and a system of values that serve him well in the various areas of experience—school or work activities, and relationships with all the people with whom he comes in contact, younger or older.

[4] Louis Kaplan, *Foundations of Human Behavior*, New York: Harper & Row, 1965, p. 18.

QUESTIONS AND PROBLEMS

1. Explain the connotation of the term *adjustment*. List some of the adjustments that you make in your daily human interactions.

2. Cite instances in which you experienced maladjustment rather than good adjustment. Explain your behavior at the time.

3. What adjustment changes have you made during the past five years?

4. Name as many as you can of the social, political, and economic changes that are taking place at present. Indicate how you, as an individual, are or can be affected by these changes.

5. Describe the two points of view concerning the process of human adjustment. Which do you prefer? Give reasons.

6. Show how the attitude of lay people toward adjustment differs from that of a trained person.

7. Give examples of differing areas of adjustment.

8. How does adjustment differ from conformity?

9. Justify the belief that adjustment is a continuing process.

10. From personal experiences, describe problems of home adjustment. Present specific ways in which these can be resolved.

11. Name some of the educational needs of an individual. In what ways are you attempting to meet your own educational needs?

12. To what extent should human welfare be a community responsibility?

13. Indicate the extent to which pressure groups known to you have attempted to influence government leaders or others.

14. Name important spiritual values that are significant in life adjustment.

15. To what extent have you achieved self-realization and contentment?

Selected Readings

Berelson, B., and G. A. Steiner, *Human Behavior: An Inventory of Scientific Findings*. New York: Harcourt, Brace & World, Inc., 1964.

Carroll, H. A., *Mental Hygiene: The Dynamics of Adjustment*, 4th ed. Englewood Cliffs, N.J.: Prentice-Hall, Inc., 1964.

Coleman, J., *Personality Dynamics and Effective Behavior*. Chicago, Ill.: Scott, Foresman and Company, 1960.

Haas, K., *Understanding Ourselves and Others*. Englewood Cliffs, N.J.: Prentice-Hall, Inc., 1965.

Hountras, P. T. (ed.), *Mental Hygiene: A Text of Readings*. Columbus, Ohio: Charles E. Merrill Books, Inc., 1961.

Jourard, S. M., *Personal Adjustment: An Approach Through the Study of Healthy Personality*. New York: The Macmillan Company, 1963.

Kaplan, L., *Foundations of Human Behavior*. New York: Harper & Row, Publishers, 1965.

Lazarus, R. S., *Personality and Adjustment*. Englewood Cliffs, N.J.: Prentice-Hall, Inc., 1963.

Lehner, G. F. J., and E. Kube, *The Dynamics of Personal Adjustment*, 2nd ed. Englewood Cliffs, N.J.: Prentice-Hall, Inc., 1964.

Nixon, R. E., *The Art of Growing: A Guide to Psychological Maturing*. New York: Random House, Inc., 1962.

Popper, K. R., *The Logic of Scientific Discovery*. New York: Basic Books, Inc., 1959.

Sarnoff, I., *Personality Dynamics and Development*. New York: John Wiley & Sons, Inc., 1962.

Sawrey, J. M., and C. W. Telford, *Dynamics of Mental Health: The Psychology of Adjustment*. Boston, Mass.: Allyn and Bacon, Inc., 1963.

Schneiders, A. A., *Personality Development and Adjustment in Adolescence*. Milwaukee, Wisc.: The Bruce Publishing Company, 1960.

Shaffer, L. F., and E. J. Shoben, Jr., *The Psychology of Adjustment*, 2nd ed. Boston, Mass.: Houghton Mifflin Company, 1956.

Shaw, F. J., and R. S. Ort, *Personal Adjustment in the American Culture*. New York: Harper & Row, Publishers, 1953.

Smith, H. C., *Personality Adjustment*. New York: McGraw-Hill, Inc., 1961.

Staton, T. F., *Dynamics of Adolescent Adjustment*. New York: The Macmillan Company, 1963.

Thorpe, L. P., B. Katz, and R. T. Lewis, *The Psychology of Abnormal Behavior: A Dynamic Approach*, 2nd ed. New York: The Ronald Press Company, 1961.

Worchel, P., and D. Byrne (eds.), *Personality Change*. New York: John Wiley & Sons, Inc., 1964.

ADJUSTMENT
AND
INTERPERSONAL
RELATIONSHIPS

FROM EARLY childhood onward an individual is concerned with the development of self-realization and self-esteem. Satisfying achievement of these personality attributes is not developed in a vacuum but depends on the amount and kind of interaction an individual experiences in relation with other individuals in the home, school, areas of occupational activity, neighborhood and larger societal group. Any attempt to explain human adjustment, therefore, must take into account an individual's interpersonal relationships.

FACTORS OF SOCIAL LIVING

Social relationships have emotional concomitants. Human beings need and desire association with other human beings, and they tend to respond to the behavior of others with similar behavior. The emotional expression of one person affects directly the emotional responses of another. Emotions in crowds are contagious and are transferred swiftly and easily from one individual to another. Most normal human beings respond to the stimulation of the crowd with keen delight. Individuals are drawn by this urge to centers where others are to be found. People go to great expense in order to provide social settings for desirable emotional stimulation.

Social Needs in Adjustment

An individual has various needs and wants. Many of these are rooted in his relationships with his associates. In order to experience a full and complete life pattern he needs to earn the respect and esteem of his associates and the affectionate regard of those who are psychologically (not necessarily geographically) close to him. He may experience the urge to be a leader of his group and display more or less dominance over their behavior and affairs. An individual tends to need the cooperation of others in his various activities, often seeking their aid in the solution of his life problems or offering them help as they attempt to solve their problems.

Wholesome competition may enter a person's relationships with others. However, the possession of too great an attitude of competition can interfere with one's development of positive and desirable social relationships. In short, few if any of an individual's needs can be met effectively except in a social setting. By connotation, *social needs* are impossible of fulfillment apart from interaction among the members of a group—be it large or small, more or less impersonal, or close and intimate.

Guilford has this to say about the factors of social needs: "Social needs require other human individuals more or less directly in their satisfaction or fulfillment. It cannot be said that they are the only needs in which other human beings are involved in some way. . . . The motives in the social-need group call for doing something *with* others, *for* others, or *to* others." He suggests four major categories of social needs, which he accompanies with examples of attitudes that are descriptive of the behavior of each.

Gregariousness: Liking to be with others, to participate in group activities. . . .
  Likes social affairs
  Likes to be with people
  Likes to have friends and acquaintances

Likes to work with others

Finds people more stimulating than anything else. . . .

Benevolence: A kindly, generous, sympathetic, and sensitive attitude toward others. . . .

Is sympathetic

Is generous

Is moral

Is sensitive. . . .

Need for discipline: Desire to have strict discipline enforced. . . .

Is severe (e.g., favors maximum jail sentences for "hit and run" drivers)

Is punctual (e.g., believes most people would not be happier if they could throw away their timepieces)

Is strict (e.g., believes that a good leader is strict)

Aggressiveness: Need to coerce others, with inclination toward physical violence. . . .

Overt aggression (e.g., believes that attack is the best defense)

Coercion (e.g., would like to make a witness talk)

Sadism (e.g., believes that husbands and wives should resort to "caveman" tactics now and then)

Biting (e.g., has had habit of chewing his pencil)

Defiant resentment (e.g., has often violated school regulations)

Indirect expression of hostility (e.g., likes to see the villain in a movie punished) .[1]

The Relation of an Individual to Society

The influence of society on an individual's chances for effective living, whether broadly conceived or narrowly defined, is tremendous. The very existence of the individual, his physical constitution and his biologically inherited potentialities, can be traced to society's standards of and attitudes toward procreation. Traditionally and socially accepted marriage regulations, educational opportunities for prospective parents, and interest in in-

[1] J. P. Guilford, *Personality*, New York: McGraw-Hill, 1959, pp. 444–446.

fant mortality either favor or militate against an individual's fundamental success in achieving effective living.

From conception to death, social forces affect a person's adjustment to life. All his experiences with the forces and factors of his environment either help or hinder his desirable progress. The individual during his infancy and early childhood is affected by home and family attitudes and habits. As he grows to later childhood, all the influences such as the school, neighborhood, community activities, religious affiliation, newspapers, radio and television, and motion pictures and travel are added to the influence of the home. As he advances into adolescence and adulthood, further molding influences are provided by his changed relations with the opposite sex, his vocational activities, his political affiliations, and his larger social experiences. His mode of response to any one of these factors causes him to achieve more or less effective adjustment to the next factor.

A person who is unable to attain the satisfactory fulfillment of his fundamental urges is likely to experience thwartings and consequent maladjustment. Personality traits, such as intellectual retardation or the lack of emotional control, may make it difficult for him to gain love and recognition from others or to experience mastery and security. Habits and attitudes resulting from ineffectual or harmful influences, economic difficulties, or social pressures may inhibit or retard his normal adaptations.

Each individual possesses many attitudes peculiar to himself that have developed from his original urges as these have been satisfied or thwarted in his daily association with other members of his group. An individual's success in his interactions with the various groups to which he is exposed depends on the extent to which his attitudes are in accordance with or in conflict with those of the group. The individual, as he progresses from babyhood to old age, is progressively stimulated by gradually enlarging group concepts. Beginning with the influence on him of his close family environment, he continues to respond by thought and action to the cultural pattern of other groups such as neighborhood, school, clubs, church, occupation, political parties, cities, nations, races, and finally the world itself as a complex of many differing cultures and patterns of group behavior.

If an individual is to be an effective member of any one of these groups he must (1) recognize and adapt himself to desirable group attitudes, (2) recognize and use whatever leadership power he possesses as he attempts to change undesirable group attitudes, (3) help other members of the group to recognize and adjust to desirable community attitudes, and (4) cooperate with other leaders of the group in making possible for all its members the achievement of satisfactory physical, mental, economic, and social adjustments. Effective living is both an individual and a community responsibility. The individual must be able and willing to use all available community opportunities of hygienic adjustment.

EFFECTS OF SOCIAL FORCES ON PERSONAL ADJUSTMENT

Desires and drives are extremely personal, but their overt expression becomes social in its effects. Each individual has a desire to do what he wants to do in the way he prefers and at the time he wants to do it. However, he also learns that he is compelled by social pressure to accept the wishes of the group relative to what he does, as well as to how he does it. The gang life of children and adolescents is filled with numerous instances in which the individuals undergo humiliation and bear hardships or even pain in order that they may become members of a particular group, gang, or clique.

An effort often is made to attract the attention of other members of one's group. A pupil may show off in class or he may exhibit unaccustomed behavior for the sole purpose of directing attention to himself. The wise leader recognizes this behavior for what it is worth and meets it in light of its intent even if the brunt of the attention-getting behavior is directed at him. Proper guidance is very important at this point. If these activities are allowed to continue, the seeds of self-centered activity may be sown. Thus the individual may develop antisocial behavior.

Growing children are constantly struggling to throw off the supervision of their behavior imposed by parents, teachers, or other responsible leaders. They want to direct their own behavior because they believe they will reap greater satisfaction thereby. Whenever adults allow them extended freedom to plan their activities, however, they often turn to these same adults for help and guidance.

The Influence of Environment on Adjustment

The environment in which a child is reared or in which an adult engages in various life activities is extremely important in his social development. The individual's personality is molded according to his experiences with the members of his varying groups. Concerning one's environmental relations to personality development, Royce says:

> *Environment* has been defined as the "sum total of stimulation received by the individual from conception until death." Life is a transactional encounter with our surroundings, both personal and nonhuman. Etiologists have shown the importance of stimuli, even in the more instinctive aspects of behavior. These stimulating experiences may influence personality development in a variety of ways. Positively, one assimilates much from his environment; negatively, one may be deprived by it of needed stimulation. One person may be trained to conform to his surroundings; another may rebel and oppose them. Of two sons of a rigidly Puritanical father, one might react and become a "Bohemian" while the other might be proud of being a good, old-fashioned Puritan. . . .
>
> Parental environment is probably the greatest single factor in personality development, including as it does both imitation and training. This is attested by the universal consensus that faulty homes or lack of any home life lie at the root of most of our psychological, social, and criminal problems. School, neighborhood, church, and wider cultural groups all play their part in shaping personality.[2]

The impact of the environment can further be understood as we observe the struggle for advancement of those individuals who live in socially disadvantaged areas of our cities. A poor, run-down neighborhood is the type of environment that does not inspire one to betterment. Yet, it is in this kind of setting that the disadvantaged live with their families. These families frequently move from one slum area to another. They seldom have opportu-

---

[2] James E. Royce, S.J., *Personality and Mental Health*, rev. ed., Milwaukee: The Bruce Publishing Company, 1964, pp. 89, 91.

nities to engage in uplifting experiences with the result that their levels of aspiration remain low. They manage to survive with a minimum of clothing, food, heat, and furniture. Often, as many as six families will live in a house that once was occupied by a single family. They survive on money received from welfare and are seldom motivated to expect to have many advantages for themselves or for their children.

Individuals who live in environments that are significantly below national standards usually have a high rate of unemployment, live in old houses with unsanitary conditions, have large families, are unable to utilize human resources, and, as a result, develop attitudes of hopelessness. Although socially disadvantaged individuals are found among all groups, the Negro and the non-English speaking immigrant are usually the greatest sufferers. They tend to find living quarters in the poorer sections of the city where they are among others who have little incentive to improve their situation.

Life in a slum area tends to be self-perpetuating. A large number of the families living here have fatherless homes. The mothers are left with the problem of assuming the dual role of coping with child-rearing problems. The absence of the father or male figure with his authority and leadership often causes the child to have difficulty in relating to other adults with whom he comes into contact. This increases the burden of the mother or grandmother who remains as the authority figure in the family situation. Also, much extramarital sexual behavior and illegitimacy, which often arises in these situations, adversely affect the growing child and make it difficult for him to rise above them.

The Influence of the Cultural Milieu on Adjustment

The socially adequate person is the one who can get along with people. He is a product of the culture in which he lives. His pattern of behavior and his attitudes are significantly influenced by the mores and customs of his group. In terms of cultural standards, he learns to recognize his own shortcomings as well as those of his associates. The socially normal person not only attempts to discover and remedy his own cultural faults but also accepts other people in spite of their personality lacks.

Cultures differ. An individual may have accepted one cultural pattern and adjusted his interpersonal relations to the demands of that culture. If, for one or another reason, he is transported to another cultural milieu, he may find it difficult to adjust to the new cultural standards. To the extent that he possesses an interest in people and their affairs and is outgoing in his reactions to others, it is probable that he can learn to reorganize his own social values; he can make changes in his social attitudes so that he becomes an accepted member of the new cultural society.

We usually accept the premise that changes in an individual's personality represent natural phenomena. Yet, it cannot be denied that throughout his life span an individual's behavior and attitudes are patterned according to cultural standards. Concerning cultural conditioning, Ruth Benedict says:

All cultures must deal in one way or another with the cycle of growth from infancy to adulthood. Nature has posed the situation dramatically: on the one hand, the new born baby, physiologically vulnerable, unable to fend for itself, or to participate of its own initiative in the life of the group, and, on the other, the adult man or woman. Every man who rounds out his human potentialities must have been a son first and a father later and the two roles are physiologically in great contrast; he must first have been dependent upon others for his very existence and later he must provide such security for others. This discontinuity in the life cycle is a fact of nature and is inescapable. Facts of nature, however, in any discussion of human problems, are ordinarily read off not at their bare minimal but surrounded by all the local accretions of behavior to which the student of human affairs has become accustomed in his own culture. For that reason it is illuminating to examine comparative material from other societies in order to get a wider perspective on our own special accretions. The anthropologist's role is not to question the facts of nature, but to insist upon the interposition of a middle term between "nature" and "human behavior"; his role is to analyse that term, to document local man-made doctorings of nature and to insist that these doctorings should not be read off in any one culture as nature itself.

Although it is a fact of nature that the child becomes a man, the way in which this transition is effected varies from one society to another, and no one of these particular cultural bridges should be regarded as the "natural" path to maturity.[3]

A culture exercises a potent influence over the behavior of those people it comprises. Concerning the importance of an individual's cultural background in his life, Allport says:

Culture is in part a set of inventions that have arisen in various parts of the world (or with subgroups of population) to make life efficient and intelligible for mortals who struggle with the same basic problems of life: birth, growth, death, the pursuit of health, welfare, and meaning. The solutions are passed on from one generation to another.

It would not be quite accurate to say that a culture is nothing but a set of devices for meeting individual needs. It does, of course, fulfill this function, telling us, for example, how to satisfy (without conflict with our fellows) the needs for food, for excretion, for mating, for affiliative relations with others. It tells us how to handle our need for recreation and for self-esteem, and our sorrow after bereavement. But in time culture also becomes a "way of life." We come to love the practices and the values and the interpretations we have learned from our culture. We desire (and need) the Hopi way, the Italian way, or the American way. At first, culture is an instrument that trains us and satisfies our needs. Gradually it becomes a value in its own right, and our love and loyalty to our culture are a prime, autonomous motive whose force we feel most keenly when we are deprived of our cultural anchorage. We come to say to ourselves, "This is the only way I can live." Thus our culture, at least those features that we "internalize," may become motivational in our lives.

Of course, we do not mean that every feature of every culture comes to be loved by its members. Many cultural practices remain peripheral habits for the person, residing

[3] Ruth Benedict, "Continuities and Discontinuities in Cultural Conditions," *Psychiatry*, Vol. 1 (1938), p. 161.

not in the appropriate but in the outer layers of personality. Perhaps it is only our own private culture construct that we have in mind when we say that we love the Hopi, the Italian, or the American way.

In terms of real culture what seems to happen is that the individual, according to his temperament and evolving sense of self, selects from the "tolerable range" allowed by his culture the features that fit best his own style of life. He may, of course, find that almost every feature suits him. If so, he becomes a full-blown conformist, a true stencil copy. Many people, on the other hand, deviate in practice and thought from cultural models and conform only within necessary limits. Some, of course, are total misfits and rebels. Most of us lie between the extremes.[4]

A culture sets language patterns for the developing child since he develops much of his linguistic ability through imitation of the language forms common to the environment in which he is reared. Beginning with family influences and continuing as a concomitant of his relationships with people outside the home, more or less correct language patterns are learned. To the extent that the younger or older person moves from one culture to another he may need to master a foreign language so that he can communicate satisfactorily with his new associates.

What has been said about language applies also to other behavioral trends. An individual adjusts his general pattern of behavior to meet cultural expectations. His mode of dress, his interpersonal relationships, even his occupational activities and other life patterns, have cultural roots.

The child from a socially disadvantaged area has many environmental hurdles to overcome if he is to be able to fully develop his potential. For example, he is often expected to assume more responsibilities in the home and is less free to participate in a social life than his more privileged peers. He resents the fact that he has home duties that many other children do not have and finds himself in conflict with members of his family or perhaps with members of his own group. Often, to compensate for his situation, he displays uncooperative behavior and, thus,

[4] Gordon W. Allport, *Pattern and Growth in Personality*, New York: Holt, Rinehart and Winston, 1961, pp. 168–169.

gives the impression that he is not interested in the activities of the group.

The child needs help to develop an adequate self-concept, which can be conditioned only by his relationships with his family as well as with others outside the home. His perception of himself—his physique, his abilities, and his surroundings—is affected by the way he is treated in his early home environment. For a child who constantly experiences failure and is criticized for it, the slightest praise can be uplifting. He has a great need for commendation for anything that he does well. This is especially essential for the colored child who learns by the time he is four that our culture favors white people. Prior to the age of three or four playmates do not even notice whether they are white or colored. But the fact that prejudicial attitudes appear at these ages suggests that self-acceptance or self-rejection begins to reflect the awareness of racial attitudes in the environment.

STAGES IN SOCIAL DEVELOPMENT

From birth onward, an individual is surrounded by other people of all ages who bear differing relationships to him but who in one way or another influence his development and help make him the kind of person he eventually becomes. The members of his family, friends, acquaintances, teachers, classmates, employers, and fellow workers all share in the process of an individual's social development. Here I shall briefly trace the characteristics of the individual's social self.

The Infant and Social Adjustment

The infant is satisfied if he is well and regularly fed, if his clothing is comfortable and warm enough but not too warm, if his crib, chair, or play-pen is interesting, if his physical activities are not restricted, and if he is given the personal attention that he craves. Any lack in his physical needs or of personal attention, or any change (such as sudden noise) causes him to be dissatisfied and produces behavior that may resemble that of fear or anger. His overt behavior in any satisfying or unsatisfying situation depends to a great extent on the kind of habit training to which he has been subjected. The primitive responses of cuddling, smiling, cooing, crying, shrinking, throwing, yelling, or resisting are modified by his early-acquired recognition of the kind of behavior that is most likely to gain for him the satisfaction that he desires.

The Preschool Child and Social Adjustment

At the end of his infancy the normal child is unself-conscious and friendly. As he begins to develop an awareness of himself as an individual among many other individuals of all sizes and attitudes, he develops a natural self-consciousness, shyness, negativism, and perhaps resistance. This is his first sign of growing ego-awareness. Unless he is badgered too much during this stage, he develops greater confidence in himself and in others, and his early friendliness returns.

Between the ages of two and three the child follows his own play interest, and although he apparently enjoys being in the presence of other children, he usually prefers playing alongside them rather than with them. Gradually this attitude changes, and he makes overtures to other children, offers them his toy (which he immediately takes back), and shows interest in the toys and activities of others. During this period he gradually learns to do things for himself and, if properly encouraged and given sufficient time, can manipulate large buttons and assist in the putting on and removing of his outer garments. He enjoys washing his hands, although much patience may be needed by the adult who permits the child to do this, as many washings and much playing with the water may be included in the process. The child is not so much interested in the result of the washing as he is in the activity itself. The same is true of his growing ability to serve himself at meals and to put away his own toys.

During his third year he is busily perfecting and refining his manipulatory skills. He gains, under patient tutelage, the ability to dress and undress himself if the process is not too complicated. Modern manufacturers are giving much attention to these matters, and the majority of children's clothes are simple and easy to manage. He can wash himself, clean his own teeth, dry dishes that are not too large or too awkward, and perform other simple household tasks. To him, life is a glorious adventure. He delights in new and varied activity but also enjoys repetitions of particularly attractive activities. He laughs, he jumps, he responds to other children. If he is not forced beyond his age and powers and if he is not allowed to engage in too strenuous exercise, he goes to sleep during his daytime rest period and at night, indulges in no undesirable sex play, and awakens the next morning ready for another day of thrilling activity with his associates.

With the fourth year comes greater language ability and interest. The child prattles, he asks questions (usually without waiting for or attending to the answer), he criticizes, and he demands praise and attention. His interest in the world of make-believe is keen. He loves stories about things that are familiar to him, but he wants to have these placed in exciting settings. To him there is little if any difference between his dream world and that of reality. He and his playmates live the lives of their elders or of the products of their childish fantasy. He must be taught the reality of his actual world. Fairy stories should not be given to children at this age but reserved until they are at least five years old and able to distinguish better between the real and the fanciful. Young children may develop secret fears of possible attack by goblins, witches, or other threatening characters of fairy-book fame.

During this period parents are often bothered by the apparent deceitfulness of their children. Falsehoods, "tall stories," like the thousand cats in the areaway, which on investigation dwindle to two cats, that, however, "made enough noise for a thousand," and similar exaggerations are common to this age. The child is not a deliberate liar. His two worlds are as one to him. However, unwise treatment of this habit may develop in the child deliberate and conscious untruthfulness as a way of meeting parental disapproval and lack of understanding of his inconsistencies.

The child's social development continues slowly but surely, and if unimpeded by poor social conditions, takes him to his elementary school period with definite motor control, with an appreciation of himself as a member of the group, having certain rights and privileges as well as responsibilities, with socialized attitudes toward other children, and with the ability to participate in free social play as well as in organized games.

By the end of the preschool period the child has a definite understanding of reasonable obedience and can derive satisfaction from participation in work projects directed toward worthy goals. His attention span has been increasing, and he is able, with little or no aid, to carry on activities that are suited to his age and ability. He is democratic and generally friendly and trusting of others. To whatever extent the child at the end of this period deviates from this general pattern, much of this deviation can be traced to unwise training during this important period of the individual's life.

The Elementary School Child and Social Adjustment

The young child is primarily an egoist. During his elementary school life he develops attitudes toward other persons that may color his permanent social relationships. The child upon his entrance into school is ready for his enlarged social horizon and, under wise guidance, usually makes satisfactory adjustments to the presence of and association with new and differing personalities. As a result of his preschool experiences, however, the child may be diffident and afraid of these larger social contacts, or he may be overaggressive and exhibit a tendency toward domination.

It is the function of the school staff to develop in these young people attitudes of cooperation, of friendliness, of generosity, of kindness, of respect for the rights and property of others as well as their own, and of a feeling of security in the social group. Unkind or sarcastic remarks by the teacher or other pupils, favoritism, lack of sympathy for the child in difficulties, and disregard of dishonest or selfish behavior on the part of any members of the group militate against the development or desirable social attitudes. The child must be made to feel that he, as well as every other child in the school, is being accorded friendly, kindly, and fair treatment and that the same kind of behavior is expected of him. The shy child must be given opportunities for social participation. The aggressive child must be trained to defer to the wishes and rights of others in the spirit of cooperative living.

Elementary school children are usually interested in their own families. They enjoy talking about their parents, their older and younger brothers and sisters, their pets, their home activities, and their possessions. This demonstrated interest in the family should be encouraged only to the extent that certain children do not develop the habit of boasting of their home associations to the resentment or envy of other children. If a child does not display this tendency to talk about his home and family, the teacher may be able to discover in this fact the basis of undesirable behavior habits in the child, and thus assist the child to effect better social adjustments.

In the past, the school was looked on as an institution the prime function of which was to assist the learner in the acquisition of a body of prescribed information and the mastery of certain definite skills. The concept of education as the adjustment of the total personality is of relatively recent origin. Incidence of juvenile delinquency and crime among young people has forced the school to appraise the extent of its responsibilities for social maladjustment among its pupils. Consequently, educators are accepting the principle that the school is charged with the development in a learner of desirable social attitudes and emotional controls that will function during his life as the means whereby he becomes an adjusted and contented citizen.

The development of desirable attitudes and behavior patterns lies outside the realm of the inculcation of factual material or of the instruction in manual competence. The subtle interactions of personality traits defy the objective techniques of formal teaching and measurement. However, the functions of the school in the education of the child must be comprehensive and far-reaching. Its influence touches every phase of the child's life. The extent to which any school is able to meet its responsibilities depends on the degree to which the community and the school personnel appreciate the breadth of the school's function and on the nature and training of the members of the school faculty.

The Adolescent and Social Adjustment

An adolescent's attitude toward his elders is strongly linked with his intellectual understanding of and his emotional adjustment to peer relationships. He is struggling to free himself from his childhood dependence on the older members of his family, but the latter are not always conscious of this struggle or of the need for it. To them, the adolescent is still a child to be directed in terms of adult ideals. Consequently, the young person either resents this adult domination and exhibits behavior that is un-warranted and socially undesirable, or he gives up the struggle and falls back on his childhood dependence, thus denying himself the possibility of advancing toward mature control of his own behavior. Either reaction represents poor social behavior.

The resentful and defiant adolescent becomes the suspicious, arrogant, and uncooperative adult who tends to dominate his own family and to accuse other members of his occupational or social group of unfairness to him. The dependent adolescent becomes the dependent adult, who seems unable to make his own decisions, who constantly calls on other persons to solve his problems for him, or who accedes to the wishes and desires of others without question and sometimes against his own better judgment.

It is only as the adolescent works and plays with other members of his group, as he plans with others for the welfare of the group, as he learns to modify his own interests so that they harmonize with those of the group, and as he gains an apprecia-tion of communal rights and duties, that he acquires the power to meet adult responsibilities and is accepted as a worthy member of the group. Home and school experiences provide opportu-nities for him to meet people and to be faced with situations that offer him the challenges that are inherent in all social relation-ships.

The Adult and Social Adjustment

An adult's interpersonal relationships are rooted in the kind of social activities he experienced during his earlier years. The societal groups with which he is associated increase in size and variety. He is fortunate if by adulthood he has learned to adjust his behavior and attitudes in such ways that he can achieve and maintain good relationships with the persons of any age group or social class with which he is associated. Friendships formed ear-lier may be strengthened; new friendships are formed. The adult probably has lost some of the self-centeredness that is charac-teristic of childhood and adolescence. To the extent that he has achieved maturity, his interests are socially relevant, his motives are positively controlled, and his behavior patterns are fairly well integrated. He should have the power to influence other persons, adults as well as young people, toward constructive and socially desirable attitudes and modes of behavior. At the same time, he should reflect in his own attitudes and behavior whatever wholesome influences by which he is stimulated as a member of a group.

Middle age is the period during which an individual is likely to become a leader in societal groups, especially those of furthering human welfare. This is the period of extreme interest in culture patterns and world affairs. The desire for extended knowledge of music, art, literature, science, economics, and politics should be met through the offerings of the various agencies of adult education. The middle-aged citizenry exerts a stabilizing influence on society. This stabilization is effective only to the extent that the individuals become stable, well-informed, and tolerant leaders through wise educational leadership.

The young adult usually finds considerable satisfaction in participating with others of the same age status in relatively strenuous physical activities. As he approaches the middle years, however, he needs to begin to limit his social activities to quieter forms of socially pointed recreation. Witness the fact that baseball players seldom have sufficient physical stamina to play the game competitively beyond the age of forty. Contrariwise, at one time a sport such as golf was considered to be an "old man's" game. Now, however, the winning professionals are under the age of fifty, although the game is played by individuals of all ages.

The senior citizen is faced with the problem of changing his pattern of social behavior. Not only must he be willing to avoid arduous physical activities but he also must realize that his relationships with other people should take into account the fact that he no longer is able to participate in the forms of social activity in which he formerly had engaged. Concerning the social needs of older persons Havighurst has this to say:

> Try as one may to keep young and to avoid being classed with the "elders," the day must come to everyone when he says to himself, "I'm not as young as I used to be. I'd better *be* my age." This day is brought on by the fact that the costs of continued participation in the middle-age group rise more rapidly than the gains. The costs consist of fatigue due to the too rapid tempo of middle life; embarrassment at

being unable to keep up, physically and financially and vocationally, with the middle-age group and a feeling of being ignored or pushed aside by younger people.

Over against these costs are the rewards of participation in the older-age group, such as a more comfortable tempo of life; ease of finding companionship among other people who have leisure time; availability of positions of prestige and leadership in organizations of older people.[5]

THE INDIVIDUAL'S ROLE IN
THE GROUP

During his lifetime, an individual is a member of different groups. In each of these groups he plays a specific role based on his position in the group. We can differentiate his position in a societal group according to age and sex. The role of an adult differs, of course, in respect to his interpersonal relationships, from that of a child or an adolescent. Society expects certain behavior patterns to be characteristic of the individual at each of the age periods. Sex also is a factor in personal-social adjustment that grows out of sex needs and interests.

In the family, an individual fulfills his or her role as a parent, son or daughter, uncle or aunt, grandparent, cousin. In school the role of the teacher differs from that of the pupil. The employer holds a position different from that of his employees. Although social groups usually are brought together according to similarity of interests, each participant has a specific role to play. He may either dominate the activities of the group or be submissive to the wishes of some or all of its members.

Norman Cameron has this to say about the social roles of men and women:

A social role is what a person *is* in relation to his society. It is not normally something that he plays at being. The general outlines of the social roles are provided by the organization of society. The individual performance of them

[5] Robert J. Havighurst, "Social and Psychological Needs of the Aging," *Annals of the American Academy of Political and Social Science*, Vol. 279 (1952), p. 13.

—the particular way that a person occupies his social role—fills in the details and gives a role the personal touch. Society provides men with a great many different roles, besides those of husband, father and head of the household. Society provides less variety for women. The vast majority of women, no matter what their social status or their education, are primarily homemakers, mothers of new human beings, and caretakers of the young, the feeble and the sick.

Although women who evade the essentially feminine roles, and compete successfully with men, are usually praised for it, their choice is often the result of an inability to fulfill a woman's socially prescribed role, rather than a sign of superiority. There is no evidence that, even though a woman can do a great many things that a man can do, she has powerful inborn needs that cannot be satisfied in our culture unless she accepts the feminine roles of homemaker, wife and mother.[6]

Groups differ in their size and in the purpose which they serve. At one and the same time an individual may be a member of a small, intimate group, such as the family, or of a large institutionalized societal unit, such as the church, government, or business corporation. A group has structural integration and cohesiveness. It possesses differing degrees of attitudinal conformity, i.e., the extent to which there is consensus among its members and an attitude of sharing. Yet it is more difficult to identify human groups than to identify an individual's role in a group. According to Newcomb, Turner, and Converse:

> The fact that there are different kinds of groups, and that some kinds have little in common with other kinds except that two or more individuals are being referred to as a single entity, means that we shall need to distinguish one kind from another, but it does not mean that groups are necessarily figments of the imagination rather than being "real." And it also means that we shall need to be careful about definitions. There is, unfortunately, no standard usage. The only unambiguous meaning of the single word group is "a set of persons considered as a single entity";

[6] Norman Cameron, *Personality Development and Psychopathology; A Dynamic Approach*, Boston: Houghton Mifflin Company, 1963, p. 197.

without any further qualification, the term thus means little more than that the speaker wishes to view two or more persons in this manner. When we wish to refer to some special kind of group we shall therefore indicate that this is the case, by such phrases as *formal membership* group, *ethnic* or *residential* group, *family* group, and so on. For most purposes we shall be primarily interested in groups of persons who have face-to-face interaction with one another over a continued period of time. We have referred to these as "interaction groups," although if the context is clear we sometimes use only the term "group." [7]

Earlier I noted that an individual's role in a group depends on his position in it. As one's position in his group changes so does his role or behavior in relationship to its members change. For example, the child grows up and becomes a father. A student, after appropriate education, may take on the role of teacher. In fact, an individual can fill two related roles at the same time. A man is the son of his father who is still living and expecting the man to continue to act the role of an obedient son, but the son is himself a father who expects filial behavior from his son. A member of a societal group may tend to dominate some members of the group and be dominated by others.

The family is a primary life group. Everyone has a specific role in its organization and conduct. Family relationships do not occupy all of an individual's time and energy, however. In fact, to be a good family member necessitates the filling of other roles in order to enhance the family role and meet a human being's other social needs.

There is great variability in light of cultural and situational factors. To achieve a full life an individual may need to meet the participation in many differing roles. Care must be taken that one does not suffer the effects of "overloading" one's roles, i.e., attempting to engage actively in the activities of so many different groups that one suffers physical, mental, or emotional strain. Allport analyzes the various roles of members of a family group, especially those of the father.

[7] Theodore M. Newcomb, Ralph H. Turner, and Philip E. Converse, *Social Psychology: The Study of Human Interaction*, New York: Holt, Rinehart and Winston, 1965, pp. 290–291.

Consider an average family in Western culture. As a general thing the father is expected to leave the home in the morning, go to work, provide for the family, discipline the children, play with them, and in various ways abet the mother. The role of motherhood comprises a multitude of prescribed duties and tasks, even appropriate thoughts and feelings, and also, perhaps, a few privileges. The child's "structure mode" is, broadly speaking, one of obedience, plus privileges of play and receiving nurture. The oldest child is expected to help care for the younger and assist in the housework. The male child soon occupies a special role appropriate to his masculinity; he is supposed to do boyish things, including fighting back if attacked by a schoolmate. The daughter is expected to learn housekeeping, and to be more modest and reticent than her brother (again speaking broadly). The interaction of all these roles is exceedingly subtle, and constitutes what we call the *family social system.*

While the child is fulfilling his own role he is also learning the roles of his father, mother, and siblings. Their roles are reciprocals of his own, but they are likewise models which he may imitate. A two-year-old after a misdeed will often call himself "naughty," just as his mother might do; a four-year-old will imitate his father's motions in driving the family car. These role-assumptions, added to the child's own role, play a large part in socializing and acculturating him for the requirements of adult life.[8]

An individual's status in a group depends on the position he holds in the group structure and the degree of success he achieves in his role as a participant in group interactions. His behavior in relation to other members of a particular group is influenced by what he conceives to be his rights and responsibilities in the management of group affairs.

Group interaction is a two-way process. An individual needs both to learn how to adjust to group prescriptions, and to help other members of the group discover and carry through their responsibilities in relation to him. The status of employer, for example, implies that the individual so designated recognizes

[8] Allport, *Pattern and Growth in Personality,* pp. 181–182.

and accepts his responsibilities toward his employees, as well as his rights in expecting them to fulfill their roles of submitting to his requirements of an honest day's work for an honest day's pay. Constructive interpersonal relations, then, rest on the degree to which each individual is willing and able to fulfill his role as other members of his group or groups fulfill theirs.

Aspects of Personal-Social Adjustment

Throughout the discussion I have stressed the interrelations that exist between an individual and the group or groups of which he is a member. At each age level he brings to his societal relationships whatever personal qualities he has developed as the result of the influence upon his inherited potentialities of his experiences in previous group situations. Every boy and man and every girl and woman reflect in their personal and social reactions the effect upon them of parental strengths and weaknesses, and of parental and marital home, educational, occupational, and recreational influences. At the same time, the individual himself, through his displayed attitudes and his behavior, exercises a more or less potent influence upon his physical and social environment. Hence personal-social adjustment represents a continuous two-way process.

CONTINUITY OF THE ADJUSTMENT PROCESS.   Adjustments vary with people and situations. They are influenced by the number and quality of environmental stimuli. Some persons adjust easily and successfully; others are motivated toward behavior which hinders their subsequent efforts at adaptation. Each new environment presents many adjustment problems. Variation to be found among people in meeting new situations is not a mere matter of chance. An individual constantly is acquiring new behavior patterns and attitudes; his adjustments are based upon specific and definite factors within and outside his own developing personality. This is true whether the adjustments are satisfying, or whether individual or social problems arise.

The strains and stresses of modern life are making it increasingly difficult for the average individual to maintain a consistently stable attitude of acceptance. Many persons who experience conflicts and difficulties, however, are able to meet such disturbances by changing their customary activities, their habitual attitudes, or their former points of view. They are flexible; they can adapt themselves to changing conditions and still maintain their self-esteem and the respect of their associates.

The maintenance of good physical health is dependent upon the exercise of sound principles of physical hygiene. The application of the principles of mental hygiene can help in the preservation of good mental health. One visit to a physician or one month of watching one's diet cannot insure continued good health; neither can a quickly broken resolution to "mend one's ways" bring about permanent control of behavior.

THE MENTAL HEALTH APPROACH. The achieving of emotional stability may be a slow process, especially if in the physical and social environment one is exposed to many conflict-arousing situations. Serious problems of personal-social adjustment have been experienced by people during every stage of civilization; they are not the concomitants only of our modern fast pace of living and confused state of world affairs. Approaches to attempted solution of problem situations vary, however.

To prevent physical or mental illness, primitive peoples employed magic; later, superstitions exercised a strong influence upon individual and group behavior. Today, emphasis is placed upon scientific methods of research and the development of various theories of cause-effect relationships. The history of the mental hygiene movement exemplifies twentieth-century interest in mental and emotional health. Increased understanding of the causes of mental and emotional breakdown has resulted in the development of functional approaches toward the maintenance of sound mental health.

An individual's developing values affect his childhood relationships with his parents, other relatives, peer associates, teachers, and other adults. During later adolescence and adulthood, his established set of values influences his attitudes and behavior in his various situational relationships, such as courtship, marriage, family rearing, occupational activities, leisure-time and recreational pursuits. At any period of his existence a person's philosophy of life constitutes the interplay of his developing set of values and his relational experiences.

To be emotionally secure, a human being needs to experience self-esteem and self-confidence. It is unlikely that he never will encounter self-reproaching and self-defensive conditions or experiences. If his attitudes in situations provocative of the loss of self-esteem are directed by positive life values, however, he is enabled to meet his problem with an insightful understanding of the basic causes of the problem. Either unaided or with the help of others, he can solve his problem and regain confidence in himself and the power to avoid or to adjust satisfactorily to similar situations.

The nature and extent of mental growth also affects the adjustments that are made by the individual. Information learned between the ages of four and twelve is most helpful to him throughout the remainder of his life. Most of this knowledge is gained through the medium of language. In his discussion of "The Course of Cognitive Growth" Jerome S. Bruner arrives at the following basic assumption:

It seems to me that growth depends upon the emergence of two forms of competence. Children, as they grow, must acquire ways of representing the recurrent regularities in their environment, and they must transcend the momentary by developing ways of linking past to present to future—representation and integration. I have suggested that we can conceive of growth in both of these domains as the emergence of new technologies for the unlocking and amplification of human intellectual powers. Like the growth of technology, the growth of intellect is not smoothly monotonic. Rather, it moves forward in spurts as innovations are adopted. Most of the innovations are transmitted to the child in some prototypic form by agents of the culture: ways of responding, ways of looking and imaging, and most important, ways of translating what one has encountered into language.

I have relied heavily in this account on the successive emergence of action, image, and word as the vehicles of representation, a reliance based both upon our observations and upon modern readings of man's alloplastic evolution. Our attention has been directed largely to the transition between iconic and symbolic representation.

In children between 4 and 12 language comes to play an increasingly powerful role as an implement of knowing. Through simple experiments, I have tried to show how language shapes, augments, and even supersedes the child's earlier modes of processing information. Translation of experience into symbolic form, with its attendant means of achieving remote reference, transformation, and combination, opens up realms of intellectual possibility that are orders of magnitude beyond the most powerful image forming system. . . .

If I have seemed to underemphasize the importance of inner capacities—for example, the capacity *for* language or *for* imagery—it is because I believe that this part of the story is given by the nature of man's evolution. What is significant about the growth of mind in the child is to what degree it depends not upon capacity but upon the unlocking of capacity by techniques that come from exposure to the specialized environment of a culture. Romantic clichés, like "the veneer of culture" or "natural man," are as misleading if not as damaging as the view that the course of human development can be viewed independently of the educational process we arrange to make that development possible.[9]

INDIVIDUAL RESPONSIBILITY FOR ADJUSTMENT. Each individual possesses specific traits and characteristics, abilities, drives, thoughts, and actions that are peculiar to himself. He experiences environmental stimulations and opportunities that differ from the life experiences of every other individual. Within the individual a constant battle rages between the urge to do and the urge to leave undone, the satisfaction of achieving personal desires and consideration for the needs of others, the drive for freedom and the habit of restraint, the desire for approval and the dread of disapproval. The individual continuously experiences the emotional strains and stresses of his loves, his fears, his dominations, his submissions, his drives toward self-glorification or self-abasement, and, finally, those innumerable behavior responses through which he strives to attain the satisfaction of his physical, emotional, and social needs.

Since the total personality is more than the complex of specific traits, the essence of personality is intangible, subtle, and undefinable. Hence it is difficult to predict with certainty the

9 Jerome S. Bruner, "The Course of Cognitive Growth," *American Psychologist*, January, 1964, pp. 13–14.

kind of adult a child eventually will become. Results of studies seem to indicate that the physical and mental health of the parents and the kind of environment in which a child develops are predicating factors of the adequacy of his personal and social adjustment. Yet, in some instances, the expected outcomes are not evidenced. Specific influences of which the significance is not recognized are the bases of deviations from what normally might be anticipated. There are certain cause-effect relationships, however, that seem to function for most individuals as adjustive or maladjustive factors.

Much of family discord can be attributed to the insistence by one or more of its members upon the fulfillment of personal wants and preconceived notions of individual rights and responsibilities. Many occupational difficulties seem to stem from personal struggles to gain money, prestige, and power. Social maladjustment is rooted in selfish interest and in competition for personal distinction or control. Political, economic, national, or international conflict can result from an overemphasis upon individual or group superiority. As emotionally mature men or women participate in family, occupational, social, and civic projects and activities they develop an inner attitude of personal sufficiency. They learn to appreciate the beauty and worth of natural, scientific, and artistic phenomena. They are capable of using the power of self-direction. Fundamentally, they are relatively unaffected by destructive forces outside themselves.

In general, a full and rich life cannot be developed in a meager and uninspiring environment. Hence, everyone needs to be stimulated by whatever is best in the way of home conditions, educational advantages, occupational opportunities, and social and civic adjustment. Mental hygiene succeeds in its function as it progressively makes possible, for every individual, equality of opportunity within personal limitations for constructive adjustment to fundamental human wants and urges. Beyond that the "good" life can be attained by an individual only through his conscious striving to achieve socially acceptable and personally satisfying attitudes and behavior patterns.

QUESTIONS AND PROBLEMS

1. Justify the statement that self-realization and self-esteem do not develop in a vacuum.

2. Discuss how social relationships have emotional concomitants.

3. Indicate the extent to which an individual needs the cooperation of his associates.

4. Discuss Guilford's four main categories of social needs.

5. Indicate specifically how social forces affect your adjustment to life.

6. Name four ways in which you can be an effective member of a group.

7. Cite instances of children resenting dominance of an adult.

8. Justify the statement that parents represent the greatest single factor in a child's personality development.

9. Compare cultural differences between the United States and one other country. Show how differences in culture affect an individual's interpersonal relationships.

10. Trace an individual's social adjustment from infancy through old age.

11. Describe your role in your family group.

12. Explain what is meant by an interaction group. Be specific.

13. Give your reaction to Allport's interpretation of the family group.

14. In what ways is group interaction a two-way process?

15. Discuss the significance of good mental health in personal-social adjustment.

16. How does an individual's set of values affect his interpersonal relationships at different stages of his development?

17. Illustrate from personal experience ways in which you are responsible for your degree of social adjustment.

18. Explain why it is believed that good adjustment concerns an individual's total personality.

19. Offer suggestions helpful to adolescents in the development of improved patterns of adjustment.

20. List adjustment problems that you are having in your student life or in your vocational activities. Suggest what you can do to resolve them.

Selected Readings

Berelson, B., and G. A. Steiner, *Human Behavior: An Inventory of Scientific Findings.* New York: Harcourt, Brace & World, Inc., 1964. Chapters 8–16.

Cohen, A. R., *Attitude Change and Social Influence.* New York: Basic Books, Inc., 1964.

Collins, B. E., and H. Guetzkow, *A Social Psychology of Group Processes for Decision-making.* New York: John Wiley & Sons, Inc., 1964.

Dalton, R. H., *Personality and Social Interaction.* Boston, Mass.: D. C. Heath and Company, 1961.

Hammond, P. B. (ed.), *Cultural and Social Anthropology: Selected Readings.* New York: The Macmillan Company, 1964.

Hare, P. A., *Handbook of Small Group Research.* New York: Free Press of Glencoe, 1962.

———, E. F. Borgatta, and R. F. Bales, *Small Groups.* New York: Alfred A. Knopf, Inc., 1955.

Hartley, E. L., and R. E. Hartley, *Fundamentals of Social Psychology.* New York: Alfred A. Knopf, Inc., 1952.

Harvey, O. J., *Motivation and Social Interaction: Cognitive Determinants.* New York: The Ronald Press Company, 1963.

Heider, F., *The Psychology of Interpersonal Relations.* New York: John Wiley & Sons, Inc., 1958.

Kelman, H. C., *Social Influence and Personal Belief.* New York: John Wiley & Sons, Inc., 1962.

Kluckhohn, C., and Henry A. Murray (eds.), *Personality in Nature, Society, and Culture,* 2nd ed. New York: Alfred A. Knopf, Inc., 1953.

Leuba, C., *Personality: Interpersonal Relations and Self-understanding.* Columbus, Ohio: Charles E. Merrill Books, Inc., 1962.

Luft, J., *Group Processes: An Introduction to Group Dynamics.* Palo Alto, Calif.: National Press, 1963.

Moustakas, C. E., *Loneliness.* Englewood Cliffs, N.J.: Prentice-Hall, Inc., 1961.

Newcomb, T. M., R. H. Turner, and P. E. Converse, *Social Psychology: The Study of Human Interaction.* New York: Holt, Rinehart and Winston, Inc., 1965.

Reissman, F., *The Culturally Deprived Child*. New York: Harper & Row, Publishers, 1962.

Schachter, S., *The Psychology of Affiliation*. Stanford, Calif.: Stanford University Press, 1959.

Smelser, N. J., and W. T. Smelser, *Personality and Social Systems*. Englewood Cliffs, N.J.: Prentice-Hall, Inc., 1961.

Stansfeld, S., and R. C. Williamson, *Social Psychology*, 3rd ed. New York: The Ronald Press Company, 1966.

Stouffer, S. A., *Social Research to Test Ideas*. New York: Free Press of Glencoe, 1962.

Verba, S., *Small Groups and Political Behavior: A Study of Leadership*. Princeton, N.J.: Princeton University Press, 1961.

Yablonsky, L., *The Violent Gang*. New York: The Macmillan Company, 1962.

Zalenick, A., and D. Moment, *The Dynamics of Interpersonal Behavior*. New York: John Wiley & Sons, Inc., 1964.

{ 3 }

MOTIVATION
IN
HUMAN BEHAVIOR

A HUMAN BEING, from birth to death, is an active, functioning organism. His activity is purposeful and continuous. An individual strives not only to satisfy his body needs but also to acquire the knowledges, skills, attitudes, ideals, and behavior habits that will enable him to function successfully as a member of each of his various life groups. Social urges have a biological basis, and human drives follow rather definite patterns of behavior adjustment.

BASIC CONCEPTS OF MOTIVATION

Motivation is closely associated with the dynamic aspect of human behavior. To the student of psychology the term *motivation* connotes psychological causation. It refers to sequence or continuity. Every human experience involves a causation factor to the extent that a motive always precedes a particular act. Cause and effect relationships in human behavior imply that every motive produces some effect and that every response or effect is preceded by a motive. It is difficult, sometimes impossible, to

[53]

trace this motive-effect sequence in the thinking or behavior of an individual. The utilization of psychoanalytic techniques of behavior evaluation, however, can help an individual gain some insight concerning deep-seated emotionalized motives that are affecting his behavior.

Motivated behavior is orderly, persistent, and energized with numerous emotional qualities. Most behavior can be explained when the reasons for it are known. The baby cries either to seek food or help, or to avoid pain or discomfort. The adolescent wears selected clothing either to gain peer approval or to avoid criticism or even ostracism. He also studies in order to win success in his schoolwork or to avoid failure. Hence human behavior not only is an active process but is goal directed. In general, human beings are motivated by a felt need (1) to satisfy bodily desires or to satisfy physiological needs, (2) to achieve a purpose or goal, (3) to gain satisfaction through social recognition of one form or another, or (4) to avoid an anticipated unpleasant experience.

The human being has a multiple of needs that must be satisfied if he is to enjoy his day-to-day living. He needs food, water, oxygen, sleep, rest, warmth, and sex. He needs to dominate, to admire, to follow, to emulate, and to be independent. He needs to accept others, to accept punishment, to avoid blame, and to be well behaved. He needs to be friendly, discriminating, sympathetic, and helpful toward others. He needs to relax, to be curious, and to give information to others. He needs to overcome obstacles, to excel, to receive praise, to dramatize his behavior, to preserve his ego, to defend himself against blame or belittlement, and to avoid failure or defeat. These and other needs help account for the physiological, psychological, and social drives of the individual.

Meaning and Characteristics of Motivation

Motivation, as an activating force, affects every area of human behavior. Its field of influence ranges from the directing of a simple act, the motive of which is obvious, to a complex, formal activity pattern, e.g., career behavior, which represents numerous detailed aspects of motivation. There is evidence that motivation is complex in its functioning, even in apparently simple activities associated with the satisfaction of body requirements such as food, water, and oxygen.

Motivation of human behavior can be better understood when the meaning of such terms as *drive, incentive* (goal), and *homeostasis* are interpreted in simple terms. I shall give brief interpretative statements of each.

Definitions of such terms as *motivation, needs, drives,* and *incentives* are given by Lindsley as follows:

> *Motivation* is generally defined as the combination of forces which initiate, direct, and sustain behavior toward a goal. This may be much too broad and inclusive to be useful, and we will see that this definition needs further qualifications.
>
> *Needs* are often dealt with under two broad categories: *Biological needs,* and *Personal-Social needs. Biological needs* are basic conditions (usually chemical) which are necessary to the maintenance of life and normal processes of health, growth, and reproduction. Specifically, these might be the need for oxygen, calcium, carbohydrates, etc. *Personal-Social* needs can be less objectively described by such concepts as personal security, self-confidence, group status, prestige, aggression, etc.
>
> *Drives* are generally defined as the internal stimuli or organic states which initiate activity and predispose an animal toward making differential responses which presumably aid in attaining satisfaction of needs but may well go beyond this. These we are told may be primary and unlearned, or secondary and acquired.
>
> *Incentives or goals* are the external stimuli (or their surrogates) toward which or away from which the animal orients himself in seeking satisfaction of needs.[1]

Human drive refers to a condition of the individual in which his behavior is activated or directed toward some goal. It is a relatively convenient term to use in an attempt to explain human behavior. An incentive or goal is that which affects the individual in such a way as to cause a reduction of the drive or its

[1] Donald B. Lindsley, "Psychophysiology and Motivation," in Marshall R. Jones (ed.), *Nebraska Symposium on Motivation,* Lincoln: University of Nebraska Press, 1957, p. 48.

elimination. Thus, food is an incentive to satisfy the hunger drive. Money is an incentive to encourage a boy or girl to perform a task, and the like.

Homeostasis can be used to describe the equilibrium-preserving function within the individual. Various biological drives are involved in maintaining this physiological equilibrium. Once an individual's physiological equilibrium has been disturbed, activated behavior ceases only when the goal is attained and the equilibrium restored. A water imbalance, for example, must be corrected in order for the individual to reduce or lose his drive for water. Proper intake of water will complete the process of homeostasis.

Lindsley has been concerned with the biologically oriented aspects of motivation. His point of view is summarized in his assumption

> that life itself, in terms of cells, tissues, organs, organ systems, and even whole organisms, implies a continual shifting of materials and energies. This process may be referred to as *homeostasis* or *regulation*, for it is going on constantly in order to maintain physio-chemical balances of smaller or larger scope within the organism and between the organism and its environment. These seem to constitute a backdrop of activity against which special increases or decreases may arise from time to time. The mechanisms underlying homeostasis appear to be built into the organism, and although subject to modification, are relatively inflexible. Their unity and integrity are products of a long history of natural selection.[2]

Then, according to Lindsley:

> Motivation requires persistence of action or its surrogates. The ARAS [Ascending Reticular Activating System] set in action manifests some persistence; the hippocampus which is activated by it may show a longer perseveration. Habits and memories established by virtue of its complementary action, and perhaps that of the hippocampus, to excitations in the cortex which are marked by discrimination, provide relatively indefinite persistence.

[2] *Ibid.*, p. 96.

Motivation *may* require direction and a goal or goal-surrogate. . . . Sheer activity, with or without direction, may be a goal in itself. The perception and definition of a goal and the establishment of direction toward it seem to call for selective discriminatory control, and imply specific alerting based on novel or unique stimulus cues. The ARAS and the diffuse thalamo-cortical projection system presumably play an important role, but the reticular formation seems to have a way of dealing with an eliminating routine and repetitive stimuli by "habituation" or "adaptation." [3]

D. O. Hebb is another authority on motivation. He has placed great emphasis on the physiological bases of motivation. In an article in which he discusses drives and the conceptual nervous system, he includes his definition of motivation and then explains his ideas fully. We present his definition and a few of the salient ideas that appear in the discussion.

Before going on it is just as well to be explicit about the use of the terms motivation and drive. "Motivation" refers here in a rather general sense to the energizing of behavior, and especially to the sources of energy in a particular set of responses that keep them temporarily dominant over others and account for continuity and direction in behavior. "Drive" is regarded as a more specific conception about the way in which this occurs: a hypothesis of motivation, which makes the energy a function of a special process distinct from those S-R or cognitive functions that are energized. In some contexts, therefore, "motivation" and "drive" are interchangeable. . . .

I find myself obliged to reverse my earlier views and accept the drive conception, not merely on physiological grounds but also on the grounds of some of our current psychological studies. . . . the same stimulation in mild degree may attract (by prolonging the pattern of response that leads to this stimulation) and in strong degree repel (by disrupting the pattern and facilitating conflicting or alternative responses) .

The significance of this relation is in a phenomenon of the greatest importance for understanding motivation in

3 *Ibid.,* p. 98.

higher animals. This is the *positive attraction of risk taking,* or mild fear, *and of problem solving,* or mild frustration. . . .

One virtue of identifying arousal with drive is that it relates differing views (as well as bringing into the focus of attention data that may otherwise be neglected). The important thing is a clear distinction between cue function and arousal function, and the fact that at low levels an increase of drive intensity may be rewarding, whereas at high levels it is a decrease that rewards. Given this point of view and our assumptions about arousal mechanisms, we see that what Harlow has emphasized is the exteroceptively aroused, but still low-level, drive, with cue function of course directly provided for. In the concept of anxiety, Spence and Brown emphasize the higher-level drive state, especially where there is no guiding cue function that would enable the animal to escape threat. . . .

Obviously these are not explanations that are being discussed, but possible lines of future research; and there is one problem in particular that I would urge should not be forgotten. This is the cortical feedback to the arousal system, in physiological terms: or in psychological terms, the *immediate drive value of cognitive processes,* without intermediary. This is psychologically demonstrable, and *has* been demonstrated repeatedly.[4]

Except for his hours of needed sleep and his other periods of quiescent behavior, the human being is active. I am interested in what causes him to bestir himself and become active, that is, the motives that underlie the desire for action. In this discussion I use "motive" to refer to those qualities that incite the individual to active behavior or that enable him to continue in that action toward a particular outcome or goal. When a squirrel is discovered burying a nut, or a child asks for candy, we become interested in the cause of the underlying motive.

Motivated behavior is activated behavior. It represents the difference between being asleep or awake, relaxed or tense. In motivated behavior the individual is in a state of readiness to

---

[4] D. O. Hebb, "Drives and the C. N. S. [Conceptual Nervous System]," *The Psychological Review,* July, 1955, pp. 243–254.

become active or to continue action. Thus is established a motivational sequence that results in the reduction or elimination of the drive. A hunger drive, for example, activates the incentive that affects the intensity of the drive that eventually reduces or eliminates it.

Motivated behavior tends to persist, to display itself in a variety of ways, and to be energized by emotional experiences. The continuity of behavior is characteristic of its persistent aspects. The stronger the desire, the more persistently will the individual pursue the goal. For example, with an increase in hunger goes an increase in food-seeking behavior; with an increase in interest to become a member of the team goes an increased cooperation in practice. Persistence in effort is closely associated with the strength of the motive.

If failure has resulted from an attempt to attain a desired goal, the motivated behavior may take the form of *exploratory variation* that continues until the goal is achieved. During his first day in school, a child who is a newcomer in the neighborhood may exhibit variations in his behavior as means of earning group acceptance. He displays his possessions; he attempts to demonstrate superior mental or physical ability. If either of these methods fails he turns to another and then another until one works, and he is accepted. By introducing the new pupil to the class members, the teacher can help lessen the child's need to engage in acceptance-seeking activities.

Exploratory variation is seen also in adult behavior, as attempts are made to be accepted by a new group. The degree of variation depends upon the speed with which the stranger is accepted and the extent of his interest in the group. The principle of exploratory variation can be put to greater use by the more able individual than by the dull person.

Emotional tonus gives power to human motives and drives. *Emotional energization* occurs in strongly motivated instances. When there is delay or resistance but the motive is strong, the organism's behavior shows increased energy through emotional tension. The behavior may take the form of anger, anxiety, fear, aggression, or some other emotional expression. If added effort results in successful achievement, great emotional satisfaction is experienced. This reaction is characteristic of the dull as well as of the bright.

TABLE 1
Appetites (Drives)

Name	Organic base	Rhythm	Sense or sense organ	Response	Social control	Maladjustment
Thirst	Reduction of fluid in tissues	Few hours	Localized in throat	Swallowing, drinking	Very little	Rare
Hunger	Metabolism	Several times daily; varies with culture	Cells sensitive to stomach contractions; appetite "gnawing"	Swallowing, eating	Foods and habits vary widely	Non-hunger (food refusals) or "gorging"
Elimination	(a) Secretion via kidney and bladder	Few hours	Cells in bladder wall	Urination	Sanitation and modesty	Enuresis (bedwetting)
	(b) Excretion via intestines	Daily	Cells in intestines and colon; "pressure"	Defecation	Sanitation and modesty	Incontinence or constipation
Rest or sleep	Chemical changes in blood, as result of muscular action	Daily	Fatigue, weariness	Lying down, relaxation, sleep (usually at night)	Time regulated by need and custom	Insomnia, nightmares
Sex	Stimulation of erogenous zones, sex organs, and glands	Glandular secretions have regular period, female has monthly cycle	Localized sensations, general tension	Manipulation, copulation	Marked social control of all aspects	Many disorders

Source: John E. Anderson, *The Psychology of Development and Personal Adjustment*, New York: Holt, Rinehart and Winston, 1949, p. 236. Copyright © 1949 by Holt, Rinehart and Winston, Inc. Reprinted by permission.

Direction and Tensions of Motivated Behavior

Inherent urges, desires, or habitual attitudes are basic to motives that serve as action stimulators. Organized behavior is directed toward goal achievement. Purpose and tensions are aspects of motivated behavior. Tensions may be established by stimuli inside or outside the body. Viewed externally, motivated behavior appears to be purposive; considered internally, motivated behavior represents attempted tension reduction. When it is set off, a tension system runs its course until it is satiated. Hence it is an energy system organized to meet some human need.

The tension systems are unified and dynamic. Their management involves intelligence and motivated behavior. These tensions not only arise from the physiological needs but also from the social culture and habit patterns of the individual. The simplest forms of tension systems are individual appetites. According to Anderson: "Each appetite has its own mode of expressing itself upon the organism, its own cycle, and its own method of satiation." His organization of the appetites is presented in Table 1.

The Acquisition of Motives

In order to discover how motives are acquired, David C. McClelland conducted extended research during which he attempted to develop the achievement motive in adults. This was undertaken for the purpose of gaining knowledge concerning how the complex human characteristics are acquired. The overall research strategy was to involve businessmen of various cultural backgrounds in learning situations over a number of years in training periods that were of short duration (1 to 3 weeks) and that were designed for groups rather than for individuals. Many factors and influences that bring about motive change were considered. As a result of the research McClelland presented the following twelve propositions:

> 1. The more reasons an individual has in advance to believe that he can, will, or should develop a motive, the more educational attempts designed to develop that motive are likely to succeed. . . .

2. The more an individual perceives that developing a motive is consistent with the demands of reality (and reason), the more educational attempts designed to develop that motive are likely to succeed. . . .

3. The more thoroughly an individual develops and clearly conceptualizes the associative network defining the motive, the more likely he is to develop the motive. . . .

4. The more an individual can link the newly developed network to related actions, the more the change in both thought and action is likely to occur and endure. . . .

5. The more an individual can link the newly conceptualized association-action complex (or motive) to events in his everyday life, the more likely the motive complex is to influence his thoughts and actions in situations outside the training experience. . . .

6. The more an individual can perceive and experience the newly conceptualized motive as an improvement in the self-image, the more the motive is likely to influence his future thoughts and actions. . . .

7. The more an individual can perceive and experience the newly conceptualized motive as an improvement on prevailing cultural values, the more the motive is likely to influence his future thoughts and actions. . . .

8. The more an individual commits himself to achieving concrete goals in life related to the newly formed motive, the more the motive is likely to influence his future thoughts and actions. . . .

9. The more an individual keeps a record of his progress toward achieving goals to which he is committed, the more the newly formed motive is likely to influence his future thoughts and actions. . . .

10. Changes in motives are more likely to occur in an interpersonal atmosphere in which the individual feels warmly but honestly supported and respected by others as a person capable of guiding and directing his own future behavior. . . .

11. Changes in motives are more likely to occur the more the setting dramatizes the importance of self-study and lifts it out of the routine of everyday life. . . .

12. Changes in motives are more likely to occur and persist

if the new motive is a sign of membership in a new reference group.[5]

Motives function continually to fulfill human needs. Some motives may be small or specific and relatively weak; others may influence the continued behavior of an individual over a long period of time. The persistence of motives is based upon human wants and human interests. The energy required sometimes works toward the attainment of a goal; sometimes expenditure of energy acts as a block. Tension systems act as forces in motivation. Anderson concludes:

A tension system involves (1) some impulsion or need within the organism, (2) an object or goal outside toward which energy is directed, and (3) some process of reduction of tension, or satiation, when the goal or object is attained. To describe goals and objects in this reciprocal relation involves the concept of *valence,* which refers to the mutual attractiveness between a need and an object or goal. The organism is within a *field of forces* which is enclosed by a boundary and which may contain both a number of objects with valences and a number of barriers which temporarily block access to them. What the person does depends upon interaction within and with the field of forces. Because he is surrounded by different objects and goals with different valences, *conflict* arises. Out of conflict comes the necessity of choice between alternative lines of action. A characteristic of the person's reactions in a conflict situation is an *oscillation,* or a shifting back and forth from one alternative to another, prior to the decision or action which terminates the disturbance between the tension systems.[6]

NATURE AND SIGNIFICANCE OF
HUMAN MOTIVES

In order to understand human motives there is needed an understanding of the basic desires that are present in all normal

---

[5] David C. McClelland, "Toward a Theory of Motive Acquisition," *American Psychologist,* May, 1965, pp. 324, 325, 327–330.

[6] John E. Anderson, *The Psychology of Development and Personal Adjustment,* New York: Holt, Rinehart and Winston, 1949, p. 256.

human beings. As an aid to the process of development from birth onward, a human being is equipped by nature with a host of potential desires and cravings that operate as the driving forces of his life activities. The amount of satisfaction or annoyance that he experiences in life situations is determined by the extent to which his interests and urges are gratified or thwarted. These urges are dynamic forces that affect thoughts, emotions, and behavior.

As a member of the Nebraska Symposium on Motivation, Edward L. Walker suggested the following concerning the nature of motivation:

> Thus innate biological motives, acquired human motives, sets, attitudes, and traits may be regarded as alike in being readinesses to respond selectively to limited classes of stimuli or to select limited classes of events by an identical mechanism. The readiness creates a condition in which a relevant stimulus produces a greater arousal reaction than it would without the readiness, the arousal reaction increases the complexity of the relevant event, and thus increases the likelihood that such an event will be nearest optimal psychological complexity. These terms differ with respect to the operations which produce them, and their endurance properties. Sets are usually of a situational character and of short duration. Motives of the biological kind have a cyclical character dependent upon a growing readiness which is reduced or eliminated by consummation. Some biological readinesses may be largely stimulus induced. Motives such as need for achievement and attitudes are indistinguishable in that both are acquired, both are enduring, but both are subject to modification. Traits are simply more permanent than any of the others.[7]

General Nature of Drives

The individual is born with certain potential urges or drives that seek expression. The way in which these inherent desires are

---

[7] Edward L. Walker, "Psychological Complexity as a Basis for a Theory of Motivation and Choice," in David Levine (ed.), *Nebraska Symposium on Motivation*. Lincoln: University of Nebraska Press, 1964, p. 90.

satisfied through overt behavior is conditioned by environmental influences and by experience. These experientially modified drives to action become the motivators of human attitudes and actions.

The relatively simple behavior drives of early childhood increase in number and complexity as an individual matures and experiences more and differing life relationships. As we are stimulated by varying social values, we attempt so to direct our interests and desires that we may achieve satisfying social recognition. Other less desirable drives may be present within us and become powerful as motivators of our behavior. However, we may refuse to recognize the presence of these drives or we may delude ourselves into thinking that our behavior is motivated by noble impulses.

Importance of Motives

Activity-arousing stimuli are supplied by the environment. Human response to these stimuli at any one time is conditioned by the particular urge that is dominant in the individual. For example, a man returns home very tired from a hard day at the office to find that he is invited to join friends in a card game. Normally, he would be delighted to accept an invitation of this kind. This evening, however, his extreme weariness stimulates him to refuse the invitation, in order that he may stay at home and rest. Inner urges determine the nature of responses.

A careful observation of human conduct leads to the conclusion that an understanding of motives is very useful to us in our daily relationships. As we are stimulated by the actions of other persons, we tend to question the motives that give rise to this or that form of behavior. In our search for the underlying motives of our own behavior, or that of other people, we are not always successful in discovering the actual motivating force that stimulates one to act as he does. Our behavior often reflects the functioning of more than one kind of urge at the same time. In general, we are motivated to satisfy bodily needs, to realize a purpose or an ideal, or to achieve personal satisfaction in a socially desirable activity.

Why do humans behave as they do? Do men play baseball because of large audiences? Do pupils conform to school rules because they are expected to do so? Why do people build different types of houses, buy different kinds of clothes, or engage in different kinds of work? In individual urges and desires, as these are modified by experience, can be found the reason for differences in the kind of activity that is personally satisfying.

Just as a child develops functional, positive attitudes of his own, becomes independent of his parents, grows active in self-interest, learns to be self-determining, and eventually outlives his parents, so it is with motives. Each motive originates in whatever inherent tendencies, organic tensions, or diffuse irritabilities man possesses. Adult purposes result from the experiences of infancy and early childhood. However, during the process of maturing, many new neural connections are formed, resulting in a better-functioning human being.

Genetic Sequence of Motives

During very early childhood our activities are generally self-centered. Later, we are motivated by the wishes of individual members of the family, or playmates. This desire to do for others is further expanded to include relatively small groups, such as the entire family, the school, or the club. As we approach adolescence and then adulthood, our activities and interests are influenced by our desire to cooperate with the large groups in which we are active. These may include religious, political, business, and community affiliations.

Individual motives are always colored by personal desires, likes, and physical urges; social level; economic status, or interest in self or in others. Nevertheless, because of the socializing influences that constantly are present, motives follow an organized pattern in the developing life of the individual as he progresses step by step from infancy to adulthood.

An individual motivated to *pretend* to be a particular kind of person may actually *become* that which he has pretended because of the force and strength of the stimulating drive or motive. Likewise, the genius is forced, through the strength of his own inner drives, toward creation in the exercise of his talents, even though no external stimulus may seem to be active. An individual's active motives may reshape his behavior.

Persistent Unconscious Motives

A vast number of human irrationalities and maladjustments are due to lack of awareness of motives. There is needed an intelligent understanding of what are the dominant motives operating in the individual, how these are interrelated, how they are affected by continuous experience, and how they organize themselves into beneficial or detrimental patterns of human adjustment. Modern dynamic psychology is gradually revealing the subtle power of unconscious motives and emotional drives to control behavior responses so as to inhibit wholesome personality development. Any effort that will bring the motives to the level of awareness is worthy of careful consideration by those who are responsible for the education of an individual.

When a country is led into war, the people usually are denied the knowledge of the real motives of the leaders that underlie the latter's decisions. Likewise, in advertising, the general public is not told of the motives that have stimulated the writers of the advertisements. More wholesome attitudes are evidenced when underlying motives are expressed and understood by all concerned. Psychiatrists, in treating a neurotic, often need to dig back into past experiences of the patient. He is unaware of his own motives, since these often are buried in an unsatisfied desire, a potent fear, or a difficult life situation.

In dealing with this problem we are in the realm of subjective phenomena. It is difficult to explain the background of a disturbing experience. What does the individual know about the affective value of this stimulus, that experience, or that drive? He needs help in attempted introspection; unaided, his attempts at analyzing his motives for behavior are likely to be affected by his mental set and his physiological condition.

THE FUNCTIONING OF DRIVES

All of an individual's behavior reflects the functioning of one or another need, want, drive, or urge. Rarely does one of the drives act in isolation; seldom can a desire or need be satisfied except in terms of existing environmental conditions. Drive to action can be described as physiological, psychological, or social; yet, the satisfying of physiological needs has social implications.

The internal conditions that motivate an individual toward attaining goals in his environment are of two main kinds: (1) *biological drives* in which there are tissue needs such as food, water, oxygen, and sleep, and (2) *psychological* and *social motives* in which there are personal needs to be satisfied. These psychological and social motives include self-esteem, recognition and approval, security, sex, and the like.

Biological Drives

Biological drives result from organic conditions in which there is aroused behavior based on change in body equilibrium. Inner imbalance of the individual arouses activity that attempts to restore homeostasis. Thus, a need for food tends to arouse the hunger drive, although the hunger drive does not necessarily become stronger as the intensity of the need increases. Hunger pangs tend to come and go when individuals refrain from eating for long periods of time, yet their food need continues.

THE HUNGER DRIVE. The origin of hunger is not fully understood although it is one drive that has received careful study. Internal changes in the region of the stomach produce mass sensations known as hunger. These hunger pangs seem to result from the contraction of stomach muscles, yet experimental evidence indicates that the hunger drive persists in the absence of these contractions. This leads to the belief that hunger may be chemical in nature and that the stomach contractions may be by-products of other organic conditions in the hungry individual.

The balloon technique has been used to study the relationship between the hunger drive and general body activity. It has been discovered that there is a close relationship between the rhythmic occurrences of hunger pangs and the rhythmic occurrences of striped muscle activity. The recording on the pneumograph indicates that the hunger pangs correspond closely to the periods the stomach contractions are at their maximum.

Hunger sensations usually are more pronounced under conditions of semi-starvation than of total fasting. An individual who has gone without food for many hours does not feel hungry all of the time. Also, the satisfying of hunger and the eating of tasty food differ in that considerable conditioning is required to develop eating habits and food tastes. For example, the frequency and the precise hour of eating are matters of custom or habit. The preparation of food and the seasoning of it may contribute to the liking or disliking of that food, regardless of its nutritional value to the individual.

There are certain food allergies, the cause of which is not known. These sometimes result from a developed attitude toward the particular food. The attitude may result from the extent to which the eating of the food causes stomach distress. Likewise, the environment in which it is eaten may cause the food to disagree with the eater. Palatable drumsticks coming from a pet chicken may be refused by the boy who raised the chicken. Individual conditioning is important in food values. Yet, if the hunger pangs are strong enough, the individual easily surmounts these psychological hazards to satisfy his hunger needs.

THE THIRST DRIVE.   Water as well as food is needed for human survival and endurance. The need for water arises earlier than does that for food. Dryness of the mouth and throat are thirst stimuli. Yet, craving for water only partly satisfies the thirst drive. In the long run, needed water intake is determined and regulated by the amount of water the body needs, not by the sensation of dryness of the mouth and throat. If the body is deprived of water for a substantial length of time, it starts to make adaptations aimed at the correction of the imbalance. Excessive loss of water damages body tissue more quickly than does loss of food. Therefore, it is believed by some that, among the biological drives, thirst is second in strength to the maternal urge.

THE NEED FOR OXYGEN AS A DRIVE.   A lack of oxygen is seldom experienced under normal circumstances, but, under certain conditions, air hunger may become an intense drive. Persons moving to a high altitude, where the oxygen content is considerably less than that to which they are accustomed, may suffer from acute oxygen deficiency without being aware of its cause. They may experience dizziness or a confused feeling; they may shout, burst into tears, or even become aggressive.

The brain is in constant need of a supply of oxygen. If the oxygen supply is cut off for even a brief period actual neural damage can result. It is believed that severe oxygen deprivation (anoxia) at birth may result in sufficient damage to the brain to be the cause of feeble-mindedness.

THE NEED FOR SLEEP. Rest and relaxation are needed to provide good conditions for homeostasis. The actual cause of sleep is not known. Certain conditions essential to sleep include a general relaxation of the body and a possible stimulation of the nerve and brain centers by a kind of chemical reaction in the body. This concept is based partly on the fact that certain drugs such as chloroform and ether produce a relaxed condition resembling sleep.

The fact of sleep is biological; the behavior patterns utilized during sleep seem to be a part of the culture of people. They also are associated closely with light and darkness and tend to alternate with them. In extremely hot climates sleeping during the heat of the day is a common practice of people living in those regions.

THE SEX DRIVE (Biological Aspects). A physiological drive that may or may not be rooted in homeostasis is the sex urge. Although this drive is associated with social living it also is closely associated with the maternal urge and the urge to experience sensory pleasure. The physical manifestations of the sex drive concern us at this point; the intellectual, emotional, and social manifestations are considered later in the chapter.

Sex activity is essential to the *survival of mankind*. Sexual satisfaction, although not essential to the survival of the individual, contributes to his physical, mental, and emotional health. The sexual life of the individual refers to all the conditions and processes that are in any way associated with interest in or desire for a person of the opposite sex who stirs him emotionally.

The sex drive is powerful and biologically important. It is so powerful that animals have been known to go through difficult pain stimulations in order to satisfy it. The human often shuts his eyes to disease possibilities or social disapproval in attempts to give unbridled expression to the sex drive. Nature uses this drive to secure the perpetuation of the species. It takes many forms in subhuman organisms, during their mating activities and the production of offspring, and in providing for the latter's growth and development. In humans, energy is produced by the physical organism in order to make possible the satisfaction of this urge.

Physical stimuli are potent motivators of sexual behavior because of the sensitivity of the genital organs and other erogenous zones. The psychological factor is extremely significant, however. Memory and imagination play their part in associating past experiences and present stimuli with romantic or sexual satisfaction. Much of a person's activity is influenced by interests and attitudes that have their bases in the sexual urge to reproduce but that have been refined and sublimated so that they express themselves in creative productions of literature, music, or art, or in activity directed toward the welfare of other persons.

This physical urge or appetite is more constant in the human than it is in animals. He differs from them in his capacity for thought and feeling, his ability to remember and to plan, and his interest in the emotions with which the physical and biological drives of sex are invested. It is the human's capacity for love that, through his work and play, has so utilized his creative abilities as to give much beauty to art and religion and to the many other aspects of his life that he has changed for world betterment.

In an advancing civilization the persistency of the sex drive makes necessary a psychological development. There is a psychosexual development that includes the thoughts, feelings, and emotional attitudes which accompany the physical maturing of the reproductive organs from birth. These mental attitudes are influenced by the inner nature of man and by environmental and educational factors, especially by the incidental sentiments and attitudes of which the child becomes increasingly aware in his enlarging environment. He develops certain mental and emotional patterns or ways of thinking and feeling that give him his social attitudes toward sex, and condition his sex drive to that extent.

It is through his early experiences in his family life that the child develops his basic patterns of love life upon which he builds his later love relationships. Given the example of desirable parental behavior and of other adult life in the home, a child can build strong, wholesome attitudes that are devoid of the "suggestive" which so fill the thinking of those who are shocked to learn that the children are imitating adult behavior. Without their realizing it, adults give children distorted attitudes in the area of sex. Many of these are difficult to outgrow.

Erotic feelings toward a member of the opposite sex may manifest themselves solely in attempts to be with and enjoy the company of the object of the erotic attraction. Usually, however, the emotional state is accompanied by a strong desire for physical contact with the other person, and/or coitus, if the conditions are favorable for sexual intercourse. It can be noted that sexual activity, in a more narrow interpretation of the term, is not necessarily a manifestation of erotic feelings. For example, an individual may engage in coitus as a means of reducing physical tensions, regardless of the presence of erotic or amatory feelings for the other person with whom sexual intercourse is being experienced.

Stimulation of Erogenous Areas. Erotic desires, feelings, or thoughts are aroused by appropriate sensory stimuli: tactile, visual, auditory, or olfactory. Bodily areas that are especially sensitive to touch and pressure stimulation are called erogenous areas. The penis of the male and the clitoris and vagina of the female are considered to be the primary areas of stimulation. Secondary areas that are common to both sexes, in varying degrees, include the nipples, the lips, the ears and the skin in back of the ears, and the flat area on the small of the back. These areas can be stimulated by pressure and touch, especially tickling. An erotic response may be aroused under some conditions, but not under others; certain skin areas are erogenic only for some persons.

The sight of a loved one or the sound of her voice may cause a man to experience erotic thoughts or feelings. The olfactory is a source of erotic or erogenic stimulation for many men. There seems to be a functional connection between the erectile tissue in the nasal passages and the erectile tissue in the genital organs. In a state of erotic excitement nasal turgescence may be so great that breathing becomes difficult. Characteristic female odors are erogenic for some men and may produce genital processes; for other men, these odors produce no erotic stimulation.

Stimulation of erotic areas may produce erotic desire, erotic feeling, or erotic thought without producing any general effects. Further, a response to a sensory stimulus is not erotic unless it produces erotic processes of some conscious sort, even though the genital processes are not involved. Sometimes stimulation of the genitalia may produce disgust instead of erotic feeling. It cannot then be called erogenic.

Erotic Perversions. A perverted desire or urge is abnormal in that it is directed away from what can be considered to be its normal object or objects. A perverted urge that becomes habitual is known as a *perversion*. Perversions may not always be harmful, yet they may be the cause of worry and maladjustment. Autoerotism and homosexuality (homoerotism) are two erotic perversions that give rise to considerable concern in some cultures. Their impact upon the individual who practices them and upon others who are affected by his behavior is discussed briefly.

Autoerotism. The production of erotic responses by oneself without stimulation by another person is known as *autoerotism*. Autoerotic activities include any type of self-induced sex pleasure in which the genital organs or other parts of the body are stimulated until an orgasm is produced. Autoerotism is more commonly known as *masturbation*. It means sexual stimulation through the use of the hand.

Autoerotism is a common practice during the period of pubescence; it may be continued through adulthood. Among the men and women interviewed by Kinsey and his staff it was found that most of the men and more than half of the women had used self-stimulation at some time in their life.

Masturbation that has its beginning during early childhood, whether discovered by the child himself or taught to him by others, is likely to become an obsessive habit. Usually, however, masturbation in the male begins shortly before puberty, when erotic responses are developing rapidly and when the orgasm becomes possible.

Symptoms of autoerotic behavior are sometimes observable by parents, but the symptoms are not completely reliable. The boy may tend to withdraw from social contacts with other children, or display psychological changes that are subtle and difficult to detect or describe. He may become moody and irritable. The frequency of the masturbation may decrease in a few years but in some cases it may continue into adult life.

Homosexuality. Homosexuality refers to the production of erotic responses through the cooperation of a person of the same sex. It sometimes is referred to as *homoerotism*. Homosexual experiences are more common than many people realize. Kinsey found that homosexuality was practiced to a greater extent by men than by women. His research revealed that, although more than half of the women studied had engaged in self-stimulation, only about one fifth of them had had sexual contact with other females. Among the men interviewed he found that at least 37 percent had had homosexual experiences to the point of orgasm. His findings are contrary to the once widespread belief that homosexual responses and completed contacts occur more frequently among females than among males.

Some persons who are homosexuals are inverts. The inversion may be physiological or it may be psychological. Some pairs of homosexuals stimulate one another with no differentiation of roles; usually, however, one of the male pair plays the role of a female and is referred to as "passive." He experiences inversion. In the case of women, the "active" person is considered to be inverted. These roles may be temporary; the inverted roles may change from time to time. Also inverts are likely to adopt the dress and mannerisms of the adopted sex.

Homosexual practices among women seem to be responsible for certain cases of frigidity. Likewise most male homosexuals who marry are usually frigid with their wives. A woman usually fails to stimulate erotic desire in a man who has for a long period obtained erotic and genital stimulation from another male. Some male homosexuals marry and force themselves to have intercourse with their wives. If the individual is a strong invert, sexual incompatibility results and divorce is the usual outcome. However, a male homosexual may marry to avert a scandal that already has reached the whisper stage.

Homosexuals are considered to be deviates in society; if they are apprehended, they become socially unacceptable. Thus homosexuals tend to be drawn closer together. If a high school boy's initial homosexual experience is discovered, for example, he is likely to want to leave school and perhaps the community in which he is known. He finds it increasingly difficult to make heterosexual contacts and seeks the company of other homosexual individuals; eventually he develops a definite homosexual pattern. In many cases the first homosexual experience has been thrust upon the individual. It is important, therefore, that a boy be removed from a situation of this kind, lest social disapproval of this one act force him into the company of homosexuals.

The theories of homosexuality usually are interpreted in light of adult homosexuality. These evolved theories are based on the assumption that homosexuality is either a psychopathic state or a result of other influences. In discussing the concepts of male homosexuality, Bieber and associates [8] present a succinct comment following a presentation of the essence of the theories of such authorities as Freud, Klein, Sullivan, Horney, Thompson, Rado, Ovesey, Kallman, Kinsey, and Hooker.

All *psychoanalytic* theories assume that adult homosexuality is psychopathologic and assign differing weights to constitutional and experiential determinants. All agree that the experiential determinants are in the main rooted in childhood and are primarily related to the family. Theories which do not assume psychopathology hold homosexuality to be one type of expression of a polymorphous sexuality which appears pathologic only in cultures holding it to be so.[9]

Other Sexual Perversions.   Adolescents often turn to behavior practices that give sexual satisfaction yet are unacceptable to society and bad for their own health. One form of sexual excitement practiced by some adolescents that may be a sublimation of the sex drive comes through the use of drugs. In writing about the effects of the sniffing of glue on sexual gratification, Winick and Goldstein suggest possible behavior outcomes of a sexual nature that may result from glue sniffing

The available findings indicated that glue sniffing is a form of passive retreat, and the personality of a sniffer is likely to display many of the characteristics found in alcoholics and drug addicts. Dr. Sandor Rado, in pioneering psychoanalytic studies of drug addiction, developed the hypothesis that the injection of a drug into the blood stream induces highly pleasurable sensations quite similar to those normally achieved through sex. Rado suggested that this by-passing of the individual's sexual system is closely related to the typical addict's retreat from any interest in outside sexual objects.

The Rado theory applies primarily to those cases in which a substance is injected directly into the blood stream, and any application of the theory to glue sniffing is speculative. But the possibility exists that, like narcotics addicts (though perhaps to a lesser degree), the practice of glue

[8] Irving Bieber, M.D., & Associates, *Homosexuality: A Psychoanalytic Study*, New York: Basic Books. 1962, Chapter I.
[9] *Ibid.*, p. 18.

sniffing represents an indirect approach to sexual satisfaction. The large majority of glue sniffers falls into an age group which is neither expected nor culturally permitted to seek direct sexual gratification through contact with the opposite sex. Many older adolescent males do occasionally engage in intercourse, but this is much less frequently the case within the younger adolescent and preadolescent age groups from which a substantial proportion of glue sniffers is derived. However, even at those age levels where overt sexual activity is culturally prohibited, various manifestations of sexual identification are culturally encouraged and form an important aspect of personality development. The development of an emotional dependence on a bizarre pattern of gratification, like the pattern presumably provided by glue sniffing, will result in a lessening of dependence on external sources of gratification, and thus interfere with the development of interest in the opposite sex. It is likely that the development of emotional dependence on glue sniffing is itself indicative of a withdrawal of interest from external objects.

In both the narcotic addict and the glue sniffer, there is likely to be a pronounced deficiency of normal sexual interest. This makes each of them particularly susceptible to modes of gratification which are indirectly rather than directly sexual. As such a pattern of indirect satisfactions is formed, it is likely to lead to a further loss of interest in normal sexual outlets. When a boy becomes psychologically dependent on glue, he runs the risk of losing any sexual interest in girls. Because he is likely to be far younger than the typical narcotic addict, it is plausible to assume that the confirmed sniffer's psychic structure is in a more vulnerable condition.

The development of anyone's traits of character and personality is not an overnight process. The point in this process at which the technique of by-passing the sexual system is first acquired is very important. The individual's most profound sexual attitudes, and for that matter his most basic attitudes toward life itself, are here most deeply concerned. It is not so much the practice of glue sniffing but rather the growth of a psychological dependence on it that presents a danger of turning the boy aside from normal sexual interests. Here it may again be emphasized that the young people most likely to develop this emotional dependence on glue sniffing are precisely those whose inner nature predisposes them to a less-than-normal interest in the opposite sex.

The available data suggest that these boys have very low opinions of themselves, and have difficulty in communicating with others. They are likely to be passive and victims of anxiety. They withdraw from social situations, tend to be disorganized, and have a weak personality which may break down under situations of stress. In large measure, glue sniffing is a reflection of a boy's susceptibility to social pressure. The high incidence of delinquency among sniffers may occur primarily among those who have been moved to it by just such pressure.[10]

Significant Findings in Sexual Behavior. The most comprehensive study of the sexual behavior of human males and females was conducted by Dr. Alfred C. Kinsey and his associates. Their conclusions were based upon data obtained from the voluntary reports of 5,300 males and 5,940 females interviewed. The studies represent an age and a geographic cross-section of American males and females. Dr. Kinsey emphasized the fact that the relatively small samplings make it impossible to arrive at a scientifically sound generalization concerning the sexual behavior of all human males and females in the United States. Moreover, the validity of the conclusions based upon the samplings is dependent upon the correctness of the voluntary reports. The ideas presented here are based on the findings of Kinsey and his associates.[11]

The public was greatly aroused by the Kinsey findings. Some of the unfortunate social outcomes of the publication of the Kinsey reports are the results of unintelligent misunderstanding

---

[10] Charles Winick and Jacob Goldstein, *The Glue Sniffing Problem,* New York: The American Social Health Association, 1965, pp. 13–15.

[11] A. C. Kinsey, W. B. Pomeroy, and C. E. Martin, *Sexual Behavior in the Human Male,* Philadelphia: W. B. Saunders Company, 1948; and *Sexual Behavior in the Human Female,* Philadelphia: W. B. Saunders Company, 1953.

of the number limitation of the studies and an unscientific proneness to draw sweeping conclusions from particular data. Regardless of the reactions of public opinion concerning the work of Dr. Kinsey and his associates, their investigation presented evidence of certain significant characteristics of male and female sexual behavior and trends in modern sex life that pose serious problems of sexual adjustment. Some of the characteristic likenesses and differences in the sex life of males and females, as reported by Kinsey, already have been referred to; certain other developmental tendencies and practices are presented here. The facts and percentages given are based upon *a limited sample that may or may not be representative of the population as a whole.*

Significant Aspects in Sexual Behavior. The Kinsey reports reveal significant data relative to sexual practices of males and females at different stages of their development and during single and married life. Kinsey emphasized the fact that all individuals differ in their sex responses and practices; no one person fits into an assumed normal or average pattern. There appears to be a considerable change in the sex habits of women since World War I; heavy petting and premarital sexual intercourse are engaged in by a larger number of girls and women; since 1900 frigidity has declined among women by about one third.

The peak of sexual strength is reached by men before the age of twenty; for most women the age is twenty-seven or twenty-eight. Once women reach their peak of sexual activity they usually maintain a steady level until their fifties, sometimes into their sixties. The male peak is far higher than that of women; male sexual activity remains higher for a longer period of time. In spite of this fact, most men are growing old in sexual capacity when their wives are becoming more interested in and often less inhibited in sex, especially if a wife is younger than her husband. The fact that women do not show aging effects may create problems of compatibility between the married partners.

FREUD'S EXPLANATION OF DRIVE. Freud held that all behavior was determined by unconscious drives, called instincts, which affected behavior in devious and disguised ways and functioned as causative forces in striving toward a goal. He viewed these drives as an accumulation of psychic energy (libido) available to and used by the individual. He believed that the newborn baby comes into the world with libidinal impulses that are unrelated to reality factors. The child is unable to distinguish between the real and the unreal and cannot inhibit impulses. It is believed that the libido, which represents the total psychic energy possessed by the individual, arises from the sexual and aggressive needs of the individual. For example, children have the urge to fight and destroy. Libidinal energy may be expressed in general excitement of the individual, or it may be associated with an object in the environment. Although psychic energy is believed to be objectless at birth, the child gradually becomes involved with other individuals and objects in his environment as he develops. Hence, any sexual and aggressive impulses of infancy and early childhood help explain important aspects of behavior.

The libido is basic to Freud's theory of psychosexual development, which the child moves through in four general stages. He considered the first three stages, which occur during the first five years of life, to be of tremendous importance. These are the *oral stage,* the *anal stage,* and the *phallic stage.* The fourth stage (the *genital stage*) is associated with sexual maturity. However, Freud believed that there is a latency period between the years of five and of early adulthood.

In the *oral stage* the child's principal sources of pleasure center in the erogenous areas of the mouth. He puts his hand and other objects into his mouth, which serves as the focus of discharge of sexual energy. He derives pleasure from biting, sucking, and eating. If he is not adequately satisfied or if he is frustrated in this gratification, he may develop patterns of passivity, dependency, or excessive oral tendencies.

The *anal stage* is reached as the focus of libidinal discharge is shifted from the mouth to the anal region. Toilet training gives the child his first real experience in which he is confronted with external regulation of instinctive impulses. What is done here is important in personality development. On the one hand, care needs to be exercised to insure that the child does not hold back his feces, for there is the danger that he may develop obstinate tendencies or even defecate at inappropriate times. On the other hand, overstrict training may lead to the development of drives toward conformity or compulsiveness.

The *phallic stage* falls between the ages of three and five when the child begins to focus on himself and his genitals as a source of libidinal gratification. The child's fantasy life, which develops at this stage, together with his physical exploration and autoerotic activity, gives rise to the *Oedipus complex*. During this developmental process, attachment to the parent of the opposite sex is formed. The mother becomes the object of the boy's sexual desires, and the father becomes the object of the girl's sexual desires. The boy may develop an incestuous craving for his mother, thus experiencing conflict because of his resentment of his father. For example, he may develop a *castration complex*, believing that his father is going to remove his genitals as a punishment for his craving. A girl, on the other hand, may develop *penis envy*, the female version of castration anxiety.

The *genital stage* is the final or mature stage of psychosexual development. It is characterized by mature and responsible social-sexual relationships that emerge from the earlier stages of sexual activity. In the genital stage the man or the woman is attracted to a partner of the opposite sex: the normal sexual behavior of adult individuals (heterosexual). However, in the process of attaining the genital stage, individuals may go through a brief homosexual experience with a person of their own sex whom they look up to. In the normal course of growth, sexual development does not move smoothly from one stage to another. The fact that there is often a residue of earlier attachments indicates that the shift from one stage to the next is not clear-cut. However, if there is a prolonged lag in normal progress from one stage to the next, the individual may need professional help to correct the problems resulting from his arrested development. Freud and his followers made use of psychoanalysis to alleviate deviate aggression and deviate sexual behavior that were expressions of these residual drives.

A CHALLENGE OF PRIMARY DRIVES AS THE BASIS FOR MOTIVATION. In an explanation of drives in the motivation of human behavior, I have joined many who hold that human drives have a physiological and instinctive basis. Robert W. White challenged these interpretations, holding that there is a deepening discontent with the drive-reduction theory of Hull and the psychoanalytic theory of Freud. White presents his arguments in a lengthy article in the *Psychological Review* of September, 1959. The entire article is provocative and worth the time of the reader. We present his summary here:

. . . there is widespread discontent with theories of motivation built upon primary drives. Signs of this discontent are found in realms as far apart as animal psychology and psychoanalytic ego psychology. In the former, the commonly recognized primary drives have proved to be inadequate in explaining exploratory behavior, manipulation, and general activity. In the latter, the theory of basic instincts has shown serious shortcomings when it is stretched to account for the development of the effective ego. Workers with animals have attempted to meet their problem by invoking secondary reinforcement and anxiety reduction, or by adding exploration and manipulation to the roster of primary drives. In parallel fashion, psychoanalytic workers have relied upon the concept of neutralization of instinctual energies, have seen anxiety reduction as the central motive in ego development, or have hypothesized new instincts such as mastery. It is argued here that these several explanations are not satisfactory and that a better conceptualization is possible, indeed that it has already been all but made.

In trying to form this conceptualization, it is first pointed out that many of the earlier tenets of primary drive theory have been discredited by recent experimental work. There is no longer any compelling reason to identify either pleasure or reinforcement with drive reduction, or to think of motivation as requiring a source of energy external to the nervous system. This opens the way for considering in their own right those aspects of animal and human behavior in which stimulation and contact with the environment seem to be sought and welcomed, in which raised tension and even mild excitement seem to be cherished, and in which novelty and variety seem to be enjoyed for their own sake. Several reports are cited which bear upon interest in the environment and the rewarding effects of environmental feedback. The latest contribution is that of Woodworth (1958), who makes dealing with the environment the most fundamental element in motivation.

The survey indicates a certain unanimity as to the kinds of behavior that cannot be successfully conceptualized in terms of primary drives. This behavior includes visual exploration, grasping, crawling and walking, attention and perception, language and thinking, exploring novel objects and places, manipulating the surroundings, and producing effective changes in the environment. The thesis is then proposed that all of these behaviors have a common biological significance: they all form part of the process whereby the animal or child learns to interact effectively with his environment. The word *competence* is chosen as suitable to indicate this common property. Further, it is maintained that competence cannot be fully acquired simply through behavior instigated by drives. It receives substantial contributions from activities which, though playful and exploratory in character, at the same time show direction, selectivity, and persistence in interacting with the environment. Such activities in the ultimate service of competence must therefore be conceived to be motivated in their own right. It is proposed to designate this motivation by the term effectance, and to characterize the experience produced as a *feeling of efficacy*.

In spite of its sober biological purpose, effectance motivation shows itself most unambiguously in the playful and investigatory behavior of young animals and children. Specimens of such behavior, drawn from Piaget (1952), are analyzed in order to demonstrate their constantly transactional nature. Typically they involve continuous chains of events which include stimulation, cognition, action, effect on the environment, new stimulation, *etc*. They are carried on with considerable persistence and with selective emphasis on parts of the environment which provide changing and interesting feedback in connection with effort expended. Their significance is destroyed if we try to break into the circle arbitrarily and declare that one part of it, such as cognition alone or active effort alone, is the real point, the goal, or the special seat of satisfaction. Effectance motivation must be conceived to involve satisfaction—a feeling of efficacy—in transactions in which behavior has an exploratory, varying, experimental character and produces changes in the stimulus field. Having this character, the behavior leads the organism to find out how the environment can be changed and what consequences flow from these changes.

In higher animals and especially in man, where so little is innately provided and so much has to be learned about dealing with the environment, effectance motivation independent of primary drives can be seen as an arrangement having high adaptive value. Considering the slow rate of learning in infancy and the vast amount that has to be learned before there can be an effective level of interaction with surroundings, young animals and children would simply not learn enough unless they worked pretty steadily at the task between episodes of homeostatic crisis. The association of interest with this "work," making it play and fun, is thus somewhat comparable to the association of sexual pleasure with the biological goal of reproduction. Effectance motivation need not be conceived as strong in the sense that sex, hunger, and fear are strong when violently aroused. It is moderate but persistent, and in this, too, we can discern a feature that is favorable for adaptation. Strong motivation reinforces learning in a narrow sphere, whereas moderate motivation is more conducive to an exploratory and experimental attitude which leads to competent interactions in general, without reference to an immediate pressing need. Man's huge cortical association areas might have been a suicidal piece of specialization if they had come without a steady, persistent inclination toward interacting with the environment.[12]

Psychological and Social Drives

Motives arising from inner urges find expression in habitual goal-attaining behavior. These active processes, originating in inherent potentialities, change with experience. During childhood, motivated behavior tends to be self-centered. Later, the individual is motivated by additional influences that lie outside himself. In his expanding desire to do for others he attempts to include small intimate groups of his own selection. Gradually, these groups reach out to embrace the entire family, schoolmates, and eventually the members of the community in which he lives. During adolescence and adulthood, his activities and interests are affected by his desire to cooperate with intimate groups and organizations.

[12] Robert W. White, "Motivation Reconsidered: The Concept of Competence," *Psychological Review*, September, 1959, pp. 328–330.

Individuals are social beings. In their relations with others they exhibit individual differences in their expression of attitudes and behavior. Either may be pleasing or annoying to others. Most social motives are grounded in physiological needs and are conditioned by the behavior of others. Some social motives are widespread in one culture and absent from another. The competitive drive is an example. Among the motives that have social significance are those concerned with success and mastery, recognition and approval, superiority, sympathy, security, adventure, and sex.

THE DRIVE TO SUCCEED AND TO ACHIEVE. The successful completion of a coveted project is an experience that is difficult to share with others. It gives inner satisfaction to the individual and serves to strengthen his bodily tonus for further activity. Although others may often give unlimited praise for an individual's successful achievement, too often they might speak otherwise if they were to express their true feelings. Nevertheless, the individual who makes progress in achieving, even to a small degree, that in which he is interested earns thereby a satisfaction that is important to him in his growth and development.

Successful effort predisposes toward continued activity. A feeling of success is an important factor in child development and emotional release. A child or an adult may strive for many hours to attain a relatively insignificant goal if it represents a satisfying degree of achievement for him. He personally experiences great satisfaction from planning an action, overcoming an obstacle, or demonstrating a skill in which he is proficient. The pleasure derived from activities that are accompanied by anticipated success is a most powerful motivating force.

Everyone needs to experience success in worth-while activity. The school should so gear its program to individual capacity as to permit constant success for each child regardless of his ability or interest. By this is meant that each child should be encouraged to achieve progressively in chosen projects. Successful activity will enable him to find himself and not be inhibited in behavior by those inner conflicts that have tended to restrict child behavior.

Since individuals differ because of inherited and environmental factors, school people can organize training in terms of the experience and ability level of the individual student so that he may be stimulated by the success drive that is so fruitful of productive activity. Just as the manager succeeds or fails in light of the spirit shown by the members of the baseball team or their belief in the cause for which they are striving, so is the child able to make progress when he is interested in the activity. We can help him keep it there when we provide stimulating and challenging situations for him to meet and solve.

THE DRIVE TO AVOID FAILURE AND DISAPPOINTMENT.   The desire to avoid failure is powerful. It is only after an individual has developed a habit of success that he is able to view unemotionally a situation that challenges mastery. Children need to be helped to appreciate the fact that even though they do not always meet acceptable standards in their work, their efforts in most instances do not represent complete failure. Some individuals, however, are so constituted that their chief concern is to push ahead regardless of the relative success of their achievement. If the leader accepts their careless work, such individuals tend to become less and less accurate and are finally unable to meet accepted standards. It is as important for a leader to require high standards of production as it is for him to cater to the interests of individuals.

All individuals cannot be expected to attain the same level of achievement or goal, but authorities should provide competitive situations that are more realistic than they have been. In this way many children can avoid the disgrace of retardation in school and at the same time be assisted in the development of skills and attitudes that are beneficial to them. The competition then need not be a matter of reaching the degree of mastery achieved by others, but competition with one's own past record in striving to attain higher goals.

Observe the behavior of a child when he fails to do that which he is striving to do. What do you observe in his behavior? Do you find him carrying his head erect or does it droop a little? The learning process can be inhibited or stimulated through teaching techniques. The school that emphasizes failure is not giving the pupil the best chance to get ahead. A teacher who emphasizes success and so individualizes instruction that the learning of the child will be a continuous process rather than a matter of mere promotion from grade to grade is giving attention to individual differences. In the name of good mental hygiene for all concerned—the bright, the average, and the dull—the system of promotions needs to be changed. Teachers then will be prepared to report on the progress of the child at any stage of his school life in terms of accomplishment and not in terms of how many subjects he has not "passed."

Some teachers allow the danger of failure to become a major fear to a learner. Failure is so powerful and so overwhelming that it often inhibits children to the extent that they lose their ability to function effectively. This denies them the success feeling that they normally would have attained had the fear of failure not been instilled.

I am not suggesting that "failure" can be eliminated from life experiences; but I do suggest that more can be done in school life to eliminate the fear effects of failure. A pattern too often has been followed that has helped make educational loafers of the bright and failures and misfits of the dull.

THE MASTERY DRIVE. The dominant drive basic to the success and happiness of human beings is considered by some to be that of superiority. Everyone has a strong desire to be superior in at least one type of activity. People crave activity, but even more do they desire to excel—to be better than other persons. An individual is not so much interested in the perfection of his product as he is in the fact that it is better than another to which he can compare his own. This attitude is based partly on the realization that he has attained a satisfactory degree of mastery as compared with other work with which he is familiar.

An awareness of ineffectual performance sometimes serves as a stimulus for additional activity in an attempt to perfect skills that are known by the person but that seem to be unattainable. Any degree of conflict that may arise in the individual as a result of such attempted mastery is detrimental to personality development if the individual is forced to achieve his feeling of superiority through evasion or other compensatory measures. A feeling of inferiority, however, may be overcome through participation in a socially desirable activity, and the total effect may be beneficial. It is unfortunate if a drive is so strong that the resulting mental and emotional conflicts can be resolved for the immediate satisfaction of the individual only by his resorting to extreme antisocial measures, such as lying, stealing, or cheating.

It is not enough simply to be doing something. The human

bcing desires to be able to do at least one thing well. Adler believed that the human being desires *to be superior* in some way and that this is the dominant motive underlying basic human behavior. There may be a question about this conclusion. Yet all will agree that "mastery" is fundamental to individual development. The human being seeks to gain attention to and approval of his ideals. When he can socialize his interests, the mastery drive becomes especially wholesome and fruitful.

Attempts by an individual to establish superiority in certain activities very often are responses to a recognition of his weaknesses. If this feeling of inferiority is compensated for through a socially valuable activity, the effect is beneficial. On the other hand, if the individual attempts to achieve superiority through an evasion or another compensating measure, the total effect will be the development of undesirable personality qualities. Or, if this person is trained to make wise use of his abilities, energies, and time, he may extend the greatest possible latitude to the urge of becoming the master of himself, of a certain field of knowledge, or of the situations in which he finds himself from day to day.

THE DESIRE FOR RECOGNITION AND APPROVAL.   The urge for recognition and approval is closely associated with the success urge, but its functioning concerns the attitude of others as well as the inner satisfaction that accompanies achievement through application of one's effort to an individual project. All people experience a feeling of satisfaction in the successful completion of tasks. However, the feeling is magnified and intensified when it is given the approval of the group. Many behavior problems in school are the direct results of the failure on the part of a teacher to give proper recognition or approval to the respective achievements of a child. When a child cannot obtain approval through desirable and acceptable means, he often uses other less desirable techniques.

A boy is careful of his English in a group because he desires approval; a girl dresses as she does because she seeks recognition; a college student conforms or does not conform in order to gain attention for himself. There are great differences among people as to the kind of approval that is desired and as to the form that the approval will take. In our daily life we take too many people for granted. A housewife works many hours preparing an attractive and well-balanced dinner, hoping for an expression of appreciation. A teacher or a student has done a good piece of work for which he desires approval. The giving of deserved praise takes little time and is productive of so much personal satisfaction to the deserving person or persons that the recognition given usually is followed by more and better efforts on the part of the individual praised.

The individual not only wants to succeed, but he wants his achievements to be recognized by others. The attention given to him and to his efforts stimulates him to further productive activity. He usually is less concerned with the sincerity or insincerity of the expressed approval than he is with the fact that it has been given. Praise is a powerful stimulator of interest that results in activity which removes many, if not most, of the conflicts that may have been latent. The individual very often needs to receive an objective appraisal of his efforts by others. He is so close to what he has been doing that he may over- or underestimate its real worth. Abraham Lincoln, for example, thought that the address which he gave at Gettysburg was a failure and was downhearted about it until he discovered that the verdict of the listeners was quite different from his own evaluation of his performance.

The wise leader appreciates also the effective use of disapproval. It is one of his strongest aids in directing behavior into the channels in which it should go. To be willing to give praise when and if deserved, to be ready to disapprove misbehavior, and to recognize and approve desirable attitudes are basic to the development of socially commendable and effective attitudes that will function in a wholesome way in the life of an individual.

THE URGE FOR SYMPATHY. Human beings crave all the attention they can obtain from others. If they injure themselves or suffer reverses, they seek someone to whom they can tell their experience. If the listener displays appreciative understanding, great relief is experienced. It is relatively easy to seek sympathy or to accept it. The transmitting of sympathy, however, is difficult. Words are inadequate to transmit the extent of one's feelings or emotions to another. Everyone has difficulty in finding appropriate words to express the sorrow he feels in the misfortune of another.

Sympathy is a dominant drive of the individual. He constantly seeks the sympathy of others. A child faced with a difficult problem needs to talk about it with a sympathetic listener in order to give support to his ego. If a child receives a scolding the sting is eased if he can talk about it to an individual who displays an understanding attitude. If a child injures himself he can endure the pain more bravely in the presence of those who show by their actions that they know how badly it hurts. This tends to comfort him and relax tension.

Any problem that requires the sympathetic understanding of a superior or of a group can be handled in the light of all the inherent factors. Sympathy can be given in a wholesome manner. It needs, however, to be given objectively, and continued so long as its effects are of positive value to the person needing it. As much harm can come from its use as can good, if the person learns to withdraw from situations just to get the sympathy of others. It may be better in that case to withhold sympathy and offer an understanding reproof.

Even though sympathy is sought by all of us in varying degrees, at different times and under different circumstances, tactful expressions of it often seem difficult. Have you ever felt helpless in trying to extend your true feelings to another? To sympathize is to experience, with the hope that the other person will appreciate your true feeling toward him in the specific situation under consideration. At a time of great sorrow we try to be sympathetic. We search for words and know that they are inadequate because we realize that we can feel so much more than we can reveal through words. Fortunately, the other person usually is able to recognize the sincerity of our affection, sympathy, or respect even though our overt expression of these attitudes may be inadequate.

THE URGE FOR SECURITY. Everyone wants to be secure in the respect of another, or to be sure that he is in favor with his parents, other relatives, neighbors, or peers. The desire for security is one of the powerful socializing urges. It assists an individual to be agreeable to others and helps him build a society with interests sufficiently similar to permit people to live together in peace and harmony. It is distasteful to be out of favor with the leader of a particular group in which the individual is extremely interested. Secret societies and college fraternities recognize the extent to which they can compel candidates to perform ridiculous stunts in order to be accepted by the membership of the organization.

To be secure in the affection of the opposite sex is an urge strong enough to cause many changes in the behavior of the adolescent. The boy begins to spruce up, to comb his hair, to brush his teeth, to wear ties without being coaxed, to shine his shoes, and to exhibit many other traits that were not apparent before his newly awakened interest or urge. A girl, with the awakening of her interest in boys, develops techniques and mannerisms that often bewilder her elders.

A feeling of insecurity is one of the most serious factors of maladjustment. An individual, in order to be satisfied with his life adjustment, needs to be sure that he has earned the respect and admiration of his coworkers, that he is secure in the affections of his family and of his intimate friends, that he is in no danger of losing his job, and that he and his family may be reasonably certain to enjoy financial security throughout their lives. The child craves the security of his parents' love and protection; the individual at any age desires to be confident that his presence is welcomed in his social group; the worker needs to be sure that his workmanship and his employer's financial stability are such that he is relatively free from the fear of adverse criticism or loss of his job.

Economic security is an important mental and emotional adjuster. An increasing number of persons are seeking affiliation with organizations that offer tenure of job and pension rights. Consequently, the number of civil-service employees has increased tremendously. Workers gradually become interested in stable and permanent though possibly lower incomes rather than in immediately higher but possibly insecure wages. Desire for security against loss of income resulting from death, disease, accident, unemployment, and similar factors of economic insecurity has materially advanced the popularity of all forms of public and private insurance plans.

All individuals are interested in financial security. Some women and men marry to satisfy this urge, and men and women work long and diligently to avoid insecurity. Worry overtakes many individuals in their attempt to satisfy this drive. Some persons worry about the loss of their jobs and its effect on them or their family, some worry about their old age, and others worry about misfortunes that never happen. Social Security, pension systems, Medicare, and insurance are based upon the strength of this urge. A feeling of security gives a confidence that is valuable hygienically and is of great benefit to the social order where it is implemented.

THE DRIVE FOR ADVENTURE. There is a persistent urge to experience the new and the different. Children have abundant opportunities to exercise this urge; yet, because so many of their activities are planned for them and carefully supervised, they often feel frustration. Children often "play school" and evolve rules that are more severe than those of an actual school situation, or they participate in imaginary activities that would be terrifying to elders.

Children find little difficulty in discovering excellent outlets for their spirit of adventure; but to the extent that the adult's regular work is routinized, he must satisfy this urge in other ways. He may turn, for relief, to gambling or to some other *undesirable* habit. This urge is sometimes satisfied through attendance at a night club, through the frequenting of the "hangout" of the gang where the adventure is largely a matter of tall stories, or through actual exploits that are harmful to the community.

Children get into trouble with their elders, boys and girls leave home, men join the army, girls and boys marry, young people plan parties or other social activities—often in the spirit of adventure. The fast pace of modern life and the excessive seeking of excitement, however, indicate the lengths to which individuals are willing to go in order to experience the new and the different. When these stimuli do not suffice, they combine the automobile and a bottle of liquor and temporarily enlarge the experience. A denial of many adolescent urges toward adventuresome behavior causes conflicts that are rarely resolved, mainly because we have not yet learned how to deal with these youthful cravings. Witness the large increase in delinquent behavior.

It is normal to want to see a new car, a new face, a new scene, a new picture, a new anything. In some people these drives are spasmodic and completely unplanned. That is, a person does not want to participate in planned activity. He wants to be free to follow his whims of the moment. He decides to do one thing today and another tomorrow. Another person develops some control of his spirit of adventure. Consequently, he eventually gains his desired experiences but is the better for it since he has cultivated the art of living and experiencing in a systematized way. He knows that he will be able to get across the river much more quickly by ferrying than by swimming.

The wise leader constantly provides situations that awaken the spirit of adventure in desirable ways, thereby satisfying the drive through exhilarating and productive activities. Awaken his interest, and a man will have as much enjoyment in working with a new idea as he will with the *new* in other situations.

THE SEX DRIVE (Psycho-social Aspects). The sex drive is one of the most important and dominating influences in the life of a person. The conflicts between this elemental urge and the restrictions and inhibitions of social conventions and moral codes are present in all lives and become pronounced in some. As a result of the many taboos connected with sex, a passing thought or a dream with sexual connotations may become emotionally charged and embedded in the conscience of certain individuals and be a cause for worry unless relieved by an understanding person.

The persistence of the sex drive makes necessary a healthful psychological development of the individual for the good of himself and of society. The psychosexual urges include the thoughts, feelings, and emotions that accompany the physical maturing of the sex glands and organs. Mental and emotional attitudes toward sex are greatly influenced by the conditioning of an individual's environment, and, therefore, each person develops certain ways of thinking and feeling toward sex which affect his sex drive.

In the integration and adjustment of personality the sex drive affects the development of ethical and social relationships. Since the meaning of sex to adolescents is still vague and sometimes faulty, they tend to expand on their real or imagined escapades. Boys use tall stories to gain prestige; girls boast about their dates and their popularity with the members of the opposite sex. Sex conflicts arise partly because of societal denials and partly because of the belief of adolescents that they should experiment in order to demonstrate their adulthood.

Today adolescents are influenced in making decisions about sex practices by changing codes of behavior and differing points of view on what constitutes desirable behavior between mature adolescents. They are faced with setting up their own standards based on the different points of view that are aired in their own groups and in books and magazine articles. Recently, the father of four preadolescent boys and a girl advocated greater freedom between the sexes, including sexual intercourse for sexually mature adolescents. He believes that educators should approve of his idea. Specifically he suggests the following:

> The present sexual code requiring premarital chastity is spiritually destructive in the strongest sense. Among other things, it inculcates the most blatant hypocrisy as a basic tenet of American civilization. The code requires boys as well as girls to be chaste; yet few self-respecting high school or college boys would admit virginity. The boy either breaks the code or has to lie to save face. Both these acts are more immoral and more dishonest than sexual intercourse. This situation also perpetuates the well-known and well-detested double standard, since girls may not admit lack of virginity. . . .
>
> The present sexual crisis among adolescents has been brought on not by a growing moral laxity in our society but by the intransient puritanical moral code. As with most of the problems of the world, it has been brought about by unthinking acceptance of assumptions that are not true: in this case the assumption that premarital sexual intercourse is intrinsically and inherently bad.[13]

After reading this article a seventeen-year-old girl sent her suggestions to the Editor of *The New York Times Magazine.* Among other things she said:

> Changing the sexual code of society "to allow sexually mature persons to engage in sexual intercourse as they choose" is ridiculous. It goes against the basis of sex in marriage as a union between husband and wife. I say this because allowing sexually mature persons to indulge in sexual intercourse with whomever they please includes husbands and wives, children of 13 and younger, the mentally

---

[13] William G. Cowan, Letter to the Editor, "Sex Among Teen-agers," *The New York Times Magazine,* March 27, 1966, pp. 90, 92.

disturbed, etc. Perhaps a boy of 15 or a girl of 16 is sexually mature. However, he or she is far from being emotionally mature for love affairs or sexual intercourse with anyone.

Of course, you can hand out contraceptives to teenagers, and teach them to use them correctly. Then what do you have at the age of 21? Thousands of people to whom sex is just something else to do. "Let's do it tonight—there are no good movies playing anywhere." [14]

Another point of view is expressed by a mother of four boys,[15] who makes several points relative to premarital sexual intercourse. It is her belief that if a boy is briefed on sex by his mother and father, he will be able to obtain a better perspective of the total problem. She accepts the fact that there is pleasure derived from the experience but calls attention to the suffering that may accompany or follow it. The societal stigma of having a child out of wedlock is borne by the girl, not by the boy who fathered it. Although the boy who impregnates a girl may seem to escape the stigma, he is deeply involved, a fact that will remain with him all of his life. The writer wants her sons to be so well informed that they can make their own decisions about premarital sexual intercourse. She hopes that if one of them decides to experience premarital sex that it will be because both he and the girl feel that it is an honorable way of participating in a "profound relationship." She wants sex behavior to be based on a full knowledge of the responsibilities and possible consequences.

During adulthood, sex conflicts arise from numerous causes. The middle-aged man who recognizes a lessened interest in sexual intercouse may accuse his wife of being unfaithful. The man may select a younger woman to satisfy his sex interest or to demonstrate his virility. The alcoholic may drink to excess to attempt to prove his potency. A young woman, as a result of too rigid training during her girlhood, may be frigid or overmodest in her sex relations. As she approaches the menopause, conflict may arise between her recognition of her changed sexual life and her sex interests or, if she still is unmarried, between her desire to

[14] Name Withheld, Letter to the Editor, "Teen-ager's View of Sex," *The New York Times Magazine*, April 24, 1966, p. 22.

[15] Arlene Silberman, "What Should I Tell My Son?" *The Reader's Digest*, May, 1966.

experience sex activity and the knowledge that she is probably
no longer sexually attractive.

Venereal Disease as a Social Side of Sex Practices. Venereal
disease is a general term that is applied to a group of extremely
contagious and serious diseases that usually are introduced into
the body through the genital organs by means of sexual contact.
Since they are likely to be contracted as a result of sexual intercourse with an infected person, they often are referred to as social
diseases.

Syphilis is induced by the introduction into the body of the
Spirochaeta pallida, a corkscrew-shaped microorganism. After infection, these germs multiply rapidly as they make their way into
the blood stream and are distributed throughout the body. The
infected individual may notice a pimple at the point of infection.
Since the pimple may disappear within a short time, he may not
realize that the germs are active within his body. The devastating
effects of the disease are experienced later in the form of severe
impairment of many vital organs. The final stage is paresis—a
destruction of the brain cells, resulting in mental enfeeblement.
The disease is highly contagious during the first and second
stages.

Gonorrhea, a disease that is more prevalent than syphilis, is
caused by a paired germ called gonococcus. Gonorrhea is a localized disease, in that it attacks the mucous membranes of the
genital organs and does not spread to other parts of the body.
The affliction may cause severe damage to the reproductive system, however. Although its total effects upon the inflicted individual may not be severe, it may cause sterility. The child of an
infected mother may be blind at birth. The germ can be killed,
however, if the newborn baby's eyes are washed with nitrate of
silver.

Occasionally syphilis is contracted by the germ entering the
body through a lesion in the skin or mucous membrane elsewhere than in the genital region. Fortunately, these germs cannot
live long outside the body. Hence there is little likelihood that a
person will acquire the disease from ordinary contacts. In order
to achieve recovery from either syphilis or gonorrhea it is essential that the symptoms of infection be recognized early and
treatment applied immediately. The germs usually can be killed
easily if they are attacked before they have had a chance to

TABLE 2

Cases of Syphilis and Gonorrhea and Rates for 100,000 Population Reported by State Health Departments, Fiscal Years 1950–1965

Fiscal Year	Primary and Secondary Syphilis		Early Latent Syphilis		Late and Late Latent Syphilis		Total Syphilis*		Gonorrhea		Total Infectious VD (P&S Syphilis & Gonorrhea)		Total VD (Syphilis† all stages & Gonorrhea)	
	Cases	Rate	Cases	Rate	Cases	Rate	Cases	Rate	Cases	Rate	Cases	Rate	Cases	Rate
1950	32,148	21.6	64,786	43.5	112,424	75.5	229,723	154.2	303,922	204.0	336,070	225.6	533,645	358.2
1951	18,211	12.1	52,309	34.7	107,133	71.1	198,640	131.8	270,459	179.5	288,670	191.6	469,099	311.3
1952	11,991	7.9	38,365	25.2	101,920	66.9	168,734	110.8	245,633	161.3	257,624	169.2	414,367	272.1
1953	9,551	6.2	32,287	20.8	100,195	64.7	156,099	100.8	243,857	157.4	253,408	163.6	399,956	258.2
1954	7,688	4.9	24,999	15.9	93,601	59.4	137,876	87.5	239,661	152.0	247,349	156.9	377,537	239.5
1955	6,516	4.1	21,553	13.4	84,741	52.7	122,075	76.0	239,787	149.2	246,303	153.3	361,862	225.2
1956	6,757	4.1	20,014	12.2	89,851	54.8	126,219	77.1	233,333	142.4	240,090	146.5	359,552	219.5
1957	6,251	3.8	19,046	11.4	96,856	58.1	130,552	78.3	216,476	129.8	222,727	133.6	347,028	208.1
1958	6,661	3.9	16,698	9.8	85,974	50.5	116,630	68.5	220,191	129.3	226,852	133.2	336,821	197.8
1959	8,178	4.7	17,592	10.2	86,776	50.1	119,981	69.3	237,318	137.0	245,496	141.7	357,299	206.3
1960	12,471	7.1	16,829	9.5	84,195	47.6	120,249	68.0	246,697	139.6	259,168	146.7	366,946	207.6
1961	18,781	10.4	19,146	10.7	80,942	45.0	125,262	69.7	265,685	147.8	284,466	158.5	390,947	217.5
1962	20,084	11.0	19,924	10.9	78,264	42.9	124,188	68.1	260,468	142.8	280,552	153.8	384,656	210.9
1963	22,045	11.9	18,683	10.1	81,736	44.1	128,450	69.3	270,076	145.7	292,121	157.6	398,526	215.0
1964	22,733	12.1	18,104	9.6	72,184	38.4	118,247	62.9	290,603	154.5	313,336	166.6	408,850	217.4
1965	23,250	12.3	17,315	9.1	67,633	35.7	113,018	59.7	310,155	163.8	333,405	176.1	423,173	223.5

* Includes congenital and other syphilis

† Excludes chancroid, granuloma inguinale, and lymphogranuloma venereum

Source: Today's VD Control Problem, A Joint Statement by the American Public Health Association, the American Social Health Association, the American Venereal Disease Association, and the Association of State and Territorial Health Officers with the cooperation of the American Medical Association.

multiply. It is important, therefore, that a person who suspects that he has been exposed to possible infection lose no time in consulting a physician for diagnosis and treatment.

Historically, the incidence of venereal disease has been high. Popular attitudes toward venereal infection have varied among differing cultures and developing stages of civilization. Venereal infection has been regarded by some cultural groups as a more or less natural concomitant of sexual intercourse. In other societies, an infected individual became a social outcast, unworthy of medical care.

A relatively recent recognition of the serious personal and social implications of these dread diseases has stimulated considerable concern over the effect of their spread upon human resources and adjustment. Vigorous campaigns are being waged to prevent their spread. Medical science is conducting extensive research that is aimed at arresting the progress of the disease or curing the afflicted person.

The fight to control the spread of syphilis and gonorrhea is far from won. States in which the number of cases per 100,000 population was the highest during 1965 are: New York, 19.4; Louisiana, 21.5; Mississippi, 22.7; North Carolina, 22.7; Georgia, 25.4; South Carolina, 33.9; Alabama, 38.6; and Florida, 38.7. States having the fewest number of VD cases per 100,000 population during 1965 were those of North Dakota, .2; Vermont, .2; Maine, .7; Kansas, .9; Idaho, .9; Wyoming, .9; Iowa, 1.2; Indiana, 1.5; and Utah, 1.6. The range for the remaining states falls between 2.0 and 19.0 per 100,000 population. Data for the country as a whole are given in Table 2.

Whether or not there should be greater premarital sexual intercourse is more than a matter of morals. The decision of promiscuity might well be made in terms of the right of one person knowingly to infect another and extend the suffering that accompanies venereal disease. Although various groups are trying to prevent the spread of VD little headway is being made. Agencies actively concerned with the VD problem include the American Public Health Association, the American Social Health Association, the American Venereal Disease Association, the Association of State and Territorial Health Officers, and the American Medical Association. Recently they sponsored a joint statement that was written and distributed by the American

Social Health Association. Among their suggestions to prevent the spread of VD are the following:

The search for syphilis through the process of interviewing and re-interviewing every person found to be infected with early syphilis, plus the cluster interviewing of suspects and associates, has been exhaustively pursued by state and city health departments during the past several years. Their goal is to identify and bring to examination and treatment every person who has been exposed to infection.

This is demonstrated by the detailed reports of 38 state and 76 local health departments setting forth the statistics recording their efforts over the two year period of fiscal years 1964 and 1965.

The staff member of the health department who interviews a patient who has been diagnosed as having infectious syphilis is sure of one thing: that the patient has been exposed to at least one other person who is infected and who was the source of his infection. The interviewer recognizes also that the chances are good that the patient may know more than one such other person, and that he may also have infected or exposed to infection one or more other persons. These are known as "spread contacts."

Armed with these facts, the interviewer points out to his patient that the other person or persons with whom the patient has had sexual contact must be alerted to their danger, must be examined and given treatment if infected. In this interview, the staff member must convince the patient of the seriousness of the disease, and of his responsibility to identify persons with whom he has had sexual contact both for their protection and for the protection of others with whom they have had sexual relations. The interviewer must convince his patient that however reluctant he may be to divulge information about his sexual activities, it is important that he do so. The promise of confidentiality as to the source of the interviewer's information and his concern only about the disease itself—not about the morals of his patient—are the key factors to a successful interview, yielding the names and addresses of his patient's sexual contact.

The interviewer also knows by experience that if his patient is a promiscuous person the patient probably knows other persons who are promiscuous, and who should be warned of the danger of becoming infected.

But long experience has taught that the patient seldom tells all in the first interview; that after a period of time has elapsed, and he has given further thought to his responsibility and is more relaxed about the interviewing experience, a re-interview will bring forth further information, such as a contact not previously "remembered," or an address of a contact which he has since been able to secure, or better identifying information on previously reported contacts. By this time the patient knows "the score" and is likely to be ready and willing to give the names of friends and acquaintances who are sexually promiscuous. The securing of this information is known as the "cluster" procedure.

Throughout this process, the patient must be assured of confidentiality about the information he gives. When he becomes convinced that strict confidentiality is being observed, his willingness to give information that will help in tracing infectious syphilis increases.

This description is an over-simplification of the interviewing process. Actually, the interviewer must probe into one of the most delicate of subjects with clients who come from a wide range of ages, experience and social status. They include teen-age boys and girls—some promiscuous, some caught in a first sexual experience, some bold and boasting of sexual prowess, some timid and fearful of their parents' reaction. They include men and women of varying social status, some unconcerned, some fearful of social disgrace if their infection should become known to their family and friends; the married man, afraid that his wife may learn of his infidelity and that he may have infected her; the married woman, perhaps even more fearful on the same basis. Perhaps the most fearful of all is the homosexual because he knows that his homosexual relations are not only socially disapproved, but also that they are illegal.

The interviewer assigned to this task must be carefully chosen for tact, sensitivity and natural ability to work with a variety of people and to adjust his approach to their personalities and backgrounds, Recruitment and training of VD interviewers is one of the major responsibilities of the VD Branch of the Public Health Service. The assignment of these interviewers to state and local health departments as a grant-in-aid from federal funds represents a contribution of first importance to the VD Control program.[16]

[16] *Today's VD Control Problem,* written and published by the American Social Health Association, New York, 1966, p. 20.

QUESTIONS AND PROBLEMS

1. By the use of illustrations, show that in motivated behavior you are in a state of readiness to become active.

2. Differentiate among the terms *drive, incentive,* and *homeostasis.* Give examples of each.

3. Discuss the interpretation of motivated behavior as exploratory variation that continues until a goal is achieved.

4. Show specifically that purpose and tensions are aspects of motivated behavior.

5. List at least five activity-arousing stimuli that are supplied by the environment.

6. Trace the genetic sequence of motives. Be specific.

7. Explain what is meant by unconscious motives. Try to recall the extent to which your behavior is motivated by them.

8. Differentiate between biological drives and psychological and social drives. Give examples.

9. Discuss the need for sleep. Try to discover the differing hours of sleep needed by you and your classmates. Explain any differences that you find.

10. Differentiate between the physiological and the psychological aspects of the sex drive.

11. How can a child be helped to break the habit of masturbation without instilling fear?

12. Discuss the possible effects upon an individual of engaging in homosexual activity.

13. Describe ways in which motives are affected by personal interests.

14. Discuss the influence of drives on overt behavior.

15. Explain the effects of imitation, suggestion, and integration on motives.

16. Study the summary of White and explain the differences that you find between his interpretation of drives and that of Freud.

17. What can the school people do to reduce the damaging effect of failure on learners?

18. In what ways may the approval or disapproval of another person become a motivating force in the life of an individual?

19. Review the social drives or urges presented in this chapter. Which of them are important motivators of your behavior? Explain.

20. Illustrate how the spirit of adventure can be satisfied in wholesome ways.

21. Explain why venereal disease is sometimes called a social disease. What can be done to curb its spread?

Selected Readings

Atkinson, J. W., *An Introduction to Motivation*. Princeton, N.J.: D. Van Nostrand Company, Inc., 1964.

Berkowitz, L., *The Development of Motives and Values in the Child*. New York: Basic Books, Inc., 1964.

Cofer, C. N., and M. H. Appley, *Motivation: Theory and Research*. New York: John Wiley & Sons, Inc., 1964.

Cory, D. W., and J. P. LeRoy, *The Homosexual and His Society: A View from Within*. New York: The Citadel Press, 1963.

Crowne, D. P., and D. Marlowe, *The Approval Motive: Studies in Evaluative Dependence*. New York: John Wiley & Sons, Inc., 1964.

Duffy, E., *Activation and Behavior*. New York: John Wiley & Sons, Inc., 1962.

Eysenck, H. J. (ed.), *Experiments in Motivation*. New York: The Macmillan Company, 1964.

Foss, B. (ed.), *Determinants of Infant Behavior*. New York: John Wiley & Sons, Inc., 1961.

Fuller, J. L., *Motivation: A Biological Perspective*. New York: Random House, Inc., 1962.

Hall, J. F., *Psychology of Motivation*. Philadelphia, Penna.: J. B. Lippincott Company, 1961.

Harvey, O. J., *Motivation and Social Interaction: Cognitive Determinants*. New York: The Ronald Press Company, 1963.

Jones, M. R. (ed.), *Nebraska Symposium on Motivation*. Lincoln: University of Nebraska Press, 1957.

Krech, D., and R. S. Crutchfield, *Elements of Psychology*. New York: Alfred A. Knopf, Inc., 1958. Part II.

Levine, D. (ed.), H. H. Kendler, R. W. Leeper, D. Premack, J. McV. Hunt, D. T. Campbell, and J. P. Guilford, *Nebraska Symposium on Motivation*. Lincoln: University of Nebraska Press, 1964.

Maslow, A. H., *Motivation and Personality*. New York: Harper & Row, Publishers, 1954.

Morgan, C. T., *Introduction to Psychology*, 3rd ed. New York: McGraw-Hill, Inc., 1966. Chapter 3.

Murray, E. J., *Motivation and Emotion*. Englewood Cliffs, N.J.: Prentice-Hall, Inc., 1964.

Rethlingschafer, D., *Motivation as Related to Personality*. New York: McGraw-Hill, Inc., 1964.

Shaffer, L. F., and E. J. Shoben, Jr., *The Psychology of Adjustment*, 2nd ed. Boston, Mass.: Houghton Mifflin Company, 1956.

Stacey, C. L., and M. F. DeMartino (eds.), *Understanding Human Motivation*, rev. ed. Cleveland, Ohio: Howard Allen, Inc., 1958.

Teevan, R. C., *Theories of Motivation in Personality and Social Psychology*. Princeton, N.J.: D. Van Nostrand Company, Inc., 1964.

Young, P. T., *Motivation and Emotion: A Survey of the Determinants of Human and Animal Activity*. New York: John Wiley & Sons, Inc., 1961.

❈ 4 ❈

IMPACT
OF EMOTIONS
ON
ADJUSTMENT

HUMAN BEINGS pride themselves on the fact that their behavior represents the activity of intellectual controls that are superior to the directive powers of lower animal forms. Observation of the ordinary activities of most individuals, however, leads to the conclusion that many human responses are influenced quite as much, if not more, by emotional urges and compulsions as by objective reasoning and judgment. Too often the emotional reaction comes first, and the intellectual justification for it either follows or is almost completely absent. We dare not minimize the effect of emotions on our behavior patterns.

THE BASES OF EMOTIONAL
EXPERIENCE

An emotion is but one phase of a comprehensive internal adjustment that takes place in order to enable higher animals to react as coordinated entities and to be more completely the master of sudden changes in their environment. An emotion is dynamic; it stimulates behavior that makes the person less rational as the emotion takes possession of him. In general, an emotion is concerned with a mobilization of available energy reserves. By utilizing necessary movements and functions, and by inhibiting or accelerating them in terms of his needs, an emotion may affect an individual's entire being.

Meaning of Emotion

In a definition of emotion the emphasis may be placed either on the bodily activities involved or on the overt behavior and feeling tones. An emotion is an affective experience that results from generalized adjustment. This affective experience is accompanied by mental and physiological stirred-up states in the individual. The result is a dynamic internal adjustment that operates for the protection and welfare of the individual. Emotions are great assets to the individual, giving richness and fullness to his life. However, if the emotions secure too great a hold on an individual, his behavior may display irrational tendencies.

Emotional expression results from the fusion of complex sensory experiences with the patterns of behavior already established as inherited or learned. Perception of the stimulus starts the emotional reaction which is not fully experienced until the feelings and other affective elements have been aroused through the operation of the autonomic nervous system. It is through the help of the endocrine system that responses are diffused and spread throughout the body, affecting the human being as a whole. Thus, emotions have both inherited and learned reaction patterns, involving visceral behavior and affective experiences that are generalized through the functioning of the vital functions: change of heart action, and release into the blood stream of energizing products of the endocrine secretions. Sartain, North, Strange, and Chapman suggest three aspects of emotion as follows:

All emotions have at least three aspects that may be analyzed and investigated. These aspects are the *physiological changes* in the body such as blood pressure and breathing; the *emotional behavior* shown by the person, such as laughing and crying; and the *personal emotional experience,* in which the individual knows and feels the emotions.[1]

Importance of Stimuli in Emotional Development

A specific stimulus is required to activate inherited potentialities and to utilize the learned patterns in the fusion of the complex experiences into what is called an emotional experience. Stimuli must be associated with interest or desire in order to become emotion-arousing factors. Any interest an individual may have in another individual, an object, or a situation is potential for an emotional reaction when and if the former is properly stimulated by an individual, object, or situation. The same external stimulus may have differing effects on different individuals or on the same individual at different times.

Certain stimuli are emotion-arousing at one time and not at other times. An object or a person in whom one is not interested may arouse no stirred-up states. Yet, if interest is developed later in the object or person, the denial of the possession of the object, or the loss of the privilege of speaking to the person is likely to result in emotional reaction. To be emotion-producing the stimulus must be associated with an interest or desire to attain the specific goal.

A stimulus will produce an emotion in terms of the interpretation of the stimulus by the individual. A stimulus that arouses one of the emotions does not arouse another emotion at the same time. A similar stimulus, however, may arouse different emotions at different times. For example, loud noises may arouse fear at one time, but later, if they are understood, may bring joy, elation, or anger. Stroking and caressing may arouse the emotion of affection but under a different setting may stimulate fear or anger. Richard S. Lazarus suggests the following in support of the cognitive appraisal of a stimulus in stress formation:

It has been shown here that threat, or at least stress reactions mediated psychologically, depend upon the cognitive appraisal of a stimulus. This is another way of talking

[1] Aaron Q. Sartain, Alvin J. North, Jack R. Strange, and Harold M. Chapman, *Psychology: Understanding Human Behavior,* 2nd ed., New York: McGraw-Hill, 1962, p. 103.

about the interpretation of the personal significance of the stimulus. Moreover, two kinds of appraisal, intellectualized on the one hand, and that based on denial and reaction formation on the other, result in the short-circuiting of the expected threat arousal. These modes of viewing a potentially threatening stimulus, based on the theory of ego defense, are not as readily accepted by all persons, but if they are, they make for a nonthreatening appraisal.

The experimental analogue involves two steps. One is the assumption that the subject, in watching a motion-picture film, identifies himself with the actors in the film as though he were one of them, and can be thus threatened by what is happening to them. The second stage in the analogue concerns the process of cognitive appraisal, in effect, that the orienting instructions and sound tracks produce varying appraisal processes of the sort involved in the concepts of denial and reaction or intellectualization, and that these, in turn, correspond to what occurs in the natural context.[2]

The duration of an emotional response is determined by the persistence of the stimuli. Evidence of good social adjustment is to be able to change the emotional experience rather rapidly if and when the stimuli that arouse these states are changed. It is possible for a person to be highly elated at one moment but, with the entrance upon the scene of a particular person, to experience quickly the emotion of hate, jealousy, fear, or envy. The normal human being, however, tends to be affected by many pleasant stimuli; the resulting emotional tension is quite satisfying to him.

The training and experience of an individual at any one time of his life influence the effectiveness of emotion-arousing stimuli. As the individual develops, as his interests and desires progress, as his health or general understanding is changed, so are his emotional reaction possibilities affected. The sick person may be aroused easily by stimuli that would not disturb him if he were well, and the healthy person may be stimulated by factors that would not affect him if he were ill.

The effectiveness of the stimulating force changes with situa-

2 Richard S. Lazarus, "A Laboratory Approach to the Dynamics of Psychological Stress," *American Psychologist*, June, 1964, p. 409.

tions. It is conditioned by an individual's desires at the moment, his state of health, and his understanding of all the attendant circumstances. The presence of a beautiful young woman may arouse emotions that are less potent in a man if he is happily married than if he is single. An undesirable social situation has little effect upon the emotional life of a person when he is not concerned with the problem. However, if he becomes actively interested in improving the situation, he is aroused by any slight comment about it that is presented.

Emotional States

The experience during an emotion is an individual one. It makes one intensely conscious of himself and tends to spread over the field of consciousness. We are "wild" with rage, "frozen stiff" with fear, "filled" with enthusiasm, "thrilled" with joy, "overwhelmed" by grief, "in the depth" of despair. Everything looks better to one who is in a cheerful mood than it does to one who has a case of the "blues." The experience that accompanies the release of energy during these bodily states can be described as representing the emotional state of the individual at any one time.

There is a continual flow of emotional experience that accompanies most of our behavior. These affective mental qualities arise from the facilitation, inhibition, and obstruction of the impulses resulting from external and internal stimuli. The resulting emotional states give richness to life and prevent monotony. Whether emotions are inherited or acquired, the long list of emotional states begins with the baser emotions, and extends through the socializing emotions to the more subtle emotions.

Factors of Emotional Growth

The feeling tones of an emotion arise during the first two years of life. Through maturation, learning, or conditioning, emotional patterns develop during babyhood to such a degree that definite emotional states are displayed. Bridges constructed a scale of possible emotional experiences to be expected during progressive stages of the first two years of the child's life. These are illustrated in Figure 1. In order for a child to experience an emotional reaction as such, he must be able to understand to

Figure 1. Changes in Emotional Behavior from Birth to Two Years

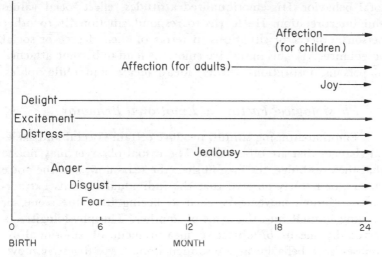

SOURCE: Based on data in "Emotional Development in Early Infancy," by Katherine M. B. Bridges, *Child Development,* March, 1932, p. 340.

some degree his own behavior and the behavior of others about him. Emotional patterns are thus established, modified, expanded, or repressed.

Some emotional patterns become relatively fixed at an early age; others undergo great refinement. With physiological growth the relationship between visceral reaction and the intensity of emotional experiences becomes more diffuse and perhaps even more persistent. The child is less likely to transfer his emotional reactions from one situation to another than is the adolescent or the adult. This may be accounted for partly by the child's inability to make abstractions. When his cortical areas are sufficiently developed, he coordinates his patterns of behavior through the inhibition, regulation, and directive control of his behavior by the active mental processes.

As an individual develops through childhood and adolescence into adulthood, his emotions assume characteristic behavior that causes the recognition of them as fear, anger, disgust, grief, hate, affection, and jealousy. As he becomes more proficient in conveying to others his true feelings, an appraisal of the emotional experience is made easier. Favorable emotional reactions usually accompany good health, attractive physical features, economic security, and satisfactory social status. The adolescent's appreciation of values, ambitions, or ideals tends to influence his total behavior. His emotionalized attitudes reflect social values and interpretation. He learns to respond emotionally to other persons, objects, or situations in terms of their degree of social acceptance. Also, his impulsive emotions tend to become attached to persons, institutions, duties, ideas, ideals, and philosophies.

Physiological Factors in Emotional Behavior

Emotion-arousing stimuli produce certain visceral and skeletal changes that are observable. The casual observer may notice that the eyes bulge, the face flushes, the tears flow, and the voice chokes, or he may observe that the individual exhibits extraordinary random movements, such as fleeing from the scene, or flinging himself into the arms of another. The physiologist observes, by means of objective measurement of emotional responses, such behavior as the sudden stopping of digestive movements, the change of blood flow from the trunk into the limbs, an increase in the blood pressure, especially in the main arteries of the limbs, increased endocrinal secretion, decreased flow of saliva, and so on.

The autonomic nervous system, affected as it is by the internal secretions of the endocrine glands, causes behavior that is physiologically significant. The emotional process is facilitated through the quick action of these glandular secretions. The secretion of adrenin helps to relax the smooth muscles, to rush blood to the surface of the body, to release glycogen into the blood stream, to increase the heartbeat, and to contract the blood vessels. Overactivity and underactivity of the thyroid gland produces, respectively, overexcitation and emotional sluggishness. Its normal functioning is required for desirable emotional stability. In general, emotional behavior is affected through the functioning of the endocrine glands, the visceral organs, the autonomic nervous system, and the lower midbrain areas, particularly the thalamus.

THE RELATION OF CERTAIN EMOTIONS
TO ADJUSTMENT

Of the numerous emotions that are associated with important problems of human adjustment, we shall discuss those adjustment problems that are associated with fear, worry, anger, jealousy, and affection. These emotional states appear so often during a person's waking hours that an understanding of their behavior and methods of controlling them becomes essential to a better understanding of the theory and practice of adjusted living.

Fear

THE INFLUENCE OF NORMAL FEAR ON BEHAVIOR.   The characteristic response of fear is that of retreat. The growing child learns gradually how to make his fears less evident to his associates. By the time he reaches adolescence, he has evolved techniques of explaining many of them away. Nevertheless, young children have many fears. They are taught to be afraid of the dark, of some animals, of noises, or of any situation that can be used to direct their behavior through the use of this negative approach. It is much better to have the child engage in positive behavior for the values to be derived from that experience. It may seem easier to direct behavior through the use of fear controls, yet the child pays the price in nervousness.

People learn to fear and avoid situations that threaten their safety, that disturb their sense of security, or that alarm. A constant state of fear may be aroused by walking on a high precipice, looking down from a height, or skating on thin ice. Persons then try to avoid such experiences; they are not at ease watching others in such situations. Increased heart action may result from watching a tightrope walker, even though he is in little danger of falling.

Perhaps the fears that are most dynamic in their functioning are those that are aroused indirectly. The child is afraid to recite in public because his father has said over and over that he (the father) was always afraid to speak in public. The child learns to have fear of snakes, of lightning, or of certain diseases because he has heard of the dangers connected with them. When the general attitude in the home is one of fear of a specific activity, the child is almost certain to fear the activity before he experiences it. Fear of the dark or of being alone is an ill-at-ease feeling for the child and is relieved by the presence of the mother or other person. Illness or nervousness increases the child's timidity.

It is a normal reaction to avoid unpleasant sensations. The

person who can let worms or caterpillars crawl up his arm is likely to be a hero to his peers. The harmless creatures are not to be feared, yet the very sight of bugs makes some people creep all over. The response is one of disgust. People avoid many things that they fear in part, such as insects, snakes, mice, or cold and clammy things. If fear is fed by an active imagination, disaster may result. A person may allow himself to anticipate robbers, contagion, ghosts, loss of investment, or anything that he would prefer not to have happen to him because it would interfere with his comfort or plans. (See Figure 2 for responses to fear-producing stimuli.)

Figure 2. Types of Responses to Fear-producing Stimuli

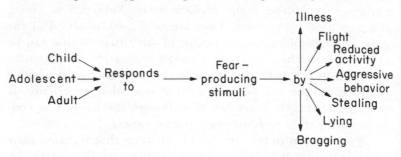

Teachers too often use the threat of failure as a device to awaken interest in schoolwork. However, instead of acting as a stimulant to the child to do his best, it may develop a fear of failure that will cause a detrimental emotional reaction. In order to promote emotional health in children, a competitive spirit is introduced so that it may function in the life of each child. Competing children, within the limits of general information and understanding for all competitive undertakings, ought to be equated in ability as closely as possible.

As the individual matures, he refines his behavior reactions to the extent that he represses many of his fear responses to the detriment of his emotional health. In his desire to conceal his fear, the adult sometimes attempts daring feats in order to impress his associates with his bravery. Fatigue may arouse fear since normal thinking is interfered with during overwork. Fatigue leads to fear, fear to worry, worry to fatigue, and thus among the nervous and physically weak the vicious cycle starts and continues. The individual needs a balance among his thinking, his feeling, and his doing.

Self-preservation is a fundamental urge in every individual; consequently, there is a tendency to avoid situations that in any way may threaten his safety or security. A person may fear animals, creeping or crawling creatures, darkness or dark places, storms, fire, closed places, high places, death, examinations, audiences, teachers, policemen, and the like. It also is possible for an individual to exhibit fear as he observes another person experience a fear-arousing situation.

Some fears are developed entirely by listening to another person recite his fear reaction in certain situations. For example, the child fears snakes because he has heard of their deadliness, or he fears to speak from a platform because he has heard members of his family discuss their fear reactions in such situations. He fears certain diseases because of the strong impression made on him by lectures or written accounts of the horrors of disease. The child is fortunate if he is surrounded in the home by parents and other relatives who have learned to meet life's problems objectively without introducing fears that detract from life's values.

The possible effect on an individual of motion pictures, radio, and television is not always fully comprehended. Thrill pictures or realistic war scenes create great emotional disturbance in children and also, though less observable, in many adults. Some years ago Orson Welles portrayed war on a radio program so realistically that many adult listeners believed it was true and became alarmed. Studies of emotional effects of motion pictures on child audiences reveal that pictures that emphasize dangerous or gruesome events stimulate the emotions of young spectators to a marked degree. During such performances on the motion-picture screen or on television, children display various types of behavior such as biting their fingernails, hiding their faces, jumping out of their seats or chairs, sliding under their seats, or dashing from the room or theater. Following this experience many of them suffer from disturbed sleep and unpleasant dreams during the night.

EFFECT OF PHOBIAS ON INDIVIDUALS.   Pathological fears, called *phobias,* are symbolic in nature. They are morbid fears and may be aroused by many situations such as dirt, crowds, high places, water, and closed rooms. An individual who has developed a phobia is unable to explain its cause or to give a clear description of his feelings during the emotional experience. Often, persistent fears that tend to control an individual's behavior are not revealed by him to others. Thus, a person who fears crowds may attempt to explain his avoidance of crowded places on the basis of a possible heart attack or his love of wide open spaces. He is often able to convince other people that the effects of placing himself in the feared situation will be extremely harmful to him —even catastrophic.

These morbid or abnormal fears should not be confused with equally strong avoidances that are more like exaggerated disgusts, such as becoming sick or uneasy in the presence of certain sights or odors. Ordinary fears may result from unpleasant or harmful experiences that stimulate toward the avoidance of or retreat from similar situations. Such fears are normal and may be experienced by all people. Phobias are more intense and persistent. They are *symbolic* of an intense fear which is connected with a feeling of guilt or of extreme anxiety. A person, alone in a small closed room, may have engaged in undesirable behavior and at the same time experienced extreme fear that his behavior might become known. Later, although the original incident has been forgotten, the fear of small rooms persists, and the individual is filled with an unreasonable dread of confinement in a small, closed room. He is reviving his former guilt or anxiety as symbolized by the present situation.

A person may suffer from a phobia, but may be normal in most situations that do not present stimuli which arouse his specific phobia. Phobias differ with people and conditions. A person may have a phobia of too close confinement in space, of open spaces, of darkness, or of disease. Phobias are built out of experience and are seldom found in children. An intense experience with prolonged fear is fertile ground for a phobia. During childhood and adolescence fear situations need to receive prompt treatment in order that a sense of guilt may not be attached to them and, at a later time, result in phobias.

VALUE OF FEAR. Fear can be a desirable human experience. Intelligent fear is both needed and welcomed. It is not an experience to be avoided completely since it does not necessarily inhibit or curtail achievement. Fear can be so utilized that it becomes a constructive force in one's life, if it is kept under control and not permitted to take the form of abnormal emotional disturbance. Fear may restrain an individual from engaging in exploits that are undesirable or that can harm him. For example, fear sometimes serves to prevent an individual from engaging in an activity that may result in a loss of prestige or position.

Fear is an effective control of behavior if it keeps an individual from doing those things that, through curiosity, he otherwise might be impelled to do. Yet, he should not exercise caution to the extent that through fear he becomes timid or shy. Thus he may be overcautious and make friends with difficulty. Or he may believe that others are taking advantage of him, not realizing that his feelings are easily hurt. Sometimes, in his attempts at overcoming his deficiencies, he becomes overaggressive and develops an overbearing attitude.

An individual often has been spurred to great accomplishment due to his fear of consequences through inaction. In these instances, the positive drives are based on anger, hate, jealousy, or affection. The balance wheel that tends to operate for the welfare of the individual during these experiences is fear. Often conservative living and the attainment of many social virtues can be credited to the constructive utilization of fear in an individual's life.

It is unwise to use the threat of fear in an attempt to awaken the interest of children in study, or of adults in work. To threaten a child with failure if he does not prepare his assignments is not the kind of positive stimulus that will lead to desirable and effective thinking. Neither is it desirable for a supervisor through the use of threats to arouse such fear in a workman that his efficiency is reduced rather than stepped up. Fear has value to the extent that it motivates people to be cautious; but when the fear becomes abnormal, it is harmful and can be dangerous. It may be a cautious fear that causes the automobile driver to stay on his side of the road, yet it is panicky fear, rather than the ability to think clearly, that gets him into trouble when he is confronted with a critical driving situation.

IMPORTANCE OF CONTROL OF FEAR. Individuals should attempt to control rather than to eliminate fear, since the good is greater than the harm done by this emotion. Any stimulus that is likely to arouse an emotional disturbance needs to be controlled and possibly eliminated. Situations that have fear-arousing elements need to be met and conquered. If a child fears the consequences of being hit by an automobile he will learn to cross the street cautiously. As he learns about the pain and damage caused by fire he avoids playing with matches that cause fire, and so forth.

Children are great imitators of adult behavior. Adults who are responsible for conditioning child behavior need to exhibit confident attitudes in situations that can serve as fear-evokers for the child. Too frequently the young child is exposed to the display of fear behavior on the part of adults. The adult, for example, who becomes frightened by thunder and lightning is likely to pass this form of fear to a child in his presence. Fear of animals also is transmitted to children in a similar manner.

SUBLIMATION OF FEAR. This emotion is usually associated with the tendency to flight. The relation of the fear response to the stimulus that causes it in sequence of time is a moot question. Whether one runs because he is frightened or is possessed with fear because he runs is considered by some psychologists to be in favor of fear because of flight. Even though fear is consciously aroused in our mental process after we flee from danger, the fear that we experience as we run contributes directly to our rate of running.

To fear is to have an attitude of avoiding, of retreating, of fleeing, or of concealing. Fear is the most persisting of the emotions and takes control of the person often to the extent of paralyzing his power of flight. Abnormal fear caused by a failure in adjustment is perhaps the most unhygienic emotional attitude.

Fear has been used as a control measure in political, religious, and other social groups. It also serves as a control of individual behavior. The inhibitions produced are often for an individual's social betterment. Fear acts as a check on development or advancement if it inhibits a person from doing the things that he should do for such advancement. He can benefit from ideas and ideals that keep him from doing personal harm to himself or to others, but it is better if his behavior is directed by forces other than those of fear.

The boy can be trained not to fear his teacher; he can be trained also to respect the rules of the school, the rights of others, and his own person. Self-control rather than fear can be developed to produce effective behavior in children. Nevertheless, fear can be used constructively. If it serves to caution the automobile driver, the pedestrian, or the bicyclist, many lives can be saved annually. Fear can be used as a protective tendency to preserve life, extend happiness, prevent pain, or alleviate suffering.

We have too many abnormal fears. It is unfortunate for a child to grow up in a home in which parents make a great fuss about the lightning that seldom strikes, the snake that never bites, the burglar that never comes, or the disease that seldom afflicts. The more valuable procedure is to instill intelligent understanding of the dangers and limitations of each of these so that proper precautions can be exercised at all times.

Parents and others need to remove from the child's environment undesirable fear stimuli over which control can be exercised. Children need to be informed on as many situations as possible. One reason that children can be so easily excited or thrilled is their lack of information. When understanding is increased, the abnormal fear elements often are removed. It usually is the *unknown* factor in a situation that is the potent fear stimulator.

Everyone who works with growing children needs to be careful about the kind of stimuli he provides in their presence. Radio, television, and motion-picture programs and other fear-producing stimuli in the home and social situations contribute to emotional development. These all can aid in the acquisition of a proper sense of values and go far toward the development of adequate fear responses.

Worry

THE INFLUENCE OF WORRY ON BEHAVIOR.   Worry affects everyone and is rooted in the imagination. It is a fear that is only partly associated with real causes. It can be more devastating than emotional reactions that result from actual fear-producing situations. It is somewhat transitory and disappears with the removal of the causal factor. It concerns a past act or a future possibility about which nothing positive is being done at present. A feeling of personal inadequacy often is associated with an attitude of inferiority, with the anticipation that adequate adjustment to the worry-arousing situation is impossible.

The factors that induce worry are always near at hand.

TABLE 3

Adolescent Worries in Various Life Areas

Life Area	Male Worries	Female Worries
School life	Homework Getting along with teachers Tests Marks Failure Reciting in class Grade for parents' sake College entrance Being accepted	Homework Getting along with teachers Tests Marks Failure Reciting in class Parents' attitude toward grades Being accepted College entrance
Home life	Arguments with sister or brother Arguments with parents Arguments between parents Strict parents Conflicts with parents Arguments about dating Treated unjustly	Younger brothers get what they want Parental domination Parents object to going steady Conflicts with parents Fear of mother Conflicts on values Arguments in home
Boy-girl relation-ships	How to get a date Girls I like don't like me Girls cost too much How to be invited to parties Mother objects to my going steady How to have a girl go steady Inability to dance Does girl love me? Girls of another religion How to forget girl who jilted me	How to meet new friends Boys I like don't like me How to be popular Boys are too demanding I would like to go steady Loss of boy friend Behavior of boy friend Sexual relations to maintain Girls who try to steal boy friend How to get over love for boy How to refuse a date tactfully
Friends	Are they true friends? Friends may not like me To be worthy of good friends How to make friends To be popular	Are they true friends? Not to let friends down To be popular How to be a leader in a group Feelings of inferiority
Vocational choice	State of indecision How to get a job	State of indecision How to get into show business
Religion	Should I marry out of my religion? Indecision Not attending religious services	Should I marry out of my religion? Doubt about religious values Fear parents will discover that I wish to change my religion

Health	How to grow more	Thinness and smallness
	How to lose weight	Fear of losing good health
	Pimples	Disease
	Disease	Illness tendencies

Source: Lester D. Crow and Alice Crow, *Adolescent Development and Adjustment*, 2nd ed., New York: McGraw-Hill, Inc., p. 145. Copyright 1965. Used by permission.

Worry precedes attempted solutions of problems for which adequate preparation has not been given. For example, students worry about passing an examination for which they are poorly prepared. Worry may be associated with all forms of life activities: vocational success, scholastic success, adjustment to members of the opposite sex, social competence, or dread of meeting situations for which one is not prepared.

Past events that have not been personally satisfying are common causes for worry. Equally important as a cause of worry is the confrontation of a situation in which there is a strong desire to succeed. Worry may appear at any age, but is prominent during the adolescent years. Adolescents are concerned about their relationships with their associates of both sexes. They have strong desires to be liked by their peers. These facts and others are revealed in the study completed by the Crows, and reported in Table 3.

SUGGESTIONS FOR THE CONTROL OF WORRY. It is easier to tell another not to worry than it is to give him the help he needs to overcome it. Confidence in oneself and preparedness are two of the best suggestions for anyone who seriously wants to reduce worry to a minimum. The uncertainty of the outcome of an activity to be completed in the future provides the basis for worry. This is the reason for being thoroughly prepared for the activity if worry is to be minimized. Self-assurance arises in proportion to the confidence one has in his ability to succeed. If worry is to be overcome, the individual must be willing to take positive action. The following suggestions can be helpful to the individual who is willing to involve himself in preplanning.

1. Deliberately plan to meet the problem with a workable solution.

2. Become informed as completely as possible concerning the factors involved in the problem and, without hesitation, ask others for information that you may lack.

3. Face the worry squarely and try to evaluate the cause of it.

4. If the cause of the worry can be discovered, do whatever is necessary to remove it.

5. Actively seek the help of others for the purpose of eliminating serious worries.

6. Be encouraged by the fact that the impact of worry actually motivates one to greater heights of achievement.

Anger

THE INFLUENCE OF ANGER ON BEHAVIOR. Anger is expressed through differing forms of behavior depending on the age and training of the individual. It is usually aggressive in its expression and is manifested by activity that tends to cast off irritating or disturbing stimuli. Thwarting of activity or desire often produces anger. During early childhood the anger emotion may be expressed by kicking, screaming, or sulking. Habits that govern anger usually are well established by the time adolescence is reached. In adulthood, anger responses may take the form of profanity, criticism, or silence. There usually is marked overt expression of this emotion. (See Figure 3 for types of responses to anger-producing stimuli.)

Figure 3. Types of Responses to Anger-producing Stimuli

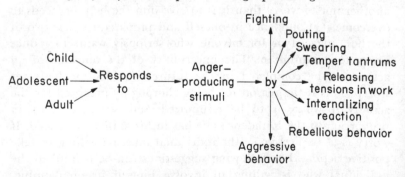

The persistence of the emotion of anger is found in the *temper tantrums* that are resorted to in order to gain one's desires. To be denied that which one wants immediately and to discover that, through persistence, the wish will be granted is an experience that may lead to the development of behavior patterns in the child, the adolescent, and the adult, of forcing gratification of desire. If, by chance, the child obtains his desired end by a display of temper, he may learn to engage in temper tantrums early in his life. The child gets his way at first because the parents are not sure about his state of health, and they give him the benefit of the doubt. Consequently, the parents give in rather easily. Later, the child persists, since he has learned that if he continues in his behavior long enough, eventually he will win out. In too many cases he is successful because the parents are tired or are afraid that personal harm will result if they do not give in to him.

The temper tantrum is based upon an inadequacy of the individual. Once a child has learned that he can intimidate his parents by temper tantrums he makes good use of them at every opportunity. Temper tantrums are modified in form as the child grows through adolescence and adulthood, but they seldom are discarded completely. Some forms of the tantrum are so subtle that they are not easily detected; an observant person is alert to their onset and deals with them in a completely objective manner. Unfortunately, grandmothers and mothers-in-law may make effective use of tantrum behavior to the dismay of those who live with them.

IMPORTANCE OF THE CONTROL OF ANGER. Anger disappears rapidly upon the removal of the stimulus that arouses it. Parents and teachers can help the individual's adjustment by recognizing and applying this simple fact, and changing the stimulus to one that will evoke a more favorable emotional response. Children need to be stimulated to action if it is socially desirable action. The suggestion of counting to ten before fighting is based on the principle that with change of stimulus comes a rapid disappearance of the emotion of anger.

Parents and teachers have daily opportunities to apply the principle of directing the attention of the individual to another stimulus when anger has been aroused by a present stimulus. A complete change of stimulus is bound to result in a new and different emotional reaction. For example, if a child shows anger because he is not given candy, it usually is desirable to deny him the candy and at the same time give him something to do that he enjoys doing. The application of the change of stimulus principle is sound for individuals of any age. It is well to keep in mind that the new stimulus needs to be one that will call forth a pleasurable response.

If the motives or reasons that underlie the behavior are known to the person who is guiding the individual, the former's task is made easier thereby. A deserved compliment given to an individual often helps him overcome his real or fancied hurt. A pleasant remark will turn away anger, but argument or attempts at reasoning often increase the emotional response. Stimuli that elicit the tender emotions are excellent to remove angry behavior.

SUGGESTIONS TO HELP CONTROL TEMPER TANTRUMS. Temper tantrums are acquired in the individual's environment and can be corrected. If a child is to be helped to recondition his tantrum behavior, he needs the guidance of someone who will deny his demands with firmness but with justice. He needs to discover that his behavior is completely understood without the adult's saying it in so many words. His ego should be maintained and his pride spared, but his wishes should be denied when they are demanded in the form of a tantrum. The child knows his mother and what he may expect from her. It is well to be known as a parent who speaks when he wishes action and gets action before speaking again. This behavior will give the child valuable training and will spare the parents much trouble in the future.

If a child develops the tantrum technique, the problem can be met by all who come into contact with him: parents, teachers, or other group leaders. An effective way of dealing with the child while he is having his temper tantrum is to ignore him. If he discovers that his behavior is not gaining the attention of the proper persons, he will allow the tantrum to subside. He then can have explained to him that his wishes will be granted on the basis of their worth and not upon the basis of his demands expressed through persistent infantile behavior.

A second method of dealing with the child while he is having a temper tantrum is isolation. This method is used in social groups and in the school. During the tantrum, the child or older person is isolated from the group. If necessary, he is removed bodily with permission to return as soon as his behavior is in conformity with the rights and comforts of others; or the group may move from the room to let him have his tantrum alone.

The individual needs to learn through hard experience that he will fare better if he behaves in an acceptable fashion in the first place. No treatment is ever permanent, however. The individual's behavior is conditioned toward the specific situation and toward the person controlling the situation. For example, a child may never throw a tantrum in the presence of one parent, yet he may do so in the presence of the other; he may never have a tantrum in the presence of one teacher, but he does have a tantrum in the presence of another one.

SUBLIMATION OF ANGER.   In sublimation an effort is made to push conflicting influences of mental and emotional life from lower levels of development to progressively higher levels where harmonious personality integration can be achieved. This process is an individual experience and can be effected through the understanding efforts of adults (teachers, parents, or counselors) in their attempts at the redirection of undesirable emotional behavior.

It is important that educational leaders recognize emotional differences among learners and then provide special attention to any emotional deviations that may interfere with desirable social adjustment. Within the limits of their emotional expression learners need to be afforded opportunities for participation in group activities that involve emotion-arousing potentialities. Stimulation by way of art, music, and other aesthetic experiences can be made available on an intellectual level suited to the age of the individual and his power to respond.

The emotion of anger has been associated with pugnacity. Pugnacity is a primary tendency that is likely to be aroused if a blocking occurs among any of the other tendencies and their associated emotions. It is basic to the fighting attitude of man, serves him in defense, and operates as a self-protective reaction. Anger is aroused when any of the inherent emotions is thwarted. The emotion of anger kills happiness, for man cannot be truly happy when he is angry. Any interference with a person's pleasures is resented. Nevertheless, anger gives us courage, determination, and endurance. It aids in concentration of effort by clearing away detrimental inhibitions.

The pugnacity in human life is to be transformed rather than reduced. The fight attitude or the will to work is needed in the complete development of man. Attention can be directed toward giving it careful direction so that it may have effective expression. Critical disapproval can be administered in ways that are socially acceptable. Both society and individuals can be trained to use effective means of expressing disapproval without the use of violence.

Every person can be trained to exercise indignation, disapproval, or a critical attitude toward certain undesirable persons or conditions in his environment. These responsibilites cannot be evaded without violation of one's own self-respect. Moral character is built upon these evaluated qualities of life. The deserved disapproval of any faults of persons or institutions can be given effectively through controlled behavior, not dissipated through blustering or other overt pugnacious acts.

We ought to be certain that our critical, pugnacious, and antagonistic attitudes are expressed tactfully. Emotionally uncontrolled and unreasonable behavior rarely brings desired results. We first are convinced that we are logical, just, and reasonable in our critical evaluation of the situation and the persons concerned. We then attempt to present our point of view constructively by offering workable suggestions for the improvement of the situation and of individual behavior. If such suggestions are given sympathetically and objectively, most individuals can be led to accept the corrections offered, and are mentally and morally stimulated by their attempts to conform to more desirable standards of behavior.

Does avoiding a fight indicate lack of courage or is it an expression of good sense? Most boys have critical judgment that tells them not to fight. Nevertheless, it needs only a little prodding from several buddies to supersede that judgment and to start a fight. Too often, in an attempt to settle these issues, adults criticize the combatants rather than the instigators on the side lines. Disapproval should be directed against all who are guilty. This will help the person who is involved in the fist fight which he has entered with the mistaken idea that, in this way, he will be able to maintain his social dignity and standing in the group.

Jealousy

THE INFLUENCE OF JEALOUSY ON BEHAVIOR. Jealousy is a deep-rooted emotion that combines the feeling of subjugation and of inferiority with the fear emotion. Also associated with it are the anger and the affection impulses. Jealousy is aroused by the loss, or the fear of loss, of affection desired from another, or of the loss of a coveted honor or recognition, and the like. The prospect of the loss or the actual loss wounds the individual's pride and self-esteem. Anger is aroused, and activities of a revengeful nature may be resorted to.

Jealousy inevitably results when a child or adolescent is denied a privilege that is granted another when he has shown an interest in it. This is characteristic behavior, whether the situation occurs in the home, the classroom, the playground, or in any other social situation. Jealousy often arises when adolescents move from larger group activities to dating. Numerous situations arise in the home to arouse the emotion of jealousy. It is interesting to note how often one sibling thinks he is the neglected one, or that his brother or sister is given preference over him in most things of value in the home.

CONTROL OF JEALOUSY. Jealousy represents a resentful attitude of one person toward another and originates in the actual or imagined loss of the good will or affection of another person, or in the fact that the other person has attained a goal much desired by the former. For example, an older child has been accustomed to being the center of parental attention until the sudden appearance of a baby sister or brother. If the child has been prepared for the arrival of the new baby, he is likely to accept him, but if not, he is likely to display jealous behavior. His behavior may take the form of refusing food when fed, demanding help in his dressing and undressing, special help with his toys, and so forth. He attempts to regress to an earlier stage of development in order to compete for a share of attention that he believes is unfairly given to the baby. He needs careful supervision in order to ensure his not hurting the helpless baby.

Sibling rivalry takes many forms. Older children engage in teasing, quarreling, ridicule, boasting, sarcasm, or even tale-bearing. These displays of behavior usually are confined to the home setting. An adolescent may criticize his brother or sister but he will defend the sibling against any criticism expressed or implied by a person outside his family.

Jealous attitudes are displayed in school in many ways. Here a jealous child may attract attention to himself through deviate aggressive behavior, loud speech, telling imaginary stories about his feats of courage or those of members of his family, or inciting classmates to participate in acts of mischief.

Affection

THE INFLUENCE OF AFFECTION ON BEHAVIOR. Affection is one of the tender emotions. Affection represents an outgoing reaction that is directed toward a person, an object, or a situation. The display of behavior that is distinguished as affectionate behavior begins during the first year of life. It is expressed in smiles, gurgles, and cooing. Later it is also expressed through various approaches in which interest is shown toward others.

Affectionate behavior is developed by the growing child as he increases his number of associations outside the home, during which time he gives affection to people who care for his needs and who are especially attentive to him. He needs this display of affectionate behavior extended toward him by interested adults. It is a pleasant realization to know that he is wanted and liked by others of his own age and by adults. Not only should he enjoy receiving affection from others; he needs to gain experience in exhibiting attitudes of love and affection toward others and to show concern for their welfare.

Parents can assist children in the development of outgoing attitudes and behavior by permitting them to assist in the care of younger children and/or pets in the home. Proper attitudes of affection developed in the home can be carried over into outside group relationships. Thus are strong friendships made in school, clubs, or other community organizations. Many friendships formed during the growing years continue throughout life. Through one's affection and respect for friends and associates, strong feelings of self-esteem and self-appreciation can be acquired.

A child needs to be afforded many opportunities to display affection-giving and affection-receiving experiences. Thus will he develop a feeling of security that will enable him to play and work with others on a cooperative basis free from serious resentment or jealousy. He needs to receive affectionate attention from others in his day-by-day living in order to acquire affectionate emotional development that is important to him throughout the rest of his life.

An adolescent needs to feel secure in the affection of another and to know that he is liked and wanted by his family and his peers. He usually does not express his affection through uncontrolled behavior but rather by desiring to be with the loved one, by acceding to the wishes of the latter, and by doing a variety of things to make him or her happy. The adolescent is stirred deeply by his affection for an admired person. He tends to feel insecure in the absence of the loved one. Thus he invents various schemes to keep in touch with him or her. These may take the form of visits, letters, telegrams, or messages sent through a third person. The objective is to continue a close relationship with the admired person.

GENERAL INFLUENCE OF EMOTIONS ON BEHAVIOR

The bright, the average, or the dull person may be maladjusted. The cause usually can be traced to an obstacle that has been faced and not resolved. Any interference of this kind should be removed, not ignored. To ignore the obstacle is to increase the difficulty that confronts the individual. It is better to face the actual conditions and to give the true cause for one's failure than to project the responsibility to a convenient person or cause. If we build up habits of running away from or of ignoring the issue, we merely permit the tension to increase until our defenses against nervous disorders are broken down.

Teachers and parents become aware of the habits and practices of children and develop an understanding of the causes of the undesirable behavior that is manifested by children. If a young person attempts to adjust through the use of bullying, stealing, sex offenses, or temper tantrums, it will not help much to administer punishment for the social behavior; adjustment is more effective if the cause of the undesirable act can be determined and controlled.

Influence of Emotions in Specific Problems

Prolonged emotional stress, regardless of age, affects the efficiency, attitude, and physiological condition of the individual. These are the symptoms through which we become aware of the emotional strain.

Retardation is caused very often by emotional disturbances which, if they could be removed, would permit the child to pass his schoolwork. He may be emotionally upset about home conditions, be filled with intense hatred for his teacher, or possessed with deep fears which will not allow him to reach the degree of efficiency that he could if desirable emotional conditions prevailed in his life.

Stammering is another unfortunate effect of prolonged emotional strain. Since few children have anatomical defects that might result in the difficulty, it is considered to be caused by emotional stress. A careful observer can detect easily that the stammerer usually has trouble only in certain environmental situations. His difficulty is greatest when he is embarrassed or excited. His speech is quite normal when he is relaxed and at ease. The school situation offers many embarrassing situations; the social consciousness of the stammerer gives added strength to the state of excitement. The trouble is started by an emotion-arousing episode which contains many complex elements.

Success. A good emotional tonus is very helpful in putting to effective use the talents, energies, and abilities of a person in the solving of problems. The working man who is sufficiently stirred but not overexcited is in a better state to do the kind of thinking that will be required than is the worker who is not so stirred. The supervisor should not instill fear of failure, since this emotional drive may become the dominant one, and the worker may become so excited that he is not able to do his best work. He should be stimulated toward success so that he will have the desire to push ahead rather than have the feeling that he wants to run away from something.

Influence of Emotions on Health

It is a well-known fact that the emotions exert a great influence upon digestion. A person's attitude at the time of eating and immediately thereafter has a decided effect upon the secretions of the digestive organs, including those of the salivary and gastric glands and the glands of the intestinal tract. Chronic fears and worries may cause subnormal secretion of the digestive system, and a consequent condition of constipation. If ill health results, a person begins treatment at the point of irritation instead of giving attention to whatever fundamental causes stimulated the arousal of the predisposing emotional state.

Physicians are becoming increasingly aware of the fact that

stomach ulcers have for one of their chief causes that of emotional disturbance. Several years ago a young woman known to the author was experiencing serious emotional disturbance. She was advised to eat proper food, secure sufficient rest, and avoid stimuli that might arouse undesirable emotions. Her intelligent adherence to this advice resulted in her complete recovery within a year. The removal of fear and worry is one of the most effective means of preserving or regaining health.

The success of the Christian Science movement results in part from the emphasis given by its advocates to the value of emotional control during illness. The attempts made by them to keep the body functioning normally at all times have significant and potent health values. The person as well as the disease must be treated.

Emotions as an Asset

The tender emotions constitute the great driving force that stimulates the human to achieve that in which he is interested and which he is capable of doing. This emotion helps him to endure hardships, to take criticism, or to work at long intervals. Fear, on the other hand, serves as a check on behavior. It keeps man from becoming too reckless, thereby saving his reputation and, sometimes, even his life.

Human beings want to be near stimuli that arouse them. They want romantic love put into storybooks and fear put into the automobile. Emotions lend color to their existence and spur them on to do many daring deeds. The human craves emotional stimulation and desires emotional experiences. He tries to get them through books, movies, radio, television, and social gatherings. Nevertheless, he needs emotional balance in all of them. Overstimulation is unhealthful.

The poet, the musician, and the artist rely upon their emotions to serve as driving forces during their creative efforts. They are able to experience emotionally much more than many others and, consequently, have the ability to translate their emotional state into words, pictures, or music. Thus, through insight and integration of ideas do they produce the new, the beautiful, and the creative work of art. An emotional state in the right setting may give one an entirely new outlook on his own life.

As the individual moves from self-centeredness that prevails in infancy to other-centeredness of adolescence and adulthood, he is growing in emotional maturity. This is a gradual process that is dependent upon both physiological maturation and learning. In his discussion of emotional maturity, including both its nature and its importance to the human being, Kaplan makes the following significant statements:

> At each stage of development the individual needs assurance that his needs will be met either through his own efforts or through the ministrations of others. He needs to feel assured of love, approval, and emotional support when he needs it. With this emotional support he can develop a sense of self-reliance and a confidence in his own ability to manage the emotional problems of living. As his personal competencies develop, he can let go of his supports and form the expanded attachments to others which the process of emotional maturity requires.
>
> This combination of emotional support and freedom is the foundation of emotional security. The emotionally secure person does not feel alone in the world, nor does he feel completely dependent upon others. He can look beyond himself and his own needs and establish rich human relationships which will be satisfying to himself and to others. He will be free to try new experiences, form new friendships, and move out into the expanding social world with zest and confidence.
>
> The person who lacks emotional security is likely to see the world as a hostile environment to which he is exposed. He is in the position of a starving individual whose first concern in the presence of food is his own desperate need. He must satisfy his own emotional needs before he can be concerned with the requirements of other people. This type of behavior perpetuates his emotional insecurity. In centering upon himself, the emotionally deprived person alienates others. He becomes so preoccupied with building his emotional defenses that he loses sight of other rewarding and pleasurable aspects of life.[3]

[3] Louis Kaplan, *Foundations of Human Behavior*, New York: Harper & Row, 1965, p. 165.

Emotional conditioning is complicated by inner conflicts and previous emotional experiences. The difficulty of the problem of developing emotional control is increased by an individual's inner drives and desires and by the respective affective qualities of his experience. Attitudes which are associated with self-interest are useful in giving positive direction to emotional behavior. As attitudes are established they produce a state of readiness that exerts dynamic influences upon the behavior of an individual. Hence an attitude toward success tends to establish success; an attitude of failure encourages failure.

Sometimes, through mental action, an individual is enabled to bring the past to the level of consciousness and, through this, secure a definite emotional discharge. This method (catharsis) is used as a means for the reduction of emotional tensions and for the avoidance of undesirable emotional reactions. Music and art sometimes are used to stimulate the emotions and at the same time to purge them of their coarser elements. Thus aesthetic expression becomes an emotion conditioner. Emotions under control add beauty to life. Hence the goal is to rule the emotions rather than to be ruled by them.

Emotions as a Liability

Excesses in the use and functioning of any of the emotions will produce a maladjusted person. Healthy emotional life is a decided asset; the emotions, when they are too powerful, can make life miserable for an individual and for those about him. Emotions become liabilities as soon as they interfere with a person's social success or work efficiency. It is because of these liabilities that education of the emotions is so necessary.

QUESTIONS AND PROBLEMS

1. Discuss emotion as a factor of human adjustment.
2. Differentiate between feeling and emotion.
3. Discuss the value of fear and anger in human affairs.
4. What fear-arousing situations have you experienced during the past year? Describe the stimuli, the situation, and the adjustments made.
5. To what extent can adult approval become a motivating force in a child's life?
6. Discuss the use of desirable incentives as behavior motivations.
7. Describe a situation in your experience that illustrates the effects of emotion-arousing in a crowd.
8. Describe some of the emotional changes that come about with increasing age.
9. What are some limiting factors in the education of the emotions?
10. How is the health of a person related to emotional experiences?
11. Discuss the relationship between avocational activities and one's emotional life.
12. Explain the relationship between social adjustment and emotional control.
13. Recall stimuli that aroused you emotionally during childhood and early adolescence. How do they compare with the stimuli to which you now respond emotionally?
14. What do you consider to be the relationship between your degree of success as a student and your emotional reactions?
15. List the characteristics of an emotionally mature person. Justify your selections.

Selected Readings

Birrer, J. E., *The Psychology of Aging*. Englewood Cliffs, N.J.: Prentice-Hall, Inc., 1964.

Cameron, N., *Personality Development and Psychopathology: A Dynamic Approach*. Boston, Mass.: Houghton Mifflin Company, 1963.

Crow, L. D. and A. Crow, *Adolescent Development and Adjustment,* 2nd ed. New York: McGraw-Hill, Inc., 1965.

Krech, D., and R. S. Crutchfield, *Elements of Psychology.* New York: Alfred A. Knopf, Inc., 1958. Part II.

Morgan, C. T., *Introduction to Psychology,* 3rd ed. New York: McGraw-Hill, Inc., 1966.

Plutchik, R., *The Emotions.* New York: Random House, Inc., 1964.

Ruch, F. L., *Psychology and Life,* 6th ed. Chicago, Ill.: Scott, Foresman and Company, 1964. Chapter 7.

Sartain, A. Q., A. J. North, J. R. Strange, and H. M. Chapman, *Psychology: Understanding Human Behavior,* 2nd ed. New York: McGraw-Hill, Inc., 1962.

Schneiders, A. A., *The Anarchy of Feeling: Man's Struggle for Freedom and Maturity.* New York: Sheed and Ward, Inc., 1963.

Taylor, E. A., *Meeting the Increasing Stresses of Life: A Multiple-Therapy in Education.* Springfield, Ill.: Charles C Thomas, Publisher, 1963.

White, R. W., *The Abnormal Personality,* 3rd ed. New York: The Ronald Press Company, 1964.

PERSONALITY
ADJUSTMENT

PSYCHOLOGISTS AND laymen alike recognize the fact that there appears to be a definite relationship between an individual's personal characteristics and his demonstrated degree of success in the various areas of his life experiences. From earliest time onward more or less adequate attempts have been made to find answers to questions such as: What is personality? What causes the personality of one individual to differ from that of another? How can personality be changed?

Exposure of physically unfit infants, use of incantations and charms, astrology, phrenology, and anthropometric measurements are examples of methods that have been employed at successive stages of cultural development in order to explain differences among people in their observable personality patterns. According to some modern media of advertisement there is supposed to be a close relationship between a man's or a woman's personality pattern and matters dealing with dress and grooming; style of clothing; hairdo; application of cosmetics; care of teeth; use of deodorants. These approaches to ways of improving personality place emphasis upon the importance of a pleasing appearance, not only as a means of attracting favorable comment from associates, but also as a way of bolstering one's own self-confidence.

If concern about them does not become an all-absorbing interest, good grooming and appropriate dress affect a person's relations with others. They represent, however, personal attitudes and values that constitute only a phase of the total personality; they are not necessarily indicative of the fundamental bases of individual personality, as viewed by the psychologist.

It is difficult for anyone to achieve an adjusted life pattern in his relationships with his fellows unless he possesses some understanding of the degree of interdependence that exists between his own personality characteristics and those of other people with whom he associates. Hence it is important that the term *personality* be analyzed carefully so that it may be understood and appreciated.

THE EGO OR THE SELF

From early childhood onward, the individual is much concerned about *himself* in relation to people, things, and conditions in his environment. Expressions such as egocentricism, selfhood, self-realization, and self-assertion are common. Utilization of these terms implies a recognition of one's *self* as different from the selves of other people. In their consideration of personality, psychologists need to understand the significance of an individual's self in the development of his personality pattern.

The Concept of the Self

The concept of the self can be interpreted roughly as the more or less gradually developed and more or less objective awareness of one's own needs, interests, attitudes, and behavior habits. The ego concept is related to factors in the physical environment and in relationships with other human beings who make up an individual's social environment.

Robert White has this to say about the concept of the self:

Taking a short historical perspective, it can be said that the self or ego has recently emerged and risen to prominence in psychology. Taking a longer perspective, the self has experienced a brief absence from the center of the psychological stage and has now returned to play the indispensable role allotted to it by serious thinkers throughout the ages. The self was placed in obscurity only for that brief period perhaps from 1880 to 1930—when psychology, fascinated by the methods and models of the physical sciences, devoted itself to experiments on elementary processes and postponed the attempt to understand the person as we know him in everyday life. From abnormal psychology, which of necessity continued to take people as its subject-matter, this concept was never really absent. The self or ego is one of the most difficult concepts in the whole realm of thought. It would simplify things if we could do without it. But no one can write sensibly about people without using this concept or its equivalent. . . .

The necessity of using the concept of the self does not confer the privilege of misusing it. As we use concepts in our thinking, they tend to get firmer and harder. Thought about fluid events tends to curdle and form solid clots. Before long we begin to think of the self as if it were a lump in the personality. It becomes an entity so sharply bounded that arguments begin as to whether a certain piece of behavior belongs in the self or out of it, proceeds across an ego boundary, or involves a collision between the ego and something else. In the end the self is standing like a solid boulder of granite in the midst of personality, and one's thinking about it is as flexible as granite. Yet perhaps a more serious danger lies in animating the boulder again in order to invest it with magic powers. . . .

NEED FOR A UNIFYING CONCEPT. In spite of its dangers we need the concept of the self. Without it we have no point of anchorage for the personal pattern of tendencies that is characteristic of each individual. When we speak of a personal pattern our phrase carries several implications. It means, first, that the individual's tendencies form an *arrangement of related strivings,* rather than a list or chance conglomeration. It means, in the second place, that this pattern has no standard form, but *differs from one person to another* according to his nature and history. It must have still a third implication if we are going to talk about living people rather than inanimate systems. It must mean that the tendencies are patterned in order to accomplish the maintenance and expansion of a living unit. They function within an organism, and they are *patterned to make that organism live and grow.* That is the principle that governs the patterning and makes it intelligible.

The concept of the self helps us to bear in mind the basic fact of the unity of the organism. If we forget this basic fact, we are apt to talk about urges and differentiated tendencies as if they were tenants in a boarding house, each leading an independent life and submitting to a pattern of rules and regulations only because the other tenants interfere so badly. In practice none of us regards either himself or anyone else as a boarding house of independent tendencies. If I lose my temper and make a childish scene, I do not blame one of my tenants, the aggressive urge. I blame myself for letting this tenant get out of hand. If my neighbor starts an uprising venture and makes a success of it, I do not congratulate his need for achievement; I congratulate the man. We think of ourselves and others not as conglomerations, not even just as patterns, but as units.[1]

A self-concept gradually emerges as the individual develops various attitudes toward himself as a result of his many changing experiences. In his discussion of the self, Kendler emphasizes the part played by learning as the child gradually achieves some degree of self-esteem.

Although we are all aware that as a child matures he is forming judgments about others, we forget that he is also learning attitudes toward himself. The concept of *the self* refers to these attitudes.

Learning about oneself is a gradual affair. The infant must first learn that he exists as an individual separate and distinct from everybody and everything around him. He has to learn, for example, that when he pinches himself he causes himself pain, but that when he pinches his toy he does not. Reacting to his bodily sensations is only the beginning

[1] Robert W. White, *The Abnormal Personality*, 3rd ed., New York: The Ronald Press Company, 1964, pp. 145–146.

of reacting to himself. Later, when the child learns reactions to the behavior of others, he learns also to respond to his own behavior. He perceives his mother as kind and gentle and his father as strong and competent. It is a truism to add that how he perceives himself becomes *his* self.

Self-evaluating reactions vary as a child matures; he learns new dimensions in judging himself. One especially important dimension concerns his own competence, or as it is often technically labeled, his *self-esteem*. A related dimension is the evaluation of his own goodness or badness. You frequently hear a child say, "I'm a good boy (or girl)" or "I'm bad." Although the specific reaction and the meaning may change, self-evaluations persist throughout life. The reader is aware, though nobody else may be, of how competent he believes he is at anything, and how generally "good" or "bad."

The reader will not be surprised to learn that people differ in their self-concepts. But most of us are not aware of how vast are the differences among individuals in their reactions toward themselves or of how wide a discrepancy often exists between individuals' reactions toward themselves and others' reactions toward them. Some individuals have great confidence in themselves; others are convinced that they are hopelessly inadequate. The people at these two extremes of self-perception may be equal in ability, or the one whose self-esteem is low may actually be the more competent. There are these discrepancies between self-evaluation and performance in all sorts of activities. For example, an individual may think he is socially popular when, in fact, others consider him a bore, and the opposite can be true.[2]

Development of the Self-Concept

The newborn infant apparently has no concept of himself as a member of a world of selves. Self-awareness develops gradually. Self-recognition and self-assertion begin with relatively vague and general recognitions of and urges to fulfill certain physical

[2] Howard H. Kendler. *Basic Psychology*, New York: Appleton-Century-Crofts, 1963, pp. 459–460.

needs, such as need for food, sleep, warmth, release from discomfort, and activity that is appropriate to the stage of maturation.

As the young child gradually comes to recognize objects and persons in his environment that are associated with his developing feelings of comfort and discomfort, he begins to enlarge his needs to include satisfying relations with these environmental factors and to discover that he is a recipient or a giver of attention. He is developing an awareness of *self*. Also in his own immature fashion, he asserts his *ego* through his attempts to fulfill his increasing needs and wants.

During later childhood and adolescence and into adulthood the developing individual comes to recognize the impact upon himself, and upon his needs and his urges, of the rules, regulations, customs, and accepted patterns of behavior that are common to the society of which he is a member. To a greater or lesser extent he achieves the ability to evaluate himself in terms of general and specific social modes, standards, and ideals. To the extent that he can measure his own self objectively in his relations with others, he experiences an increasingly accurate appreciation of himself. He also develops the ability to adjust himself and his needs and urges in such a way that he can become an accepted member of his group.

Control of the Ego

As the child achieves increasingly greater social consciousness, he is developing egoistic tendencies. Not only does he need to have his personal needs fulfilled but he also is conscious of other people's urges and drives, and attempts to accede to them in so far as he recognizes their rights in relationship to his own wants and needs.

Fundamentally, to a greater or lesser extent, everyone is egocentric. The degree of control exercised by an individual over his display of self-regarding behavior depends upon the attitudes toward his personal rights and responsibilities that he has been helped to achieve during his formative years. What is generally referred to as *conscience*, and by the Freudians as the *superego*, is the self-restraining power that is an attribute of an individual's total personality pattern. In order to achieve positive self-satisfaction as well as the approval of those with whom he associates, he constantly seeks to set up an *ideal self* through the activation of success-acquiring behavior patterns. According to White:

> Ego-ideal means simply the self that one wants to become. It may take the form of an ideal of personal conduct: to be an upright man, a charming woman, an altruistic person, a topnotch gangster. It may be identified with desired accomplishments: the person wants his life to mean clean city government, freedom for artistic expression, a world without alcohol, a world-wide fascist revolution. Our examples are chosen to suggest that the concept of ego-ideal is important, regardless of the wisdom and ethical character of the self one wants to become. Like the ego itself . . . the ego-ideal is an integrative concept. People may have what others consider to be conflicting aims. But they rarely think of the "selves" they would like to become. Their ideals are linked to one organism, one ego, one personal identity, integrated somehow into a single ego-ideal.
>
> When we think of idle and drifting lives, or of lives so bound by circumstances that they seem to run themselves out as a matter of routine, the concept of an ego-ideal may appear superfluous. It is needed, however, perhaps even to understand these lives, and certainly to understand those contrasting lives that achieve things of importance and change the world. It is not necessary to conceive that an effective ego-ideal must be conscious and communicable in words. Sometimes an outside observer can say more clearly than you yourself what you seem to be living for, even though he does not have the advantage of introspection. An ego-ideal can be functionally effective without being consciously formulated. In fact, when a person can formulate his ego-ideal too readily, we may suspect that the verbal statement is drifting loose from the functionally effective guides of his behavior and is being used to impress, if not to deceive, himself and others.
>
> Ego-identity refers to the self we feel ourselves to be. Ego-ideal is the self we would like to be. In the forming of these two establishments, a similar part is played by identification. To the actual people the child may be moved to imitate, the culture adds a large variety of ideal models.

From the time when the little boy is urged to act like a big boy to the time when, let us say, he enters a religious order that patterns its activities on St. Francis of Assisi or a political group that espouses the philosophy and program of Lenin, he is proffered an array of more or less ready-made ego-ideals. He may reject most of them, but the accepted ones may have an important influence upon him. Images of living or once-living people quicken his imagination and enlist his energies more strongly than would otherwise be possible. The concept of ego-ideal emphasizes the forward movement that is characteristic of human behavior. We are rarely satisfied with ourselves as we are, always trying to make things a little better.[3]

THE CONCEPT OF PERSONALITY

Any attempt to define *personality* categorically is impossible. There probably is a general agreement, however, that every individual possesses many characteristics that are inherent in his physical appearance, gestures, speech, gait, ideas, knowledge, aptitudes, skills, habits, and emotional reactions. Some of these characteristics are innate; others result from learning and experience, and are more subject to the possibility of change than the inborn. All of these characteristics tend to interact with one another. Hence they function as a more or less integrated whole.

Definitions of Personality

Although it is difficult to define personality, there are at least fifty such definitions extant. We shall cite a few of them.

One of the earliest definitions is that of Prince: ". . . the sum total of all the biological innate dispositions, impulses, tendencies, appetites, and instincts of the individual, and the acquired dispositions and tendencies—acquired by experience." [4]

The structural aspect of personality is stressed in the following definition: "Personality is the entire mental organization of a human being at any stage of his development. It embraces every

[3] White, *The Abnormal Personality*, pp. 178–179.
[4] M. Prince, *The Unconscious*, 2nd rev. ed., New York: The Macmillan Company, 1924, p. 532.

phase of human character: intellect, temperament, skill, morality, and every attitude that has been built up in the course of one's life." [5]

The subjective cognitive factor is emphasized in the conception of personality as stated by Lecky: ". . . a unified scheme of experience, an organization of values that are consistent with one another." [6]

McClelland presents personality as "the most adequate conceptualization of a person's behavior in all its detail that the scientist can give at a moment of time." [7]

Included among some of the more recent definitions are "*An individual's personality*, then, *is his unique pattern of traits*" [8] and "Personality is the unique organization of all man's habit systems whereby he is related to his environment." [9]

Kendler's concept of personality is embodied in the following: ". . . the organization of behavior patterns which characterize a person as an individual in a variety of situations." [10]

According to Allport, "There is, of course, no such thing as a correct or incorrect definition. Terms can only be defined in ways that are useful for a given purpose. For the purposes of the present volume we require a definition of personality that is 'essentialist.' We shall treat personality as a unit 'out there,' possessing internal structure in its own right." His definition, which probably is the most workable statement of the meaning of personality, follows: "Personality is the dynamic organization within the individual of those psychophysical systems that determine his characteristic behavior and thought." [11]

Personality Traits

Human characteristics usually are called aspects, components, or traits of personality. Some psychologists prefer to limit the term

[5] H. C. Warren and L. Carmichael, *Elements of Human Psychology*, rev. ed., Boston: Houghton Mifflin Company, 1930, p. 333.

[6] P. Lecky, *Self-consistency: A Theory of Personality*, New York: Island, 1945, p. 90.

[7] D. McClelland, *Personality*, New York: W. Sloane, 1951, p. 69.

[8] J. P. Guilford, *Personality*, New York: McGraw-Hill, 1959, p. 5.

[9] James E. Royce, S.J., *Personality and Mental Health*, rev. ed., Milwaukee: The Bruce Publishing Company, 1964, p. 43.

[10] Kendler, *Basic Psychology*, p. 445.

[11] Gordon W. Allport, *Pattern and Growth in Personality*, New York: Holt, Rinehart and Winston, 1961, p. 28.

trait to a characteristic that is associated with abilities, powers, attitudes, or behavior, rather than physical structure and appearance, or physiological function. Moreover, increasing emphasis is being placed upon the totality of personality. An individual's personality pattern is more than the combination of his many characteristics and traits. The continuous interaction of these components results in a general personality pattern that is unique to the individual, and that constitutes his *whole* personality. Temporarily, one trait may so dominate behavior that others may seem to be less significant. The dominance of the one affects not only the functioning of other specific traits but, during that period, alters the entire personality pattern. An example follows.

A successful middle-aged businessman has demonstrated, through his behavior, that he possesses personality characteristics that consistently have gained for him the respect and admiration of his associates. At home, in school, and in his business and social relationships he has given evidence of cheerful, cooperative, sincere, industrious, and ambitious attitudes. As a result, he has achieved a position of leadership, especially in his business dealings. His devotion to his wife and growing family always has motivated him to provide generously for their welfare. Now, he is eager to make available for his adolescent children superior educational and social advantages. He is unable to achieve his aim, as his financial earnings are not sufficient. His ambitions which, to the present, have been kept under intelligent control, now run rampant.

This man is determined to improve his financial status. It has become an obsession. So intense is this urge that all other areas of his life pattern are subordinated to it. Although he has not become definitely dishonest, he has begun to engage in what may be termed "sharp bargains" with his business associates. His constant concern with making money results in the development of harassed, antisocial attitudes. He is becoming an impatient, noncooperative member of the family for whose benefit he believes he is engaging in his present business activities. His whole personality seems to have undergone an undesirable change. Whether his present drive to accumulate money will continue to dominate his attitude and behavior-motivating traits depends upon factors within and outside himself that may lessen or increase the strength of the ambitious urge of which he now is a victim.

According to dictionary definition of terms, there can be said to be about 1,800 words that describe personality. Most of these are adjectives, many of which duplicate one another. Others represent pairs of opposites. Some are doubtful, such as *spring-like,* or represent temporary qualities: *alarmed, afraid;* still others describe other people's attitudes toward a person, rather than his personal traits. Smith has this to say about traits.

We should select traits that are independent. Unless a group of traits are actually independent of each other, we are unnecessarily burdening ourselves with the same trait under different names. We should select traits that are stable. It would be of little value for us to know how high a person's self-confidence was today if it should turn out to be quite different tomorrow. Most important of all, we should select traits that are significantly related to the task of understanding people. Psychologists work in different areas of this task. Consequently, physiological psychologists tend to deal with *drive* and *temperamental* traits; psychologists interested in *perception* emphasize traits in this area; clinical psychologists concern themselves with traits relevant to the *self* and to *problem solving;* and social psychologists emphasize *value* and *human-relations* traits.

The following twenty-five traits have been selected. . . .

Drive traits: activity, sensory awareness, and sexuality
Temperamental traits: emotionality, optimism, and expressiveness
Perceptual traits: thinking, extroversion, speed and flexibility of closure
Self traits: self-extension, self-confidence, and self-insight
Value traits: economic, religious, scientific, aesthetic, and liberal values
Problem-solving traits: ambition, emotional control, orderliness, and intelligence
Human-relations traits: gregariousness, dominance, warmth, and conformity.[12]

[12] Henry C. Smith, *Personality Adjustment,* New York: McGraw-Hill, 1961, p. 31.

Socially Effective Behavior

Certain personality traits as expressed in habitual patterns of overt behavior receive universal approval from society, unless the desirable behavior is colored by the influence upon it of other socially undesirable traits. Among the qualities that tend to earn for the person who possesses them the respect and admiration of his associates can be included neat, well-groomed, and attractive appearance; originality of ideas; punctuality in keeping appointments and in performing assigned tasks; cheerfulness; a sense of humor; good sportsmanship; sincerity; trustworthiness; generosity; kindness and sympathy; cooperation; modesty; loyalty, and ability to keep confidences.

This list of characteristics indicates that, in order to be liked by or popular with his fellows, an individual needs to shift the center of attention from himself and his own wants and desires to the interests of other persons with whom he is associated. The behavior pattern itself is satisfying only to the extent that in its expression may be recognized underlying selfless or social motives. For example, the individual receives disapproval from his group if it is evident that his cooperation or generosity is based upon ulterior motives of personal gain from such behavior; if the sincerity takes the form of an expression of personal feelings or opinions, without regard for their possible effect upon other people; if the sympathetic verges on the sentimental; if the cheerfulness is of the "Pollyanna" type; if the time and effort required to maintain an attractive appearance prevent the individual from participation in other socially approved activities. Successful group living represents intelligently balanced behavior patterns that are the expression of well-integrated, socially directed personality traits. Although certain characteristics appear to have universal significance, specific behavior is conditioned by societal standards of acceptability. For example, modesty is an admired trait. Yet, certain forms of behavior might be regarded by one group to evidence modesty but by another group to indicate lack of self-confidence.

The relationship of socially significant traits in personality is described by Munn. He says:

> [Traits that have] social significance contribute more weight than others to the personality as others see it. From the

standpoint of how others regard him, for example, his intelligence and his scholastic aptitude may be overshadowed by such social considerations as how well he gets along with others, how susceptible he is to irritation because of what people do and say, how he dresses, his manners, and how closely his behavior conforms with what is generally conceded to be moral and good. . . .

The aspect of the personality picture that predominates is always the *social* aspect. Those who say, quite incorrectly of course, that someone "has no personality" are saying, in reality, that they do not like him, or that they are indifferent to him. When they say, on the other hand, that someone "sure has a personality!" they are actually saying that they like him—that they are attracted to him rather than repelled or left indifferent. Popular terms like "sex appeal" further illustrate the point that, whatever personality may be in cold abstract scientific terms, to others it means the social self; the role played in social relations.[13]

Traits are inferred not observed in an individual's behavior. A general trait is one that pervades all or most of an individual's behavior patterns. Concerning the generality of traits, Guilford says:

By the generality of a trait, we mean the extent to which it is exhibited in the behavior of a person. Some traits are evident in almost everything a person does while others are exhibited in only a limited range of his behavior. To state it another way, the generality of a trait is proportional to the number of different trait indicators that apply to it.

Examples of broadly generalized traits would be nervousness, general-activity level, and restraint or self-control. Other traits enter into determination of certain areas of behavior but do not affect all or nearly all behavior. In this connection, we might mention the traits of endurance, interest in art, and affectionateness. There are only certain kinds of situations in which we should be able to detect any evidence as to a person's trait positions for these traits. We

[13] Norman L. Munn, *Introduction to Psychology*, Boston: Houghton Mifflin Company, 1964, p. 235.

should expect to see individual differences with respect to endurance only when there is need for individuals to persevere in an activity in the face of discomfort or pain. Interest in art would be best exhibited in behavior in the presence of art objects or implements or places of exhibit. Affectionateness would show itself in the presence of other persons or in letters or conversations.

Even less-generalized traits would be platform shyness, which is confined to appearing before groups, fear of cats, or fear of some particular cat. With these last examples, we see the continuity between the generality of traits and the phenomenon of generalization in learning. This does not necessarily mean that transfer of learning is the only basis for generalization of traits. Some of them, particularly the most widely generalized traits, could be determined by broadly effective hereditary dispositions.

Some traits, as we have seen, are restricted in their manifestations by reason of the range of situations in which the trait can operate. Other restrictions occur because the person himself has not generalized the trait. Traits of honesty, loyalty, and cordiality may be given as examples. The person who has not developed clear and strong principles of honesty that make him respond in the honest manner in many types of situations does not have a very generalized trait of honesty. He discriminates more sharply than do most people between different kinds of situations and needs for honesty. Similar statements could be made with regard to loyalty and cordiality. Thus, we can state two general principles with regard to generality of traits: there are some traits that tend to be more or less general among most people; there are also variations in generality of the same trait in different individuals.[14]

Although personality functions as a generalized whole, the effect upon behavior of its various components is worthy of study. Certain qualities or traits display themselves more or less strongly in an individual's behavior. Hence they may seem to be predictive of expected behavior in various situations. Since the display of a particular trait or characteristic *describes* but does

[14] Guilford, *Personality*, pp. 74–75.

not explain behavior, any prediction concerning its functioning in every situation may be inadequate. A businessman, for example, may be extremely cooperative in his business relationships but dictatorial and ungracious in his attitudes toward his family. The underlying causes of the differences in attitude probably lie in the total reaction pattern of the man in his various relationships. Personality traits may be deep-rooted in the personality structure, or their manifestation may depend upon definite environmental situations.

Woodworth and Marquis observed that among the large number of trait names in common use, many come in pairs of opposites. They suggest that the way to utilize the everyday vocabulary of names is to "place a pair of opposites at the ends of a line and regard this line as a dimension of personality, with individuals located at different parts of the line." They prepared a list of twelve of the most clearly established primary traits and placed their opposites alongside of them. A primary trait includes several specific traits which have much in common. The twelve primary traits, however, are relatively independent. The primary traits and their opposites as presented by Woodworth and Marquis are presented here.[15]

	Primary Traits	*Opposites*
1.	Easygoing, genial, generous, warm	Inflexible, cold, timid, hostile, shy
2.	Intelligent, independent, reliable	Foolish, unreflective, frivolous
3.	Emotionally stable, realistic, steadfast	Neurotic, evasive, emotionally changeable
4.	Dominant, ascendant, self-assertive	Submissive, self-effacing
5.	Placid, cheerful, sociable, talkative	Sorrowful, depressed, seclusive, agitated
6.	Sensitive, tenderhearted, sympathetic	Hard-boiled, poised, frank, unemotional
7.	Trained and cultured mind, esthetic	Boorish, uncultured

[15] R. S. Woodworth and D. G. Marquis, *Psychology*, 5th ed., New York: . Holt, Rinehart and Winston, 1947, pp. 91–92.

8. Conscientious, responsible, painstaking	Emotionally dependent, impulsive, irresponsible
9. Adventurous, carefree, kind	Inhibited, reserved, cautious, withdrawn
10. Vigorous, energetic, persistent, quick	Languid, slack, daydreaming
11. Emotionally hypersensitive, high-strung, excitable	Phlegmatic, tolerant
12. Friendly, trustful	Suspicious, hostile

SIGNIFICANT COMPONENTS
OF PERSONALITY

Although I regard personality as the integrated whole of all of an individual's traits, certain components of personality tend to be active in all of his reactions, and set the pattern for his general behavior and attitudes. Included among these components and discussed here are *intellect* and *intelligence, temperament,* and *character.* We shall consider others such as physique, constitution, and emotion elsewhere.

Intellect and Intelligence as Components of Personality

The terms *intellect* and *intelligence* often are used interchangeably. There is a difference, however, in their connotation. Royce distinguishes between the terms in this way.

Intellect is a qualitative term: the power or ability which makes man a certain kind of being, i.e., a rational animal; intelligence is a quantitative term, and refers to the amount of measurable operation we can expect from this power. Intellect as such cannot be measured, but there is no difficulty in expressing mathematically the external effects of this immaterial power. The problems are those of seeing that we measure nothing else, and that we catch the intellect when operating to its fullest capacity, i.e., under optimum conditions.

The intellect is the power of knowing the essence or

being of things; the ability to have universal ideas, judgments, and to reason (which operations are more than mere "verbalization"). It is often defined as the ability to utilize past experience in the solution of new problems. This is ambiguous, since it may include sensory association. Correctly taken, it comes down to the definition both Terman and Binet reached after spending most of their lives pioneering in intelligence tests: the power to abstract. This means the power to sift out from concrete sensory data the principles of things, and thus to deal effectively with one's environment, which is essentially Wechsler's definition. Intelligence seems to comprise this general ability plus various more specialized aspects or functions of it. Hence we speak of different kinds or factors of intelligence.[16]

Guilford explains the structure of intellect in terms of *operations, products,* and *contents.* Concerning these three kinds of classification he says:

> The three kinds of classifications of the factors of intellect can be represented by means of a single solid model [shown in Figure 4]. In this model, which we call the "structure of intellect," each dimension represents one of the modes of variation of the factors. Along one dimension are found the various kinds of operations, along a second one are the various kinds of products, and along the third are various kinds of content. Along the dimension of content a fourth category has been added, its kind of content being designated as "behavioral." This category has been added on a purely theoretical basis to represent the general area sometimes called "social intelligence." [17]

Mental ability or intelligent behavior may be explained briefly as rooted in the native ability of the organism to adjust to novel situations. Alertness of response to a situation for which there has not been developed a definite habit pattern depends upon the plasticity and permeability of the nervous system. Al-

[16] Royce, *Personality and Mental Health,* pp. 70–71.
[17] J. P. Guilford, "Three Faces of Intellect," *American Psychologist,* August, 1959, p. 471.

Figure 4. A Cubical Model Representing
the Structure of Intellect

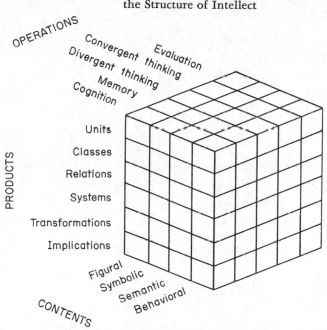

SOURCE: J. P. Guilford, "Three Faces of Intellect," *American Psychologist*, August, 1959, p. 471. Reprinted by permission.

though the general health state of neurons is important, the original constitution of the nervous system is biologically inherited but is more or less adaptable to environmental stimulation. Even the slow reactor has potentialities that he does not ordinarily exercise, since modern civilization has developed a routine of life that allows for the survival of less able individuals. Adjustments, in order to be permanently satisfying, however, must be within the limits of mental capacity for adjustment.

Spearman [18] described intelligence as a unitary or *general* process (the *g*) but recognized the presence of specific factors or *s*'s. Other psychologists, although admitting a general thread of intelligence running through all of man's mental abilities, have claimed that certain characteristics are common in intelligence.

[18] C. Spearman, *Abilities of Man*, New York: The Macmillan Company, 1927.

Thurstone,[19] factor-analyzing test items of intelligence to isolate specific abilities, developed the concept of the following primary mental abilities:

Verbal comprehension
Word fluency
Number
Space
Memory
Perception
Reasoning

Guilford and Zimmerman [20] stated that the basic elements of intelligent aptitude are:

Verbal comprehension
General reasoning
Numerical operations
Spatial orientation
Spatial visualization
Mechanical knowledge

Regardless of how we classify the components of mental ability, we realize that intelligence is a prime component of man's personality. An individual's behavior is influenced by his intellectual status. In any unselected group of individuals can be found persons of superior intelligence (the bright), the normal or average (constituting the major part of the population), and the mentally retarded (the dull). Individuals are not divided into three distinct categories, but represent a range of mental abilities from the very superior to the extremely retarded, each experiencing specific problems of adjustment.

The demands of the present social order are geared to the abilities of normal and superior individuals—those who have an intelligent quotient between 90 and 150. Other factors being equal, the average group is able to make a fairly satisfactory adjustment to existing life conditions. This adjustment is possible for the normally intelligent person only when he is not

---

[19] L. L. Thurstone, *Primary Mental Abilities*, Psychometric Monograph, No. 1, 1947.
[20] J. P. Guilford and W. S. Zimmerman, "The Guilford-Zimmerman Aptitude Survey," Beverley Hills: Sheridan Supply Co., 1947.

forced into fields of activity beyond his mental capacity. Too often parents whose children give evidence of normal or slightly below normal intelligence desire that their children prepare for vocations in which competition with more alert young people may lead to failure, discouragement, and emotional disturbance.

The very bright child may experience difficulties of adjustment in his relations with the less bright, especially if adults place too great emphasis upon his mental superiority. Parents and teachers sometimes are unwise in their laudatory comments to the child that nothing is required of him except to excel in competition with less able children. Since he does not have to exert himself unduly to uphold this slight superiority, he may develop habits of laziness and attitudes of mental snobbishness.

Unless an intellectually superior young person is brought into competition with his peers, there is no opportunity for the proper development of inherent potentialities. Even then the young person needs wise guidance, lest other difficulties of adjustment develop. An active, alert young person may be overstimulated by his elders. Too much may be expected in too short a time. The activities of a bright child may be controlled by his momentary interest to such an extent that no one activity is carried to a logical conclusion; he may become "jack of all trades and master of none" with an accompanying lack of joy in accomplishment.

If a superior individual or a group of superior individuals is kept aloof from less able individuals, there may result a lack of understanding of different types of humans. Such understanding is essential in a world in which no one group can live satisfactorily if it is completely isolated from all other and different groups. Relative values can be learned only through experience.

The problem of the mentally slow individual is different from that of his brighter brother, but it is equally serious. Disapproval from his family, failure to be accepted socially, and unequal competition in school or on the job may result in antisocial attitudes. An individual's inherited potentiality of intelligent response to his environment is an important factor of his personality adjustment. Just as important is his ability to recognize the adequacy of his adjustment and his ability to initiate desirable changes in those behavior patterns that need improvement. The person who possesses superior intelligence has a decided advantage over the less able person in the adjustment of his personality to social demands.

Temperament as a Component of Personality

Another significant component of an individual's personality is his temperament. One's temperament is closely associated with his emotional status, except that temperament refers rather

TABLE 4

A Matrix of Temperament Factors

Kind of Dimension	Areas of Behavior Involved		
	General	Emotional	Social
Positive vs. negative	Confidence vs. inferiority	Cheerfulness vs. depression	Ascendance vs. timidity
Responsive vs. unresponsive	Alertness vs. inattentiveness	Immaturity vs. maturity	Socialization vs. self-sufficiency
Active vs. passive	Impulsiveness vs. deliberateness	Nervousness vs. composure	Social initiative vs. passivity
Controlled vs. uncontrolled	Restraint vs. rhathymia	Stability vs. cycloid disposition	Friendliness vs. hostility
Objective vs. egocentric	Objectivity vs. hypersensitivity	Poise vs. self-consciousness	Tolerance vs. criticalness

Source: J. P. Guilford, Personality, New York: McGraw-Hill, Inc., p. 431. Copyright 1959. Used by permission.

to his emotional disposition as this has become habitualized than to his actual emotions. The individual develops certain emotionalized habits of behavior that differentiate him from other people. One person's emotional tone may differ from that of another. One is easily irritated and another is even-tempered; one is interested in his environment and seeks to explore it, but another is concerned only with self—responses differ; one becomes excited about a situation or condition, and the other is not affected by it—people differ in their susceptibility to emotional stimuli. According to Guilford:

> Among the better-known dimensions of temperament are the factors of confidence vs. inferiority feelings, restraint vs. rhathymia, objectivity vs. hypersensitivity, cheerfulness vs. depression, emotional immaturity vs. maturity, nervousness vs. composure, stability vs. cycloid disposition, ascendance vs. timidity, socialization vs. self-sufficiency, friendliness vs. hostility, and tolerance vs. criticalness.[21]

Guilford tabulates the factors of temperament in three columns of a matrix with headings of General, Emotional, and Social.

Character as a Component of Personality

Too often the terms *personality* and *character* are used as though they were synonymous. There is a difference between their connotations. Personality is used to describe all of an individual's behavioral reactions; character refers to his habit systems that are related to the functioning in his behavior of generally accepted ethical standards. Royce defines character as "the set of will-habits by which one is disposed to act according to principles." [22] To the extent that an individual consciously molds his behavior according to ethical principles, he can be said to exhibit *virtuous* traits. The person who acts on impulse, thereby satisfying his needs and wants without consideration of the "rightness" or "wrongness" of his behavior and its undesirable effect on himself and others, is engaging in so-called *vices*. Virtues and vices represent character components of personality. In this connection, Royce carefully describes the man of character (good character). "He is marked by those habits called virtues, either natural or supernatural. These include principles of wisdom, understanding, prudence in the intellect, and especially the very constituents of character, justice, fortitude, and temperance in the will." [23]

CHARACTER IN RELATION TO MENTAL ACTIVITY. A healthy-

---

[21] Guilford, *Personality*, p. 431.
[22] Royce, *Personality and Mental Health*, p. 74.
[23] *Ibid.*, p. 76.

minded person tends to respect the truth. The attitude of wanting to tell the truth dominates the life of such an individual. Since character traits are built early in life, parents and other adults are responsible for the development of a child's habits of truthfulness or dishonesty. This is true of all personal attitudes and behavior patterns that can be referred to as character traits. Sometimes we tend toward a self-righteous criticism of a person who is engaging in undesirable overt behavior. Too often, as we criticize, we fail to recognize the fact that we have contributed to the development of the undesirable behavior pattern.

A quantitative description of one's behavior indicates the relative strength or weakness of certain character traits. "Virtues and vices" are important in all social relations. The character of an individual determines for the individual his ultimate success and happiness so far as social values are concerned. The laws of learning and habit formation are of prime importance in the formation of character. Many a person's character qualities are results of imitation, either conscious or unconscious. Suggestion also is powerful and contributes in various ways to the ultimate mental attitudes and character traits that are potently active in the dynamic life of an individual.

ATTITUDES AND CHARACTER FORMATION. The attitudes displayed by an individual's associates do not necessarily give a true picture of his character. Although the terms *reputation* and *character* are closely related, they are not synonymous. We usually differentiate between reputation and character by saying that reputation refers to what people think you are but that character is what you really are. One's character traits soon stand out as those that are a part of his consistent behavior. Character education includes the development of right attitudes as well as the acquisition of behavior habits that are socially desirable. Not only can rules and regulations concerning good conduct be taught, but they can be understood and appreciated in the light of their values to the individual and to society. The child can be aided in making deliberate choices of behavior in harmony with his own and social betterment.

Attitudes toward people, events, or things are molded by what is said about them. Truth is often helpless when confronted by convincing misrepresentation. If a person who is known to have a good character is accused falsely of wrongdoing, he can save himself from undesirable penalties for the act only when the public emotional tide is moving in the right direction.

The Dynamic Aspect of Personality

In this discussion I have stressed the fact that one's personality pattern is relatively consistent throughout his life, except in so far as it may be strengthened, weakened, or changed as a result of experienced situations or conditions. Moreover, no personality trait functions in isolation, but represents interaction with other traits or integration. In addition, an individual is a living, functioning organism. He usually is sensitive to all the stimulating forces about him, and is more or less able to respond to them in a desirable fashion. The effect upon himself of the degree of success of his reactions aids or hinders the desirable development of all his personality traits. The effect of the overt expression of his personality traits upon other members of his group is in direct ratio to the personality patterns of the others. The adjustment of one's personality, therefore, is an outgrowth of the satisfaction or the lack of satisfaction to himself and to the members of the group that results from the interaction of whatever personality traits dominate individual and group interrelationships.

Personality is not static; it is a dynamic, ever changing expression of an individual's adjustment to changing factors in his environment. The effects may be far-reaching. Even the satisfaction of his fundamental physical wants cannot be divorced from his relations with other members of his group. He possesses many wants and interests. His social ego as well as his physical self must be satisfied. He craves recognition and approval from his associates. Consequently, he attempts to adjust his behavior in whatever way he considers appropriate to receive self-satisfying social approval.

PSEUDOSCIENTIFIC EXPLANATIONS
OF PERSONALITY

Many techniques have been devised and are still being used by pseudoscientists for the interpretation of personality traits. Among these are included phrenology, physiognomy, astrology, numerology, graphology, and palmistry. In each, a specialized procedure has been prepared, and individuals showing certain behaviors, traits, physical characteristics, lines of demarcation, or general tendencies are identified as belonging to certain types of personality in terms of the symbols devised for the respective forms of analysis. We shall describe these techniques briefly.

Phrenology

The underlying theory of phrenology assumes that the controls of an individual's personality traits are localized in definite areas of the brain. For example, phrenologists believe that such traits as love, musical ability, sympathy, and honesty result from the influence of certain specific areas. The degree of possession of a specific trait is thus dependent upon the degree of development or formation of the controlling brain area. The adherents of this theory fail to recognize the fact that, according to modern psychology, the brain cells and the number of brain convolutions are more important as directors of behavior than are the bumps on the head. Nor do the phrenologists recognize the fact that emotions and sentiments are the results of experiences that are gained through daily stimulation rather than results of the shape or size of the head.

Physiognomy

The adherents of the effect of a person's possession of certain physiological characteristics place great emphasis on the existence of a definite relationship between personality traits and such physical characteristics as head measurement, skin and hair texture, size and shape of the nose, ears, and eyes, muscular set and bone structure, height of brow, formation of chin, set of the jaw, and other physical characteristics. Such differences are supposedly regulated by the glandular secretions. Consequently, temperament and emotional constitution are presumed to be reflected in the physical form and features.

The Italian criminologist Lombroso, who developed an elaborate theory of criminal types based on physical measurements with emphasis on facial peculiarities, was an outstanding proponent of this theory. However, a study of criminals negates rather than supports his theory.

Astrology

As early as 300 B.C. the Egyptians had divided the zodiac into twelve signs and had mapped the stars. There is evidence that whole nations, such as the Babylonian, the Chinese, the Greek, and the Roman, believed strongly in the influence of the stars on man's life and destiny. Medieval universities included astrology among their studies. At present there are ardent supporters of the theory that the positions of the sun, moon, and planets at the time of an individual's birth exercise a potent effect on his behavior and experience.

A person's month and day of birth place him under the influence of a particular sign of the zodiac. The probable influence of his sign on the individual is called his *horoscope*. Each sign represents certain general characteristics that one may expect to find in a person born under its influence. The specific date of birth is accompanied by the possession of certain specific characteristics pertinent to the day. Elaborate systems of prediction are based on such further data as year, day of week, and hour of birth.

Numerology

Interest in numbers has come to us from ancient times. Mystic numbers such as *three* or *seven* have their roots in religious beliefs and rituals. *Thirteen* is a number to be avoided, according to many people. *Friday the thirteenth* is a day that augurs no good. However, such number combinations have come and gone with no particular ill luck for the majority of people. An accidental fulfillment of an expected event connected with one of these prophetic numbers is likely to be remembered, but similar experiences connected with less significant numbers usually are forgotten. Scientific study has revealed no appreciable connection between number significance and experimental expectancy.

Graphology

Characteristic handwriting long has been a stimulator of pseudoscientific attempts at character analysis. Size and shape of letters, intensity of stroke, and similar handwriting peculiarities lend themselves to this type of unscientific prediction. The open *o*, the pointed *m* or *n*, the dot on the *i*, the length of loop of such letters as *f, l,* or *g,* the direction of the final stroke of a word, or the formation of capital letters are all assumed to be connected with definite personality trends, such as generosity or meanness of disposition, mental acuity, emotional control, or executive ability. The general form and appearance of handwriting may indicate a certain degree of carelessness or precision, yet little beyond that can be predicted with certainty.

Palmistry

Second only to astrology, palmistry has had an interesting history as a pseudoscientific predictor of personal characteristics and future events. The study of palmistry goes back to antiquity but flourished particularly during the days of Greek civilization. The general disposition or character of a person is implicit in the descriptive adjectives assigned to his particular type of hand. Unfortunately for the accuracy of this theory, many hands follow no specific type and consequently indicate a mixture of personality qualities. The lines of the palm include the line of the heart, the line of fate, the line of health, the line of marriage, and those of children, besides other minor lines.

THEORIES OF PERSONALITY TYPES

There is a tendency to label an individual's personality in terms of a type description. An apparently dominant trait is emphasized as characteristic of the total personality with a disregard for other qualities. These attempts to group human phenomena into obvious and easily achieved categories are understandable. Some groupings are helpful to psychologists, psychiatrists, and others who are involved with the problems of personality adjustment while others come to us from earliest times and appear ridiculous to us now. All are associated with physical, mental, or emotional qualities.

The Four Temperaments

One of the earliest groupings of human traits is based on "humor" or disposition. About 400 B.C., Hippocrates attempted to classify personality according to body humors. Later, Galen (A.D. 150) became interested in a similar theory of personality types. The types and characteristics of body humors are given here.

Type	Characteristics
Sanguine	Quick, gay, not stable
Choleric	Easily angered
Melancholic	Pessimistic
Phlegmatic	Slow, unexcitable

Physical Types

Kretschmer was interested in discovering the extent to which the behavior of 400 individuals having mental disorders was related to their physical constitution. As a result of his study, he concluded that there can be found among all people two general types of disposition—*cycloids* and *schizoids*. The former tend to be good-natured, volatile, and socially inclined. The latter exhibit tendencies toward timidity, nervousness, reticence, and extreme sensitivity, but are kindly in their attitude toward others.

According to their physical form and stature, individuals were classified by Kretschmer as *athletic, asthenic, pyknic,* and *dysplastic.*[24] *Athletic* individuals are muscular and tend to be responsive to desirable adjustments, little concerned with serious thinking, and interested in activity and other people. *Asthenics* are likely to be tall and thin. They tend to be sensitive to criticism of themselves but critical of others. They are not particularly interested in physical activity or in the affairs of other people but devote their time and interests to intellectual pursuits. Physically, the *pyknic* tends toward shortness and stoutness. In disposition, he is easy-going and gets along well with other people. The *dysplastic* has an abnormal build with characteristics growing out of the abnormality.

Somatotypes

Sheldon, Stevens, and Tucker undertook to study some 4,000 male individuals by means of photographs of back, front, and

[24] For a more complete description of these types consult E. Kretschmer, *Physique and Character,* New York: Harcourt, Brace & Company, 1925.

side views. These findings became the basis of the groupings (*somatotypes*) into which the authors classified individuals. According to them, individuals fell into one of three general types: *endomorphic, mesomorphic,* or *ectomorphic.*

The *endomorphic* individual is characterized by softness and roundness of body. His behavior is dominated by massive digestive viscera. In the *mesomorphic* individual, muscle and bone predominate, the physique is usually hard and heavy, and the skin is thick. An *ectomorphic* individual tends to be fragile, and, because of his great surface area, is sensitive to exposure to the outer world.

The authors [25] present a 3-degree scale to allow for the dominance of one type over another. For example, the extreme endomorph would be described by the numerals 711, the extreme mesomorph by 171, and the extreme ectomorph by 117. The somatotype then results from the patterning of the morphological components. The authors suggest that the respective somatotypes have different needs and require different treatment if they are to become socially adjusted. Their food, dress, and mating require individual treatment. They believe that there are many types of body build, and that more than seventy can be distinguished.

Sheldon, Stevens, and Tucker held that associated with each somatotype is a basic temperament pattern. Associated with the endomorphic build is the *viscerotonic* temperament: amiability, love of comfort and of eating, sociability, and deep sleep. Associated with the mesomorphic build is the *somatotonic* temperament: love of physical adventure and dominating, assertiveness and courage, directness of attitude and general noisiness, need for action in adjustment. Associated with the ectomorphic build is *cerebrotonic* temperament: anxious, intense, secretive, inhibited, poor sleeper, in need of solitude when faced with problems of adjustment.

Endocrine Types

The secretions of endocrine glands affect the body indirectly through the distribution to all parts of the body of their secre-

[25] For a complete description and discussion of somatotypes consult W. H. Sheldon, S. S. Stevens, and W. B. Tucker, *The Varieties of Human Physique,* New York: Harper and Brothers, 1940.

tions via the blood stream. Each endocrine gland secretes one or more chemical agents known as a *hormone*. Because of their secondary effects on personality these glands are of special interest to psychologists. Attempts have been made to associate the variations in human behavior with the secretions of these glands. For example, personality qualities were believed to vary with the extent of the functioning of these glands.

Endocrine Type	*Characteristics*
Parathyroid	Explosive, aggressive
Hyperthyroid	Overambitious, domineering
Hypothyroid	Lazy, intellectually dull
Pituitary	Good-humored, patient, considerate, docile, diffident, tolerant of pain
Gonads, hyper-active	Very aggressive
Gonads, hypo-active	Less aggressive, interested in art, literature, and music.

Sociological Types

Individuals can be classified according to their reactions toward other people. The following classifications with their characteristics were suggested by Spranger.[26]

Sociological Type	*Characteristics*
Theoretical	Metaphysical, scientific
Economic	Very business-like
Esthetic	Sensuous, unreliable
Social	Interested in fellow beings and social movements
Political	Desirous of power over others
Religious	Either mystic and pietistic or missionary

[26] For a complete discussion of sociological types, consult E. Spranger, *Types of Men*, Halle: Niemyer, 1928.

Introvert, Ambivert, and Extrovert Types

According to Jung,[27] individuals can be classified into two psychological types, *introvert* and *extrovert*. Since all individuals do not seem to fit definitively into these two types, a third type, *ambivert,* was later added to the classification. The mixed type or ambivert includes the largest number of individuals. In fact, the introverts and the extroverts constitute only the extremes of a group.

The introvert is sensitive and shy and desires to be alone as much as possible. The extreme introvert directs his thinking toward himself and is ever fearful that other persons are commenting adversely about him and his behavior. He is afraid of people and finds it difficult to make friends. His feelings of inferiority may cause him to develop a definite antisocial and annoying attitude. However, the introvert may develop excellent habits of study and may exhibit inventive tendencies of great human value.

The extrovert directs his thinking away from himself and is less subjective than is the introvert. He is interested in his group and adjusts readily to group interests and wishes. He influences others and is influenced by them. He is willing and ready to take his share in social activities. He is not sensitive to criticism of his mistakes and failings and is usually popular among his fellows.

Too often the term *introversion* or *extroversion* assumes the extremes of behavior characteristics. As a matter of fact, there are relatively few cases that exemplify the extreme characteristics of either type of personality. The majority of individuals exhibit characteristics of both the introvert and the extrovert, and are accordingly classified as *ambiverts*. An ambivert may display introvert tendencies in one situation and extrovert tendencies in another situation. A good leader needs to possess both qualities. Characteristics descriptive of each are usually in contrasts. For example, the extrovert is relatively free from worry, the introvert inclines toward worry; the extrovert is friendly, the introvert tends to be reserved; the extrovert likes to work with others, the introvert likes to work alone.

---

[27] For a more complete discussion see C. Jung, *Psychological Types,* New York: Harcourt, Brace & Company, 1923.

Psychoanalytic Types

In their development of the psychoanalytic theory of personality types, Freud [28] and his followers appear to stress the effect on personality of environmentally stimulated satisfactions and frustrations as related to psychosexual development. These types represent abnormal rather than normal adjustment. The Freudian classification of types includes the following categories:

THE ANAL-EROTIC TYPE.   This type is characterized by obsessions related to such traits as parsimony, obstinacy, and orderliness. All of these usually are displayed in an extreme form.

THE ORAL-EROTIC TYPE.   The oral-erotic type of individual may be an active, "biting" type or a passive, "sucking" type. The oral-active type is characterized by obsessions of chewing and biting as escapes from feelings of frustration. He is pessimistic, suspicious, and malicious. The oral-passive type attempts to find escape from frustration by a return to infantile patterns of behavior. He is optimistic, but dependent and immature. He shirks responsibilities and expects others to care for him and satisfy his needs.

THE GENITAL TYPE.   In the genital types we find two classifications: (1) the phallic type characterized by exhibitionism, over-ambition, boasting, and narcissism (self-admiration); and (2) the normal development of gential-sexual maturity. The latter includes many individuals who have achieved a desirable balance between ambition and restraint, dependence and independence, and selfishness and altruism.

Value of Theories of Personality Types

Any one of the aforementioned classifications is open to criticism. It is difficult to find individuals who fall completely into any one of the groupings of many of the categories used. Individuals tend to be alike in the kinds of traits that they possess, but they differ in the degree to which they possess them. Human beings and their traits are so complex that is it impos-

---

[28] For a more complete discussion of Freud's analytic types see Sigmund Freud, *An Outline of Psychoanalysis,* New York: W. W. Norton & Company, 1949.

sible to classify them without excluding some of the very obvious characteristics. Classifications are possible if we are willing to ignore some personality factors. Crude as the types are, they tend to place individuals into groups for purposes of better remedial treatment. As the measuring instruments are refined, there may be developed means of better classification.

THE ADJUSTING PERSONALITY

A person's life consists of a series of physical, mental, and emotional responses that are conditioned by the effect upon him of the people and objects in his environment. Fundamental to every stage of his changing life adjustments is the fulfillment of his needs as these are associated with physical welfare, freedom of activity, and attainment of economic and social security.

Concomitant with the struggle for the achievement of his basic life requirements, an individual experiences many changing but vital desires, urges, and ambitions that take on, at each stage of his development, characteristics which are peculiar to his age level. Successful adjustment to human relationships at any age level is conditioned by the degree of success attained at earlier levels.

Personal Habits and Adjustment

During the first six years of his life the child, mainly through imitation, acquires a system of habits that are necessary for survival. If he is physically and mentally normal, he learns to walk, eat, talk, and care for his needs according to the patterns of behavior by which he is surrounded and that are accepted by his group. He may acquire a complex of characteristics that show good integration or coordination of habits and impulses. This adjustment will continue just *so long as the child's environment remains relatively fixed.*

As soon as new elements enter the environment, or the child enters a new environment for which his habit patterns are not ready, his former satisfactory adjustment suffers, unless he is able to change some of his existing habits of response or unless new habits are learned. The first day at school may be a bewildering experience to the six-year-old child. The child who enters this larger social group by way of the nursery school and the kindergarten usually is much happier in his adjustment to elementary school life than is the child who goes directly from the sheltered environment of the home into this new and strange world. The experiences of childhood are repeated more or less gradually throughout an individual's life. Learning to adjust to changing stimuli from within and without the organism is a continuous process. Maturing organic functions stimulate the individual in such ways that new responses are needed. An example of this is the adolescent's changed attitude toward his relationships with members of the opposite sex.

More or less frequently during his life the individual meets new social demands: he goes from elementary school to high school and perhaps to college; he enters upon his lifework; he moves from one neighborhood to another; he loses old associates and gains new ones; his economic or social status changes; he is called upon by society to assume new responsibilities; he earns social condemnation or acclaim. All these new and varied experiences require new and varied responses.

Wholesome Adjustment

As an individual matures, he retains certain fundamental attitudes and behavior patterns. The developing personality displays a continuous underlying purpose that leads to consistency of behavior, no matter how changed the overt expression of the personality may be. As his experiences increase, the individual develops, in light of his success and failure, certain desirable habits of adaptability. He meets each new situation in terms of responses that are a part of his behavior pattern but that are modified in whatever way may seem necessary. The individual has learned to adjust. He possesses, in consequence, a stable integrated personality that is at all times capable of desirable adaptation.

Healthful adjustment results in effective and socially accepted behavior responses which, in turn, result in satisfaction and mental health for the individual. The fact that a person fits the requirements of a situation makes it easier for him to adjust to another situation that is not too different from the one previously experienced. In this way forward-looking, persistent drives are established. A succession of satisfactory responses stimulated by these drives develops habits which in their strength and effectiveness bring about smoothly running adjustments.

Because of a harmonious interaction of his personality traits, the mentally healthy person is able to adapt a generally stable and persistent series of consistent values to the solution of the specific and varied problems with which he is confronted daily in his associations with other more or less stable individuals, groups, or environmental situations. His behavior is consistent and positive; his personality is wholesome, integrated, and socially valuable.

Inadequate Personality Adjustment

Inadequate personality adjustment may limit itself to the inability of one trait to function satisfactorily in any situation by which it is stimulated. For example, the tendency to fear is normal. If, because of unfortunate childhood experiences or as a result of even one such experience, an individual has developed a timid or fearful attitude, he may fail to meet adequately any situation that presents stimuli which for him are fear-arousing. Each such failure reduces his ability to adjust successfully to similar, ensuing situations. In spite of the possession of other very desirable qualities, the fearful individual may become disorganized and unstable.

Maladjustment may result also from a lack of harmony among an individual's various personality traits. In any given situation his behavior may be affected by conflict between two opposing inner drives, both of them desirable. The resulting behavior may be negative or inhibited; it may be vigorous or uncontrolled, and unfitted to the demands of the situation. Because of this conflict, tension develops and the individual does not have the power to adapt himself to the experiences of the situation.

A man who is alert and scientifically trained has developed a general attitude of fair-mindedness, honesty, and objectivity in his relations with others. He is generous and sympathetic. He finds himself, however, in a situation that involves two other persons, both of whom are dear to him and each of whom desires his attention to the exclusion of the other one. The man is torn between his intelligent understanding of the need for objective, fair treatment of the situation, and his urge to refrain from hurting the feelings of either of the two persons. The conflict that arises may drive the man to withdraw completely from the situation. Because of economic or social reasons this action may be impossible. He may engage in a series of behavior responses that alternately favor one and are unfair to the other. In any case, the stress elements of the situation may be so great that the whole pattern of this man's relations with his associates is so colored by his conflict that he becomes socially maladjusted.

Specific personality characteristics are developed by individuals as adjustments to their environments. Although extreme personality disorders are discussed in Chapter 11, I shall present at this point a few of the basic factors involved in individual maladjustment. Personality is the resultant of the interaction of organism and environment. An individual's personality components may take on an exaggerated form. They became fixed to the extent that they interfere seriously with the capacity of the individual to adjust to his immediate environment, to new situations, or to his family or social relationships. For example, daydreaming or fantasy may result in a complete flight from reality. Alcohol, first used as a means of escape from conflict, becomes a mode of life that results in asocial behavior. When these symptoms are severe, the individual is incapable of making new adjustments; he is badly maladjusted or even mentally ill.

Personality Adjustment Versus Maladjustment

Maladjustments may grow out of constitutional defects, environmental deficiencies, educational inadequacies, or sudden or unexpected shocks or thwartings which themselves may be the result of one or more of the first three. Physical characteristics, degree of capacity for recognition of the significance of stimuli, ambition, emotional drives and excitations—all present possibilities of adjusted or of unadjusted responses. Habits begun in early childhood and persisted in during the lifetime of the individual lead to the development either of good mental health or of mental illness.

The well-adjusted person attacks problems objectively and intelligently. He is able to recognize the significance of his behavior as related to that of other people. His emotional reactions to a problem and its possibility of solution do not interfere with his accustomed habits of meeting difficulties with confidence, born of past experience, in his power to adjust the difficulty with a relative degree of success. If he is not able to achieve complete satisfaction in his solution, he is able to accept the partial failure without undue emotional disturbance. He is prepared to meet other problems which may arise with an equally intelligent and unemotional attitude.

The maladjusted person is a prey to his own emotional instability. If he is confronted by a problem, he becomes so disturbed in its presence that he is unable to organize his thinking processes toward a sane solution. He may attempt to dodge the issue or to resort to tricks or subterfuges, in order to give the impression that he has met the situation adequately. He may attempt to ignore the difficulty and to retreat into a subjective and self-satisfying state of emotionalism. Such behavior causes the solution of subsequent problems to be increasingly difficult. Thus the illusory, irrational dreams of fulfillment cause him gradually to develop habits of irresponsibility and of seeking security in the figments of his own imagination.

Personality is a complex of dynamic, more or less flexible components which are modifiable. At any stage of his development an individual's personality represents a total pattern or *configuration* that is something more than the combination of all the traits that comprise it. Hence it is extremely difficult to isolate, for the purpose of evaluation, the functioning of any one trait or quality. The extent to which and the ways in which psychologists have attempted to devise valid and reliable techniques of personality evaluation are described briefly in the next chapter.

QUESTIONS AND PROBLEMS

1. Report on the relationship between intelligence status and personality adjustment.

2. Show how an individual's personality is affected by changes in the environment.

3. Describe a social environment favorable to personality development.

4. Justify the statement that an individual has personality. Also that he is a personality.

5. Discuss adjustment differentiation and integration in relation to personality and its development.

6. How can restrictions be placed on human behavior and still allow for freedom of individual initiative?

7. What is your attitude toward pseudoscientific personality evaluation?

8. According to the descriptions of the various personality theories, make an evaluation of your own personality pattern.

9. To what extent are you influenced in your evaluation of another's personality by his physical appearance?

10. Indicate personality qualities or traits that predispose toward success in each of the following fields: social work, scientific research, teaching, salesmanship, parenthood.

11. Explain and justify this statement: No two persons have identical personalities.

12. What do you consider to be your most desirable personality trait? The least desirable?

13. To what extent does the adjustment of one person to another depend on the extent to which they are similar?

14. Explain: "Self-evaluating reactions vary as a child matures."

15. Explain what is meant by *self-concept,* and indicate ways in which it is developed.

16. Study the various definitions of personality given in this chapter. Indicate, with reasons, the one you prefer.

17. Name personality traits that lead to popularity among one's peers. Justify your choices.

18. Why do displayed traits describe rather than explain personality?

19. Differentiate between personality and character.

Selected Readings

Allport, G. W., *Pattern and Growth in Personality*. New York: Holt, Rinehart and Winston, Inc., 1961.

————, *Personality and Social Encounter*. Boston, Mass.: Beacon Press, 1964.

Bandura, A., and R. H. Walters, *Social Learning and Personality Development*. New York: Holt, Rinehart and Winston, Inc., 1963.

Bischof, L. J., *Interpreting Personality Theories*. New York: Harper & Row, Publishers, 1964.

Bloom, B. S., *Stability and Change in Human Characteristics*. New York: John Wiley & Sons, Inc., 1964.

Dreger, R. M., *Fundamentals of Personality*. Philadelphia, Penna.: J. B. Lippincott Company, 1963.

Edelson, M., *Ego Psychology, Group Dynamics and the Therapeutic Community*. New York: Grune & Stratton, Inc., 1964.

Gordon, J. E., *Personality and Behavior*. New York: The Macmillan Company, 1963.

Guilford, J. P., *Personality*. New York: McGraw-Hill, Inc., 1959.

Lazarus, R. S., *Personality and Adjustment*. Englewood Cliffs, N.J.: Prentice-Hall, Inc., 1963.

Lindzey, G., and C. S. Hall (eds.), *Theories of Personality*. New York: John Wiley & Sons, Inc., 1965.

Lundin, R. W., *Personality: An Experimental Approach*. New York: The Macmillan Company, 1961.

Mussen, P. H., J. J. Conger, and J. Kagan, *Child Development and Personality*, 2nd ed. New York: Harper & Row, Publishers, 1963.

Royce, J. E., S.J., *Personality and Mental Health*, rev. ed. Milwaukee, Wisc.: The Bruce Publishing Company, 1964.

Sahakian, W. S. (ed.), *Psychology of Personality: Readings in Theory*. Chicago, Ill.: Rand McNally & Company, 1965.

Sappenfield, B. R., *Personality Dynamics: An Integrative Psychology of Adjustment*. New York: Alfred A. Knopf, Inc., 1956.

Sarason, I. G., *Personality: An Objective Approach*. New York: John Wiley & Sons, Inc., 1966.

Schneiders, A. A., *Personality Development and Adjustment in Adolescence*. Milwaukee, Wisc.: The Bruce Publishing Company, 1960.

Sears, P. S., and V. S. Sherman, *In Pursuit of Self-Esteem*. Belmont, Calif.: Wadsworth Publishing Co., 1964.

Smelser, N. J., and W. T. Smelser, *Personality and Social Systems.* New York: John Wiley & Sons, Inc., 1963.

Smith, H. C., *Personality Adjustment.* New York: McGraw-Hill, Inc., 1961.

Southwell, E. A., and M. Merbaum (eds.), *Personality Readings in Theory and Research.* Belmont, Calif.: Wadsworth Publishing Co., 1964.

White, R. W., *The Abnormal Personality,* 3rd ed. New York: The Ronald Press Company, 1964.

⚜ 6 ⚜

PERSONALITY
EVALUATION

ANY PROGRAM of personality adjustment or readjustment undertaken by the individual himself or by those interested in his
welfare must begin with an analysis of his inherent attitudes and
his behavior patterns. Considerable time and effort have been
devoted to the measurement of personality through the years.
During this time some progress has been achieved, mainly
through the ability to quantify the results and to exercise some
control over the situation and the conditions in which the measurements are being taken.

APPROACHES IN PERSONALITY
EVALUATION

It is difficult to achieve an adequate evaluation of an individual's developing personality. The subtle interactions among
the many phases of the total personality pattern may so affect the
attitudes and behavior of a developing individual that major
changes may appear from one week to another. Personality evaluation, therefore, can be expected to yield reliable data in so far as

it represents what the individual is like at the time the measurements are taken.

Scope of Personality Evaluation

An evaluation of the various areas of an individual's personality is concerned with the measurement of such personal characteristics as physical and mental status; special abilities and aptitudes, attitudes; kind and extent of achievement; and nature and extent of emotional reactions. Attention needs to be directed as well to an evaluation of the total behavior pattern of an individual that commonly is included in the concept of the term *personality*.

All measuring instruments that attempt to evaluate an individual's motivating interests, drives, and behavior are measures of personality. In a narrower sense, the term personality evaluation involves the measurement of the affective phases of an individual's personality. Measurement of his attitudes toward himself and others, his degree of adjustment as indicated by his report on preferred activities, people, and places, his fears, his worries, his likes and dislikes, and his understanding of socially desirable behavior can be discovered by means of well-constructed and properly administered measurement devices

An individual's personality patterns are not static but adapt themselves to factors within and outside himself. Hence personality measurement yields ratings that may vary with the time, techniques, and conditions of the testing. The emotional state of the individual, his relationship to the tester, and his attitude toward the test itself are factors that may influence the results of a test administered at a given time. The emotional factor, the deliberate intention to falsify, and the inability to recall past experiences and attitudes may adversely affect the accuracy of personality measurements.

In his discussion of "Homogeneity and Variation in Measuring Personality" Donald W. Fiske outlines three common models in the measurement of personality traits, as follows:

> Let us consider some types of definitions for personality traits and the corresponding psychometric models involved in test operations. Three common models are found in the

measurement of traits. One approaches a trait in terms of *pure relative frequency*. It asks this question: Without regard to the particular stimuli and situations confronting a subject, how often does he manifest a particular kind of behavior? Thus talkativeness could be defined as the proportion of time a person talks (when he is with other people).

A variant on this model is measurement with standard stimuli such as inkblots. From the same set of responses, we can determine the frequency for several characteristics: movement, human, popular, etc. In this procedure, the stimuli are the same for all subjects and the situation is more or less constant. Note, however, that in such tests, we do *not* select one set of stimuli to be used for measuring this variable, another set for that variable, and so on.

Another model is based on relative frequency for relevant stimuli. We can label this approach *specific relative frequency*. Here the stimulus items are selected from those identified or implied by the definition of the variable. This is the most commonly used model today. We find it not only in timed tests of abilities or achievement but also in interest tests and personality inventories. Thus neurotic tendency is indexed by the number of symptoms a subject reports in his responses to a neurotic inventory.

For such a test, the score is the number of positive or keyed responses, regardless of the items to which they are made. The model and the test constructor do not differentiate among the multitude of items which are clearly within the relevant domain. In principle, any such items will do.

A third major model is the *cumulative homogeneity* one, so named by Jane Loevinger (1948). It is best illustrated by power tests of intelligence, especially individual tests. Thus vocabulary is measured by the number of items the subject can define, the items being of increasing difficulty, that is, having decreasing frequencies of correct responses in the general population. . . .

So one recommendation which I wish to make for improving our measurement of personality variables is more work along the same general lines that we have been following, but with particular emphasis on stratification of items and on reduction of person-item interaction. It seems quite possible that increased effort devoted to the creation and testing of items may produce considerably improved tests of the conventional type.

But such hard work will produce only a partial solution to the problem. What is also needed is ingenuity, creativity, and a willingness to try something new. I think we should try to make personality tests less peculiar and unusual. Instead of asking questions about which the subject has never thought, we might find ways of tapping well-practiced responses.

Another promising direction is to develop measures based on meaningful tasks. While the task itself may be novel, it can be simple enough so that the subject readily grasps what he is expected to do. Examples are the tests of what Thurstone called temperament, and those currently categorized as cognitive style. Some of these get at consistent perceptual tendencies, dispositions to see things in certain ways. More generally, I believe it will be profitable to concentrate on tests where the subject's response is based upon his immediate experience, his reactions in the laboratory or testing room, rather than on his perceptions of his prior experiences mediated by his interpretation of the requirements of the testing instrument.[1]

Special Methods of Personality Evaluation

There are many methods of arriving at an evaluation of an individual's personality pattern. Some of these techniques are used by people in their everyday relations with others. Some techniques should be employed only by trained experts. Since personality and personality traits are subjective and modifiable there probably is no one reliable yardstick by which they can be measured. Evaluating techniques are valuable, however, in that they seem to indicate certain tendencies or trends, the presence of which in some instances appears to be linked with observable forms of behavior disorder. The extent to which such a situation exists for one individual at one specific time is a matter of

[1] Donald W. Fiske, "Homogeneity and Variation in Measuring Personality," *American Psychologist*, October, 1963, pp. 644, 651.

conjecture to be checked by means of all the obtained data that are available for study.

Various techniques are employed by psychologists, psychiatrists, sociologists, and educators as they attempt to evaluate individual potentialities, achievements, attitudes, and general behavior. These techniques include observation; the use of questionnaires, standardized tests (especially intelligence and aptitude), rating scales, inventories, projective procedures, and sociometric methods; the interview; and the construction of a case history. The data thus obtained have value to the extent that they are interpreted intelligently and utilized in such a way that the individual concerned may benefit from them.

EVALUATION THROUGH OBSERVATION. Unless an individual is completely self-involved, he is sensitive to the behavior or the displayed attitudes of people whom he encounters in his daily-life activities. Trained persons who, for one or another reason, are especially interested in evaluating an individual's behavior may give careful attention to what that person says and does. Hence observation of other people can be considered to be either casual or controlled.

Casual Observation. As we sit in a streetcar or a train, or in a lecture hall, or find ourselves in any other group situation, we tend to evaluate the personalities of the people around us. Such casual observations often are wholly or partially inaccurate because of the observer's inability or unwillingness to recognize correct relationships. Prejudice, carelessness in noting details, or lack of experience may invalidate the observation.

Controlled Observation. Effectively controlled observation is definite, specific, and well organized. The subject's behavior is recorded during the period of observation; it then is analyzed without prejudice, and the results of the observation intelligently interpreted. The trained observer begins his observation with a carefully planned list of items to be observed.

Controlled observation may be *vertical,* i.e., the observer studies an individual over a period of time, with special attention given to development changes that may be occurring during the period of observation. The process of observation sometimes is *horizontal,* i.e., the observer studies the reaction of a particular age or developmental stage group, in order to discover the extent to which and the ways in which the members of the group give indications of similarity and/or difference.

The two methods of approach may be combined. The members of a group are observed, according to a well-planned program of observation, intensively, over a period of time. Not only is each member of the group observed and studied, but group interaction is watched all along the way. The California study of bright children, for example, included observation of the behavior of all the members of the group included in the project from the beginning of the study through the ensuing twenty-five years of their life.

Specifically directed observation is an excellent method of studying behavior patterns of various age, racial, or occupational groups. In order to result in scientifically accepted conclusions, these observations must cover a reasonable number of cases, be reported accurately, and be interpreted unemotionally.

Utilization of Questionnaires in Personality Evaluation

Individuals have been studied through the use of the questionnaire since the end of the nineteenth century. This device can be used to gain information from the individual (self-rating) or by ratings of others. In either instance, subjective elements are involved. Data gathered need to be interpreted in light of the raters as well as the nature and extent of the questionnaire utilized.

Questionnaires can be used to obtain self-ratings concerning such personality factors as interests, attitudes, emotional states, temperament, personal reactions. They also can be used by teachers, psychologists, or other interested persons to formulate judgments concerning personality characteristics of selected individuals. Many questionnaires are so devised that the items can be answered by "Yes" or "No." The *Bernreuter Personality Inventory* provides for three categories in the answer: "Yes," "No," or "?." By the administration of six different keys to the same answer sheet, measurement is provided for six different aspects of personality: neuroticism, self-sufficiency, introversion, dominance, confidence, sociability.

The value and usefulness of questionnaires depends on their validity and reliability. Those in use today represent a wide range of validity and reliability. Questionnaires having good validity are those whose items have been preselected experimentally. Otherwise they must rest on *a priori* assumptions of validity. Their reliability is considered to be satisfactory if they yield consistent results when administered in comparable situations. Applications of the questionnaire will be demonstrated when we discuss the rating scales and inventories.

QUESTIONNAIRES THAT MEASURE EXTENT OF ADJUSTMENT. So-called adjustment questionnaires include questions concerning fears, worries, dreams, social maladjustment, likes and dislikes, and physical symptoms. Discovered deviations from normal emotional attitudes and responses are assumed to be indicated by the number and type of responses that deviate from what is generally considered to be normal behavior.

An early form of adjustment questionnaire is Woodworth's Psychoneurotic Inventory, commonly known as the *Woodworth Personal Data Sheet*. The inventory contains questions such as "Do your eyes often pain you?" "Have you ever lost your memory for a time?" Many modifications of this inventory have been devised. The *Laird-Colgate Test of Emotional Outlets* employs a form of graphic rating scale in order to determine the degree of desirable or undesirable behavior of personality types such as psychasthenoid, schizoid, neurasthenoid, and hysteroid. Allport and Allport's *Ascendance-Submission Reaction Study* attempts to measure the extent to which one tends to dominate another in a face-to-face relationship. Chassell in her *Experience Variables Record* emphasizes childhood and family relations.

The *Minnesota Multiphasic Personality Inventory* (MMPI), consisting of 550 statements, has been carefully standardized to compare the responses of individuals having psychiatric diagnoses with those of normal individuals. Keys have been prepared to measure such reactions as Hypochondriasis, Depression, Hysteria, Psychopathic Deviate, Paranoia, Psychasthenia, Schizophrenia, Hypomania, and Masculinity-Femininity. Through the years this test has proven valuable as an aid in differentiating disturbances of personality. The MMPI seems to have acceptable potentialities for clinical use, since it correlates well with an individual's anxiety and academic achievement in high school.

The *Pressey X-O Test* attempts through the technique of crossing out significant words to discover an individual's abnormal fears, worries, likes and dislikes, and sex tendencies. These tests have been widely used. Form B, adapted for use with relatively normal individuals, especially adolescents, gives an interesting picture of the individual's acquired attitudes toward common elements of his environment. For example, in Test 1 the subject is asked to cross out everything he thinks is wrong in each of twenty-five lists of terms, as *begging, smoking, flirting, spitting, giggling.* In Test 2 he crosses out everything he has ever worried about or felt nervous or anxious about, as *loneliness, work, forgetfulness, school, blues.* In Test 3 he crosses out everything he likes or is interested in, as *fortune-telling, boating, beaches, mountains, vaudeville.*

Techniques for the measuring of extroversion (the tendency to make adjustments by turning the attention outward to the situation) and introversion (the tendency to make adjustments by turning the attention inward and withdrawing from the external world) have been constructed by Heidbreder (*Minnesota Personal Traits Rating Scales*), Marston (*Personality Rating Scale*), Neymann and Kohlstadt (*Introversion-Extroversion Test*), and others.

QUESTIONNAIRES THAT MEASURE ATTITUDE. A commonly used technique for the determination of attitudes is the Thurstones' *Personality Schedule,* which consists of 223 questions drawn from the questions of Woodworth, Laird, Allport, and other workers in the field. Some of the most significant questions of this schedule include: "Are your feelings easily hurt?" and "Do you frequently feel grouchy?"

Attempts also have been made to measure such attitudes as moral, political, religious, economic, social, and so forth. Among the questionnaires used to measure various attitudes are included Allport and Vernon's *A Study of Values;* Bell's *School Inventory;* Hill's *Civic Attitude Test;* Watson's *Public Opinion Test;* Thurstone's (*et al.*) *Specific Attitude Scales;* Thurstone's *Measurement of Social Attitudes;* Downey's *Will-Temperament Test;* Williamson and Darley's *Minnesota Inventory of Social Attitudes;* Pressey's *Interest and Attitude Test;* Guilford-Zimmerman's *Temperament Survey;* and Johnson's *Temperament Analysis.*

Care must be exercised in the use of these tests and their results. Whether attitudes are measured directly or indirectly, it is important that behavior be evaluated in terms of contributing factors. For direct measurement of attitudes, the cooperation of the testee is essential in order that honest responses may be obtained. This is not always easy to achieve. However, for the obtaining of objective measures of individual attitudes these standardized approaches are more reliable than any questionnaires that may be devised by the evaluator.

INTEREST QUESTIONNAIRES OR INVENTORIES. The extent to which measures of interest are reliable indicators of an individual's actual interests is dependent on the sincerity of his responses to the questions posed in the inventory. Unless he is willing to report what he actually thinks or feels, rather than what he believes he should report, his responses are valueless.

Children tend to be influenced by environmental stimuli toward temporary periods of intense interest in one form or another of personal or recreational interest. An interest inventory is valuable to the extent that it discloses a continuity of general interest trends. Such techniques used in connection with other measuring instruments such as intelligence tests, aptitude tests, achievement tests, and other forms of personality tests are of value in the advancement of the guidance services for individuals.

Vocational interest inventories are useful to the extent that they reveal indications of behavior habits, interests, and attitudes that point to fitness for one vocational field, such as science, rather than for another that requires literary interest and achievement as a prerequisite. The most widely used instrument for measuring vocational interests is Strong's *Vocational Interest Inventories,* available in five forms. The subject is given an opportunity to indicate his attitude toward 100 occupations, 36 school subjects, 49 recreations, 47 peculiarities of people, and 48 activities. These interest blanks cover a wide and comprehensive field of individual interests. Other vocational interest inventories include Cleeton's *Vocational Interest Inventory,* Gentry's *Vocational Interest Inventory,* Hepner's *Vocational Interest Quotient,* Freyd's *Occupational Interest Blank,* Roeder's *Aptitude Tests for Occupations,* and Kuder's *Preference Record.* The last named has had wide application although its usefulness is now being questioned.

In Chapter 5 I presented twenty-five personality traits that I wish to emphasize here in a discussion of personality. These personality traits have been organized in table form by Smith according to personality traits measured by the Edwards' *Personal Preference Schedule,* Cattell's *Sixteen Personality Factor Questionnaire, and* Gough's *California Psychological Inventory.* They are presented in Table 5.

TABLE 5

Traits Measured by Inventories

Trait List of This Book	Edwards' Personal Preference Schedule, 1954	Cattell's Sixteen Personality Factor Questionnaire, 1956	Gough's California Psychological Inventory, 1954
Activity	Endurance	Nervous tension	
Sensory awareness			
Sexuality	Heterosexuality		
Emotionality		Emotional sensitivity	
Optimism		Surgency	
		Calm trustfulness	
Expressiveness	Exhibitionism		Impulsivity
Thinking extraversion			
Speed of closure			
Flexibility of closure			Flexibility
Self-extension		Sophistication	
Self-confidence		Self-sufficiency	Self-acceptance
			Social presence
Self-insight			
Economic values			
Religious values			
Scientific values	Intraception		
Aesthetic values			
Liberalism		Radicalism	
Ambition	Achievement		
Orderliness	Order	Positive character	
	Change		
Intelligence		General intelligence	Intellectual efficiency
Emotional control		Emotional stability	
		Will control	
Gregariousness	Affiliation		
	Autonomy	Adventurous cyclothymia	Social participation

TABLE 5 (*continued*)

Trait List of This Book	Edwards' Personal Preference Schedule, 1954	Cattell's Sixteen Personality Factor Questionnaire, 1956	Gough's California Psychological Inventory, 1954
Warmth	Nurturance	Cyclothymia Accessibility	Tolerance
Dominance	Dominance Deference Abasement Aggression	Dominance	Dominance
Conformity		Bohemianism	Social responsibility Delinquency

Source: Henry C. Smith, *Personality Adjustment*, New York: McGraw-Hill, Inc., pp. 64–65. Copyright 1961. Used by permission.

Smith also presents a comparison of the views of Sigmund Freud and William James on the twenty-five personality traits listed. The ratings of these two men were based on studies of their specific works, as well as on statements made by Freud. The result is shown in Figure 5.

THE MEASUREMENT OF ABILITY, APTITUDE, AND ACHIEVEMENT

School people are particularly interested in discovering a student's potential abilities and aptitudes and the extent to which he displays his degree of these in the kind of achievement ratings he demonstrates. Some young people are high achievers because of their urge to succeed. They usually perform as well as is expected. Others do not measure up to their potential and need to be encouraged to develop a greater interest in scholastic work. They often need help in the development of good study habits.

Measurement of Ability in Personality Evaluation

Mental competence is an essential factor of mental health. There is probably no more significant cause of mental and emo-

Figure 5. Trait Ratings of Freud and James

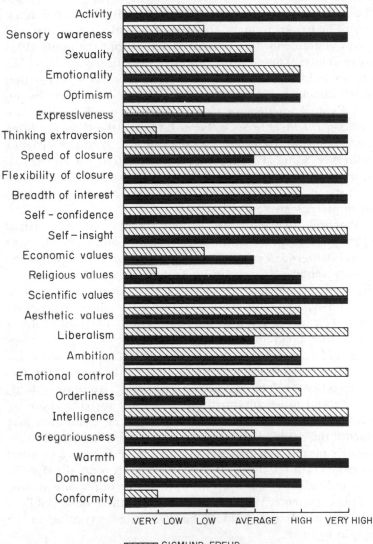

SOURCE: Henry C. Smith. *Personality Adjustment.*
New York: McGraw-Hill, p. 34.   Copyright 1961.
Used by permission.

tional maladjustment than an attempt to compete in any given activity with individuals who possess greater capacity for successful achievement. Promise of competence in specific areas appears to be in direct ratio to degree of mental acuity. Each individual needs to be helped to make the type of life adjustment that will be most desirable for him and for society within the limits of his mental acuity. The administration of intelligence tests, either group or individual, will provide information for a comparison of one individual with another individual or group of individuals. Individual intelligence tests include Terman-Merrill's *Stanford-Binet Intelligence Scale,* Form L-M, and the *Wechsler Intelligence Scale for Children* (WISC), or the *Wechsler-Bellevue Intelligence Scale* (WBIS). The Wechsler tests include verbal and performance subtests. Individual tests of intelligence can be administered and interpreted adequately only by carefully trained psychologists and clinicians.

Practical intelligence tests include verbal group tests, such as Haggerty's *Intelligence Examination,* Delta I and Delta II, Otis's *Group Intelligence Test,* Terman's *Group Test of Mental Ability,* Henman-Nelson's *Mental Ability Test,* Kuhlmann-Anderson's *Intelligence Test,* and Sullivan-Clark-Tiegs' *California Test of Mental Maturity,* 1963 edition. The Pintner-Cunningham *Primary Mental Test* can be given to the young child. This will enable a school testing program to start early for each child.

In order to yield results that are valid, all tests of intelligence must be administered strictly in accordance with the specific directions of the particular test used. Accurate timing, objective and quiet administration, and careful correction are essential. The subject's familiarity with testing techniques may influence the results slightly. However, since intelligence tests are primarily measures of reaction rate in the performance of novel arrangements of relatively familiar material, it is usually difficult for an individual to speed up his normal rate of response during a testing experience. When careful testing of the general public is done, mental abilities tend to be distributed according to the graph in Figure 6.

Recent attacks on the value of intelligence tests in identifying gifted children have produced arguments in defense of the IQ. Tests of creativity are now suggested for use to identify the gifted child. Even though these tests are of unknown validity, the results of creativity tests are considered by some to be superior to

Figure 6. Distribution of Mental Abilities, with Intelligence Quotients Superimposed

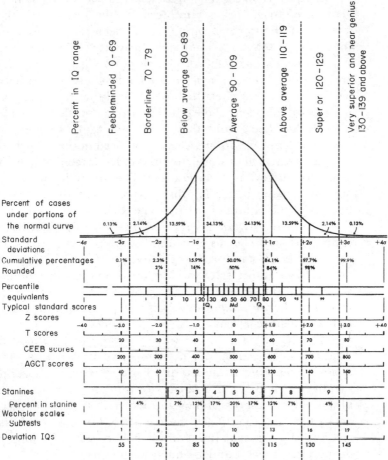

SOURCE: *Test Service Bulletin*, January, 1955, p. 2, and Lester D. Crow and Alice Crow, *Adolescent Adjustment and Development*, 2nd ed., New York: McGraw-Hill, 1965, p. 114. Courtesy of The Psychological Corporation and McGraw-Hill Book Company.

those of intelligence tests. The arguments advanced by Quinn McNemar are presented here.

The recently renewed interest in "gifted" children, along with the flurry of creativity studies, has led to a reexamination of methods for identifying the gifted. It has long been recognized that identification in terms of high IQ is too narrow—those gifted in such areas as art and music would be overlooked. The argument against the IQ is now (Torrance, 1962) being reinforced by the claim that the selection of the top 20% on IQ would mean the exclusion of 70% of the top 20% on tested creativity. This startling statistic, which implies a correlation of only .24 between IQ and creativity, is being used to advocate the use of creativity tests for identifying the gifted. Be it noted that these creativity tests will also miss those gifted in art and music.

We are being told that it is important "to identify creative talent early in life," hence you need not be surprised that the search goes down to the kindergarten level, with claims of successful identification. The creativity tests are presumed to be better for this purpose than the IQ tests because of the failure of the IQ to be constant, an argument that completely overlooks the fact that the IQ does have some constancy whereas absolutely nothing is known about the stability of standings on creativity tests. The IQ tests, known to be imperfectly valid as predictors of outstanding achievement in life, are to be replaced by the creativity tests, known to be of unknown validity as predictors. Anyway, progress, defined as change, is in the offing.

The IQ is being linked with *learning* as an outmoded educational objective; the new objective involves an emphasis on *thinking*. Somehow or other creativity, not general intelligence, is being associated with thinking. The horrible idea of underachievers and overachievers, in terms of expectancies based on the IQ, will be abolished. But no thought is given to the fact that the use of creativity tests will simply define a new crop of under- and overachievers.

In an apparent zeal to rid us of general intelligence, it is argued that measured creativity is significantly related to ordinary school achievement. Maybe so, but never, never does one find complete data reported as to the relative sizes of validity coefficients. And, as we have seen, the technique being used will show that equal coefficients are unequal. Why not the full facts, free of fantasy?

An additional difficulty is not being faced by those who would replace IQ tests by creativity tests, or creative-thinking tests. The factor-analytic studies indicate either no, or a trivially small, general creativity factor in these tests, yet these self-characterized "bold, adventurous" reformers (see Torrance, 1963) do not hesitate to advocate a total score which is nearly devoid of meaning. Changing the curriculum to the teaching of creativity and creative thinking will not overcome this measurement difficulty. Again, I express the hope that the IQ is replaced by something better rather than by something worse.[2]

Aptitude Measurement and Personality

Intelligence tests are designed to measure an individual's degree of *general* alertness without emphasis on any specific form or ability. An individual may be generally slow in his mental reactions, but he may possess better than average ability in one particular form of response. In the same way, a mentally superior person may possess outstanding or relatively inferior ability in one form of activity. In order to determine the kind or extent of an individual's potentiality for success, apart from training in any one field, a specific form of measurement known as an aptitude test must be administered. The kind of test used for this purpose depends on the connotation of the term *aptitude*. Aptitude can be considered to be that quality of a person that exists apart from training. It may or may not be inherited.

The need for aptitude measurement is paramount. Yet, the construction of valid aptitude tests is still in its infancy. However, beginnings have been made in various fields that are worthy of consideration. Among significant aptitude tests are the Segel-Raskin *Multiple Aptitude Tests*. This test battery consists of four factorial areas: verbal comprehension, perceptual speed, numerical reasoning, and spatial visualization; nine test scores; and a Scholastic Potential score that combines the verbal comprehension and numerical reasoning factors. Another important general aptitude test is the Bennett-Seashore-Wesman *Differential Aptitude Test* (DAT) consisting of eight tests: verbal reasoning, numerical ability, abstract reasoning, space relations, mechanical reasoning, spelling, speed and accuracy, clerical, and grammar.

---

[2] Quinn McNemar, "Lost: Our Intelligence? Why?", *American Psychologist*, December, 1964, p. 880.

In addition to the eight scores is a ninth: an index of scholastic ability obtained by summing the verbal reasoning and numerical ability scores. This test has great respectability.

Numerous aptitude tests have been constructed in various areas. Included among them are clerical tests, stenographic and typing tests, manual dexterity tests, mechanical aptitude and engineering tests, language aptitude tests, music tests, art tests, and multiple aptitude tests.[3] The Armed Services of the United States also has developed several classification instruments that have proven useful with their personnel. These include the *Army General Classification Test* (AGCT) and the *Armed Forces Qualification Test* (AFQT).

Achievement Measurement and Personality

The types of tests discussed in the foregoing have been designed to measure inherent ability apart from directed or conscious training. Achievement tests differ from those tests in that achievement tests have for their purpose the assessment of extent of learning. An achievement test presupposes instruction in the definite field for which the test has been constructed. An achievement test may serve one of the following functions: (1) survey the level of achievement attained by a learner; (2) discover the degree of readiness of a young person for entrance into one or another area of learning (reading readiness test) ; or (3) diagnose the specific learning difficulties of an individual in a particular field of learning. In general, the survey achievement test still is the type that is most often used on all school levels. A commendable increase of interest, however, is being evinced in readiness and diagnostic tests.

At present there is a trend in achievement testing away from specific tests in isolated areas of learning toward general achievement batteries and comprehensive examinations. A battery of tests, especially on the elementary school level, includes a series of tests representing pupil achievement in the various subject areas studied. Scoring and interpretive norms or standards follow a general pattern that makes possible an equivalence of perform-

---

[3] Names of specific tests can be obtained from such publishers as California Test Bureau, The Psychological Corporation, or Houghton Mifflin Company.

ance evaluation of all areas of learning included in the battery. *The Metropolitan Achievement Tests* (Grades 1 through 9), *The Stanford Achievement Tests* (Grades 2 through 9), and the *California Achievement Tests* (Grades 1 through 12) represent three of the most commonly used achievement batteries.

Comprehensive examinations, such as the *Cooperative General Achievement Tests* (CGAT), the *Iowa Tests of Educational Development* (ITED), and the *Tests of General Educational Development*, developed by the United States Armed Forces Institute (USAFI GED) are designed to evaluate general achievement progress on the secondary and higher school levels. The present trend toward the utilization of test batteries and comprehensive examinations gives evidence of an increased emphasis upon the general integrated resultants of learning.

Validity and Reliability of Personality Trait Measurement

The evaluation of personality traits is difficult because of the complexity of the personality pattern. It probably is impossible to rate a person *entirely satisfactory* or *entirely lacking* in the possession of a characteristic or quality in any situation that may arise. For example, a man may be extremely honest in his home relationships, but his business ethics may be questionable.

It is difficult to divorce completely one phase of personality from another, either in the individual's rating of himself or in an evaluation of himself by another. An evaluator may be influenced by his motives in rating. A school executive who is called upon to submit to another school or to a business house a personality rating for one of his students may be convinced that his students are better than are those of any other school. Hence he is unable to rate this individual objectively and thus admit that the young person possesses any undesirable qualities.

The self-rater may wish to give a good account of himself. Therefore, he responds to individual items of a test or scale as he believes he is expected to respond. Unreliable as the results of various instruments of personality evaluation may be, if an individual portrays certain tendencies as measured by different techniques periodically, some trait consistencies may be assumed for the purpose of evaluation. Some constructors of rating scales attempt to check consistency of response by presenting a single concept in two or more differently worded items.

PERSONALITY EVALUATION THROUGH PROJECTIVE TECHNIQUES

No matter how carefully the rating of personality traits is done or how many traits are rated, a total personality evaluation includes more than the rating of one trait. The subtle interaction and interinfluence of those traits which make for the integration of personality cannot be discovered through the administration of the paper-pencil variety of trait measurement. For example, people in general cannot be catalogued into rigid classifications such as ascendant or submissive, introvert or extrovert. Consequently, recently there have been developed certain forms of evaluation that permit the subject to *project* his habitual attitudes, hopes, ideas, aggressions, fears, or worries. These evaluating instruments are known as *projective techniques.*

Characteristics of Projective Techniques

In the administration of a projective technique the subject is presented with more or less unstructured situations to which he responds freely. He may give a variety of possible responses. As he describes, explains, or evaluates the "situation," he supposedly is giving overt expression to the inner attitudes and ideals that are characteristic of his general personality pattern.

An increasing number of projective measuring instruments are being made available. Among the various types that are most frequently applied are Verbal Techniques; Drawing and Painting; Play and Dramatic Techniques; the Rorschach (Inkblot) Technique, and Pictorial Techniques.

The Utilization of Verbal Techniques

Word-association tests, often referred to as "free association tests," serve as media for discovering an individual's thoughts, associations, and specific emotional states. These tests were sponsored during the nineteenth century by Francis Galton and Wilhelm Wundt. In its early form, the word-association test consisted of a list of words to each of which the subject was asked to respond with the first word that came to his mind. Each word reaction was timed. Both the response itself and the length of time between stimulus and response were considered to be significant.

This form of verbal technique is used sometimes to discover whether an individual has any knowledge concerning a situation about which he claims to know nothing. It is presumed that a subject will fumble for a response and take more time to respond to a stimulus word that may indicate personal guilt or guilty knowledge.

The presentation to the subject of incomplete sentences which he is expected to complete is another of the verbal techniques. A subject's completion of sentences similar to those presented below would seem to give a clue to his attitudes, opinions, or emotional states.

My job _____.

America's problem is _____.

The place of women in our society _____.

A liberal _____.

Young people today _____.

The way in which a sentence is completed can be indicative of the subject's relations with his associates, his breadth of understanding, or his social philosophy.

At the present time various forms of the verbal technique are being experimented with. The lie-detector technique is rela tively well known. Story-completion tests are administered to children as well as to older persons. Their purpose is to discover an individual's creative potentialities, the logical sequence of his ideas, and the extent to which his mental processes respond to realistic continuity or to flights of fancy.

The Utilization of Drawing and Painting in Self-expression

Emphasis is being placed in early education upon encouraging a child to express his interests, creative abilities, and inner tensions through the media of finger painting, crayon drawing, and easel painting. The child is encouraged to give free expression to his interests and urges. Another form of this technique is to have a child produce a picture of a person or a house as he images it.

The utilization of the drawing and painting techniques has diagnostic value. Through them may be discovered inner motives, ideas, attitudes, or resentments of which the subject himself may be unaware. These techniques also have projective application in dealing with individuals of any age who appear to be suffering an emotional disturbance. Because of the subjective factor inherent in this form of diagnosis, interpretation of the product is difficult and should be attempted only by trained and experienced test administrators. Only they are able to apply existing norms to an individual's performance. This caution holds for the administration and interpretation of all types of projective techniques.

Play and Dramatic Techniques

Play therapy has received considerable attention among psychologists as a means of releasing tensions among emotionally disturbed young children. A child is allowed to handle freely, play with, and perhaps throw on the floor and stamp upon, one or more members of a doll family. It is supposed that he thereby is giving evidence of his attitude toward, or his feelings of resentment against, the various members of his family. His comments about and to the dolls as he plays with them enable a trained counselor who is listening and watching to diagnose more or less adequately the child's emotional state.

From this beginning has developed the utilization of toys, figures, and similar materials for diagnostic purposes. The *World Test* consists of one hundred or more toy pieces which the subject is encouraged to arrange according to his interest. Such projective "toy tests" presumably indicate the possession of personal characteristics, such as aggressive rigidity, disorganization, or other symptoms of emotional disorder. Shneidman's *Make-a-Picture Story* (MAPS) is used as a storytelling device about a scene which the subject has constructed with materials consisting of various backgrounds, people, and animals.

Attitudes displayed by a subject in either of the projective techniques described in the foregoing may offer clues concerning the emotional difficulties suffered by him, and serve as the basis for reconditioning. The behavior of adolescents and adults who participate in *psychodrama* also may be enlightening. When the subject enacts one or another role on a stage, as he participates in artificially constructed scenes, he is likely to project his inner feelings and attitudes into the role which he is playing. Because of the various factors that may influence the subject's performance, conclusions concerning the emotional state of the subject may or may not be valid.

Utilization of the Rosenzweig Picture-Frustration Technique

A test devised to measure emotionalized attitudes is that constructed by Rosenzweig. In his *Picture-Frustration Test,* Rosenzweig undertook to measure three types of reactions to frustration: extrapunitive, intropunitive and impunitive. The test consists of a series of comic-strip-type pictures. Each of the individual sketches depicts a possible frustrating situation to which the subject responds by entering his actual expression in the space provided. The subject is invited to write "the first reply which comes to mind," and to "avoid being humorous." Figure 7 illustrates how the test is used. In general, the test helps to determine whether the subject attacks his environment, blames himself, or quietly ignores the problem.

Utilization of the Rorschach Technique

The Rorschach inkblots (see Figure 8) are used widely as a projective approach in personality evaluation. This technique is an excellent device to discover personality characteristics of adolescents and adults. The subject is asked to look at each of ten cards containing inkblots of various forms. Five of these forms are in shades of black and gray and five others are in two or more colors.

As the subject examines a card he reports to the examiner what he sees in the whole blot or in any one or more segments of it. In a second showing of the cards, the subject points out as exactly as he can the area or areas which represent the various objects or situations that he had seen in the first showing.

Figure 7. Picture Association Study for
Assessing Reactions to Frustration

SOURCE: Copyright, 1948, by Saul Rosenzweig. Reproduced by permission.

Figure 8. Example of Inkblot

The interpretation of a subject's performance is difficult and should be attempted only by a thoroughly trained administrator. Since no two individuals are likely to report similarly, many variations and combinations need to be considered and interpreted in order to achieve some understanding of the subject's performance.

Ames, Metraux, and Walker completed a study of 700 Rorschach records of subjects between the ages of ten and sixteen. They studied fifty boys and fifty girls at each age level. The subjects were relatively homogeneous. They report on two types of trends: "over-all direction of change for the whole period, and the changes from age to age."

> The over-all trends of change are not generally very large. In our earlier study covering the first 10 years of life, it appeared that developmental changes, as reflected in the Rorschach, tended to occur more and more slowly. Changes for the major variables were proportionately less in the years from 5 to 10 than in the years preceding.
>
> This slowing down continues in the years from 10 to 16. The values for nearly all variables are closer to adult expectation at age 16 than they are at age 10, but the rate at which they approach adult values is more rapid in the period from 5 to 10 than in the period from 10 to 16. The degree to which 16-year-old values approximate the values commonly expected from normal adults differs considerably for the different variables. . . .
>
> Sex differences in the Rorschach responses in the years from 10 to 16 appear to be marked and relatively consistent. In fact, by contrast with the years preceding 10, the difference in typical performance of boys and of girls is one of the most striking characteristics of this age range.[4]

Utilization of the Thematic Apperception Test (TAT)

A projective technique to evaluate personality by means of selected pictures is the *Thematic Apperception Test*. This test is

[4] Louise Bates Ames, Ruth W. Metraux, and Richard N. Walker, *Adolescent Rorschach Responses: Development Trends from Ten to Sixteen*, New York: Hoeber Medical Division, Harper & Row, 1959, pp. 289, 291.

especially used by clinicians to evaluate the functioning of an individual's total personality. This projective technique consists of nineteen cards, each of which represents a situation involving one or more persons against a more or less vague background. One card is blank. The subject is asked to tell a story about each of the pictures, and then to imagine a picture on the blank card and tell a story about it.

The TAT and other pictorial techniques, such as the *Children's Apperception Test* (CAT), and the Symonds *Picture Story Test for Adolescents,* are being used in school and private practice. As the techniques are improved clinicians are gaining greater insight into the significance of client responses. As a subject is motivated to tell story after story concerning the respec-

Figure 9. Example from the *Thematic Apperception Test*

SOURCE: Reprinted by permission of the publisher from Henry A. Murray, *Thematic Apperception Test,* Cambridge, Mass., Harvard University Press. Copyright 1943 by the President and Fellows of Harvard College.

tive pictures, certain attitudes continue to show themselves throughout the administration of the test. One boy, for example, to whom this test was administered, displayed a combination of fear and aggression as he attempted to interpret the pictures. An example of a picture in the TAT is given in Figure 9.

The Utilization of Puppetry

Children respond in interesting ways to the action of puppets. Among a group of children viewing a puppet show, depending on the type of exhibit, one child becomes wild with excitement, while another tends to hide his head. One child shadowboxes or moves his hands as if to fight and another tends to shrink away from the situation. In either instance, each child tends to identify himself with the puppet characters and the actions that are being portrayed by them. Each child follows through by projecting his personal feelings, desires, and hopes into the puppet show.

Puppets are classified according to the method used to manipulate them: shadow, string, and glove. The *shadow puppet* is held close behind a translucent screen in such manner that a shadow is thrown on the screen. The viewer then sees the shadow and not the puppet. The *string puppet* (marionette) is a doll so joined that the head, arms, and legs can be moved by a human operator. The *glove puppet* or *hand puppet* utilizes the anatomy of the hand to provide a three-dimensional head with a garb attached to it, and is manipulated by the hand of the performer.

Little is known concerning the validity and reliability of the therapeutic value of puppetry. The limited use that has been made of puppetry suggests that it can serve a valuable purpose in the understanding of some of the maladjustments of childhood. It shows promise of becoming a valuable therapeutic technique to be used in the study and analysis of deviating childhood behavior.

THE USE OF THE INTERVIEW IN
PERSONALITY EVALUATION

There usually are certain personality facts that can be understood and evaluated properly only through the intimate and informal relationship that is possible in a well-planned and sympathetically conducted interview.

Purposes of the Interview

The purpose of an interview may be one of the following: to obtain information about the interviewee; to give him information; or to assist him in the resolution of more or less serious problems or conflicts. An information-receiving or information-giving interview generally uses what is referred to as the *direct counseling* approach. When an individual needs and/or seeks assistance in dealing with personal difficulties of adjustment the counselor's or interviewer's approach is indirect. The problem to be solved is the client's; only the client himself can reach a self-satisfying resolution of his problem. The function of the counselor is to keep himself out of the situation as much as is possible, except as he motivates the client to "talk out" the difficulty, evaluate its seriousness, discover possible causes, and finally arrive at a possible resolution of it.

Nondirective counseling may require many sessions between counselor and counselee. The difficulty may be so deep-rooted or so serious that no one but a well-trained analyst or psychiatrist is able to gain an understanding of the client and his problem and his need for assistance. A seriously disturbed person requires more help than can be given him even through intelligently trained nondirection in counseling. The person so afflicted may need the kind of therapy that can be given only in a hospital for the mentally ill.

Problems arise in the lives of individuals that require intimate personal consultation with others who are qualified to assist in the resolution of the difficulties. The trained and skillful interviewer is able, tactfully and sympathetically, to deal with the delicate emotions of the human being. He is sensitive to fine and sometimes subtle nuances of the complex personality. Vocal and overt body expressions give him material that is helpful in the counseling role.

The more thorough is his background of knowledge concerning the client, as the result of the study of accumulated data dealing with the personality, conduct, and surroundings of the latter, the better prepared the interviewer will be to understand and interpret the difficulties of the client. Although the questionnaire is more objective than the interview, the latter has distinct advantages over the use of the questionnaire in that a skillfully conducted interview affords great opportunity for amplification, specification, and interrelation between the client and the counselor.

Effectiveness of the Interview

It is the function of the interviewer, by tactful questioning and intelligent listening, to probe beneath the mass of material already obtained by other techniques of evaluation and to discover the fundamental bases of the individual's personality status. In this way, whatever adjustment or readjustment is needed may begin at the core of the difficulty, and not concern itself merely with superficial behavior.

To the extent that the interview or interviews accomplish that which they purport to achieve they are of inestimable value to all persons who are responsible for the guidance of individuals toward the achievement of desirable personal and social goals. The teacher, the social worker, the personnel worker, the employer, the doctor, the psychoanalyst, the psychologist, and the psychiatrist are motivated by different objectives as they conduct interviews. In each case the effectiveness of the interview is dependent upon the spirit in which and the skill with which the interview is conducted.

The individual who needs guidance toward better educational adjustment, the family that needs help in the solution of financial or other family problems, the worker who is experiencing difficulties on the job or with his fellow workers, the applicant who is seeking employment, the patient who is suffering from mental or physical ill health—all come to the interview with a specific need for help. They best can achieve their own self-realization and their own self-direction if the assistance offered them is objective, tactfully and sympathetically given, and based upon a counselor background of thorough training and broad experience. The interview is pre-eminently a medium for wholesome and healthful interaction of human personalities. Regardless of the purpose of an interview, good rapport between the interviewer and the interviewee is needed to accomplish the desired goal.

Although there should be no indication of hurry during the

interview, rambling should be discouraged. Frankness and ease of relationship should prevail, and the interviewee should be encouraged toward freedom of expression of his inner motives, interests, and attitudes, but he should not feel that the interviewer is prying unduly and without good reason into his private affairs. The client should leave when the interview is completed with a desire and willingness to return for further discussion if needed.

In order to illustrate the techniques used in interviewing we present the essentials as outlined by Alpine, Chester, Kaufman, Matsumuro, and Cunningham in "Interviewing Techniques for Social Work Student Training." They suggest three basic reasons for this type of interview: (1) to give factual information to clients, (2) to gather information from clients, and (3) to modify behavior. Their suggestions follow:

TECHNIQUES TO BE USED IN THE BEGINNING

Setting the client at ease: One of the most helpful techniques to remember is to be a human being. Be relaxed. Any tenseness on your part will be sensed by the client. Be sure to introduce yourself. If it is a nice, bright day, say so. If the weather is terrible, say so. If the client has come to you, request that he explain in his own words what he sees as his problem or situation, or how and what services he expects. If you have requested the appointment, explain to him why the interview is being held. Thus, in the beginning the client knows he is a participant in the treatment process and that his thinking and feelings are important.

Exploring in a meaningful manner: Let the client know you want to help by asking pertinent questions. To relieve his anxiety, share with him the purpose of the interview. Have a purpose for each question you ask. Clarify where there is doubt as to the meaning of what the client says.

Listening: Listen to the tone of voice and note the manner of speaking, as well as noting the exact words said. By listening, you are less apt to draw erroneous conclusions or shut off the client so that meaningful material does not come out.

Silence: Although this appears an easy technique to master, it is not. It can be used to give the client enough time to muster his own thoughts. It can be helpful to the student, preventing his speaking too soon or jumping to a conclusion. It can lead to empathy, or it can be agonizing to both the client and the student.

Summarizing: Periodically summarize what is said to help crystallize your own thinking, as well as the client's.

Structure the interview: Once treatment starts, the use of time can be an important technique in the casework process. Any attempt by the client to leave early or to prolong the session may be meaningful behavior. If so, it can be dealt with. The student should feel free to accept this fact and not be bound to keep the client longer than necessary and thus create undue anxiety for the client himself.

Convey interest: The student can do this by the tone of voice he uses, his facial expression, gesture, posture, attentiveness. Remember that the client is human and that you should treat him as such. Neglecting to get across your warmth, acceptance and understanding makes the caseworker's job more difficult because of the resistance it usually creates.

The above-mentioned techniques are means of letting clients know that you are trying to help. These also help the student in setting goals and formulating treatment plans for the client. Summarizing the interview focuses on the progress made and helps the client to see where he is. Whether to focus on immediate or long-range goals is a decision which varies with agency purpose, expectations of the client, the student's techniques and the client's level of functioning.

However, it is important to have a common goal on which the worker and client can focus and attempt to attain. This results in the client's being willing to accept treatment through an ongoing casework relationship. How successful ongoing casework treatment is depends upon the student, the interviewing techniques used and the client's ability to accept help. In order to secure meaningful, workable information about the client's social and emotional life, the student needs a method of having the client reveal specific information in order to diagnose and treat.

It should be kept in mind that the casework process is in a constant state of flux, and that we always need to know areas of anxiety and difficulties, as well as the patient's resourcefulness and strength. This helps to set the casework treatment as a two-way process of effecting the client's ability to handle and verbalize about his problems, and allowing ourselves to be affected by the impact of his difficulties so that we can think with empathy.

TECHNIQUES TO USE DURING TREATMENT

The group of techniques in this area of interviewing activity can be defined as helping the patient to concentrate on the relevant aspects of his conflict (internal) and problems (external). Also, the complement of this process is to help the client let go of the irrelevant (symptoms) misdirection, confusion, etc., in order to grasp the full meaning of his difficulties.

Allow the client to tell his own story: Try to structure the interview so that you can find out from the client why he is seeing you and what the circumstances are which led to his request or need for help. This is of diagnostic value in terms of telling you how a client views people and problems, and also what his perceptual distortions and blank spots are. If you requested to see the client, after you have explained your reason, let him relate in his own words his thinking and guilt.

Reinterpret what the client says: Reinterpret what the client says so that you can gauge his capacity to view the problem with a different slant. This will tell you about the client's flexibility of ego and help you to determine a mutually agreed upon area of concentration. Otherwise, uncalled confusion and resistance may crop up.

Avoid generalization and particularize the problem with the client: Ask for a specific example of what the client means. You can thus get a better idea of the client's feelings as he relates the story and what part he or others play in the difficulties. Generalization can often serve to avoid problems and portray a fatalistic attitude. People usually have specific feelings about a problem in spite of their denial. For instance, you can ask, "At whom were you angry, and about what?"

Universalize or use analogy: When necessary and appropriately used, this is a way of adding humor to a situation or taking the onus out of the client's catastrophies. For example, one might tell the client an incident or story about other people.

Repeating the last word of the sentence: Do this with an inflection of a question. This is a way of avoiding a cross-examination kind of tone in the interview.

"*Oh!*"

This can be uttered in such a way as to indicate to a client that he should talk more or explain more fully.

Use a puzzled or questioning facial expression: This is used to indicate to the client that what he has said is not understood and that further clarification is needed.

Never agree with or attack a client's distortion: A client's prejudice or distorted perception usually serves a purpose for his mental equilibrium. The student should inquire into the background history of the prejudice or distortion so as to understand why the client is the way he is. Generally, the student never directly attacks or agrees with a client's prejudice or distortions.

Say words the client has been hinting at but needs license to use: This will help to break down resistance the client may have in discussing difficulties.

Avoid stereotyped responses: Such responses usually lead up a blind alley. They do not help the patient to think more flexibly. They may also be a sign of your own anxiety prejudice. Repeatedly asking "How do you feel about it?" "Think about it," and "Aha" can be frustrating to the client and create the feeling that the student is avoiding the issue or problem with the client.

Avoid being stingy about advice: Give advice and information if the client is specifically asking for it. However, try to get him to talk about what he really may be wanting to say or know. He may be knowingly or unknowingly requesting something more than advice, and the student should be aware of it.

Be alert to one-word answers: When the client uses the word "upset" or "nervous" what emotional significance does this have for him? Does he mean he is losing control of himself? Is he fearful of being harmed by his fellow man? Is he indicating incoherence and helplessness, or is he blocking?

He may not be clear himself as to what he does mean. The student should help him clarify.

Set the stage for a dialogue: Explore with the client what he reports. For example, "What did she say?" and "What did you say?" until the event in its entirety is clarified,

Be careful when asking for explanations of behavior: Such statements as "Why did you do that?" may put the client on the defensive.

Avoid moralizing or overidentifying: Avoid moralizing or overidentifying with the hospital administrative procedure or the agency structure. When hearing about an injustice done to a fellow patient or client, don't jump to the defense or explain why this is done. Open the door for further communication by saying "I feel that you don't like the way it was handled. Can you tell me more about the way it affects you?" The client may be expressing significant feelings or attitudes about authority or dependency needs.

Motivating: These interviewing techniques are used to try to help the client to increase his desire for helping himself.

Explaining: This technique is the use of the student's professional awareness of person situation configuration and his use of this knowledge to help the client gain understanding and control of his total situation.

Clarifying: This is helping the client to see his distortions and destructive use of self which operate on a conscious or preconscious level and to see his responsibilities for functioning in relation to his social problems. This of course has to be done partially with one attitude at a time and repeatedly done as it crops up in different situations. For example, when the client states that he always gives in to his wife or father, he may have previously stated in relation to others that unless you give in to people or help them, then they don't do anything for you. It becomes a student's job to help him see what reaction he has to it, such as later taking a drink or "blowing his top."

TECHNIQUES TO USE DURING TERMINATION

The following interviewing techniques are suggested for use in ending an interview and/or termination of treatment which has encompassed many interviews:

Summarize: Try to end interviews by summarizing the material covered, particularly when concrete material is covered. For example: referral, things to do, action to take. The emotionally charged material need not be summarized. Ask the client to think about new material until the next interview. If new material does not penetrate (for example, denial of feelings of hostility and aggravating situations), ask the client to keep it in mind when the situation arises again, and to discuss it again in the next interview.

Ask the client if he has any questions: This is a culturally developed means of termination, as we all know that questions come last.

Walk toward the door after the summary: This is generally considered rude. Do not do this unless all else fails. Walking to the door is a strong indication of ending the interview, and may be resorted to only with the most stubborn client who refuses to leave.

Prepare client for termination: Long treatment interviews are not fruitful. There is a limit on how much emotional material can be covered in an hour, and extended interviews are largely a waste of time. Watch the time and start preparing the client for termination 10 minutes earlier. Start going over previous material as a means of summary and do not go into new material.

Separation anxiety: Usually this is best handled by preparing the client well in advance for separation. Bring up the subject of termination four to six interviews before actual termination. Thus, the client has a chance to work through the anxiety of termination.

Leave the door open for future contacts: Try to handle termination so the client does not feel abandoned or that termination is final. You might terminate on a positive note of progress and competency, that he can function alone, but also assuring him that he may come back to the agency or that the agency will be ready to accept him again.

The varied methods and techniques of interviewing offered in this article were not meant to be all-inclusive. However, it is hoped that the student's learning process will be more meaningful when he sees these techniques and explanations. This is our attempt to catalogue interviewing techniques commonly used in daily practice. It is hoped that this article will stimulate others to compile further techniques.[5]

Evaluation of Social Adaptability of Psychotic Patients

The Social Adaptability Test has been developed to assist the physician, the psychiatrist, or any member of a therapeutic team to evaluate the social integration of mental patients who have recovered from their emotional disorders. It is specifically devised to assist the therapist in physical medicine to evaluate the social adaptability of psychotic patients in order to reduce the time of their hospital stay and enable them to be returned to their community and family. The development of this type of measuring instrument has been the concern of medical and paramedical personnel for many years. The purpose of the Social Adaptability Test is to discover the extent to which the patient has gained sufficient social integration to exhibit effective interpersonal relationships. Accompanying the rating scale are the directions for its use, along with the author's summary and conclusions.[6]

This test has 56 items, in the three broad categories of (1) *Speech,* (2) *Behavior,* and (3) *Personal Appearance and Hygiene.* It is designed for use by the physical medicine and rehabilitation therapist to measure the recovery of the neuropsychiatric patient. All 56 factors are designated in hours-per-week and compared to the total hours-per-week in the therapy. Social adaptability, as used in this discussion, refers to the degree of a person's emotional tolerance for different physical activities and environmental hazards he may encounter personally, occupationally, or socially. The basic objective should be consideration of the patient's abilities for activities around the clock—for the waking

[5] George C. Alpine, Robert Chester, Nathan H. Kaufman, John K. Matsumuro, and Murry K. Cunningham, "Interviewing Techniques for Social Work Student Training," *Mental Hygiene,* January, 1965, pp. 127–131.
[6] Herman Blustein, "The Evaluation of Psychiatric Recovery: The Social Adaptability Test," *The American Journal of Occupational Therapy,* March–April, 1961, p. 65–66.

hours of the twenty-four-hour day. This is predicted from the attendance in a clinic or activity in physical medicine and rehabilitation where he spends the major part of his time. A zero or blank indicates no social activity of this kind. An entry in the area of negative characteristics indicates the residual of disease or disability when the patient has achieved maximum recovery.

SUMMARY AND CONCLUSIONS

The purpose of this paper has been to suggest methods, in keeping with the modern trend of rehabilitation among the medical and paramedical professions, to extend therapeutic goals from treating disease and disability to include procedures for utilizing abilities, and improve ways of medical evaluation of social adaptability. The need is for an evaluation of the emotional assets of the whole person for activities-around-the-clock as well as for duties of daily living. Regardless of the diagnosis or status in life, the basic question remains the same for each person. How can each person utilize his emotional assets to get the most out of life without hurting himself?

The danger of using the *rating method* with its prohibitions of *no* or *limited* or *light engagement in activities* results in misunderstandings which result in economic and social misfortune to the individual. Equally harmful is the *disability method* in which evaluation is based on disability instead of ability pertaining to disease of the individual. The *specific method* (The Social Adaptability Test) has been devised to avoid these pitfalls. It is positive, individual and specific for the person's abilities. In the *specific method* an objective unit, the hour, is used to express the duration of the activity evaluated as compared to the total period under observation and treatment in the physical medicine and rehabilitation clinics.

This is an objective means of expressing an opinion, not an absolute fact. An opinion so expressed can be readily understood by others thus preventing the serious misunderstanding that often results from the use of subjective terms. The *specific method*, moreover, permits the evaluation of each person's abilities on a strictly individual basis and thus

Figure 10. Evaluation of Social Adaptability

Page 1

NAME			HOURS PER WEEK	
			DATE 3-8-60	DATE 3-17-60
REG. NO				
WARD NO.				
CLINIC				
DAYS OF WEEK IN CLINIC	5			
HOURS PER WEEK	15			
DATES OF STARTING				

SPEECH	HOURS PER WEEK	
	DATE 3-8-60	DATE 3-17-60
Normal intensity	15	15
Understandable	15	15
Applicable to situation	15	15
Connected in logical sequence	15	15
Communicates needs	15	15
Asks for help in task	15	15
Can answer questions	5	5
Can respond to others	15	15
Socially acceptable	15	15
Gives information	15	15

Page 2

SPEECH (cont.)	HOURS PER WEEK	
	DATE 3-8-60	DATE 3-17-60
Reports observations	15	15
Favorable regard of self	15	15
Desires to leave hospital	15	15
Would leave if had a job	14	14
Intense	10	10
Very loud		
Repetitious		
Are barely audible		
Talks to self		
Swears		
Teases others		
Irritable	5	5
Ideas of reference		
Ideas of persecution		
Anticipates disasters		
Indecisive		
Perplexed		
Fearful		
Preoccupied with illness		
Inferior self regard	1	1
Grandiose self regard, unacceptable socially		

Page 3

BEHAVIOR	HOURS PER WEEK	
	DATE 3-8-60	DATE 3-17-60
Likes to be with others	15	15
Relates well to others	15	15
Cooperative with others	15	15
Aware of roles in setting	15	15
Recognizes if annoying others	15	15
Reacts in appropriate fashion to others	15	15
Shows interest and enthusiasm	15	15
Takes criticism in friendly fashion	15	15
Tries to do what is expected	15	15
Obeys instructions	15	15
Is safety conscious	13	13
Takes pride in activities	15	15
Confident about abilities	15	15
Original and creative	12	12
Able to assume responsibility	15	15
Punctual in activities	10	10
Participates in group as leader	15	15
Participates in group as active participant	15	15
Capable of tolerating competition	15	15
Socially acceptable behavior	15	15
Inappropriate gestures		
Inappropriate grimaces		

BEHAVIOR (cont.)	HOURS PER WEEK DATE 3-8-60	DATE 3-7-60
Manneristic movements		
Bizarre postures		
Restlessness	5	5
Broad changes in mood		
Apathetic constantly		
Euphoric constantly		
Depressed constantly		
Disoriented		
Sitting unoccupied		
Socially unacceptable behavior		
PERSONAL APPEARANCE & HYGIENE		
Decorum in choice of clothing	15	15
Ability to dress self well	15	15
Maintains clothing, clean and repaired	15	15
Uses clothing in accord with weather and task	10	10
Able to groom self well	15	15
Proper toilet functions	15	15
Social awareness	15	15

PERSONAL APPEARANCE & HYGIENE (cont.)	HOURS PER WEEK DATE	DATE
Bizarre choice of clothing		
Resistive to dressing		
Untidy in clothing care		
Unaware of weather and task in choice of clothing		
Unaware of self grooming		
Untidy in toilet function		
Social unawareness		
THERAPIST OR AIDE		

SUMMARY:

Patient's behavior is hyperactive. Frequently patient must be slowed down through use of activities involving use of bodily muscles. At times, reference is made to mistreatment by stepfather. Extreme interest in securing employment: is expressed. Patient is likeable and is able to integrate self with care in clinic. He is easily offended by references to ethnic group to which he belongs (Spanish American).

SOURCE: Herman Blustein, "The Evaluation of Psychiatric Recovery: The Social Adaptability Test," *The American Journal of Occupational Therapy*, March-April, 1961, p. 82. Reprinted by permission.

avoids the danger of evaluations based on favored, average persons in the respective disability groups, as in the *disability method*. The positive individual qualifications of the person at hand are always emphasized, not the negative characteristics of groups or persons. In the evaluation, only the degree of emotional fitness for human activities and hazards is important, not the diagnosis. The specific questions to ask about the person at hand should be: Socially fit for what? What activities can this person perform and for how long? What hazards can he tolerate with reasonable safety?

To help the physician answer these questions the Social Adaptability Test is provided. A completed profile not only serves an employer in working out a safe adjustment for the person both on the job and in the home, but when placed in the hands of a housewife or person not gainfully employed it becomes equally valuable as a personal prescription for safer living to guide such a person throughout his daily activities.

Thus, in addition to treating the diseases and disabilities of his patients, the physician, by means of the specific method for evaluating social activity, can help the patient both to utilize and protect his abilities for a more rewarding and fuller life.

THE CASE HISTORY IN PERSONALITY EVALUATION

The case-study method involves the case history of a person, including a description of his development and the influence of the environmental factors on him. Information concerning every phase of an individual's personality—physical, mental, emotional, all obtainable factors and influences of his past or present environment that in any way have a bearing on the situation, and demonstrated behavior patterns—must be determined in order to complete the picture of the total individual. Any one or more of them may have precipitated the present difficulty.

The information suggested above can be obtained through the administration of appropriate physical, mental, and personality measuring devices, from records of school progress, from health records and charts, from controlled observation of the individual and his surroundings, and from interviews with him, his family, his teachers, and if employed, his employers and other associates. All data gathered should be organized and recorded, and interpretations and recommendations made only by experts. The case study or case history, besides containing the information suggested above, should include a systematic record of the remedial and advisory techniques employed and the progress of improvement.

Outline for Case Study

Case histories may be relatively simple or extremely elaborate, but they should be meticulously accurate, definite, objective, and unbiased. Since they deal with human factors and subjective relationships, it is difficult for the untrained person, even though he is honest in his intentions, to avoid the inclusion of prejudice, opinion, fantasy, or unconscious exaggeration. A case history should be used with discrimination since the making of *no* compilation of data concerning an individual is preferable to conscious or unconscious falsification of data.

Case-history outlines used by social and clinical workers, psychiatrists, school people, or personnel workers may vary somewhat in form as a result of variation in their specific requirements, but in general, case histories include many or all of the following items in more or less detail in their subdivisions:

Identifying data
Present difficulty (reason for referral)
Family background
Birth conditions
Health status and history
Home conditions
Social and economic status
Neighborhood conditions
Cultural deviation and conduct
Intellectual ability
Emotional development
Personal attributes
Interests, hobbies, and recreations

Achievement progress in school
School adjustment
Work history
Social behavior and interests
Sexual development and behavior
Social adjustment

When all data have been assembled, the clinic staff interpret them and offer recommendations for treatment. These recommendations may necessitate cooperation by the home, school, or place of employment. If special therapy is needed, this is administered by a psychiatrist or at a psychological clinic.

No matter how many or what agencies are involved in the readjustive process, progress needs to be reported. Also, after a client has made desirable adjustment, or if maladjustive factors in his environment have been removed or improved, a follow-up of the client's condition is an essential part of the study and therapy.

QUESTIONS AND PROBLEMS

1. Why should a psychologist be acquainted with the techniques of personality measurement?

2. Justify the statement that one's personality is not static.

3. Summarize Fiske's statements concerning the common models in the measurement of personality.

4. Distinguish between casual and controlled observation of behavior.

5. Give the values and dangers of using the observational approach in personality evaluation.

6. Analyze Table 5: "Traits Measured by Inventories."

7. Study, at first hand, interest inventories. Your instructor may be able to administer one to your class for this purpose.

8. Why is it difficult to evaluate personality?

9. Indicate the relationship, if any, between intelligence testing and personality evaluation.

10. Study the relative test ratings of Freud and James. Indicate the personality components in which they agree and in which there is considerable disparity. Report your findings.

11. Report on McNemar's arguments pertaining to an IQ obtained by the administration of intelligence tests.

12. What is an individual's best age for discovering inherent aptitude? Justify your answer.

13. Present reasons for an able young person's failing to achieve to his measured capacity.

14. Discuss the importance of validity and reliability in the measurement of personality traits.

15. Give the strengths and weaknesses of using projective techniques in personality evaluation.

16. Explain how play and dramatic techniques can serve as measures of personality.

17. Present the differences between the Rorschach technique and the *Thematic Apperception Test*.

18. What factors of personality can be discovered through the use of the interview?

19. Indicate how the case study can be used in personality evaluation.

20. If possible, administer a standardized personality test to a group of young people and interpret the results. (Exclude any projective tests.)

Selected Readings

Alcock, T., *The Rorschach in Practice*. Philadelphia, Penna.: J. B. Lippincott Company, 1964.

Ames, L. B., R. W. Metraux, and R. N. Walker, *Adolescent Rorschach Responses: Development Trends from Ten to Sixteen*. New York: Paul B. Hoeber, Inc., 1959.

Anastasi, A., *Psychological Testing*, 2nd ed. New York: The Macmillan Company, 1961.

Anderson, H., and G. L. Anderson (eds.), *An Introduction to Projective Techniques*. Englewood Cliffs, N.J.: Prentice-Hall, Inc., 1951.

Cattell, R. B., *Personality and Social Psychology*. San Diego, Calif.: Knapp, 1964.

Harrower, M., *Appraising Personality*. New York: Franklin Watts, 1964.

Hollis, F., *Casework: A Psychosocial Therapy*. New York: Random House, Inc., 1964.

Klopfer, B., and H. H. Davidson, *The Rorschach Technique: An Introductory Manual*. New York: Harcourt, Brace & World, Inc., 1962.

Maher, B. A. (ed.), *Progress in Experimental Personality Research*. New York: Academic Press, Inc., 1964.

McKinney, F., *Understanding Personality*. Boston, Mass.: Houghton Mifflin Company, 1965.

Messick, S., and J. Ross, *Measurement in Personality and Cognition*. New York: John Wiley & Sons, Inc., 1962.

Rethlingschafer, D., *Motivation as Related to Personality*. New York: McGraw-Hill, Inc., 1964.

Sarason, I. G., *Contemporary Research in Personality*. Princeton, N.J.: D. Van Nostrand Company, Inc., 1962.

Smith, H. C., *Personality Adjustment*. New York: McGraw-Hill Inc., 1961.

Vernon, J. M., *Personality Assessment; A Critical Survey*. New York: John Wiley & Sons, Inc., 1964.

≼ 7 ≽

FRUSTRATION
AND
CONFLICT

SINCE THE MENTAL and the emotional reactions of an individual
are very closely related, it is difficult to discuss the one without
implying a function of the other. A normal person possesses
interests, desires, and drives that impel him to participate in
many and varied activities. Moreover, he finds himself in a relatively complex environment to which he must adapt himself,
both mentally and emotionally. As he lives and adjusts, he is
constantly compelled to decide among situations, issues, and
opposing forces of one kind or another, or is thwarted in what he
does.

FRUSTRATION AS A HUMAN
EXPERIENCE

It is difficult for any one of us to engage in activity without
meeting an opposing force of one kind or another. The interests
of other people, rules and regulations, social codes, unfulfilled
desires, goals beyond achievement, and competitive situations are
some of the social and individual factors that cause mental and
emotional disturbance.

Fundamentally, a baby's wants are centered in the achieving of physical needs. At one time he wants food; at another time he needs sleep. A healthy baby also wants to engage in kicking, cooing, and other forms of active behavior. At all times he wants to be comfortable—free from tight clothing and other restrictions. When or if any one of these wants (which are recognized by the young child only in a relatively vague and diffused manner) is not satisfied, he engages in one or. another form of disturbed behavior, such as crying, holding his breath, stiffening his little body or tossing it about. Even at this early age the child can be said to be *frustrated* in the achieving of his felt needs.

When an individual is blocked in his pursuit of a goal, frustration results. This is easily illustrated in Figure 11. When

Figure 11. How Frustration Is Experienced by an Individual

Individual ——→ Interference ——→ Denied goal ——→ Frustration

an individual is motivated to reach a particular objective or goal, but in so doing has his course of action temporarily or permanently blocked, he experiences an emotional reaction known as frustration.

Frustration is believed to be involved with three components: the situation, the overt response to the blocking, and the internal state of the individual at the time of blocking. The component with which we are most concerned here is the state of frustration that takes place within the individual. In the internal phase the blocking element arouses the emotion that is accompanied by tension or stress. Thus is aroused anger, and sometimes anxiety. Anger especially is directed at the blocking person or object, resulting in behavior that is aggressive toward the person or object.

Numerous experiments have been designed to study the results of frustration. One such study was conducted by Levy.[1] This involved two puppies that were breast fed, two that were fed by nipples with large holes to enable the puppies to obtain the food within five minutes, and two that could get all the food in two minutes. The last two puppies became tense and restless and

[1] D. M. Levy, "Experiments on the Sucking Reflex and Social Behavior of Dogs," *American Journal of Orthopsychiatry*, Vol. 4, pp. 203–224.

engaged in almost continuous sucking activities. They displayed angry and aggressive behavior and lost weight. The first two displayed normal behavior.

Another study designed to discover the effects of keeping a group of college students awake all night was designed by Sears, Hovland, and Miller.[2] The purpose of the study was not revealed to the students. They were led to believe that the purpose was to measure the effect of fatigue on specific tests. The subjects were exposed to various types of thwarting. They were not permitted to smoke or to converse among themselves. Neither were they provided with promised games and food. The resulting behavior to this type of thwarting showed active aggression directed toward the psychologists who were conducting the experiment.

The intensity of internal frustration varies with the need or desire, and the duration of the blocking of the drive. A hungry person will experience greater frustration if denied available food than will a person who has eaten recently. A continuation of the denial of food is likely to increase the frustration experience. The person who fails to secure the type of employment he seeks experiences frustration. Likewise, the employee who tries but cannot attain advancement in his establishment develops internal tensions of frustration.

In general, a frustration can be defined as an unsatisfied need or desire. Throughout his life an individual encounters many frustrating situations. Some of the frustrations are relatively mild and can be overcome easily; others may be so serious, or seem so to the individual, that he comes to believe that there can be no satisfying way out of the difficulty.

Behavior properties associated with frustration tend toward aggression, regression, or fixation. All of these behavior responses are quite different from those associated with motivated learning. Among the differences to be found between the experience of frustration and motivation, Hall lists the following:

1. A problem situation produces stereotyped behavior in the frustrated organism whereas it produces variable behavior in the motivated.

[2] R. R. Sears, C. I. Hovland, and N. E. Miller, "Minor Studies of Aggression: I. Measurement of Aggressive Behavior," *Journal of Psychology,* 1940, pp. 297–300.

2. Responses produced under frustation, in so far as they show fixation, are rigid and stereotyped to a degree that exceeds responses produced by rewarded learning. Thus, the motivated organism is characterized by plasticity—the frustrated organism by rigidity.

3. Responses produced during frustration are not responsive to alteration by punishment although reward-learned responses can be so altered.

4. Punishment may serve as a frustrating agent, and when this happens, a learned response may be replaced by a characteristic frustrated response.

5. Frustration-induced responses seem to be an end in themselves. Motivated responses are a means to an end.

6. The method of guidance is highly effective for altering frustration-produced responses, but it has no great value for replacing reward-learned responses.

7. Frustration-instigated responses are compulsive in nature whereas responses appearing in motivation situations are choice reactions.

8. The degree of frustration can be relieved by the expression of responses, regardless of whether or not the response is adaptive. Responses expressed by a motivated organism are satisfying only when the responses are adaptive.

9. Frustration-instigated responses are either nonconstructive or destructive in nature whereas motivated responses are constructive.

10. The reponse expressed during frustration is influenced to a great extent by its availability to the organism, whereas the response expressed in the state of motivation is influenced more by anticipated consequences than by availability.

11. Learning takes place under motivation and permits an increase in the number of differentiations the organism can make, whereas frustration leads to dedifferentiation (regression) and in some cases convulsive or mass behavior.[3]

[3] John F. Hall, *Psychology of Motivation,* Philadelphia: J. B. Lippincott Company, 1961, pp. 247–248.

SOURCES OF FRUSTRATION

In an individual's striving toward goal attainment, many and various types of obstacles are confronted. Some of these obstacles are easily surmounted and others appear to defy removal. They are found both in the physical and social environment and in personal inadequacies. Thus the individual's physical environment, his cultural and economic setting, and the individual himself are important factors or sources of frustration.

The Physical Environment as a Source of Frustration

Many experiences that appear to an onlooker to be no more than petty annoyances may be productive of frustration. Any strong emotional tension that results from the blocking of a drive usually is considered to be a frustration. These emotional stresses may be induced by what to many are trivial incidents. For example, frustration may result: if a shoestring tears when the individual is in a hurry to catch a train; if a short circuit develops in his television set when he is viewing an enjoyable program; if a newly painted window sticks when he attempts to open it; if an automobile splashes dirt on his clothes; if he misses his train by only thirty seconds and is late to work because the next train does not arrive for another twenty minutes; if a child bounces a ball out of his recovery reach and must wait for an adult to rescue it for him.

Situations similar to the ones listed are frequent occurrences in the daily life of most individuals; their frustrating effects usually are temporary, however. At the time of their occurrence they create definite stress and strain, and we become emotionally upset; later, after they have been met more or less satisfactorily, we can laugh at the strong emotional reactions aroused by them. Moreover, one such annoying incident seems to be followed by others of its kind. At times it seems as if everyone were conspiring to interfere with our planned activities. However, individuals can surmount many obstacles in meeting sources of frustration by adapting new forms of approach in these frustration-producing situations.

Social Sources of Frustration

Unfortunately, not all thwartings and annoyances are overcome easily. Sometimes frustrations have their roots in environmental conditions that act as obstacles to the fulfillment of strong
interests or desires. If the frustrating situations lie outside an
individual's power to control, he may experience even greater
emotional stresses and strains. To be caught in a sudden hurri-
cane, to be affected by a contagious disease, to learn of the death
of a close relative or friend, to have a chair pulled out from
under one as he is about to sit, to be called to serve in the armed
forces during a time of war—all represent environmentally stimulated frustration situations. The emotional reactions aroused by
their occurrence varies with the degree of emotional stability
possessed by the respective persons directly affected by them.

Other sources of frustration are associated with the cultural
and social aspects of experience. Laws and codes of behavior are
established for the general welfare; yet they interfere seriously
with an individual's desires or interests. For example, if we
accept the findings of the Kinsey report of sexual behavior,
according to a strict interpretation of existing laws a large percentage of women and men could be jailed for their sex acts.
Some people have no awareness of the fact that their accustomed
sexual activities may be contrary to law, however.

Many frustrating situations probably would appear if behav-
ior-restricting laws were known and followed. For example, every
driver of an automobile is expected to know and to obey traffic
regulations; in an emergency, a person believes that he has a
good reason for breaking one or more of them. Also, a businessman may be tempted to disregard restrictions on unfair business
practices if these restrictions interfere too much with his ambition to achieve financial gains.

The fact that groups vary in their social customs may become a factor of frustration to a person who moves from one
group to another. Especially is it possible for a person to experience a strong feeling of thwarting if he is eager to gain favor in a
new group, but discovers that his habitual behavior in social
situations differs from group custom. An ardent bridge player is
expected to play canasta; a vegetarian cannot find a vegetarian
restaurant; a family that has lived in a small neighborly town

moves to an apartment house in a large city and cannot become accustomed to the fact that no other family in the house seems to know or care about next-door neighbors; a person who had lived in a city where he had been accustomed to a great deal of personal freedom in his choice of activities is annoyed by the fact that in his new small-town home everything that he does is known to his neighbors and openly approved or disapproved.

To the adaptable person the situations listed may seem to represent unimportant social differences to which one can learn to adjust easily. Yet some less emotionally controlled individuals may consider them to be obstacles to the achieving of desired social acceptance. In a graduate college class, for example, a discussion concerning appropriate dress for high school students and college undergraduates caused the display of emotional tension on the part of one of the younger members of the class.

This young man attempted to defend young people's "sloppiness" of dress; older members of the group disagreed with his expressed opinion, to the point of implying that he was exhibiting an immature attitude toward accepted social custom in matters concerning appearance and that, with increasing maturity, his opinions would change. His retort to the effect that, even though some of his classmates considered him to be a child, he would never become a social snob, led to a heated discussion concerning what constitutes social snobbery. It was asserted that sloppy dressers represent a group of social snobs to the same extent as do those who advocate greater conservatism in dress.

By the end of the session several members of the class gave evidence of strong feelings of frustration. Moreover, since all the members of the group were leaders of young people, many of them expressed their uncertainty as to what their attitude should be toward changing social custom.

Economic Sources of Frustration

There are few individuals who, at one time or another, do not experience strong desires to possess luxuries similar to those enjoyed by more affluent friends. Inability to satisfy this urge can become a strong frustration arouser. For example, a woman whose husband's salary is sufficient to supply necessities but few luxuries is motivated by a strong urge to compete with her neighbors. If one neighbor's house is painted, she wants her house painted; if another has a television set installed, she wants a television set; if an automatic washer is purchased, she wants the same kind of washing machine. Any luxury obtained by any neighbor impels this woman to prevail upon her husband to make a down-payment on a similar article. This woman constantly indulges in self-pity because of her inability to compete in every way with her neighbors. Apparently, she cannot or will not recognize the fact that relatively few of her neighbors have all the things that she wants. They are selective in their interests, in terms of their financial ability to satisfy them.

In cultures where competition is between individuals of similar economic status rather than between members of differing financial levels the economic factor is less active as a frustration inducer. The frustration is experienced by the individual who attempts to rise from his economic group to one that is considered to represent a higher level of society. The democratic ideal, based upon the concept of equality of opportunity within individual limitations to attain desired goals, has tended to eliminate class distinctions in matters dealing with material possessions. For the able person, class leveling is an excellent stimulator of ambition to achieve a satisfying economic status. It is a frustration arouser for the individual who cannot meet competition.

Often an individual believes that if he were on a higher-income level than he now is he would not experience feelings of frustration associated with material possessions. He probably would discover, however, that his ambitions would induce him to strive toward still higher economic levels. Wants seem to increase with increased power to achieve them. The goal then becomes the achievement of superior business or social prestige. Anyone who becomes too involved in this kind of competition is likely to suffer feelings of frustration that are damaging to his total personality pattern.

Personal Sources of Frustration

The fundamental sources of frustration usually lie within the person himself. The level of his aspirations and the attitudes he develops in his daily living determine his degree of adjustment. Frustration arises if a person sets for himself the attaining of goals that cannot be achieved because of personal deficiencies.

The handicapped person becomes an easy victim of frustration. To the extent that his handicap denies him participation in activities common to those engaged in by the normal person, he is likely to experience discontent, resentment, and frustration. He needs to possess sufficient emotional stability to combat the warping effects of these maladjustive factors.

As a result of his limitations, a mentally subnormal child or adult may not become frustrated unless he is brought into unfair competition with his mental superiors. A mentally normal but slow individual has enough intelligence to attempt to imitate the behavior of his more able associates. He fails in competition because he is unable to recognize and evaluate differences between himself and those who succeed. As a result, he may place the blame for his failure on factors outside himself. He becomes the victim of deep feelings of frustration. He does not have sufficient mental acuity to understand complex conditions and situations that are understood by his more able associate. This lack of understanding becomes for him the basis of emotional disturbance.

The intellectually superior young person or adult also may suffer feelings of frustration. His deeper insight and his exceptional powers of discrimination may lead to his evaluating conditions, situations, or other people more quickly and more accurately than can his less able associates. This is satisfying. If he attempts to explain his evaluation, however, he is likely to discover that his less able associates cannot understand his reasoning. This may be a frustrating situation. An intellectually gifted person often becomes impatient when his associates reject his conclusions as fantastic, and present what to him are specious arguments or evaluations.

The emotional development of the gifted does not always keep pace with their mental progress. Sometimes an extremely bright young person, whose thinking and reasoning ability already have reached adult level, cannot realize the fact that to the average adult the young person still is a child whose behavior and attitudes reflect lack of adult experience. The gifted child or adolescent attempts to perform duties beyond those expected of him by average adults. Consequently, if he is reprimanded by parents or teachers for assuming responsibility without adult invitation to do so, he is bewildered by and resentful of apparent discrimination against him. He may suffer intense feelings of frustration.

To suffer seemingly unjust reprisals for attempts to satisfy impulses and desires is frustrating; to develop an attitude of believing that one cannot attain a goal because of inherent personal lacks may be the cause of even deeper frustration. Feelings of personal inferiority can cause an individual to refrain from attempting to achieve in any area of activity, because he believes that he is doomed to failure. An attitude of superiority, unless it is an accompaniment of superior achievement, may lead to the display of aggressive behavior that eventually also may induce the experiencing of frustration situations. An attitude of inferiority is certain to intensify feelings of frustration.

Merely to have a feeling of inferiority does not necessarily arouse emotional disturbance. It may take only one failure experience to cause loss of self-respect and to arouse strong emotional reactions, however. The failure situation may have a lasting effect upon the individual, without his awareness of the fact that it is the cause of his lack of self-confidence. Nevertheless, he tends to avoid similar challenging situations in order not to become involved in another disagreeable experience. The unpleasant incident may be forgotten; yet the resulting feeling tones remain as a part of the individual's attitude pattern. Childhood experiences often are reflected in adult behavior. For example, a shy adult may be exhibiting attitudes that were developed during childhood. He fears failure in areas of activity in which his earlier experiences were unsuccessful. Hence he tends to avoid frustration-arousing situations.

Other Sources of Frustration

Four important factors that influence an individual's response to frustration are (1) age, (2) health, (3) past experience, and (4) the nature of the motive that causes the frustration. Each factor exercises a specific effect upon the behavior reaction of the individual concerned.

The influence of the age factor can be illustrated by reference to reaction patterns at different age levels. The infant tends to display "angry" behavior when his desires are thwarted; he expresses his anger immediately; restraint of muscular activity induces tantrum behavior. Later, manifestations of emotional reaction become attached to many situations and considerations other than muscular restraint. The child struggles openly to remove any condition or object that to him represents an obstacle to the satisfaction of a desired activity or motive. The socially responsive adolescent or adult, however, has learned to control his inner annoyance and to direct his emotional responses in such a way that he may continue to receive the approval of his associates. The young person or adult learns that to avoid rejection by his peers, the anger factor serves him best when it is subdued or sublimated. People soon lose patience with an adolescent or adult who has a temper tantrum whenever his motives or wants are thwarted. The relatively mature individual is expected to inhibit overt symptoms of frustration when he cannot get his own way immediately.

A second important determiner of an individual's response to frustration is his physical health. Physical illness predisposes toward emotional disturbance; it sometimes becomes exceedingly difficult to control the emotions when one is ill. Although an individual exercises emotional control when he is well, a slight thwarting may provoke a temper tantrum if he is ill. A prolonged illness, an excessive number of colds, and even a period of loss of sleep may constitute conditions that are favorable to the arousal of feelings of frustration.

The third important factor that influences an individual's responses to frustration situations is his past experience. To experience the gratification of too many expressed desires predisposes toward the use of tantrums when or if the fulfillment of a desire is denied. The children of overindulgent parents become emotionally disorganized in frustrating situations. The helplessness of an infant or of a crippled or frail child may stimulate parents and other adults who are responsible for his welfare to adopt an oversolicitous attitude toward him. Thereby he is denied the opportunity to develop gradually a reasonable control of his desires and an attitude of self-dependence. If or when he reaches the stage of needing to assume personal responsibility for his welfare, he is likely to encounter many frustration situations with which he will not be able to cope.

The nature of the motive itself is the fourth factor in determining an individual's response to a frustration. When a person's wishes and desires are of minor or of transient importance, he may adjust rather easily to their denial. If a strong desire so motivates the individual that he is determined to find a way to gratify it, failure to do so results in deep-rooted frustrations. His feeling of frustration intensifies his determination to satisfy his wishes: sometimes through direct means; sometimes through substitute gratifications, such as reading novels, attending motion pictures, joining clubs, or indulging in excessive daydreaming. Or he may attempt to reduce his state of frustration by seeking business, social-group, or community status. He runs for politial office; he strives to become a high executive in a club; he fights for power in business or industry. Through intense concentration upon ego aggrandizement in one or another such area of activity he hopes to reduce the emotional stress and strain that have been evoked by his frustrating experience.

Individuals of any age differ temperamentally. A person who has a generally cheerful outlook on life may not recognize a situation as a source of frustration. He takes the good with the bad. In either situation he does the best that he can; he does not worry too much if the results are not completely satisfactory. The kind of individual a person is and the strength of the motive basic to the frustration influence the possible reactions that result.

In their discussion of sources of frustration, Maslow and Mittlemann give attention to *situational frustration* and *internal frustration*. Their ideas are presented here.

> *Situational frustration.* Invariably in everyone's life there are situations which are extremely depriving; it is impossible to live without going through such situations. Thus illness represents not only a threat, but also a frustration, for it may make the individual stop certain activities— such as the pleasures of eating—although he may not have lost the desire for them. The death of anyone close to him may likewise be a severe frustration apart from all other aspects. Death may mean deprivation of bodily needs, as in the case of a married couple; but there is always also a frustration of emotional needs, of the need for closeness, affection, support, and dependence. Unrequited love is like-

wise a frustration of both bodily and emotional needs. Furthermore, reality always sets limitations and in that sense causes at least some blocking of the individual's goals and desires. No one can succeed in everything that he aims at, although often what he aims at is very dear to him. A scientist may invest time, energy, and emotion in a piece of research and then fail. Such an experience, of course, is disappointing, and it may be frustrating. Such situations are significant because a breakdown frequently occurs when they arise; they do not, however, necessarily lead to the breakdown. Situational frustration is commonly referred to as external frustration.

Internal frustration. By the term "internal frustration" is meant the inability of the individual, for psychological reasons, to gratify an urge or a desire or a need when he has the opportunity to do so. This factor is very important in psychopathological reactions; as a matter of fact, internal frustration is present in every patient with these reactions. We have said repeatedly that in every significant activity of the individual his evaluation of himself (self-esteem) and of other persons (feeling of security) is involved. This evaluation concerns his general strength and his body and its activities. The causes of internal frustration are conflict, inhibition, condemnation, fear. If the patient feels helpless in a situation, if he condemns and rejects a part of his body and its function, if he expects disapproval for an activity when approval is vital to him, he cannot adequately engage in that activity even if he has the opportunity. Furthermore, every activity means attitudes toward other people and assumptions regarding their attitudes toward him. Physical intimacies have the connotation of emotional intimacies. If, because of his basic character, the patient expects rejection, humiliation, and injury from the other individual, this fear will make adequate gratification impossible. The patient may have conflicting attitudes and needs in regard to the measures which he uses to save himself from a catastrophic situation. Thus he may want to be dependent but at the same time to respect himself; he may want to dominate and subjugate his partner. The result may be that he is internally frustrated in his dependency longings and experiences.

All the phenomena mentioned here may be—and, as a rule, are—largely unconscious. Thus a distinction must be made between conscious and unconscious frustrations. Even when the frustration is conscious, a great many aspects of the experience may be unconscious. Or a conscious deprivation may also be unconsciously frustrating.[4]

REACTIONS TO FRUSTRATION

Frustration and Aggression

Reaction to frustration by aggressive behavior of an individual takes the form of attacking the obstacle (or its substitute) that blocks the individual from attaining his goal. Throughout the years, aggressive behavior has tended to help man solve his frustrations. However, with the present need for good social interaction, overt aggressiveness must give way to behavior that is more suited to social living. Aggression is usually not a satisfactory form of human adjustment because, in the long run, it does not reduce the resulting physical, mental, and emotional tensions. Direct combat with the obstacle may give temporary satisfaction but is likely to meet with social disapproval and, in turn, continue the frustration in a new form.

A major contribution emphasizing aggressive responses in frustration was made some years ago by Dollard, Doobs, Miller, Mowrer, and Sears of Yale.[5] They argued that a state of frustration existed when an organism was interrupted in its making of a goal response. Hence these authors believed that aggressive behavior tends to result in frustration. In discussing the hypothesis of these authors, Hall suggests:

The authors recognized that other psychological factors, in addition to frustration itself, needed to be taken into account in order to obtain a better understanding of the aggressive response. As a result, a series of corollaries were formulated relating this response to other variables. More specifically, they posited that aggression was a function of:

[4] A. H. Maslow and Bela Mittlemann, *Principles of Abnormal Psychology*, rev. ed., New York: Harper & Row, 1951, pp. 63–64.

[5] J. Dollard *et al.*, *Frustration and Aggression*, New Haven: Yale University Press, 1939.

(1) the strength of the motivation for the blocked response, (2) the degree of blocking the instrumental response, (3) the frequency with which instrumental responses are blocked, as well as (4) the anticipation of punishment for the aggressive response. Finally, they proposed that the expression of any aggressive act was a catharsis which reduced the instigation to all other acts of aggression although a footnote limited the generality of this position. Aggression, it was here indicated, would continue if the original frustration persisted, or if the aggressive response became a learned one.

An impressive amount of evidence was obtained to support these corollaries, although much of it was either anecdotal or in the form of questionnaire studies in which the subjects reported what they had done, or would do when in a frustrating situation.[6]

During aggression there may be a transfer of hostility from the object or person causing the frustration. This occurs when the individual attacks or criticizes another person rather than the actual force responsible for the blocking. This displaced aggression usually is directed toward less threatening persons not responsible for the frustration. Thus, the office manager who is dominated in his home may snap at an employee who makes a minor error or is a few minutes late for work. This is a form of scapegoat.

In their discussion of frustration and aggression, Shaffer and Shoben offer the following pertinent suggestions on the relationship between aggressive behavior and frustration.

The persecution of minorities has been attributed to a displaced aggression resulting from social and economic frustrations experienced by the dominant group. The aggression of a warlike nation, such as Germany from 1932 to 1945, has been blamed on internal frustration which results in displaced aggressiveness toward external "enemies." Such generalizations are true to some extent, but they are probably not the entire explanation of complex social phenomena. Exceptions are conspicuous. For example, a persecuted mi-

[6] Hall, *Psychology of Motivation*, p. 236.

nority is certainly a most frustrated group, but it is generally meek and fearful rather than itself aggressive.[7]

In clinical studies of individual persons, aggression is found to be a frequent response to frustration, but it is only one of several possible responses. A person may react to frustration by withdrawing or by compromising as well as by aggression, depending on the intensity of his thwarted drive, the strength of the frustration, the threat of punishment for aggression, and his past habits of adjusting. Not all aggression comes from frustration. Sometimes it is the rewarded attitude in a social group, as may be seen in certain primitive societies and in some gangs of boys.[8]

Frustration and Regression

Regression is the process by which an individual of any age unconsciously reverts to an earlier, less mature form of behavior for the purpose of escaping from present threats or conflicts. It is characterized by infantilism during which the individual under frustration is likely to exhibit more primitive and less mature behavior. Or regression may take the form of rigidity in which the individual may continue attempting a solution already found impossible, such as tugging at a locked door without attempting to explore other ways of opening it. Fortunately, either is usually a temporary form of adjustment to the frustrating situation.

The nature and extent of regression in frustration among thirty children was studied by Barker, Dembo, and Lewin [9] in a carefully planned and conducted experiment. In this experiment, each child's ability to play constructively with different toys was ascertained by close observation of each during free play for a thirty-minute period. Following these experiences, the children were shown and permitted to examine attractive new toys which interested them very much. Then the frustration situation was

[7] G. K. Morlan, "A Note on the Frustration-aggression Theories of Dollard and His Associates," *Psychological Review*, 1949, pp. 1–8. [Shaffer and Shoben]

[8] Laurence F. Shaffer and Edward J. Shoben, Jr., *The Psychology of Adjustment*, 2nd ed., Boston: Houghton Mifflin Company, 1956, p. 102.

[9] R. Barker, T. Dembo, and K. Lewin, "Frustration and Regression: An Experiment with Young Children," *University of Iowa Studies in Child Welfare*, Vol. 1 (1941), pp. 1–314.

introduced by returning the children to their old toys and deny-ing access to the new toys, even though the new toys were within the vision of the children.

Again, careful observations were made of the behavior of the children. During this period the children spent considerable time trying to get to the new toys, pleading with the experimenter or seeking ways to leave the room. Striking examples of regressive behavior were displayed. On the average, the children regressed to a play level that represented that of children approximately fourteen months younger. Only five of the children exhibited no overt aggressive behavior.

Although this experiment was conducted with children, re-gression as a response to frustration can be found among individ-uals of any age. This is illustrated by the homesickness experi-enced by the adolescent who is away from home or by the adult who becomes unreasonable in his attitude when thwarted.

In his general comments on the characteristics of the re-gressed response as related to frustration, Hall makes the follow-ing observations:

> The experimental findings of both animal and human stud-ies indicate that when an organism is frustrated in a given situation, a type or kind of behavior which is different from that just previously found in the experimental situation frequently occurs. If this kind of response change is all that is meant by regression, there would be little argument, for most of the experimental evidence indicates it to be a real phenomenon. Unfortunately, the term used to describe be-havior in clinical as well as experimental situations has acquired surplus meanings which have resulted in consider-able confusion.
>
> One source of controversy has to do with the charac-teristics of the "regressed" response. Lewin has hypothesized that such behavior has not been previously learned, but in most of the animal studies which have presumed to demon-strate regression, such behavior has been experimentally "placed" in the organism's response history.
>
> A related difficulty has to do with the strength of the motivational antecedents which are presented following the frustration experience. Presumably, in addition to the origi-

nal motivational antecedent, a second, arising from frustration, is present. How these interact will be an important determinant of the organism's behavior in the test situation. McClelland (1951), for example, has pointed out that behavior which is used as a defense against the anxiety which has arisen out of the frustration will undoubtedly be found to obey laws different from those in which behavior is a means of obtaining some form of the original frustrated goal response. A careful classification of the variables operating in the situation, as well as the varying types of responses, is needed in order to help clarify the situation.[10]

Frustration Tolerance

The way in which a person tends to meet thwarting or frustration represents what can be termed his *frustration tolerance*. The extent to which an individual is able to endure a frustration without becoming emotionally disorganized is considered to be his *frustration tolerance*. Frustration tolerance is individual. Individual differences in frustration tolerance are related to early experience. Some people seem to experience many disappointments, thwartings, and frustrations in their observable attitudes and behavior; other people appear to display freedom from involvement in frustration situations.

A certain situation may be a source of annoyance to each of two people; the reaction of either one in the situation is an indication of his degree of frustration tolerance. For example, two equally busy men are called for jury duty. The first reaction of one of the men is to attempt to be excused from his civic duty; his business would "go to pieces" if he were unable to give it daily direction. The second man recognizes his civic responsibility; he immediately starts plans for the maintenance of his business during his absence from it. This man gives evidence of high frustration tolerance; his responses are adequate and efficient in the presence of a frustration situation.

Most human beings experience frustration, and attempt to utilize one or more methods of escape. People differ, however, in the frequency and intensity of their utilization of any one method to resolve their difficulties. The kind and size of obstacles

[10] Hall, *Psychology of Motivation*, p. 245.

that are encountered and overcome give indication of an individual's degree of frustration tolerance. Individual degree of frustration tolerance can be illustrated through examples taken from any area of activity. Equally able high-school or college students are assigned the same problems to solve. The problems are difficult. Some of the students persevere until the assignment is completed, displaying a high frustration tolerance; others complete part of the assignment; still others look at the assignment, decide that it is too difficult, and give indication of their low frustration tolerance by their failure to attempt to solve any of the problems.

Similar examples could be cited from other areas of activity: business and industry, home responsibilities, social and community projects. There are many people who are sincere in their intention to do a good job and to be cooperative in their personal interrelationships. Whether these people carry out their good intentions depends upon the extent to which they are able to persist in an activity or remain in a situation when factors of annoyance, disappointment, thwarting, or frustration interfere with self-satisfaction.

CONFLICT AND ADJUSTMENT

It is the capacity of the human being to respond in different ways to the same situation that provides the basis of conflict. If, in every situation, an individual was able to behave in only one way, conflict would not be experienced. It is the presence of more than one habit pattern competing for use that provides the conditions for conflict. When a choice is to be made, only one set of habit patterns can function at a time, thus arousing some form of conflict and producing a feeling of frustration. Hence conflict is rooted in habit patterns and frustration.

The effect of conflict upon behavior was studied by such men as Freud, Pavlov, and Lewin. Freud believed that disturbed patients were profoundly affected by conflict. Pavlov confined his studies to the behavior of dogs. He believed that conflict is capable of producing neurotic symptoms, is continuous with normal learning, and can be studied in the laboratory. Lewin believed that conflicts can be reduced to two polar opposites in an environment. Thus, he suggested the three classifications of conflicts: *approach-approach, avoidance-avoidance,* and *approach-avoidance*. The significance of this classification is discussed later in the chapter.

Causes of Mental and Emotional Conflict

An unsatisfied need or desire, or a frustration, may be the cause of mental or emotional conflict. The incompatibility of opposing desires sets up tension that often is increased by a repression of the unsatisfied drive, because of continued frustration. If these tensions are not properly resolved, many adjustment problems may arise in the mental and emotional life of the individual.

Meaning of Conflict

Mental conflicts are associated with the fact that the intellect of man is not a psychic unity. The human mind is developed through many thousands of more or less individualized experiences trying to find a place in the *psyche*. Mental conflict occurs when a person's ideas, feelings, and emotions, respectively, are pursuing their own outlets in the psychic life. This entails conflict. Adjustments are made to resolve the conflict. Some attempts at adjustment are helpful; some, called maladjustments, are harmful to the individual.

Most conflicts are undesirable because they are detrimental to the well-being of the person, dissipating his energy and creating emotional turmoil. They may be beneficial, however, if they serve to motivate behavior toward adjustment, provided that the emotional disturbance is not too severe.

Mental conflicts sometimes take the form of a combat with reality. When the demands of nature are too severe for the person, he begins to develop neurotic tendencies and tries to continue his life in a world of fantasy. It is easy for him to satisfy his desires in this dream world. Some persons find it difficult to subject themselves to the hardships encountered in routine activities, or they are unwilling to submit to any form of authority. Their emotions are highly sensitized; they dislike everything that interferes with their desire to assert their individuality or that increases the difficulty of dominating their associates or surroundings.

Areas of Conflict

The child endows each new experience with feeling and emotional values. Each day he utilizes behavior patterns that already are established; his daily experience is colored by the feeling tones of earlier experiences. The nature of these patterns determines the nature of the individual's ability to adjust to the many diverse conflicting forces and interests of his life.

Childish interests usually are fleeting. At one moment a child is deeply interested in his teacher, the next moment finds him interested in a classmate. Consequently, during these early years conflicts are of short duration and can be resolved easily by an effective change of stimuli. The wise mother does not talk about an injury done by another boy, but directs the child's attention to something else, thus reducing the emotional tension experienced by the child at this critical time. Later, she can help the child better to understand the problem in its proper setting. With the young person's increasing maturity, conflicts may become fewer in number but may tend to last longer. Older children learn to get along well together. Yet if they continually are thwarted they may develop a resentment of or a hatred of their young associates. These experiences then become the bases of subsequent conflicts. An increased appreciation of the respective rights and responsibilities of all individuals and groups that are concerned gradually will lessen the tension and modify demands.

Classification or Grouping of Conflicts

According to Lewin [11] and others there are three types of conflict situations that can be experienced by an individual. In one, the individual is subjected to two positive response tendencies that are incompatible. This is called the *approach-approach* conflict. In another, the individual is subjected to two repelling (negative) response tendencies. This is the *avoidance-avoidance* conflict. In the third, the individual is subjected to both attracting and repelling response tendencies. This is the *approach-avoidance* conflict.

Cameron suggests that conflicts can be grouped as *adient-*

[11] Kurt Lewin, *A Dynamic Theory of Personality*, New York: McGraw-Hill, 1935.

avoidant, double-adient, and *double-avoidant* reactions. After giving his interpretation of the meaning of conflict, he discusses his groupings of conflicts as follows:

When we speak of *conflict,* we mean *the mutual interference of competing reactions which prevents the adequate development, continuation or consummation of ongoing motivated behavior.* The competing reactions may be conceived of (a) as overt or covert attitudes and responses, (b) as antagonistic patterns of change in muscle tension and relaxation, or (c) as mere shifts in action, potentials, demonstrated or inferred. . . .

Adient-avoidant conflicts. The typical adient-avoidant conflict consists of two incompatible reactions, arising in the same act, one of them directed toward an object, activity, or goal (adient), and the other directed away from it (avoidant). Adient-avoidant conflicts appear early in childhood when punishment or restraint prevents the adequate development, continuation, or consummation of an act, but does not terminate it. If, for example, each time a child reaches toward some object, an adult slaps his hand, restrains him or scolds him, he may develop an avoidant reaction without, however, losing his original adient one. If reaching and withdrawing tendencies are approximately equal, the child's hand may remain suspended part way to the object or execute oscillatory movements toward and away from it, until fatigue, distraction, or a rage response tips the balance. The reverse situation develops when an adult coaxes or compels a child to face something toward which the child's original reaction, still present, is one of avoidance.

However, as every mother knows, even the certainty of punishment does not always prevent an adient reaction from going on to consummation, nor will the most attractive reward always overcome a child's avoidant reaction. Both children and adults do or refuse to do many things in spite of their accurately anticipating painful retaliation. One reason for this, of special importance in behavior pathology, is that the sustained tensions of conflict can become in themselves so intolerable that they make one reckless of consequences. The normal small child may terminate his conflict in an outburst of rage or aggression against an interference or an offending object. In young and old alike, an outburst has the immediate, though unplanned, effect of reducing the tensions of conflict. But as a child grows older, this technique becomes less and less successful in getting rid of conflict, because of society's rising scale of taboos against temper tantrums with increasing biosocial maturity.

Among children and adults, prolonged adient-avoidant conflicts are prime sources of anxiety, and anxiety is a prominent constituent of many behavior disorders. Thus, sustained conflict often leads directly into anxiety disorders, anxiety attacks, and panic reactions. The anxiety of adient-avoidant conflict may under some circumstances lead instead to phobic, compulsive, or hysterical reactions. These often protect the individual from direct anxiety at the high cost of chronic neurosis, but they do not actually resolve the conflict situations. What we call *guilt* is a special case of adient-avoidant conflict. The temptation to do something forbidden is the adient tendency while the partial inhibition of that forbidden adience, derived perhaps indirectly from previous punishment or threat, is the avoidant tendency which prevents or delays the adient consummation. The adient-avoidant conflict of guilt is clearly responsible for many delusional and hallucinatory developments, such as those we shall meet in paranoid disorders, in schizophrenia, and in mania, depressions, and delirium.

Double-adient conflicts. The typical double-adient conflict consists of two incompatible reactions arising in the same act, both of which are directed toward the same object, activity, or goal *(convergent adience)*, or each of which is directed toward a different object, activity or goal *(divergent adience)*. In *convergent adience* there is one object, activity or goal, but two competing, incompatible attitudes are aroused toward it. In *divergent adience* there are two objects, activities or goals, and one's adient attitude supports competing responses toward both at once.

Double-adient conflicts of both kinds develop in numerous common ambivalent situations. Convergent adience is seen, for example, in the simultaneous appearance of hostile aggressive attitudes and affectionate accepting attitudes toward one's parent, one's beloved, or one's child.[12] Divergent adience appears in situations that offer a person parental reward, filial, community, or celestial reward, in exchange for abandoning something else which he dearly wants. No matter which adient reaction he begins, he will find that he cannot escape the pull of the other adient-reaction tendency.

Double-avoidant conflicts. The typical double-avoidant conflict consists of two incompatible reactions, arising in the same act, each of which is directed away from an object, activity, or goal. The man in double-avoidant conflict is like a tennis ball in play; whichever way he travels he gets hurt. This is the dilemma of the child or adult who, for example, is threatened with pain, privation, or rejection if he does not go through with a disagreeable, humiliating, or frightening situation. It also was Hamlet's dilemma and the one confronting a great many suicides. Hysterical disabilities are not uncommonly the outcome of double-avoidant conflicts. Faced with the social demand that he perform some dangerous or distasteful duty, a person may be unable to escape it without incurring social retaliation and disgrace, unless there are extenuating circumstances. As we shall see, the momentary tremor, paresthesia, or paralysis that develops in the anxiety of such conflict may persist indefinitely thereafter, as an hysterical symptom, which provides an extenuating circumstance acceptable to the patient and his associates.[13]

Significant Aspects of Conflict

Conflict is an inevitable concomitant of human action and interaction. The intricate pattern of human nature and the complex character of human relationships preclude the possibility of anyone's achieving even for a short period during his lifetime a completely placid, non-thwarted state of self-satisfac-

---

[12] *Adience* should not be confused with the so-called "pleasure principle." Adience refers to relative *direction*. A hostile aggression is adient in the same general sense that a loving approach is adient. [Cameron]

[13] N. A. Cameron, *The Psychology of Behavior Disorders*, Boston: Houghton Mifflin Company, 1947, pp. 131–134.

tion. A continuous vegetative existence or bovine calmness probably would become extremely boring to most, if not all, human beings.

During discussions concerning the emotions, the author is accustomed to ask his students whether the latter would prefer to go about their affairs unhampered by emotional excitation. Student reaction always takes the form of a definitely negative response. They agree that their joys, sorrows, disappointments, frustrations, and conflicts give zest to life. The tragedies of childhood become the subject of adolescent amused retrospection. Upon the frustrations of adolescence are built adult emotional controls. Conflict situations during adulthood serve as proving grounds to develop strength of character.

Many of our unpleasant, thwarting, and frustrating experiences are relatively unimportant, temporary, and easily overcome. Hence they represent desirable elements of personality development and adjustment. Poor adjustment or maladjustment is a resultant of the inadequately resolved conflicts that tend to recur or of persistent conflicts that continue to defy attempts to resolve them.

The introduction of new interests, changing conditions, or participation in unaccustomed activities may weaken the force of a conflict situation. Although the conflict situation cannot be attacked directly and consequently resolved, its effect upon the individual wanes and the conflict situation eventually is forgotten. Later, however, a similar conflict situation may arise. The detrimental effects of the new conflict are intensified by the emotional residuum of the former experience.

For example, a college junior experienced a conflict between his desire to continue his education and his equally strong interest in marrying. To marry meant to leave college for a job. Before he made a decision he was called to service in the Armed Forces. He had not resolved his original conflict but he gained satisfactory recognition of his military activities which prepared him for successful civilian employment. He married, enjoyed a happy home life, and continued to achieve successfully in his vocational work. Some years later he received an offer of a job that had challenging possibilities. Acceptance of the offer necessitated his spending several years in a foreign country but leaving his family at home. This was a conflict situation that brought to memory his conflicting interests as a college student. This time, however, no outside factor could remove the need for decision-making. The new venture would give him added prestige and increased financial remuneration. His family left the decision to him. He thought through the situation, weighing its advantages and disadvantages; he could not sleep or eat; he suffered strong emotional stress; he wished that something might happen (as it had years earlier) to relieve him of the responsibility to resolve his conflict. So devastating were the effects upon him of his struggles that on the final day for his acceptance or rejection he suddenly became extremely ill. Attending physicians feared that his illness would be fatal. By the time he recovered from his illness the new job no longer was available. From a practical point of view, the man's illness had resolved his conflict. The emotional aftermath of the experience seriously affected his self-regarding attitudes, however. He continued alternately to re-proach himself for his indecisiveness, to resent the job's not being held for him, and to accuse his family of failing to meet their responsibility in helping him resolve his conflict.

An unresolved conflict may persist in varying forms and differing situations. Unless the victim of the conflict finally can attack the conflict and achieve a reasonable resolution, he may be driven to escape from the situation by one of several avenues: withdrawal from group living by becoming a hermit; attempted suicide; aggressive criminal acts; retreat from reality into a world of self-preoccupation. Unresolved conflicts affect the victim's entire personality. To a more or less serious degree he suffers from personality or behavior disorders that appear to be unresolvable and that may predispose toward disintegration of personality.

Arousal of Conflicts

Conflicts arise out of failure to adjust. If an individual's desires are blocked and he is unable, because of established habits or interests, to pursue another course of action, there is developed an inner disturbance that affects his mental and emotional life. The resultant conflicts function reciprocally between the external situation and the inner reaction. External conditions may interfere with an individual's ability to achieve at a time when he is most eager to succeed. The resulting conflict may have its roots in the thwarting of individual satisfaction or social ambition.

Every individual has his characteristic behavior patterns of conflicts. These usually arise out of specific environmental conditions. They originate to a large extent in the consequences of an evaluation of one's desires and attainments in relation to behavior expected by society. Hence a conflict is a pattern of mental activity characterized by unpleasant emotional attitudes in which the desires of the individual are not socially acceptable.

The individual may find his interests and desires so consistently and continuously interfered with that the thwartings may seem to overwhelm him. His own desires, the interests of others, established codes, rules and regulations, or laws arouse mental or emotional conflicts. A teacher or a parent is a constant stimulus for the arousal of such conflicts in the mind and emotions of the child or adolescent. The adult is the immediate cause for the denial of children's wishes. The adult may be disliked for this, but the antagonism usually is temporary since children eventually realize that there is value for them in this denial even though it affects them unpleasantly. However, if they believe that injustice is associated with the denial of their desires, they acquire resentments that may become permanent. The struggle between opposing forces continues. It begins in the home between the child and his parents, is continued in the school between the child and his teacher, and progresses through life between the individual and the social order.

ATTITUDES IN RELATION
TO CONFLICT

An attitude is personal. It relates to the way a person feels, thinks, or behaves in specific situations. A person is reputed to be kind, tolerant, friendly, or critical, as he displays one or another of these behavior traits in his habitual relationships. An individual's feeling tone or affective experience when he is stimulated by a person, an idea, an activity, or an object is a specific response of approval or disapproval. This acceptance or rejection is aroused within the individual by the total situation and is based upon his previous experiences. Every human experience is accompanied by a feeling tone or affective experience. This affective experience or attitude, in turn, influences an individual's thoughts, interests, and behavior.

Attitudes and interests may be quiescent (latent or potential), or active (kinetic). The active attitude or interest may function as a force by itself or as a part of the total dynamic behavior of the person at the time.

The Nature of Attitude

All daily experiences that become a functional part of life have an affective side. The accompanying sensations possess feeling aspects of pleasantness or unpleasantness, satisfyingness or annoyance. A composite of these qualities that forms a part of every experience constitutes a feeling tone or affective quality.

Attitudes are, in effect, certain kinds of habit patterns. They result from learning and are subject in their formation to the accepted laws of learning. Attitudes operate in behavior patterns, become a part of the rich mental and emotional life of an individual, and give him his joys and his sorrows or both.

Dynamic interrelationships between situations and desires give rise to attitudes that are important in the functional organization of emotional patterns. The attitudes that result from values relating to self are quite subjective. A person is concerned about his problems, his worries, his behavior, or his possessions. The mother is subjective in her attitude toward her own children but evidences a fundamentally different affective response toward the children of another family. Each individual evalutes every situation in terms of his training and experience. The resulting attitudes and affective qualities determine his behavior.

In their interpretation of attitudes Sherif, Sherif, and Nebergall state:

> *Attitudes* refer to the stands the individual upholds and cherishes about objects, issues, persons, groups, or institutions. The referents of a person's attitudes may be a "way of life"; economic, political, or religious institutions; family, school, or government. We are speaking of the individual's attitudes when we refer to his holding in high esteem his own family, his own school, his own party, his own religion, with all the emotional and affective overtones these terms

imply. We refer to his attitudes when we say he holds other groups, other schools, other parties or religions in a less favorable light or at a safe distance (as "safe" is defined by his attitudes) .

The process whereby an individual *becomes* a member of the X family, a Baptist, an American, a Democrat (or Republican) consists in acquiring appropriate attitudes about these institutions. A newborn baby can be objectively identified as the offspring of the X family, whose parents are white, American, Methodist, and so on. But, as every parent knows, the baby does not behave by heredity as a *member* of these classifications. The process by which he comes to behave and to consider himself as a member is accomplished through acquiring the attitudes appropriate for each.

To say that attitudes are *learned* implies neither mechanical imprinting nor formal instruction, necessarily. From early childhood on, an integral part of an individual's interaction with adults and with other children important in his eyes is labeling the objects, persons, events, and groups he encounters in approving, disapproving, or other affective tones. This labeling process involves words, gestures, and actions of other people. But it is not a one-way affair. As he learns labels, the individual develops the desire to belong, to be accepted, and to prove himself among those identified as his own. Henceforth, these desires cannot be ignored in the learning process.

Whether the individual's attitudes are formed primarily in interaction with others to whom he is attached emotionally or primarily by exposure to dictums, pronouncements, and printed and spoken exhortations, they constitute what makes him, psychologically, a member of the groups and institutions in his social world. Conversely, they define for him what he is not. Thus, they express the end products of the socialization of the person in so many roles—as a member of a family, school, church, political party, adherent of an ideology, citizen of a country, and so on. They express his psychological reference to these groups and institutions.

Social attitudes, therefore, have motivational and emotional properties. They are not momentary or transitory. Other, more transitory psychological states that give directionality and selectivity to behavior for a time should be given other labels, e.g., "set" or "expectation." [14]

The Influence of Mental Qualities

The development of wholesome attitudes and good habits is important for mental health and efficiency. An attitude gives mental tonus or set to experience—real or anticipated. Personal problems and conflicts are definitely supporting stimuli for attitudes. The more intense is the desire or the conflict, the stronger is the accompanying attitude. Attitudes are closely associated with specific experiences and are difficult to generalize. Thus a person has a habitual attitude toward his work, toward other people, toward authority, toward parents, or toward world conditions.

An individual's conscious attitudes do not always remain consistent toward any of the above-mentioned persons or situations. He may show one attitude at one moment and an entirely different attitude at the next, when or if conditions or an understanding of the situation changes. However, some persons are set in their attitude toward some things. For example, regardless of the existing conditions, they always vote the Republican ticket or the Democratic ticket. Yet the election is carried by one political party this time and by another party next time, by those voters whose attitudes are changed by changing conditions.

Physical Constitution and Attitudes

The actual attitudes that constitute the affective side of man's nature result from his living in his particular environment. The trend of his established attitudes—his attitude toward others and their attitude toward him—is rooted in his own personal constitution. Such factors as size, physical uniformity, physical disability, health, potent drives, degree of emotional stability, and potential energy, are significant because of their possible effect upon the individual himself and upon other persons. The proper functioning of the nervous, glandular, or circu-

[14] Carolyn W. Sherif, M. Sherif, and R. E. Nebergall, *Attitude and Attitude Change: The Social Judgment-Involvement Approach*, Philadelphia: W. B. Saunders Company, 1965, pp. 4–5.

latory system is conducive to the development of positive attitudes. A malfunctioning of one or all of these systems may result in socially undesirable attitudes and personality traits.

An individual's physical features may become very important as attitude directors, especially if too much attention is given to an apparently undesirable characteristic. A girl may admire small, smooth hands, but her own hands may be large and rough. Consequently, an attitude of shame is developed. During a visit to a friend's home the first thing that an adolescent girl called to the visitor's attention was her chapped hands. Had she not mentioned them the probabilities are that they would not have been noticed. A boy may desire a thick, bushy head of hair, but his hair may be thin and sparse. The physical trait in and of itself may not be important. It is when the person is possessed with a strong wish to be different that undesirable attitudes are strengthened. Consider the possible attitude of the boy who, as a result of a severe case of typhoid fever, lost his hair and returned to college baldheaded. The fact that he could do so was proof that he possessed certain inner attitudes that helped him during that trying time. It is this kind of experience, however, that often is the beginning of attitudes that lead to maladjustment and that are difficult to correct.

It is not the malformation itself that affects attitudes, but the way in which people react to the peculiarity. The girl who is six-feet-three is not aware of her height in the same painful way if her height is near the norm of the group, rather than the exception. To be tall when tallness has value is desirable. It is satisfying to a young woman to be tall and slender if it shows how well she can wear evening dresses; it is quite unsatisfying if she wishes to become an air hostess, since that position usually calls for the small, petite type.

Attitude and Age Levels

In general, children's attitudes are imitative, and not based on reasoning. A child tends to fall in line with accepted group attitudes. He acts with little understanding of the reason for his behavior; what he does often is divorced from his best interest.

An adolescent's attitudes are more personal and are directed by his own individual drives. Behavior on the part of elders that

interferes with his freedom may stimulate adolescent antagonisms. The teen-ager tends to feel that adults are intolerant and
nonunderstanding. He considers himself to be "broadminded,"
but his attitudes actually are biased in terms of his personal
wishes and felt needs. He is interested in trying the new—anything that is considered "taboo" by his elders. His behavior may
be motivated by an attitude of self-sufficiency or a belief in his
own personal power and rightness.

In general, an adolescent's attitude is hopeful and forward-
looking. He is driven by an urge to reform the world. Although
his attitude toward an individual child or a particular old person
may be one of impatience, he has a kindly attitude toward
children as a group, and pity or sympathy for those who are very
much older than himself. Toward the members of his own age
group his attitude is conditioned by his relationship with them.
He may be resentful of those who possess superior advantages or
who seem to receive more attention than he does. He may exhibit
an attitude of superiority toward those other young people who
appear to be less able or less successful than he is.

The attitudes of adults are colored by their own personal
whims and selfish interests; by their work and family experiences; by their social status; by the recognized degree of success
that they have achieved; by all other factors that affect their life
patterns. They want recognition from others; consciously or unconsciously, they give expression to this attitude. If they are
thwarted in the realization of their desire for attention, they may
develop an attitude of bitterness toward their associates or an
attitude of personal futility.

Attitudes offer great possibility for achievement in life. They
are important in every activity and affect all human values.
Efficiency results when a person is impelled to continue and
complete an activity, rather than to avoid an unpleasant task. A
child need not be permitted to do completely as he wishes;
usually he can be stimulated toward desirable activity through
the arousal of interest in worth-while projects. Constructive attitudes, developed during childhood, serve a person well during
his adolescence and adulthood.

If a person believes that no one cares for him, he experiences
a loss of relationship with other human beings. He needs the
sympathetic understanding of others. This desire appears early in

life and continues throughout life. The child, the adolescent, or the adult wants to feel that he belongs. He wants to identify himself with a group or with groups in which he recognizes the fact that he is important, that he is well thought of, and that he is a person. This bolsters his ego, since thereby his strong points are emphasized and his shortcomings are discounted.

Attitude affects the entire nature of an individual at any age: his learning, his thinking, his emotions, and his overt behavior. A person's attitude also exerts a powerful influence upon other people who associate with him. Much of the directing and controlling power or influence of one human over another is based upon attitudes.

Influence of Unconscious Attitudes

Our behavior is influenced by mental states of which we may not be fully aware. We do many things without an understanding of the reasons that prompt our behavior. These unconscious attitudes provide the basis for much of our unexplainable conduct and inner conflict. The effect of these attitudes is not fully appreciated by us because we do not realize the effect of our behavior upon others and, consequently, do not recognize the fact that our actual motives may be very different from those believed to be ours by other persons who observe our behavior.

A person's actions, for example, may exhibit attitudes of selfishness, insincerity, domination, or self-interest; the person himself might be very much surprised if he were accused of possessing any such attitude. A grandmother may believe sincerely that the advice and help given by her are best for a child. A mother-in-law does not always want to interfere, but her unconscious attitudes sometimes affect her behavior. The drive to have things done in the way that she considers best is so strong that she cannot yield to those who have the right to plan their own lives. Parents, in their desire to help their children, often inhibit desirable self-direction. Such parents are not aware of their underlying self-centered attitude. A father may want his son to be a doctor, a teacher, a lawyer, or an accountant. It takes more than the wish of a parent, however, to arouse an interest on the part of his child. If the parent is too persistent in his expressed attitude he may help develop strong antagonism in the child toward parental choice of vocation.

If a person admires another for one outstanding personality trait, he is likely to accept all of the other person's behavior. In the same way, if one personality trait is disapproved of, other desirable traits of the person are not recognized. If a person loses at cards he feels that someone else is at fault. Moreover, if the opponent who has won begins to gloat over his success, a deep-seated attitude may be expressed in the words "I don't mind losing but I don't like to have it rubbed in." Many examples could be cited to illustrate the influence of unconscious attitudes upon our relationships with our associates.

We should strive to keep unsocial attitudes as dormant in the unconscious as possible. Hates, prejudices, and resentments are encouraged by these attitudes as the latter find their way to active consciousness. The real motive for our behavior often is so subtly disguised that we honestly believe that our attitudes are wholesome and aimed at socially desirable goals. What widowed mother who has given much possessive love to her son can see anything of worth in any girl who may take her son away from her? This mother honestly may believe that her attitude is aimed at assuring for her son a happy life. Actually, the woman is motivated by self-interest. Overt expression of felt attitudes often presents a truer picture of underlying motives to those who observe the behavior objectively than it does to the one who is trying unwittingly to satisfy unconscious attitudes.

The skilled and proficient worker builds into his habit pattern many attitudes that become a part of his everyday living. He gains satisfaction from plans well made and work well done. However, as he works from day to day, he dreams of the time when he may retire from active service and enjoy the leisure that will be his. Too often, when this man does retire, he realizes that he has lost not only his work but also the satisfying attitudes that accompany successful achievement. It is in retrospect that we often really appreciate the satisfactions that were ours during former experiences.

Attitudes and Values

Direction is given to attitudes in terms of our interests and values. If an obtained object or goal has little value, the effect upon our attitude is negligible; if the article is lost or is easily replaced, attitude changes are slight. If, however, we are emotionally involved with an object, person, or situation, and we hold it in high esteem, we are moved deeply when it is lost or destroyed. The writer recalls the emotional turmoil suffered by a young girl who had lost, through fire, her prized possession—her diary. At that moment this girl considered the diary to be extremely important; yet, later, when she no longer was emotionally involved, she remembered little that was written in it. When its replacement or duplication is difficult or impossible, the attitude of an individual toward an object or situation approaches that of an emotional stress.

An individual's attitudes usually reflect the traditions and customary thinking of his group. His attitudes, when he attempts to solve a personal problem, may become emotionally charged because of the conflict between his habitual attitudes and his momentary interest. A student, as a result of his training, may have developed an attitude of honesty, but if his graduation depends upon his passing a test for which he is not adequately prepared and if cheating is possible, he at once faces a conflict between his habitual ideals and his immediate need. To the extent that conflicts of this nature continue, emotional strain increases. If an individual always could be certain of what is socially right and socially wrong, positive attitudes could be developed and conflicts avoided.

Emotional disturbance of one kind or another is likely to be the cause of an undesirable attitude. The person who is emotionally stable and who is able to adjust to his daily activities with reasonable success is not likely to develop antagonistic attitudes toward those who may seem to achieve greater success or recognition than he does. The boy or the girl who enjoys security in his home is not tempted to run away or to engage in one or another form of delinquency. The antagonistic or unduly critical person engages in asocial behavior as a means of fighting his own feeling of inferiority or insecurity; he is attempting to impress others with his superiority.

If undesirable attitudes are to be improved, the emotional disturbances that cause them need to be resolved satisfactorily. Unless the individual can gain the security which he craves, any attempt to redirect his attitudes is likely to result in still greater conflict.

Factors Involved in Change of Attitude

Once set, attitudes are basic aspects of personality and difficult to change. Factors involved in achieving change in attitudes are well expressed by Sherif *et al.* as they react to the question:

> What is it that is to be changed by communication aimed at attitude change? We have answered that what is to be changed is the individual's evaluative categories for appraising some class of persons, objects, ideas, or events and his own relationship to them. His attitudes thus are constituents of his self system, varying in their priority in his personal scheme. They are inferred from the characteristic and consistent patterns of his stated opinions, his expressions, and other behaviors.
>
> A change in attitude, therefore, implies a change in his categories for evaluation, which amounts to changing a part of himself; and it implies manifest change in the patterned behaviors from which they are inferred. The frame of reference for studying attitude change, therefore, includes the individual's stand and his degree of involvement in it, which affects the extent to which it is the major anchor in a communication situation. It includes the communication itself, its form, and the order of arguments. It includes the communicator and the source, both of which affect the extent to which the position presented in communication anchors the individual's subsequent appraisals of the issue. Thus, a source and speaker with high standing or prestige in the person's eyes, in effect, enhances the anchoring function of the advocated position. Similarly, any event or procedure that successfully involves the individual in a position presented to him, such as the necessity of doing a good job of presenting it or defending it himself, increases the salience of that position as an anchor when he subsequently evaluates the issue.
>
> The first and foremost implication of the present approach is that susceptibility to change decreases with increased ego involvement in [one's] own stand. Thus, persons who are noncommittal to few if any positions on an issue and have a very broad latitude of rejection at the outset are particularly likely to displace a discrepant communication

away from their own stand and less likely to change toward the position presented. The typical person with an extreme stand on the presidential election, or right to work, or a farm policy issue is an example. In fact, the enhanced discrepancy felt from communication because of the contrast effect in placement is likely to lead to reaffirmation of his own stand and even change away from the communication, if the discrepancy is extreme and if there are available positions for the individual to endorse in that direction.

Susceptibility to change is initially greater on the part of less-involved persons, including the majority of those who endorse moderate points of view on an issue. With their broader latitudes of noncommitment, less-involved persons assimilate communications over a wider range and are more likely to change toward it, since their own stand is less salient as an anchor. Similarly, the effects of variations in the communication situation, such as primacy-recency effects, are greater for less involved persons than for those strongly committed to a position.[15]

UNDESIRABLE BEHAVIOR RESULTING FROM CONFLICT

An individual's past experiences and his attitudes toward them are mental and social factors that may cause feelings of insufficiency. In his daily experiences the child finds that he is scolded for his mistakes or ridiculed for his shortcomings more than he is praised for his accomplishments. If he is clumsy and needs assistance, he is likely to be scolded or snubbed, or his behavior criticized. He is constantly being denied the doing of the things he wants to do. Parents, teachers, playmates, and other persons inhibit him in one way or another. This kind of conditioning imposes handicaps that are difficult to overcome for the already inhibited and timid person. Later adjustment to social situations is difficult for the child who develops feelings of insecurity. If he learns during early years to meet, evaluate, and attempt to solve the simple problems that confront him, he is helped thereby to adjust to problems on the adult level.

Conflict is not easy to endure. Adolescents or adults can overcome or escape it more easily than either can meet thwarting

---

[15] Sherif *et al.*, *Attitude and Attitude Change*, pp. 242–243.

or continued delayed action. Some matters may not be resolved for a long time; in fact, they go on and on indefinitely. For example, ethical or moral matters may be considered overtly or covertly over a long period. This continued indecision only serves to make the person more unhappy. In extreme instances the conflict and the indecision end abruptly in suicide or homicide. An individual in conflict needs to carry through to apparent consummation in order to reach full satisfaction and thereby experience the gratification that results.

Patterns of Inferiority and Insecurity

A feeling of insecurity is likely to be developed in children if they are permitted to attempt tasks beyond their age and ability. For a child to engage in schoolwork that is too difficult for his experience and ability level usually is disastrous. He seems to be destined to fail; he is likely to interpret the failure as something peculiar to himself. Consequently, he imagines that he is labeled by others as a failure; he develops strong feelings of inferiority.

Many persons feel that they have little chance to progress vocationally as a result of the fact that they entered industry without first having attended college. Even though they have engaged in self-education they still feel the lack of that academic label which the college degree can give them. A woman had completed only three years of college study before her marriage. On one occasion she was a member of a group of relatives and friends who were discussing the colleges from which each had been graduated. Embarrassed by the fact that she could not report the holding of a college degree, she withdrew from the group. She had reared two fine sons and had organized a successful nursery school, yet she experienced a feeling of inferiority in the presence of the degree-holding members of the group. Later she continued her studies. The eventual earning of a college degree was an ego-satisfying achievement that exercised a tremendous influence upon her attitude. She now feels secure among groups of college graduates.

THE RESOLUTION OF CONFLICTS

There is no standard remedy that can be administered to a person who is suffering from a state of conflict. It is possible, however, for parents, educators, employers, and other community leaders to help young people develop attitudes and behavior patterns that will lead to the achievement of self-building experiences. In this way conflict-arousing interpersonal relations can be prevented. Moreover, community leaders can do much to help the individual who already is experiencing a conflict situation.

School Factors

Schoolmen who know the content of education better than they do the psychology of the educand often are heard to say that any one who uses *common sense* as a means of assisting high school students in their adjustment problems is applying basic psychological principles. I do not object to this belief, but I know that some advisers are more successful than are others in helping high school students. Can this greater success be explained only in terms of greater common sense? Is there any teacher who will admit that he does not make considerable use of common sense in his dealings with his learners? Common sense becomes a significant factor of counseling, if the term is interpreted to include a consideration of the problems of the student in light of his background, his interests, his limitations, and his attitudes. To help a confused adolescent resolve his conflicts, a counselor needs *uncommon sense* that is the resultant of intense training, broad experience, and adequate personal adjustment.

Social Factors

On the social level the life-adjustment program has three objectives. First, the individual definitely needs to gain all those positive attitudes, ideals, practices, beliefs, and habits that are essential to his becoming an efficient member of the social groups of which he forms a part. Such qualities as cooperation, geniality, generosity, kindness, and courtesy are socially acceptable traits that, as they are born of experience, become effective agents in preventing and resolving mental and emotional conflicts. Second, it is important that care be exercised to eliminate or minimize all social influences that tend to produce major conflicts in the respective groups and institutions that form the framework of social experiences.

Finally, when maladjustments already have been acquired, attempts can be made to determine the social nature of the causative factors. Efforts then can be made to remove the social irritants and to change the social situation, or to correct the individual's attitude. The preventive program is confronted with innumerable problem possibilities on the social level. With an increase of interest among adults in the development of better-adjusted children may come a more successful functioning of preventive measures.

Work Factors

There probably is no more hygienic method of resolving conflicts than participation in interesting and challenging work. Every adolescent dreams of the time when he will be a successful economic factor of society. In fact, a college senior was heard to remark that every high school graduate should have a year of work experience before continuing his education on the college level; thereby he can enrich his college life.

Too ambitious occupational aims, parental opposition to personal vocational interests, lack of opportunity to train adequately for a chosen vocation, or insufficient need of workers in a desired occupation for which ability and training are adequate are fundamental sources of youthful conflicts. Young persons who, for the reasons stated, see no hope of a satisfying occupational ambition may develop antisocial attitudes and actions. If young people recognize that they are being thwarted in their normal urge to be gainfully employed according to their interests, they tend to resolve their conflict by placing the responsibility for their failure upon the inadequacy of the society that they believe to be the cause of their unfortunate situation.

Recently some students of a trade school neglected their studies yet refused to withdraw from school, although they were over the compulsory school age. When they were asked their reasons for neither studying nor quitting, their answer was that there was no reason for them to learn a trade since they were just "sticking around" until they were eighteen, at which time they would let the government take care of them in the armed services. There is evidence here of an attempt to resolve conflict through *flight* from purposeful activity.

Several brilliant and well-educated young college tutors who were among a group of college teachers accused of un-American activities began their careers as enthusiastic and loyal Americans. Because of their ability, they had been encouraged by their college advisers to prepare themselves for college teaching, and were given part-time jobs in teaching and assisting in the college. Confident of an eventual appointment, these men, at great sacrifice, continued their graduate studies and then married. Budgetary cuts interfered with their receiving permanent college appointments. They became embittered by what they considered false encouragement followed by unfair discrimination. Hence they were motivated to *fight* against the, to them, existing intolerable social order.

Quite different from these young people who resolved their vocational conflicts in an antisocial manner are those young adults who are strong enough emotionally to accept failure in the achievement of their desired vocational aims, and who are ready and able to engage in whatever work is available—doing an honest job, but alert to more desirable work possibilities. Many of these young people are so successful in their "forced" work that they not only develop an interest in it but also win promotion and economic security. Others are able, eventually, to achieve their original aims. Consequently, they believe that their temporary disappointment has made them more appreciative of their final success.

Numerous conflicts among workers are mitigated through the efforts of industry itself. Many firms are discovering that it is a good common-sense procedure to provide better working conditions, to permit rest periods, to arrange shorter hours, and to plan recreational programs for their workers. It took many years for the more foresighted companies, stimulated by the demands of organized labor groups, to demonstrate the benefits of these methods of satisfying workers.

The Individual and His Conflicts

Society has a major responsibility for the prevention of and resolution of conflicts experienced by individuals or groups. In the final analysis, however, the individual who is experiencing a conflict is the one who must attempt to resolve that conflict.

To the extent that a younger or older person who finds himself in a frustrating or conflict-arousing situation possesses habitually stable emotional qualities, he usually can resolve the difficulty in a manner that will be satisfying to himself and acceptable to others. The emotionally insecure person is likely to attempt a resolution of an existing conflict in such a way that the situation becomes more serious. He may even come to lose whatever degree of stability he once possessed.

A conflict may be rooted in two or more warring urges or desires within the individual himself, or it may arise out of a frustrating situation which involves persons or conditions in his environment. Whatever the source of the conflict may be, the person who is experiencing it can approach the problem situation in one of three ways. (1) He decides that he no longer can endure the conflict, so he attacks it *directly*. He does something definite about it. (2) He recognizes the fact that the conflict situation does not permit an "all or nothing" approach. Compromise between the elements of the conflict situation appears to be the most effective means of resolving his emotional stresses and strains. (3) His conflict has become so severe that there appears to be no reasonable way of resolving it. He becomes the victim of the conflict situation and withdraws completely from realism; he becomes mentally ill.

We know that mild or more severe conflicts are common. A young man has an intense desire to be the proud possessor of a high-priced automobile; he also wishes to marry. His financial status does not allow him to do both. A young woman was teaching in the elementary school after the completion of a three-year teacher-training course. She had saved enough money to make a fourth year of study possible, but she was responsible for the support of a widowed mother. If neither became ill, her savings would take care of both of them while she was not earning any money. A man who was earning a relatively small salary fell in love with a girl whose parents were wealthy. The girl wanted the man to give up his job and work for her father. The girl's father was willing to give the young man a high salary, but the young man was not interested in the work and had no training background for it. Moreover, he enjoyed his present work. Hence he felt that accepting this man's proposition verged on the parasitical.

Many more instances of similar conflict situations could be cited. In any case, something needs to be done to preserve mental health. The person involved is the one to decide whether he should employ the direct approach or attempt to compromise. In the first case cited the man married, hoping that eventually he might be able to afford an expensive automobile. His hope was realized. The young teacher compromised. She continued to teach and earned her degree from a university at which she could complete her college work after regular school hours. The man gave up the girl, and remained in his chosen occupational field. He reached this decision, however, only after much conflict and some guidance. He still is not certain that he made a wise decision.

Relative Value of Direct Action and Compromise

Various factors need to be considered before a conflict situation is approached either by way of direct action or by compromise. Direct action may be impulsive, it may not take into consideration all of the factors that are basic to the conflict situation. An immediate solution to a problem is satisfying only if the person has an intelligent understanding of the whole situation and is certain that the action that is decided upon will resolve the conflict. For example, a woman teacher lives with her aged mother in an apartment house in a large city. Because of her mother's ill health the woman devotes all of her time to her schoolwork and to the care of her mother. She lacks opportunity to engage in relaxing social activities. Hence she is under continual pressure.

Although the woman can retire from teaching, she is very much interested in her schoolwork; but her mother resents her daughter's absence from the home during school hours and feels that she is being neglected. Here is a conflict situation that needs resolution through direct action. The daughter realizes that retirement means a reduction of income, but that careful planning will make it possible for the two of them to live comfortably on her pension. Hence she retires; she and her mother leave the city for a small town in a warm climate. The woman does not regret her decision. Her mother's health and attitude have improved and the daughter is enjoying the social relaxation which had been denied her for so many years. Moreover, since they are living in a college town, the teacher probably may do some part-time teaching for personal satisfaction.

Too often a person takes direct action to solve a conflict situation and later regrets his decision. A high school girl was undecided about her plans for the future. She was a good student who would have gained much from a college education. She believed, however, that her family needed the money that she would earn if she went to work directly after graduation from high school. Consequently, in spite of the attempts to dissuade her by both the family and the school officials, she elected the commercial course. This action did not solve her conflict, however. By the time she was graduated, she knew that she wanted to go to college but did not meet college entrance requirements. At this point she compromised by working during the day and completing her college entrance requirements in the evening division of the high school. This meant at least two years of evening study, but she persisted. She then entered college and worked during the late afternoons and evenings in order to support herself financially. Although this heavy program was difficult, she felt that she finally had resolved her conflict. She found further satisfaction from the fact that, upon graduation from college, she was able to enter a professional field in which she was successful.

Compromise usually is the first approach for a person who can meet his conflict situation with some intelligent understanding of its fundamental factors and who is willing to give a little rather than to demand the complete satisfaction of his own wants. At one time or another every person is faced with a situation in which there are present more or less serious elements of conflict. He does something to free himself from the problem situation. Any action that relieves tension is better than passive acceptance of emotion-disturbing conditions. If an individual is unable to resolve his conflict by means of satisfying direct action or intelligent compromise, he may attempt to settle the struggle for adjustment by adopting one or another unrealistic approach to his problem, or he may withdraw completely from the demands upon him of a realistic situation which he believes he cannot meet successfully.

A successful executive is invited to address a national gathering of important men in his field. Although he is an excellent organizer, he always has had an abnormal fear of public speaking. He believes that a refusal to speak before the group would be interpreted as an admission of weakness. He withdraws from the situation honorably (as he believes) by suddenly losing his voice. He is not shamming; he attempts to speak but no sounds emerge. Apparently his vocal cords have become paralyzed. It may take considerable therapeutic treatment to help him regain his power of speech, especially if normal speaking ability were to be associated with recurring invitations to address large audiences. Other conflicts that involve fear of engaging in a particular situation may cause a person to lose the power of locomotion or the ability to use one's hand for writing, for example.

Some of the more common devices referred to as unrealistic approaches are presented in the following chapter. The complete or almost complete repudiation of reality is discussed in the chapter that deals with mental illness.

An excellent summary of frustration and conflict as organized by Sappenfield is presented here.

Frustrations may be classfied in a number of ways. *Primary frustrations* involve the sheer continuation of needs, while *secondary frustrations* involve the perception of some particular interference with gratification.

Passive frustrations involve the mere perception of an interference with gratification, while *active frustrations* involve a threat to the individual's safety; in other words, active frustrations involve a larger pattern of motives than is involved in passive frustrations.

Need frustrations involve the temporary or permanent prevention of gratification; *instrumental act frustrations* involve interference with a particular mode of achieving gratification; *object frustrations* involve interference with gratification in relation to a particular cathected object.

Frustrations may also be classified, in terms of their source, as *external* and *internal;* external and internal frustrations may be further subdivided into *privations* (lacks or defects), *deprivations* (losses), and *obstructions* (barriers between the individual and his goals). Internal obstructions are termed *conflicts*.

Conflicts may be classified in terms of the possible combinations of valence or cathexis—in terms of whether they are predominantly plus-plus, plus-minus, or minus-minus.

Plus-plus conflicts require a choice between incompatible goals that are positively cathected. Plus-plus conflicts are usually relatively minor, since either choice will bring some gratification; they may, however, be of major importance when they require a relatively permanent or irrevocable choice.

Plus-minus conflicts require a choice between losing some desired goal in order to avoid its negative features and accepting the negative features in order to attain the desired goal. Immobility and vacillation frequently occur in response to plus-minus conflicts. Plus-minus conflicts are likely to be of severe intensity, since they are difficult to resolve, and since either solution will involve frustration.

Minus-minus conflicts require a choice between negatively cathected goals; in order to escape one frustration, the individual must become the victim of another. The typical reactions to minus-minus conflicts are withdrawal and vacillation. Minus-minus conflicts are typically severe; they are difficult to resolve, since escaping one frustration will involve being trapped by another.

Conflicts usually involve complex combinations of positive and negative cathexis; the above classification of conflicts, therefore, should be regarded as an oversimplification.

Conflicts may also be classified in terms of the origin of the motives that conflict with each other. *Id-id conflicts* involve the operation of two or more incompatible biogenic motives. *Id-superego conflicts* involve the operation of psychogenic motives that are incompatible with biogenic motives. *Superego-superego conflicts* involve the operation of incompatible psychogenic motives. Id-id conflicts are usually of minor significance, but id-superego and superego-superego conflicts may be at the root of most instances of human maladjustment.

Human living is beset with frustrations that are typical at different stages of development. Among these typical frustrations are loss of love, feeding frustrations, exploration restrictions, cleanliness training, rivalries within the family, lessening dependence, sexual restrictions, sex patterning, school frustrations, adult frustrations in striving for economic security and social status, death of family members and friends, and failures in various enterprises.

Frustration involves all of the principles that relate to motives. The concepts of discomforting stimuli, increased muscular tension, increased activity, and unconscious motivation apply as much to frustration as to the original motives that are frustrated.

For a frustration or a conflict to be significant, it must involve relatively strong motives. Both the motive and its frustration—both of the incompatible features of a conflict —must be of equal strength if the frustration or conflict is to become significant for adjustment. Of the motives involved in conflict, those which are prepotent will eventually win out. If prepotent motives are frustrated by agencies other than incompatible motives, the frustration is likely to be severe. The response to a series of minor frustrations may be similar to that which is induced by a single major frustration.

Frustrations are dynamically interrelated. The severity of the total interacting pattern of frustrations will not necessarily be equal to the summation of the separate strengths of each component frustration; the strength of the total pattern of frustrations will sometimes be less than, sometimes more than, and sometimes equal to, this sum.

In a complex society, contradictory demands may be made on the individual; he may introject values that are mutually conflicting, or he may introject ambitions, ideals, or standards that are incompatible with the resources available in his environment.

Frustrations may generalize from one situation to another. On the basis of previous frustrations, the individual may develop a low level of confidence in himself or in his environment, and he may become less than normally efficient; therefore he will be more likely to perceive any given situation as frustrating.

Since many motives operate on a relatively unconscious level, the frustration of relatively unconscious motives will occur; the individual may be aware that he is frustrated, or merely aware of anxiety, without knowing what motives are being frustrated.

Frustration tolerance (or need tolerance) is defined as the individual's capacity to delay gratification. It will develop most adequately when the frustration required of the individual increases gradually within the limit of pre-existing tolerance. Too little frustration or too much frustration at any given time will interfere with the development of frustration tolerance.

General reactions to frustration include the direct removal of frustration through gratification of the original motive, the development of aggressive motivation, and the development of anxiety.

The principles of frustration have the following adjustive implications: (1) that frustration is unavoidable; (2) that frustration is necessary for learning; (3) that the level of aspiration should be maintained reasonably near the level of the individual's previous achievement; (4) that persons in authority over others should be sensitive to the frustration tolerance of those who are subordinate to them, and should strive to socialize, teach, or supervise in such a manner that the induced frustration will be within the limits of frustration tolerance; and (5) that many conflicts are readily resolved, and many frustrations rendered unimportant, if the individual has developed a stable hierarchy, or ordered system, of values.[16]

16 Bert R. Sappenfield, *Personality Dynamics: An Integrative Psychology of Adjustment*, New York: Alfred A. Knopf, 1961, pp. 120–122.

QUESTIONS AND PROBLEMS

1. List situations which, during the past month, have aroused a feeling of frustration within you. Indicate why this is so.

2. Indicate the relationship that exists between frustration and conflict.

3. Describe cases known to you in which desirable personal adjustment followed relatively severe conflict.

4. Describe a study in this chapter that deals with frustration and conflict.

5. Name and discuss some of the sources of frustration.

6. Distinguish between situational frustration and internal frustration.

7. Report ways in which aggressiveness is related to frustration.

8. What is meant by frustration tolerance? Illustrate through examples from personal experience.

9. Enumerate some of the conflicts that arise between parents and their children; between teachers and their pupils; between employers and their employees. What can be done to resolve them?

10. In what ways do unconscious attitudes affect human behavior?

11. Why are some teachers disliked and others liked by their pupils?

12. Reflect on your behavior when experiencing a conflict. Report your feelings and overt behavior.

13. Describe your behavior when you are frustrated in the achievement of a goal.

14. How do you meet situations in which you feel inadequate?

15. List at least two things that you are expected to do but believe yourself incapable of doing successfully.

16. Explain the statement that conflicts are rooted in habit patterns.

17. Differentiate among these types of conflict: approach-approach, avoidance-avoidance, and approach-avoidance.

18. Justify the statement that conflict is an inevitable concomitant of human action and interaction.

19. Explain the statement that conflicts arise out of failure to adjust.

20. Show the relationship that exists between attitude and conflict.

21. Outline a program for the resolution of conflicts.

Selected Readings

Berlyne, D. E., *Conflict, Arousal, and Curiosity.* New York: McGraw-Hill, Inc., 1960.

Coleman, J. C., *Abnormal Psychology and Modern Life,* 3rd ed. Chicago, Ill.: Scott, Foresman and Company, 1964.

Coser, L., *The Functions of Social Conflict.* New York: Free Press of Glencoe, 1964.

Dollard, J., L. W. Doob, N. Miller, O. H. Mowrer, and R. R. Sears, *Frustration and Aggression.* New Haven, Conn.: Yale University Press, 1939.

Festinger, L., *Conflict, Decision and Dissonance.* Stanford, Calif.: Stanford University Press, 1964.

Hilgard, E. R., *Introduction to Psychology,* 3rd ed. New York: Harcourt, Brace & World, Inc., 1962.

Horney, K., *Our Inner Conflicts.* New York: W. W. Norton & Company, Inc., 1945.

Kendler, H. H., *Basic Psychology.* New York: Appleton-Century-Crofts, Inc., 1963. Chapter 12.

Maier, N. R. F., *Frustration—The Study of Behavior Without a Goal.* Ann Arbor: University of Michigan Press, 1961.

Munn, N., *Introduction to Psychology.* Boston, Mass.: Houghton Mifflin Company, 1962. Chapter 8.

Shaffer, L. F., and E. J. Shoben, Jr., *The Psychology of Adjustment,* 2nd ed. Boston, Mass.: Houghton Mifflin Company, 1956.

Sherif, C. W., M. Sherif, and R. E. Nebergall, *Attitude and Attitude Change: The Social Judgment-Involvement Approach.* Philadelphia, Penna.: W. B. Saunders Company, 1965.

Smith, H. C., *Personality Adjustment.* New York: McGraw-Hill, Inc., 1961.

Washington, B. B., *Youth in Conflict: Helping Behavior-Problem Youth in a School Setting.* Chicago, Ill.: Science Research Associates, 1963.

Yates, A. J., *Frustration and Conflict.* New York: John Wiley & Sons, Inc., 1962.

⚜ 8 ⚜

DEFENSE
MECHANISMS IN
ADJUSTMENT

HUMAN DRIVES and urges impel man to activity of one form or another. The form and direction that this activity takes depend on the forces of cooperation and opposition to which an individual is exposed, on his intelligence, and on his interests. As an individual begins his struggle for existence, he is interested primarily in self-preservation. His other desired satisfactions are secondary. He makes whatever adjustment is necessary to preserve himself in his complex environment. The influences in his environment have resulted from the accumulation of social traditions to which he has fallen heir. In this society he strives to maintain his individuality and at the same time to conform to the interests and wishes of the members of his group, since, if he is to survive in the group, some conformity is essential.

Human drives and urges serve as bases of ideals and actions. Any inner drive that motivates an individual to engage in activities that are unsuccessful in their self-regarding effects is likely to cause him to seek a more satisfying form of behavior. This pattern of behavior may be considered to be a learned set of reactions that tends to reduce the force of the stresses and strains resulting from the nonfulfillment of an urge.

An individual's behavior patterns act as mechanisms of adjustment. Thus, he tends to reduce the force of the drives that are calling for action. If an individual is inherently good, for example, he may discover in his competitive struggle for a place in the group that his progress is slow. Consequently, he may take short cuts in the forms of lying and cheating in order to excel in the achievement of a coveted goal. His imagination may work overtime in helping him to invent ways and means of circumventing the rules and regulations of the established group. This type of behavior is a common method used to attain a desired aim or purpose, but an individual needs to be helped to understand that not all compensatory behavior is desirable.

The normal individual is usually able through the exercise of socially accepted means to achieve his goals in his struggle for the satisfaction of various wants and urges and for survival. The habit patterns thus established attain for him not only individual satisfaction but also the approval of his fellows. The individual's concept of and evaluation of the goal itself may be incomplete or faulty; his appreciation of his ability to achieve may be inadequate. If either of these two situations exists, it is difficult for him to achieve personal satisfaction through participation in ordinary or realistic experiences. Hence he attempts to adopt an adjustive form of behavior that satisfies his impulse to satisfactory achievement. This substitute behavior continues until he no longer feels the need to achieve the desired goal, or until the actual achievement of the original goal can be realized. His constant effort to vary his behavior so as to achieve his desired goal demonstrates the use of one or another of the mechanisms of adjustment.

I now shall describe briefly some generally recognized substitute forms of behavior, including their significance as adjustment-seeking techniques and their relationships to maladjustment.

Although psychologists, psychiatrists, and mental hygienists are not in general agreement concerning a classification of the various mechanisms of adjustment, they do agree that substitute activity may take many forms. The adjustment approaches commonly utilized by individuals in their attempts to make adjustments include the following:

Introjection Criticism Negativism
Compensation Sympathy and refusal
Displacement Daydreaming and Retrogression
Identification fantasy Repression
Rationalization Idealization Neurotic
Projection Conversion behavior
Sublimation Withdrawal Delinquent
Malingering behavior: behavior
Egocentrism Shyness and
Attention-getting seclusiveness

Introjection

Introjection is defined as the process by which an individual unconsciously acquires ideas, emotional attitudes, and ideals from the people around him. Emotional attitudes, ideals, and feelings are absorbed as an individual lives with his parents and others during his growing years. Ideals and standards of behavior are developed in this way. The beliefs and ideals of parents regarding morals, education, and social values become the beliefs of the growing child. As education and experience are acquired there is an interaction that helps the individual to develop values of his own and become less dependent on the forces that affect him during his early years.

Most of our ideas are garnered from others. The home environment is the important factor that determines the politics of the individual. Our prejudices, for example, are likely to be similar to those of our parents and/or close friends. Attitudes or points of view that differ from those held by parents usually result from resentment toward parents or defiance of parental authority.

The process of introjection is automatic and operates below the level of consciousness. It is seldom recognized as an experience. For example, it is easy to accept and agree with the ideas of someone we like, but difficult to accept new ideas from a person we dislike. Attitudes of objectivity should be practiced even though it is difficult to accept another person's point of view.

The value of introjection is predicated on the basis of a rich environment. The adjustment and learning problems faced by the culturally deprived child illustrate the dangers of introjection. Because of introjection a poor environment in the home and neighborhood is self-defeating. The many programs that are being planned for individuals in this type of environment are essential in the adequate acculturation of the children who reside therein. The enrichment of their experiences through early attendance at school will help do much to give these children better opportunities to profit from introjection.

Compensation

Compensation may be defined as the utilization of extra energy in the development of a trait to alleviate the tensions caused by a real or imagined defect. It is an attempt to adjust to a failure or an inadequacy, real or imagined, thus reducing tensions that result from a recognized shortcoming of some kind. For example, an individual often emphasizes the functioning of another trait or characteristic that is likely to distract the attention of associates from the real or imagined defect. The substitute or compensatory behavior may or may not receive approval.

Those individuals who overact in the same general functions in which they have defects display the most common and perhaps the simplest form of compensation. The short girl attempts to accentuate her height by wearing extremely high-heeled shoes. The fat boy overexerts himself in order to direct attention away from his size toward his ability to do things or to get about as others can. In like manner the cripple offers to help others as a means of diverting attention from his handicap.

Transferred compensations or compensations in which the overactivity is of a function other than the one of felt deficiency are also common mechanisms of adjustment. An individual who cannot succeed in abstract, academic activity may be able to perform physical feats that give him desired recognition. On the other hand, he may substitute mental superiority as a transferred compensation for physical deficiencies that account for attitudes of inferiority. If the mental ability of this person is high, he may attain scholarly achievement, but, if his intellectual ability is average or lower, he may become a "wisecracker" or display another form of behavior in his efforts at compensation.

Some individuals develop specific traits to a high degree of perfection in order that they may surpass others who are compet-

ing with them. Those who develop specific skills for the purpose
of compensation are usually unwilling to compete in games or
other activities that do not give an advantage to their highly
developed trait. The collecting of objects as substitute achievement for social recognition is a mechanism of compensation, the
importance of which is in direct ratio to the value placed on the
collection by the group.

SOME COMMON FORMS OF COMPENSATORY BEHAVIOR. Many examples could be cited of the utilization of compensatory behavior. A throat difficulty interfers with the continuance of a singer's
musical career. To compensate for the disappointment, he either
develops his histrionic talents or becomes a teacher of music. A
boy who cannot excel in study may aim consciously to become a
successful athlete.

Sometimes the adoption of this kind of behavior is unconscious. Small men often tend to become assertive or aggressive.
They may develop superiority in a special skill whereby they
gain social approval, in spite of their small stature. They may
become meticulous in dress and grooming.

Some parents attempt to compensate for their own inadequacies through the achievement of their children. These parents
want to make available for their child the opportunities that they
themselves had desired but were denied. They insist upon selecting the child's career, his associates, and his mate, in terms of
their own thwarted interests. The socially unpopular adolescent
or adult may adopt a hobby, such as collecting stamps, signatures
of well-known persons, rare coins, or other objects. The pride
that he develops in his collection and the social recognition that
he receives compensate for his social inadequacies. A childless
woman may become concerned about the welfare of all young
people and engage in some form of social work.

INEFFECTIVE COMPENSATORY BEHAVIOR. A compensatory activity may be unrealistic, such as exaggerated manner, affected
speech, or ultramodern dress. The individual may tend to compensate for a defect by overaggressiveness, bullying, false submissiveness, or overzealousness in denunciation of social or individual inadequacies. These compensatory habits are expressions of
the individual's denial to himself of his own inadequacy. Ineffectiveness of compensation is illustrated by the behavior of M. Z.
and J. L.

M. Z. is twenty-three years old. She is extremely conscious of the fact that she is only five feet tall; she complains that her friends seem to tower above her and call her a "shrimp." Her dress is very peculiar; her use of cosmetics seems to be directed toward compensating for her short stature. Her nails are very long and very red, her hats have tall crowns, and her heels are extremely high. When she was in her second year at high school she joined a liberal youth group, as a revolt against general peer attitudes. Since then she has been intolerant of all people who do not share her views; she constantly asserts that she is proud of the fact that she is different from the "common crowd."

J. L., a college student, is shy and ill at ease with members of the opposite sex. As a result of this attitude she refuses to attend any mixed gatherings. She gives as her reason the fact that she is engaged to a young man in the army. Since he is gaining promotion rapidly, she must devote all of her time and energy to study so that he will not be ashamed of her. She is a brilliant student but is beginning to show the strain of overwork. Her classmates suspect that she is not truthful concerning her engagement. They are worried about her physical and mental health but are unable to help her make a better social adjustment.

There is danger in overcompensation. An individual may not be content to develop normal competence in the substitute activity but may strive for complete mastery. The energy expended in this way may be too great; the individual may break under the strain. Moreover, the substitute attitude or behavior pattern may be socially disapproved. Inner tensions are thereby increased rather than reduced.

Displacement

Displacement represents an effort on the part of an individual to adjust to a frustration-provoking situation by releasing, in overt behavior, the pent-up emotions experienced at the time. It usually is more temporary than compensation, yet somewhat similar to it. Displacement shows itself in an individual as he taunts a smaller classmate following a reprimand by his teacher for his misbehavior. He attacks or criticizes the smaller individual rather than the teacher who may be the source of the frustration. Thus he releases his emotional tension. If he talks back to the teacher or otherwise displays resentment, he fears further punishment, which tends to intensify rather than alleviate his emotional stress. A mother who is kicked by her young child uses displacement to reduce the tension that has been building up to cause the bad behavior. This substitute approach is better than spanking the child to deter further behavior of this type. The teacher who relies on punishment to correct behavior is likely to see emotional tension build up rather than be released by the individual involved. Threats of punishment by anyone in authority tend to increase the emotional stress rather than reduce or release it. Attitude changes are influenced more by a display of understanding than by attempts to deprive the individual of a privilege or to administer a severe form of punishment.

Identification

The attempt of an individual to identify himself with another successful individual or a desirable situation is referred to as identification. It reduces personal tension through the achievements of other persons in whom the individual is keenly interested. The baseball fan, for example, identifies himself with his favorite team; he regards the home runs hit by his team as personal victories. This satisfaction is achieved more easily than one that is earned through personal endeavor. Moreover, in case of failure on the part of one's chosen idol, it is relatively easy to satisfy one's desire to experience success by switching one's allegiance from the failing individual, team, or group to another more successful one, and then identifying with the latter.

DEVELOPMENT OF IDENTIFICATION PATTERNS. This is a common and relatively harmless form of adjustment. Most of us belong to a small group within a larger social group. It is usual for us to identify ourselves with or to experience pride in the achievement of noteworthy members of this select group. Such identification may interfere with an individual's active participation in group activity, however; it is easier to overcome a feeling of inferiority by basking in the reflected glory of the exploits of the other person than to gain recognition for personal achievement. Still, this diverted attention may prevent the arousal of emotional stress.

Identification as a means of compensation may begin very

early in life. The small child identifies himself with his parents of whom he usually is proud. "My father can lick all your fathers put together"; "my mother is the prettiest woman in the world—my father says so"; "my father knows everything"—are remarks frequently made by children of well-adjusted parents. Because of this hero worship the child tends to imitate his parent's behavior so that someday he may be as fine as the adult is.

As children proceed through school and college they identify themselves with their various "adored" teachers or campus heroes. Witness the mannerisms of the little girl playing school and imitating her teacher. The child has so carefully observed gestures, intonations, and even vocabulary, that her teacher is given a chance—and sometimes not a flattering one—to see herself as others see her. The boy lives the life of his storybook or television hero—it may be an Indian chief or it may be Willie Mays. The girl temporarily may be Red Riding Hood, Cinderella, or a glamorous motion-picture star.

A bright little girl, who was an ardent reader of well-chosen children's books, each evening became a different storybook character. This interest activated a game between herself and her father. When he arrived home from business she was accustomed to greet him with an imitation of the day's heroine. His part in the game was to address her by her heroine's name and to carry on with her an appropriate conversation. So good was her imitation, which at the time was not acting but living, that the practice thus acquired did much to help her later to become a famous character actress.

As the individual grows older he tends to identify himself with special groups: fraternities, select clubs, and civic and business organizations. He takes great pride in the good reputation of his organization. The more highly selected it is and the less outstanding his participation in the group activities, the greater is his tendency to boast of his group's achievements. Usually those persons who are responsible for maintaining the standards of the group are too busy to talk much about their achievements. Members of outstanding families, who themselves are relatively mediocre, have an inordinate pride in the family's history.

An individual's identification with a person who is worthy of imitation or with a group that has high ideals may develop into a desire to become like these leaders. Gradually the individual, within his limitations, may imitate his heroes as the child imitates his parents. In this way he may acquire personality traits that cause him to be a model for others to imitate.

EFFECT OF IDENTIFICATION UPON PERSONALITY. Parents who have a feeling of personal failure sometimes identify themselves with the success of their children to an extent that exceeds justifiable parental pride. An individual may identify himself with his possessions to so great a degree that he boasts of his home, his automobile, his clothes, his jewelry, etc., as though his possessions were endowed with qualities of excellence that cannot be found elsewhere. Identifications of the types described are undesirable: first, because too much bragging becomes boring to listeners and so interfers with an individual's normal associations with his fellows; second, because the individual may waste his time in boasting rather than in doing. One criticism of American sport is that too many Americans are bleacher-seat athletes who exercise their lungs in yelling and their arms in waving hats rather than participating in healthful games. Another criticism of Americans is that they think more of what they have than what they are.

IDENTIFICATION AS MALADJUSTMENT. Identification is undesirable when the person so loses his individuality in that of his ideal that he is no longer conscious of himself as a person, but takes on in thought and in action the personality of his hero. Since his background and environment may be very different from that of the hero, the results may be disastrous.

If normal boys identify themselves with the heroes of undesirable motion pictures or thrilling badmen stories, their identification with the characters may go no further than the mental reliving of exciting exploits. No more serious effects may result than a waste of the time that should be given to study, or a reduction of power to meet routine duties. In its extreme form this identification may result in an attempt to emulate the behavior of the hero, with consequent danger to other persons or penalties to himself.

Among the mentally ill this form of compensation is quite common and may be one of the first observable symptoms of a mental disorder. The kindly, moral, and religious but ineffectual man suddenly becomes God; the brilliant, diligent student of history now is Napoleon; the derelict who is picked up on the park bench tells the policeman about the treasure which he has hidden safely at the bottom of the Pacific Ocean and which, as soon as he has finished his nap, he will have brought to the surface and distributed among his friends.

A young woman had been brought up very carefully by an uncle and an aunt. Because of their attitude against continued education for girls, she was not allowed to enter college or to study music. She resented her relatives and her enforced idleness. Finally, she left home and started on a trip to Europe. All her clothes and accessories were white. During the trip she informed fellow passengers that she was a princess who was returning to her native country to claim her fortune. She asserted vehemently that most of this fortune would be given to her uncle and aunt who had been good to her but whom she had treated badly.

Her behavior gave evidence of her identification with heroines of the historical novels and operas of which she had been exceedingly fond. She was returned to America and committed to a hospital for the mentally ill, where she is confined for life. She refuses to see any of her former associates; she devotes most of her time to reading and rereading historical romances. On occasions she is a brilliant conversationalist. She has lost her own identity in that of fictional heroines. She does not answer to her name.

Rationalization

Rationalization includes those thinking processes by which the individual deceives himself through the concealment of the real bases of his thought. He justifies his beliefs or actions by the presentation of reasons for his behavior other than those which actually motivate it. It is an attempt to excuse behavior that is recognized by the person engaging in it to be undesirable or foolish, yet produces certain emotional satisfactions. Since there is no valid reason for the self-satisfying behavior, there must be conjured an apparently sensible justification of it.

A common rationalization mechanism is the sour-grapes attitude. If a person fails in an activity, he may declare that he does not wish to succeed. He usually finds fault with the situation before the failure is experienced. The losing card-player hastens to remark, "Unlucky in cards, lucky in love." He may reverse the order of the excuse if he wishes to belittle the opponent's success. An individual may be aware of much that is inconsistent in his behavior; yet, he may dislike to resolve his conflicts, harmonize his disagreements, or in general, put his thinking in order.

BASES FOR THE UTILIZATION OF RATIONALIZATION. It is difficult for an individual always to admit to himself the true reasons for his acts or the real motives behind his behavior. The higher his standards of conduct and the finer his ideals, the greater may be his attempted self-deception. It is almost unbearable to admit that one's behavior is actuated by unworthy motives. Hence, the average man is given to excusing his socially undesirable conduct by justifying it in terms of highly commendatory though false motives. Usually he is deceiving no one but himself. If he rationalizes his behavior too often, there is danger that he is not believed even when he gives an honest explanation of his behavior.

Anyone dealing with young people knows the difficulty encountered in obtaining from them straightforward accounts of the reasons for their misdeeds. One high school dean has developed a relatively successful technique of dealing with this problem. She listens courteously to the student's explanation of nonconforming behavior. Then she remarks in a conversational tone, "Now let us get the real reason." Usually, after a few pointed questions by the dean, the student admits the real motive for the infraction. After a few such experiences a student meets a situation of this kind by saying, "I thought that I was doing it for this reason but I guess I had better find the real reason before you find it for me."

Many rationalizations have become almost social traditions and are used and accepted without much thought of their connotation. Some of these are: genius never could spell; great people write unintelligibly; the man who does things has no time to bother about superficial matters; attention to petty details is the sign of a small mind. The inference in each case is that if an individual has failed in one of these specific forms of desirable behavior, the failure itself is the sign of the possession of a more worthy quality. Many more such forms of self-justification are common. Our likes and dislikes; our fears; our tendencies to indolence, to selfishness, to jealousy, to spitefulness and envy, to extravagance or miserliness, to too great interest in or too little interest in appearance, to too much or to too little time spent in recreation or in work—all lend themselves to plausible and self-satisfying explanations.

Our consideration for the feelings or for the plans of other people, our sense of duty, our good manners, or our heavy responsibilities are favorite forms of excuse for failure to meet the ordinary daily demands of life. If with the rationalization goes the determination not to repeat the conduct that needs to be excused, the results are not serious.

EFFECTS OF RATIONALIZATION.   An individual's associates accept his occasional utilization of rationalization, since they themselves sometimes may experience a similar self-bolstering need. If this device is utilized consistently as a means of self-justification, however, the group soon learns to resent its implication and the individual's social adjustment is hindered by the unfriendly attitudes of his associates.

The persistent use of rationalization may lead to the development of a false appreciation of one's own personality. For example, an elderly man was so absent-minded that he rarely did what was expected of him and almost never kept appointments. Consequently, he developed the habit of inventing startling and seemingly convincing alibis for his memory lapses. So fixed had become this habit that it was almost impossible for him to tell the truth. Occasionally he recognized his defect, and urged his listeners not to believe the story he had just told them; whereupon he would proceed to regale them with another tale no more truthful than the one he had branded as a falsehood.

As a result of extreme utilization of this device, reality becomes less and less a part of the mental content; delusions are imminent. A serious form of projection may accompany the rationalizing habit to the extent that the reasons for an individual's failures are completely divorced in his thinking from inability to achieve. He places the blame for his inadequate adjustments upon conditions outside himself, or upon other persons or groups. In extreme cases this shifting of responsibility for personal inadequacies develops into strong feelings of persecution.

Projection

In his use of projection, the individual either attempts to place the blame for his failure on the undesirable behavior of another person or the latter's unwillingness to cooperate with him; or he calls attention to the shortcomings of another person in order to divert attention away from his own undesirable behavior, motives, or traits. Projection is akin to rationalization to the extent that an individual uses it to place blame for his own failure to achieve on the shoulders of others or on unfavorable factors in his environment.

BASES OF PROJECTION. Examples of projection are common. The child fails in his test because the teacher gives the wrong questions or marks his paper unfairly. The cook's cake falls because someone shakes the stove by slamming the door. The adolescent girl is a wallflower because her mother makes her wear an unbecoming dress, or because boys have poor taste or want something for nothing. One's car hits the post because the road is not level.

Such projected reasons could be true, but in most instances the use of them is an excuse—a kind of grabbing in a specific situation at a straw of possibility that is not a probability. For most people the temporary conscience-salver is accompanied by a suspicion that the fault lies in the individual himself. Usually, after an experience of projecting blame, a person will attempt to meet a similar situation with a form of behavior that will give more satisfying results. Yet the attitude of projection may be used for the justification of other personal mistakes. Used in this way, projection protects the individual from the feeling of futility that might result if he were affected too seriously by all of his minor behavior mistakes.

UNFAVORABLE EFFECTS OF PROJECTION. When projection becomes a habit, when all one's failures are blamed on others, when a deep-seated and unreasonable attitude of projection is developed toward a particular person or group, the resulting emotional state of bitterness may become a factor of mental disturbance. The habitual integration of projection results from conflicts that are induced by a recognition of personal failure, and attempts to explain failure in such a way that the personal fault will be minimized. An attitude of inferiority may dominate the experiences of an individual academically, economically, politically, and morally.

In connection with conflicts on the academic level I have referred to a student's tendency to blame his teacher for his failure. More serious is the "self-made" man's denunciation of a college education, and his campaign against public support of parasites who have learned the easy way and who are being paid by public funds to continue ineffectual methods of superficial education. If a coveted position is won by a college graduate, the reason for the choice is not to be found in the superior ability and training of the person chosen but in the false standards of an effete civilization. The disappointed candidate may become so bitter that he withdraws from his group and goes to an unspoiled community where real merit is appreciated. He stays there until he loses out in competition. A series of such experiences, instead of convincing the man of his own need of self-improvement, may so exaggerate his feeling of thwarting that he develops a delusion of persecution.

An individual who is economically inferior to others may attempt to compensate for his inability to achieve desired financial or social status by engaging in the promulgation of radical ideas concerning political or social justice. For example, he believes that the cause of his obscurity or poverty lies not in his own lack of power to achieve but in the unfair competition to which he is subjected.

This man becomes the advocate of the thesis that all men are equal and should share equal rewards and recognition. He fails to appreciate differences in ability or willingness to achieve, or in the social value of the achievement. The radical thus projects the blame for his own incompetence upon an unfair and prejudiced social order of which he is an innocent victim. He often is unaware of his own power to achieve, and fails to recognize opportunities for success that may be offered to him. In fact, he may have become so imbued with attitudes of economic or social martyrdom that any attempt to change his status would be regarded as further evidence of political or social injustice. Moreover, it sometimes happens that in those cases where economically or socially underprivileged radicals have later become members of the group of "the overprivileged oppressors" they then have become bitter opponents of the "grabbing lower classes" who interfere with their progress, through unreasonable economic or social demands.

Most individuals dislike admitting their errors of judgment or their inability to perform successfully. It is much more satisfying to project the blame for failure on other persons or objects in the immediate environment. Another person is to blame for the failing marks of a student; the stone should not have been in the way, the ice should not have been left on the sidewalk, or the nail should not have been on the street to puncture the tire. If the projection used is understood by the person, the results may be a source of amusement and not serious. Yet, if the resulting behavior takes the form of irrational ideas of false persecution, it becomes a maladjusting influence to the individual.

Sublimation

If an individual's conduct meets with interference, it may be possible to lessen the resulting conflict by guiding him toward the use of a substitute form of activity. The utilization of a substitute activity is called sublimation. It is a form of conscious substitution of desirable behavior practices for those that may be considered to be socially undesirable or that may be impossible to achieve. Sublimation is utilized to redirect natural impulses of individuals that are based on desires and emotions into ideals of higher thinking. An individual has a strong desire for activity. His energy can be diverted, tranformed, and transmuted. Thus an individual can be encouraged to become active along socially desirable paths. When behavior is raised from lower to higher levels of integration, provided there is harmony in the process, the resulting behavior is referred to as sublimated activity.

If an individual's fulfillment of a strong interest or a desired activity is thwarted, he is likely to display emotional stresses unless the interest or activity can be diverted or sublimated toward achievable ends. According to the Freudian interpretation, the thwarting that needs to be sublimated is limited to the undesirable expression of the sex urge or the *libido*. For a person living in our present culture to avoid emotional stress, the primitive form of sex expression must be diverted toward higher, socially approved forms of behavior. The individual may be unconscious of the force of the original drive; he is unaware of the indirectness of his interest in the substitute activity. He honestly may believe that his "substitute" activity is motivated directly by highly social attitudes.

THE FUNCTIONING OF SUBLIMATION. Sublimation has social significance. There is value in the sublimation of one's primitive urges or selfish desires toward behavior that will benefit other members of the group or of society at large. It is an excellent method of releasing human energy into channels of the kinds of activity that are satisfying both to the individual himself and to those who are affected by his behavior.

The substitution of behavior may be conscious, in that the individual, recognizing a certain ability in himself, definitely directs this talent toward humanitarian ends, e.g., a man who possesses persuasive powers of speech becomes the leader of propaganda for worthy social causes. Sublimation, in its strict interpretation, however, implies that the transference of interest or of activity is on the emotional rather than on the intellectual level.

Sublimation is used as a means of adjustment when, temporarily or permanently, a strong drive cannot be translated into drive-satisfying activity. Consequently, there may occur a gradual, unconscious change from interest in self-gratification toward concern with the welfare of others. If the enlarged activity is successful, feelings of thwarting or of personal tension are modified or eliminated, and the person becomes a well-adjusted member of society. A boy is larger and stronger than his schoolmates; instead of using his strength to plague his fellows, he may become the champion of smaller boys or of girls and fight their battles for them against other boys who have not sublimated their primitive fighting tendencies.

Much of literature, art, and music may be explained as the outpouring of emotional energy into creative compositions. The man or woman who, because of circumstances beyond his control, is denied the opportunity of having children of his own, may adopt all children and become active in fighting for their health and safety. The childless woman or the woman whose children have died or have grown up and moved away from her may direct her maternal urge into social-service work, teaching, or similar activities.

VALUE OF SUBLIMATION. Many primitive inner urges or drives that motivate an individual to activity are concerned with the survival of the self. In so far as the realization of a drive is not antisocial, this is desirable. When society is harmed by an individual's satisfaction of such inner urges, however, functioning of sublimation becomes an excellent form of adjustment. Some writers claim that the progressive improvements in civilization constitute forms of sublimation. By nature, the individual is antisocial rather than social; all basic motives are directed toward selfish ends. Although one may not agree with this evaluation of human nature, to sublimate often has personal and social value.

Since sublimation is a tension-reducing form of behavior that gives opportunity for desirable or even highly commendable activity, it usually leads away from rather than toward inadequate adjustment. It is only when the sublimated behavior pattern becomes extreme that maladjustment is possible. The humanitarian may become a rabid emotional propagandist or a weak sentimentalist. The artist may try for the bizarre in his creation. The social "uplifter" may develop into an aggressive fanatic. In such cases the individual concerned probably is suffering extreme emotional imbalance that would make normal adjustment of any kind difficult if not impossible.

Malingering

Malingering represents a retreat from meeting the situation. There is little or nothing about it that has positive value. In fact, it usually results in harm to the individual. An example is an attempt to feign illness to avoid an unpleasant situation. The individual tends to focus his attention on illness, and this becomes a mental set to guide his behavior. He thus acts under negative suggestion that provides the basis for the development of some psychosomatic disorders.

Teachers and therapists should be aware of malingering, but should avoid pressing the individual into activity when he is physically ill. Each should be on the alert to discover any attempts to feign illness. An individual who is active and happy when he is not being observed and who shows symptoms of illness only when observed may properly be viewed with suspicion as experiencing some form of malingering. Help for a malingering person may need to take the form of denial of activities he enjoys doing, unless he has other behavior problems.

Egocentrism

Behavior that has developed as a result of constant attention and praise characterizes egocentrism. Children early become accustomed to receiving attention to their demands and, when this behavior becomes habitual, the individuals who exhibit it use many devices in order to continue their position as the center of interest and attraction. Various techniques are used to gain attention of this kind. Temper tantrums are examples of the more extreme cases. Another form of this mechanism is the expressed desire of parents that their child lead in all areas of competition.

Egocentrism is especially bad when a child attempts to gain the satisfaction of his requests by the use of prolonged temper tantrums. Also, if egocentric traits are highly developed, the individual may experience serious frustration in his relations with the members of his social group. One should not expect greater consideration from his associates than he is willing to give to them.

Attention-getting

Thwarted egocentrism develops behavior that produces attention-getting responses. Many attention-getting devices are learned in infancy. The baby sometimes cries to receive the kind of attention that he craves. The older child asks questions, romps, gets in the way, or sulks just to get attention. Each is ingenious at inventing behavior responses to attract attention.

The desire for attention is strong in individuals of all ages. To receive social approval, for example, is more satisfying than to be ignored by others. When one's usual behavior fails to gain approval from others, he may strive to bring attention to himself by the display of unconventional behavior. If children do not receive the praise they desire, they may try deliberately to be disobedient in order to be reprimanded. Any display of excessive attention-getting behavior on the part of a child should be ignored. Normal children soon learn to change these antics to more acceptable behavior.

ATTENTION-GETTING DEVICES. Crying without physical cause, throwing things, strutting, imitating Mother's use of rouge and lipstick, among young children; boasting of personal or of family prowess, displaying bad manners of speech or writing, among adolescents; engaging in hobbies and collections and affecting peculiar dress or manner, among adults—these are only a few of many attention-getting techniques that are utilized when ordinary behavior does not gain for the individual the amount and kind of recognition he desires. Even though an individual is successful in his daily activities, his success may be taken for granted by his associates. Since this passive approval is not completely satisfactory he may strive to force a more active recognition of himself.

An amusing story is told of a six-year-old boy who started his school career in the same building in which his older brothers and sisters had received their early schooling. During his first few school days the family evinced fluttering interest in his enthusiastic reports of his good work. Since his experiences were no different from those of the older children who also had shown superior ability in their schoolwork, displayed interest in his achieved "stars" and success stories gradually lessened. He announced to the family one day that his teacher had scolded him. This announcement was received without much comment, whereupon he reported that his teacher had not only scolded him but had hit him. He could give no reason for his teacher's behavior but continued to bring home stories of undeserved punishment. Puzzled by the situation, an older sister, who knew his teacher well, visited the school to discover what this small child was doing. To her surprise, the teacher insisted that he was a model boy; he had not been punished; actually, he had received more commendation than had any other child in the class. Asked to explain his conduct, he burst out, "I tried to tell you all the nice things that I was getting but no one would listen to me. I said that my teacher was hitting me so that *you would pay attention to me.*"

A person may have won considerable public recognition because of unusual achievement in art, music, literature, or other activity. After his reputation has become established as that of an accepted artist, his performance no longer is regarded as sensational. He then may begin to display odd mannerisms, unusual style of dress, or other personal peculiarity. People notice these and often imitate them. His behavior becomes a "fad": he temporarily relives the thrills of his early triumphs.

An individual may use this form of adjustment in order to divert attention from one factor of his personality and focus it upon another. B. L. is an intelligent college graduate. As the result of an accident, one side of his face is badly scarred. Although he is conscious of this physical shortcoming and tends to be shy in social situations, he is an excellent salesman. He attributes his success to the fact that he always is ready with a laugh, a joke, or a quip. Since his humor is clever, the listener attends to what he says and is diverted from giving too much attention to his physical defect.

Many of these simple attempts at attention-getting represent innocuous, possibly helpful adjustment techniques. For example, a boy is in a class with children mentally superior to himself. He is able to pass in his work, but is not good enough to win honors. Hence he tries to gain the attention of his classmates by collecting unusual specimens of whatever the current interest of the group may be: campaign buttons, shells, stones, marbles, or pictures. The approval that he receives acts as an impetus toward further achievement in this kind of activity. Although most children do some collecting, this specially motivated activation may be the start of a profitable adult career.

OVEREMPHASIS UPON ATTENTION-GETTING. The normal desire for attention may be so stimulated through the exercise of otherwise praiseworthy activities that maladjustment may result. For example, it is desirable to develop in young people a habit of thrift; the school bank is an excellent means to achieve this purpose. Yet if too much attention is given to the individual or to the group that deposits the most money in the bank there is danger that a child may become so interested in the size of his account that he develops miserliness, or is tempted to obtain the money for deposit in dishonest ways. Hence school leaders are careful not to emphasize class competition unduly.

The individual's desire for attention may be so strong that he is stimulated toward abnormal and socially undesirable means of satisfying his urge. There are many causes for the lies of children, among which are included that of attention-getting. In order to gain prestige, the young person who believes that he is inferior to the other members of the group in commendable achievement regales his pals with tales about his great prowess or his unusual experiences. If the story is not convincing enough, he is forced to bring evidence of his "crime." Consequently, he is impelled to justify his boastings by participation in delinquent activities.

Other forms of attention-seeking behavior may be displayed. For several years the author worked with a high school girl who displayed symptoms of emotional disturbance. Her difficulty started with certain phobias that made her unwilling to come to school. As the result of the attention given her by her teachers, the girl's early fears were modified and she gradually made a good adjustment to her schoolwork. It was no longer necessary for her teachers to single her out for special attention. However, she still craved the attention from the author that had been given consistently in the form of approval of her school success and of her improved cooperation at home. This general approval did not satisfy the girl. She needed special attention.

Criticism

Consciousness of inadequacy in one's ability to meet social demands often results in the development of an attitude of criticism toward other persons, especially if the latter appear to be well adjusted to situations in which the individual is experiencing failure. The discovery of weaknesses in the successful person mitigates the lack of self-esteem of the failing person. Gossip has its foundation in this attempt at adjustment. Although this attitude is found among normal persons, it may be a symptom of serious maladjustment.

KINDS OF CRITICISM. Tactful criticism *to* an individual of an observable fault usually is appreciated as a sign of friendly interest. Criticism *of* an individual to others generally is motivated by a feeling of inferiority to the person criticized. This feeling may be very slight; implied and expressed criticism in the form of gossip usually is not malicious. Since no one is perfect, it is taken for granted that the faults of an individual are proper material for common discussion. No matter how harmless the criticism is, however, any emphasis upon the weakness of another person arouses in the critic a comforting feeling of virtue.

A child often uses this method (which he has learned from listening to his parents discuss their friends) to counteract the effect of having other children held up to him as models to be imitated. He resents the fact that his parents appear to like another child better than they do him. Therefore, he looks for faults in the other child and consoles himself with the thought that he excels the other in the display of certain desirable qualities. He may strive toward personal improvement in these respects. The child is helped to overcome his original lack; his criticism of the model may have desirable rather than undesirable effects. He no longer resents the model child, but feels equal to him or even superior to him. Instances have been known in which the child or young person actually has tried to help his former object of criticism to overcome the faults that he has recognized in him.

Self-criticism, if based upon a normal desire to improve behavior, is desirable. However, self-criticism may be a form of adjustive behavior. The expected response of the listener to a person's belittling his own achievement is praise. If the listener seems to agree with the self-critic, the latter starts to justify his own degree of achievement in comparison with that of others. Unusual displays of modesty often follow this pattern. Persons who employ this technique are not sure of their status; they are attempting to bolster their ego.

INEFFECTIVE ADJUSTMENT THROUGH CRITICISM. Carried to an extreme, criticism may develop definite maladjustment. A father who was overzealous concerning his young daughter's deportment was accustomed to point out to her certain faults in the behavior of other girls. His purpose was to encourage her to refrain from behaving in a similar manner. The effect of this training was twofold. It helped her develop a keen power of observation, but it also cut her off from free associations with her peers. She constantly watched them for possible faults lest she imitate their behavior and receive reproof from her father for conduct unbecoming a lady. Her father's death during her adolescence stopped this training before she had developed a critical attitude that might have interfered seriously with her social adjustment.

Unless his energies are redirected into other channels, a person who develops the habit of gossiping as a self-bolstering device may become so intent upon picking up choice tidbits that he will lean more and more upon this method of self-realization. His chief desire is to be the first to thrill his associates with a new bit of scandal. His listeners' reaction to his tales is to him a most satisfying form of social approval. If actual facts are not available or not spectacular enough, he almost unconsciously embroiders the truth or resorts to the manufacture of stories based upon very slight threads of fact. These tales may be extremely damaging in their implications. The individual no longer is rational; he believes the stories that he has invented. The realization that his listeners come to discredit his gossip may have serious effects upon his mental health.

Sometimes the listener to criticism of another person encourages this criticism in order to convince himself that the speaker approves of him (the listener) or he would not take him into his confidence. A pathetic case of this kind is that of a mother whose love for her only child was extremely possessive. She resented any attention that the girl might give to friends, regardless of sex or age. If the girl praised anyone in her mother's presence the latter would use every means at her disposal to break up the friendship. The situation became so intolerable that the daughter found it necessary to meet her friends away from the home, or to satisfy her mother's ego by discovering real or imaginary faults in these young people. If she chose the latter course, her mother would become the stanch advocate of the criticized person and reprove her daughter for not recognizing the person's sterling qualities. The daughter could then agree that her mother's judgment was better than hers. The girl could not be too enthusiastic about the person or find virtues other than those that had been pointed out to her by her mother. In this way the mother satisfied her urge to maintain first place in her daughter's affection. As a matter of fact, however, the girl, as a result of her training and experience, was a much better judge of people than was her mother.

Sympathy

One of the significant defense mechanisms is that of the human being striving for sympathy. To attempt to secure the sympathy of others in order to avoid a problem or obstacle is known as the mechanism of sympathy. Children often are given too much assistance. When denied this help they seek the sympathy of others by indicating how hard they work, how tired they are, how unfair their parents are, or how rigid are their teachers. They turn to others for solace when they have a feeling of inadequacy.

Daydreaming and Fantasy

Daydreaming and fantasy represent the imaginary satisfactions that are not attained in real experience. Problems are solved in imagination, and escape from reality is made possible. The imagination often is used as a means of escape if an individual is confronted by a perplexing problem. It is relatively easy to retire from the factual world, where problems must be solved in terms of reality, to an imaginary world, where imaginary successes are easy to achieve. If started early in life this habit may cause much trouble later. The individual is likely to carry over into adult life any confusions between fact and fantasy.

Daydreaming is one of the functions of the mind and is not harmful to the healthy child or adolescent. An individual is in a constant state of awareness, but if his thinking concerning a particular topic or problem follows ideas unrelated to the problem, the possible results of a more or less permanent flight into fantasy may become serious. The danger is not in the mental wandering but rather in the fact that the mind does not or cannot return to the problem at hand. Hence there is a fluctuation among ideas and images, and a consequent interference with the solution of the problem.

To gain satisfaction from imaginary achievement of success and approval when these are not possible of actual attainment is a popular form of self-satisfying adjustment. There are very few persons who, at some time during their childhood, adolescence, or adulthood have not experienced the thrill of imaginary success achievement.

PURPOSES SERVED BY DAYDREAMS. Daydreaming represents a tendency to allow the imagination to play with ideas that are satisfying realizations of desired goals or purposes. If an individual recognizes the ephemeral character of his dreams or uses these dreams as preparation for actual accomplishment, this form of adjustment is helpful. It is only when the world of fantasy is divorced completely from reality that the utilization of this self-satisfying device leads to inadequate adjustment or maladjustment.

A great work of pictorial art, music, or literature is conceived and brought to the level of expression through the imaginative dreams and flights of fantasy of the creator. The author, the painter, the engineer, the architect, or the composer uses his daydreams as the means of building real and appreciated masterpieces. He is able to combine constructive imagination with practical realization. The imaginative meanderings of his childhood and adolescent daydreaming experiences constitute the background of his controlled utilization of revery as the basis of creative activity.

There is no definite line of demarcation between a child's dream world and his actual world. To him fairies, goblins, giants, brave princes, and beautiful princesses are as real as are his living associates. In his early life he may become too engrossed in fairy tales because he does not have sufficient opportunity to play with children of his own age. Consequently, these mythical figures are more real to him than are living people. Moreover, experience with his family and little friends may not always bring him desired satisfaction, but his book friends never fail him. Hence the young child may identify himself with a mythical hero or heroine; he creates highly satisfying stories of his own prowess and achievement.

During the child's school years, especially if he is brighter or slower than the average student in his class, actual classroom work may become boring to him; his early habits of telling himself stories may return in the form of daydreams. His apparent inattention to classroom routine may earn the disapproval of his teacher, in which case he may become more dissatisfied with the situation and, consequently, intensify his habit of daydreaming.

The healthy child is in no way harmed by his youthful dreams or fantasies, if he is given plenty of opportunity for successful achievement within his abilities. For example, the young child's supreme belief in Santa Claus as a giver of gifts to good children stimulates him to merit the approval of the donor. His discovery that his parents and friends are the givers of the gifts helps him to shift his loyalty from his childish ideal to his real associates.

During early adolescence dreams of adult accomplishment are common. The majority of young people are stimulated by stories of adult success long before they are old enough or sufficiently trained to experience similar successful achievement. A normal girl dreams about Prince Charming. A boy envisions himself as a noted physician, a stalwart policeman, or a successful businessman. Unless an adolescent's dreams of conquest are too unrealistic, they stimulate him toward the achievement of constructive goals. This is especially true if the dreams grow out of successful activities and are followed by continued success in the stimulating activity.

The more challenging an adult's program of activities is and the more opportunities it offers for further achievement, the more likelihood is there that each step in his career may be followed by dreams of further achievement. His dreams of future success act as an incentive for further activity and are, at the same time, an indication of lack of satisfaction with his present accomplishment. This is sometimes referred to as "noble discontent." The well-adjusted person knows when to transfer his dreaming into productive activity.

If the past experiences of an aging adult have been relatively satisfying, he tends to give much of his time and attention to retrospective dreaming of his past achievements. He again is telling himself stories; he is returning to the fairy-tale level of imagination, except that now his memories are embroidered in such a way as to make himself the hero of previously experienced feats of performance. In each reliving there is an increase in the glorification of the real experience as he had lived it earlier.

Besides these organized, continuous dreams or fantasies that have their foundations in an imagination permeated by romantic tales of achievement, every individual indulges in idle dreaming of the kind that is common to the man who may be sitting in a comfortable armchair, facing a friendly fire and puffing at his favorite pipe. His thoughts wander idly from one half-formed dream to another; he is only mildly conscious of his surroundings. His dreams have little or no basis in reality; he is enjoying the satisfaction that comes temporarily from losing oneself in the world of make-believe.

INEFFECTIVE UTILIZATION OF DAYDREAMS AND FANTASY. Daydreaming or fantasy may be a symptom of inadequate adjustment or of serious mental illness. The individual who finds himself unable to make adequate adjustments to life situations gradually develops the habit of dream adjustment, almost to the point of losing complete contact with reality.

The child whose normal activities are unsatisfactory may become so engrossed with his dream world that failure to adjust in his actual experiences is no longer significant. He "sits through" his class periods, to the dismay of his teacher, who is unable to stimulate him to activity through any ordinary means of encouragement, scolding, or shaming. Disapproval from his parents for his lack of cooperation has no effect upon him; he is scarcely conscious of it. Examples of this extreme form of fantasy are relatively uncommon, however.

Adolescents and young adults often use this type of escape technique as a compensation for unsatisfactory sex adjustment. Too strict parental control or awareness of personal unattractiveness may lead to the thwarting of normal sex impulses. Satisfaction is sought through erotic dreams. As these dreams become increasingly systematic, the likelihood of normal sex adjustment decreases. Similarly, failure or inadequate achievement in school or business may motivate an individual to seek self-realization in a dream life or world of fantasy. His power to improve his inadequate adjustment in realistic situations thereby is lessened or completely lost.

Idealization

Idealization means that, for personal satisfaction, an individual places a far greater value on something than its real worth. This mechanism is used by an individual to idealize himself or others. Idealization is exemplified by exaggerated expressions concerning the beauty of things or people. For example, the individual with whom a young person is in love becomes the most beautiful or most handsome person in the world.

Idealization within desirable limits is wholesome. If one idealizes himself or other persons or things too much, he may be considered by others to be conceited. Success is achieved, in part at least, by one's faith in his ability to succeed. This gives sufficient confidence to attack a problem of adjustment. Poise and perspective result from a proper balance in idealization. To be unable to see one's faults or admit one's mistakes is the wrong application of idealization, however, and may lead to serious emotional disturbance.

Conversion

If an individual transfers the energy of a desire that he cannot express otherwise into a physical symptom or complaint, he is making use of the mechanism of conversion. There often is conflict between the ideas and wishes that come from the unconscious and have no outlet in the conscious. Such ideas and wishes possess considerable emotional force. They can be helpful to individuals during developing periods, and can be tension-reducing, but they also can be responsible for emotional stress.

The utilization of the mechanism of conversion helps to transfer the emotion attached to the idea or wish into a substitute idea or form of behavior. The latter usually is a complaint of a physical ailment. Headaches that cannot be explained often are overt expressions of these drives. Stomach trouble that results from homesickness is another example. Conversion symptoms are developed by everyone and usually are not serious. However, in difficult situations an individual utilizes every outlet during his responses in adjustment.

Withdrawal Behavior

The behavior of an individual who retreats from participation in life experiences exemplifies the mechanism of withdrawing. Most individuals are timid in at least one life situation, especially if they are not adequately prepared to meet it. The withdrawing attitude is a maladjustment only when its use interferes with social effectiveness. Shy and timid persons are not usually disturbing to others. As they are not active competitors with their fellows, their real maladjustments often go unnoticed. If the individual develops the habit of retreat from active participation in life situations, he is too easily frustrated, and the functioning of this adjustment mechanism is unwholesome for his personality development.

In their social relationships some persons appear to be more outgoing in their attitudes than are others. Natural tendencies and environmental experiences cause individuals to differ from one another in their degree of ascendance or submissiveness in social situations. Withdrawing tendencies are rooted in temperament, personal interests, and ambitions and situations. An attitude of self-sufficiency may have little or no effect upon an individual's adequacy of adjustment. On the other hand, extreme withdrawal may be symptomatic of inadequate adjustment or severe emotional disorder. We shall consider briefly three forms of withdrawal: shyness and seclusiveness, negativism and refusal, and retrogression.

SHYNESS AND SECLUSIVENESS.   Because of overprotectiveness or too strict discipline on the part of parents, or because of a lonely childhood, a child may become very shy in the presence of strangers. He takes refuge in a passive attitude that deceives the unobservant adult into thinking that the child is well adjusted. The youngster is not naughty, nor does he indulge in temper tantrums. Yet beneath his quiet, unassuming exterior the child may be experiencing feelings of tension and frustration. The disturbed emotional state is the result of a conflict between his desire to participate in the activities of his peers and his fear that he may not be accepted by them. A continuance of the conflict state leads to still greater withdrawal.

The shy child often is hindered in his normal development by lack of activity. He possesses too many fears and is unable to share his difficulties with another person because he lacks the courage to discuss his problems with anyone. The "only" child needs careful induction into group life if he is to become an active member of his special group. He may have a hidden desire to lead but may withdraw or shrink from participation in any of the activities in which other children actively engage. These individuals have a strong tendency toward daydreaming.

NEGATIVISM AND REFUSAL.   Negativism is a common child-hood mechanism in which the individual deliberately refuses to recognize the real situation, pleasant or unpleasant, and displays behavior that is characteristically rebellious against authority or suggestion. The child passes through the stage of saying "No" to any request even though later he may carry out the assignment. If these refusals persist and are accompanied by temper tantrums, there is danger that a permanent mechanism of negativism is in the process of development. Negativism usually does not persist in an individual unless parents and teachers overtax his physical strength or mental ability. However, when invited to perform tasks beyond his capacity he may refuse to participate without giving any real reason for his decision.

Serious patterns of negativism or refusal are manifested by the older child or the adult who has developed habits of contradictory attitudes, stubbornness, and rebellion against authority. Such behavior patterns often are the behavior resultants of physical or mental weakness that has made it impossible for an individual to perform successfully the tasks assigned him. Neither he nor other persons in the situation understand the cause of his difficulty; the victim's only adjustment seems to be that of refusal. If these conditions continue, the individual becomes suspicious of the intent of any requests or suggestions made to him by his associates. He is likely to develop habitual antagonistic attitudes.

An example of the functioning of negativism is the habitual attitude of a brilliant educational leader. She admits that, as a student, she worked hardest for those instructors whom she suspected of disliking her. Her purpose was to show them that they were wrong in their judgment of her. Her life has been one of challenge. If the members of her family wish her to agree with any of their plans or decisions, they suggest the opposite of their real interests. She is dogmatic, stubborn, and strong-willed. She does not recognize her own faults and is annoyed by the stupidity and lack of cooperation of her professional associates. She also is a lonely and unhappy woman. Her superior ability sets her apart from her peers. She has not learned to adjust to a society composed of her inferiors.

RETROGRESSION. The utilization of the mechanism of adjustment that achieved satisfaction during an earlier developmental period is descriptive of the behavior of an individual who displays the use of retrogression, sometimes called regression. This is a type of withdrawal behavior in which the individual retreats to an inferior type of adjustment and does not strive to meet directly his present difficulties. The individual who has derived great satisfaction from the experiences of his sheltered life during his infancy and early childhood may prefer, when he is called on to make decisions for himself, to retreat to the protection of his earlier satisfying adjustments.

Retrogression may show itself in the life of a child who is two or three years of age. If the attention that he covets is given instead to his newborn brother or sister, he may so resent the transfer of the affection of his parents that he allows himself to become helpless in the performance of many customary activities, such as feeding himself, putting on shoes and stockings, or caring for his toilet needs.

Those persons who are able to master their daily problems do not have occasion to resort to the use of retrogressive behavior. Habits that have been successful in the past are resorted to only when individuals face new and trying situations in the meeting of which they experience either actual or feared frustration. The fact that memory of the pleasant is more lasting than is that of the unpleasant makes possible the reverting to the past for the comfort and satisfaction that may seem to be lacking in the present. However, the individual who is trained for adult responsibility is in little danger of developing retrogressive tendencies, because he thinks of his past joys only in desirable retrospect.

Adolescents who leave home for college or a job miss the family attention to which they are accustomed. A feeling of homesickness results. A young married woman is expected by her husband to be proficient in certain routine activities. He does not give her the praise that she feels is her due, or he is not properly sympathetic about burned fingers or a disagreeable tradesman. She reverts to an earlier stage of development. She either finds an excuse for returning to the shelter of her mother's protective care or she develops symptoms of illness that compel her husband to expect less from her or give her the attention that she craves.

These examples represent regressive attitudes that can be overcome through the experiencing of satisfying success in activities that are appropriate to the age and ability status of the individual. Retrogression may be a symptom of extreme withdrawal when or if an individual will not or cannot meet the demands of his life situations.

Repression

Repression is the deliberate thrusting aside of present desires or drives for emotional expression because of social inhibitions. Most people evidence a forgetting of the unpleasant to a striking degree. The individual seems to avoid any situation that may be associated with a painful memory, and seems to be able to inhibit any inner stimulation that might help to recall it. It is a normal tendency to avoid places and people that are associated with unpleasant experiences. The individual who uses repression or inhibition limits or inhibits his power of adjustment to ordinary unpleasant situations. Usually repression is an unfortunate form of adjustment, as it affords little opportunity for the reduction of emotional tensions. The use of the repression is itself often a tension-arousing experience.

Repression is different from failure to recall that is caused by lack of sufficient associations, or from temporary forgetting that results from the interference of distracting stimuli. Repression means that the individual *wants to forget*, although he may not be conscious of his desire to do so. This attitude tends to increase rather than decrease tensions. The memory of the unfortunate occurrence persists in its attempt to come to the foreground of attention; consciously or unconsciously, the individual wills it back to forgetfulness.

THE BASES OF REPRESSION. Repression, the forgetting of the unpleasant, has been the subject of much controversy. The followers of Freud use the term to designate the relegation of an unpleasant memory into the "unconscious"; other psychologists who deny the existence of an unconscious mind attempt to explain repression as an element of attitudes. Regardless of the point of view of any particular school of psychology, reports of experiments dealing with the effects of pleasantness or unpleasantness upon retention seem to indicate that unpleasant experiences are forgotten more readily than are pleasant ones. Although there are individual differences among people in this respect, there is reason to believe that it is normal to forget or to try to forget an experience that arouses a feeling of shame, embarrassment, or extreme annoyance.

Individuals tend to relive mentally those personal experiences that are self-satisfying. This mental repetition of the experience fixes it in the memory. Ordinarily, a man or a woman dislikes thinking or talking about unpleasantness that is associated with personal inadequacy. He, therefore, does not fix any such experience in his thinking; he may forget it entirely. If he possesses a sufficient number of self-regarding memories to take the place of these "forgotten" ones, he is spared thereby the feeling of failure or of conflict that otherwise he might experience. For no apparent reason, however, a similarity between the repressed or forgotten experience and a non-conflict-arousing experience may cause him to forget the details of the second experience.

THE EMOTIONAL CONCOMITANTS OF REPRESSION. An individual may avoid, or become emotionally excited in, an apparently normal situation because of a suddenly aroused fear that seems to have no basis in fact. Although an earlier fear- or embarrassment-producing experience is forgotten, its emotional coloring and attendant tension are still present. A tension of this kind is reduced through the continued placing of oneself in such situations with satisfying results and with an understanding of the basic cause of the fearful attitude.

For example, a young couple were strolling along a sandy beach under a boardwalk. The young people failed to notice that the rising tide apparently had cut off any means of exit from the beach. Not until they had crawled and dug their way through the sand were they able to get out from under the boardwalk. No physical damage was done and no reference was made by either one to the seriousness of their predicament, except a laughing remark concerning the narrowness of their escape. The memory of her undignified crawling and digging remained a source of embarrassment to the girl, however. Finally, the incident was forgotten, but for many years the girl could not tolerate being in a crowd or in a small room. Intelligent efforts to discover the original cause of her phobia combined with pleasant experiences in former fear-producing situations have helped her overcome the stresses associated with her early fear-producing experience. She has continued to dislike low ceilings, however, but understands the reasons for her attitude.

Emotionally unstable persons often become the prey of intense and abnormal fears and phobias. These fears or phobias arise out of unpleasant or shameful experiences that are characteristic of this kind of personality. The result may be a form of maladjustment that is difficult to recondition. The tendency to repress the undesirable memory struggles with the recurrence of fear in any stimulating situation. The conscious recall to memory of the repressed material may bring about an adjustment. Contrariwise, such recall may intensify the fear of the actual situation. Moreover, a symbolic fear caused by the combination of a desirable and an undesirable experience may be so great that the fear response spreads to many stimuli.

Neurotic Behavior

Neurotic behavior is often displayed by an individual in an attempt to escape from the frustrations of reality through the utilization of illness or disease. Persons who use illness or physical incapacity in order to avoid meeting a definite duty or responsibility often simulate the sudden onslaught of a headache or a more serious form of hysteria involving psychic inability to walk, talk, or hear. These represent the extremes between which are to be found varying degrees of more or less serious use of this mechanism.

The child or adult who announces his illness in the morning and who later makes a miraculous recovery is allowing his real or imagined suffering to help him evade a disagreeable school or work situation. Although no organic difficulty is discernible, the individual may be experiencing actual suffering. This situation is too often treated with indifference and impatience by parents and associates. Often, the individual has witnessed many examples of similar behavior in the home before he himself makes use of it for his own retreat from meeting responsibility. He has observed others invent fictitious excuses or has seen them simulate illness for the purpose of evading unpleasant duties or responsibilities.

Neurotic behavior may show itself in many forms. A person may become a victim of hysteria, which is a functional nervous disorder that has no organic base. Hysteria may take the form of emotional outbreak, swooning, blindness, temporary paralysis, loss of memory, feelings of unreality, loss of will power, catalepsy, delirium, or other forms of behavior. Neurotic symptoms are frequently symbolic and difficult to understand, either for the victim or for those who wish to help him.

Delinquent Behavior

Delinquencies as defense mechanisms often originate in other mechanisms such as attention-getting and compensation. Delinquent behavior often takes the form of aggression or antisocial behavior. Some delinquent behavior is motivated for the purpose of recognition and admiration by others. Mistakenly, adolescents sometimes are impressed by the overt, independent deviant behavior of their peers. A youth who has had the experience of living a satisfactory home life rarely seeks peer prestige in this fashion.

Some individuals whose abilities do not permit of continued school success want to compensate for their inferiorities by aggressive behavior that will prove their superiority to their associates. They may attempt it in at least one area. Also, those children who have developed a deep hostility toward their parents deliberately practice one or another form of delinquent behavior, for the purpose of punishing their parents. This is characteristic of many girls who become sexual delinquents. They want someone to love them and to give them the attention they desire. In discussing some factors that influence delinquent behavior Shaffer and Shoben offer the following suggestions:

> Reactions to frustration and conflict are not the only causes of delinquency, of course. Otherwise, all thwarted people would become delinquent. There are other factors that determine whether the outcome of conflict will be delinquency or some other form of adjustment. Perhaps the most significant determiner is a person's degree of socialization, the extent to which he has internalized as his own the ethical standards of a law-abiding culture. That in turn depends on his parents' attitudes, and on the quality of the relationship that he has with them. A strong, mutually understanding parent-child relationship almost excludes the possibility of delinquency, unless the parents themselves have and teach criminal attitudes. A second basic factor in delinquency is the culture pattern of the other persons in a youth's immediate community. If the main sport of youngsters of an area is to fight, steal, and run from the police, a youth will fall in line with the practices of his fellows. The family and community socialization factors are related to a number of variables that have been studied statistically: the effects of broken homes, of parental criminality, of gangs, and of "delinquency areas" in cities. The psychology of delinquency is a complex subject with a large literature of its own. No attempt can be made to present it fully here, but only to show some of its relationships to the psychology of adjustment.[1]

[1] Laurence F. Shaffer and Edward J. Shoben, Jr., *The Psychology of Adjustment*, 2nd ed., Boston: Houghton Mifflin Company, 1956, p. 184.

QUESTIONS AND PROBLEMS

1. Describe a case in which a mental conflict has been the cause of physical breakdown; of mental breakdown.

2. Present examples to illustrate each of the mechanisms of adjustment discussed in this chapter.

3. What experiences have you had that contributed to self-deception?

4. Analyze the reasons given by a friend for his apparent failure to meet a responsibility.

5. An adolescent girl desires to wear a certain dress to a party and her mother disapproves. How can the girl solve her problem?

6. Report a personal experience in connection with joining new groups. What were some of the specific problems that you faced? How did you proceed to deal with them? If you failed to solve them, what did you do?

7. List three experiences through which you have passed recently that threatened your self-respect. How did you meet these situations?

8. Observe a small child, and note as many expressions of attention-getting as you can. Which of these are undesirable?

9. What rationalizations do you practice that you should discard?

10. Give as many examples as you can of daydreams that resulted in productive creation.

11. Analyze your motives for criticizing others. To what extent does your criticism tend to help or hurt the other person?

12. Should children be taught the Santa Claus myth or the story of the stork? Justify your answer.

13. Discuss the effect of fairy stories upon the mental and emotional development of the child.

14. What can be done to help a person who exhibits a form of withdrawal behavior?

15. If you have an abnormal fear, indicate what you can do to try to resolve it.

16. Describe a case in which the individual was able to adjust to the trying conditions of a situation in which the conflict was pronounced.

17. To what extent do you practice the mechanisms of compensation? Of repression? Of projection?

18. If you have a younger brother or sister, try to recall your first reactions to his or her birth. How well did your parents prepare you for the birth of the baby? What was your attitude toward him or her after a period of a year or two?

19. Describe the characteristics of any "hero" or "heroine" that you have or may have had.

Selected Readings

Cameron, N., *The Psychology of Behavior Disorders.* Boston, Mass.: Houghton Mifflin Company, 1947.

Crow, L. D., and A. Crow, *Readings in Abnormal Psychology.* Paterson, N.J.: Littlefield, Adams and Co., 1958.

Eysenck, H. J., *Crime and Personality.* Boston, Mass.: Houghton Mifflin Company, 1964.

Gold, M., *Status Forces in Delinquent Boys.* Ann Arbor: The University of Michigan Press, 1963.

Jourard, S. M., *Personal Adjustment,* 2nd ed. New York: The Macmillan Company, 1963.

Laughlin, H., *Mental Mechanisms.* Washington, D.C.: Butterworth, Inc., 1963.

Lazarus, R. S., *Personality and Adjustment.* Englewood Cliffs, N.J.: Prentice-Hall, Inc., 1963.

Lehner, G. F. J., and E. Kube, *The Dynamics of Personal Adjustment,* 2nd ed. Englewood Cliffs, N.J.: Prentice-Hall, Inc., 1964.

Miller, D. R., and E. G. Swanson, *Inner Defense and Conflict.* New York: Holt, Rinehart and Winston, Inc., 1960.

Morgan, C. T., *Introduction to Psychology,* 2nd ed. New York: McGraw-Hill, Inc., 1961. Chapter 5.

Sappenfield, B. R., *Personality Dynamics: An Integrative Psychology of Adjustment.* New York: Alfred A. Knopf, Inc., 1954.

Shaffer, L. F., and E. J. Shoben, Jr., *The Psychology of Adjustment: A Dynamic and Experimental Approach to Personality and Mental Hygiene,* 2nd ed. Boston, Mass.: Houghton Mifflin Company, 1956.

9

ANXIETY
IN ADJUSTMENT

FEARS ARE THE bases upon which anxieties are developed. Fear as an emotion is discussed in Chapter 4. Although the terms *fear* and *anxiety* are related, one difference is that the object of fear is clearly perceived but feelings of anxiety tend to be vaguely disclosed or unknown and include all degrees of fear. Anxiety may run a course from relatively mild anxiety to severe panic. So severe may the anxiety state become that it takes on the nature of a form of neurosis. It may serve as a predisposing factor of psychotic reactions, although the patient may not recognize the presence of the anxiety.

SIGNIFICANCE OF ANXIETY

A fear, when its cause is recognized, can be removed. If the anxious state tends to persist, however, it may color the individual's continued attitudes and behavior. Strong anxiety lessens the power to recall, lowers the attention span, and interferes with efficient reasoning.

Interpretation of Anxiety Reaction

Anxiety is experienced directly by individuals who have a long history of unsolved conflicts. It tends to be free-floating and thus can be distinguished from other neurotic reactions. An anxiety reaction is characterized by a constant state of tension and restlessness. It tends to cause insomnia and generalized irritability and to interfere with effective concentration. It is not ameliorated by the development of phobias, compulsions, or other defense reactions. Hence the individual experiencing an anxiety reaction is more or less at the mercy of his anxiety. Anxiety states usually are accompanied by visceral and motor symptoms of distress.

In anxiety reaction the individual usually finds it difficult to make decisions and constantly fears that he may make a mistake. He may experience abnormal heart action such as palpitations when there is no organic reason for them. His blood pressure also may fluctuate widely. Because of a loss of appetite, he may lose weight and experience a feeling of nausea. These reactions are evidence of a chronic state of fear that has overtaken him.

Most individuals feel uneasy at times and may even experience an occasional mild anxiety attack. Anxiety behavior reflects the individual's acute feelings of inadequacy in response to stress situations that are threatening. A severe anxiety reaction, for example, may be precipitated in a relatively stable person by a severe stressful experience. A normal state of anxiety may be experienced by an individual who has a severe financial setback or loses his job. Anxiety states are associated with the reaction of an individual when there are threats to status or when he worries a great deal about making a decision that he faces.

Effect of Anxiety on Mental Activity

Various investigations have been conducted to discover the effect of anxiety on mental activity. Two interesting studies of the relationship between anxiety and taking tests or examinations are described briefly here. Mandler and Sarason [1] studied

[1] G. Mandler and S. B. Sarason, "A Study of Anxiety and Learning," *Journal of Abnormal and Social Psychology*, 1952, pp. 166–173.

the reactions of two groups of students with widely differing anxiety effects. The two groups were told whether they had done very poorly or very well in a previous test prior to the administration of a new test. The results were significant. The pressure on the high-anxiety students resulted in a lowering of performance on the new test. Contrariwise, low-anxiety subjects improved their performance on the test in spite of the applied pressure.

Another study concerned with the arousal of feelings of anxiety and the concomitant performances on course examinations was made by Paul and Eriksen. From a class of 250 female students enrolled in a course in introductory psychology, 100 were selected for the study. The students were given an examination in the course on the morning of the experiment. Later, they were told that the purpose of the study was to ascertain the feelings, attitudes, and reactions of people to different examination situations. They then were asked to complete a Test Anxiety Questionnaire (TAQ) and to take another short examination covering the course material on which they were tested that morning.

Paul and Eriksen report the following conclusions:

> For the sample as a whole the relationship between anxiety level and differential performance on the anxious and nonanxious examinations was not significant. However, if the 70 percent of the sample which comprise the broad middle range of scholastic ability was examined, significant relationships were obtained between TAQ measures of anxiety and differential examination performance. The Ss above the median on the TAQ obtained as good or higher scores on the experimental examination relative to the regular examination whereas Ss below the median on the TAQ showed poorer performance on the experimental examination. When the experimental examination scores were compared with the second mid-term and the final course examinations the same pattern of differences between high- and low-anxiety Ss was found, suggesting that whatever anxiety contributes to course examinations remains relatively constant throughout the duration of the course.[2]

[2] Gordon L. Paul and Charles W. Eriksen, "Effects of Test Anxiety on 'Real-life' Examinations," *Journal of Personality*, September, 1964, p. 493.

In her discussion of "symptomatology" of the anxiety state, Bosselman had this to say:

Anxiety is a familiar experience to all human beings and presumably to non-human animals as well. Obviously it is not necessarily pathologic. It may, however, be an expression of neurosis in so far as it is realistically excessive and occurs in the absence of recognizable external danger. The mother who is anxious about her severely ill child is reacting normally in a generally understandable cause-effect manner. The woman who is tormented by feelings of apprehension and their somatic concomitants for no reason known to herself is reacting to turmoil within which is understandable if one understands the conflicts, conscious and unconscious, with which she is burdened. She would therefore be considered to be suffering from neurotic anxiety.

The symptomatology of anxiety state is identical with reactions of fear. The somatic and subjective responses which are characteristic of any human being confronted by danger are here expressed in response to a threat which has no apparent external cause. Anxiety differs in this respect from fear. It is not stimulated by a clearly tangible, external threat but rather by an internal danger, the nature of which the person does not consciously perceive. In each case the reactions are essentially a biologically-determined, violent defense. The patient suffering from an anxiety state, not being aware of the nature of the internal threat which arouses his anxiety, is confused by his own disturbed reactions. They seem to him to orginate for no reason, and he is inclined to interpret the condition by assuming that he has some mysterious physical illness or that he is "going crazy."

The symptoms of anxiety state may be either largely somatic or largely subjective or a combination of the two. The somatic symptoms involve the vegetative nervous system and, therefore, have to do with the organs of internal integration. They may be diffuse or may be limited largely to one organ-system. Some patients, for example, describe attacks of tachycardia as outstanding; others have nausea, diarrhea or other gastro-intestinal symptoms. Dyspnea with air hunger is a common manifestation, as is dizziness. In other patients, however, the physical symptoms are vague and diffuse, expressing a general sense of weakness and imbalance.

The symptoms may come on suddenly, in which case the attack is known as an anxiety panic. Such a panic state usually occurs in a patient who has been aware of being uneasy and "nervous." However, it is sometimes described as being precipitated without any apparent conscious relationship to the previous state. The patient may have difficulty in describing the onset of an anxiety panic, but will often speak of a characteristic feeling of spasm or weakness in the abdomen "as though something gripped me," which is apparently identical with the feeling described as a reaction to sudden danger. The popular expression, "He hasn't the guts," is no doubt related to the universality of this fear-reaction.

The symptoms which follow the acute onset of panic may, as has been indicated, center in one or another vegetative organ system. If the manifestation is cardio-vascular, as in dizziness or tachycardia, it almost certainly leads to development of a secondary fear of heart disease. Sometimes the anxiety may not be clearly expressed somatically, but may rather be described by the patient as an overpowering sense of terror and confusion: "As though I were losing my mind." He feels as though something were happening within himself which he cannot understand or control. He feels dazed, cannot concentrate his thoughts, and fears he may behave irrationally.

The acute anxiety panic usually clears up within a few minutes or a few hours, but it leaves the patient shaken and apprehensive, and may be followed by a more or less chronic state of anxiety. Appetite and sleep are interfered with and there is to a varying degree loss of interest and enjoyment in life. The patient dreads the occurrence of further panics, feels restless and insecure, and develops fears about his physical or mental health. A mild sense of unreality is often a distressing and persistent feature. It may be characterized as a "far away feeling" or as haziness of vision—though orientation and perception are, of course, undamaged.

In some anxiety states, acute panics are lacking or unrecognized, and the onset of symptoms is more gradual. In these chronic, insidiously-developing disorders, the emphasis is on diffuse somatic symptoms with a vague sense of physical weakness and disequilibrium. Subjectively there is "free-floating anxiety" which attaches itself in an undifferentiated way to the environment. The patient worries about trifles, fears disaster, is unsure of his own decisions.[3]

Most forms of nonintegrative behavior are rooted in anxiety. In his striving for satisfying a drive the individual finds it difficult to find an adjustment mechanism that adequately can meet the situation to reduce the tension. The result is that the unreduced drive causes the anxiety that maintains the emotional tension. The effect of anxiety on the individual depends largely on the extent to which he is successful in reducing tensions associated with the anxiety state.

An individual may exhibit in his behavior evidence of a persistent reaction that seems to defy adjustment. He may remain stirred up and express his anxiety overtly. This often is the result when he is confronted with an insistent and difficult-to-resolve conflict situation for which he is unable to find a ready solution. Individuals who are unable to find a way to cope with their conflicts continue to be stirred up or exhaust themselves in their inability to find mechanisms to reduce the tensions engendered by conflict situations.

Vague fears and feelings of apprehension are not uncommon experiences. So great and so persistent may be the anxiety state that the individual is unable to sleep, or his pulse rate rises. During the anxious state he seems to be unable to concentrate; his mood alternates between depression and excitement, and he may be irritable or easily angered.

The victim of irrational anxiety usually possesses fear of inadequacy, especially in his strivings for security or self-assertion. For example, a man's business is prospering; vicariously gained knowledge of the effects of economic instability upon his business conditions causes him to worry about possible disastrous conditions. He develops a persistent anxiety state that hinders his gaining any satisfaction from his present business success. A possessive mother exhibits irrational anxiety if her daughter does not return home from school or business at the usual time. By the

[3] Beulah C. Bosselman, *Neurosis and Psychosis,* 3rd ed., Springfield, Ill.: Charles C Thomas, 1964, pp. 11–13.

time the daughter arrives, this mother is displaying symptoms of physical illness from which she recovers only after her daughter explains the reason for her delay, expresses regret, and applies remedial measures to relieve the mother's suffering.

Mild anxiety or concern about conditions that affect an individual's safety, his plans, or his ideals may be a normal reaction; but if the tendency is carried to excess and the causes of this unnecessary anxiety are exaggerated, the emotional condition becomes pathological. These conditions may show up in the form of (1) a morbid fear of the future, (2) a state of indecision, (3) extreme feelings of helplessness, or (4) deep resentment.

The morbid tendency that accompanies the anxiety state may cause the individual to expect the worst. Since he is under great tension he may become irritable, pessimistic, and sometimes panic-stricken. He is likely to question the wisdom of any decision made by himself. If the anxiety pertains to matters of health, the individual, in severe cases, is unable to reduce his emotional tension and attempts to gain relief by attending to his bodily symptoms. In his effort to escape anxiety he may attempt to use compensation or rationalization; he may try to deny its existence; he may turn to drugs, or he may direct his thinking to stimuli that do not arouse it.

Worry and Anxiety

Worry affects everyone and differs from anxiety only in degree. It is more transitory and disappears with the removal of the causal factor. It concerns a past act or a future possibility about which nothing is being done at the present. There is often a feeling of personal inadequacy, which is associated with an attitude of inferiority and a realization that adjustment to the worry-arousing situation is impossible. Worry precedes the attempted solution of problems that must be faced without adequate preparation. Individuals worry often because they are unprepared to meet situations adequately.

Worry can be alleviated. To do so the individual must take positive action. He needs to have a plan of action to attack a problem that is basic to the worry state. The utilization of the following may prove fruitful in the reduction or alleviation of worry.

1. Deliberately plan to meet the problem with a workable solution.
2. Become informed as completely as possible concerning the factors involved in the problem and do not hesitate to ask others for needed information or help.
3. Face the worry squarely and try to evaluate the cause of it.
4. If the cause of the worry can be discovered, do whatever is necessary to remove the cause.
5. Seek the cooperation of others (trained experts) for the reduction of serious worries.

The Threat of Danger and the Anxiety State

The development of anxiety reaction is related to the recognition of a danger that threatens the individual's equilibrium. White has this to say about the effects upon behavior of a real or imagined danger leading to an anxious state.

It is important to notice that the presence of danger tends to restrict behavior. Attention is concentrated upon possible sources of threat; spontaneity is lost; certain features of behavior are exaggerated in order to maintain control. The effects of anxiety are for a while uniformly in the direction of lessened flexibility.

As danger mounts, control becomes increasingly difficult. The person's mind begins to be occupied incessantly with the danger. He can no longer inhibit the bodily signs of anxiety: perspiration, tremor, restlessness, fast-beating heart, quickened breathing force themselves upon him. Thought and judgment deteriorate, actions are erratic and poorly controlled, new acts are started before old ones are completed. As he finds it impossible to pull himself together, the person "experiences an extremely unpleasant sensation of losing his mental balance" (Mira). Danger seems to be everywhere. When panic begins to reign, the conscious state resembles a nightmare, "consisting of a peculiar, irregular stream of delirious, distorted mental images, most of which are forgotten when the subject returns to normal." Scarcely aware of what he is doing, the panic-stricken person may rush wildly about, laughing, shouting, crying in rapid succession. These reactions sometimes lasted many days in soldiers exposed to prolonged fire. In some cases a stuporous and comatose state follows the peak of panic.

It is clear that the fully developed fear reaction has no value for continuing existence. It represents the collapse of everything that might serve to extricate a person from danger. The trembling musculature and clouded memory are of little service; above all, the mental confusion, the failure to observe and to test reality correctly, is a fatal handicap to further adaptive efforts. The experience of intense fear thus seems to accompany a more or less complete breakdown in the ordering of behavior.

The Experience of Panic. Everyone knows what fear feels like when experienced in slight or moderate intensities. Few people, however, can remember the full force of their childhood panics, and fewer still, even of those who have been in great danger, can report the contents of acute anxiety in adult life. If we are to appreciate the dynamic role of anxiety in neurosis, we must realize the overwhelming nature of the experience of panic.[4]

White also indicates the need of recovering from a frightening experience in order to avoid disastrous aftermaths. His suggestions follow:

Relearning after Fright. Following a fright, the overwhelming impulse is simply to avoid the whole frightening situation. Perhaps the danger is so great that no other response is possible. Very often, however, the danger was only momentary (like a motor accident) or is such that, given a second chance, the person could really cope with it perfectly well. Furthermore, many dangers are incurred in the pursuit of vital interests which the person cannot sacrifice. The pilot whose plane crashes cannot afford to give up his livelihood. The active child does not want to surrender his explorations and adventures because on one occasion he has been frightened. Pride may be involved: the person is ashamed to continue being afraid. Then there are incubation and generalization to consider. If no action is taken, the anxiety may

---

[4] Robert W. White, *The Abnormal Personality,* 3rd ed., New York: The Ronald Press Company, 1964, pp. 193–194.

be experienced as getting worse and as spreading to so many related stimuli that the whole world seems to be unsafe. One has to come to terms with the circumstance of having been frightened. This means acting in direct opposition to the impulse to avoid. It means *renewed contact* with the threat, a *new appraisal* of its threatening character, and *new actions* to cope with it. It means, in short, new learning in the face of a strong motive to avoid new learning.[5]

SELF BOUNDARIES AND ANXIETY

Functional boundaries in the developing individual need to be established to protect the preconscious and the conscious self from those influences that might be disintegrating. According to Cameron, there are four general conditions that are basic to the development of anxiety: impossibility of overt escape, strong anticipation of punishment, separation from emotional support, and absence of opportunity to carry through an approach reaction. Freud first conceived of anxiety as dammed-up libido, resulting from repression. Later he regarded anxiety as a signal to warn the ego of impending danger and to prepare a defense.

Regarding the relation between repression and the id, ego, and superego, Cameron says:

> *Id-derivatives and the Repressed Unconscious Ego.* Man never achieves a corresponding mastery over id-derivatives, and over the repressed unconscious ego functions which go to join them in the primary process. The best that he can do is to develop defense mechanisms which exclude them sufficiently to prevent their disintegrating secondary process perception, cognition and motor coordination. These defense mechanisms apparently do not prevent a continual interchange from taking place between preconscious organizations and the unconscious ego and id-derivatives, whose products appear in full preconscious during the night as dreams. We have already said that a night's dreaming is prepared in part during the preceding day, and that it usually includes residues of the day's preconscious and even conscious experiences. . . .
> *The Superego and Its Precursors.* Stable self-control is

[5] *Ibid.,* p. 209.

impossible without a superego, and yet the introduction of a superego organization within the psychodynamic system leads inevitably to new sources of conflict and anxiety. In the preceding chapter we discussed the functions of the superego, and of its precursors, as internal representations of the parents and other authority figures. To the extent that a child's parents and parent figures are themselves socially organized, and succeed in passing on socially acceptable standards to him, the child will develop his own standards, with their gradients or hierarchies, which help him to structure his experience and behavior in socially acceptable ways.

As a scanning and evaluating system, the superego operates for the most part automatically at unconscious levels. When things go wrong, or we feel in need of moral or ethical guidance, the superego may become conscious and function as our conscience. The rest of the time it is unconscious, but still effectual. As we have said before, the superego makes use of an ego-ideal as its yardstick in evaluating ego performance, including ego perception and thought as well as action. The ego-ideal, unfortunately for some persons, tends to be not only perfectionistic and unrealistic, but also often primitively narcissistic, with infantile components. It can then become the source of much real dissatisfaction and unhappiness, especially if the superego exercises punitive parental functions when ego achievement falls short of the narcissistic ideal, or when *ego interests* are also infantile, but far from ideal.[6]

In her discussion of ways of escaping anxiety, Karen Horney suggests four that are effective. After naming them she then explains them, in part, as follows:

> The first method—rationalization—the best explanation for evasion of responsibility. It consists in turning anxiety into a rational fear. . . .
> The second way of escaping anxiety is to deny its existence. In fact, nothing is done about anxiety in such cases

[6] Norman Cameron, *Personality Development and Psychopathology: A Dynamic Approach,* Boston: Houghton Mifflin Company, 1963, pp. 228–229.

except denying it, that is excluding it from consciousness. . . .

The third way of finding release from anxiety is to
narcotize it. This may be done consciously and literally by
taking to alcohol or drugs. There are, however, many ways
of doing it, without the connection being obvious. One of
them is to plunge into social activities because of fear of
being alone; it does not alter the situation whether this fear
is recognized as such or appears only as a vague uneasi-
ness. . . .

The fourth way of escaping anxiety is the most radical:
it consists in avoiding all situations, thoughts or feelings
which might arouse anxiety. This may be a conscious process, as when the person who fears diving or mountain climb-
ing avoids doing these things.[7]

CHANGES IN PATTERNS
OF ANXIETY

The need for security is especially present in the young child's
relations with his mother or a substitute figure. The mother's
overwhelming show of affection for her child may lead to his
struggles for independence. An attitude of rejection on the
part of a mother may cause an infant's normal, healthy responses
to be seriously interfered with. In introducing his treatment of
the infant experiences (basic anxiety) Garre says:

> . . . it can be said that, to the degree that the mother ex-
> periences the infant as an encumbrance, she must unavoid-
> ably be pervaded by resentment and by the wish, of which she
> may or may not be aware, to be rid of the child. The infant,
> although only on an emotional level of course, will be per-
> vaded by the feeling that its existence is threatened. It will
> fear death to the degree that it senses its mother's resent-
> ment. We should not underrate the infant's perceptivity.
> Tests have shown that newborn infants in nurseries react
> differently when in the care of nurses who are generally
> considered motherly as opposed to those who perform their

[7] Karen Horney, *The Neurotic Personality of Our Time*, New York:
W. W. Norton & Company, 1937, pp. 48, 49, 52, 53.

duties in a perfunctory or even resentful manner. When we consider human development in terms not only of weeks and months but of years, we can see the cumulative effect of basic attitudes and can sense the total amount of resentment and rejection an infant is exposed to. It is clear that this amount will vary according to the individual case. To the degree that the infant is pervaded by this feeling that its very existence is threatened by the significant person, it will fear death. Physiologically, danger is normally met only through the well-known mechanisms of fight or flight. Threat must be either overcome or avoided. The anxiety that the infant must feel to some degree at least I call the "basic anxiety," and it will be the task of this book to show the extent to which this basic anxiety is the key to personality adjustment, the focal point of our difficulties in orientation, the cause of our diseases and maladjustments, and in fact the central point in the adaptation of humans to life. I postulate that basic anxiety must be present in every human infant. It will vary only in degree, depending on the degree to which the mother or significant person basically rejected the infant. It is obvious that the infant although pervaded by fear for its very existence and reacting basically in the physiological pattern of fight or flight can do neither one nor the other. . . .

The basic anxiety in the human infant is also sensed primarily and initially as an external stress. This basic anxiety becomes the source of subsequent disturbances, and these disturbances can manifest themselves in different ways. If the fear remains unaltered, the individual will be pervaded with free-floating anxiety, unrelated to any object, person, or occurrence. We still then recognize an anxiety neurosis. However, since unadulterated anxiety in itself is just about intolerable, some process is likely to take place by which this basic anxiety is converted into a more bearable form, although even after conversion it will interfere materially with the pursuit of happiness, health, and success.[8]

In his discussion of changes in the pattern of childhood anxiety, Cameron distinguishes between *primary* and *secondary* anxiety.

[8] Walter J. Garre, *Basic Anxiety: A New Psycho-biological Concept,* New York: Philosophical Library, 1962, pp. 3–4, 4–5.

Primary anxiety.   The pattern of anxiety which is normal for adults is absent during early infancy. Its precursor in the early weeks is an irresistible need to discharge tension under any stress, which occurs in such activities as crying and generalized hyperactivity. We call this *primary anxiety.* [9] Usually the child is suffering from some identifiable stress, such as that coming from hunger, pain, discomfort, loud noise or rough handling.

Early in life, the tensions arising from stress cannot be tolerated. Their immediate discharge is imperative; and the discharge may continue after the source of stress has been removed. This continuation seems to be a *secondary reaction* to the *experience* of the primary anxiety. Sudden stress sometimes produces a gasp and a vigilant pause before the tension discharge occurs. [10]

Secondary anxiety is a reaction to the disintegrative effects of primary anxiety, which both neurotic and psychotic patients may experience. In *anxiety reactions,* for example, something of which the patient may have been unaware precipitates an anxiety attack—which is a resomatization and a dramatic, infantile discharge—and the patient is then terrified by the attack itself. The latter is *secondary anxiety.* [11]

Cameron also says:

As everyone knows, the infant gets an enormous amount of help in alleviating the stresses of need to which he is exposed; and he soon learns to anticipate help. He becomes quiet, for example, when he hears and sees preparations being made to feed him, even though nothing has entered his hungry mouth. Whether or not the anticipation involves imagery, it obviously reduces the stress effect of the internal need without satisfying it. An organized expectation takes the place of the previously diffuse, overwhelming tension, and this expectation or anticipation becomes itself an organized response which can absorb free energy.

[9] M. Schur, "The Ego in Anxiety," in R. Loewenstein (ed.), *Drives, Affects, Behavior,* New York: Internat. Univ. Press, 1953, pp. 67–103. [Cameron]

[10] Cameron, *Personality Development and Psychopathology,* p. 222.

[11] *Ibid.,* p. 231.

We adults, when we are injured, in pain, or suddenly taken ill, experience fully the calming effect of anticipating help as soon as we are told that help is on its way. Nothing in the objective situation may have changed, but the unbearable tension from our inner need for help gets channeled into an organized anticipation. . . .

Something like this experience seems to develop during early infancy as his mother appears and the child's sense of being overwhelmed disappears. There is no need to assume that at first the child recognizes any connection between his mother's appearance and the reduction of stress. The infant's first ego-defense is thus really his mother; his first adaptive mechanism for escaping from his overwhelming tensions is that of crying and becoming hyperactive ("restless," "fussy," "fretting") so that his mother will come. There may be anticipatory imagery involved in the child's growing ability to tolerate delay—what Freud called "the hallucinated breast"—or there may not. It is most probable that some kind of central representation of expected relief develops, and that this is one of the precursors of organized fantasy and of secondary process thinking which fills in the delay. . . .

As an infant matures perceptually and cognitively, he at the same time develops many motor coordinations which help him to tame his primary anxiety. The things that an infant is able to do need not in themselves be useful; but they are more organized, specific and complex than a primitive, generalized tension discharge. Their very organization, like that of perception and imagery, absorbs or "binds" free energy and thus reduces the sense of being overwhelmed and helpless.

During periods of unrelieved stress, we adults experience something similar when we busy ourselves with some activity or other. Even though we achieve nothing else, the activity soaks up some of the tension engendered by the stress. It helps calm our apprehensions further while we wait for relief. Thus, for example, men pace up and down to no purpose and swear, while women rock and sew or talk.

The child who has a few infantile activities in his repertory is far better off than he was when all he could do was to be restless and cry. For a time at least, he may find relief in sucking, watching, searching, fingering, babbling, playing and imagining, while he waits for the specific satisfaction of some specific pressing need. With these more structured outlets for free energy he can now tolerate delay still better, and fill in the time with ego activity.

A further help in controlling anxiety will come when the infant has matured and developed sufficiently, in perception, in motor coordination and in imagination, to be able to experience *primary identification,* the kind of experience that structures the mother-child symbiotic unit. At first, we assume, the infant cannot experience his own individuality or identity, the kind of individuality that you and I experience as separate persons. Neither can he experience a unity with anyone else, the kind of oneness that we experience in intimate personal relationships and deep emotions, when we seem for the moment to lose our boundaries and merge with others or with the infinite.

The experience of unity appears to come first. The infant at first has developed no boundaries between himself and others. He has no recognition of himself as an individual, and no recognition of others as individuals separate from himself. Therefore it is easy for him to identify with a stable, reliable, trustworthy mother figure. It is easy for him to experience things as his that we recognize as actually his mother's, to experience her achievements, her movements, sounds, warmth, embrace and ministrations as somehow belonging to the fused unity of mother-child.

In some such way, through the lack of separation, through the confusion that we call primary identification, a child's experiences are enormously enriched, and his sense of power and security are greatly enhanced, as long as he has the mother figure within his orbit. He is experiencing in a direct, primitive way the kind of enrichment, the kind of enhancement of security and power that we adults experience at a more sophisticated level when we surrender some of our individuality and identify emotionally with a powerful group or a powerful cause, or even when we share with others some tremendous disaster.[12]

12 *Ibid.,* pp. 223-224.

Anxiety and Hostility

Basically, anxiety is a fear in which a subjective factor is involved. The individual has deep feelings about confronting powerful dangers from which there seems to be no escape. The anticipated danger and his accompanying feeling of helplessness toward the meeting of the situation are reinforced by his own impulses. Inherent in these impulses is the potential for a build-up of feelings of hostility. In this connection, Karen Horney says: "hostile impulses of various kinds form the main source from which neurotic anxiety springs." Horney states further:

Repressing a hostility means "pretending" that everything is all right and thus refraining from fighting when we ought to fight, or at least when we wish to fight. Hence the first unavoidable consequence of such a repression is that it generates a feeling of defenselessness. . . .

That a repression of hostility leads with inexorable logic to the generation of anxiety does not mean that anxiety must become manifest every time the process takes place. . . .

There are infinite variations in the forms of anxiety which may ensue from the process of repressing hostility. For the sake of a better understanding of the resultant pictures I shall present the different possibilities schematically.

A: The danger is felt to arise from one's own impulses.
B: The danger is felt to arise from outside.

In view of the consequences of repressing hostility, group A appears to be a direct outcome of the repression while group B presupposes a projection. Both A and B can be subdivided into two subgroups.

I: The danger is felt to be directed against the self.
II: The danger is felt to be directed against others.

We would then have four main groups of anxiety:

A. I: The danger is felt to come from one's own impulses and to be directed against the self. In this group the hostility is turned secondarily against the self. . . .
A. II: The danger is felt to come from one's own impulses

and to be directed against others. Example: phobia of
having to injure others with knives.
B. I: The danger is felt to come from outside and to concern the self. Example: fear of thunderstorms.
B. II: The danger is felt to come from outside and to concern others. In this group the hostility is projected to
the outside world and the original object of hostility
is retained. Example: the anxiety of oversolicitous
mothers concerning the dangers menancing their
children.[13]

Anxiety and Age Levels

As was indicated earlier, an individual, from birth onward,
tends to experience feelings of anxiety that can range from those
rooted in mild, more or less temporary fears to severe states of
panic brought on by exposure to real or imagined threats of
danger to the life pattern. We know that the arousal of anxiety is
associated with hereditary factors: high or low anxiety tolerance.
Also, some elements of an individual's environment are more
conducive to the experiencing of anxiety than are others.

Moreover, strength of resistance to these elements differs
both from individual to individual and within any one individual. With developmental changes from infancy to adulthood and
increasing degrees of maturity, differences are apparent not only
in kinds of stimuli basic to anxiety states but also in the degree to
which an individual reacts unfavorably to anxiety arousers.

It would seem that practically with his first breath an infant's needs include provision of his physical wants, protection
from danger, and security in the love of those who surround him.
Another cause of the arousal of anxiety in an infant is a possible
separation from his mother for an extended period of time. This
state is called *separation anxiety*. The infant seems to sense that
he thereby is in danger of losing the care and protection her
presence assures him.

Throughout childhood and adolescence and even during
adulthood, long-term separation from beloved relatives or friends
can cause emotional disturbance. The fear of loss through death
of a mate, a parent (especially the mother), or a son or daughter

[13] Horney, *The Neurotic Personality of Our Time*, pp. 63, 64, 72-73.

can lead to the development of deep feelings of anxiety. For example, a woman known to the author was an only child. After the death of her father during her adolescence the bond between herself and her mother became extremely close. Although this woman, an intelligent and well-educated person, recognized the inevitability of death, she could not tolerate any thought that her mother might die. Even as an adult who was objective in her professional relations, this woman would "go to pieces" if her mother were suffering a slight illness, such as a head cold. She could not sleep, she trembled and broke out in a cold sweat. When the mother finally died at the age of eighty, however, the woman was very calm. The mother had suffered extreme pain before she died and the daughter was thankful that her mother was relieved of her misery.

The preschool child's anxieties are usually centered around members of the family and family life. One little four-year-old seemed to be in a state of "constant worry" lest his two-year-old brother hurt himself unless he, the older brother, watched carefully the baby's every move. In fact, the four-year-old was observed standing at an open window and asking God to keep his brother good so that he would not have to worry so much about him.

Again, a five-year-old girl, whose father was very strict in his treatment of her behavior, displayed definite signs of an anxiety state when she inadvertently broke a strap on a valise which he had just fastened. Fortunately, no damage had been done and the child's anxious feelings abated. Many incidents occur daily in the life of the young child (in fact in the lives of individuals of all ages) that combine to develop a more or less constant state of anxiety. Too often parents are not aware of the highly emotionalized state the young or older child may be experiencing. Also, as I noted earlier, the less normal (either too great protection or almost complete rejection) the parents' reactions to the child may be, the more numerous and deep-rooted the child's anxieties may become.

Beginning at about six years of age or earlier, the area of anxiety suffered by the child increases as a result of his entrance into school life. The school situation can function as a basis of new causes of anxiety-arousal that may continue throughout his educational experiences: adjusting to the personality patterns of a succession of teachers, attempting to achieve success in school studies, and developing constructive social relations with school-mates. Sources of anxiety still may be rooted in family life but expand to include increasingly large and different kinds of experiences outside the home.

During adolescence, an individual's anxiety pattern continues to include family, school, and neighborhood factors but widens to incorporate his relationships with members of the opposite sex. Boy-girl relations can be the focus of much anxiety, both general and specific, for the young people involved. A strong urge to be attractive to and liked by members of the other sex may lead to participation in many anxiety-filled activities. Adolescence may not be a period of "storm and stress" but many stressful situations can be present.

The normal life pattern of the adult usually includes such areas as marriage, rearing of a family, occupational activities, and enlarged social realizations. The person who does not experience at least mild anxiety in his various life activities is indeed fortunate. Too many individuals suffer serious emotional upset as they endeavor to meet their many responsibilities. It should be expected that with increasing maturity, an individual should be better prepared to meet more efficiently the demands upon him of all the anxiety-producing stimuli by which he is surrounded. His power to meet such situations may differ with his natural propensities and his age status.

In his discussion of the role of deviant maturation in the pathogenesis of anxiety, Caplan offers valuable suggestions. Concerning maturation and age status Caplan says:

> Where maturation occurs within the proper rate and proper sequence, personality grows along lines which have to some extent been studied and partly understood. The dynamic relationship between the external environment and the growing child, the role of the family, the dominating, rejecting, overprotective or intellectual "refrigerator" mother, have all received attention. But how much thought have we given to the following questions? What happens when growth and development are deviant because of basic primary biological factors? What significance does deviant development have for the child's ego, his mother, his

teacher? What happens to the drive to live, to be normal, to reach maximum potentialities when deviant maturation disturbs the equilibrium within the personality and sets up a stress in the external environment?

Factors that impair the drive for normality or frustrate the maturational sequence may create a basic primary stress which is biologically determined. This may at times, either of itself or when reinforced by secondary environmental stresses, seriously weaken the ego. These primary disturbances may so challenge the child's environment by placing a strain on his family, his school and his contemporaries that they in turn further aggravate the basic defect because of the anxiety induced in the organism. Thus a vicious cycle is set up, often very early in childhood, whereby primary tensions are constantly fed by secondary ones. The latter may be perpetuated long after the primary maturational defect has been overcome and subsequent normal growth and development have taken place. Adults may present a picture of personality dysfunction where the pathology at that time can only be seen in id drives and environmental relationships and where the basic primary disturbances which precipitated the cycle have long ceased to exist. We have recently heard much that is relevant to the point in "feed back mechanisms" and changing concepts of causality. Moreover, in the adult where the problems of motility control, language acquisition, visuomotor perception and reading conflicts are no longer to the fore, the therapeutic management consists largely of integration of past life experiences. The ability to recognize these deviations early in the life of the child and to interpret them adequately to the parents, the educator and society may prevent secondary reverberating tensions and hence may facilitate growth and development to their fullest inherent potentialities. Can further research perhaps in the area of obstetrics, pharmacology, education, etc., help control the rate and sequence of maturation? To date more of our energies have been devoted to a study of how the environment affects the child. Too little attention has been given to how the child affects his environment. Every child exerts a consistent and persistent influence on the total life of every member of the family. . . .

Early childhood is normally accompanied by sudden

spurts in growth and development. A great many vectors in maturation may make their appearance. Language, motility, perception and "intellectualization" set up within the child forces leading to new self-awareness and new facilities for object relationship. All this brings with it, for the child, new problems in mastery and self-control; for the parents, new adjustments to the changing child. The rapidity of movement creates, at least temporarily, a disequilibrium in the system. The resulting anxiety is the basis for the frequent comment that every child goes through a "neurotic stage" at one time or other. Where there is neurotic disturbance, the symptomatology varies in severity with the duration and depth of the disequilibrium and is often related to the state of psychobiological maturation reached at the moment of crisis. In the first year of life, symptoms center around oral and respiratory activities, such as crying, sucking, feeding problems; ages one to two years focus on posture and motor control and are related to irritability, restlessness, rhythmic muscular activities and the beginnings of somatization reactions; ages two to three years show an increasing preoccupation with sphincter control, language and motility; ages four to five years bring with them problems around interpersonal relationships, e.g., the mother, the sibling, the contemporary, and so on.

Adolescence too is a period of rapid growth and development. Changes occur at different rates in different areas. It is commonly accepted that marked anxiety may be found where maturation is either too precipitous or overly lagging. The adolescent is therefore typically anxious. Often this may be so acute and overwhelming that the picture simulates a complete psychotic breakdown. One must be very cautious in the diagnosis and prognosis, as equilibrium may be restored fairly quickly. What is most important, however, is how the environment deals with the organism at its stage of rapid flux.[14]

In conclusion, I wish to emphasize the significance of anxiety in an individual's life pattern. Causes of the various forms of anxious states which different persons display are rooted in the

[14] Hyman Caplan, "The Role of Deviant Maturation in the Pathogenesis of Anxiety," *American Journal of Orthopsychiatry*, January, 1956, pp. 96-98.

patient's natural constitution, his rate and kind of maturation process, his experiences, and the environmental factors by which he is stimulated. In tracing the developmental aspects of anxiety in an individual's life it seems that anxiety feelings generally begin in the home during the early life of a person. The extent to which children receive training in anxiety is indicated in the following:

Children can be *trained* to be tense and anxious by parents who are not themselves especially anxious persons. An overprotective parent, for example, may train a small child to be habitually apprehensive by making sudden protective lunges and by giving continual warnings of danger. Adults who, for cultural or personal reasons, are especially alert to strange noises and strange people, or who are too dramatic about ordinary precautions, such as crossing the street when there is traffic, may instill chronic anxiety in a child long before he is able to identify what the danger is about which his mother is warning him. Horror stories, ghost stories and tales of disaster and destruction can have similar effects upon the very young if they open up frightening dangers against which the child feels powerless to defend himself.

Older children are sometimes *taught systematically to ferret out* in imagination every hidden danger that might conceivably lurk in an apparently innocent situation. They learn to think always in terms of the future but never to have confidence in it, to cross bridges before coming to them, and to imagine each bridge collapsing the moment they give it their full weight. By such procedures growing children build into their personality structure tense, uneasy attitudes of anticipation which may interfere with their seeking out the activities they need to become socially mature.

Some parents make the mistake of trying to foster social maturity in their child by *parading adult problems, uncertainties* and *disillusionments* continually before him— doubts concerning food and shelter, financial and business worries, adult social strivings, and parental discord that divides his loyalties and threatens his most fundamental source of security. The child has many difficulties of his own to work out, difficulties that belong to his own age. He needs *protection* from adult uncertainty and adult disappointment so that he may be free to build his security in relation to childhood responsibilities among his elders and his peers. Otherwise a child grows into adulthood prematurely frightened by its threatening aspects and overwhelmed by its burdens. He has learned adult apprehensions before acquiring the strength, social skill and emotional maturity needed to meet and to master the problems of adulthood.[15]

[15] Cameron, *Personality Development and Psychopathology*, pp. 268–269.

QUESTIONS AND PROBLEMS

1. Differentiate between fear and anxiety. Also show the relationship between the two.

2. To what extent and how does anxiety affect mental activity?

3. Describe your behavior prior to the taking of an important test or examination.

4. Prepare a list of symptoms of anxiety. Identify those which you may have experienced.

5. If you have ever experienced panic, try to recall your physical and mental reactions. Describe any overt behavior displayed during the experience.

6. Indicate ways in which fear of inadequacy is related to anxiety.

7. To what extent are you a worrier? List the kinds of situations or problems about which you tend to worry.

8. Evaluate the various suggestions to prevent worry that are given in this chapter.

9. What are some of the dangerous situations you have experienced that have been basic to the development of an anxious state? What did you do about them?

10. Discuss the need for and the difficulties involved in relearning after being frightened.

11. Explain what is meant by "self boundaries and anxiety."

12. How is repression related to the id, ego, and superego? Be specific.

13. Present the therapeutic measures for anxiety suggested by Karen Horney.

14. Discuss anxiety in the infant, and trace the patterns of anxiety from infancy through adulthood.

15. In what ways are anxiety and hostility related?

Selected Readings

Craison, M., *Illusion and Anxiety*. Translated by B. Murchland. New York: The Macmillan Company, 1963.

Freud, S., *The Problem of Anxiety*. New York: W. W. Norton & Company, Inc., 1963.

Garre, W. J., *Basic Anxiety: A New Psycho-biological Concept*. New York: Philosophical Library, Inc., 1962.

Goodstein, M. J., and J. C. Palmer, *The Experience of Anxiety: A Casebook*. New York: Oxford University Press, 1963.

Haring, N. G., and E. L. Phillips, *Educating Emotionally Disturbed Children*. New York: McGraw-Hill, Inc., 1962.

Horney, K., *The Neurotic Personality of Our Time*. New York: W. W. Norton & Company, Inc., 1937.

Kisker, G. W., *The Disorganized Personality*. New York: McGraw-Hill, Inc., 1964.

May, R., *The Meaning of Anxiety*. New York: The Ronald Press Company, 1950.

Rosen, E., and I. Gregory, *Abnormal Psychology*. Philadelphia, Penna.: W. B. Saunders Company, 1965.

Ruitenbeek, H. M. (ed.), *The Problem of Homosexuality in Modern Society*. New York: E. P. Dutton & Co., Inc., 1963.

Sappenfield, B. R., *Personality Dynamics: An Integrative Psychology of Adjustment*. New York: Alfred A. Knopf, Inc., 1954.

Shaffer, L. F., and E. J. Shoben, Jr., *The Psychology of Adjustment*, 2nd ed. Boston, Mass.: Houghton Mifflin Company, 1956. Chapter 10.

Thorpe, L. P., B. Katz, and R. T. Lewis, *The Psychology of Abnormal Behavior: A Dynamic Approach*, 2nd ed. New York: The Ronald Press Company, 1961.

White, R. W., *The Abnormal Personality*, 3rd ed. New York: The Ronald Press Company, 1964.

MENTAL
AND
EMOTIONAL
DISORDERS

IN CHAPTER 7 are described some of the devices that are utilized by frustrated or thwarted individuals in their struggle for adequate adjustment to conditions or people who constitute their daily environment. Inner controls may be lacking to overcome what appears to be an unsurmountable obstacle, however. The conflict may be so severe that its victim can find no way to resolve it in a socially satisfactory fashion. Consequently, his attitudes and behavior become increasingly unrealistic and unacceptable to his associates.

Mental illness has been recognized as one of the most mysterious of human ills. In the past, ignorance concerning its significance gave rise to the superstitions and prejudices that surrounded all forms of mental disturbance. The sudden strange behavior of the victim, who seemed to be physically well, was ascribed to the fact that evil forces had gained possession of him. With the advance of scientific knowledge, however, there has slowly evolved an understanding of symptoms, and psychiatrists have discovered the causes of many forms of mental disorder.

Scientific knowledge has progressed to the extent of prevention, treatment, and sometimes cure of many mental diseases that heretofore were little understood and were considered incurable.

BASIC ELEMENTS OF
MALADJUSTMENT

A severe emotional strain may interfere with an individual's habitually well-adjusted reactions to function adequately. The death of a member of his family, a severe illness, a serious disappointment, or any other emotion-disturbing or frustrating situation may lead to poor adjustment. Extreme maladjustment usually is associated with generally inadequate emotional control. Yet the effect of a conflict situation upon a generally stable person may be so overwhelming that he suffers a temporary or more permanent mental or emotional disorder.

It would be difficult, if not impossible, to list all of the factors in which are rooted an individual's development of maladjusted behavior. White suggests the following situations or conditions as some of those that are basic to the onset of maladjustment.

Failure to outgrow the dependent tendencies of childhood, failure to achieve a working compromise between disciplinary requirements and autonomy, difficulty in guiding one's sexual and aggressive tendencies into socially workable channels, warping by the effects of the family constellation, unusual patterns of ability, troubles in establishing self-esteem based on competence and its recognition by others, insufficient or unfortunate social experiences both with groups and with close friends, conflicts among socially expected roles, an unabsorbed super-ego, unfortunate options in the way of identification figures, weakness of ego-identity, failure to internalize an effective hierarchy of strivings and a guiding ego-ideal—each of these maladjustive possibilities exists and plays a significant part in one life or another.[1]

[1] Robert W. White, *The Abnormal Personality*, 3rd ed., New York: The Ronald Press Company, 1964, p. 188.

Behavior Trends

A person experiences various interpersonal relations with his fellows. Leary classifies these into sixteen mechanisms or reflexes as shown in Figure 12. Any one of these forms of interpersonal behavior may be fraught with factors of maladjustment, varying from slight deviation to serious emotional strain.

The first failure to make a satisfactory adjustment to an emotion-disturbing situation is likely to become the basis of continued failures and of decreasing power to withstand the unwholesome effects of maladjustment. The child of emotionally unstable parents is affected by his parents' maladjusted behavior. Regardless of the stabilizing influences to which this young person may be exposed outside the home, the effect upon him of conflict in the home makes it difficult for him to free himself completely from experiencing overemotionalized attitudes and behavior.

Inability to master a disturbing situation may result either in flight from the annoying condition or in an unwarranted and abnormal attack upon the situation. An example from everyday life is that of a young woman who anticipates happiness in her married life. She believes that she is failing to achieve this desired goal. She may return to her sheltered girlhood home or she may launch a continued verbal attack upon her mate. Her attitude becomes so unbearable that her mate attempts to escape from the unpleasant situation through drink, extramarital relations, or complete repudiation of his home responsibilities.

Flight is characterized in varying degrees by retreat from the situation, self-dissatisfaction, abnormal envy, alcoholism, drug addiction, neurotic or psychotic state, or suicide. The *fight* response to failure may take the form of grouchiness, brutality, physical combat, juvenile delinquency or crime, or some other form of aggressive personality disorder.

In their milder forms, mental and emotional disorders usually are recognized by psychiatrists and many psychologists, but are little understood by the average person. The layman becomes aware of abnormal attitudes and behavior in another person only after these have reached a well-developed stage. Hence a person who is afflicted with a less easily recognized form of disturbance may remain in his home environment. Little or no attention is

Figure 12. Classification of Interpersonal Behavior into Sixteen Mechanisms or Reflexes

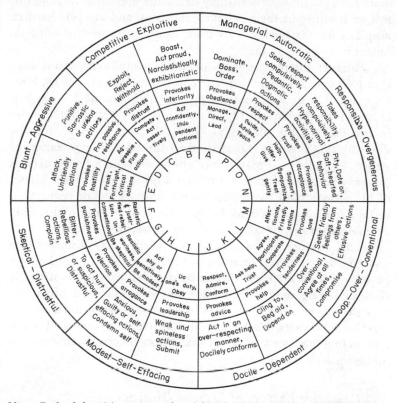

Note: Each of the 16 interpersonal variables is illustrated by sample behaviors. The inner circle names adaptive reflexes, such as *manage.* Proceeding outward, the next ring indicates the type of behavior that this interpersonal reflex tends to 'pull' from the other one; thus the person who uses the reflex A tends to call up in others *obedience.* These findings involve two-way interpersonal phenomena—what the subject does and what the other does in return—and are therefore less reliable than the other interpersonal categories presented in the inner and outer rings. The next circle illustrates extreme or rigid reflexes, such as *dominates.* The perimeter of the circle is divided into eight general categories employed in interpersonal diagnosis. Each of these general categories has a moderate (adaptive) and an extreme (pathological) intensity, such as *managerial-autocratic.*

SOURCE: Timothy Leary, "The Theory and Measurement Methodology of Interpersonal Communication," *Psychiatry,* May, 1955, p. 152. Copyright 1955 by William Alanson White Psychiatric Foundation, Inc.

given to his abnormal state except that his family or friends consider him to be "queer." As a matter of fact he may suffer more than do those who display decidedly abnormal attitudes of fear or hostility in their behavior patterns, and are protected in hospitals for the mentally ill from emotion-arousing stimuli inherent in everyday living.

Fatigue, disappointment, or other emotional strains may lead to temporary mental disturbance. The majority of us, however, are able to attain and maintain a wholesome mental balance. It is the persistence of a disturbance that places the disorder in the field of the abnormal. This, in part, accounts for the difficulty that often is experienced in the legal interpretation of sanity. An individual may evince abnormality in a few situations but may be able to achieve rational adjustments in most phases of his personal and social life. Furthermore, with the removal of certain stresses and strains he may be able to regain desirable normal adjustment in all phases of his behavior patterns.

The advance of psychiatric knowledge has dispelled the concept that irrational or antisocial behavior is an indication of a pathological disorder. Abnormal behavior during an emotionally disturbed state may be the resultant of social and other life experiences, or of ineffectively functioning inherent traits and reaction tendencies. Many mental disorders originate in thought and feeling and need to be treated through constructive mental and emotional stimulation.

Causative Factors of Mental Disorders

A serious disorder may result from a failure to attain socially acceptable outlets for a primitive urge. An individual may suffer from sexual frustrations and inhibitions, or from an inability to satisfy a strong urge for superiority and power over animate and inanimate factors of his environment. His conflicts reach the surface of consciousness but the underlying causes may be unknown to him. He may not realize, for example, that fixed parental attitudes and prejudices or rigid disciplining experienced in his childhood may have caused the development of certain severe repressions, thereby weakening his mental and emotional immunity.

In general we may classify the causes of serious maladjustment as *predisposing* and *exciting*. Personal inability to adjust can be considered as a predisposing factor. Predisposing causes of disturbed states are built into the personality of an individual. They grow out of a conflict between his psychobiological drives and the restrictions of his environment. This conflict and its resolution determine the course of his personality development. Social, occupational, and sexual readjustments are significant barriers that call for a detour into another path which often is the path of least resistance.

Predisposing causes of abnormal behavior may be biological, psychological, or sociological in origin. Rosen and Gregory suggest basic conclusions in each of these areas of influence, as follows:

BIOLOGICAL PREDISPOSITIONS TO ABNORMALITY

The belief that predisposing biological causes are real, that "something must be there," is not unwarranted despite the relatively weak results to date. First, since the organism is an interrelated system of biological and behavioral processes, it is plausible to assume that there *must* be biological predispositions to disturbed behavior. Second, since the existence of hereditary predispositions to certain behaviors is fairly well established, it follows that structural or functional dispositions should also exist, as connecting links between heredity and behavior. Third, although the results are weak, they have some degree of consistency: the studies have repeatedly demonstrated that, at the very least, there are biological correlates of disturbed behavior. Some of the correlations that have been found undoubtedly reflect causation and some do not. The problems to be solved consist of determining which biological factors are predisposing causes as well as correlates, precisely which disorders are influenced by such biological causes and just how the biological causes interact with other etiological agents.

PSYCHOLOGICAL PREDISPOSITIONS TO ABNORMALITY

The experimental and clinical data, both animal and human, are consistent enough to permit a series of general conclusions.

1. Psychopathological behavior results from learning under conditions of frustration, conflict and deprivation. If all other variables such as heredity were to be held constant, then the more stressful these conditions were the more severe the subsequent psychopathology would be.

2. Early experience is crucial. Severe and possibly irreversible damage may result from early childhood experiences; at a later period the same experiences have less serious effects.

3. Within childhood there are several critical developmental periods and several critical types of stimulation and experience. In the critical oral phase the infant is particularly sensitive to oral stimulation or deprivation (as well as to body contact) ; in the critical anal phase he is sensitive to the discipline of toilet training; and so forth. Specific types of stimulation in specific phases mold subsequent behavior.

4. Lasting psychopathology is less likely to result from a single traumatic event than from prolonged stress.

5. For normal development, children require close and enduring relationships with a parent or parent-substitute of each sex and with peers of both sexes. Deprivation of these relationships is an unquestionable cause of emotional disorder.

6. Parents and siblings may condition inappropriate effects or reinforce maladaptive behaviors by a variety of obvious and subtle means including nonverbal communication. Any parental attitude that deviates from acceptance of a child—overt rejection, perfectionism, inconsistency and overdominance—increases the probability that the child will develop an emotional disorder.

SOCIOLOGICAL INFLUENCES THAT ACT AS DETERMINANTS OF ABNORMAL BEHAVIOR

Social disorganization, cultural conflict and economic deprivation and other undesirable aspects of membership in the lowest socioeconomic class are the major sociocultural variables affecting various mental disorders, including schizophrenia. For manic-depression, however, a correlation with neighborhood disorganization has not been demonstrated. A mechanism by which social disorganization seems to conduce to schizophrenia is that of social isolation and withdrawal.

10. Minority status and family instability—both of which are known to be associated with disorganization, low socioeconomic status and cultural conflict—are inimical to mental health.

11. Stressful and critical situations—unemployment, family disintegration due to divorce or death, rapid technological change and residential mobility—have negative effects on emotional functioning.

12. Finally, since sociocultural determinants act on an individual with a given heredity, constitution and learning experiences, it follows that genetic, biological nongenetic, psychological and cultural factors always interact in the etiology of abnormality.[2]

If his life is relatively free from unusual stresses or strains, even a relatively unstable person can achieve a satisfactory pattern of adjustment in his daily relationships with his associates. Conflict situations may arise in the person's life, however, that act as *exciting* causes of more or less serious mental and emotional disorders. Some exciting causes may result in no more than a temporary form of mental disturbance. Others, through their persistence, may lead to disturbed conditions that cannot be remedied or alleviated except by way of hospitalization and appropriate therapy.

Psychogenic Disorders

Organic or mental disorders that are rooted in emotional disturbances, severe frustrations, or unresolvable mental and emotional conflicts can be referred to as psychogenic disorders. I already have listed some causative factors that underlie the onslaught of one or another form of illness. For discussion purposes I first am classifying roughly the various forms of disorder into two groups: (1) psychosomatic illness and (2) personality disorders. Since personality disorders differ in degree of seriousness, we can subdivide them into what are termed neurotic tendencies

[2] Ephraim Rosen and Ian Gregory, *Abnormal Psychology*, Philadelphia: W. B. Saunders Company, 1965, pp. 124, 149, 171.

and psychotic states. I now shall consider briefly some of the causes and symptoms of psychosomatic illness, neurosis, and psychosis. Suggested therapies for the treatment of mentally and emotionally disturbed individuals are presented in Chapter 12.

PSYCHOSOMATIC ILLNESS

The term psychosomatic implies an interrelationship of mind and body, with especial reference to disease. The diagnostic and remedial techniques employed by the Armed Forces in their care of servicemen who became "mental" patients were instrumental in bringing to public attention the close interrelationship that exists between emotional status and health condition. A psychosomatic disorder may be a manifestation of anxiety. White distinguishes between this form of disorder and a somatopsychic disorder as follows:

> Disturbances in which emotional maladjustment leads to chronic dysfunction in some organ system are nowadays referred to as psychosomatic disorders. As so often happens, the title is not particularly suitable. The term appears to include every disorder in which psychological and somatic factors both play a part, but in practice no one intends to give it such a sweeping meaning. It is best to limit it to those disorders in which chronic maladjustment is the primary process and somatic dysfunction the result or by-product. One might keep in mind the opposite term, *somatopsychic disorders*—though it is not widely used—for those cases in which bodily disorder is primary and psychological changes secondary. Such a term could be applied to head injury or encephalitis, for example, in which dysfunction of the cerebral cortex produces the result of impulsiveness and poor control so that the person has difficulty in accepting social restraints.[3]

Psychosomatic Reactions

It is a recognized fact that a disturbed emotional state is accompanied by various physiological changes, e.g., increased heartbeat, gastronomical changes, and increased muscular

[3] White, *The Abnormal Personality*, p. 391.

strength during extreme anger or rage. Usually these bodily changes or emergency states return to their normal functioning with the reduction of emotional tension. The victim of a persistent fear or rage condition is unable to cope with the conflict situation, however. He may be more or less unaware of the strength of his emotional state; yet he continues to suffer physical discomfort or pain, which he interprets to be symptomatic of a diseased condition.

The mental and emotional conditions include fears, anxieties, compulsions, delusions, or hallucinations. The physical symptoms may be one or more of the following: aches and pains (especially visceral), sleeplessness, poor appetite, constipation, tics, labored breathing, and feelings of fatigue. Some physical disorders that formerly were considered to have an organic origin now are regarded as psychosomatic in that they involve emotional factors. Among the more common types of psychosomatic disorders or diseases are included ulcers, asthma, hay fever and other allergies, the common cold, colitis, eczema, arthritis, disorders of circulatory system, obesity, and sterility.

Bosselman outlines both negative and positive symptoms of psychosomatic disturbances:

> Some of the symptoms of psychosomatic disturbance are negative ones. A common complaint of these patients is excessive fatigue. This is an objective manifestation of a state subjectively described as "feeling inferior" or "feeling inadequate." Such patients are conflictually tied up. The energies which should be flowing outward are blocked, either because they have no opportunity for expression or because the patient's internal conflict will not allow it. He complains of exhaustion, often is sleepy and apathetic. Every small effort tires him, and he may react to exertion as does the asthenic patient, with breathlessness, tachycardia, and trembling. These patients give an original impression of suffering from a debilitating condition, and such conditions should always, of course, be ruled out. Physicians, however, tend to be overly cautious in this respect and even in the presence of a negative examination persist in restricting the patient's activity, thus arousing secondary anxiety and favoring a tendency to invalidism.
>
> The fatigue reaction is a relatively simple and direct

expression of conflict and often clears up promptly as the patient gains insight into its meaning and finds acceptable outlets for his dammed-up energies. The condition is a common one among women who are sexually stimulated but not satisfied; it is often seen in men as an expression of unacknowledged wishes for dependency.

The more positive psychosomatic disturbances may follow a non-specific pattern of expressing anxiety. A chronic stimulation by undischarged emotion disrupts the normal function of organs concerned in emotional expression. The rapid heart, pain and heaviness in the chest, dizziness and shortness of breath which simulate cardiac disease are an exaggeration and prolongation of symptoms anyone feels in states of grief, fear, or anger. Diarrhea and/or constipation, anorexia, nausea are well known also in such states.[4]

Beginnings of Psychosomatic Reactions

Organic changes that result from emotional stimulation of organic dysfunctioning differ between young children and older persons. The very young child who is exposed to a situation that gives evidence of emotional stress components may experience a generally reduced power to function physiologically. For example, an infant's separation from the mother or mother substitute denies him the loving care and the warm interpersonal relations that are experienced by the child whose mother is with him. The emotionally "neglected" baby may give evidence of the symptoms of marasmus: apathy, listlessness, a general physical "wasting away" that results in an early death. An increasing understanding of a young child's emotional as well as physical needs has resulted in a definite decrease of this form of psychosomatic disorder. Certain prenatal and postnatal factors may predispose toward psychosomatic reactions.

PRENATAL FACTORS. The first modification of an individual's overt behavior may result from disturbances during his prenatal life. It is an accepted fact that there are no communicating fibers between the nervous system of the mother and that of the fetus. The fetus is an intimate part of a "total" psychoso-

[4] Beulah C. Bosselman, *Neurosis and Psychosis*, 3rd ed., Springfield, Ill.: Charles C Thomas, 1964, pp. 174–175.

matic organism, however; therefore it is probably influenced by its emotional and metabolic processes.

Through the endocrine organs and cell metabolism emotions change the composition of the mother's blood, either momentarily or for longer periods. This proves irritating to the fetus as evidenced by increased bodily activity. It appears that the fetus is modified to the degree of the mother's somatized anxieties or fears.

This irritability may carry over to postnatal life along with hyperactivity, exaggerated bowel and gastrointestinal activity, and a higher fluctuation of heart rate. Physical symptoms of cardiospasm and rejection of food either by regurgitation or passing it as undigested curds may be of psychic origin.

POSTNATAL FACTORS. When a child's growth in height, weight, intelligence, maturation of emotional processes, and sexual maturation does not develop evenly, certain psychosomatic reactions are likely to arise.

Retardation in sexual growth, as in the Froelich syndrome, is another example of the interrelationships between the psyche and soma. The patient becomes effeminate in appearance, obese, and generally infantile. Besides feelings of inadequacy and inferiority, such individuals develop deep-seated anxieties which in turn produce significant degrees of somatic dysfunctioning.

A severe illness or generally poor health can change the factors of the child's environment or the position of the child in it. It causes the withdrawal from normal social situations and from contacts and competition. If the child is acutely ill he becomes the center of attraction, is frequently spoon-fed by the mother or nurse, and is more or less pampered. The child gradually regresses or retreats to the infancy level. His modified patterns and the regression of his process of socialization are psychosomatic aspects of illness.

Since a balanced diet is necessary for mental growth and energy levels, poor eating habits tend to create anxiety in parents. The child, unaware of his needs and physical standards, sees pressure being put upon him to eat when he may be neither hungry nor like the food placed before him.

Some individuals have a constitutional ease of conformity while others seem to be entirely lacking in this quality; each child is endowed with certain constitutional characteristics and qualities which determine his potential resistive or reactive responses to environmental pressures. The strong, highly active, mentally alert child may respond to a restrictive parent with open rebellion, while his brother may make a passive adjustment, withdrawing from new or anxiety-producing situations.

In all cases this potential or energy is subject to modification through nutrition, disease, and the pressures of environment. This modification is not limited to childhood, but is extremely important during the early years. This is the period in which the individual is most rapidly expanding his social sphere. As he grows older, he comes in contact with an increasing number of people and an increasing number of expectations and demands. These pressures may be opportunities for rebellion both in overt behavior and in terms of somatic function.

Enuresis, encropresis, and vomiting are common means of expressing aggression or hostility, or of getting attention. The symptom does not necessarily mean organic defect or weakness. A child learns early that physical hurts or pains receive prompt and satisfying adult sympathy and attention.

In the home and the school many concessions are made for the sick child. He is excused from the fulfillment of home duties and preparation of homework. A child's emotional difficulties may be disregarded by adults, or may be interpreted as signs of stubbornness, lack of cooperation, laziness, or "naughty" behavior.

The tendency learned in childhood to emphasize the suffering of physical pain rather than to call attention to his experiencing of emotional stress can influence an adult's reactions in similar situations. Moreover, to complain of symptoms of physical illness is less embarrassing than it is to let it be known that one is suffering from mental or emotional disturbance.

DISORDERS OF PERSONALITY

Disorders of personality represent maladaptive behavior and attitudes. The behavior disorders resulting from serious conflict situations are relatively set and require therapeutic treatment. The disorder may require temporary or prolonged treatment or hospitalization. Rehabilitation may be complete or partial. In the more serious cases, rehabilitation or cure may be doubtful, or the patient may never recover. Bosselman traces the arousal of disorders as shown in Table 6.

It is estimated that in the neighborhood of 18,000,000 persons suffer at one or another time in their life from a relatively

TABLE 6

Arousal of Disorders

When Inherited Capacities
    based on variable
    intelligence,
    physical efficiency,
    energy,
    capacity for adaptation,

Are Subjected to Early Environmental Difficulties
    such as
        lack of acceptance,
        over-intimidation,
        discouragements to maturation,

And These Lead to Rigid Defensive Personality Patterns
    such as those of
        retreat,
        projection,
        over-compensation (reaction formation)

Which Are Later Subjected to Acute Situations of Stress and Strain
    which either strengthen repressed forces, or weaken
    the repressive capacity,

Neurosis or Psychosis May Result.

Source: Beulah C. Bosselman, *Neurosis and Psychosis,* 3rd ed., 1964, p. 3. Courtesy of Charles C Thomas, Publisher, Springfield, Ill.

serious form of mental and emotional disorder. About half of all hospital beds are occupied by disturbed patients. In Table 7 are presented the mental patient data for fiscal years 1954, 1962, and 1965.

Classification of Personality Disorders

The main types of personality disorders can be classified roughly as: psychoses, neuroses, psychosomatic disorders, delinquent and psychopathic personalities, and lesser maladjustments. The last two categories are referred to in other sections of the book. I also have considered psychosomatic illness. Now I shall discuss neurosis and psychosis briefly.[5]

The term psychotic is applied to those persons whose behavior disorders are so serious that they are legally committable to a hospital for the mentally ill. Neurotics or psychoneurotics are permitted to be free, but receive expert care or treatment.

Difficulties arise when we attempt to distinguish between these classifications from the point of view of symptomatic behav-

TABLE 7

Mental Patient Data for Fiscal Years 1954, 1962, and 1965

Item	1954 351 of 352 Hospitals	1962 285 of 285 Hospitals	1965 289 of 289 Hospitals
First admissions	121,430	129,698 *	144,042 *
Readmissions	50,252	90,843 †	115,486 †
Discharges	115,196	216,383	286,989
Deaths in hospitals	42,652	49,563	44,270

* Classified as No Prior Admission to any inpatient psychiatric facility.
† Classified as Prior Admission to hospitals in same state system.
Source: Patients in Mental Institutions, Part II, 1954 and 1962, U.S. Dept. of Health, Education, and Welfare, Public Health Service, Mental Health Statistics Current Reports, Series MHB-H-10.

ior. Psychoneurotics and psychotics are maladjusted persons. They attempt to solve their serious frustrations and conflicts through the display of unrealistic behavior. In extreme cases of the psychoses, the personal struggle for adjustment to accustomed life activities becomes a losing battle: the patient succumbs to his disordered state. Personality disorders require the services of trained therapists.

According to Freud, a neurosis is a physical process associated with sexual adjustment; a psychoneurosis represents mental disorientation. At present the terms *neurosis* and *psychoneurosis* are used interchangeably. Neurasthenia, described by Beard as weak nerves, and psychasthenia, associated by Jung with a weak psyche, are today considered to represent forms of psychoneurotic behavior.

Listed in Table 8 are terms that represent the various types of neurotic and psychotic disorders from which individuals may suffer.

[5] A more detailed discussion of these appears in Chapter 11.

TABLE 8

Statistical Classification of Mental Disorder

1. Acute Brain Syndromes, Associated with:
   Epidemic encephalitis
   Other intracranial infections
   Systemic infections
   Alcohol intoxication
   Drug or poison intoxication, except alcohol
   Trauma
   Circulatory disturbance
   Convulsive disorder
   Disturbance of metabolism, growth or nutrition
   New growth
   Other diseases and conditions, NEC (not elsewhere classified), or unspecified disease or condition

2. Chronic Brain Syndromes with Psychotic Reaction, Associated with:
   Conditions and diseases due to prenatal influence
   Central nervous system syphilis
   Epidemic encephalitis
   Other intracranial infections, except syphilis
   Alcohol intoxication
   Drug or poison intoxication, except alcohol
   Birth trauma
   Other trauma
   Cerebral arteriosclerosis
   Circulatory disturbance other than cerebral arteriosclerosis
   Convulsive disorder
   Senile brain disease
   All other disturbance of metabolism, growth or nutrition
   New growth
   Other diseases and conditions, NEC, or unspecified disease or condition

3. Chronic Brain Syndromes with Neurotic Reaction, Associated with:
   Conditions and diseases due to prenatal influence
   Central nervous system syphilis
   Epidemic encephalitis
   Other intracranial infections, except syphilis
   Alcohol intoxication
   Drug or poison intoxication, except alcohol
   Birth trauma
   Other trauma
   Cerebral arteriosclerosis
   Circulatory disturbance other than cerebral arteriosclerosis
   Convulsive disorder
   Senile brain disease
   All other disturbance of metabolism, growth or nutrition

TABLE 8 (continued)

New growth
Other diseases and conditions, NEC, or unspecified disease or condition

4. Chronic Brain Syndromes with Behavioral Reactions, Associated with:
   Conditions and diseases due to prenatal influence
   Central nervous system syphilis
   Epidemic encephalitis
   Other intracranial infections, except syphilis
   Alcohol intoxication
   Drug or poison intoxication, except alcohol
   Birth trauma
   Other trauma
   Cerebral arteriosclerosis
   Circulatory disturbance other than cerebral arteriosclerosis
   Convulsive disorder
   Senile brain disease
   All other disturbance of metabolism, growth or nutrition
   New growth
   Other diseases and conditions, NEC, or unspecified disease or condition

5. Chronic Brain Syndrome without Qualifying Phrase, Associated with·
   Conditions and diseases due to prenatal influence
   Central nervous system syphilis
   Epidemic encephalitis
   Other intracranial infections, except syphilis
   Alcohol intoxication
   Drug or poison intoxication, except alcohol
   Birth trauma
   Other trauma
   Cerebral arteriosclerosis
   Circulatory disturbance other than cerebral arteriosclerosis
   Convulsive disorder
   Senile brain disease
   All other disturbance of metabolism, growth or nutrition
   New growth
   Other diseases and conditions, NEC, or unspecified disease or condition

6. Psychotic Disorders
   Involutional psychotic reaction
   Affective reactions
   Schizophrenic reactions
   Paranoid reactions
   Psychotic reactions without clearly defined structural change other than above

7. Psychophysiologic Autonomic and Visceral Disorders

8. Psychoneurotic Disorders

9. Personality Disorders
   Alcoholism (addiction)
   Drug addiction
   All other personality disorders

10. Transient Situational Personality Disorder

11. Mental Deficiency

Source: Committee on Nomenclature and Statistics of the American Psychiatric Association, *Diagnostic and Statistical Manual: Mental Disorders,* American Psychiatric Association, Washington, D.C., 1952, pp. 75–77. Reprinted by permission.

Effects of Social Change on Mental Health

The evidence of social change or the inability of a society to continue to be completely stable, exercises a potent effect upon an individual's power to maintain positive mental health. Among the types of social change effects are the individual's degree of readiness to change, his resistance to therapeutic applications, and his responses as well as those of different groups and subgroups to social change. In this connection Fried says:

> Analysis of social change must be filtered through a variety of individual and mass experiences of change; and an approach to mental health must be derived from data on emotional impairments. To make these transformations, we can conceive of change experiences as a range of events that may affect only isolated individuals, discrete groups, widespread populations or an entire society. And we can use a model of mental health that implies a spectrum ranging from the optimally healthy to the extremes of illness. This model is too crude to carry us very far, but it has the distinct advantage of simplicity and a gross correspondence to observable phenomena.
>
> The observable phenomena are the variations among people in the range of situations, of stresses, of frustrations, of crises they can tolerate with little disruption in functioning. Individuals who seem able to handle most situations with manifest evidence of mastery (if not with equanimity) are at one extreme. These individuals are unlikely to show all the attributes any group of judges would define as "optimally healthy." But there is apparently a relatively small

array of characteristics frequently allocated to health in our society.[6] Achievement, cognitive clarity, competence, executant ego functions, ego strength and self-actualization vie with one another only within a narrow, if rather culturally limited, range.[7]

In his concluding analysis of the effect of social change on mental health, Fried presents profound suggestions for further thinking. He says:

In view of the complex set of biological, intrapsychic, interpersonal, social and cultural factors implicated as sources of disturbance by the many studies of social change and experiences of change, it seems essential to expand our definitions of health and illness. The persistence of individual attributes and orientations is a function of the continuity of sociocultural patterns and of an ongoing system of social positions and roles, as well as of personality. Even if we designate mental health status on the basis of these individual attributes and orientations, it becomes increasingly clear that *mental health does not inhere in the individual but in the relationship between the individual and his immediate environment*. Mental health appears to be a *process* that involves the fulfillment of individual needs, wishes and goals, but this also implies a *relationship* of interaction, participation and commitment with others whose needs, wishes and goals are fulfilled or frustrated by the reciprocal patterns of interpersonal and role contact. Mental illness is similarly an adaptive or a maladaptive process based on the relationship between the individual and others with whom he shares reciprocal patterns of interpersonal and role interaction. Too often, in considering mental illness, we use the model of the most severe, incapacitated and chronically disturbed individuals who tax this view to its utmost. But in

[6] F. Barron, *Personal Soundness in University Graduate Students*, Berkeley: University of California Press, 1954. M. Jahoda, *Current Concepts of Positive Mental Health*, New York: Basic Books, 1958. D. C. McClelland, *The Achieving Society*, Princeton: D. Van Nostrand Company, 1961. R. W. White, "Motivation Reconsidered: The Concept of Competence," *Psychological Review*, 66 (5) (1959) , 297–333. [Fried]

[7] Marc Fried, "Effects of Social Change on Mental Health," *American Journal of Orthopsychiatry*, January, 1964, p. 6.

these extreme instances, probably far less frequently than the diagnosis of schizophrenia would suggest, the relative imperviousness of the individual to adaptive change is a product of the ready assimilation of potential objects and experiences to a restrictive past. It is also in part an effort to resist the attractive but threatening possibilities of new opportunities for adaptation. It is a limiting case of adaptive relationships that depends on a gross persistence of "unresponsive" social relationships to support the persistence of fixated goals and restrictive defenses and does not challenge the conception of illness as a maladaptive process involving *both* the individual and his environment.

We do not really know the necessary and sufficient conditions for producing such structural, intrapsychic rigidities that seem impervious to any modest change experiences. The vast majority of any population, however, has a much broader range of potential adaptive resources and few situations of social change are so traumatizing as well as constricting that widespread mental disorder can be anticipated. Mental disorder and the entire range of emotional impairments, of course, hardly exhaust the significant effects of social change. In examining emotional impairments, however, we become particularly cognizant of certain features of social change and its effects. Social change involves *disorganization* as well as *reorganization* and *reintegration*. And some form of persisting disorganization, within personality or within social roles and relationships, seems to be a necessary intervening factor in those social changes that lead to increased frequency of mental disorders. Disorganization produces serious problems for some individuals and is more disturbing for certain types and groups than for others. But the normal course of social change, even very rapid social change, appears as frequently to lead to adaptive achievements as to adaptive failures. And we can only account for these variations if we consider the mutual relationships between an individual and his environment in which failures in adaptation at one source can be compensated and their direction of movement reversed by appropriate changes at the other source.

Crises in societal patterns or in individual experience

that involve important losses, separations or disruptions and are not compensated by new social resources and a new sense of belonging and commitment are particularly significant for mental health and illness. But even the effects of these crises are not necessarily limited to impairments, despite their potential for disorganizing consequences. For some people these situations open the way to a new and more meaningful life. In fact, *the most general conclusion we can draw regarding the effects of social change on mental health and illness is that, despite the disturbance of adaptation entailed, there is a wide range of alternative methods of coping with change experiences.* At the same time, the evidence of constellations associated with change, constellations leading to more effective functioning and those more frequently related to impairment, suggests that it is possible to facilitate the successful patterns and to modify the patterns of failure. More effectively planned social action and more broadly conceived psychotherapeutic intervention provide opportunities for achieving greater and more widespread well-being in the face of inevitable and persistent social change. This is a major challenge to both the investigative and the preventive service potentialities of the behavioral sciences, a challenge to adapt more effectively to the complexities of an urban industrial civilization.[8]

SYMPTOMS OF MENTAL DISORDER

The symptoms of serious mental or emotional disturbance differ in degree rather than in kind from those experienced by most of us. Furthermore, to determine whether apparently serious symptoms are real, imagined, or feigned requires trained insights. Not all of the symptoms listed below are characteristic of every form of mental illness; neither can they be classified into definite patterns. They may show themselves in varying interrelated combinations.

Commonly experienced symptoms of mental disorder fall into four general categories: physical, mental, emotional, and behavioral. The various categories include the following:

[8] *Ibid.*, pp. 22–24.

1. PHYSICAL SYMPTOMS:
   a. Excessive or loss of appetite.
   b. Deviations in pulse rate, respiration, and body temperature.
   c. Abnormal weight changes.
   d. Headache, dizziness, nausea, vomiting.
   e. Abnormal pupillary activity, coughing, and real or imagined pain or fatigue.

2. MENTAL SYMPTOMS:
   a. Loss of memory (*amnesia*).
   b. Inability to perceive realistic relationships (*agnosia*).
   c. Failure to understand or produce language (*aphasia*).
   d. Delayed or retarded mental association, mental blocking, flight of ideas and distractibility.
   e. Phobias.
   f. Obsessions or fixed ideas that often take the form of unrealistic attitudes or beliefs (e.g., a close relative is planning the death of the patient; or the human race will be destroyed by insects).
   g. Strong compulsions to engage in antisocial behavior.
   h. Extremely unrealistic perceptual illusions resulting from an abnormal mind set toward sensory stimulation (e.g., a stranger is mistaken for a close relative who has been dead for many years; an inanimate object is recognized as an attacking enemy).
   i. Hallucinations or imaginary perceptions (e.g., the seeing of objects, hearing of sounds, tasting of food, etc., that are nonexistent except in the imagination of the individual).
   j. Delusions or false judgments beliefs that have no factual basis, are unrelated to personal experience, and defy appeal to reason. They usually take the form of delusions of grandeur, delusions of persecution, and delusions of melancholia.

3. EMOTIONAL SYMPTOMS:
   a. Emotional apathy or indifference, expressed through crying, constant sighing and gloominess, brooding, and/or almost complete silence and refusal to eat.
   b. Emotional exhilaration and freedom from care or

worry, expressed through excited talking, singing, dancing, and uncontrolled laughter.

4. BEHAVIOR SYMPTOMS:

   a. Excessive psychomotor activity that impels toward abnormal shouting or whispering, laughing or crying, and constant motion.
   b. Retarded psychomotor activity, inducing hesitation or indecision (*abulia*), halting speech or refusal to talk, body rigidity, and a general slowdown of motion.
   c. Abnormal impulsiveness or suggestibility (e.g., doing the reverse of what might be expected, persistently repeating the words or actions of another person).
   d. Continued, unreasonable repetition of the same movement or act (*stereotypy*).
   e. Nonhabitual behavior reactions (e.g., shuffling walk, facial grimaces, and other peculiar body mannerisms, unaccustomed use of profane or vulgar language).

General Physical Symptoms

Physical symptoms should not be disregarded in the observation of mental patients for a diagnosis or understanding of their illness, since the patient either does not know or will not admit that he is mentally ill and, consequently, will not cooperate in the diagnosis of his case. Many such persons not only deny that they are ill but also resist treatment. This behavior is conditioned by the existing social attitude toward persons suffering from mental disorders. If this attitude can be corrected, the discovery and treatment of mental ill health will be accelerated. Society counts it no disgrace to be physically ill but apparently attaches personal responsibility and disgrace to mental disability.

Among the physical symptoms that require close observation and study are changes in temperature, the pulse and respiration rate; nausea; vomiting and headache; dizziness; loss of or abnormal appetite; loss of weight; coughing; pain; fatigue; speech disturbances; writing peculiarities; abnormal pupillary activity; and motor incoordinations. Any deviation from the normal in one or more of such behavior patterns may be symptomatic of mental disorder and should receive careful attention from properly trained persons.

Temperature changes during changing mental states. Anxiety and overactivity cause an increase in body temperature, and sadness and inactivity tend to lower it. Likewise, the pulse may be affected; it may change from regular to irregular, from strong to weak. Fear may accelerate the pulse or may temporarily paralyze heart action. During the emotional states of fear, joy, and elation the pulse is usually strong, but it tends to be weak during depressed states. The time of the day at which vomiting occurs, its regularity, and the extent to which food-taking is accompanied by nausea should be noted. Attention also should be given to the onslaught of a headache—time of occurrence, location in the head, and type of activity that caused it.

Peculiarities of eating, loss of appetite, and overeating may be indicative of mental disturbances. Signs of fatigue should be recognized. These include irregular eye movements, dark coloration beneath the eyes, irregular pulse, headache, and general appearance of exhaustion. Lisping, slurring, stuttering, stammering, hoarseness, and very rapid or very slow speech may be significant. Unusual dilation or contraction of the pupils of the eyes should be noted and the causes determined.

General Behavior Symptoms

The person who has become mentally ill soon exhibits deviations from his habitual behavior patterns. The mental patient may show ability to use his memory, but other actions or modes of response may indicate that he is different from his former self. The patient's display of vulgarity or of profane language may be a definite change from his accustomed behavior. Increased psychomotor activity indicates emotional excitement. The patient seems to be impelled toward constant motion accompanied by whispering, shouting, crying, or laughing. Emotional depression tends toward decreased psychomotor activity or the slowing down of the individual's movements and speech.

The behavior of the mentally ill is often impulsive and responsive to external suggestion. The patient may repeat the words or imitate the movements of another, or maintain a given muscular position; he may reverse his behavior and either refuse to respond or do the exact opposite of what is expected of him. The behavior of mental patients also includes abulia (hesitation and indecision), and many other peculiar mannerisms such as queer movements of the hands, the shoulders, or the mouth.

General Mental Symptoms

Among the mental symptoms are those of flight of ideas, distractibility, blocking of the thought processes, and retardation or delay of mental associations. The patient shows that he is unable to continue systematic and logical thinking, is distracted by respective stimuli, and allows the expression of his ideas to follow a consequently disorganized sequence because his thinking has been blocked; he may develop his ideas slowly and arrive at decisions with extreme difficulty. Among the more abnormal mental symptoms are to be found fixed ideas, obsessions, compulsions, phobias, delusions, illusions, hallucinations, delirium, aphasia, and agnosia. Many of these are widely used terms and should be understood by laymen as well as the professionals.

Illusions, Hallucinations, and Delusions

Illusions and hallucinations are caused by disturbances in perception. In *illusion* the perception is faulty, and objects are not perceived as they really are but are distorted by mind-set or imperfections in the receptors. Illusions may be associated with any of the sense organs, although illusions of sight are most commonly recognized.

Hallucinations represent disorders of the imagination. They are imaginary perceptions—those that have no immediate sensory foundation. In the past it was believed that persons who had illusions or hallucinations were hopelessly disturbed. The individual who sees an object when no object is present, who hears voices, bells, or other sounds when others cannot, who experiences taste sensation without food, or who believes that his body has changed position as a result of disturbances in the sensory areas of the muscles, joints, and tendons is suffering from a mild form of hallucination, which through experience has become systematized and controlled. The autosuggestive technique enables the individual to think that he sees or hears things that are really only transitory hallucinations.

In discussing the meaning and function of illusions and

hallucinations, it should be emphasized that both forms of irrational behavior result from identical mental processes. At times the actual stimulus that gives rise to an illusion affects the mental processes so differently that the resulting false perception almost assumes the nature of an hallucination. The mere mention of a certain kind of food may arouse in the thinking of the disturbed person a conviction that he is being forced to eat this food and that it will poison him. Consequently, he may exhibit behavior of violent refusal of food that is not actually present.

Some hallucinations are artificially produced through the use of drugs and alcohol, as is illustrated in delirium tremens. In general, hallucinations are expressions of thought content that normally would be controlled by habits of repression or inhibition. If there occurs a relaxing of the mental or emotional control, repressed desires, urges, or interests come to the surface in one of several forms of morbid behavior (sex indulgences, or abnormal curiosity concerning physical functions), or direct the content of the dream life of the individual.

A patient may recognize his own susceptibility to hallucinatory experience, but he may be unable to resist his response to the imaginary stimuli. He may attempt to explain the causes of his difficulty in terms of normal reactions, or he may accept his hallucination and make no attempt to justify the fact that he is responding in any other than normal behavior patterns.

Delusions are significant disorders of judgment. They are false beliefs and are characterized by the following: (1) An appeal to reason will not correct them. (2) They have no basis in fact. (3) The experience of the individual does not justify them. They do not harmonize with the individual's ability or training, and he holds to the ideas in the face of evidence to the contrary. They are of three kinds: persecution, grandeur, and melancholia.

Delusions of *persecution* are mental states in which the individual misinterprets events in his environment by imagining that they are the result of malicious influences that are acting to interfere with his welfare. The individual maintains the truth of his delusion in spite of contradictory evidence. He may accuse others of attempts to hurt him, to take away his possessions, to call him names, or to poison him.

Delusions of *grandeur* are mental states in which the individual imagines that he possesses great influence and power. He believes that he has great wealth, that he is a superior student, that he is Napoleon, Churchill, or Johnson, or that he has attained specific accomplishments such as great inventions, or similar powers, that will transform the world.

Delusions of *melancholia* are mental states in which the individual accuses himself of wrongdoing or thinks that he is suffering from a serious illness. He may believe that he has committed a great sin, has caused suffering to others, or has contracted an incurable disease.

Other symptoms of mental disorders may involve a clouding of the consciousness with possible illusions; stupor in which awareness is interfered with and activity retarded; or delirium in which there is confusion, temporary delusion, or hallucination. The general disturbance of consciousness is usually accompanied by lack of normal motor control and by speech difficulties and incoherencies. In these clouded or stuporous states the patient is likely to suffer from disorders of memory. He may lose his memory completely (amnesia), he may seem to possess a very high degree of retentiveness (hypermnesia), or he may seem to recall events which have never occurred (paramnesia).

General Emotional Symptoms

As most physical functions are influenced by emotional states, emotional abnormalities are among the first symptoms of mental disorder. Close observation of the patient may show an emotionally aroused attack of indigestion, headache, flushing of the face, acceleration of the pulse, perspiration, or increased blood pressure. The patient may exhibit a state of emotional indifference or apathy, or he may exhibit an unnatural state of happiness. His elation may be accompanied by much self-expressing activity in the form of singing, dancing, laughing, and talking. He may become morbid and depressed; he may be gloomy and exhibit the traits of the downhearted. He may worry, sigh, speak very little, or refuse to eat. Such indifference on the part of the individual indicates that there is a deterioration of his mental states and that his feeling powers are greatly weakened. Changes of stimuli that ordinarily would cause feelings of surprise fail to do so, and it is evident that deterioration has set in.

The emotions play an important role in the behavior of the disturbed individual even though the basis of his disorder may seem to be largely of mental origin.

A delusion probably constitutes one of the most striking psychotic symptoms. Because of inadequate knowledge, a normal person may give expression to a false belief, but his error of judgment can be corrected through the acquisition of factual information. A completely unrealistic delusion suffered by the mentally disturbed tends to persist in spite of anything that may be done to change the patient's belief.

As a compensation for his basic, unsatisfactory adjustment, the tendency to daydream characteristic of normal individuals becomes an intense divorce from realism. The individual may come to imagine that he is superior to other humans, or is superhuman. His delusion of grandeur is a fixed belief that he possesses great authority of power and that others are or should be subservient to him. He demands that he receive the kind of treatment commensurate with his exalted state. At the same time he may display an extremely altruistic and beneficent attitude toward many or all his "inferiors."

The psychotic, unable to face the fact that he is responsible for his maladjusted state, may project the blame to others to so great a degree that he develops a delusion of persecution. He is convinced that one, a few, or many of his associates, especially relatives and close friends (sometimes his physician or psychiatrist) are plotting against him because of their jealousy or envy, or their false belief that he has harmed them. Contrariwise, an appreciation of personal inadequacy may cause a disturbed individual to believe that he has committed an unpardonable sin, or that he has contracted an incurable illness because of his own shortcomings. A victim of the delusion of melancholia, suffering remorse for wrongs he has not committed, tries to compensate to others for hurts he believes he has inflicted, engages in acts of self-abasement, and is convinced that there is no hope for him in this world or in any other.

QUESTIONS AND PROBLEMS

1. Differentiate between functional and organic mental disorders.
2. Discuss the causes and factors that result in the development of personality disorders.
3. Why is *mental ill health* a better term to use than *insanity?*
4. Describe the symptoms of hysteria.
5. Why do some people regard mental illness as a disgrace? What can be done to change this thinking?
6. Describe the behavior of anyone whom you know who displays any of the following symptoms: negativism, stupor, depression, delirium.
7. What are some of the things that the Federal government has done to help the mentally ill?
8. Describe a program of education that is aimed at the prevention of mental and emotional illness.
9. Enumerate factors in family life that might lead to emotional disturbance.
10. What is being done in your community to help individuals who have some type of personality disorder?
11. Explain what is meant by *illusions, hallucinations,* and *delusions.* How do they differ from one another?
12. Name and discuss the basic elements of mental illness.
13. Interpret Leary's classification of interpersonal behavior.
14. Give examples of *flight* and of *fight* as symptoms of mental disturbance.
15. What are the basic causes of psychosomatic illness? How can psychosomatic illness be treated?
16. Name common examples of extreme aggressive behavior.
17. Study the data to discover the extent of the problem of mental illness in the United States. Report your findings.
18. List terms that are used to represent various types of neurotic and psychotic behavior.

19. Discuss the relationship between social change and mental health.

20. List commonly experienced symptoms of mental disorder. Discuss one type.

Selected Readings

Allport, G. W., *Pattern and Growth in Personality*. New York: Holt, Rinehart & Winston, Inc., 1961.

Cameron, N., *Personality Development and Psychopathology: A Dynamic Approach*. Boston, Mass.: Houghton Mifflin Company, 1963.

Coleman, J. C., *Abnormal Psychology and Modern Life*, 3rd ed. Chicago, Ill.: Scott, Foresman and Company, 1964.

Crow, L. D., and A. Crow (eds.), *Readings in Abnormal Psychology*. Paterson, N.J.: Littlefield, Adams and Co., 1958.

Hahn, M. E., *Psychoevaluation: Adaptation-Distribution-Adjustment*. New York: McGraw-Hill, Inc., 1963.

Kaplan, B. (ed.), *The Inner World of Mental Illness: A Series of First-person Accounts of What It Was Like*. New York: Harper & Row, Publishers, 1964.

Kisker, G. W., *The Disorganized Personality*. New York: McGraw-Hill, Inc., 1964.

Lehner, G. F. J., and E. Kube, *The Dynamics of Personal Adjustment*, 2nd ed. Englewood Cliffs, N.J.: Prentice-Hall, Inc., 1964.

Nunakawa, W. D., *Human Values and Abnormal Behavior: Readings in Abnormal Psychology*. Chicago, Ill.: Scott, Foresman and Company, 1964.

Rosen, E., and I. Gregory, *Abnormal Psychology*. Philadelphia, Penna.: W. B. Saunders Company, 1965.

Royce, J. E., S.J., *Personality and Mental Health*, rev. ed. Milwaukee, Wisc.: The Bruce Publishing Company, 1964.

Stern, E. M., *Mental Illness: A Guide for the Family*, 4th ed. New York: Harper & Row, Publishers, 1962.

Stern, P. J., *The Abnormal Person and His World*. Princeton, N.J.: D. Van Nostrand Company, Inc., 1964.

Strange, J. R., *Abnormal Psychology: Understanding Behavior Disorders*. New York: McGraw-Hill, Inc., 1965.

Thorpe, L. P., B. Katz, and R. T. Lewis, *The Psychology of Abnormal Behavior: A Dynamic Approach*, 2nd ed. New York: The Ronald Press Company, 1961.

Zax, M., and G. Stricker (eds.), *The Study of Abnormal Behavior: Selected Readings*. New York: The Macmillan Company, 1964.

⁋ 11 ⁋

THE
PSYCHONEUROSES
AND THE
PSYCHOSES

A PSYCHONEUROSIS or minor personality disorder may result from a failure to attain socially acceptable behavior in the satisfaction of a primitive urge. A person may suffer from frustrations and inhibitions or from an inability to satisfy his natural wants and inner drives. Predisposing causes operate when the restrictions of the environment set up conflicts as precipitating causes of the disorders. Even though the conflicts reach the surface, the underlying causes may remain unknown.

Fixed parental attitudes, prejudices, denials, and shocks experienced during childhood may have produced devastating repressions that serve to weaken the individual's mental immunity and to pave the way to disassociation. Temporary mental disturbance may be the result of fatigue, disappointment, or other emotional stress or strain. In general, however, the psychoneurotic has ambivalent emotional attitudes toward conflict situations and often feels trapped by these attitudes.

The most serious forms of mental and emotional disorders are known as the *psychoses*. The psychotic person rejects the world of reality and builds a dream world to meet his own unconscious needs. He is as handicapped emotionally as a person suffering from a fracture of the leg is handicapped physically. He usually is misunderstood by the mentally and emotionally normal person, especially since most individuals have abnormal tendencies of one kind or another.

THE PSYCHONEUROSES

The term *neurosis* or *psychoneurosis* is used to designate a serious form of maladjustment that generally is milder in form than a psychosis. A psychoneurotic patient rarely is hospitalized. Estimates indicate that between 10 and 20 percent of patients admitted to general hospitals have psychoneurotic tendencies; the majority of psychoneurotics do not require hospitalization.

A psychoneurosis is not a disease but rather represents a range of maladjustments that can affect an individual's behavior and make it difficult for him to lead a "normal" life and carry on successful relationships with his fellows. Ginsberg distinguishes between normal and neurotic behavior as follows:

> To be "normal" is to be able to hold a job; have a family; not get in trouble with the law; enjoy the usual opportunities for pleasure; and be free of anxiety or symptoms which would prevent one's usual round of duties and commitments.
>
> Such timeworn clichés as "Everybody is a little crazy" or "There are as many nuts outside as inside the asylums" suggest the common recognition of the fact that the borderline between normal and "sick" is indeed vague and ill defined. It is not accurate, of course, to say that everyone is "neurotic" if that term is to have any usefulness. But two things can probably be said with considerable validity.
>
> First, all individuals possess what has been termed a "neurotic potential," which means that under certain circumstances everyone will experience feelings and display behavior which may be quite accurately termed neurotic (reflected in the Army's now familiar contention that "every man has his breaking point") .
>
> Second, everyone has some quirk of behavior, some

habit of thought, some conflict in emotions, which of itself is of small consequence but which, theoretically at any rate, may be considered abnormal. An increase in the intensity of any such pattern of behavior or thought, or the combination of a number of such deviations, may lead to a clinically significant neurosis. The executive who must have all his pencils neatly and freshly sharpened before he can begin work; the housewife made unnecessarily and often acutely uncomfortable by an unemptied ash tray or an unexpected guest; the compulsive smoker; the incessant doodler—these and many other such attitudes and patterns of behavior familiar to each of us in others and, on a moment's reflection, in ourselves illustrate this point.[1]

A psychoneurotic disorder usually is caused by a conflict between an individual's strong desires or ambitions and the restrictive force of society's accustomed standards of conduct. The thwarted urges or wants may represent highly personal attitudes or faulty habits that were developed during childhood. These attitudes or habits serve as predisposing conditions of emotional disturbance. Definite symptoms of mental disorder are displayed when the individual meets a shock-inducing situation or no longer can repress successfully his conflict condition. Concerning this conflict state, White says:

> Even if a person's life history loads him with overdriven strivings, he will try his best to achieve some kind of workable integration. He is under the same influences that prompt a healthy person to function as a unified and harmonious individual. His task, however, is much harder. Because of their compulsive intensity, overdriven strivings tend to block and exclude other tendencies. As Horney pointed out in her discussion of moving toward, against, and away from people, neurotic trends are incompatible with good social adjustment. If any one of these three attitudes is lifted to neurotic intensity, it more or less wrecks the chances of using the other two. Yet because the other two represent more or less universal human needs, it is not really possible to subordinate them completely. A person whose anxiety in human

[1] Sol W. Ginsberg, "The Neurosis," *Annals of the American Academy of Political and Social Science*, 1953, pp. 55–56.

relationships can only be held in check by an overdriven striving for seclusive withdrawal does not thereby obliterate his wishes for affection, esteem, and glory. These wishes needle him from time to time; he cannot feel satisfied with the limitations imposed by his chief defense. If a second trend is also reinforced in the interests of defense, the situation is still more difficult. He feels anxious if he cannot have seclusion and he feels anxious if he cannot have competitive success. The very intensity and indiscriminateness of over-driven strivings make it almost impossible to harmonize them with each other and with the rest of the person's tendencies. The result is chronic conflict: *neurotic conflict,* because one at least of the conflicting tendencies is an insatiable neurotic trend.[2]

The psychoneurotic needs affection and power. He strives for superiority but tends to feel inferior to others. Especially during adolescence the disturbed person attempts to inhibit his feelings and dislikes any show of feeling in others, and attempts to avoid any sign of impulsive behavior. He is concerned with maintaining rigid self-control. Repression is characteristic of the psychoneurotic.

Freud emphasizes the presence of repression in emotional disorders. His point of view has been generally accepted. A repressed emotion cannot run its natural course and tries to achieve an escape along a different path. According to Terruwe:

> A simple and frequent case may illustrate this. A boy experiences a sexual urge, but has a great fear of impurity and believes that the fact of experiencing this sexual feeling is in itself already sinful. Therefore, that fear will want to obliterate the sexual feeling immediately, something which is obviously entirely irrational. The sexual feeling is then repressed and disappears from consciousness, but it contin- ues to exist in his unconscious emotional life.
>
> This repression, then, is the cause of the neurosis. It is clear that a single repression cannot cause this lasting illness, but it never remains a single repression. The reasons why the

[2] Robert W. White, *The Abnormal Personality,* 3rd ed., New York: The Ronald Press Company, 1964, p. 228.

repression occurs are usually permanent; for instance, a mistaken understanding of sexual matters will continue to exert its influence for years and years. This results, on the one hand, in a hypertrophy of the repressing utility appetite which then will dominate the emotional life far beyond the normal limits, thus giving rise to a typically neurotic attitude toward reality. On the other hand, the ever repeated repression causes an accumulation of tensions until altogether they reach such an intensity that they break out in an illness, in a neurosis. According to experience, in the case of a true neurosis, this process of repression begins already in childhood, and the earlier the repression begins, the deeper the neurosis will be. In very serious cases one may even have to go back to infancy.

Another result of this repression in childhood is that the emotional life develops no further, but remains in the state in which it was at the moment of repression. The emotional life of the child has to grow, has to unfold, but when put under pressure it is incapable of doing so. This is the cause of the infantile characteristics which occur so frequently in the neurotic; as far as the somatic and intellectual development is concerned he is an adult, but in his emotional life he is still a child. This may sometimes give the impression that one is dealing with a psychopathic personality, but it would be entirely unjust to label such a person that way. The neurotic is healthy as far as his constitution is concerned; the abnormality is acquired in the years of growth as a result of an unnatural interference in the emotional life.[3]

Psychoneurotic behavior may be characterized by the overt expression of differing symptoms. There are many differences of opinion concerning possible classifications of psychoneurotic disorders. Coleman presents a summary of symptoms of psychoneuroses in Table 9.

Some writers are inclined to believe that we should attempt no classification. For purposes of discussion we shall consider that psychoneurotic disturbance falls into the following groups in

[3] A. A. Terruwe, *Psychopathic Personality and Neurosis*, tr. by Conrad W. Baars, ed. by Jordon Aumann, New York: P. J. Kenedy & Sons, and London: Burns & Oates (*The Priest and the Sick in Mind*), 1958, pp. 96–97.

TABLE 9

Summary Chart of Psychoneurotic Disorders

Reaction	Major Symptoms	Basic Dynamics
Anxiety	"Free floating" anxiety, usually punctuated by acute attacks.	Handling of internal or external threats by simple repression. Anxiety not yet "bound" or controlled by ego defenses.
Asthenic	Feelings of weakness, fatigue, lack of enthusiasm; somatic complaints.	Protection of self from anxiety aroused by unsatisfactory life situation in which individual feels trapped. Utter discouragement— feels too tired and sick to continue fight.
Conversion	Simulation of actual "organic" illness—may involve varied sensory, motor, or somatic illness symptoms.	Getting sick to escape from anxiety-arousing stress situation.
Dissociative	Amnesia, fugue, multiple personality, somnambulism.	Escape from anxiety-arousing conflicts by isolating or dissociating opposite poles of the conflict; in fugue reaction, for example, the conflict between fighting and withdrawal is solved by becoming amnesic and running away.
Phobic	Irrational fears which individual realizes are irrational but which lead to anxiety if not heeded.	Persistent conditioned fear or defensive reaction to protect self from anxiety-arousing stress by displacing anxiety from the actual danger to some symbolically related aspect of it which then protects patient from having to face the stress situation itself.
Obsessive-compulsive	Persistent thoughts or impulses which the individual realizes are irrational but which he cannot avoid.	Defensive reactions which protect the individual against internal and external threats by substitutive activities, reaction formation, isolation of anxiety-arousing desires from their affective base, counteracting of fears

TABLE 9 (*continued*)

Reaction	Major Symptoms	Basic Dynamics
		by compulsive rituals and by an obsessive "ordering" of the situation so that everything is under control and nothing can go wrong.
Neurotic-depressive	Feelings of dejection, discouragement, self-depreciation.	Extreme discouragement resulting from environmental setbacks with part of the anxiety aroused by these setbacks allayed by intropunitiveness (self-punishment).

Source: By permission of Scott, Foresman and Company from *Abnormal Psychology and Modern Life*, 3rd ed. by James C. Coleman. Copyright © 1964 by Scott, Foresman and Company, p. 228.

terms of similarity of symptoms in each of the respective groupings: phobias, obsessions, and compulsions (formerly grouped under the general class of psychothenia); neurasthenia, anxiety states, hysteria, and character neurosis. I already have discussed anxiety states (see chapter 9); I shall now discuss the other types.

Phobias, Obsessions, and Compulsions

Phobias or abnormal fears were referred to in the discussion of emotions. Emotionally disturbed states aroused by possible phobia-inducing situations seem to originate in remembered childhood experiences that at the time of their occurrence produced strong fear reactions. A phobia is associated with various conditions or situations that are related to earlier unpleasant incidents, such as fear of high places (*acrophobia*), fear of closed places (*claustrophobia*), fear of open places (*agoraphobia*), fear of pain (*algophobia*), fear of the dark (*nycophobia*), fear of animals (*zoophobia*), fear of the new (*neophobia*), and fear of strangers (*xenophobia*).

A person may not be able to free himself from an idea that he recognizes to be irrational. The idea or *obsession* usually is morbid. It persists against the individual's wishes. The obsession may lead to the development of compulsive behavior. A *compulsion* can be regarded as a tendency to perform meaningless motor acts that are recognized to be irrational. The engaging in compulsive behavior cannot be controlled, however. In order to avoid the recurrence of an obsession or to substitute for activity associated with it the individual may experience one or another compulsive tendency. Obsessive-compulsive neurosis represents a regressive and elaborate pattern of the basic defenses characteristic of the anxiety state. Obsessive ideas and compulsive behavior may function to a mild degree among many individuals, especially children.

Obsessions may be mild, such as mental repetition of relatively innocuous ideas, or they may represent irrational beliefs such as that the world is coming to an end before the year is over, that people who live in large cities are unfriendly, self-centered, or downright dishonest; that a particular political party or religious group is noneffective. Compulsive behavior may be no more serious than, for example, to throw a pinch of salt over one's shoulder if salt has been spilled, to attempt to divide the words of a sentence into groups of three words, or to compensate for an obsessive fear of failure by carrying a rabbit's foot in one's pocket and stroking it in a possible failure-producing situation. Some compulsions are extreme. The compulsive act may be personally or socially harmful, e.g., the impulse to steal (*kleptomania*), the compelling urge to drink liquor (*dipsomania*), or the impulse to set fires (*pyromania*).

Neurasthenia

The neurasthenic seems always to be suffering from feelings of physical and mental fatigue. He is self-preoccupied and depressed. He is also greatly concerned about the state of his health, although there may be no evidence of organic disorder. Certain areas of his body may be hypersensitive to pain; other areas may be insensitive. He tends to be irritable; his attention may be limited, and he may lack normal flow of ideas. He is likely to complain that he is suffering from one or another physical ailment: indigestion, constipation, heartache, eyestrain, spots before the eyes, shortness of breath, palpitation, hot or cold flashes, inability to swallow, or general aches and pains.

A neurasthenic recognizes the fact that he cannot cope with his problems. As an escape from meeting social or work demands he concentrates his attention upon his bodily processes. In rare cases this form of disorder is a result of overwork; it is more likely to be rooted in feelings of inadequacy. It may be possible that the inherited nervous system cannot meet successfully the demands upon it of complex modern life.

Hysteria

In some ways hysteria is similar to psychosomatic illness. The patient reports that he is suffering from one or another form of physical difficulty and demands immediate treatment. Sometimes it is difficult for the diagnostician to discover whether the symptoms have an organic basis or are imagined. The hysterical patient often suffers severe disorder, although his symptoms tend to be variable and inconsistent.

The hysteria-induced symptoms may be associated with any area of physical and physiological functioning—sensory, mental, or motor. Apparently, hysteria is caused by unconscious attempts to escape an unresolvable conflict situation, to adjust to a partial repression of a real or fancied sexual shock or trauma (the current viewpoint of psychoanalysts), or to compensate for hereditary inability to develop a normal personality synthesis.

Whatever the cause of the hysterical condition may be, the patient complains of one or more of the following disorders: partial or complete inability to hear or to see; muscular habits such as tics or tremors or spasms; prolonged periods of forgetting (*amnesia*); ambulant behavior during sleep (*somnambulism*); clouded states of awareness of self and surroundings (*trances* or *fugues*); and apparent epileptic seizures (*idiopathic epilepsy*). Hysterical symptoms differ in form and intensity, but the development of a symptom represents a struggle to escape a conflict situation or a means to achieve the fulfillment of strong wishes or desires.

Character Neurosis

Character can be defined as an individual's habitual adaptive reactions to environmental conditions and situations and to his relationships with the members of the various groups with which he is associated. Many neurotic disorders show themselves as distortions of conduct or behavior. The sexual pervert, the alcoholic, and the drug addict are examples. The development of character traits is healthy if maturation progresses with a minimum of anxiety or conflict. Desirable character formation is encouraged when the child is motivated early to achieve commendable self-discipline.

We experience cultural contradictions, such as religious emphasis upon tolerance and submissiveness and actual acceptance by society of ruthlessness and competition, or verbal adherence to a strict code of sexual behavior and generally accepted disregard of sexual control. Such contradictions between what we preach and what we practice can cause an individual to experience conflict in his thinking and doing, and a character neurosis is suffered by him.

The person suffering from a character neurosis may become withdrawn. This is especially found among adolescents. They find it difficult to integrate their recognition of the need to follow a moral code and their self-satisfying impulses. They may become daydreamers who retreat from any situation demanding competition or the assuming of responsibility. They may attempt to be socially competent through the carrying on of noncompetitive activities such as science, art, music, or writing.

Character neurotics may become antisocial, developing a sociopathic personality. Acts of delinquency or crime are common among them. They fail to recognize their duty to society; rather they seem to believe that other people are responsible for them and their welfare. According to Stern:

> The extreme type of the sociopath, often designated as "psychopath," with his blithe irresponsibility and apparent freedom from anxiety and guilt, has always aroused a certain horror. This type of person is often found among confidence men, chronic perpetrators of fraud, forgers, and other practitioners of nonviolent forms of criminality, whose actions cannot be explained in terms of want or need or other rational considerations, and who are characterized by extreme impulsivity and incorrigibility by experience. Because the behavior of the psychopath flouts the usual standards

of rational calculation and even of unconscious motivation, the attempt has been made time and again to account for the etiology of psychopathy in terms of extrapsychic, organic factors. . . .

The most important feature of the psychopath is his monumental irresponsibility. He knows what the ethical rules are, at least he can repeat them, parrot-like, but they are void of meaning to him. He blandly makes promises which he has no intention of keeping; he signs checks in the full knowledge that they are going to bounce; he gets married, or commits himself to some other major obligation, yet sees himself as unhampered as before. And he does all these things with the mien of entire righteousness, with all the indication of a conscience so clear that other men might envy him for it. No one can so well tell colossal lies while looking the person to whom he is talking straight in the eye. No one wears the mask of normality in so convincing a fashion. He is strikingly cool and sure of himself in situations where others would tremble and sweat with fear. Even when he has talked himself into obvious contradictions, even when a discovery of his misdeeds is imminent, he retains a superhuman composure. His personality seems to have been especially designed to mock our ideals of stoic self-mastery and unshakable superiority.

The psychopath has a cavalier disregard for the distinction between reality and fantasy. He is almost always an inveterate liar, for whom the distinction between truth and falsity is irrelevant. His lies tend to be an art for art's sake, and are often perpetrated without visible advantage to him. He exhibits a childish delight in fabrication, and shows an ingeniousness in the process which would be worthy of a better cause.[4]

THE PSYCHOSES

The psychotic suffers from the most serious type of mental and emotional disorder. His behavior usually represents complete or almost complete withdrawal from reality. He appears to

[4] Paul J. Stern, *The Abnormal Person and His World; An Introduction to Psychotherapy*, Princeton: D. Van Nostrand Company, 1964, pp. 136–138.

have given up the struggle for normal adjustment. The bases of some psychoses have been demonstrated to lie in bodily dysfunctioning (*organic psychosis*). For some psychoses there still is not known predisposing bodily cause. Hence these varieties of insanity or psychoses are regarded as functional disorders.

Causal Factors

The basic causes of functional disorders constitute a complex hierarchy of factors that have their beginnings in native constitution and environmentally stimulated experiences. Some causes can be regarded as predisposing; others are exciting in that a disturbing or conflict situation may give rise to relatively sudden disintegration and disorientation. In general, the cause of a psychosis or mental illness differs in strength and potential rather than in form from a condition or situation that arouses a relatively less serious personality disorder or psychoneurotic state. Common predisposing and exciting causes of temporary or persistent personality disorders are:

1. Shocks experienced during childhood, or habitual parental denials or prejudices.
2. Extreme worry, anxiety, fatigue, or boredom.
3. Exhaustion and toxemia produced indirectly by climatic conditions.
4. Lack of ability to satisfy a fundamental desire, such as the sex urge, according to social standards of conduct.
5. Stresses caused by unsettled social, economic, or political conditions.
6. Diseases (especially syphilis) ; trauma (especially spine or head injuries) ; toxic infections caused by narcotics, alcohol, or body poison usually forming in the gastrointestinal tract.
7. Periods of physiological change, such as puberty and the menopause.
8. Great emotional shock brought about by an extremely frightening experience, the sight of the wounded or dying (as in war or a serious accident) , sudden death of a close relative or friend, and similar situations.

Rarely does a psychotic patient pass through a psychoneurotic stage. Thorpe, Katz, and Lewis list in Table 10 the significant differential factors between psychoses and psychoneuroses.

The general characteristics of a psychosis include such factors as: the patient loses contact with reality; he needs to be hospitalized; he does not understand the nature of his illness; he

TABLE 10

Principal Differential Factors Between Psychoses and Psychoneuroses

Factor	Psychoneuroses	Psychoses
General behavior	Affect only part of the personality; the socially organized individual is not deranged; in contact with reality.	Affect the whole personality; the socially organized individual is completely disorganized; not in contact with reality.
Nature of symptoms	Usually transitory and stationary; only mildly incapacitating for social participation; speech disturbances infrequent.	Usually lasting and progressive; usually incapacitating for social participation; speech disturbances frequent.
Orientation	Patient rarely loses orientation to environment.	Patient frequently loses orientation to environment.
Insight	Patient usually has insight into nature of his behavior.	Patient rarely has insight into nature of his behavior.
Social aspects	Behavior rarely injurious or dangerous to patient or to society; patient rarely needs institutional care.	Behavior frequently injurious or dangerous to patient or to society; patient frequently needs institutional care.
Treatment	Patient usually easily managed; permanent cure therefore more readily attained.	Patient usually difficult to manage; permanent cure attained with difficulty.

Source: Louis P. Thorpe, Barney Katz, and Robert T. Lewis, *The Psychology of Abnormal Behavior*, 2nd ed., New York: The Ronald Press Company, p. 376. Copyright © 1961.

displays symptoms of hallucinations, delusions, or violent behavior; his behavior may be dangerous to himself or others. Coleman presents a summary chart in which he outlines the psychotic disorder, the general symptoms, and tentative psychodynamics or behavior. We present his chart in Table 11.

The frequency of occurrence of six different psychoses among first admissions to mental hospitals is presented in Table 12.

TABLE 11

Summary Chart of Functional Psychoses

Psychotic Disorder	General Symptoms	Psychodynamics (tentative)
Schizophrenic Reactions		
Simple reaction	Reduction of external interests and attachments, impoverishment of interpersonal relationships, neglect of hygiene and appearance. Apathy and indifference common, but not conspicuous delusions or hallucinations.	Simple retreat from anxiety-arousing stress to lower level of psychobiological functioning involving emotional indifference and lowered aspiration.
Hebephrenic reaction	Shallow, inappropriate emotional responses, silliness, mannerisms, bizarre delusions, stereotypes, unpredictable hollow giggling.	Severe personality decompensation with fragmentation of thought processes, loss of faith in self and world, social withdrawal, and surrender to disintegration.
Catatonic reaction	Conspicuous motor behavior, with either generalized inhibition (stupor, mutism, negativism, waxy flexibility) or hyperactivity.	Individual momentarily overwhelmed by problems but struggling desperately to find some system of beliefs, some faith on which he can build.
Paranoid reaction	Delusions of grandeur and/or persecution; hallucinations, usually with constant attitude of suspiciousness and hostility. Sometimes expansive delusional system predominates, with delusions of omnipotence, remarkable talents, and high social status.	An attempt to maintain ego integrity by projecting blame for difficulties onto "enemies" and/or by compensating grandiose delusions However, individual so overwhelmed by reality that delusions are not well systematized and personality disorganization is severe.
Childhood schizophrenia	Withdrawal, disorganization of thought processes, distorted emotional reactions and fantasy. Hyperactive, autistic.	Atypical psychological development with marked disturbances in parent-child relationships. Frequently evidence of constitutional abnormalities.

TABLE 11 (continued)

Psychotic Disorder	General Symptoms	Psychodynamics (tentative)
Paranoid Reactions		
Paranoia	Systematized delusions of persecution and/or grandeur with rest of the personality remaining relatively intact.	Defense against self-devaluation resulting from feelings of failure; blame is projected on others. Imagined persecution seen as proof of own importance.
Paranoid state	Delusions of grandeur and/or persecution—not so well systematized as in paranoia but without bizarre fragmentation and deterioration of the paranoid schizophrenic. Hallucinations common.	Similar to above but less systematized and usually precipitated in predisposed individual by particular anxiety-arousing stress situation. Usually transient, with spontaneous recovery.
Affective Reactions		
Manic-depressive reaction	Exaggerated mood swings with elation and overactivity or depression and underactivity or a combination or alteration of these. Bizarre, poorly systematized delusions and hallucinations.	Attempts to cope with anxiety-arousing feelings of failure by a "flight into reality" or by intropunitiveness with self-recrimination and self-punishment to "undo" or "pay price" for failure.
Psychotic depressive reaction	Similar to depressive pattern above, but not cyclical.	Similar to depressive pattern above, with external precipitating factors more common.
Involutional psychotic reactions	Depression, usually with agitation, in absence of history of manic-depressive reaction. Two main types: those characterized chiefly by depression, with predominant mood of hopelessness, and guilt; self-recrimination; and those centering around paranoid delusions.	Overreaction to feelings of failure to achieve goals and to approaching old age with no hope of future attainment. Allays anxiety in part by self-punitiveness but anxiety-arousing stress remains too great, leading to severe personality disorganization without spontaneous recovery.

Source: By permission of Scott, Foresman and Company from Abnormal Psychology and Modern Life, 3rd ed. by James C. Coleman. Copyright © 1964 by Scott, Foresman and Company, pp. 342–343.

TABLE 12

First Admissions* to State and County Mental Hospitals in the United States
by Selected Psychoses, 1960–1964

Psychosis	1960 249 of 280 Hospitals	1961 268 of 285 Hospitals	1962 271 of 285 Hospitals	1963 262 of 284 Hospitals	1964 256 of 289 Hospitals
Meningoencephalitic syphilis	531	459	306	195	154
Acute brain syndromes, alcohol intoxication	3,320	3,890	3,648	3,497	3,026
Cerebral arteriosclerosis	18,137	19,428	16,577	16,141	14,973
Senile brain disease	9,179	9,474	7,482	6,768	5,969
Manic depressive and psychotic depressive	4,331	4,829	4,120	3,984	4,214
Schizophrenic reaction	29,224	31,687	25,698	24,463	23,308
Total	64,722	69,767	57,831	55,048	51,644

* Beginning with 1962, this category was changed to Admissions with No Prior Psychiatric Inpatient Experience.
Source: *Patients in Mental Institutions,* Part II, State and County Mental Hospitals, 1960–1964,
U.S. Dept. of Health, Education, and Welfare, Public Health Service.

BRIEF INTERPRETATION OF
CERTAIN PSYCHOSES

Whether the cause of a mental disorder is a single factor or a
combination of factors, persistent abnormalities of behavior are
organized by psychiatrists into certain major classifications. In
order to acquaint the reader with some of the more common
forms of mental disorders a brief interpretation is given of each
of six of the types. I shall consider the acute brain syndromes, alcoholic psychoses, manic-depressive psychoses, senile brain disease,
cerebral arteriosclerosis, and schizophrenia (dementia praecox).

Acute Brain Syndromes

A brain or head injury may produce mental disorders that
are accompanied by certain characteristic symptoms. Brain inju-

ries vary in form and effect. There may be extensive destruction of tissue or a simple concussion that accompanies the physical shock, whether or not the skull is fractured. The immediate symptom may be delirium followed by hysteria, with a gradual development of memory defects and general mental deterioration. An injury of this type may lead to dementia praecox, paresis, and manic-depressive psychoses. Cerebral birth trauma may result in left-handedness, convulsions, stuttering, enuresis, or dull or subnormal intelligence.

ALCOHOLIC PSYCHOSES. These psychoses develop as a result of excessive or continuous use of alcohol. There are different forms of alcohol-induced disorders that have their roots in the personality of the individual, his relative resistance to alcohol, and the extent of his indulgence. These forms are delirium tremens, Korsakow's psychosis, acute hallucinosis, and alcoholic deterioration. In delirium tremens, the patient may be restless and irritable, exhibiting varying hallucinations, as of snakes and worms. In acute hallucinosis, the hallucinations of hearing and the delusions of persecution are very acute, often driving the patient to suicide.

The symptoms of Korsakow's psychosis include paralysis of the extensor muscles, disorientation, lack of retention, suggestibility, mental fatigue, and sometimes hallucinations. Alcoholic deterioration caused by excessive and continued indulgence results in disturbances of motion, sensation, and intellect. If the patient cannot be cured of his indulgence in liquor he will show a history of progressive mental impairment.

The use of alcohol may be incidental to other psychoses. It may accompany general paralysis, manic-depressive psychosis, or epilepsy. If the patient has a psychopathic personality, however, and is not a chronic drinker, he may develop an alcoholic psychosis as a result of a few drinks during a relatively short spree.

MANIC-DEPRESSIVE PSYCHOSES. Mental disorders traceable to emotional disturbances of a functional nature may be characterized by emotional oscillations and recurrences. A patient, however, may continue to display continued manic behavior, or give evidence of a consistently depressed state. The manic phase is characterized by overactivity and restlessness; slightly elevated temperature, and increased pulse rate; emotional elation; flight of ideas; violent or impulsive behavior. There may be little or no impairment of memory or clouding of consciousness, except in periods of great excitement during which time ideas seem to flow too rapidly for coherent expression. The patient is noisy, boisterous, and uncontrollable in his exuberance. He may quote poetry which he cannot recall during his normal periods, or repeat vulgar jokes or risqué stories which normally would be most distasteful to him.

During the depressed phase these symptoms are reversed. The pulse and temperature may be slightly subnormal, the skin feels cold and dull, and headaches may be common. The patient is emotionally depressed, and neither talks nor responds to questions, unless forced to do so. His answers to questions are given either by a movement of the head or in monosyllabic whispers. His mood is sad, hopeless, uneasy, or anxious; he seems to have a sense of physical and mental insufficiency and often exhibits suicidal tendencies. Extreme depression may be characterized by qualities of almost complete stupor similar in their appearance, although different in nature, to the catatonic type of dementia praecox. The patient usually suffers from ideas of death and self-destruction.

In the mixed phase, the respective symptoms of the other types are so mixed that the resulting state cannot be classified properly as belonging to any one of them. For instance, the patient may exhibit symptoms of depression with flight of ideas, agitated depression, or maniacal stupor. A patient may exhibit the symptoms of the manic at one time and those of the depressed at another, recurrently in circulatory fashion.

SENILE PSYCHOSES. As the name suggests, senile dementia is a disease of old age in which there is brain atrophy, progressive mental deterioration with loss of memory, and physical deterioration. The patient loses his accustomed acuity of sensation and keenness of perception, and may become disoriented. His memory is defective for the immediate past but may be unusually clear concerning details of his earlier experiences. Attention wanders and ideas become limited and fixed; illusions, hallucinations, and delusions are common; irritability, suspicion, quarrelsomeness, abusiveness, and resistance may be marked.

CEREBRAL ARTERIOSCLEROSIS. Patients suffering from cerebral arteriosclerosis represent about 14 percent of admissions to hospitals for the mentally ill. It sometimes is difficult to distinguish between arteriosclerosis psychosis and senile psychosis, except that in the former the individual's personality pattern is better preserved than in the latter, although the sclerotic patient may suffer more from such symptoms as dizziness, difficulties of coordination, and headaches. The onset of this disorder may be sudden but recovery is more likely than in senile psychosis.

In arteriosclerosis the supply of blood to the tissues becomes inadequate as a result of the hardening and thickening of blood vessels, especially of the arterial walls of the brain, affecting in particular the occipital and temporal areas. This brain damage may cause, in addition to the neurological symptoms, incoherence, cloudiness, restlessness, and loss of contact with the environment. There may be displayed delusions of persecution or of grandeur similar to those found in general paresis but usually far less developed than in paresis. The older person becomes relatively confused and somewhat depressed and agitated. The younger person who is afflicted with the disorder tends to manifest compensatory behavior; his delusions take on the nature of delusions of grandeur in order to counteract feelings of personal incompetencies.

Schizophrenia (Dementia Praecox)

Included in schizophrenia are mental disorders that usually occur during adolescence or early adulthood and that are characterized by a number of symptoms. The main categories of schizophrenia are: *simple type* (heboidophrenia), *hebephrenic type*, *catatonic type*, and *paranoid type*. The exact causes of these disorders have not been determined. Yet, the basis for the disturbance usually is found in unstable personality development that may result from any of many factors—physical weakness, inherited tendencies, unhealthful responses to inherent urges and desires, and consistent failure to adjust successfully to changing demands of childhood and adolescence.

Although schizophrenia is perhaps the most common form of mental and emotional disorder, the early symptoms are difficult to recognize. The social importance of this psychosis, however, can be recognized from the fact that it represents about one fourth of the incidence of mental disorders. Many normal young people tend to exhibit behavior traits such as occasional resentment, suspicion, uncooperativeness, and a retreat into dream fulfillment of desires and ambitions. It is not always easy to determine with any degree of certainty whether the individual's behavior is a normal striving for self-realization or an abnormal inability to meet the problems that are inherent in the maturing processes.

Schizophrenia is characterized by a seclusive type of behavior, by indifference, silliness, blunting of the emotions, fantastic ideas, autistic thinking, a belief that other persons are attempting to control the individual's behavior, and similar traits. The onslaught is generally slow but persistent and progressive. The symptoms of this particular psychosis are many. The patient cannot hold a job, withdraws from reality, and becomes generally inactive and given to daydreaming. He may become rigid and stubborn, his eyes may dilate, his body may quiver if he is forced to do something, and he may reach the point where he has little interest in his appearance or in what is happening about him.

SIMPLE TYPE (*heboidophrenia*). The simple type of schizophrenia is characterized by idleness, daydreaming, lack of interest in others, and gradual development of an apathetic state. The individual becomes indifferent to his family and friends and, even though he has been doing well in school, loses interest in scholastic success and becomes indifferent to what others think about him.

HEBEPHRENIC TYPE. Hebephrenia is characterized by a more abrupt onset than is found in simple dementia, although the beginning of hebephrenia may remain unnoticed for several months. Individuals so affected show a persistent tendency toward silliness, grimacing, smiling, laughing, and other grotesque behavior. Their hallucinations are fleeting, and the delusions are changeable and fantastic. There is great emotional deterioration. The fantastic ideas may be neurotic or religious, or may center in self-destruction. The patient's listlessness and lack of interest in the world about him gradually may develop into a retreat from the world of reality into a world of dreams or fantasy.

CATATONIC TYPE. In the catatonic type of schizophrenia, symptoms of headache, insomnia, confusion, and listlessness may precede the chronic onset. The patient exhibits a prominence of negativistic reactions accompanied by stupor or excitement. The latter includes hallucinations and peculiar behavior.

Muscular tension and negativism are associated with the cata-tonic stupor. Patients have been known to retain for long periods of time any position of the body in which they have been placed.

The patient may become mute and refuse to talk, or he may show extreme excitement and inflict injury upon any person near him or break any object within his reach. During a visit of the writer to the home of a person who was suffering from this disorder, the afflicted person was outwardly calm although he exhibited body tremors. Shortly after the departure of the writer, the patient attacked his brother with great strength. His mental and emotional deterioration had become so great that he lost all interest in work, family, and social life. He had to be hospital-ized.

PARANOID TYPE. The paranoid type of schizophrenia is char-acterized by delusions and by ideas of persecution or grandeur, which are somewhat systematized and accompanied by halluci-nations. During the early stages of this type of disorder it is often difficult to determine whether it is the paranoid type of schizo-phrenia or a paranoia psychosis. In the latter the symptoms are confined to the development of a delusional system. It does not involve hallucinations as is characteristic of the paranoid type of schizophrenia.

The patient often not only believes that others are persecut-ing him, but imagines that they perform many activities such as whispering about him, spying on him, or poisoning his food. He hears voices directing him to perform great feats or telling him he is an important world figure. Early in the illness the patient appears to misinterpret reality and his own emotional reactions. In later stages the delusions tend to become more disorganized. He experiences mental images that represent magical powers and he may be able to make detailed drawings of some of them. His entire world image becomes increasingly complicated for him. In general, he displays a loss of interest in people, objects, and reality. There seems to be a far-reaching disintegration of person-ality.

Recently there has developed an interest in schizophrenia that occurs in childhood. Concerning the onset of schizophrenia in childhood years Lauretta Bender says:

After twenty years on the Psychiatric Division of Belle-vue Hospital, recognizing, describing, and treating schizophrenic children 2 to 12 years of age, viewing their life course longitudinally by follow-up studies up to the age of 30, I have arrived at the following definition: Childhood schizophrenia involves a maturational lag at the embryonic level characterized by a primitive plasticity in all areas from which subsequent behavior develops. It is genetically determined and activated by a physiological crisis such as birth. Anxiety is both the organismic and psychological response calling forth defense mechanisms. Three types of clinical pictures are presented depending in part upon the defense mechanisms: (1) the pseudodefective or autistic, retarded, inhibited child; (2) the pseudoneurotic with any number of neurotic mechanisms and evident anxiety; (3) the pseudopsychopathic with paranoid ideation, and a tendency to act out in antisocial behavior.

Schizophrenia is a disorder of the whole organism and when it appears in early childhood it persists for the lifetime of the individual. Schizophrenia so viewed should not be equated with psychosis. The child who presents the picture of the pseudodefective type is typically autistic and may have been retarded in maturation from the beginning or may have regressed after an early normal or even precocious development. He is repressed, inhibited, withdrawn, often mute and incapable of adequate object relationships. Physically he has labile and inadequate homeostasis, inadequate muscle tone which does not respond to stimulation although he may be hypersensitive, and his postural and motor behavior retains immature features even at an embryonic level.

Children with the pseudoneurotic response present the picture of a pan-neurosis with anxiety, phobias, obsessions, compulsions, hypochondriacal or psychosomatic defenses, concern about body boundary, body image, identity, and orientation in time or space. They have disturbed thought processes, disturbed speech, sensory distortions, exaggerated or unusual introjections and projections; they often have exaggerated insight, and an exaggerated capacity to relate and often with high verbal, graphic capacities and other symbol formations and high intelligence. Such children are most frequently recommended for psychotherapy.

Children with the pseudopsychopathic behavior present a picture in late childhood or early puberty of paranoid ideation and difficulties in identifying with or relating to peers, and negativism to authoritative figures. They tend to aggressive and antisocial acting-out behavior. They wander about aimlessly or with compulsive and obsessional patterns such as counting street numbers, following the sky line of the city or riding all the subways. They feel persecuted and "fight back" often on command of voices; they are impulsively aggressive, fire-setters, and nonconformists. They lack insight and feel no guilt or anxiety.[5]

[5] Lauretta Bender, "Schizophrenia in Childhood—Its Recognition, Description, and Treatment," *American Journal of Orthopsychiatry*, July, 1956, pp. 499–500.

QUESTIONS AND PROBLEMS

1. Discuss the causes of a psychoneurosis; of a psychosis.

2. Show that a psychoneurosis represents a range of maladjustments.

3. Justify the statement that everyone has some "quirk" of behavior. Illustrate.

4. Prepare a list of psychoneurotic needs.

5. Show the relationship between repression and psychoneuroses.

6. Discuss the symptoms of psychoneurosis.

7. Show that anxiety states are related to the psychoneuroses.

8. Discuss obsessions and compulsions in human behavior. Give examples.

9. If you have an obsession or a compulsion, indicate how it affects you.

10. Differentiate among neurasthenia, hysteria, and character neurosis.

11. What are the characteristics of a psychopath?

12. List and describe briefly the various types of functional psychoses.

13. Study Table 12 showing first admissions of psychoses to state and county hospitals from 1960 to 1964. What conclusions can you formulate? Be specific.

14. Compare symptoms of alcoholic psychoses, manic depressive psychoses, senile psychoses, and cerebral arteriosclerosis.

15. Name and describe the main characteristics of the various types of schizophrenia.

16. If possible, visit a mental hospital and observe psychotic patients. Report your findings.

17. Discuss childhood schizophrenia.

Selected Readings

Arieti, S. (ed.), *The American Handbook of Psychiatry.* New York: Basic Books, Inc., 1959.

Beck, S. J., *Psychological Processes in the Schizophrenic Adaptation.* New York: Grune & Stratton, Inc., 1965.

Bergler, E., *Parents Not Guilty of Their Children's Neuroses: New Concepts in the Psychology of Human Behavior*. New York: Liveright Publishing Corporation, 1964.

Bosselman, B. C., *Neurosis and Psychosis*, 3rd ed. Springfield, Ill.: Charles C Thomas, Publisher, 1964.

Dorcus, R. M., and G. W. Shaffer, *Abnormal Psychology*, 4th ed. Baltimore, Md.: The Williams and Wilkins Company, 1950.

Hollingshead, A. B., and F. C. Redlich, *Social Class and Mental Illness: A Community Study*. New York: John Wiley & Sons, Inc., 1958.

Horney, K., *Self-Analysis: Neurosis and Human Growth*. New York: W. W. Norton & Company, Inc., 1942.

Kasanin, J. S., *Language and Thought in Schizophrenia*. New York: W. W. Norton & Company, Inc., 1964.

Laughlin, H., *The Neuroses*. Washington, D.C.: Butterworth, Inc., 1965.

Maslow, A. H., and B. Mittlemann, *Principles of Abnormal Psychology*, rev. ed. New York: Harper & Row, Publishers, 1951.

Masserman, J. H., *Behavior and Neurosis*, 2nd ed. New York: Hafner, 1964.

Mental Disorders (Diagnostic and Statistical Manual). Washington, D.C.: American Psychiatric Association, 1952.

Myers, J. K., and B. H. Roberts, *Family and Class Dynamics in Mental Illness*. New York: John Wiley & Sons, Inc., 1959.

Opler, M. K. (ed.), *Culture and Mental Health: Cross-Cultural Studies*. New York: The Macmillan Company, 1959.

Putney, S., and G. J. Putney, *Normal Neurosis: The Adjusted American*. New York: Harper & Row, Publishers, 1964.

Strecker, E., *A Basic Psychiatry*. New York: Random House, Inc., 1952.

Terruwe, A. A., *Psychopathic Personality and Neurosis*. Trans. by C. W. Baars, ed. by Jordan Aumann. New York: P. J. Kenedy & Sons, 1958.

THERAPEUTIC
TREATMENT
OF PERSONALITY
DISORDERS

THE SITUATION of individuals suffering from mental and emotional disorders is not completely hopeless. Many patients respond well to existing therapeutic techniques. It can be hoped that scientific study will continue to advance knowledge concerning the causes and the prevention of emotional disorders and the eventual cure of serious mental illness.

For the well-trained physician the diagnosis and treatment of physical disorders are relatively simple in comparison with the diagnosis and treatment of mental and emotional disorders. The inner reactions that comprise human personality and the subtle interactions that constitute human interrelationships make it difficult for therapists to diagnose behavior disorders correctly and to apply appropriate therapeutic measures successfully.

The degree of successful rehabilitation that can be expected from the utilization of remedial or therapeutic techniques depends in large measure upon fundamental personal factors. Progress toward ultimate recovery is possible for the disturbed person when his difficulty is recognized early and appropriate treatment administered. The development of the mental hygiene point of view and growth in scientific understanding of mental illness are reflected in improved methods of treatment. Some of the more commonly utilized modern therapeutic techniques for the treatment of mental and emotional disorders include psychosomatic medicine, psychotherapy, psychiatry and psychoanalysis, group therapy, and occupational and recreational therapy.

ATTITUDES TOWARD PERSONALITY DISORDERS

Our modern complex civilization is extremely challenging to young and old alike. It is difficult for even an intelligent, well-intentioned individual to remain thoroughly well adjusted in all the trying situations in which he may find himself. He constantly is beset by a host of stimuli that interfere with his accustomed patterns of response. The effect upon him of these emotion-disturbing factors depends in good part on his own attitudes toward himself and his problems, as well as the attitudes of those who share with him the responsibility for his welfare.

There is probably no person who at every moment of his life is completely sane, emotionally stable, and entirely controlled and objective in his behavior. Everyone, either temporarily or for long periods during his life, exhibits modes of behavior that display more or less deviation from the accepted normal pattern. Peculiar mannerisms, irrational fears, uncontrollable compulsions, fixed ideas, inconsistent likes and dislikes, emotional outbursts, retreats, and other abnormalities are common to a greater or lesser degree.

Therapy of Minor Disturbances

There is danger in too much introspection or self-criticism. If the daily routine of life is met with an average amount of self-satisfaction and social approval, there is probably little evidence of maladjustment. Some habits of behavior may need redirection, but for the majority of people therapy is possible outside the walls of a hospital for the mentally ill. What is needed by the layman, therefore, is some understanding of the causes and symptoms of mental illness and a willingness to accept himself and others with all their possibilities of "queer" behavior without too much concern.

The responsibility of parents in this matter is great. A child is entitled to be born of emotionally stable parents and to experience a home life that affords him opportunities for adequate personality adjustment. Furthermore, his parents should be on the alert for any behavior manifestations that deviate from the usual range of childhood aberrations.

Too often parents refuse to recognize peculiar characteristics in their child's attitude and behavior. They minimize or resent any suggestions made by counselors or friends that the child may need to be examined by an endocrinologist or a psychiatrist. A high school student, for example, began to exhibit unusual reactions such as writing meaningless jingles, playing with dangerous laboratory equipment, and bursting into recitation rooms without adequate reason. The parents refused to respond to suggestions offered by the school counselor. The girl eventually wandered away from home but was returned. In this episode the parents were more concerned about the possible disgrace to the family in any discussion of their daughter's conduct than they were about her emotionally disturbed condition.

The beginnings of mental disorder should be recognized by teachers, counselors, employers and others. Parents should be helped to accept the reality of the situation. The emotionally disturbed person needs to be helped to resolve his conflicts and develop a constructive attitude toward himself in his relations with others. There is a point, however, beyond which the layman should not attempt to apply therapy. The services of the trained specialist are needed if the individual does not seem to respond effectively to skillfully administered lay or semi-professional treatment.

Personnel Involved in Treatment of Personality Disorders

Some forms of mental illness appear to be relatively quick in their onslaught and can be cured by the application of appropriate therapy. Others, although their symptoms may seem to be slower in making their appearance, may be difficult, if not impossible, to cure. Excellent facilities and highly trained specialists are needed for effective therapy. Scientific knowledge has progressed so that the prognosis for some of the psychoses is good.

Many schizophrenic patients and those with manic-depressive psychoses have excellent chances of recovery if skilled people get to them in time.

The physician, the psychiatrist, the psychoanalyst, and the clinical psychologist share the responsibility to help the mentally ill regain their health. At one time the physician attempted to combine mental therapy with the treatment of physical illness. Unfortunately, the medical practitioner is not equipped in his preparation to do more than bolster the morale of his patient. He is particularly unprepared to help in cases of functional psychoses, as he is likely to look for an organic base for the disorder. Hence the mentally ill patient should be, and usually is, referred by the physician to a psychiatrist for treatment.

Psychiatrists are generally successful in their treatment of individuals with mental and emotional disorders. This is true especially if the disturbance is associated with organic difficulties and the patient gives evidence of physical symptoms of disturbance.

A well-trained psychoanalyst utilizes the functional approach in his therapy. As originated by Sigmund Freud, psychoanalysis employs methods such as free association, catharsis, dream analysis, and transference. Through analysis, the patient can be helped to gain an understanding of the roots of his present disturbance. Although this method may necessitate long periods of treatment, the patient may gain sufficient insight to readjust his thinking and behavior.

The clinical psychologist is pre-eminently successful in his treatment of functional psychoses. He understands the ways in which these difficulties are developed. Through the utilization of psychoanalytic techniques, directive and nondirective interview approaches, and testing techniques, he is enabled to study the fundamental bases of the mental disorder and to motivate the patient toward readjustment.

The work of the psychiatric social worker is invaluable as a means of obtaining objective and accurate data concerning the life history of the patient. The nurse also serves an important function. The hospital or public health nurse can do much to help build the client's morale. The nurse in a mental hospital works closely with her patients. Thus she is enabled to study reactions which, when reported by her to the doctor, can be of inestimable benefit to him in the application of appropriate therapies. Trained occupational and recreational therapists are gaining for themselves respected places in mental hospitals.

THE APPLICATION OF THERAPY

Victims of mental and emotional disorders can often be helped through the application of somatic treatment or/and psychotherapy. Epilepsy, for example, responds to the application of specific medicines and what can be referred to as "practical management," such as hospitalization of the patient or the sending of children to foster homes, camps, or suitable schools.

The therapist must maintain an objective, nonmoralistic attitude toward his patient. His primary aim is to aid the patient in such a way that the latter will develop patterns of satisfactory behavior, both now and in the future. To achieve this, various techniques are utilized.

The Utilization of Psychosomatic Medicine

The combining of scientifically acquired knowledge concerning psychiatric and clinical treatment with an improved understanding of the significance of psychogenic illness has resulted in an increased appreciation of the importance of psychosomatic medicine. In this area of therapeutic treatment emphasis is placed upon the relationships that exist between emotional reactions and the onset and course of a physical disease.

According to estimates, from one third to one half of all persons who believe they need medical care exhibit symptoms of physical disorder that are rooted in emotional disturbances. These patients are not hypochondriacs to the extent of imagining symptoms of illness. They may suffer as much pain as does the victim of a purely organic disorder. The physician or psychiatrist recognizes the fact that psychosomatic illness requires treatment of the organism as a whole. It is impossible to separate the *psyche* from the *soma*. The classification of ailments as either functional or organic is outmoded. Diseases and disorders involve the whole personality and, consequently, the whole personality needs to be treated.

It is difficult to explain to an individual that his illness may have an emotional origin. At the same time, he can be helped to understand (1) that emotional maladjustments and illnesses are not evidences of weakness, (2) that much of behavior, even the functioning of body organs, is motivated by strong forces of unconscious origin, and (3) that these forces often are beyond the influence of consciousness. The individual then can be assured that he has a strong and normal mind, but that he needs help so far as his emotions are concerned. The person who helps him readjust his emotional life needs to possess a reassuring personality.

IMPORTANCE OF THE PHYSICIAN'S PERSONALITY. The physician who deals with a psychosomatic patient not only has an understanding of disease but also displays a sympathetic attitude toward the behavior of sick people. He is concerned with the emotional reactions of the patient as well as challenged by the patient's physical disorder. To a certain extent he identifies himself with the emotional pain which his patient suffers. He understands psychopathology as well as tissue pathology. Most important of all, he realizes that his patient is an emotionally disturbed person who is expressing emotional pain in physical form.

Physicians and nurses recognize the effect of the emotions upon a patient who is suffering from a physical ailment. A patient's chances of recovery are associated closely with his attitude toward his illness, his degree of cooperation with the physician and nurse, and the kind and amount of worry caused by the temporary interruption of accustomed activities. The onslaught of a serious disease may cause an emotionally unstable person to become so depressed that he is unable or unwilling to cooperate with the physician toward an amelioration of the disease condition or to help in the fight for recovery. According to Vaughan:

The value of the psychosomatic approach is in its emphasis upon the treatment of the *whole* person, involving a study of his *physical* condition *and* an exploration of his *mental* outlook. The traditional medical concentration upon the organic will be corrected by the psychosomaticists who call attention to the importance of including the psychological angle too. The doctor who is wise will consider the personality of the sick person in addition to taking his temperature, thus obeying the famous dictum of Sir William Osler: "It is more important to know what kind of patient has a disease than to know what kind of disease a patient has." [1]

CLOSE ASSOCIATION OF BODY AND MIND.   There are certain illnesses in which there is no question concerning the existence of a physical cause of the disorder. Numerous attempts have been made to demonstrate the presence of a psychogenic element in certain bodily disorders. Among these are such body conditions as ulcers, asthma, skin diseases, arthritis, and migraine headaches. Although the symptoms are real, psychological measures are needed in their effective treatment. The psychogenic factor, however, lies in the personal history. The body organ that breaks down does so because it has been unable to meet the stressful conditions that have affected the individual continuously over a period of time. Full recovery can be obtained only when the psychogenic irritants have been discovered and removed; otherwise there is likely to be a temporary recovery followed by relapse.

The close association of the body and mind in psychosomatic medicine is clarified by Stern when he says:

> In a new guise the old body-mind problem bedevils psychosomatic medicine. To some extent, the inadequacy of our clinical formulations may simply reflect the philosophical perplexities in this field. Seemingly transparent conceptual formulas become obscure and enigmatic as soon as we probe deeper into their meaning. What do we really mean and imply when we talk of the psychic causation of a somatic event or when we talk in terms of body "acting on" mind? Many workers who use these and similar formulas appear to conceive of body and mind as quasi-autonomous objects, capable of exerting effects on one another (*interaction model*). Such a model, however, leads to manifest philosophical absurdities. [2] Other workers, in an attempt to avoid the philosophical fallacies inherent in the interaction model,

---

[1] W. F. Vaughan, *Personal and Social Adjustment*, New York: The Odyssey Press, 1952, p. 210.

[2] K. Jaspers, *Allegemeine Psychopathologie*, 6th ed., New York: Springer, 1953, p. 223. [Stern]

espouse a *double aspect* theory according to which physiology and psychology study different aspects of one and the same thing.[3] This formula also involves us in philosophical difficulties. Mitscherlich [4] attempts to solve the problem by diluting the notion of psychosomatic etiology to a concept of *psychosomatic simultaneity* which limits itself to stating purely temporal relationships (simultaneity, antecedent-consequent) between observed bodily and mental events. Dunbar [5] takes a somewhat different tack. She wants to formulate psychosomatic events in terms of a physicalistic *field concept*. Field theory regards any phenomenon "as an event taking place in a field, an event on which every force in the field may have a bearing, be it active or relatively inert. This field is a complex of forces and conditions which may be plotted by uses of axes and coordinates. Time is regarded as one of the relevant factors." [6] It is dubious whether Dunbar's field theory amounts to much more than a fanciful way of restating the familiar notion of a multiplicity of determining conditions, which, in the case of psychosomatic disease, would be partly "organic" and partly "psychic."

More interesting is the position adopted by Merleau-Ponty.[7] According to the French author, the terms "body" and "mind" describe different levels of integration or signification. It is meaningless to talk of causal operations between different planes of integration. The only legitimate meaning to be assigned to the statement that, in a given instance, mind has "acted upon" body is that we are describing human conduct which has been integrated at such a level that it has rational signification and cannot be accounted for in physicalistic or biological terms. Inversely, to say that body has acted on mind can only mean that one deals with less integrated behavior that can be understood without residue

[3] F. Alexander, *Psychosomatic Medicine: Its Principles and Applications*, New York: W. W. Norton & Company, 1950, p. 36. [Stern]

[4] A. Mitscherlich, "Contribution à la Théorie Psychoanalytique des maladies psychosomatiques," *L'Evolution Psychiatrique*, Fasc III, 529 ff. [Stern]

[5] F. Dunbar, *Psychiatry in the Medical Specialties*, New York: McGraw-Hill, 1959. [Stern]

[6] *Ibid.*, p. 4. [Stern]

[7] M. Merleau-Ponty, *La Structure du Comportement*, Paris: Presses Universitaires de France, 1953. [Stern]

in terms of mechanistic or biological notions. Only at these lower levels of integration, which usually reflect deficiency or pathology, do causalistic notions apply.[8]

Psychotherapeutic Techniques

The utilization of psychotherapeutic techniques is expanding rapidly. Yet there is still a gap between the needs of human beings for aid in re-establishing adequate individual and social patterns of behavior and the application of scientifically evolved therapeutic techniques. Psychotherapy is marked by direct interaction between the therapist and the patient. In so far as it is possible, the therapist helps the victim of a mental or emotional disturbance to rid himself of what have become unnatural fears and worries, obsessions, compulsions, or more or less deep-seated abnormal states.

PSYCHOTHERAPY AND PSYCHIATRIC TREATMENT. It is important to distinguish between psychotherapy and psychiatric treatment. Too often their meanings are confused, or the terms are used synonymously. Essentially, the confusion stems from the fact that the difference in emphasis between the two is not generally understood. Therapeutic or mental hygiene approaches are utilized in situations that represent a wide range of individual and social maladaptations which are not forms of serious mental illness. Moreover, it often is difficult to achieve a clear-cut differential diagnosis of the disturbed condition, and to select an appropriate form of therapy. For cases of relatively mild disorder, rehabilitation probably can be brought about through the utilization of one or more of the following types of community-service agencies: medical, psychological, social, educational, religious, and recreational. All of these community agencies utilize the resources of one another as ancillary services when the nature of the individual's adjustment problem seems to require such cooperation. Many of these community services utilize psychotherapeutic techniques to aid an individual resolve his conflicts. If a person is the victim of a severe mental disorder, however, he needs the services of a psychiatrist. Psychiatric treatment involves

[8] Paul J. Stern, *The Abnormal Person and His World: An Introduction to Psychotherapy*, New York: D. Van Nostrand Company, 1964, pp. 128–129.

the utilization of various types of intensive therapy, including the administration of appropriate drugs.

Psychotherapy can be defined as any "non physical" technique that is aimed at the improvement of the client's attitudes, emotional reactions, and overt behavior. The utilization of this technique implies the treatment of mental and emotional disturbances through suggestion and re-education. The sufferer may not be so ill that he needs to be treated by a psychiatrist; he can be helped by a physician or another trained service worker in whom he has confidence. Similarly, a mentally ill patient's confidence in his psychiatrist often is as effective, if not more so, than is prescribed medication.

Suggestion and reassurance can relieve tensions. Whenever it is possible, the psychotherapist appeals to the intelligent understanding of the patient by explaining the relationship that exists between physical illness and emotional disturbance. If a patient, for example, believes that he has a cancer, the use of X-ray, in addition to reassurance, helps the individual understand that he is physically sound. The therapeutic treatment may take the form of repeated encouragement that reassures the patient who seeks help because he believes he is suffering from one or another ailment.

Most physicians, psychologists, and social workers apply therapeutic techniques in several ways. According to Maslow:

> . . . psychotherapy takes place in six main ways: (1) by expression (act completion, release, catharsis) as exemplified in Levy's release therapy; (2) by basic need gratification (giving support, reassurance, protection, love, respect) ; (3) by removing threat (protection, good social, political, and economic conditions) ; (4) by improved insight, knowledge, and understanding; (5) by suggestion or authority, and (6) by positive self-actualization, individuation, or growth. It is probable that all systems of psychotherapy use all these basic medicines in varying proportions.[9]

It may be difficult for an emotionally disturbed person to gain an adequate appreciation of the origin of his existing conflict situation. He needs to evaluate, in light of his total experi-

[9] A. H. Maslow, *Motivation and Personality*, New York: Harper & Brothers, 1954, p. 306.

ence pattern, his fears, anxieties, feelings of insecurity, and general lack of adjustment. Some insight can be achieved through his informal, permissive talks with the psychiatrist. Some psychologists, physicians, and psychiatrists believe that self-understanding is achieved best through psychoanalysis, a technique that has been used extensively by Sigmund Freud and his followers.

PSYCHOTHERAPY AND LEARNING.   The utilization of psychotherapy connotes direct interaction between the therapist and the patient and stresses the value of the learning process rather than that of environmental conditions or the state of the body tissues. It represents new learning or relearning by the patient. He is helped to gain a new perspective on his habituated behavior reactions. Psychotherapy aids in the removing of blocks in his understanding of himself and his actions, and differs from education as such and persuasion.

The psychotherapist avoids the teaching of subject matter. He is concerned with encouraging positive and socially acceptable adaptations in, or adjustments of, the patient's abnormal state, thereby stimulating the return of good and satisfying mental and emotional health. Successfully applied psychotherapy is an aid in increasing the patient's insights. Its application represents a process of mental and emotional growth as the patient with the therapist engages in appropriate learning activities. Holland has this to say concerning the relationship between psychotherapy and learning:

> The objective of psychotherapy is to change the habit structure of a person so that his behavior will result in more pleasant and fewer unpleasant experiences. The means by which this change is to be achieved is an effective communicative relationship between the person and the psychotherapist.
>
> Freud suggested three specific objectives for psychotherapy: catharsis, the achievement of insight (especially into unconsious processes), and the working through of the transference neurosis. Although any or all of these experiences may occur in psychotherapy and have some therapeutic value, these objectives, singly or together, still leave the psychotherapeutic process inadequately defined and conceptualized.

I believe that any adequate conception of psychotherapy must begin with the assumption that it is a learning
process. This implies that the psychotherapist must be concerned with *all* the conditions necessary for learning, un-
learning, or relearning. These conditions are: motivation,
cue, response, and reinforcement.[10]

Although psychotherapy is usually conceived as a learning
process, the implications of this idea have not been fully accepted. It is believed, however, that human behavior is modifiable
through the application of psychological procedures. Based on
the fact that psychotherapy rests on the assumption that psychological approaches affect human behavior, Bandura, in discussing
"factors impeding integration," says:

> . . . the deliberate use of the principles of learning in
> the modification of human behavior implies, for most psy-
> chotherapists, manipulation and control of the patient, and
> control is seen by them as antihumanistic and, therefore,
> bad. Thus, advocates of a learning approach to psychother-
> apy are often charged with treating human beings as
> though they were rats or pigeons and of leading on the road
> to Orwell's 1984.
>
> This does not mean that psychotherapists do not influ-
> ence and control their patients' behavior. On the contrary,
> in any interpersonal interaction, and psychotherapy is no
> exception, people influence and control one another.[11] Al-
> though the patient's control of the therapist has not as yet
> been studied (such control is evident when patients subtly
> reward the therapist with interesting historical material and
> thereby avoid the discussion of their current interpersonal
> problems) , there is considerable evidence that the therapist
> exercises personal control over his patients. A brief examina-
> tion of interview protocols of patients treated by therapists
> representing differing theoretical orientations, clearly reveals
> that the patients have been thoroughly conditioned in their
> therapists' idiosyncratic languages. Client-centered patients,

10 Glen A. Holland, *Fundamentals of Psychotherapy*, New York: Holt,
Rinehart and Winston, 1965, p. 56.
11 J. D. Frank, "The Dynamics of the Psychotherapeutic Relationship,"
Psychiatry, Vol. 22 (1959) , pp. 17–39; and B. F. Skinner, "Some Issues
Concerning the Control of Human Behavior," *Science*, Vol. 124 (1956) , pp.
1057–66. [Bandura]

for example, tend to produce the client-centered terminology, theory, and goals, and their interview content shows little or no overlay with that of patients seen in psychoanalysis who, in turn, tend to speak the language of psychoanalytic theory. Even more direct evidence of the therapists' [12] controlling influence is provided in studies of patient-therapist interactions.[13] The results of these studies show that the therapist not only controls the patient by rewarding him with interest and approval when the patient behaves in a fashion the therapist desires, but that he also controls through punishment, in the form of mild disapproval and withdrawal of interest, when the patient behaves in ways that are threatening to the therapist or run counter to his goals.

One difficulty in understanding the changes that occur in the course of psychotherapy is that the independent variable, *i.e.*, the therapist's behavior, is often vaguely or only partially defined. In an effort to minimize or to deny the therapist's directive influence on the patient, the therapist is typically depicted as a "catalyst" who, in some mysterious way, sets free positive adjustive patterns of behavior or similar outcomes usually described in very general and highly socially desirable terms.

It has been suggested, in the material presented in the preceding sections, that many of the changes that occur in psychotherapy derive from the unwitting application of well-known principles of learning. However, the occurrence of the necessary conditions for learning is more by accident than by intent and, perhaps, a more deliberate application of our knowledge of the learning process to psychotherapy would yield far more effective results.[14]

[12] R. W. Heine, "An Investigation of the Relationship Between Change in Personality from Psychotherapy as Reported by Patients and the Factors Seen by Patients as Producing Change," unpublished doctoral dissertation, University of Chicago, 1950. [Bandura]

[13] Albert Bandura *et al.*, "Psychotherapists' Approach-avoidance as a Process of Incidental Learning," *Journal of Consulting Psychology*, 1960, pp. 1–8; E. J. Murray, "The Content-analysis Method of Studying Psychotherapy," *Psychological Monographs*, 1956, Whole No. 420; J. M. Rogers, "Operant Conditioning in a Quasi-therapy Setting," *Journal of Abnormal and Social Psychology*, Vol. 60 (1960) , pp. 247–252. [Bandura]

[14] Albert Bandura, "Psychotherapy as a Learning Process," *Psychological Bulletin*, March, 1961, pp. 154–155.

THE THERAPEUTIC INTERVIEW.   If skillfully handled, psychiatric interviews afford the physician an opportunity to gain an understanding of his patient's difficulties. The interviewer carefully participates in the interview and observes the patient's reaction. During a series of interviews, there usually develops a close personal interaction between the client and the psychiatrist.

Psychiatric interviews have cathartic value. The patient is motivated to talk about his troubles. As he repeatedly recounts his experiences and gives overt expression to his fears, frustrations, and conflicts, the patient comes to minimize the importance to himself of his pent-up feelings. Gradually, new insights into his condition are achieved. If the emotional disorder is not too fixed, the individual can come to understand and accept his condition, and gradually he makes desirable changes in his behavior.

Psychotherapeutic interviews have for their aim positive and desirable modifications of the client's attitudes and behavior. An interpersonal relationship develops between the interviewer and the interviewee which is marked by the possession of certain attitudes by the therapist and the client. Shoben describes the therapist's attributes as (1) *concern* for and interest in his client, (2) *nonretaliatory permissiveness,* that permits the client to discuss any topic he desires, including his attitudes toward the counseling situation, (3) insistence on an increasing degree of candor and self-exploration. He tries to encourage *honesty* and *understanding.*[15]

The therapist's attitude toward the patient, especially in the initial interview is very important. He should have a receptive attitude. Holland says about the initial interview:

> The psychotherapist's playing a predominantly receptive role in this initial contact may be considered another means by which he enhances the patient's feeling of value or importance. The patient may indicate that he does not know what to say. By telling him that whatever he wants to say will probably be of value, we indicate confidence in his intelligence and judgment.

[15] Edward J. Shoben, Jr., "A Theoretical Approach to Psychotherapy as Personality Modification," *Harvard Educational Review,* Vol. 23 (1953), pp. 128–142.

Actually we have rather effective means of controlling the content of the patient's communication without obviously correcting or redirecting him in a manner that may tend to make him feel inadequate or "in the wrong." The communicative techniques of reflection, restatement, and summarizing are very useful at this stage for this purpose. By these means we can indicate what we are more interested in by including such material in our reflection, restatement, or summary and not including in such responses that information which we consider less relevant.

More directly, but in a positively reinforcing way, we can use evaluation, for example: "What you were just saying about your relationship with your boss is very interesting. I would like to hear more about that." In this manner we can elicit particular information that we may want for our preliminary evaluation while still complimenting the patient on his discernment in bringing the topic into his conversation.

Generally we avoid more active intrusions into the communication during the middle part of the initial appointments. I have found that inclinations to evaluate (prematurely), interpret, share, give information or make suggestions at this time are likely to be due to feelings somewhat threatened in our own ego-evaluation as compared with our evaluation of the patient. We interpret our own impulse to intervene in these ways as indicating that we are anxious to do something to assert or establish our own value. Such competitive impulses are injurious to the relationship (status of the psychotherapist in the patient's eyes) in any event.[16]

The interview has value as a means of helping an individual bring about personal adjustments in his various life areas. There are two generally accepted approaches to the interview situation, *directive* (counselor-centered) and *nondirective* (client-centered) . According to E. G. Williamson [17] and other clinical psychol-

[16] Holland, *Fundamentals of Psychotherapy*, pp. 254–255.
[17] E. G. Williamson, *Counseling Adolescents*, New York: McGraw-Hill, 1950.

ogists who advocate the direct approach, the therapist assumes leadership during the interview. The counseling technique includes the following steps: *analysis, synthesis, diagnosis,* and *prognosis.* Before and during the interview, the therapist arranges to have the client take tests, etc., that will supply pertinent data. Although the therapist may make judgments about needed treatment, he accepts the client as he is. Both the therapist and the patient (if possible) accept responsibility for the course of action to be taken. In directive counseling, the therapist may include statements such as "If I were you I would . . ." and "It would seem to me that the best thing for you to do would be. . . ." The weight of decision-making would thereby be placed on the shoulders of the therapist.

In the nondirective approach the role of the counselor primarily is that of a listener as he attempts to help the client. The client is responsible for gaining insight into his basic difficulty and for arriving at a possible solution. The therapist helps the client clarify his thinking by injecting an occasional comment such as "You have found that . . ." or "You therefore believe that. . . ." A well-known client-centered therapist, Carl Rogers, explains the purpose of this form of psychotherapy thus:

> It aims directly toward the greater independence and integration of the individual rather than hoping that such results will accrue if the counselor assists in solving the problem. The individual and not the problem is the focus. The aim is not to solve one particular problem, but to assist the individual to *grow,* so that he can cope with the present problem and with later problems in a better-integrated fashion. If he can gain enough integration to handle one problem in more independent, more responsible, less confused, better-organized ways, then he will also handle new problems in that manner.[18]

In his discussion of the characteristics of a helping relationship such as exists between the psychotherapist and the client,

[18] Carl R. Rogers, *Counseling and Psychotherapy,* Boston: Houghton Mifflin Company, 1942, pp. 28–29. Also, for application of the nondirective approach, see Carl R. Rogers, *Client-Centered Therapy,* Boston: Houghton Mifflin Company, 1951.

Rogers [19] interprets this relationship as one that brings about "more appreciation of, more expression of, more functional use of the latent inner resources of the individual." After describing certain studies [20] dealing with the nature of the helping relationship, Rogers raises questions concerning ways in which he can create a helping relationship. Roughly stated, these questions deal with such elements as (1) consistency and dependability of attitude, (2) expressiveness without ambiguity, (3) the experiencing of positive attitudes toward the other person, such as liking, respect, and interest in, (4) strength as a separate person, (5) personal security that permits separateness, (6) a feeling of empathy toward the other individual's feelings and personal meanings, (7) acceptance of the other person as he is, (8) sufficient sensitivity so as not to become a threat to the individual, (9) the freeing of the individual from a fear of external evaluation, and (10) the viewing of the individual as a person in the process of becoming rather than in light of the therapist's and the patient's past.

Rogers summarizes his treatment of the helping relationship with these words:

> If I see a relationship as only an opportunity to reinforce certain types of words or opinions in the other, then I tend to confirm him as an object—a basically mechanical, manipulable object. And if I see this as his potentiality, he tends to act in ways which support this hypothesis. If, on the other hand, I see a relationship as an opportunity to "reinforce" *all* that he is, the person that he is with all his existent potentialities, then he tends to act in ways which support *this* hypothesis. I have then—to use Buber's term—confirmed him as a living person, capable of creative inner development. Personally I prefer this second type of hypothesis.

CONCLUSION

In the early portion of this paper I reviewed some of the contributions which research is making to our knowledge *about* relationships. Endeavoring to keep that knowledge in

[19] Carl R. Rogers, "The Characteristics of a Helping Relationship," *Personnel and Guidance Journal*, September, 1958, pp. 6–15.
[20] *Ibid.*, p. 6.

mind I then took up the kind of questions which arise from an inner and subjective point of view as I enter, as a person, into relationships. If I could, in myself, answer all the questions I have raised in the affirmative, then I believe that any relationships in which I was involved would be helping relationships, would involve growth. But I cannot give a positive answer to most of these questions. I can only work in the direction of a positive answer.

This has raised in my mind the strong suspicion that the optimal helping relationship is the kind of relationship created by a person who is psychologically mature. Or to put it in another way, the degree to which I can create relationships which facilitate the growth of others as separate persons is a measure of the growth I have achieved in myself. In some respects this is a disturbing thought, but it is also a promising or challenging one. It would indicate that if I am interested in creating helping relationships I have a fascinating life-time job ahead of me, stretching and developing my potentialities in the direction of growth.

I am left with the uncomfortable thought that what I have been working out for myself in this paper may have little relationship to your interests and your work. If so, I regret it. But I am at least partially comforted by the fact that all of us who are working in the field of human relationships and trying to understand the basic orderliness of that field are engaged in the most crucial enterprise in today's world. If we are thoughtfully trying to understand our tasks as administrators, teachers, educational counselors, vocational counselors, therapists, then we are working on the problem which will determine the future of this planet. For it is not upon the physical sciences that the future will depend. It is upon us who are trying to understand and deal with the interactions between human beings—who are trying to create helping relationships. So I hope that the questions I ask of myself will be of some use to you in gaining understanding and perspective as you endeavor, in your way, to facilitate growth in your relationships.[21]

In his efforts to bring about modifications of the client's behavior, the therapist needs to gain the confidence and coopera-

[21] *Ibid.,* p. 15.

tion of the client. It may happen that the latter fails to give full cooperation; he may resist the therapist and his attempt at bringing about changes in attitudes and behavior. Knight has this to say about resistance on the part of the patient.

> All of the major psychotherapies—i.e., those which aim at significant alterations in personality structure rather than at symptomatic relief—have encountered the phenomenon discovered by Freud and termed by him "resistence." This refers to those partly conscious and partly unconscious tendencies in patients to resist self-knowledge and change, as manifested in their inability to remember the past or to capture for therapeutic use the current unconscious content. Resistance produces a marked slowing down of progress, often approaching stalemate, while symptoms continue unaltered. Technical problems of resistance are among the most difficult to solve, and the long duration of major psychotherapy is attributable chiefly to this phenomenon.[22]

Comment and Recapitulation

The successful utilization of psychotherapy depends upon the kind and degree of verbal communication that is established between the patient and the therapist. The therapist is concerned with the development by the patient of a "hierarchy" of behavior responses that will enable him to function adequately in his various human relationships. Through techniques, such as summarizing, reflecting, restating, and interpreting, the patient is helped to make positive adjustments in his life experiences. Psychotherapy is a helping technique intended to enable the patient to achieve emotional stability. The psychotherapist's own emotional status is an important factor in the patient's behavior pattern. The process of psychotherapy is succinctly stated by Rogers in his recapitulation of ideas in one of his articles. It follows:

> I have tried to sketch, in a crude and preliminary manner, the flow of a process of change which occurs when a client experiences himself as being received, welcomed, un-

[22] Robert P. Knight, "A Critique of the Present Status of the Psychotherapies," *Bulletin of the New York Academy of Medicine*, Vol. 25 (1949), p. 114.

derstood as he is. This process involves several threads, separable at first, becoming more of a unity as the process continues.

This process involves a loosening of feelings. From feelings which are unrecognized, unowned, unexpressed, the client moves toward a flow in which ever-changing feelings are experienced in the moment, knowingly and acceptably, and may be accurately expressed.

The process involves a change in the manner of experiencing. From experiencing which is remote in time from the organic event, which is bound by the structure of experience in the past, the client moves toward a manner of experiencing which is immediate, which interprets meaning in terms of what is, not what was.

The process involves a loosening of the cognitive maps of experience. From construing experience in rigid ways which are perceived as external facts, the client moves toward developing changing, loosely held construings of meaning in experience, constructions which are modifiable by each new experience.

The process involves a change in the self. From being a self which is not congruent with experience, the client moves through the phase of perceiving self as an object, to a self which is synonymous with experience, being the subjective awareness of that experience.

There are other elements, too, involved in the process: movement from ineffective to effective choice, from fear of relationships to freely living in relationship, from inadequate differentiation of feelings and meanings to sharp differentiation.

In general, the process moves from a point of fixity, where all these elements and threads are separately discernible and separately understandable, to the flowing peak movements of therapy in which all these threads become inseparably woven together. In the new experiencing with immediacy which occurs at such moments, feeling and cognition interpenetrate, self is subjectively present in the experience, volition is simply the subjective following of a harmonious balance of organismic direction. Thus, as the process reaches this point, the person becomes a unity of flow, of motion. He has changed; but, what seems most significant, he has become an integrated process of changingness.[23]

In his discussion of psychoanalysis, Rosen provides us with an excellent summary of psychotherapy.

The psychotherapeutic relationship has several distinguishing features. First, it is openly and deliberately concerned with this problem of wish-fulfillment, of emotional relief. The individual says, in effect: "I need help." And the psychotherapist says, in effect: "I am going to help you." Second, the relationship is deliberately intended to be one-sided. Ideally, at least, the psychotherapist is not supposed to be seeking his own emotional relief from the individual whom he is treating. He may incidentally benefit himself by giving help—but he is not supposed to be seeking any emotional benefits for himself, under false pretenses. Third, the psychotherapeutic relationship is deliberately controlled and guided from start to finish, by the psychotherapist. He does not let the individual run away with the treatment. Nor does he expect that psychotherapy will just "happen" in the course of many treatment sessions. Psychotherapy is not to be defined as self-help or as accidental help; any such definition would make the relationship indistinguishable from the various kinds of social relationships that the individual could develop elsewhere. Fourth, the psychotherapeutic relationship is *therapeutic*. It does something, it gives relief to the individual, it fulfills or modifies the wishes that finally drove him into the "before" and "after" pictures that an observer might see. There should be change in the individual's behavior, in his self-concept, in his conceptions of other individuals. If these changes have not occurred, then the whole purpose of treatment has been defeated.[24]

PSYCHOANALYSIS

Sigmund Freud can be called the "father of psychoanalysis." As a physician he found that many of his patients were suffering

---

[23] Carl R. Rogers, "A Process Conception of Psychotherapy," *American Psychologist*, April, 1958, p. 150.
[24] John N. Rosen, *Psychoanalysis: Direct and Indirect*, Doylestown, Penna.: The Doylestown Foundation, 1964, pp. 35–36.

emotional inadequacy as well as physical ailment. Freud first experimented with hypnosis as a means of helping these patients to regain emotional normalcy. He found, however, that he could achieve as good results by permitting his patients to talk about their difficulties in a relaxed state as could be obtained by the use of hypnosis.

Freud explained personality as consisting of the *id, ego,* and *superego.* The id, the fundamental basis of personality, may be suppressed by the ego. The superego or *conscience* manifests itself in attempts to raise personal behavior to higher levels. Freud is also credited with the development of the *libido* theory, according to which pleasant stimulation of sensitive parts of the body has an erotic base. Erikson [25] claims that the development of the ego stresses the interactive nature of behavior. Psychoanalysis stresses the fact that the ego is responsible for the organization of behavior in its relationship to environmental conditions and situations. Self-understanding is needed and is achieved best through the application of psychoanalytic techniques.

After Freud's introduction of the concept of psychoanalysis, proponents of this theory (neo-Freudians) built upon his original thesis. According to Holland,

> Among those who parted from Freudian psychoanalysis before 1940, Adler, Rank, and Horney represent important additional aspects of development that pose a marked challenge to the individual's ability to adjust. These center around inferiority feelings, dependency needs, and problems of handling hostility, respectively. Jung was among the first, but by no means the last, to differ fundamentally with Freud on the sexual aspects of his motivational theory. Klein (and Anna Freud) extended psychotherapeutic techniques into the years of childhood and stressed the significance of very early emotional trauma. Reich indicated that the total "character structure" of the patient is his problem, so that it is impossible to deal with "the problem" as an isolated entity.
>
> Among the later neo-Freudians, Fromm represents the social critic who discusses the "sick" aspects of society as well as the "sick" aspects of the individual's attempts to adjust to society. Franz Alexander has worked for greater efficiency and

[25] E. H. Erikson, *Childhood and Society,* New York: W. W. Norton & Company, 1950.

flexibility in psychotherapeutic techniques. Rosen has presented drastic new departures in means of communicating with and relating to the patient. Szasz has finally separated psychotherapy from the model presented by the medical treatment of organic conditions. Harry Stack Sullivan has presented a theoretical orientation that differs markedly from psychoanalytic thinking on certain points regarding both the therapeutic relationship and therapeutic communication, at least so far as emphasis is concerned.[26]

The importance of the value of psychoanalysis in the study of the origin of human values continues unabated. The extent to which many basic values have their origin in childhood has become an area of study. An investigation of the use of psychoanalysis to discover the origins of values in children was undertaken by Rudolf Ekstein in the Reiss-Davis Clinic for Child Guidance, Los Angeles. His summary statement is given here.

In summary, psychoanalysis suggests that the origin of all values, moral and otherwise, rests in the early child-parent situation. The teacher is much like the gardener who gets the small seedling from the nursery. He must find ways to make values continue to develop and he will do so best if he can help the child to see what is full of meaning of skill and knowledge. This capacity on the part of the teacher depends on a stable committed professional self and on an institutional atmosphere in which the professional self can function in such a way as to fulfill the individual values of the teachers. The origin of value then is the need of the helpless, met by the constant fulfillment of the trustworthy.

The transmitting mechanism of value is the child's identification with the adult generation. The survival of values rests on available opportunity for their fulfillment. Our school system then must accept the need, provide the opportunity and the techniques for identificatory learning, and offer the skills and the knowledge which will maintain the continuity of the individual and the society within our value system, which guarantees life, liberty and the pursuit of happiness.[27]

[26] Holland, *Fundamentals of Psychotherapy*, pp. 30–31.
[27] Rudolf Ekstein, "Psychoanalysis Looks at the Origins of Values in Children," *Educational Leadership*, May, 1964. p. 526.

Psychoanalysis is the process of eliciting from a patient a body of significant information concerning his past emotional and mental life. The client discloses past incidents in his life that may have continued to exert a potent influence upon his emotional reactions. The psychoanalyst hopes to discover through psychoanalytic techniques the ways in which a pathological state has been produced. He then attempts to offer suggestions concerning definite methods of treatment.

A fundamental distinction between psychoanalysis and other procedures, somatic or psychic, is that it attacks the underlying emotional conflict rather than symptomatic behavior. In psychoanalysis, little attention is given to the symptoms as such. It may be comparatively easy to remove a particular symptom by suggestion; but if nothing is done about the underlying causative conflict the patient soon displays a new symptom. An example of this is the "eternal patient" who, as soon as he apparently is cured of one symptom, is back with another.

Freud was convinced that the symptoms of neurotic patients were in reality the expressions of mental conflicts. Emotional impulses were transformed into abnormal physiological functions through a process which was called conversion. Consequently, an hysterical paralysis was called a conversion symptom, since it represented an unconscious resolution of mental conflict of which the patient was completely unaware. The emotional catharsis, under hypnosis, of the original traumatic memories and their attendant emotions brought relief only temporarily since it was not fused with the consciousness of the patient when he was brought out of the hypnotic state.

Consequently, Freud cast about for another method of securing the recall of repressed memories in the waking or conscious state. He essayed a direct attack upon this problem by utilizing direct suggestion. He assured the patient that he could recall the past if he tried. Freud soon discovered that this frontal attack was futile. He then developed a new technique called *free association* which remains the cornerstone of the psychoanalytic procedure.

Freud reasoned that ideas were associated in the mind in two ways: (1) by logical relationships and (2) by emotional relationships. It was the latter type of association in which Freud was particularly interested. By having the patient recline on a couch with back to the physician, it was possible for the patient to relax and to speak his mind freely, i.e., to say whatever came to him. It did not matter whether it made sense or not, whether it was conventional or objectionable. The important principle was to report anything and everything that came to mind.

Freud evolved the theory, which has been confirmed by countless analyses, that the patient is relieved of the necessity for logical thinking; he reacts to the pressure of feelings and emotions rising to express themselves. Hence he reveals, through a free association of ideas and feelings, those clues which provide the analyst with the content of the deeper layers of the motivating factors. Through this method the patient gradually brings into consciousness the repressed memories and emotions which had been prevented from being recalled into consciousness because of resistances. This finally was the technique utilized by Freud to unlock the unconscious mind while the patient was conscious. The major problem, however, was how to overcome habitual resistances so that repressed memories could flow into consciousness.

In this connection Freud made an important discovery, which he called the *transference neurosis*. This was the essential dynamic mechanism for the resolution of resistances. Transference is a powerful instrument in accomplishing this end, since the patient inevitably transfers to the analyst his neurotic behavior patterns. Essentially, the patient relives his neurotic past in his present relationship. It is a type of *facsimile* of the patient's real-life neurosis of which the patient is cured step by step, as he is led through it with insight from one growth-stimulating experience to another. This aspect of the analysis came to be called *emotional re-education*, since it was a procedure arrived at for establishing permanent changes in the personality.

In this process of uncovering repressed material Freud found that his patients frequently reported dreams. The utilization of free association was an excellent technique for making an intensive study of these dreams as they related to the mental and emotional life of the patient. Repeatedly he discovered that a dream essentially was a "wish fulfillment." Like neurotic symptoms, it had definite meaning; it was a conscious expression of unconscious wishes or fantasies. By the skillful application of free association to the *manifest content* of the dream (which almost invariably was a disguise for the *latent content* or meaning), he was able to elicit the actual meanings which the censorship of the unconscious prevented from coming into waking life, except as they were disguised or masked in symbolic form.

Psychoanalysis, both as a depth psychology of personality and a therapeutic method, has had a pervading influence upon the development of psychotherapy and upon the course of psychological theory in general. Its most fundamental contributions have been the introduction of a dynamic approach to the study of personality, and the elaboration of a systematic theory of personality and behavior which encompasses the human personality in all its aspects, and throughout its life span. Moreover, Freud's theories were singularly fruitful in that they led coworkers and students to further discoveries and to the elaboration of additional psychotherapeutic methods and psychiatric techniques.

The Psychoanalytic Process Shared by Patient and Analyst

In psychoanalysis both the patient and the therapist share responsibility in the psychoanalytic process. The success of the therapy depends on the work done by the analyst and that of the patient as they interact in the situation. The outcomes are influenced by the fact that there are two persons involved in the interaction. Each person in the situation exerts considerable influence on the work of the other. The work of the patient is three-fold. According to Horney:

> There are three main tasks that confront the patient. Of these the first is to express himself as completely and frankly as possible. The second is to become aware of his unconscious driving forces and their influence on his life. And the third is to develop the capacity to change those attitudes that are disturbing his relations with himself and the world around him. . . .

Suggestions pertaining to the work of the analyst also are succinctly given by Horney in the following:

> The analyst's general task is to help the patient to recognize himself and to reorient his life as far as the patient

himself deems it necessary. In order to convey a more specific impression of what the analyst does in pursuing this goal, it is necessary to divide his work into categories and discuss these individually. Roughly, his work can be broken down into five divisions: observation; understanding; interpretation; help in resistance; and general human help.

To some extent the analyst's observations are not different from those of any observant person; to some extent they have a specific character. Like everyone else, the analyst will observe general qualities in the patient's behavior, such as aloofness, warmth, rigidity, spontaneity, defiance, compliance, suspicion, confidence, assertiveness, timidity, ruthlessness, sensitivity. In the mere process of listening to the patient he will, without direct effort, gain many general impressions: whether the patient is able to let himself go or is tense and constrained; whether he talks in a systematic, controlled fashion or is jumpy and scattered; whether he presents abstract generalities or concrete details; whether he is circumstantial or to the point; whether he talks spontaneously or leaves the initiative to the analyst; whether he is conventional or expresses what he really thinks and feels.

In his more specific observations the analyst learns, first, from what the patient tells him about his experiences, past and present, his relationships with himself and others, his plans, his wishes, his fears, his thoughts. Second, he learns from observing the patient's behavior in his office, for each patient reacts differently to arrangements concerning fees, time, lying down, and other objective aspects of analysis. And each patient reacts differently to the fact that he is being analyzed. One patient regards analysis as an interesting intellectual process but refutes the idea that he really needs it; another treats it as a humiliating secret; while a third is proud of it as a special privilege. Moreover, patients exhibit an endless variety of attitudes toward the analyst himself, with as many individual shades as exist otherwise in human relationships. Finally, patients show innumerable subtle and gross vacillations in their reactions, and these vacillations themselves are revealing.[28]

[28] Karen Horney, *Self-Analysis*, New York: W. W. Norton & Company, 1942, pp. 101, 123–124.

Evaluative comments pertaining to direct and indirect psychoanalysis are set forth by Rosen in the closing remarks of his recent discussion of the topic. They are presented here.

According to Eissler, psychoanalysis "offers at the social level" a therapy. I am inclined to object to this offering, on the grounds that it cannot be made good. I regard indirect psychoanalysis as a process of investigation, not as a therapeutic process. If it is true that the conventional psychoanalyst has as his goal the discovery and imparting of information—"self-knowledge"—to the individual, then conventional psychoanalytic investigation would seem to be the indicated procedure for him to follow. Perhaps I can focus my objections on the social offering, the promise of treatment. Why does the indirect psychoanalyst make this promise? Why does he make it, if he privately considers "therapy" to be a superficial kind of goal? Why does he not simply offer a course of self-exploration that might possibly lead to self-knowledge?

I suspect that the indirect psychoanalyst would not be able to stay in business if he openly disavowed his interest in treatment, if he ceased to hold out the promise of cure. As I mentioned earlier, in my experience it is a rare occurrence for an individual to prefer self-knowledge to treatment. If my experience is any sample of the usual psychoanalytic experience, then there must be a shortage of sincere seekers after self-knowledge.

I will never forget, or try to deny, the extent of my obligation to Freud. After all these years, we can still say that we owe our progress in psychotherapy largely to him. His investigations made psychotherapy possible. What I am saying is that investigation *per se* does not constitute psychotherapy. The therapeutic process is not a matter of impartial and detailed study. On the contrary, it is a matter of intense subjective involvement. The psychotherapist must intervene, he must make himself a prominent figure in the realities and unrealities of the individual whom he is treating, in order to have the necessary impact upon the individual's ego and superego. Only by bolstering the ego and ameliorating the superego can he break up the vicious cycle of need and frustration that originated in the individual's early maternal environment. Only by creating a new maternal environment can the psychotherapist make it possible for the individual to become adult psychologically, and to survive in adulthood, against the stresses of the present or the pressures of the past.[29]

GROUP THERAPY

There is an increasing need for help in resolving problems of adjustment. Moreover, there exists a serious dearth of psychotherapists for individual treatment. Hence professional workers have been experimenting with other ways of dealing with maladjustments. A practical answer to the quest for rehabilitating techniques to be applied to mentally disturbed men during World War II was found in *group psychotherapy*. The first conscious and deliberate utilization of group psychotherapy, however, was not included in the treatment of neurotic or psychotic patients. It was used with tubercular patients by Dr. Pratt, in Boston, about 1905. He called it class treatment, but it was the first attempt to apply group influences aimed at specific therapeutic goals.

Group Therapy in Action

The conducting of group therapy sessions requires considerable preplanning by the therapist. Although the sessions themselves may seem to be no more than a getting together of individuals to discuss topics of common interest to the group, there needs to be considerable structuring of the experience before the session begins. The procedure may reflect the nondirective permissiveness approach propounded by Rogers or it may adhere more closely to psychoanalytic techniques with emphasis on the transference factor in the meetings. Some therapists tend to be somewhat directive in their attitude toward the conduct of the sessions. If the nondirective approach is used, the group, as is true of individual therapy, may find it difficult to adjust to it. They look to the leader for guidance of their discussion.

[29] Rosen, *Psychoanalysis*, p. 49.

The number of patients involved may range from two to eight. Some therapists consider that best results are obtained with five or six participants. It is important for the success of this type of therapy that the members of the group represent similarity in the kind of emotional difficulty they are suffering. Sessions may be held once or twice a week, and usually continue from about five to ten months, although some therapists believe that a year or longer may be needed to achieve desired results.

The therapist, especially if he uses the nondirective approach, acts as an interpreter. He attempts to develop for the group what can be termed a constructive social experience. Although the leader may need to start the ball rolling at the initial meeting, the success depends upon his ability to motivate the various members of the group to carry on the discussion without intervention from him except as he may find it necessary to summarize what has been said or to redirect what may have become senseless rambling. An attitude of permissiveness is most desirable except with seriously disturbed patients where a more directive approach may be needed.

The topics of discussion in the group are many and varied, although they usually revolve around a discussion of the members' problems and recognized symptoms. Care must be taken that the more aggressive members do not monopolize the conversation and the withdrawn individuals become listeners rather than participants. As the sessions continue under flexible leadership, however, all of the patients become increasingly articulate and become less eager to look to the therapist for leadership. In fact, one topic of discussion may become the leader himself; the patients engage in discussing freely his attitudes and motives. They also may talk about the ways in which they affect one another as they compare the relative seriousness of their respective difficulties.

Personal Qualities of the Therapist

The personality characteristics of the therapist exert a significant influence on the reactions of the group. Fundamental qualities probably include a quiet approach to the situation and friendliness, as well as an accepting attitude toward the members of the group. He should exhibit no disapproval of what they may say or do. Corsini describes the personal qualities of the ideal leader in a group as follows:

Patience.   The first quality that comes to mind is patience. Above all the therapist must have a high tolerance for boredom, frustration, and delay. He must have the ability to proceed doggedly in the face of disappointments and failure under conditions that induce anxiety, anger, and unrest. Patience should be the resultant of a deep conviction, amounting to faith, in oneself, the group, the method, and the theory. The patient therapist combines a feeling of assurance, security, determination, confidence, and hopefulness about himself and others. He must have an optimistic outlook on life.

Courage.   Somewhat related to the concept of patience is that of courage. The therapist must have the capacity to act on his convictions and not be swerved by immediate events. He needs faith to hold on with great tenacity to his convictions, to follow with determination his line of attack, and to meet in a serene manner the opposition, which at times may explode with some violence. Courage is needed to penetrate, sometimes blindly, into new areas, or to meet crises with aplomb. The therapist must have inward qualities of fortitude of the kind possessed by martyrs.

Flexibility.   Courage does not mean rigidity, for while the therapist must hold on to basic principles with tenacity, he must nevertheless be able to modify tactics without changing strategy. He needs extraordinary flexibility to go rapidly from topic to topic, emotion to emotion, from person to person, keeping meanwhile a sense of the needs of the group as a whole. He must be sensitive to the moods of the group, and to the needs of the individuals, but he must also be alert to the demands of society, the desires of patients' families, and ethical issues.

Warmth.   The ideal therapist is a warm person, with a genuine liking for people, who really wants to see others improve. While he may have preferences among the patients, he must value them equally as striving individuals in trouble. He must be ready to give of himself fully.[30]

[30] Raymond J. Corsini, *Methods of Group Psychotherapy*, Chicago: William James Press, 1964, p. 125.

Behavior of Members of the Group

Each member of the group brings his behavior potentials acquired earlier. The patterns he has developed to relate to others have been developed through the years. He also has anticipatory attitudes that he displays during the group process. These may hinder or facilitate his progress. According to Eiserer:

> The response repertoire of a person is utilized selectively in relation to events in a group. Hostility, anger, affection, love—any emotion may be evoked by events in the group. Whatever happens, however, is grist for the therapeutic mill. Reactions are reflected, examined, evaluated, denied, rejected—perhaps all—by various members of the group. What is most important to the behavior generally is how the leader reacts to him. From him the behavior usually gets his clues as to limits, what is preferred, valued, accepted or rejected.
>
> The individual soon learns that he is not alone in the group and that he has perceptions and feelings about other members of the group as well as the leader. He learns that different people perceive him differently.
>
> A common phenomenon reported by therapists of every persuasion is the tendency for members "to behave like therapists." They project upon the group what they perceive to be the role of the therapist—they probe, advise, exhort, question, offer solutions to problems. One might say that they behave like "poor therapists." This phenomenon should be distinguished from the fact that as the group develops members may be more helpful toward one another. They may help one another explore problems, listen empathically, provide provisional explanations. This kind of behavior on the part of members may result in the identification of attitudes and behavioral dynamics which escape the therapist. It is commonly observed that persons are often more sensitive toward others in areas of mutual concern. Thus a member may sense a need or problem more deeply than the therapist and respond to it helpfully or hurtfully.[31]

[31] Paul E. Eiserer, "Group Psychotherapy," *Journal of the National Association of Deans of Women* (now the *Journal of the National Association of Women Deans and Counselors*), March, 1956, pp. 120–121.

Various studies have been conducted to illustrate group therapy in action. I shall present two of these briefly. Manny Sternlicht undertook to initiate a program of group psychotherapy with several groups of institutionalized mentally retarded adolescents who exhibited serious acting-out behavioral difficulties.

In one group, Sternlicht started the project by asking at the first meeting for the "strongest" member. As a result fighting took place among those who considered themselves to be the strongest in the group. The therapist selected the boy who, as a result of these fighting matches, appeared to excel in strength. In order to demonstrate his superior physical ability, Sternlicht then had an Indian hand-wrestling match with him and was the victor. This victory not only enhanced the therapist's authority but led to another result which Sternlicht describes as follows:

> As a consequence of this rapid and "easy" victory, the group responded to the therapist with undisguised awe and admiration, thus permitting the therapist to introduce those minimal limits considered necessary for therapeutic success with such a group, i.e., that there will be no damage to person and no purposeful damage to property. This feeling of awe and admiration lasted for two or three sessions, after (and during which) a working therapeutic relationship developed with no undue difficulties. It is felt that this was made possible as a result of the tremendous diminution of the usual initial acting out and testing-of-the-limits behavior characteristic of such groups.[32]

A study of group psychotherapy with delinquent adolescents is reported by Marvin Hersko. This report is based on Hersko's three years of experience in carrying out group psychotherapy with adolescent girls in a training school setting. As a result of his experiences, the therapist arrived at these findings:

> It is difficult to develop a sense of group unity with adolescents. The group members fear that the fact that they are receiving psychotherapy means that they are crazy.

[32] Manny Sternlicht, "Establishing an Initial Relationship in Group Psychotherapy with Delinquent Retarded Male Adolescents," *American Journal of Mental Deficiency*, July, 1964, p. 40.

Hence, they are dubious about their own participation in the group and reluctant to identify with other members. Also, adolescents are always afraid of losing status with their peer group. They fear that others will interpret their involvement in therapy as weakness and dependency upon an adult, both of which are contrary to adolescent values and particularly to delinquent values. . . .

In discussion of their interpersonal relationships, the conflicted self concepts of the group members will gradually become more apparent and of more concern to them. The members can be expected to show extreme sensitivity in this area so that a great deal of tact, support, and patience will be demanded of the therapist. Free discussion of the diffuse and conflicting self concepts of the group members is essential. Some of the important subjective dimensions within which the adolescent must locate herself are: dependency vs. self-sufficiency, good vs. bad, masculinity vs. femininity, and lower class vs. middle class. It is reassuring to the group for the therapist to point out that these are a universal problem of adolescence. . . .

With adolescent delinquents, the acting out of sexual and aggressive impulses is the chief resistance to the therapeutic process. Acting out signifies that the anxiety of the group has risen to a disruptive level. The acting out serves both to lessen awareness of painful emotions and to defend against getting close to the therapist. The relatively unstructured nature of therapy arouses anxiety about the adolescents' ability to control themselves and concern about whether the therapist is strong enough to control them. Acting out is also used by the group to test the therapist's affection and dependability. Its most common use, however, is that of diverting the group discussion from a subject that is too threatening.[33]

PSYCHODRAMA

The application of group psychodrama in the field of mental disorders began in 1911. Dr. Moreno encouraged children to participate in what he has called psychodrama, in which they

[33] Marvin Hersko, "Group Psychotherapy with Delinquent Adolescent Girls," *American Journal of Orthopsychiatry*, January, 1962, pp. 170, 172, 173.

were encouraged to act out their fantasies in groups. Since then several "spontaneity" theaters have been constructed for psychodramatic use. It is Moreno's view that all the important elements of psychotherapy are available through psychodrama, with the additional advantage of reaching the larger group of the audience as well as the cast. For both cast and audience there is cathartic aid in different degrees. Both in an analysis of acted-out events as well as in subsequent discussion there is re-education value.

According to Moreno, psychodrama employs five instruments: the stage, the subject or patient, the director, the staff of therapeutic aids or auxiliary egos, and the audience. The first instrument is a stage because it provides the patient with a living space which is multi-dimensional and flexible to the maximum. The second is the subject or patient who is asked to be himself on the stage, to portray his own private world. The third is the director who has three functions: producer, therapist, and analyst. The fourth is a staff of auxiliary egos who have a double significance. They not only are extensions of the director but of the patient, and they portray actual or imagined personae of their life drama. The fifth is the audience which has a dual purpose. It may help the patient, or the audience itself may be helped by the subject.

After describing briefly the significance of the Greek drama, in a paper he read at the American Psychiatric Association Meeting in 1946, Moreno concluded his paper with the following statements:

> We may be credited to have put the psyche itself on the stage. The psyche which originally came from the group—after a process of reconversion on the stage—personified by an actor—returns to the group—in the form of the psychodrama. That which was most startling, new and spectacular to see and to feel on the stage appears to the participants after thorough exposure as a process which is familiar to them and intimately known—as their own selves. The psychodrama confirms their own identity as in a mirror.[34]

Helen Hall Jennings, another recognized authority on psychodrama as well as in the area of sociometrics, has provided the

[34] J. L. Moreno, M. D. (ed.), *Sociometry*, Vol. 9 (1946), Beacon, N.Y.: Beacon House, Inc., Publishers, pp. 249–253.

author with an excellent capsule description of the process of psychodrama. Jennings literally makes the process of psychodrama come alive when she states:

> The process of psychodrama is an action portrayal of the personality dynamics of the protagonist (patient) in a setting of others (a group) who are sensitive to respond to the needs of the protagonist so that he gains a wider and deeper psychological view (insight) into the nature of his needs in relation to an understanding of the needs of others.
>
> Such a setting is not always possible to create for the protagonist. In this case the therapist comprises the prototype of the group. In either event ideally there are present those who are trained to act as auxiliary egos to the individual in treatment to aid him fully to express the nature of his problem and to gain an inter-personality global view of it under such conditions as necessary to produce catharsis.[35]

The most important dynamic concept involved in psychodrama is that of the auxiliary ego. A child is dependent upon his mother who, as an auxiliary ego, assumes full responsibility for him until he begins to share with her this responsibility for his behavior. Finally, he matures and contributes to the welfare of others.

The psychotic and the neurotic cannot meet their life problems on a mature adult level. Hence the attempt is made to wean them from dependency by gradual steps, and to bring them to maturity in easy stages, through the efforts of trained personnel as auxiliary egos. The procedure includes the interviewing of all patients who will participate; an analysis of data about each one (in order to plan the action), and a classification of each patient according to his dominant psychopathological pattern. This type of therapy, Moreno indicates, is of greatest value in cases of neurosis, incipient neurosis, and simple interpersonal conflicts.

HYDROTHERAPY, HYPNOSIS, DRUGS, AND SHOCK THERAPY

The treatment of mental and emotional disorders can utilize one or more of the following: hydrotherapy, hypnosis, adminis-

[35] Helen Hall Jennings. Professor of Education, Brooklyn College, 1965.

tration of drugs, and "shock" therapy. I shall discuss each of these briefly.

Hydrotherapy

The relaxing effect of a warm bath after hard work is known to most of us. A mentally ill person who is tense or wrought-up experiences a similar relaxation through the application of hydrotherapy. The patient may be wrapped in wet sheets, placed into a continuous-flow bath of warm water, or given a spray or shower bath. So effective is this technique in the treatment of actively disturbed states that the "strait-jacket" technique is being discarded in its favor. Patients have been known to request a "bath" when they recognize the approach of a disturbed state.

Hypnosis

In hypnosis the therapist induces a deep hypnotic sleep during which past experiences can be recalled and present feelings disclosed. The therapist may suggest certain acts which the patient should perform during the post-hypnotic state. These are then carried out according to directions. Before he developed the technique of psychoanalysis, Freud was intensely interested in hypnosis and used it to explore the hidden memories of the patient and to help in the abreaction of suppressed feelings.

Through hypnosis, hysteria or such symptoms as hysterical blindness can be induced. Hypnosis can give rise to the feeling of pain through the suggestion that a hot metal object has been placed on a subject's arm, for example. Hypnosis also can bring about insensitivity to pain. The carrying out of hypnotic suggestion is an example of the unconscious denying the sensation. It can be used by the therapist to encourage the patient to talk about himself.

At one time hypnosis was extremely popular; later it lost its appeal. It was found that it did not always function successfully; either the patient could not be hypnotized or he did not fall into a sleep deep enough to make its utilization helpful. Modern therapists are beginning to use hypnosis as an adjunct to other forms of therapy, in that it can help in clarifying the memory of the patient and cause him to express his feelings freely. Thorpe, Katz, and Lewis give the following as helpful uses of hypnosis:

The classical uses of hypnosis include breaking through amnesias, posthypnotic suggestion, the creation of analgesic states in which surgical operations may be performed, and the removal of hysterical symptoms. Its more functional uses, so far as substantial psychotherapeutic procedures are concerned, may, however, be summarized as follows:

1. A combination of hypnosis and psychoanalytic techniques offers many possibilities. So far such an approach has shortened the time required for therapy, as well as making possible the integration of more remote repressed incidents with the individual's current ego-defense system.

2. Hypnosis seems to produce relatively permanent results (so far as present evidence goes) when used in combination with progressive relaxation.

3. Hypnosis is valuable as a tool with which to gain a clearer understanding of the dynamics of a particular neurosis. Information gained from the trance may serve to increase the clinician's insight into a situation even though such information is in itself of no therapeutic value to the patient.

4. Age regression under hypnosis may serve as a valuable analytic tool in the determination of the probable etiology and approximate time of onset of an emotional conflict or neurosis.

5. The capacity for auto- or self-hypnosis may be initiated by the therapist and later utilized by the individual to "recharge" himself periodically with temporary personality qualities which he has been unable to develop in a permanent way.

6. Hypnosis has a promising future in the treatment of children. Evidence seems to indicate that only one or two in five adults can be placed in a deep trance, whereas it is believed that four out of five children of elementary school age are susceptible to deep hypnosis. At this age the personality is relatively plastic and the symptom patterns less rigid and protective to the patient.[36]

[36] Louis P. Thorpe, Barney Katz, and Robert T. Lewis, *The Psychology of Abnormal Behavior*, 2nd ed., New York: The Ronald Press Company, 1961, p. 565.

The Administration of Drugs

Certain drugs known as tranquilizers have a soothing effect on patients suffering from mental and emotional illness. Some drugs help to hasten recall and abreaction having effects somewhat similar to those induced by hypnosis. Many "wonder drugs" have been found to be antirepressant. Their application can shorten a patient's stay in the hospital as they tend to lessen the distress suffered by him. It must be kept in mind, however, that their effect is palliative rather than fundamentally curative. Their effects are somewhat irregular and they may have undesirable side effects.

Chlorpromazine, reserpine, and similar drugs have some value in the reduction of anxiety and agitation that are characteristic of manic disorders. The application of chlorpromazine is also helpful in cases of schizophrenia.

Fever therapy and the administration of tryparasmide and penicillin have effected encouraging improvement in cases of general paralysis or paresis. Dilatin and tridione are helpful in the treatment of epileptic seizures. Sodium pentothal and sodium amytal are used in psychiatric therapies known as narcoanalysis, narcosynthesis, and twilight sleep. The withdrawn, inhibited patient appears to emerge from sleep produced by one of these drugs in a relaxed condition that temporarily stimulates greater clarity of thinking. He becomes more accessible for therapeutic treatment. Patients suffering from involutional disturbance may be helped to achieve relief from mild depression by the use of a combination of benzedrine sulphate and small doses of barbiturate.

The foregoing represents the use that is being made of a few drugs for therapeutic purposes. Further scientific research and study should result in the advancement of medicinal therapy. It should be emphasized, however, that the administration of such drugs is the function of the trained specialist. The layman should never attempt to experiment with them. Great as their therapeutic value may be, inexpert or unadvised use of them is extremely dangerous.

Shock Therapy

In this form of treatment, insulin or electricity is administered to quiet the patient's emotional or nervous condition. Insulin shock treatment, introduced in 1933 by Dr. Manfred Sakel of Vienna, later gained great popularity, especially in the treatment of schizophrenia. In this treatment, coma is induced by the reduction of the sugar content of the blood over a period of two to three months. The insulin shock treatment is terminated by supplying a sugar solution to the body by way of mouth, vein, or nasal tube. Improvement is not likely to be apparent until a minimum of fifteen shocks have been induced. The result may run the gamut for recovery through some improvement to partial improvement and no improvement. It is considered inadvisable to administer more than fifteen shocks if no improvement has been noted.

Electric shock treatment is used extensively in mental hospitals. Electroshock is used especially in the treatment of depressive and manic disorders. In this treatment (electroconvulsive therapy) mild electric currents are passed through the brain by electrodes attached to the head. The patient responds with a convulsion. Unfortunately, in too many cases the success of the therapy is only temporary. The patients have relapses after a longer or shorter period of time. Also, patients who show recovery without shock treatment are less likely to reappear in the mental hospitals. It has been found, however, that the involutional depressions respond best to electroconvulsive therapy.

QUESTIONS AND PROBLEMS

1. Review various attitudes disclosed toward personality disorders.

2. Indicate ways in which minor personality disorders can be treated.

3. List the kinds of personnel involved in the treatment of personality disorders, and discuss the functions of each.

4. Explain what is meant by psychosomatic medicine.

5. Discuss the psychogenic elements in certain bodily disorders.

6. Give examples of adjustment through the application of psychotherapy.

7. Suggest ways in which learning is related to psychotherapy.

8. Discuss the effect of the personality of the therapist on the patient.

9. Outline the functions of the therapeutic interview.

10. Differentiate between the directive and the nondirective approach in psychotherapy.

11. Why is verbal communication between therapist and patient important?

12. Describe the process of psychoanalysis. Report on the value of using psychoanalysis.

13. Give the names of important psychoanalysts, and report their respective contributions to the field.

14. Explain what is meant by group therapy. Illustrate how it is used.

15. Compare Sternlicht's and Hersko's use of group therapy.

16. Discuss the use of psychodrama; of play therapy.

17. Explain the value to the psychotic patient of the use of hydrotherapy, hypnosis, and administration of drugs, or shock therapy.

18. If possible, visit a hospital for the mentally ill and observe therapies applied for patient improvement.

19. List shortcomings of a physician as a therapist.

20. What are some of the existing limitations to the cure of mental illness? What can be done to overcome them?

Selected Readings

Corsini, R. J., *Methods of Group Psychotherapy*. Chicago, Ill.: William James Press, 1964.

Crockett, R., R. A. Sandison, and A. Walk (eds.), *Hallucinogenic Drugs and Their Psychotherapeutic Use*. Springfield, Ill.: Charles C Thomas, Publisher, 1963.

Dewald, P. A., *Psychotherapy: A Dynamic Approach*. New York: Basic Books, Inc., 1964.

Eysenck, H. J., *Behavior Theory and the Neuroses*. New York: Pergamon Press, Inc., 1960.

———— (ed.), *Experiments with Drugs: Studies in the Relation Between Personality, Learning Theory and Drug Action*. New York: The Macmillan Company, 1963.

Fairweather, G. W., *Social Psychology in Treating Mental Illness: An Experimental Approach*. New York: John Wiley & Sons, Inc., 1964.

Fish, F. J., *Schizophrenia*. Baltimore, Md.: Johns Hopkins Press, 1962.

Foulkes, S. H., *Therapeutic Group Analysis*. New York: International Universities Press, Inc., 1964.

Friedman, A. S. et al., *Psychotherapy for the Whole Family*. New York: Springer Publishing Company, Inc., 1966.

Ginott, H. G., *Group Psychotherapy with Children: Theory and Practice of Play Therapy*. New York: McGraw-Hill, Inc., 1961.

Holland, G. A., *Fundamentals of Psychotherapy*. New York: Holt, Rinehart and Winston, Inc., 1965.

Hollis, F., *Casework: A Psychosocial Therapy*. New York: Random House, Inc., 1964.

Horney, K., *New Ways of Psychoanalysis*. New York: W. W. Norton & Company, Inc., 1939.

Kahn, S., *Psychodrama Explained*. New York: Philosophical Library, Inc., 1964.

Luchins, A. S., *Group Therapy*. New York: Random House, Inc., 1964.

Menninger, K., *Theory of Psychoanalytic Technique*. New York: Harper & Row, Publishers, 1964.

Rosen, J. N., *Psychoanalysis: Direct and Indirect*. Doylestown, Penna.: The Doylestown Foundation, 1964.

Rosenbaum, M., and M. Berger, *Group Psychotherapy and Group Function*. New York: Basic Books, Inc., 1963.

Singer, E., *Key Concepts in Psychotherapy.* New York: Random House, Inc., 1965.

Theron, A., *Psychotherapy in Our Society.* Englewood Cliffs, N.J.: Prentice-Hall, Inc., 1963.

Wahl, C. W. (ed.), *New Dimensions in Psychosomatic Medicine.* Boston, Mass.: Little, Brown and Company, 1964.

White, R. W., *Ego and Reality in Psychoanalytic Theory: A Proposal Regarding Independent Ego Energies.* New York: International Universities Press, Inc., 1963.

❧ 13 ❧

ADJUSTMENT
AND
MENTAL HEALTH

THE INDIVIDUAL who has achieved successful adjustment in his relationships with people and conditions in his environment can be described as possessing good mental health. Community agencies, such as the home, the school, and business and industrial organizations are becoming more and more concerned about the mental health or adjustment of all people—children, adolescents, and adults. At least they are manifesting an interest in the application of mental health principles to human behavior.

CONCEPT AND SIGNIFICANCE
OF MENTAL HYGIENE

Early in the twentieth century there became apparent a commendable interest in the problem of mental illness. This attitude encouraged the application of scientific knowledge to the therapeutic treatment of inmates of mental hospitals. This interest in human adjustment has progressed to include not only the cure of mental illness but also the development of ways and means to preserve mental health and thereby prevent the on-slaught of mental illness.

Growth of the Mental Hygiene Movement

In 1900, twenty-four-year-old Clifford Beers, a Yale graduate, attempted to commit suicide by jumping out of a fourth-story window of his home. His apparently disturbed mental condition caused him during the next three years to be confined in various institutions for the mentally ill. Beer's experiences in these institutions, his eventual recovery, and his recognition of the indifference toward, and cruel treatment accorded to, mentally ill patients in these institutions motivated him to report his experiences in a now famous autobiography, published in 1908 under the title of *A Mind That Found Itself.*[1]

The publication of this book stimulated a movement that was destined to affect the lives of many people both in and outside the United States. Adolph Meyer, a leading psychiatrist, helped Beers to launch the new movement. It was Meyer who suggested that the term *Mental Hygiene* be applied to it.

These two men were able to rally many humanitarians to their cause. In 1908, they were successful in establishing a state committee of mental hygiene in Connecticut. This action was followed in 1909 by the organization of the National Committee for Mental Hygiene (now known as the National Association for Mental Health) and numerous state committees. These committees are voluntary organizations of physicians and interested laymen. Early activities were directed toward giving medical and psychiatric assistance to patients in mental hospitals. During the past sixty years, however, the work has expanded gradually so that at present mental health principles exert a significant influence on most educational activities, organized or unorganized.

Mental health principles have been drawn from such fields of knowledge as psychology, biology, physiology, sociology, and medicine. Although the specific subject matter has not yet been definitely determined, it has shifted its emphasis from that of *cure* to that of *prevention* and *preservation.* As a result, the mental health attitude has motivated the establishment of child-

---

[1] Clifford W. Beers, *A Mind That Found Itself,* 5th ed., New York: Doubleday & Company, 1953.

guidance clinics, has led to the inclusion of mental health courses in most schools of higher education, and is having an impact on educational theory and practice. With the advance of knowledge in the behavioral sciences has come not only greater success in the treatment of mental illness but also more skillful techniques in the desirable adjustment of developing individuals.

The Meaning of Mental Hygiene

Mental hygiene (mental health) is a science that deals with human welfare and pervades all fields of human relationships. Its three major purposes are (1) to prevent mental and emotional disorders through an understanding of the relationship that exists between wholesome personality development and life experiences, (2) to preserve the mental and emotional health of the individual and of the group, and (3) to discover and utilize therapeutic measures to cure mental illness.

Mental health as *cure* utilizes principles of mental and emotional adjustment that have been derived from scientific findings in the fields of the behavioral sciences. Any advance in these fields necessitates change of emphasis in the treatment of respective cases of mental illness. Mental health as *prevention* and as *preservation* provides opportunities for an individual to cultivate desirable attitudes and to make adequate adjustments in his various life situations. He is thus enabled to avoid conflicts that bring about maladjustments and is helped to resolve constructively his specific problems of adjustment. Also, since adjustment problems are closely allied to emotional reactions, the nature, development, and control of the emotions constitute a significant area of study in mental health.

It is difficult to define the term *mental hygiene* exactly. A working definition should include the concepts of *prevention, preservation,* and *cure.* Wallin combines these concepts in a terse statement:

> Mental hygiene represents the application of a body of hygienic information and technique, culled from the sciences of psychology, child study, education, sociology, psychiatry, medicine, and biology, for the purpose of (1) the preservation and improvement of the mental health of the

individual and of the community, and (2) for the prevention and cure of minor and major mental diseases and
defects and of mental, educational, and social maladjustment.[2]

THE MENTAL HEALTH APPROACH

Attitudes toward mental illness or less serious maladjustment arc changing from what they once were. In the past, persons whose behavior differed markedly from what was accepted as
normal were adjudged to be "insane" or "crazy" and, for the
safety of others, were incarcerated in institutions where they
received minimal care. At present, we are (1) attempting to so
regulate the experiences of young people that they can preserve
good mental health, (2) adjusting environmental conditions in
such ways that the onslaught of mental illness may be prevented,
and (3) instituting programs of mental therapy in order to help
rehabilitate those individuals who, in spite of our best efforts,
have developed one or another form of mental illness.

To achieve the above goals, all who are concerned with the
mental health of the citizenry need to gain an understanding of
what constitutes mental illness and the therapeutic practices to
be utilized. This is not an easy task. Altrocchi and Eisdorfer
attempted to discover ways in which attitudes toward mental
illness can be changed. In their summary statement they say:

> Three studies were carried out to assess changes in favora-
> bleness of attitudes toward mental illness as a function of
> increased information about mental illness and psychothera-
> peutic training. Attitudes were measured by a semantic
> differential. In the first study with three small summer ses-
> sion classes, attitudes toward concepts of "Neurotic Man,"
> "Neurotic Woman," "Insane Man" and "Insane Woman"
> did not change in the favorable direction. In the second
> study with 75 nursing students undergoing training in psy-
> chiatric nursing, a number of significant changes in the
> favorable direction were found for attitudes toward the same
> concepts.

[2] J. E. Wallace Wallin, *Personality Maladjustment and Mental Hygiene*,
2nd ed., New York: McGraw-Hill, 1949, p. 3a.

In a third study with 48 similar nursing students, but assessing attitudes toward personality sketches of people with emotional problems, a number of significant changes were found again. In both studies changes were most apparent in the understandability and evaluative factors of the semantic differential.

It is postulated that, with people in the advanced stages of college and nursing training who are relatively well-informed, favorable changes in attitudes toward mental illness are not likely to result from increased information alone but may result from training which also includes contact with patients and the learning of psychotherapeutic behavior.[3]

The Problem of Mental Illness

The incidence of mental and emotional disturbance in the United States is high. Available data indicate that during the past eighty years the rate of mental and emotional disturbance has been on the rise. The number of patients in state and county mental hospitals in 1880 was less than 41,000, or about 64 persons per 100,000 population; in 1945, the number of such patients was approximately 625,000, or about 360 per 100,000 population; in 1963, the number had risen to approximately 660,000, or about 365 per 100,000 population. Furthermore, more than 132,000 new patients enter mental hospitals annually.

A good estimate is that one out of every twenty persons may be expected to become a patient in a mental hospital at some time in his life, and that one out of ten will suffer from some form of mental disturbance during his lifetime, even though he is not hospitalized. The increase in incidence of mental illness may be caused partly by the complexity of modern civilization and partly by ignorance concerning the predisposing factors of the emotional disturbance.

Mental Health Status

Not all mentally ill persons are in mental hospitals or receiving therapeutic treatment. Many individuals of all ages are at-

[3] John Altrocchi and Carl Eisdorfer, "Changes in Attitudes Toward Mental Illness," *Mental Hygiene*. October, 1961, p. 569.

tempting to carry on a normal pattern of daily activities in spite of the fact that they are suffering from a relatively serious emotional disorder. There is no sharp line of demarcation between positive and negative mental health, however. Rather do we find among the members of any societal group varying degrees of mental and emotional stability, varying from high positive adjustment to maladjustment.

The mentally healthy or well-adjusted individual has a mature attitude toward his life experiences. He is socially sensitive, recognizing the rights of other people and his responsibility, as an older child, adolescent, or adult, for their welfare. He displays a cheerful, friendly, and outgoing attitude in his relationships with other people. He is self-reliant, demonstrating his ability to manage his affairs wisely and to the benefit of all concerned. He can be depended on to meet his daily duties and obligations conscientiously and successfully.

In general, the mentally and emotionally healthy individual is a happy person who can meet his frustrating experiences calmly and intelligently. Contrariwise, the seriously disturbed individual suffers many frustrations in his daily experiences. He is dependent on others for the fulfillment of his wants and needs. He often gives evidence of moodiness and may be antisocial in his relationships with other persons. Between these two extremes can be found varying degrees of adjustment to home, school, vocational, and social conditions and situations.

Preservation of Mental Health

What can be done to prevent the onslaught of mental ill health or to preserve emotional stability among our young people? An efficient, happy, and contented person possesses habit patterns that free him from emotional and nervous tensions, conflicts, discords, and inconsistencies. He welcomes change and develops an attitude that will bring about satisfactory adjustments to the constantly changing forces and stimuli of his environment. Anything that can be done to encourage wholesome behavior at every stage of a person's life represents the positive approach of mental hygiene.

If mental hygiene is to function in the lives of people, we need to do more than gather and master information about the subject or its related fields. We need to concern ourselves with the effect of the selected information on an individual, the direction that his overt behavior takes under any given influence, the purpose and value of drives, the effect of an individual's emotions on himself, and the permanency of personality development and adjustment. We need to determine (1) the character traits that a leader or teacher needs to be of greater assistance to the learner, (2) the traits that are to be developed by the learner for his effective living, (3) the measuring instruments to be utilized for effective evaluation of successful adjustment, and (4) the criteria to be devised for the formulation of sound general conclusions.

An individual's self-realization will be strengthened if he

1. Has insight into his basic reactions and adjustment problems.
2. Maintains a wholesome attitude toward life.
3. Attains the goals that he seeks.
4. Experiences satisfaction in his many activities.
5. Keeps his wants and desires within the limits of social approval.
6. Adapts easily to social situations.
7. Engages in desirable emotional experiences.
8. Displays a normal drive to work or to play.
9. Forms habit patterns that are beneficial to himself and others.

James E. Royce suggests the following practical rules for preserving mental health:

1. Live one day at a time. "Sufficient for the day is the evil thereof," contains the same practical wisdom as the adage which members of Alcoholics Anonymous use when they remind themselves that anybody can live without drink (or whatever) for just 24 hours. Deal with problems as they come up. Forget the past; don't cross future bridges before you come to them.
2. If you cannot change a situation, adapt to it. Or as the old saying goes, "If you can't lick 'em, join 'em." There is great wisdom in knowing when we must hold to principles, and when we are just batting our heads against a stone wall. Face your problem squarely; either

solve it or decide it can't be solved and forget it. Don't detour around sorrow; live through it with calm acceptance.

3. Get interested in others. Adler saw the "will to community" as the only salvation from ruin by the "will to power"—echoing the theme of "love thy neighbor" in a document nineteen centuries older. Happiness is like a soap bubble; if you try to grasp it, you destroy it; leave it alone and it is there to be enjoyed. Most people who are unhappy are those who are clutching at happiness, thinking about whether they are happy; those who are absorbed in working for others don't need to stop and analyze their happiness.

4. Life is what you make it. To a great extent, we get what we really want out of life. Make up your mind that your goal is worth while and have confidence in your natural powers of attaining it. (Decide that you are going to be miserable and you most certainly will be—and make everyone around you miserable, too.)

5. Cultivate a sense of the ridiculous. Develop the habit of looking for the funny side of every situation. There always is one; sometimes it's on you.

6. Don't take yourself too seriously. Accept yourself for what you are, and you're not God. If you feel sorry for yourself, nobody else will; if you blow your own horn, others will not be disposed to toot it for you.

7. Remember that *perfect* happiness is unobtainable in this life. As Browning says, "A man's reach should exceed his grasp, or what's a Heaven for?" Success does not consist in not having troubles, but in bearing them well.

8. Cultivate high ideals.

9. Relax.

10. Don't act on emotion: wait.

11. Cultivate an interest in your work and develop good hobbies. Broaden your interests.

12. Maintain a confidential relationship with some reliable (preferably older) person to whom you can safely unburden yourself.

13. There is no substitute for peace of conscience.[4]

---

[4] James E. Royce, S.J., *Personality and Mental Health*, rev. ed., Milwaukee: The Bruce Publishing Company, 1964, pp. 163–164.

Significance of Mental Activity

Desirable mental adjustment is closely associated with the belief that, beginning with inherited qualities and potentialities, an individual can be helped, through proper education, to bring about changes in his habit patterns essential to his adequate adaptation to all life situations. The hope of mental hygiene lies in the possibilities of an individual's progressive development through his day-to-day living toward a well-integrated personality.

Mental experiences result when stimuli activate our sensory apparatus. We develop certain traits and soon are known by these characteristics. To try to be different would cause us to become confused, ill at ease, or nervous. We become creatures of habits that simplify our behavior when correctly formed. Through proper habits we become proficient workers and express ourselves intelligently.

The individual who in his youth acquires the scientific approach is establishing habits of thinking that will be of great value to him as he progresses through school and, later, as he struggles with the problems of adult life. Consider the experiences that accrue to the growing child. His interests, his wants, and his attitudes fluctuate as he interacts with his environment. Through their influence he builds mental habits that determine the integration, the adjustment, and the unity of his mental life.

The point of view enunciated in the foregoing is detailed by Eric Berne in his book *Games People Play*. Berne believes that individuals "play games" with one another as expressions of their experiences or lack of them, their interests, and their goals. Important games played by individuals include life games, marital games, party games, and sexual games. The extent to which an individual may need therapy depends upon the personal qualities he has acquired through the years and the kind of social intercourse he activates. For example, infants need fondling and handling in order to gain adequate emotional stimulation for the development of effective social relations with others. More important, if an infant has been denied certain stimuli, the effect may be devastating to his mental and emotional development. Any sensory deprivation may be the root of temporary mental and emotional disturbance. An extreme example is the case of individuals who have been placed in solitary confinement displaying a transient psychosis.

The infant needs to be stroked so that stimulus-hunger will not be experienced. According to Berne:

> The social psychiatrist's concern in the matter is with what happens after the infant is separated from his mother in the normal course of growth. What has been said so far may be summarized by the "colloquialism": "If you are not stroked, your spinal cord will shrivel up." Hence, after the period of close intimacy with the mother is over, the individual for the rest of his life is confronted with a dilemma upon whose horns his destiny and survival are continually being tossed. One horn is the social, psychological, and biological forces which stand in the way of continued physical intimacy in the infant style; the other is his perpetual striving for its attainment. Under most conditions he will compromise. He learns to do with more subtle, even symbolic, forms of handling, until the merest nod of recognition may serve the purpose to some extent, although his original craving for physical contact may remain unabated.[5]

Berne further states:

> The advantages of social contact revolve around somatic and psychic equilibrium. They are related to the following factors: (1) the relief of tension, (2) the avoidance of noxious situations, (3) the procurement of stroking, and (4) the maintenance of an established equilibrium. All these items have been investigated and discussed in great detail by physiologists, psychologists, and psychoanalysts. Translated into terms of social psychiatry, they may be stated as (1) the primary internal advantages, (2) the primary external advantages, (3) the secondary advantages, and (4) the existential advantages. The first three parallel the "gains from illness" described by Freud: the internal paranosic gain, the external paranosic gain, and the epinosic gain, respectively. Experience has shown that it is more useful and enlightening to investigate social transactions from the point of view of the advantages gained than to treat them as defensive

[5] Eric Berne, *Games People Play: The Psychology of Human Relationships*, New York: Grove Press, 1964, p. 14.

operations. In the first place, the best defense is to engage in no transactions at all; in the second place, the concept of "defenses" covers only part of the first two classes of advantages, and the rest of them, together with the third and fourth classes, are lost to this point of view.[6]

MENTAL HEALTH AGENCIES

Public concern over the problem of mental illness and an increasing interest in the preservation of good mental health with a consequent emphasis on the prevention of mental disorders has resulted in the establishment of various agencies dealing with the problems involved in the mental health status of all individuals—children, adolescents, and adults. The efforts of Beers and Meyer to establish a mental hygiene committee in Connecticut (1908) led to the organization of other state committees and the organization of the National Committee for Mental Hygiene (1909), now called the National Association for Mental Health, a privately endowed organization.

The National Association for Mental Health

The parent association was instrumental in awakening the American people to a recognition of mental illness as a national health problem, and not only has been active in its efforts to provide more hospitals for the mentally ill and to improve conditions in such institutions, but also gradually has come to emphasize the prevention of mental disorders and the preservation of good mental health. Although its work has been hampered by insufficient funds and personnel to carry on its program, it established in 1949 (1) a division of education, and (2) a division of state and local organization. The functions of these two divisions are to disseminate mental hygiene principles and to assist in the strengthening of mental health organizations already in existence as well as to establish more such groups.

Government Agencies

By 1946, public interest in mental health had progressed to the point that Congress passed the Mental Health Act. This act

[6] *Ibid.*, p. 19.

gave impetus to the organization of various national groups and
further assistance to the cause by the national government. In
1949, the National Institute of Mental Health was established.
The work of the Institute is providing widespread service. It
offers direct help to communities for the establishment of clinics,
for research projects, for the education of professional groups,
and for planning various educational services. The Institute also
conducts research and clinical programs of its own. Funds made
available to the National Institute of Mental Health have been
increased annually during the past twenty years. Legislation enacted in 1965 made available $188 million for distribution to
various states on a matching basis, and for its own research and
clinical programs.

Other agencies that attempt to deal with the problem of
mental ill health include the United States Office of Education,
the Department of Labor, the Department of Agriculture, the
Children's Bureau, and the National Institute of Child Health
and Development. These and similar organizations allocate funds
for the establishment of agencies to improve health services and
help in other more direct ways.

Child-guidance Clinics

Child-guidance clinics began in Chicago under the direction
of William Healy. They undertake, through the cooperative
effort of a competent staff which includes physicians, psychiatrists, psychologists, and psychiatric social workers, to discover
the child's difficulty and then as far as is possible through changes
in the child's home conditions and school program, medical
attention, and personal work with the child to adjust his difficulties. The child is usually referred to the clinic by the school or
the home, and the clinic works in close cooperation with these
two agencies.

Child-guidance clinics tend not to treat children who are
definite hospital cases. Clinic efforts are directed toward the
readjustment of children before incipient difficulties become too
serious. The clinics also serve as educational media for the dis-
semination of mental health principles and practices to parents
and school people. Unfortunately, the work of these clinics, since
it is individual and since each case needs the services of a staff of

experts, is expensive, and few, if any, communities have adequate facilities to meet the needs.

There is a trend to establish educational clinics in institutions involved with the preparation of teachers. Such clinics serve two purposes: (1) diagnosis and therapy for maladjusted children, and (2) orientation to clinical procedures for prospective teachers. These clinics contain well-equipped reception rooms, offices for the staff, and one-way-vision observation rooms. The staff includes a director, psychologists, clinical assistants, social workers, a pediatrician, and a psychiatrist.

MENTAL HEALTH AS RELATED
TO LIFE AREAS

The application of the principles of mental hygiene touches every phase of an individual's life. Hence such principles need to function in his home, school, and industrial and social activities. In the following we consider the place of mental health in any program of life adjustment.

Mental Health and Physical Health

Is physical health a condition that may be influenced by mental factors? Is there any relationship between the mind and the healing of the body when it is impaired? The answer to both these questions is in the affirmative, but the potential relationship between physical and mental health is not yet fully known or utilized. The attitudes, the behavior, the relative buoyancy, and the effect on others of the healthy individual are quite different from those of the sickly person. An individual during illness often displays personality characteristics that are absent from his accustomed role. An excellent doctor, an efficient nurse, proper diet, and rest are essential in any healing process, but an attitude of wanting to recover will stimulate the patient to respond to treatment and is usually as efficacious as the treatment itself.

Neither the parent nor the teacher should so overemphasize the value of good health that the child becomes emotionally disturbed concerning the state of his own health, but the observance of good health habits should become a matter of daily routine. The child should be taught that occasional illnesses are inevitable and need prompt and efficient treatment, but he should not be exposed to constant and detailed adult discussion of pains, aches, and disease symptoms.

Many young people are the victims of their elders' inordinate interest in their own health problems. Detailed and over-frank descriptions of real or imagined symptoms of ill-health, expressions of self-pity, shirking of responsibilities because of ill-health, or unwise emphasis on unnecessary health precautions on the part of parents or other adults may develop in the child exposed to such experiences an undue and possibly morbid self-consciousness concerning his own health. Intelligent care of one's health and the avoidance of foolhardy exposure to contagions or other unhealthful conditions are desirable. Such health habits should be fostered as early as possible in the developing individual.

Mental Health and the School

In the past, the elementary school was satisfied to teach the "three R's." The success of the school was determined by the number of children who could learn to read, write, and do arithmetic. The child who failed was allowed to leave school and to devote his energy to the learning of his father's trade or to another activity of his own choosing. The school accepted little responsibility for the social adjustment of such pupils. Children were expected to become law-abiding citizens even though they had received little formal education in this field.

Many experimental techniques in social education have been tried. Since most of these significant techniques demand teachers with competencies quite different from traditional teacher preparation, progress has been slow, however. Various plans are now in operation to prepare teachers to meet these changing conditions. Attention is given to the needs of the culturally disadvantaged child. Teachers are being helped to understand and meet the needs of these learners.

Unless children can be given a more functional education than is now generally available, they are likely to emerge from this training poorly fitted for their adult responsibilities. Retarded and slow learners need educational stimulation that will interest them and offer them opportunities for mental growth. Their limited capacities cannot respond to the techniques of motivation that stimulate successful learning in more able pupils. They must be motivated on their experiential level.

Teachers need to be trained to enable them to understand the problems of children, to know how to implement individual instruction, and to be sympathetic toward those who have experience lacks. Teachers cannot be expected to understand the physical, mental, social, and emotional needs of children if they have not been educated so to do. The teachers of today need broadened insights, perfected skills, and workable techniques. They must be encouraged to proceed with their work without interference from administrators.

Mental Health and Religion

As a person enlarges his perspective, he achieves an increasingly healthy state of mind. Many positive values come to him who is keenly aware of and sensitive to the spiritual values about him. He is aware of subtle influences to which only man can respond. He reacts to these with a hope that impels him to do the better things. The instrument he uses is that of prayer, which represents an invisible emanation of man's worshiping spirit and which generates a most powerful form of energy. The scientist, Dr. Alexis Carrel, believed in the power of prayer. He believed that through prayer it is possible to "achieve that complete and harmonious assembly of body, mind and spirit which gives the frail human reed its unshakable strength." [7]

If religion is to function in the lives of people, it must do so through established organizations or through those that may be established. The child needs early training in these values and he needs also the religious experiences that accompany religious education. It is recognized that these experiences are caught as well as taught. Religion gives an individual a chance to face life's problems with greater confidence and develops an attitude that will serve in time of crisis. Many conflicts need to be resolved in order to attain and appreciate higher values. This is often done through the conversion experience, as a result of which an indi-

[7] Alexis Carrel, "Prayer Is Power," *The Reader's Digest*, March, 1941, p. 35.

vidual may develop a confidence that enables him to achieve greater harmony between himself and his environment.

Religion need not develop a narrow but rather a broadened emotional and intellectual outlook. It should not be lived solely on the emotional level but should aid in the adjustment process through mental insights. Faith should supplement, not contradict, reason. There are values that we have been unable to reduce to logical or scientific terms; yet there is a faith that should have an important influence on our rational thinking.

Mental Health and the Courts

The advances of the behavioral and natural sciences have done much to develop a new point of view toward the juvenile who falls into the hands of the law. Until recently all such cases were treated from a strictly legal point of view. Since the establishment of adolescent courts in New York, special consideration is given to the individual with the hope that he may be rehabilitated. It is believed that it is better to save juvenile offenders from the influence of hardened criminals than to penalize all of them with severe sentences because a few continue to run afoul of the law when they are given a second chance. Proper behavior cannot be legislated, but can become a life pattern of boys and girls through adequate training.

Mental Health and Industry

The employer knows that a trained and skilled worker is more valuable to him than is an untrained person. He also knows that it costs much in time and money to train a new employee to gain desirable efficiency. From a purely dollar-and-cents point of view, the employer is interested in keeping his workers happy and well. Also, even though he must treat impersonally many of his employees, he has a personal, human interest in them.

Although expensive, personnel departments are demonstrating their value through the mental satisfaction to both employer and employee. The dissatisfied worker is often made happy by another assignment where he is given an opportunity to do work for which he is better fitted. The mental health practices that have been introduced into many business establishments, such as rest periods, comfortable lounging rooms, canteens, sanitary eating places, and coffee breaks, add to the happiness and efficiency of the worker.

Mental health practices can be of value if applied to the many difficult problems of industry. For example, an increased understanding of the problems of the firm, the goals to be achieved, the conditions of employment, the desirability of rest periods, the need for rules to govern all who function in an organization, gives the employee a new perspective. It is basic in changing attitudes of antagonism to those of cooperation.

It is estimated that about 20 percent of business or industrial workers are misfits. These persons are liabilities or potential liabilities to their employers. These are the workers who require the services of personnel departments and who must be transferred from job to job or eventually dropped if they do not resign. Their problems fall usually into one of the following types of difficulties: inefficiency, physical illness, mental illness, irregular attendance, uncooperative attitude, deliberate obstinacy, or home worry. Many of these adjustment difficulties can be helped by the application of proper therapeutic techniques. The help is worth the cost in terms of the happiness engendered to the individual, to his family, and to the industrial organization.

Mental Health and Public Opinion

It is through the individual experiences which we gain in our daily living that we develop our attitudes of social relationships. Attitudes are contagious and move from the behavior of one person to the experience of another as people associate with one another.

Attitude qualities are not found in isolation but are interrelated, and possess emotional and mental qualities. They affect opinion and direct it toward the personal interest of the individual. The attitudes aroused in a group or crowd help us understand social behavior. Our interests tend to establish certain set attitudes that operate in given situations. We are constantly adjusting to the opinion of the group, and we fear the criticisms of the individuals of the group. It is this constant struggle to seek approval that gives us an impetus to do what is desired and to achieve success in a project of which the group will approve. It is difficult for any one of us to stand alone against the adverse attitude and opinion of the group with which we are associated.

MENTAL HEALTH AND THE
DEVELOPING INDIVIDUAL

From birth onward, the individual meets situations and conditions that tend to impair his mental health. During each age period he experiences wants and needs that are to be fulfilled if he is to achieve an adjusted life pattern. In addition to physical, emotional, and social needs an individual can be said to have *ego needs*. These are of two kinds, such as need for self-confidence, independence, and achievement; and need for status, recognition, and appreciation. The former refers to one's self-esteem and the latter to one's reputation. We now shall discuss briefly those factors and influences that affect attitudes and behavior from the preschool years through old age.

Adjustment Problems of the Preschool Child

The term preschool is used to describe the child between the ages of eighteen months and five-and-one-half years or the ages from two to six. Whichever age span is preferred, the preschool period represents roughly the developmental years between the end of infancy and the normal child's entrance into school.

The infant lives an egocentric life. The world about him is relatively nonexistent for him except in so far as it provides or fails to provide for his urgent physical wants. If these wants are supplied satisfactorily, his behavior exhibits characteristics that may be referred to as contentment, happiness, and peace; the overt expression of this inner state takes the form of coos, gurgles, smiles, and muscular relaxation. If his needs are not satisfied, if new and strange elements enter his environment, or if his little body is not physically fit, the infant is unhappy or fretful; his behavior exhibits responses such as crying, tensing, beating with his little fists, kicking, or screaming; responses which, in modified forms, are generally associated with fear or rage in an older person.

As the child matures, similar states and overt expressions of these states are evidenced. The causes of such behavior, however, are not limited to the satisfaction or denial of physical wants but may have their roots in psychological experiences, such as successes or thwartings. Since the child in the process of satisfying his physical wants is dependent on the ministrations of other people, he cannot avoid the acquisition of habits of response to the human beings who surround him. His social consciousness is at first vague and indefinite, but continuing experience teaches him the value of self-assertion, submission, obedience, or consideration for others. At this time he begins to develop the habits of cooperation, thoughtfulness, respect, and self-awareness as a member of the group. These habits must be guided into desirable paths if the child is to mature into a well-adjusted and adaptable adult.

The child's emotional life does not appear to follow the consistent pattern of development that can be expected (with minor variations) in other phases of his growth. The infant in his behavior gives indications of feelings of strong satisfaction or annoyance. Many of his overt responses seem to justify their being referred to as those of fear, anger, jealousy, or enjoyment. It is not until the child is able to talk, however, that behavior that approximates adult forms of emotional expression is found.

The child's increased power of speech and of understanding the speech and behavior of others exposes him to an increasing number of emotion-arousing stimulations, both pleasant and unpleasant. Adult approval expressed through gesture, facial expression, words, and actions gives great joy to the young child. Disapproval may arouse in the child fear, anger, bewilderment, or resentment, and may affect his behavior to such an extent that his actions become the bases of further adult disapproval.

The child's social development continues slowly but surely, and if unimpeded by unhygienic social conditions takes the child to his elementary school period with definite motor control, with an appreciation of himself as a member of the group, having certain rights and privileges as well as the ability to participate in free social play and in organized games. By this time the normal child has a definite understanding of reasonable and reasoning obedience and can derive satisfaction from participation in work projects directed toward envisaged and attainable goals. His attention span has been gradually increasing, and he is now able, with little or no aid, to carry on activities that are suited to his age and ability. He is democratic and generally friendly and trusting. To whatever extent the child at the end of this period deviates from this general pattern, much of this deviation can be traced to unwise education during this very important period of the individual's life.

Adjustment Problems of the Elementary School Child

The normal six-year-old has attained certain physiological and psychological powers and abilities that can and should be strengthened and refined during his approaching stage of later childhood. Although before this period the child has developed many behavior patterns and has attained some understanding of his environment, his learning has been for the most part incidental and without any real awareness of or desire for learning. He now is activated by a conscious urge to discover and to master elements of his enlarged environment.

Whether or not a child is normal in all phases of his early development, at this age a new attitude toward learning is apparent to a greater or lesser degree. However, before he is subjected to the routine of elementary school procedures, it is important to determine the extent to which the six-year-old child is physically, mentally, and emotionally ready for school entrance.

If the child is to be successful in his new school environment, he must be emotionally and socially ready for the stimulation afforded him by the enlarged social horizon. The socially and emotionally immature child is at a serious disadvantage among his more adequately adjusted associates. He is unable to meet the requirements of satisfactory participation in group living. Unless a child has attained a reasonable amount of independence from adult care, he will be embarrassed among his new schoolmates by his relative inability to perform such activities as dressing himself, traveling to and from school unaccompanied, expressing himself intelligently, and participating adequately in the regular school routine of work and play.

The elementary school child requires opportunities for the expression of his emotional drives. He wants to participate and to compete in activities with his associates. He wants to feel secure in the affection and respect of his classmates as a result of his successful accomplishments and adjustments. He wants to give expression to many facets of his maturing personality. His thinking and behavior are displaying a conscious striving toward this goal.

During his first three years in elementary school, the child's learning experiences, though different in content and degree of difficulty, are similar to those that will follow, but attendance at a nursery school and kindergarten may help him meet his learning needs with commendable success. The older child's urge for security, self-expression, and socialization is usually satisfied if his school and home environments are healthful. The well-adjusted child at this age is trusting and friendly. He feels secure in the affection and esteem of his associates. If he has been well stimulated, he accepts his world as a delightful place in which to live.

The upper-grade child is developing conscious beginnings of religious faith, aesthetic appreciation, and respect for civil authority. He is not disturbed by doubts; yet his acceptance of people and things is not altogether the blind faith of his earlier childhood. His appreciation, reasoning, and judgment are childish and incomplete but personally satisfying. He is intensely aware of other human beings. His interest in them is usually a corollary of his interest in himself, but he is habitually democratic in his attitude toward others.

During the upper-grade period the young person needs the companionship of people of all ages and especially of his own age. This is the *gang* age. His interests have been shifting from concern with the activities of his immediate family circle to the challenge of the more novel interests of his school associates. It is in his gang activities that the preadolescent or early adolescent may find his greatest chances of self-expression and education in socialization. In his relationship with a congenial group of his own age, he receives practice in the art of sharing similar interests and activities.

Historically, the home has been the primary agency for the direction and adjustment of a child's personality. Many of the original functions of the home, however, have been assumed by the church and, more recently by the school. No longer is the goal of formal education the provision only of mental stimulation. The development of desirable attitudes and behavior patterns lies outside the inculcation of factual information or the training in manual competence. The school shares with the home and the church the responsibility of influencing every phase of a child's life. Education for the development of desirable attitudes is one of the most important phases of the school's functions.

Attitude patterns become habits that determine behavior habits. Hence the child needs to be encouraged to develop healthful attitudes toward mental and physical health, work, recreation, and other persons. Moreover, he can be trained in an attitude of respect for authority and in an appreciation of and obedience to civil and school laws that have been devised for the protection of himself and his fellows. The extent to which he develops socially acceptable attitudes and behavior patterns determines in large measure his degree of success in meeting life's demands on him as an adolescent and adult.

Adjustment Problems of the Adolescent

Adolescence begins with puberty and ends with the acquisition of full physical growth, increased capacity for intellectual activities, and mature emotional control of behavior. The physical, mental, emotional, and attitudinal phases of personality do not mature simultaneously. The teenager is passing through a difficult period of adjustment. Adults often fail to recognize or understand the problems encountered by the young person as he struggles to fit himself to undertake adult responsibilities.

During the years between twelve and twenty-one, an individual is experiencing all the inner and outer stresses of growing up. He needs to learn to adjust to his own changing body; he is assailed by new desires and yearnings; he is stimulated by a constantly changing, enlarging, and sometimes bewildering environment; life is presenting new and different values, and he is becoming increasingly aware of his own relationship to society as his social status changes from the dependence of childhood to that of adult independence. The struggle within himself between his early habits of dependence on others for the fulfillment of his desires and his recognition of these new-found urges toward freedom from adult restraint and control often creates problems of adjustment. Many of these feelings of restlessness, ambition, disappointment, resentment, and discouragement often are expressions of restrictions imposed on his freedom of choice.

An individual attains his full mental growth during the

adolescent years. A factor that influences the mental development of adolescents is their degree of curiosity concerning their relationship to the social group. This interest may show itself in any one of several forms of behavior, each of which is motivated by the young person's appreciation of his own importance as a member of his community or of his country. He feels an urge to do something unusual and in this way to make a contribution to human welfare or to gain fame and fortune for himself and his family.

The gifted adolescent is usually aware of his need for education in order to accomplish his purpose in life. This type of adolescent, therefore, is likely to be an excellent student, often making personal sacrifices in order to achieve the education necessary for his career. Adolescents who are mentally less able may be eager to achieve. Their limited ability, however, may cause their educational progress to be less satisfying to them. This situation often leads to a type of daydreaming in which the young person substitutes fancied success in imaginary exploits for real success in schoolwork. The satisfyingness of these illusory feats of accomplishment distracts from his efforts at mastery of actual study material. Thus his failure and consequent discouragement go on unabated. He becomes the despair of his parents and teachers. He dislikes school and resents any attempts to force him to attend to his school duties.

Emotional experiences constitute an important accompaniment of the growing-up process. Well-adjusted adolescents have their stresses and strains as well as their satisfying and thrilling experiences. Often they fluctuate between withdrawing, pessimistic depression and optimistic cooperation. They want to love the entire world but become easily and intensely annoyed by a grandparent, a parent, or sibling.

Adolescents seek social approval yet cannot tolerate any thwarting of personal interests. They are stirred to become unduly submissive or aggressive. They are stimulated to become affectionate or jealous, approving or disapproving, tolerant or intolerant. They are seriously concerned about the approval of their peers. The emotionalized attitudes of adolescents are outgoing, wholesome, and subject to intellectual control. Those that are unhealthful require the patient assistance of wise and sympathetic adults to ensure improvement. Adolescents seek and want the guiding hand of parents, teachers, and others as they strive for self-realization.

The adolescent tends to analyze his own behavior in terms of its possibilities of gaining for him desired self-satisfaction and security in the affection of his peers. He also evaluates the behavior of others in light of expressed or implied attitudes toward him. He is sensitive to real or imagined slights to his developing maturity and eager for recognition, approval, and affection; sometimes his desire for such favorable attention is so strong that he may actually appear to avoid or resent it. He clothes himself in a protective covering of apparent indifference or even shows contempt for approval or affection. He may be able to accept criticism of his actions; yet rarely can he tolerate disapproval of himself as an individual.

An adolescent's attitude toward his elders is strongly linked with his intellectual understanding of and his emotional adjustment to age relationships. He is struggling to free himself from his childhood dependence upon the older members of his family, yet the latter are not always aware of this struggle or of the need for it. To them, the adolescent is still a child to be directed in terms of adult ideals. Consequently, the young person either resents this adult domination and exhibits behavior that is unwarranted and socially undesirable, or he gives up the struggle and falls back on his childhood dependence, thus denying himself the possibility of advancing toward mature control of his own behavior. Neither type of reaction is likely to result in the development of wholesome adult attitudes.

The resentful and defiant adolescent becomes the suspicious, arrogant, and uncooperative adult, who tends to dominate his own family and to accuse other members of his occupational or social group of unfairness to him. The dependent adolescent becomes the dependent adult, who seems unable to make his own decisions, who constantly calls on other persons to solve his problems for him, or who accedes to the wishes and desires of others without question and sometimes against his own better judgment.

Childhood patterns of response no longer give satisfaction. The adolescent is extremely self-conscious and is uncertain in the face of many new social stimuli. He struggles for self-assurance and recognition of his approaching adulthood, thus arousing emotional disturbances that vary in intensity with his own aims and ambitions, and with the extent of the emotion-arousing stimuli for which he has no habitual response.

Adolescents differ in their overt behavior signs of inner stress and strain. Apathy, daydreaming, withdrawal from school activities, apparent inability or unwillingness to take part in classroom discussions are significant signs of emotional maladjustment. Some of the more spectacular forms of maladjustive behavior are open defiance of the teacher, temper tantrums, quarrels with other students, lying, stealing, destruction of school property, hysterical crying, and fainting.

The normal adolescent is likely to exhibit an occasional form of abnormal behavior, which should be watched but not taken too seriously. An attempt should be made to discover the cause of the difficulty and then to do whatever is possible to relieve the underlying factors. Much of adolescent unpredictableness can be avoided if sympathetic help is given early. Expert and tactful guidance is necessary for the adolescent whose emotional disturbance has been caused by a recognized physical or health deficiency, who is faced with a difficult home situation, who is unable to make satisfactory progress in his studies, who is uncertain about his vocational choice, or who fails to achieve desirable adjustments to his peers of the same or opposite sex.

Adjustment Problems of College Students

The first and fundamental problem of adjustment of the college student may arise out of his basic fitness for college entrance. Parental ambition may force into college a young person who by temperament and developed interests is neither ready nor ambitious for the kind of education that will be afforded him on the college campus. Not included in this discussion is the plight of those other young people who are both qualified and eager for the privilege of securing a college education but who, because of financial inability or prejudices of parents, are denied the opportunity to attend college upon graduation from high school.

Some of the common problems faced by college students include lack of self-control, new environmental stimulations, sexual immaturity, or unequal competition. The adjustment to be made to any one of these factors may be slight and the disturbing states temporary and easily remedied. If the college entrant is mentally qualified, the problems that confront him on the college campus are no more serious than those experienced in other social situations. To the extent that he is below normal in any phase of his development and is thereby a victim of more than one of the types of adjustment problems listed above, his power of adaptation may be lessened and successful college adjustment threatened.

Unexpected trouble, illness, death in his family, personal illness, or accident may interfere temporarily with the student's progress. The arousal of a vocational interest apart from that for which he may be preparing, an unusually fine business opportunity offered to the student prior to his completing his college degree, and home changes may cause temporary conflict within the individual. Such incidents are common. The extent to which college students are able to meet these or any other problems depends on the young people's inherent and acquired abilities to recognize their problems and on the kind and amount of help and guidance available to them.

ORIENTATION NEEDS. The college student needs assistance, first of all, in satisfactory orientation to his new environment and mode of life. Many colleges have established a service of this kind. However, undue enthusiasm of the faculty in introducing the college entrant to his new experiences and insufficient understanding of an individual's capacity for absorbing the new and the different often result in an orgy of rapidly changing stimulations that leave the entering freshman in a state of bewilderment and confusion that may hinder rather than help his early adjustment to the situation. Wrong values may be stressed, rules and regulations emphasized out of proportion to their actual importance, or too much social participation suggested. Many of these may or may not be experienced by the individual student. Orientation of students to college should not be only a freshman week affair but should be a continuous process.

The new student needs help toward social adjustment. Not only should the college provide and encourage opportunities for social and recreational activity in the form of clubs, dances, parties, sports, and projects, but college leaders and advisers need to make sure that *all* students are encouraged to participate in one or more of these activities. Too often the more extrovert or aggressive students participate in an undue number of college activities at the expense of the more retiring or socially inexperienced students. College advisers also need to be alert to any excesses such as drinking, gambling, petting, or loafing that may become a part of campus life.

MENTAL HEALTH SUGGESTIONS. The program of mental health in college should function both indirectly and directly. The preventive program should include the establishment of hygienic environmental conditions and work and play activities, and the practicing of examples of good campus living by the faculty and upper-class students. There should also be provided opportunities for all students to receive personal advice on any problem with which a student is confronted. In brief, the college should provide a place of learning that will motivate the student toward successful achievement.

Among individuals at this stage of their development a certain amount of deviate behavior is an indication of normal growth. Such deviations from desirable behavior cannot be adjusted successfully through denial of freedom, harsh reprimands, severe penalties, or expulsion. Sympathetic and constructive redirection of behavior, administered objectively and intelligently, usually earns the students' cooperation.

The essentials of a mental health program in college may be summarized as follows:

1. Careful selection of students admitted to college
2. Adequate orientation program
3. Flexible and pertinent curriculums
4. Mental health-minded faculties
5. Clubs for desirable social activities
6. Program of recreational activities
7. Attention to physical health needs
8. Psychological and psychiatric assistance available for all students who may need it

Adjustment Problems of the Adult

By the time he reaches adulthood the individual has developed behavior patterns, reasoning ability, attitudes, and emotional controls that should fit him for adult experiences. As he begins his adult career as a homemaker, as a worker, and as a citizen, he brings to his mature life the results of the education and adjustment that have been made possible for him in his earlier years. The extent to which he can assume adult responsibilities successfully depends partly on the adequacy of his previous development and partly on the favorableness of the changing environments to which, as an adult, he will be exposed. New stimulations and new conditions challenge him to make new responses and adjustments. The preparation with which the adult starts his mature pattern of life, no matter how thorough and desirable that preparation may have been, is no guarantee of complete adjustment in all phases of his adult career.

If the adult is to experience satisfactory and continuous adjustment to the many possible changes that he may be called on to face as he progresses through the remainder of his life, he must continue to be a learner, to gain understanding of the problems that confront him in his personal, occupational, social, and civic life, and to seek improved methods and techniques of adjusting to his changing and challenging interests and duties.

Between the ages of eighteen and thirty-five full growth is attained and an individual is at the peak of his physical vigor. He can endure more physical strain, run faster, wrestle better, play strenuous games more effectively, dance longer, and in general be more active than will be possible at any later period in his life. Also, since mental maturity reaches its height during this period, much of the individual's creative thinking is done at this time. As a high school student, the individual may have lacked persistency in the solution of mental problems, but he now finds that he has more endurance and is better able to face and resolve difficulties. As he acquires habits of thinking, he exhibits mental patterns that can be of great help to him unless their adequacy has been inhibited by insufficient or faulty training.

Emotionalized habits are fairly well established by this time and are either well controlled or unstable, as a result of the adequacy of their education. Positive or negative appreciation is keen. The days of puppy love are passing, and emotionalized drives toward mating are showing themselves. The psychological weaning that has been slowly taking place in the life of the growing individual should be relatively complete by this time.

The person who has sublimated his primitive responses of anger, love, hate, rage, and jealousy to higher levels is likely to be welcomed by any group with which he chooses to associate. The individual should have developed a desirable degree of independence of thinking and behavior.

COURTSHIP AND MARRIAGE. Various problems of adjustment are encountered by the young adult. The drive for mating is powerful during this period. Our present society makes it possible for the young person to find and select his mate. Courtship can be a delightful experience. However, many forces interfere with the continuance of youthful enthusiasm and fervor, such as the behavior of relatives, petty misunderstandings, money, attempts by one individual to change the behavior of the other (especially after marriage), and dissimilarity of interests.

At best marriage is a difficult relationship. Many young people enter into it with no training for adjustment to the problems that must be met and the responsibilities that must be assumed. Before marriage the individual's goal was to stimulate in the other person an interest in himself, but after marriage too many people disregard that goal. Marriage offers many and varied tests of character in the meeting of new situations. Too many young people derive their concept of the marital state from their acquaintance with romantic novels and motion pictures that describe in detail the premarital adjustments of the hero and heroine to each other and then end abruptly with the assumption that continuous happiness and contentment will be their marriage lot.

The youth of eighteen or twenty-two, whether he is a high school or college graduate, faces the problem of securing employment in an occupational field that will offer him opportunities for advancement in work in which he is interested and for the doing of which he is prepared. The young person's attitude toward his work life is an important factor in the adjustment pattern of early adulthood. He may be too ambitious and thus miss excellent work opportunities because he is unwilling to begin with more or less routine work at a moderate salary. Later, a man may be prejudiced against the idea of a married woman's continuing in her occupation, and, if he is unable to advance quickly enough in his vocation so that he can support a wife, he may become resentful and emotionally disturbed.

ADJUSTMENT PROBLEMS DURING MIDDLE AGE.   During the ages from thirty-five to sixty-five the courage, strength, and health of an individual usually are excellent, although he is gradually losing some of his earlier buoyancy and exuberance. If he has not established a desirable balance between his less active life and the kind and the amount of food he eats, he tends to add weight and thereby experience a greater slowing down of his activities. A diet adjusted to the activity and to the age of the person accounts for desirable physical adjustments during this period.

If the individual has been consistent in the enlargement of his experiences and his powers of performance, he is capable of continuing his learning; with proper utilization of his energy he can engage in productive thinking that is as effective as it was during his earlier years. His judgments are as sound as the background of experience on which they are based. His intellectual achievements reflect his mental habits, degree of skill, adaptable attitudes, and creative processes acquired through the years.

Emotional responses should indicate stability of personality. Those persons whose emotional control has developed well as a result of favorable environmental conditions and whose nervous system has suffered no severe shocks are well equipped to meet emotional crises. On the other hand, the individual who has experienced one emotionally disturbing experience after another is developing a nervous system that will surely disintegrate if he is exposed to any sudden or extreme change in his mode of living. Systematic training in emotional control is helpful in meeting stimuli that may cause maladjustive responses.

The man or woman who has acquired gradually the habit of adaptability is not too much disturbed by any changes in his life patterns during this period. If the habits of life are well established by this time, however, it is difficult for the individual to make changes in them even if they would be beneficial to him. Although each person is an individual and functions as such, the fact that many of the habits of life tend to follow socially accepted patterns makes it necessary that his behavior exhibit some degree of similarity to that of his associates. Thus, conventionalized behavior is an expression of fixed behavior habits that are not easily broken.

Middle age is the period of extreme interest in culture patterns and world affairs. The desire for extended knowledge of music, art, literature, science, economics, and politics should be met through the offerings of the various agencies of adult education. The middle-aged citizen exerts a stabilizing influence on society. This stabilization is effective only to the extent that the individuals who compose this group have themselves become stable, well-informed, and tolerant leaders through wise educational leadership.

ADJUSTMENT PROBLEMS DURING OLD AGE. By this time body adjustments are fairly well completed. The average life span for Americans extends to approximately seventy years, but we find that more and more individuals are living longer and that as a result, desirable adjustments are increasing in number. Speed of reaction and motor agility have been considerably reduced. Individual differences show themselves at this time in ways that were not apparent earlier. Some individuals are as old physiologically at sixty-five as others are at eighty. There seems to be a high correlation between mental ability and physical agility during these older ages. The body tends to shrink and stoop, and the pace of walking to slow down. The heart requires careful attention, as it is not able to make the rapid adjustments that are often required of it.

IMPORTANCE OF ATTITUDES. As the age for usefulness nears its end, the desire for continuance in active work increases. The healthy person of seventy years does not want to retire since he believes that he is still as efficient as he was twenty years earlier. Often he has been kept on the job out of respect for his former efficiency, but he may falsely believe that he is still indispensable.

Desirable attitudes toward retirement need to be established. If we expect the person who is about to retire to enjoy that retirement, we must educate him for his new-found leisure. To change suddenly from a life of activity to one of idleness is difficult without preparation, if hygienic values from this new form of life are to be gained. He should be helped to plan his retirement so that he can turn from one kind of activity to another rather than to mere idleness.

This discussion has been directed toward the more fortunate few (although the number is increasing) who enjoy a retirement income. In spite of Federal aid in one form or another, many older people are dependent on their children or some form of welfare for their care and subsistence. This usually means that they return to live with a son or daughter and thus create an emotionally charged atmosphere. No one is satisfied with the relationship, as both the elder and the younger members of the family feel that their rights and privileges are being interfered with by the others. This situation can be alleviated through a well-functioning plan of old-age security that provides the aged with a modest but comfortable subsistence independent of their relatives. In this way, bitter resentment-arousing conflicts could be avoided by our senior citizens. They deserve a happier ending to their useful lives.

VALUE OF PREVENTION OF MENTAL ILL HEALTH IN CHILDHOOD

Any help that can come early in the life of the child to assure the prevention of mental illness is welcome. The close association of mental illness with such social problems as delinquency, poverty, and alcoholism has alerted professional people to the need for correcting these conditions. Even though mental well-being cannot be assured by the functioning of all the available services, the early application of mental hygiene principles can do much to alleviate the situation.

In his discussion concerned with the prevention of mental illness during early childhood, Ivor Kraft offers salient suggestions worthy of our attention.

In discussions of physical and mental illness it is common to distinguish between three levels of prevention: primary, which is the prevention of occurrence of the illness; secondary, which is the early diagnosis and treatment of an ailment to prevent its worsening and its progression to more aggravated states; and, finally, tertiary prevention, which is the control of mitigation of advanced conditions of illness, or rehabilitation when a disease has run its course or has been arrested. Some authorities also consider postponement of death as an aspect of tertiary prevention. . . .

Over and over again, no matter how earnestly we may try to discuss prevention by confining it to the biological and psychological sectors, we are compelled to confront the sociological influences. Over and over again, in the studies, researches, and reports on primary prevention, there loom in the background the mundane and inescapable conditions under which mothers, fathers, and children live out their lives. We confront problems of housing, jobs, travel, money, prejudice, the struggle for status and security. Over and over again, the ponderous and learned discussions on anxiety, guilt, shame, self-concept, aggression, negativism dissolve into the daily facts of daily living. . . .

Our society is so constructed that it deliberately violates one of the basic insights about human nature. There is nothing new about this insight. It is as ancient and venerable as the roots of scientific medicine and the origins of systematic philosophy. It was known to Hippocrates and is embodied in the oath which carries his name. It was known to Plato and Epictetus, to Avicenna and Maimonides, to Johann Weyer and Philippe Pinel. It was made the cornerstone of Harry Stack Sullivan's psychiatry, although Sullivan certainly did not invent it.

This powerful insight asserts that it is the relationships which prevail among men as individuals and as members of a structured society that ultimately determine their basic states of mental health and spiritual well-being. It is possible to have a strong and healthy mind in a weak, even a tortured and devastated human body. The example of Helen Keller comes to mind. But to have strong and healthy *collectivities of minds* we must have healthy social relationships.

To have societies where creativity and vigorous altruism prevail, we must have a social structure which fosters altruism. To have free, strong and happy men and women, we cannot tolerate social conditions which breed inferiority, insecurity and systematic exploitation of certain segments of society by other segments. . . .

The primary prevention of mental ill health does not have one precise locus. We cannot point to one action, one event, one mechanism, one area of intervention and say: this is the danger spot; this is where we do the preventing.

Indeed, in the final analysis we cannot prevent mental dysfunction in the way we speak of preventing typhus or polio, with inoculations or public health measures. There are no inoculations or public health measures that yield a healthy mind or a tranquil, loving soul. We prevent mental ill health through acts of universal promotion—through promoting social relationships and social structures which yield physical well-being, the general security and creative living patterns for all of mankind.

We shall be forever doomed to failure if we persist only in seeking to invent techniques of prevention, only in weaving subtle theories of human personality that will reveal the vulnerable crisis points, only in forwarding still newer and more fanciful fashions in psychotherapy. We are merely reshuffling the deck; the cards remain the same. Until we learn to prevent as well in the social order, there will be no real primary prevention.

In the United States today we do not yet possess a true philosophy of primary prevention, because we do not yet have clear convictions on how we must prevent in the social order. We do not yet have genuine programs of primary prevention because we are so committed and over-committed to symptomatic treatment methods.

We seem powerless, each of us in our own professional identities, to move in the direction of collective efforts, to regroup social forces with fearlessness and selflessness. At bottom, with the prominent exception of certain vital social security measures inaugurated in the 1930's, we in the United States are still operating in a framework of nineteenth-century concepts of charity, although we heatedly deny this.

What is needed is the strength, the audacity and the courage to sustain the broadest possible vision of man's ultimate potentialities, of his proved capacity to remake his own nature,[8] while at the same time working within the contemporary framework and its incredible flexible limitations. So much is possible, and so much is impossible.

We must have the courage to plunge into action despite the waves of ignorance and despair which pound all around us, despite our painful awareness that it is the destiny of man not to leap from ignorance and evil to wisdom and

[8] G. Murphy, *Human Potentialities*, New York: Basic Books, 1958.
[Kraft]

goodness, but rather to traverse an unknown road from error and limited vision to less error and less limited vision.

As teachers, nurses, counselors, parents, physicians, we too plod along this endless path which began in the times when the ice covered our planet and a frail thinking creature emerged to fashion tools and to be fashioned by them. It is our task to carry this creature another step along the path and, while so doing, to diminish pain, to remove obstacles, to forestall error and failure.

But this is work not of prevention but of promotion. In the last analysis we will prevent those nonbiological failures, dysfunctions, errors and miseries of behavior which we lump together and call mental illness only if we are bold and courageous in promoting those still tenuous and primitively developed capacities of man for tenderness, sympathy, altruism and selflessness.

What, then, is true prevention? It is the continual creation and re-creation of a world which fosters these capacities among men.[9]

[9] Ivor Kraft, "Preventing Mental Ill Health in Early Childhood," *Mental Hygiene*, July, 1964, pp. 414, 418–419, 419–420, 421–422.

QUESTIONS AND PROBLEMS

1. Discuss the concept and significance of mental hygiene.

2. Trace the history of the mental hygiene movement.

3. Differentiate among the concepts of prevention, preservation, and cure of mental ill health as used in mental hygiene.

4. Evaluate the contribution of the National Association for Mental Health to the problem of mental health in your community.

5. Discuss the value of a well-planned schedule of activities to mental health.

6. How widespread is the problem of mental illness in the United States?

7. List and explain the concomitants of good mental health.

8. By what means can an individual's self-realization be strengthened?

9. In what ways are mental activities related to mental health status?

10. List government agencies concerned with the problems of mental health.

11. Show the relationship that is believed to exist between physical and mental health

12. Discuss the responsibility of the school and the home for the mental health of young people.

13. Personal human values can result from religious beliefs. Explain.

14. Explain the value and effectiveness of juvenile courts.

15. Explain the extent to which and the ways in which your opinion differs from your attitude.

16. Recall a crisis you have experienced. Report on what you did to meet it.

17. What provisions does industry make for the continuance of good mental health among workers?

18. Trace applications of mental health principles in the developing individual. Give examples of problems associated with different age levels.

19. Differentiate among the mental health problems of young adults, middle-aged individuals, and older persons.

20. Summarize Kraft's suggestions concerning the value of preventing mental ill health during childhood.

Selected Readings

Berne, E., *Games People Play: The Psychology of Human Relationships*. New York: Grove Press, Inc., 1964.

Carroll, H. A., *Mental Hygiene: The Dynamics of Adjustment*, 4th ed. Englewood Cliffs, N.J.: Prentice-Hall, Inc., 1964.

Crow, L. D., and A. Crow (eds.), *Mental Hygiene for Teachers: Readings*. New York: The Macmillan Company, 1963.

Hountras, P. T. (ed.), *Mental Hygiene: A Text of Readings*. Columbus, Ohio: Charles E. Merrill Books, Inc., 1961.

Jourard, S. M., *Personal Adjustment: An Approach to the Study of Healthy Personality*, 2nd ed. New York: The Macmillan Company, 1963.

Katz, R. L., *Empathy: Its Nature and Uses*. New York: Free Press of Glencoe, 1963.

Kemp, C. G., *Perspectives on the Group Process: A Foundation for Counseling with Groups*. Boston, Mass.: Houghton Mifflin Company, 1964.

Langner, T. S., and S. T. Michael, *Life Stress and Mental Health*. New York: Free Press of Glencoe, 1963.

Lehner, G. F. J., and E. Kube, *The Dynamics of Personal Adjustment*, 2nd ed. Englewood Cliffs, N.J.: Prentice-Hall, Inc., 1964.

Levinson, H. *et al.*, *Men, Management and Mental Health*. Cambridge, Mass.: Harvard University Press, 1962.

Lindgren, H. C., *Psychology of Personal and Social Adjustment*, 2nd ed. New York: American Book Company, 1959.

Redl, F., and W. W. Wattenberg, *Mental Hygiene in Teaching*, 2nd ed. New York: Harcourt, Brace & World, Inc., 1959.

Rogers, C. R., *On Becoming a Person: A Therapist's View of Psychotherapy*. Boston, Mass.: Houghton Mifflin Company, 1961.

Sawrey, J. M., and C. W. Telford, *Dynamics of Mental Health: The Psychology of Adjustment*. Boston, Mass.: Allyn and Bacon, Inc., 1963.

Schneiders, A. A., *Personality Dynamics and Mental Health*, rev. ed. New York: Holt, Rinehart and Winston, Inc., 1965.

Stern, E. M., *Mental Illness: A Guide for the Family*, 4th ed. New York: Harper & Row, Publishers, 1962.

Stern, P. J., *The Abnormal Person and His World*. Princeton, N.J.: D. Van Nostrand Company, Inc., 1964.

Sullivan, J. S., *The Fusion of Psychiatry and Social Science*. New York: W. W. Norton & Company, Inc., 1964.

Taylor, L., and S. Chave, *Mental Health and Environment*. Boston, Mass.: Little, Brown and Company, 1964.

Thorpe, L. P., *The Psychology of Mental Health*, 2nd ed. New York: The Ronald Press Company, 1960.

❧ 14 ❧

ADJUSTMENTS
TO
FAMILY LIFE

OF PRIMARY importance to the degree of successful adjustment achieved by an individual in his continuing experiences with people, things, and conditions are the attitudes and behavior patterns he develops gradually as a member of his family group. These adjustive experiences begin early in the home of his parents and continue later as an adult in his own home.

THE SIGNIFICANCE OF THE HOME

The home is the first and probably the most significant agent in the adjustment of any individual toward successful living. In his family relationships he develops adjustment patterns that are basic to his larger social interactions. It is in the well-organized and hygienic home that the individual receives fundamental training in the development of desirable social attitudes and habits of behavior. It is in the close and intimate relationship of family life that he gains a desirable understanding of individual rights and responsibilities, the use and abuse of authority, and the principles of organized group living. It is in the home that he first experiences his joys and his sorrows, his enthusiasms and his disappointments, his pities and his resentments.

The fact that family life influences and is influenced by affective responses is itself a significant cause of the difficulty experienced by many individuals in their attempt to achieve satisfactory family adjustments. It is relatively easier to be objective and impersonal in one's general social relationships than it is to be so in the intimacy of family experiences. The affection that is so important a factor of these intimate relations is itself the stimulator of subjective, often unreasonable, and frequently disturbing conflicts within the individual himself and between the members of the family.

Man's relationship to his home and his emotional reactions to all that it signifies to him are traditional themes of prose, poetry, and song. The importance to humans of their home associations is reflected in such well-known expressions as "home, sweet home," "home is where the heart is," "homesickness," "home cooking," and "I want to go home." No matter what the actual living conditions in the home may have been, memory tends to keep green only those incidents of past home life that cause desire for the reliving of the remembered happenings. The possession of a home with all its opportunities for self-expression and development appears to be a general human urge.

THE FAMILY AND
SPECIAL ADJUSTMENT PROBLEMS

In its broadest connotation, the family can be interpreted as including all those individuals who are related to one another by heredity or marriage: husband and wife, parents and children, sisters and brothers, aunts and uncles, nephews and nieces, cousins, and in-laws. More narrowly interpreted, the family consists of a married couple and their child or children. In our present discussion we shall stress the adjustment factors in light of the second meaning of the term. The relative success or failure of the more intimate family unit depends primarily on the habitual attitudes and behavior patterns of the man and woman who marry and become parents.

The success or failure of the family as a social unit is, to a high degree, dependent on the success or failure of the husband

and wife as individual members of society, and on the success or failure of the interaction of these two individuals with each other, with their children, and with other members of their respective families. The physical health of the husband and wife, their mental efficiency, and their emotional stability are basic factors of family adjustment and of effective family living.

Beginning in adolescence and continuing through young adulthood, the individual becomes increasingly concerned with the problems of family living. He senses various problems of adjustment and decision-making in areas such as mate selection, and the achievement of emotional and financial security. His attitudes and ideals for his future home are influenced positively or negatively by those displayed by his parents.

A study of some factors of marital adjustment faced by college students who were married and one or both attending college was conducted by Florence D. Aller. The purpose of the study was to find the extent to which 100 couples (at least one member from each couple was enrolled at the University of Idaho) were "achieving harmony and mutual satisfaction in the marriage relationship." The median ages of husbands and wives were 23.9 and 22.2 years, respectively. The results are summarized in Table 13.

Another influence on marital adjustment is the birth of the first child. A study of middle-class parents was completed by Everett D. Dyer, and some of his significant findings are reported here.

> The husband-wife courtship and pre-parenthood marriage relationship has become routinized and satisfying to the couple over the years, and then the intrusion of a third member (non-socialized and all-demanding) calls inevitably for substantial readjustments in the husband-wife interaction patterns. Will the child's claim of priority on the mother make the husband feel he is the third party in the trio, a semi-isolate perhaps, as LeMasters suggests? Or, in some instances, does the wife come to feel that her husband is more interested in the child than in her now?
>
> The present findings supported this hypothesis in some degree. While 37 percent of the husbands felt their wives never neglected them for the baby, 50 percent felt she

TABLE 13

Causes of Serious Difficulty in Own Marriage as Indicated by
59.5 Percent of Subjects *

Problem Causing Difficulty	Men		Women		Both Sexes	
	N	Percent	N	Percent	N	Percent
Stubbornness	34	59.5	31	50.0	65	54.6
Nagging or criticism by spouse	21	36.9	21	33.8	42	35.3
In-laws	8	14.0	17	27.4	25	21.0
Selfishness	11	19.3	13	21.0	24	20.2
Jealousy	8	14.0	9	14.5	17	14.3
Spouse does less than (his, her) share of "family chores"	4	7.0	13	21.0	17	14.3
Health problems	9	15.8	6	9.7	15	12.6
Spouse "gets on my nerves"	5	8.8	7	11.3	12	10.1
Dishonesty	6	10.6	2	3.2	8	6.7
Disagreement on rearing of children	6	10.6	2	3.2	8	6.7
Other causes of difficulty	2	3.5	6	9.7	8	6.7
All causes	114		127		241	
Mean number of difficulties	2		2		2	

* There were 57 men and 62 women who indicated they had serious problems.

Source: Florence D. Aller, "Some Factors in Marital Adjustment and Academic Achievement of Married Students," Personnel and Guidance Journal, March, 1963, p. 611. Reprinted by permission.

sometimes did, and another 12 percent said she often did. Recall that among the more frequently mentioned "crisis" problems of the wives were such items as "husband grew tired of being second," and "less time to give to my husband," etc. Only 12 percent of the wives felt their husbands sometimes neglected them for the child, however.

LeMasters suggests "that parenthood (not marriage) marks the final transition to maturity and adult responsibility in our culture. Thus the arrival of the first child forces the young married couples to take the last painful step into the adult world," jarring them out of the honeymoon stage of marriage, as it were.

In the present study 50 percent of the husbands and 87

percent of the wives felt that parenthood had indeed been a maturing experience.

Indication of the maturing function of parenthood, and increased awareness of adult responsibilities, may be seen in the comments and advice they offer to other young couples expecting their first child, e.g.: (1) "Realize your life will be different because of addition of the baby, but it will be a better and more complete life"; (2) "If the husband and wife want the child and will share the responsibilities, I think they will be happier, and the child will deepen their love for each other. It is a new but very rewarding experience." There were many other similar expressions. All of the husbands and all but two of the wives said they now felt much better prepared for any subsequent children they might have.[1]

Adolescent Attitudes Toward Marriage

Adolescent attitudes toward marriage and the beginning of a family differ from one another although certain trends can be found. For example, Harold T. Christensen conducted a study to discover answers to the question, "What do high school students plan for the approximately sixty years of life left to them following graduation?"

As a result of the study of the replies of 2,000 tenth, eleventh, and twelfth grade high school students concerning their marriage and family plans, he drew the following conclusions:

1. On the average, males wanted to marry 3.9 years after graduation and females 3.0 years. Both sexes thought the first child should come about 1.6 years from marriage. Thus, the males of the sample planned to start their families about five and one-half, and the females about four and one-half, years following graduation.

If high school graduation can be assumed to take place at age eighteen, the average male in our sample wanted to marry at age twenty-two and to have his first child by the time he was twenty-three and one-half. Respective ages cal-

[1] Everett D. Dyer, "Parenthood as Crisis: A Restudy," *Marriage and Family Living*, May, 1963, p. 201.

culated for the female are twenty-one and twenty-two and one-half.[2]

2. Males and females who planned to marry either during or very soon after high school were predominantly from low income and low educational level homes. And, as might be expected, they viewed themselves as discontinuing school and entering either jobs, military service, or homemaking (females) immediately following graduation.

3. An insignificant number of females (2 percent) but almost one-tenth of the males (9 percent) stated that they planned not to marry at all. These non-marriage oriented males were predominantly from the lower social classes and they intended, more than did other males, to discontinue school following graduation.

4. Approximately one out of every ten in our sample (10 percent of the males and 11 percent of the females) declared that they would "let nature decide" when the first child was to be born. In general, these were the ones who expected a child during the first year of marriage. They were predominantly Catholic and from the lower income classes.

5. Male and female respondents differed in their conceptions of woman's role. For example, only 10 percent of the females expected to be in homemaking the first year following graduation, whereas 25 percent of the males thought that the girl they eventually married would be in homemaking immediately following her graduation. Similarly, 62 percent of the females, as compared with only 37 percent of the males, named either full or part time jobs as an activity for the female during this first post-graduation year.[3]

Courtship in Mate Selection

The wise choice of a mate should be of pre-eminent importance to every man and woman contemplating marriage. The

[2] Obviously high school students are not entirely realistic, since on the average U.S. marriages *actually occur* at about ages 23 for the male and 20 for the female and the first birth *actually* takes place about one year after marriage. [Christensen]

[3] Harold T. Christensen, "Lifetime Family and Occupational Role Projections of High School Students," *Marriage and Family Living*, May, 1961, pp. 181–182.

reports of the United States Census Bureau indicate that at present not only are more persons marrying but that they are marrying at an earlier age. Unfortunately, it also is a fact that the rate of divorce is alarmingly high, indicating that too many men and women either are not taking marriage seriously or are unprepared to meet the responsibilities of family life.

Marital success seems to be associated with similarity of mental status, cultural background, religious affiliation, and life interests. Modern culture, however, tends to accept the basis of marriage to be romantic love. Sexual attraction alone cannot be expected to ensure marital bliss and effective parenthood. Help ful experiences in their parents' home and constructive education for home and family life are needed to ensure for a young couple the achieving of desirable family adjustment. As a result of a study to determine teen-agers' attitudes toward child rearing, the evidence indicates that the kind of parents teen-agers will become depends on the training they received both in their homes and in the school.[4]

The impulsive nature of romantic love may blind the young person to the importance of other factors as determiners of a successful marriage relationship. The emotional factor is important in mate selection, but good marital adjustment requires that the man and woman recognize their marital responsibilities and are prepared to meet them. Early home training, the relationship of parents to one another and to their children, and the training, stability, and ability of a young person exercise a definite influence on his own attitude toward the choosing of his mate.

Occupational or educational association, or neighborhood propinquity may be a determining factor of one's "falling in love." An individual tends to be attracted toward a member of the other sex who is like himself in disposition, ability, or physical constitution. His choice of mate is influenced also by similarity in personality characteristics, economic status, and social class. There is probably more chance of marital success between persons of similar interests, culture, education, religion, and traditional background than is possible if the mates are so different from one another in any of these respects that understanding and tolerance of such differences are not possible.

---

[4] Evelyn Mills Duvall, "What Kind of Parents Will Today's Teen-agers Be?" *Marriage and Family Living*, August, 1960, pp. 264–266.

Adjustment Problems of Courtship

The nature and intensity of the adjustment problems that may arise during the period of courtship are closely related to personality characteristics of each of the two persons concerned and the bases upon which mate selection is founded. The term *courting* can be interpreted to include an older adolescent's or an adult's relationships with members of the opposite sex which may eventuate in mate selection and marriage. In a narrow connotation of the term, courtship refers to behavior during the period of time between final mate selection and marriage, commonly referred to as *the engagement period*.

In either case, the length of time that elapses between first acquaintance with the future mate and marriage and the extent of knowledge about each other that is achieved during that period of time are important factors of marital adjustment. Some research studies in this area of human relationship yield results that would seem to indicate that the optimum period is at least one year in length. According to statistical data, a whirlwind courtship followed by marriage after a brief period of acquaintance is provocative of marital incompatibility. Regardless of the cause, an engagement period that is prolonged beyond the point of emotional involvement also constitutes inadequate preparation for successful marriage relationships. These conclusions apply generally; yet, in some instances, too short or too long a courtship period in no way interfered with the success of the marriage.

Intensity of sexual attraction is closely related to the effectiveness of courtship as preparation for marriage. Petting is coming to be considered a normal accompaniment of courtship. Holding hands, embracing, and occasional kissing are accepted activities of young people who think that they are "in love." Such physical contacts can arouse strong sexual urges unless both individuals possess considerable self-control. To control further erotically stimulated physical activities short of the point of coitus is a tension-arousing and frustrating experience. The exercise of sexual control is particularly difficult for the engaged couple.

The engaged man and woman desire physical contact with each other. They become emotionally and physically stirred through their petting activities. Then arises the question concerning the possible harm of coitus, especially if the marriage date has been set for the immediate future. There is difference of opinion concerning premarital sexual intercourse. Its advocates assert that the young couple thereby can discover the extent to which they are sexually compatible. On the debit side, however, must be taken into account the possible results of coitus: arousal of guilt feelings, fear of pregnancy, repulsion, or lack of interest in the experience on the part of one of them. Strong feelings of frustration may result if the situational factors make coitus impossible or unsatisfying; the frustrated partner may decide that he or she is sexually impotent or unfitted for marital sexual relations.

There are other problems that are associated with engagement: what one should tell the other concerning his past, whether an engaged person should limit his or her social activities to those which can be shared with the other, the extent to which the engaged couple should plan ahead concerning income and budgeting, the continuation after marriage of the present occupational activity of the woman, the bearing and rearing of children, the kind of home which they shall establish, and the elaborateness of their wedding. The final decisions vary with conditions and individual interests of the couple. To attempt a satisfactory settlement of these issues becomes a test of the ability of each to cooperate and to compromise. It provides each with an opportunity to evaluate the other's degree of emotional control and intelligent approach to problem-solving, and alerts each to what may be the marital attitude and behavior of the other.

Mate Selection

The selection of a marriage partner has had an interesting history. Respective cultures have imposed specific regulations concerning who shall marry. Political, religious, economic, and family restrictions of one kind or another have controlled and still control mate selection among differing societal groups.

MARRIAGE CONCEPTS. Polyandry (one woman with several husbands) and polygamy (one husband having several wives) still are conventional forms of marriage among some of the more primitive peoples. The so-called civilized world, however, is committed to the concept of monogamy, or one mate for each person. Moreover, in those cultures in which only the monogamous form of marriage has legal status most marriage rituals imply, through the words "till death do us part," that the one marriage shall be a permanent relationship until the death of one of the mates.

Traditionally, the female mate was expected to be chaste before her marriage. The discovery by her husband, during the couple's first sexual intercourse, that his wife's hymen had been broken was legal cause for an annulment of the marriage. Real or imagined evidence of a wife's infidelity to her husband also constituted grounds for the husband's dissolving the marital relationship.

With a few exceptions societal groups always have and still continue to display a generally accepting attitude toward male sexual activities. This attitude probably is rooted in a traditional belief that for the male sexual intercourse is a necessary activity for the maintenance of good health, strength, and virility. The female, as was noted earlier, was expected to be the passive recipient of the male's sexual aggression; she subjected herself to, rather than desired, the sex act. We now know, of course, that the sex desire is as strong in the female as in the male.

There still are parents who attempt to guard jealously the chastity of their unmarried daughters, but they prefer sons-in-law who have had considerable experience in sexual activity or "have sowed their wild oats." The implication of this expressed parental attitude was the fact that an "experienced" man probably would be less likely to engage in extramarital sex relations. The possibility of the man's having contracted a venereal disease before his marriage was not considered a significant factor of suitability for marriage. Many states, however, have enacted legislation requiring that both the man and the woman submit to a premarriage physical examination to detect symptoms of venereal disease.

TRADITIONAL BASES FOR MATE SELECTION. In many of the older cultures marriages were arranged by parents on the bases of parent-determined suitability of the match. Socioeconomic status and degree of prestige of the families concerned often were considered to be the determining factors of suitability; the girl's parents supplied the dowry, the man's contribution was his superior social status. In many instances the man had the privilege of selecting a girl to whom, at the time, he was sexually attracted or who would be likely to bear him children and establish a comfortable home environment. Whether the girl was emotionally stirred by her suitor was not important. It was taken for granted that the marriage relationship would stimulate in the woman the development of wifely attitudes of loyalty to and respect and liking for her husband.

In spite of traditionally established controls over mate selection, many young people managed to marry persons of their own selection. History has given us stories of great lovers, either married or unmarried. Romantic love, as a generally accepted basis of mate selection, however, is a relatively recent concept. At present a mate may be selected for reasons other than strong emotional attachment; yet it is customary for friends and relatives of the couple to express the conviction, at least superficially, that the contemplated marriage be based on "true love." Many problems of marital adjustment stem from this sentimental attitude toward the marriage relationship in conjunction with the social acceptance of freedom in mate selection as a democratic ideal.

MODERN BASES OF MATE SELECTION. Each state enacts legislation concerning the age at which a young person may marry without parental consent. When a young man or woman has reached the legal status of an adult, as prescribed in his or her state, the person is at liberty to marry and to be unrestricted in the choice of mate. In fact, except in cases of extreme sex perversion or of venereal-disease infection, much latitude is permitted an individual in connection with his sexual activities and relationships.

Thoughtless mate selection and "quick" marriages are the resultants of various sex-stimulated phases and conditions of modern life. However, not all young people are motivated toward hasty, nonconsidered mate selection and marriage. Stabilizing factors can offset the effects of unwholesome or abnormal sex-stimulating situations, conditions, or experiences. It cannot be denied, however, that changes are taking place in man-woman relationships, bases of mate selection, premarital attitudes, and marriage status.

The equalization between the sexes of educational, occupational, and political opportunities and freedom of behavior has led to the development in members of each sex of a better understanding of and respect for members of the opposite sex. The "veil of mystery" in which one sex was enshrouded for the other has given way to the possibilities of objective evaluation of one another. During the early days of the feminist movement some older, conventionally minded men and women expressed the fear that equalization of the rights of men and women would cause women to lose their femininity and men to become less masculine. Inherent physical and temperamental differences between the sexes are such, however, that, with few exceptions, each sex apparently is continuing to maintain his or her particular sex role.

PROBLEMS OF MATE SELECTION. From the societal and religious point of view the fundamental purpose of marriage is to establish a home and raise a family. In earlier times the selection of a mate and consequent marriage followed this pattern. An important factor of the woman's choice of mate was the man's ability to provide a good living for his family; the man sought a woman who would bear him many children, and be an efficient wife and mother. When the home constituted the center for the provision of life necessities, a large family was an asset. Especially was this the case on a farm. Religious teachings encouraged this attitude toward the function of marriage; among some societal groups a large family was also regarded to be parental insurance against a destitute old age.

During the past half century or more the marriage function changed. Life necessities were made available through mass production outside the home; as a result of their increased educational and career opportunities, women no longer accept marriage as their only ultimate destiny. They have come to exercise greater freedom of choice concerning mate selection and marriage. Successful career achievement and economic independence, especially among more able women, have altered the bases of mate selection, marriage relations, and size of family. For the economically secure woman, the choice of a mate who will be a good provider is not imperative. Moreover, a woman who can or wishes to continue to be gainfully employed after marriage usually is interested in having a small and planned family. This attitude is strengthened by the fact that many couples believe that they owe their children whatever luxuries and success-achieving educational and vocational opportunities are available. Hence, in urban areas especially, there are many childless couples or families that consist of two gainfully employed parents and one or two children.

In rural areas the establishment of a home that contains a large family, financially provided for by the father and cared for by the mother, continues to be a purpose of mate selection and marriage; at present there is also an observable trend in this direction among city dwellers. Various personal desires, interests, or conditions determine an individual's decision to marry and the choice of mate.

Among the factors that are basic to mate selection in our modern American culture can be included one or more of the following: sexual attraction, romantic love, companionship, emotional security, desire for home and a family, escape from an unsatisfactory home situation, parental influence, loneliness, adventure, social position and prestige, financial security, gratitude, urge to reform (especially among women), notoriety, example set by members of one's intimate social group, premarital pregnancy, self-assertion in face of parental opposition, military or occupational pressure, and a felt need to regain self-esteem that may have been lost or severely damaged by being "jilted" by the first selected mate.

Unless the mate has been selected in terms of mutual attraction and respect, and similarity of interests and ideals, the chances are slim for the achievement of marital adjustment. If other factors are favorable, it is generally believed that a marriage is likely to succeed: if the woman is younger than the man (optimal age for the woman is between 20 and 25 years, actual median age is 21.6 years at marriage; for the man it is between 22 and 27 years, actual median age is 24.3); if both have the same religious affiliation; if they have equal intelligence and educational status, or if the man's is slightly higher than the woman's; if the couple became acquainted in educational or occupational surroundings rather than in a social situation only; if the marriage represents freedom in mate selection; if the parents of either mate accept the other mate, and if the socioeconomic level of both mates is similar.

Important as these factors may seem, many marriages have been successful regardless of the lack of one or more of the favorable factors listed. The possible marital problems that might arise from differences in age, socioeconomic or educational status, religious affiliation, parental attitudes, or any other differences can be recognized before marriage by both the man and the woman, discussed frankly by them, and agreement reached concerning their solution. Marriage counselors have discovered that the primary cause of marital discord and mate incompatibility appears to be rooted in the personal inadequacies of either or both mates.

The emotionally uncontrolled, self-centered, and self-indulging child and adolescent becomes the uncooperative, adversely critical husband or wife who displays an inconsiderate and rejecting attitude toward the mate. As we have said earlier, sexual incompatibility or an abnormal attitude toward marital sex relations is conducive to sexual unfaithfulness to the spouse. Too great difference in ideals, interests, or behavior habits may give rise to feelings of boredom, lack of respect, or disgust. It is during the period of courtship that the couple can evaluate each other's personal characteristics and decide whether they can be tolerated. If not, a broken engagement is better than an unhappy marriage or a marriage that ends in separation or divorce.

In his study, "Dating Maturation of Children from Happy and Unhappy Marriages," Landis [5] found significant differences existing between children from happy and unhappy marriages. This is especially true in their self-evaluations and indicated confidence in their heterosexual relationships. However, children who believed the marriages of their parents were happy indicated higher self-evaluations and greater confidence in heterosexual behavior than did children who believed the marriages of their parents to be unhappy.

Special Considerations

In order to discover the relationships that may exist between mate selection and social class, a study was made of 2,706 marriage license applications issued in Columbus, Ohio, during four months (March, June, September, and December) of four years

[5] Judson T. Landis, "Dating Maturation of Children from Happy and Unhappy Marriages," *Marriage and Family Living*, August, 1963, pp. 349–353.

(1933–1938, and 1957–1958). The names, addresses, ages, and occupations of the marriage applicants were placed in their appropriate files. The findings are reported as follows:

> The results of this study are more provocative than conclusive. Two major developments in mate selection patterns in metropolitan Columbus, Ohio, appear to have occurred in the last quarter of a century. On the one hand, there has been a tendency for maximally endogamous marriages to decline. On the other hand, and as originally suggested, there has been an equally significant decline in widely disparate marriages. In short, both extremes have declined, and marriages contracted by persons of relatively similar socio-economic status and tract residences have increased.[6]

If an individual hopes to achieve effective family living, he must approach the question of his marital choice intelligently, thoughtfully, and objectively. Although marriage is no longer viewed as a business arrangement, the individual dare not allow himself to be swept off his feet by a sudden and unreasonable passion for a member of the opposite sex whom he finds later to be entirely unsuited to himself in attitudes, ideals, interests, or behavior habits. The basis of marriage needs to be affection and a desire to be with the other person; however, unless the man and the woman have been prepared through education and control of emotions to face this momentous decision with reasonable calmness and forethought, the success of the mating is unpredictable.

The age at which to marry, the kind of person to marry, the length of the courtship, and similar considerations can be decided by each individual in terms of his personality qualities, degree of maturity, and economic and social status. The choice, however, is one to be made carefully. An individual should not give more time and thought to the selection of a garment to wear, an automobile, or a house than he does to his choice of a mate.

The length of the courtship depends on the individual's readiness to marry and on his or her other responsibilities. Too short a period of time between the agreement to marry and the

---

[6] Simon Dinitz, Franklin Banks, and Benjamin Pasamanick, "Mate Selection and Social Class: Changes During the Past Quarter Century," *Marriage and Family Living*, November, 1960, p. 349.

marriage itself does not allow the couple to become acquainted with one another, unless the engagement follows a long friendship. Too long an engagement may introduce factors of boredom, may cause the relationship to become a habit, or may impose too great strain on the emotional control needed during this prenuptial intimacy if conventional standards of behavior are to be adhered to.

The behavior of engaged persons toward one another may create difficult situations. Society disapproves of premarital sexual intimacies. If such practices are engaged in, there is danger that the marital relationship will thereby be hurt. It is generally agreed that the most desirable length of an engagement is between six months and one year. This gives the pair an opportunity to become accustomed to each other's habits. The period is short enough so that they may bring to their marriage the freshness and expectancy of the love experience. It is important and in some states obligatory that a physical examination precede the marriage so that each individual may bring to the marriage state a physical constitution basic to a successful and happy marriage.

The extent to which husband and wife achieve a personally and socially satisfactory marriage depends on their ability, singly and together, to fulfill adequately the responsibilities and functions of the marital state. Willingness and ability to have children in accordance with the mate's hopes and desires, a sane and adult attitude toward the sexual relationship, sexual harmony, emotional maturity, mutual understanding and tolerance, desire and ability to cooperate with each other toward socially desirable goals, and similarity of interests are the keystones of marital happiness. If there is disharmony or an unresolvable difference in any of these factors, marital conflict and disorganization are almost inevitable.

Marital Adjustments

If a marriage is to be successful, the two persons concerned need to know one another well before they enter into the marriage relationship. They should have discussed frankly and come to an acceptable agreement concerning important factors of marital adjustment such as: attitude toward the sex relationship, desire to have a family, arrangements concerning budgetary matters, religious beliefs, social and recreational interests, and the extent to which the two will participate alone or together in leisure-time activities. Moreover, the wife-to-be should be certain that she is interested in and possesses some understanding of the man's occupational activities so that she can evince an intelligent interest in his work.

The young couple also should come to an agreement concerning the attitude that each will have after marriage toward friendships made and social activities engaged in before marriage. If marriage is to be a workable partnership, the man or woman usually should give up his or her earlier interests unless the mate can be brought into the situation in a wholesome and satisfying way. Otherwise, petty jealousies or serious marital conflicts may result. Misunderstanding and recriminations are likely to follow if either mate insists on continuing social relationships with members of the opposite sex that were established before marriage. The wife becomes jealous of the girls that her husband knew well before he was married, especially if he continues to see them or expects his wife to accept them as welcome guests in her new home. She may come to believe that her husband regrets his choice of her as a mate. She may become inordinately sensitive of anything he says or does that would seem to indicate that he still admires one of his former women friends.

Similarly, a man is likely to be wary concerning the men with whom his wife associated before marriage and who still are counted among her friends. He tends to compare himself unfavorably with these others. He especially resents those who seem to be more successful financially than himself. He feels inadequate. He comes to believe that his wife is dissatisfied with what he can offer her in the way of comforts and luxuries. He may decide that his wife regrets her marriage to him rather than to one of her other admirers. No matter whether or not the husband or wife is correct in this attitude toward the mate's former friends, the relationship between the two becomes strained. They tend to lose that close understanding so necessary to marital adjustment, unless each can assure the other, both before and throughout their married life, by word and deed, that the past is a closed book and that henceforth they belong only to each other.

Marital differences are bound to occur. It must be remembered that each mate is an individual with a developed pattern of habitual attitudes and behavior. No matter how good a job of becoming well-acquainted with each other the man and woman have done before marriage, adjustment is a continuous requirement. The day-by-day intimacies of married life are accompanied by differences of opinion concerning minor or serious matters that may cause friction between the two. Also, either one may become emotionally disturbed by factors outside the home and "take it out" on the mate.

Each needs to bring to a real or a fancied difficulty an intelligent desire to solve the problem constructively. For the wife to run home to her mother or the husband to spend the night away from the home in order to "bring the other to his or her senses" is an immature way of trying to settle the difficulty. The intellect and not the emotions should control. If there must be a quarrel, it should end constructively so that the marriage bond is stronger when it is over. If too many disagreements are allowed to interfere with marital faith and love, it is almost impossible to close the rifts successfully.

It is relatively easy to say what should be done to effect a well-adjusted marriage relationship; to so regulate one's attitudes and behavior that the marriage will be successful is a difficult task that requires constant thoughtful attention. Bowman presents basic ideas on the attitude of adjustment.

In marriage the concept of adjustment is fundamental. But adjustment to what? Two personalities must adjust to each other, to the marital situation in both the narrow and the broad sense, and to social conditions in general. All these elements are continually in a state of flux. Marriage is a process, not a constant. Marital adjustment is, therefore, dynamic rather than static. It does not imply one person's adjusting to another as if the other person were a fixed point and both were seeking to reach a dead level of changeless equilibrium. Being dynamic, it implies a developing mutual relationship in which resources for satisfaction are more and more fully drawn upon. Preparation for marriage is of necessity generalized. In marriage, adjustment becomes particularized through knowledge, love, discovery, effort, and ingenuity.

Adjustment does not imply that one person must do all

the adjusting or that there shall always be compromise. There may be situations in which no compromise is acceptable, as for instance, in cases of excessive alcoholism or infidelity. Even in such cases, however, a study of causes is important and readjustment may be possible.

Every problem of marriage adjustment or human relationships, with a few possible theoretical exceptions, is two-sided and occurs in a milieu, against a background of the marital and social situation. Adjustment may be achieved by one person's changing his behavior, by the other's changing his attitude, by a change in the elements that compose the situation—such as income, housing, or proximity to relatives.

Adjustment implies relief from tension. The only complete relief is death. All life involves tension, some of which is never completely relieved, while some may be temporarily relieved. In marriage there is always some tension because marriage involves the relationship of two persons of opposite sex. A perfect adjustment, with complete relief from tension, could be achieved only by sexless automata. Continual adjustment to tension infuses zest into marriage. When adjustment does not eventuate, that same tension may produce dissatisfaction or failure.[7]

Effective Parenthood

The birth of a child brings with it many changes in the relationship of husband and wife. By the time the first child is born, they probably have become adjusted to their new life together. They have effected an economic program of living, they have adjusted to their daily schedule of activities, and they have developed satisfactory social relationships. Now the pattern of life is disturbed. The financial budget requires reorganization, the daily program must be changed, and social activities are interfered with, sometimes unduly so by the wife. The attention and care that the young husband has learned to expect from his wife suddenly must be shared with the child. The wife's health

---

[7] Henry A. Bowman, *Marriage for Moderns*, 4th ed., New York: McGraw-Hill, 1960, pp. 287–288.

may suffer. The parents may not agree on the proper care and training of the child. The home has changed in its function, and adjustments to the changed conditions must be made.

As other children are born, as all the children develop and make new and constantly increasing demands on their parents' time, attention, and money, this adjustment process must keep pace with the new demands. A different relationship develops between the parents. They must learn to face their increasing responsibilities together, and they must consider not only their adjustment to their children but also to one another.

The responsibility of the parents is not only to care for the physical needs of the young people but also to provide their children with a healthy environment, to inculcate healthful ideals, attitudes, and interests, and to encourage their children toward desirable educational progress, socially acceptable behavior, and emotional control so that the young people may benefit from them. Finally, they must prepare their children for future family responsibilities by setting an example of harmonious, contented, and stimulating marital adjustments and by providing adequate and intelligent sex education.

Education toward the development of desirable attitudes concerning physical structure and physiological functions should, ideally, begin early in the home and continue there during the child's preadolescent and adolescent years. However, the school can do much to supplement the home in various matters dealing with sex. Many parents and religious groups, on the whole, oppose the schools' teaching sex, while more enlightened adults readily admit the value of the school's usefulness in this area of education. Suitable courses are now being introduced into the curriculum on various school levels.

Children who spend their childhood and youth in a well-organized and harmonious environment, who have not been retarded or inhibited in their development by family conflict, who respect and love their parents, who have learned to recognize their own rights and responsibilities as well as those of other members of the family are more than likely to become effective parents in their own homes. Such children tend to bring to the solution of their youthful and adult problems a capacity for intelligent thinking that they have attained through the observation of their parents' behavior in difficult situations.

THE INDIVIDUAL, HIS HOME, AND
HIS FAMILY

Family life embodies human craving for security, understanding, sympathy, privacy, and intimate relationships. The home environment is a molder of human habits, ideals, and attitudes. It is supreme in its opportunities for self-development, self-realization, and social interaction. In the home, the individual first learns to appreciate himself as a member of a group bound by ties of kinship and by similarity of interests and abilities. Here, too, he meets his first conflicts between rights and responsibilities. In his home an individual may experience his greatest thrills of successful achievement or his most serious thwarting. The individual is fundamentally a reflection of his home environment.

Concept of Home and Family

Although it is possible for an individual to regard as *home* that place in which he lives alone, the word *home* usually implies the presence of other persons who generally are referred to as the *family*. All members of a family, however, need not at any one time live in the same home. The term family sometimes is limited to those immediate relatives who share with an individual his place of residence and general plan of life, but it also is used to include all persons who are related to the individual by birth or marriage.

The average family reflects in its accustomed behavior and interactions the standards and ideals of the social group or community of which the family is an integral part. On the other hand, in the family itself as a primary social unit are developed those attitudes, ideals, and practices that the members of the family carry into their associations with other members of the social group. These later become the bases of the general cultural ideals and standards of that group. In this way a family's attitudes and ideals tend to mold not only the customs and traditions of the community in which it functions but also predetermine to a great extent the traditional and cultural patterns that govern the behavior and ideals of succeeding generations. No family or community can be evaluated apart from its debt to the past or its effect upon the future. Anyone interested in the problem of adjustment cannot treat lightly the influence of the home and of the family in the development of well-adjusted or inadequate behavior patterns.

Individual Rights and Privileges in the Family

One of the basic causes of family adjustment or maladjustment is found in the type of relationship which exists among the various members of any specific family. Inherent in every normal individual are two fundamental urges—one for power and the other for personal freedom of thought and of action. If the members of a family are to live together amicably there must be a complete understanding concerning the extent to which each member of the group assumes specific responsibility for the well-being of himself and of his kin, and the amount of and direction of his own freedom of behavior in relation to the rights and responsibilities of the other members. The history of family development gives indication of the fact that there have been varying emphases upon the authority and freedom within the family group. The modern family exemplifies remnants of traditional attitudes combined with struggles for emancipation from one or another earlier custom. The family of today as compared with the family of the past is independent, loosely integrated, and democratic rather than dependent and closely knit; it is small rather than large, and democratic rather than autocratically controlled. Demonstrated affection is more common than was the case in earlier family relationships. Also with the decrease in the authority of the father has come an increase in family freedom.

There are apparent in modern family relationships, however, sufficient remnants of older traditions and mores to cause dissatisfaction with the newer family concept. Conflicts arise between struggles for authority and demands for further freedom from actual or imagined family controls. It is in these conflicts and struggles that the seeds of family maladjustment lie. In differences of individual interests are found the psychological bases for these conflicts. Hence we need to determine as scientifically as is possible the relative value of the old versus the new in the meeting of fundamental human needs. This could lead to the development of a program of education in family life that (1) can function as a basis for family adjustment; (2) can be psychologically and socially sound; (3) in its successful application can encourage a healthy and happy family life upon which can be built a well-adjusted and harmonious society.

FUNCTIONS OF THE FAMILY

As the family is, so will be society; contrariwise, what society is, so will be the family. Since the family is a primary social unit, attitudes and behavior patterns that are characteristic of family interrelationships will be carried over into larger group relationships. At the same time family members are responding constantly to the societal influences by which they are surrounded. A child's first educational experiences are centered in the home; his teachers are the older members of the family; their ideals, attitudes, and general pattern of behavior are the resultants of their own childhood rearing and the effect upon them of the social, religious, economic, and educational influences of their out-of-home experiences.

Patterns of Family Life

Primarily, the family is a social institution that is concerned with the care of the young. The extended period of human growth and development is basic to the significant position of the family as a social unit. The concept of home and family relationships has varied with different cultures and stages of civilization, however.

Although the pattern of marriage and home relationships differed among various primitive peoples, family life was characterized by strict patriarchal or matriarchal authority, rigorous systems of taboos, and pride in clan or entire family accomplishments and relationships. The modern American home reflects the influence upon family members of successive stages of societal development: Greek, Roman, and Hebrew stress upon patriarchal rule; monogamy and exogamy; Christian emphasis upon an individual's responsibility for his acts; the production of life necessities, as an outgrowth of the Industrial Revolution, and the ideal of democratic rights and responsibilities upon which our form of government was founded.

Factors of the Home in Society

The complexities of modern civilization have given rise to a kind of social climate that, according to some writers, is unfavorable to the development of wholesome home life and good personal and social adjustment of the individual members of the group. It cannot be denied that the characteristics of modern society include some undesirable aspects. Practically every day one can read newspaper reports of antisocial behavior that is rooted in extreme self-interest, jealousy, impetuosity, intolerance, fearfulness, or unintelligent loyalties. Unfortunately, emotionally controlled, adequately adjusted behavior and constructive attitudes do not produce exciting newspaper headlines. It probably is not being too optimistic to believe that most American homes represent wholesome family and social adjustment, in spite of an increasing concern about the possible disintegration of the home.

In his home a young person can learn early to respect the rights of others, to develop an understanding and accepting attitude, to gain satisfaction from participation in the cooperative efforts of his family toward a common good, to tackle difficult problems unemotionally and purposefully, and to weigh decisions before he acts. A child who achieves emotional security in his family relationships probably will be enabled thereby to make satisfactory adjustments in his larger group experiences.

Whether or not the family of the present produces individuals who will be healthy, intelligent, and emotionally controlled citizens of the future depends upon society's present standards for the family. It is necessary to find answers to questions such as these: Who shall marry and bear children? What responsibility do parents have for the rearing of their children? What are the economic and social needs of a family? What are the rights of the individual members of a family? What especially can organized society do to encourage and assure socially desirable child inception and life?

Marital Function

The sex urge and the desire for the companionship of the opposite sex are inherent human drives. History has shown that experiments in segregated living have been unsuccessful except for a very few individuals. The two sexes so complement each other that an individual of either sex finds his complete self-realization only in harmonious association with and stimulation by a member of the opposite sex.

Extramarital sexual experiences in the satisfaction of the sex urge can be unsatisfying to the individual who practices it. The marriage relationship gives a couple a better opportunity for stability in the satisfaction of this normal drive. Although the gratification of the sex urge is not generally accepted as the sole basis of the marital relation, the marital state affords a relaxation of sex tension and a socially approved avenue for the satisfaction of a normal need.

Intellectual parity, similarity of interests, dispositional likeness, and sufficiency of activity provide for husband and wife the fundamentals of cooperative living and companionship in the atmosphere of which there can be experienced desirable individual growth accompanied by healthful relaxation and freedom from strain. The mutual interest in and care of children fit into this pattern of marital life, enriching it and giving to it a purpose beyond that of individual development and self-satisfaction. Although the complete family unit presupposes the presence of children, the marital function of the family can be achieved by the childless couple if they project their abilities and their energies into activities outside their own personal interests, and work together toward the realization of a wider social good.

FACTORS INFLUENCING FAMILY LIFE

Perhaps the most outstanding characteristic of modern family life is its variation. In America today there is probably no "typical" family. The family may be large or small; it may include in its immediate circle only the members of the immediate family, or it may have added to it, in the same home environment, other relatives. The family may be rural or urban; it may represent a high degree of education and wide culture, or its members may be relatively uneducated and crude; its members may be engaged in highly trained professions or may earn their livelihood in unskilled occupations. The family members may be closely knit by similarity of interests and well adjusted to one another, or the members of the group may be indifferent to or antagonistic to the interests and activities of other members. In short, the complexity of modern civilization is reflected in many different kinds of modern American homes.

Factors of Acculturation

It is a proven fact that people who come to America from other countries and who have been reared in cultures different from our own seem to be able easily and often quickly to assimilate American ideals and customs. However, certain Old World attitudes that are hard to change tend to persist in family relationships. Traditionally, parental authority is greater than now is customary in the American home. The young person's choice of a mate or of a vocation, leisure-time activities, religious affiliations, friends, foods, and speech are influenced by the wishes and the habits of his foreign-born parents. Since the older members of the family tend to associate with persons of their own kind or nationality, they cannot understand or tolerate the desire of the younger members of the family to drift away from family friends and customs.

This situation gives rise to family conflicts which may disrupt the family, cause suffering to all its members, and result in socially undesirable behavior. Each successive generation feels less of the compulsion of the foreign tradition. If other factors are favorable, the assimilation of the traditions and ideals of the adopted country leads to their becoming the dominating influence not only upon the individual's relations with persons outside his home but also upon his family attitudes.

Influence of Economic Status

Economic status exercises a potent influence upon family adjustment. The members of a financially affluent family may not experience any need to participate in constructive, socially beneficial activities; habitual self-indulging attitudes and behavior can result eventually in boredom, restlessness, feelings of frustration, or emotional disorders. Even more serious are the maladjusting effects of the limitations of activity imposed upon the members of an economically underprivileged family. There probably is a medial economic status that can ensure for all the members of a family the self-satisfying comforts and luxuries that have personal and social value.

For the underprivileged, the struggle for mere existence may be so difficult and the financial returns so meager that all members of the family except the very young need to expend most of their energy in uninteresting work. There is little time left for participation in relaxing social activities. Discontent, irritation, and feelings of insecurity and of resentment may cause family dissension and unhappiness. Fortunately, public interest and legislation are bringing about some amelioration of the maladjustive conditions caused by extreme poverty.

Maladjusting factors can be found in some homes of the economically privileged or overprivileged. The responsibility for supplying an abundant family income may be the lot of one member of the family, usually the husband and father. The other members may indicate through their attitudes and behavior that it is their right to spend money lavishly for the satisfaction of self-centered interests. In a family situation of this kind the father may break under the strain of attempting to meet the extravagant demands of his wife and children; they may succumb to the effects of boredom caused by their aimless activities, or may continue feverishly to seek new and thrilling experiences. No close family unity is developed; family friction, discontent, and conflict are likely to characterize home relationships.

Best adjustments in family life seem to be established (1) if one or more members of the family are supplying adequately the fundamental needs of the group; (2) if all members understand and appreciate the occupational activities of those who are gainfully employed; (3) if there is time, opportunity, and money enough for the family to take part in socially desirable activities, sometimes together and sometimes apart; and (4) if each member of the group feels a personal responsibility for the family money, either through successful earning or by intelligent spending.

The kind of home in which a family lives, the neighborhood of this home, the satisfactoriness of clothes and of food, and the type of cultural and recreational activities in which the members participate depend to a great extent upon the economic status of the family. Ordinarily, we are not much concerned with the activities of persons far removed from us in geographic distance or social status. We very definitely are interested in the activities and possessions of our immediate associates. Family accord or discord may be based upon no more important factor than the extent to which the members of the family are economically able to afford those privileges which are enjoyed by their neighbors.

Occupational Influence

Apart from the financial success of occupational activity, the form of occupation itself has an effect upon the lives of all the members of the family. It influences the family's interest in, and the attitude expressed by the family toward, social, political, and economic conditions of the country. If the father is an employer, the family attitude toward labor and labor legislation and toward class distinctions is different from the attitude of the family of an employee. The social level of the occupations in which members of the family are employed affects the social status of the entire family, and, consequently, the attitude of its members toward persons in their own social class and in other classes. The length of the work day and of the work week affect not only the leisure-time activities of the worker himself but also those of the other members of the family.

If the mother is gainfully employed outside of the home, the organization of home activities and responsibilities must be adjusted to meet her work program. Often the circle of friends and acquaintances reflects the occupational interests of the family. Parents' choice of a vocation for their children and the children's own vocational choices may be influenced by the family attitude toward the occupations of the various members of the family. A parent who is dissatisfied with his own vocational life may be willing to make many sacrifices in order that his children can be prepared to enter vocations that seem to be more desirable than his own. A parent who enjoys his work may try to force his children to enter the same field, even though their interests and abilities lie in other directions. The children themselves may be influenced toward or away from the occupational work of their father, as a result of the attitudes which they have developed toward it.

The status of the home as the center for the provision of

food necessities is found at present only among families who still live on the farm. The increasing trend toward specialized farming, however, makes it not unusual for the farm wife and mother to buy her vegetables, milk, and other food products in town or from various other farmer specialists. Hence even the modern farm child fails to experience those forms of cooperative family life that were common in the past.

In general, city children are denied the experience of working with other members of the family in the care of the home. Even in humble homes, the laundry is sent out; canned and preserved foods are used; mechanical devices minimize the time and energy required to keep the home clean, and, in many cases, the meals are eaten away from the home. Girls, as well as boys, are accustomed to earning the money required to provide for the needs of the family by working away from the home rather than providing these necessities directly in the home. In this way, instead of the members of the family being drawn together by cooperative activities, they are forced apart by their separate vocational interests and activities.

Educational Influence

The child's first training is received in the home, and his early and permanent habits are established through this training. The educational level of the members of the family who are responsible for this early education is reflected in the habits and attitudes of the children. The family's attitude toward the value of systematic education affects the attitude of the children toward their educational ambitions. Important factors are the parents' interest in the school progress of their child, their cooperation with school authorities, their efforts to provide time and a suitable place for the child's home study, their understanding and willingness to accept their child's mental limitations, and their efforts to provide sufficient and suitable education for their child. The extent to which these factors become functional indicates not only parents' attitude toward the value of formal education but also their interest in providing a home environment that will ensure good educational opportunities for their child.

Some American families still exhibit a traditional attitude of differentiation of educational opportunities for boys and girls.

Parents may be willing to make tremendous sacrifices for the education of their sons. At the same time, they not only may deny similar privileges to their daughters, but expect and demand that the girls of the family leave school as early as the law will permit and go to work. The girls then can assist their brothers to acquire an expensive college education. This attitude may prevail in spite of the fact that the girls have demonstrated their ability to profit from further educational opportunities to a much greater extent than can their brothers. A situation of this kind has its roots in the belief that the girl should and will marry early and that she needs only the minimum of formal education in order to be a successful wife and mother.

Cultural Influences

The cultural atmosphere of the home has a potent effect upon the developing personality of a child. The child reared in an apartment house in the center of a crowded city has an outlook upon the relative values of life different from that of the child who spends his early life in a suburban home, or the child who has learned early about the beauty of nature in his home on the farm.

The kinds of books read by the family; the conversation of elders; the religious affiliations and practices of the family; their tastes in music, art, clothes, and furniture affect the child's interests. The family choice of leisure-time activities influences the recreational habits of the child. His behavior both in and out of the home will reflect the social standards that govern the conduct of the family. Wealth or poverty alone cannot be accepted as a criterion of the cultural influences to which the young members of the family may be exposed.

Among potent cultural influences are the experiences of children who grow up in disadvantaged homes. Great mobility, poverty, and broken homes cannot help but have a debilitating influence on the growing child. For example, Susan is a child in a one-parent family; the family consisting of a mother and seven children has moved four times in the past three years. Linda's father deserted her mother and three children when she was four years old; they subsist on welfare. Lawrence lives in an institution among other children of divorced or separated parents; here he experiences much frustration and inadequate attention to his needs. It is little wonder that such children do not have the energies or motivation for cultural attainment of children from stable and secure families.

Influence of Intra-family Relations

The children of a family usually reflect in their behavior and attitudes the attitudes of husband and wife toward each other, the attitudes of both toward their children, the relationships that exist among the children themselves, and the attitudes of grandparents, aunts and uncles, and cousins. We find in any family a subtle interplay of varying mental appreciations, of emotional drives, and of habitual modes of response that may effect desirable adjustment, or may cause unhappiness and failure in family relationships.

The displayed attitude of the husband and wife toward each other probably exercises a most potent influence upon general family behavior. The wholesomeness of their influence depends in great measure upon the extent to which they respect and admire each other, the satisfaction which they derive from their physical life together, their similarity of educational background and of interests, their accord in matters dealing with the rearing of their children, their willingness to defer to each other's wishes, their relations with their own and their mate's family, their religious accord, and their relative degree of independence of and dependence upon one another.

If children are aware of a close, intelligent, and emotionally stable relationship between their parents, they cannot avoid being influenced by it in their own relationships with their parents, with their brothers and sisters, and with their other relatives. Good social adjustment usually is achieved by young people, if these ideals are characteristic of family life: parents evidence a tolerance and an understanding of the rights of others; they accept their family responsibilities and expect others to assume theirs; the children are held to the high standards of conduct which the parents themselves practice; other family relatives are treated with consideration and respect but are expected to know and to observe their rightful place in the family; affection and care are given by the father and mother, and encouraged but not demanded from the other members of the family. It is equally true that the members of a family in which such attitudes prevail carry over to their other social associations the same understanding appreciation of their place in the larger group as they exhibit in their more intimate family relations. According to Schneiders,

> A summary of the characteristics of the ideal home includes the following: (1) minimum amount of friction between parents, and between parents and children; (2) opportunities to utilize the home for expression of legitimate desires (as in the entertainment of friends) ; (3) family affection; (4) minimum amount of strict discipline; (5) opportunities for independence of thought, feelings, and action; (6) confidence in parents, and mutual respect between parents and children; (7) family conferences regarding difficulties; (8) companionship between parents and children; (9) emotional stability of parents; (10) economic adequacy; and (11) a wholesome moral and religious environment.[8]

MALADJUSTMENTS IN THE FAMILY

Maladjustments in home and family relationships may result from the predominance of any one of many personal factors that may be present, regardless of the economic, occupational, educational, or cultural status of the home. Many of the maladjustments could be avoided if the members of a family were led to recognize the serious consequences of undesirable attitudes and behavior, and were helped to prevent the development of them. Domestic relations courts are filled with persons who, if they had used foresight instead of hindsight, might have avoided the humiliation of bringing their troubles to public notice. A complete survey of the many petty and relatively unimportant causes of family discord is impossible, but a few of the major maladjustive factors in family life are described here briefly.

Emotional Immaturity

Too often young people enter into marriage with little or no appreciation of the responsibilities inherent in their new life together. Marriage, especially for a young woman, may seem to

---

[8] Alexander A. Schneiders, *Personality Development and Adjustment in Adolescence*, Milwaukee: The Bruce Publishing Company, 1960, p. 405.

be an easy way out of an intolerable or unsatisfactory home, school, or occupational situation. The writer recalls a high school girl who was not succeeding in her studies, who was very much dissatisfied with her mother's overreligious strictness, and who saw no prospect of obtaining a desirable job. She informed the writer that she just did not want to be bothered by any attempts to adjust her school program, insisting that she expected to leave school on her seventeenth birthday and marry. She admitted that she had no particular boy in mind, but that the finding of a husband would be easy and that then she would be able to enjoy life. Since she would be careful to pick a man who had a good job, she would have no further worries. The attitude of this girl gave evidence of unrealistic romanticism born of too great concern with motion pictures, light fiction, and daydreaming.

This concept of marriage as a way out of existing difficulties is not confined to the young and immature. Adults often display the same lack of understanding of the meaning of marriage. They enter into the relationship without planning beyond the honeymoon. When they awaken to the realities of adjusting to the idiosyncrasies of their mate, and recognize the need of establishing an orderly and well-regulated life with the person who was a comparative stranger before marriage, they cannot accept the prosaic aspects of married life. They fall back upon their former discontent with life. They may neglect their responsibilities, hurl recriminations upon their mate, or withdraw completely from the marriage relation through a tacit agreement to live apart or by a legal separation or divorce.

Adjustment Problems of Unwed Mothers

The problem of illegitimate pregnancy is an increasing one. Because of human drives and cultural inhibitions it captures the imagination. Although vicarious gratification is aroused in the individual who has not breached the social code or at least has not "been caught," illicit sexual behavior, pregnancy, and childbirth arouse in most human beings repressed wishes, frustrations, and anxieties. Thus are the attitudes of society conditioned toward the unwed mother and her child. Florence Clothier, M.D., gives insight into the adjustment problems confronted by the individual so involved and indicates something about the reaction of the other adults in her environment.

In cultural groups where rigid patterns of morality prevail, repressed impulses for sexual gratification run in a strong current. Individuals, to protect the social structure against their own submerged desires for forbidden sexual gratification, direct aggression and punishment against the unmarried mother and her child who have mobilized those wishes. The "fallen woman" and the "bastard" are viewed by society not as individuals but as projections of strong desires and even stronger defenses against those desires. Because women even more readily than men are threatened by identification with the unmarried mother, they are usually the more vociferous in their condemnation and more cruel in their punishment. Though churchmen, educators, social workers, and parents may consciously deplore it, mankind likes its wrong-doers whose acts give them indirect satisfactions while at the same time providing an opportunity for righteous indignation and even at times relief of tension through aggressive expression. The unmarried mother, herself a part of the cultural background, readily allies a part of herself with the punishing public and often welcomes ways of expiating her guilt, which lies deeper than her offense against the cultural mores. . . .

Unmarried motherhood in our culture almost always represents a distorted or unrealistic way out of inner difficulties. It is thus comparable to a neurotic symptom on the one hand or to impulsive delinquent behavior on the other. The adolescent girl who has sexual relations with men or boys is lacking in a capacity to protect herself. Her reality sense is not sufficient to cope with her biological drives or with her conflicts centering around her struggle for emancipation. Wishes, conflicts, or phantasies are acted out and by accident or design the girl may become pregnant. . . .

Married or unmarried, these immature girls make poor mothers. They transmit to their children through the emotional climate they provide for them the same primary emotional disturbances which crippled their own development. The indication would seem to be to make it easy for them to give up their babies in the hope that better provision can be made for the baby than was made for its child-mother. Society's traditional punishing attitude that keeping the baby will force responsibility on the mother and make her "settle down" is doomed to bring only tragedy to the baby and the young mother whose fundamental needs are still unmet. . . .

The adolescent girl, unprotected by a firm reality sense, is predisposed to sexual relationships and illegitimate pregnancy by her biological sexual drives and by the conflicts stemming from her struggle to integrate new standards with old. Where infantile needs have remained unsatisfied, or where infantile conflicts are still unresolved, adolescence is disturbed and an illegitimate pregnancy may be a particularly virulent symptom of that disturbance. A predisposition to a disturbed adolescence fortunately does not mean that illicit sexual relationships or unmarried motherhood will occur. Pregnancy out of wedlock is always overdetermined and both sexual and nonsexual motivations play important roles. The adolescent girl, driven by sexual feelings, may attempt to meet long-standing nonsexual needs through promiscuous relationship with boys or men, or through motherhood. . . .

As an attempted solution for frustrated love and security needs, or as a way out of neurotic conflict, unmarried motherhood is doomed to hopeless failure. To the girl's original frustration and confusion are added stupendous responsibilities which she inevitably will have to evade. Her old feelings of rejection, "Nobody likes me," are given a firmer reality base. She has lost her "ghost lover" and society has branded her a bad woman. The symptom "unmarried motherhood" has numerous highly individual psychodynamic determinants. Particularly in the case of the adolescent girl it has also important psychodynamic consequences affecting not only the future adjustment of the baby but also of the mother—herself a child. [9]

Inadequate Sex Adjustment

For many years there has existed among religiously minded persons a constant struggle between their natural urges and their religious teachings. Although the sex act is admitted to be neces-

[9] Florence Clothier, "The Unmarried Mother of School Age as Seen by a Psychiatrist," *Mental Hygiene*, October, 1955, pp. 631–646.

sary for the continuance of the human race, it seems difficult for society to agree on the kind of training to be given to young people in preparation for marriage. As a result, much of the information which individuals have received concerning their sex life has come to them indirectly or in undesirable ways.

Parents are embarrassed by questions about sexual matters. This conspiracy of silence has affected girls even more than boys. Combined with the double standard of morality, it has been one of the most serious causes of marital incompatibility. Very often the husband and the wife exhibit very different attitudes toward sex relations. The husband does not always understand his wife's attitude and mistakes her fear and ignorance for frigidity. The husband does not know the art of love-making or the preparation for the sexual act. Hence he either adds to the fear of the wife or arouses her disgust. The modern tendency toward smaller and planned families has further increased this tension between husband and wife. Psychologists, psychiatrists, and mental hygienists are attempting to develop a more rational attitude toward sexual relations. They are hampered in their efforts by a certain amount of social disapproval, and by their recognition of the possible difficulties inherent in the development of an adequate program of sex education.

Unless parents have achieved a normal and satisfying attitude toward their own sex relations, their children recognize the sex tension between their parents and are affected by it. Not only does the home life of the family suffer, but the children carry into their own adult sex lives an inadequate sex adjustment which may cause serious conflicts in their own marital and family relations.

Influence of Parents on Homosexual Behavior

The influence of a parent on the development of homosexual behavior in children may be significant. In families, for example, where the father is absent or is considered to be a nonentity or is inadequate in some way, the behavior of either the mother or the father may be important. Westwood [10] believes that the lack of relationship between the father and son may be

[10] Gordon Westwood, *A Minority—A Report on the Life of the Male Homosexual in Great Britain*. London: Longmans, Green and Co., 1960.

as important as an overdeveloped relationship between the mother and son. Bieber and collaborators report:

> Our data strongly support these findings; in fact, the fathers we studied were more actively and destructively involved with their homosexual sons than is indicated in Westwood's study. The greater degree of aggression against the son apparent in our group of American fathers may be an indication of a national characteristic; or, it may be that our investigation into the relationship between H-fathers and *siblings* delineated the aggression more clearly. Now, why were the homosexual sons in our sample so unpopular with their fathers? Was it because they were inadequate and unattractive as children? Their mothers obviously did not find them undesirable—in 63 of 95 families the patients were their favorite sons (11 were only children). Of the 42 H-sons who were least favored by their fathers, 29 were preferred by their mothers in contrast to only 10 of 19 C-patients who were preferred by their mothers and least favored by their fathers. A child's status of "least preferred" is as pathogenic in personality development as is preference over other siblings—even more so—and is as much an indicator of parental psychopathology. Were the father's antagonism and aversion provoked by the close, intimate, sexually colored relationship between the mother and her preferred son? The close maternal-filial bond may have played an important part in arousing paternal resentment but, where it did, it seems merely to have reinforced pre-existing paternal psychopathology. A reasonably "normal" father protects his child from destructive maternal influences. He will step in as an interceding agent against undue "coddling," overprotectiveness, seductiveness, and so forth.[11]

In their conclusions Bieber *et al.* combine their suggestions with those of Ford and Beach [12] and those of Hooker [13] and report on the homosexual problems as follows:

[11] Irving Bieber, M. D., & Associates, *Homosexuality: A Psychoanalytic Study*, New York: Basic Books, 1962, pp. 124–125.

[12] C. S. Ford and F. A. Beach, *Patterns of Sexual Behavior*, New York: Harper & Row, 1951.

[13] Evelyn Hooker, "The Adjustment of the Male Overt Homosexual," *Journal of Projective Techniques*, Vol. 21 (1957), pp. 18–31.

Ford and Beach, in accord with Kinsey *et al.*, also imply that homosexuality is not pathologic but that "the basic mammalian capacity for sexual inversion tends to be obscured in societies like our own which forbid such behavior and classify it as unnatural." The authors compare the sporadic and indiscriminate "homosexual" behavior frequently observed among infrahuman species (though heterosexual behavior is not extinguished in hardly any instances and is reinstated with no apparent change), with human homosexual behavior where cognitive and highly complex patterns are involved and where, at least in our society, fear of heterosexuality is salient. Based on the frequency of homosexual phenomena, the authors state, "The cross-cultural and cross-species comparisons presented . . . combine to suggest that a biological tendency for inversion of sexual behavior is inherent in most if not all mammals including the human species." Following their logic, one might assume that any frequently occurring sexual aberration may be explained by postulating an inherent tendency. A pathologic formation, i.e., homosexuality, viewed as an inherent tendency points to a confusion between the concept of adaptational potential and that of inborn tendency.

Ford and Beach do not distinguish between *capacity* and *tendency*. Capacity is a neutral term connoting *potentiality* whereas *tendency* implies the probability of action in a specific direction. In our view, the human has a capacity for homosexuality but a tendency toward heterosexuality. The capacity for responsivity to heterosexual excitation is inborn. Courtship behavior and copulatory technique is learned. Homosexuality, on the other hand, is acquired and discovered as a circumventive adaptation for coping with fear of heterosexuality. As we evaluate the maturational processes, a homosexual phase is not an integral part of sexual development. At any age, homosexuality is a symptom of fear and inhibition of heterosexual expression. We do not hold with the now popular thesis that in all adult males there are repressed homosexual wishes. In fact, most adult heterosexual males no longer have the potential for a homosexual adaptation. In the comparison sample one-fourth of the cases revealed no evidence of homosexual propensities—conscious or unconscious. If we assume that homosexuality is a pathological condition, and our data strongly support this assumption, we would no more expect latent homosexuality to be inevitable among well-integrated heterosexuals than we would expect latent peptic ulcer to be inevitable among all members of a healthy population.

Another approach to the question of homosexuality as behavior within a normal range is found in Hooker's work. In this investigation projective techniques were utilized to determine whether homosexuality and homosexual adjustment could be distinguished from that of heterosexuals. It was found that the differences sought between the two populations could not be reliably distinguished. The conclusion was that "homosexuality may be a deviation in sexual pattern which is within the normal range psychologically." Since the tests and adjustment ratings were performed by competent workers and the implication of the findings and conclusions are at marked variance with those of our own and other studies, we suspect that the tests themselves or the current methods of interpretation and evaluation are inadequate to the task of discriminating between homosexuals and heterosexuals.

Still another type of argument is that homosexuality in certain individuals is related to genetic factors. In Kallman's twin studies,[14] homosexuality among monozygotic twins was investigated. Each sibling of forty pairs was found to be homosexual. Kallman placed enormous emphasis on genetic factors; yet he contradicted his own position by stating that the sexual impulse is easily dislocated by experiential factors. Even assuming a genetic determination, it cannot be strongly operative if sexuality responds so sensitively to non-genetic influences. We propose that the study should have included psychoanalytic treatment for at least some of the pairs studied. Had a shift to heterosexuality occurred in the course of treatment, as it had in one-fourth of the homosexuals in our sample, the reversibility would have cast doubt on the significance of genetic determinants in homosexual-

[14] Franz Kallman, "Comparative Twin Studies on the Genetic Aspects of Male Homosexuality," *Journal of Nervous and Mental Disorders*, Vol. 115 (1952), pp. 283-298. [Crow]

ity. Though reversibility in itself is not a sufficient argument against the genetic position, there is so much evidence on the side of the nurture hypothesis and so little on the side of the nature hypothesis, that the reliance upon genetic or constitutional determinations to account for the homosexual adaptation is ill-founded.[15]

Parental Rejection of Children

Children are aware of parental attitudes toward them and, in their behavior, respond to this awareness. It is normal for an individual to crave approval from the members of his group; it is imperative that a child recognize that he is "wanted" by his family, and that he is accepted as a desired and respected member of this close social unit. If he fails to gain this assurance, the effects upon his developing personality are serious.

Rejected children tend to exhibit behavior characterized by indifference, lack of emotional control, social antagonisms, and undue motor activity. Such behavior requires wise treatment. These children may seek, outside the home, the attention and love which they fail to obtain from their parents. Usually, however, they are unfriendly, and may be rebellious, confused, discontented, and discouraged. Parental attitude is responsible for these maladjustments and it is only through a correction of the parents' attitude that these undesirable traits in children can be overcome.

A child may be unwanted for one of several reasons. The coming of the child may interfere with other parental plans, or the family already may be larger than the parents desire or feel that they can care for adequately. Child rejection by one or both of the parents may be caused by lack of harmony between the parents themselves, resulting from inadequate sex adjustment or from undesirable family background of one or both of the parents. Whatever the cause of the rejection, the results are dangerous enough to engage the attention of all persons concerned with the wholesome development of our citizens. Prospective parents need to understand what the outcomes of their parental attitude may be.

[15] Bieber *et al.*, *Homosexuality*, pp. 304–306.

Parental Overprotection of Children

Almost as serious as rejection is the situation which results from parental overprotection of their children. A child born after many years of married life without children may be so overwhelmed by the solicitous care of his parents that normal tendencies toward personal independence have little or no opportunity to develop. A mother who is dissatisfied with her married life may transfer to her child the love which she once felt for her husband and which she believes is no longer welcomed by him. This is especially true if the child is a boy. An only girl in a family of boys (especially if she is the youngest child) may become the apple of her father's eye and the center of his life.

The overprotected child does not lead a normal child's life. Usually his activities and his companions are hand-picked. He may be sheltered from any normal childhood difficulties, and granted all of his whims or wishes. The household revolves around the child. Such parental attitudes not only affect the "spoiled" child unfavorably but also may arouse resentment and jealousy among other children in the family. Overprotected children tend to display infantile, withdrawing types of behavior and to need assistance from others in meeting school or social situations.

Parental Domination or Submission

Related to the difficulties in family life that result from overindulgence or rejection of the child are those which arise from overdomination by or oversubmission of parents in relation to their children. Overdominance or oversubmissiveness of a parent may result from unadjusted marital relations, from the early training of the parent, or from the possession of a generally dominant or submissive nature. Such parents usually display similar attitudes toward other members of the family.

Parental domination tends to develop apparently desirable social attitudes in children. As a result of their home training they are able to adjust successfully to their school responsibilities. Because of their lack of freedom in the home, however, they may exhibit inability to express themselves, shyness, self-consciousness, seclusiveness, and general submission to authority.

In general, the characteristics of children of submissive parents are the opposite of those displayed by children of dominant parents. Children who enjoy great freedom in the family exhibit tendencies toward disobedience, irresponsibility, and uncooperativeness. They may lack the power of concentrated and systematic work, and be careless, lazy, unpunctual, and stubborn. Yet they usually are well poised, and possess adequate powers of expression. They are generally untractable and defiant of authority.

Conflicting Ideals

If parental attitudes differ greatly as a result of early childhood training, educational advantages, intellectual ability, religious affiliation, or recreational interests, resulting conflicts may be the causes of family disharmony and disruption. The husband or wife who is mentally superior to the mate is likely, after the first thrill of the marital relationship, to find that he or she is bored by the other. The fact that the children themselves may inherit the intelligence level of one or the other of the parents may lead to further difficulties. Parental ambitions may be thwarted, or the less able parent may tend to protect the less able child from the ire of the other parent, resulting in resentments and possible family cleavage.

As a result of their own early experiences, parents may disagree concerning the training of their children. One parent may favor a strict upbringing; the other may desire a more lenient treatment. Young children soon recognize this difference in parental philosophy and learn to capitalize upon it, if assured of the ready sympathy and protection of the less strict parent. Family deceits are practiced, habits of "getting out" of expected duties or responsibilities are common, and family loyalties are strained.

Whether or not persons of different religious affiliations should marry is a much discussed question. Many examples can be cited of instances in which such marriages have been very successful, and the children have made desirable religious adjustments. Unless the couple have given the matter serious consideration before marriage and have agreed upon a policy for the religious training of their children, however, a marriage of this kind often results in the development of an indifferent or nonreligious life for the family.

Golf widows and bridge or canasta widowers have been the subjects of much good-natured and humorous sympathy. Extremes of difference between husband and wife in their recreational interests subtract from the kind of companionship that is vital to family well-being. There is likely to be some resentment against the mate's interest in an activity which takes him away from the home and the family circle during leisure time. The neglected mate tends to exhibit an antagonistic attitude toward the other's absorbing interest. He is bound to reflect this attitude in his relations with his mate, his children, and other close associates of the family. Again, family loyalties may center around the apparently neglected mate.

Very serious are the effects of conflicts between the traditional ideals of parents and those which their children meet in their associations with other families. This situation is especially difficult for adolescents. If the parents have certain Old World attitudes toward the social activities of their children, it is difficult for both them and the young people to have the latter denied privileges which are accepted as a matter of course in other homes.

Anyone who has been closely associated with these rebellious adolescents cannot refrain from sympathizing with them when they raise questions similar to the following: "Why must I be home before eleven o'clock at night?" "Why am I not allowed to go out with boys?" "Is it wrong for a girl to smoke an occasional cigarette?" These questions usually are followed by the statement that other nice young people are allowed to do these things. Resentment toward the parents for their "intolerant" attitude often is accompanied by a lack of respect for the parents' judgment and, in many instances, the practice of the forbidden activity without parental knowledge. This struggle between the urge for individual freedom and respect for authority may result in an apparent victory for the latter, but the attitude of thwarting or the sense of guilt which may accompany defiance of authority interferes with the young person's normal social development.

Family Relatives

The presence of relatives in the home is a well-known source of family conflict. Temporary or more permanent misunderstanding of feelings of hostility may arise between husband and wife or between parents and children that are caused by the presence in the home or close to the home of the domineering mother-in-law, the fussy father-in-law, the indulgent or critical grandparent, the hanger-on brother of a mate, and the self-sacrificing sister or aunt. Any one of these can damage the feelings of security among the members of a family unit which help family life become a welcome relaxation from more formal social relationships. Interference with parental rearing of children can lead to a display of bad manners and a lack of proper restraint and reticence on the part of the offending relatives, the parents, and the children.

Relatives may take it for granted that their kinship gives them special privileges. They seem to feel that they are justified in interfering with matters which are no concern of theirs. In fact, they appear to believe that it is their responsibility not only to give advice but also to insist that their counsel be accepted and followed. These persons would hesitate to attempt to control the behavior of persons not related to them or to ask special consideration from them; but the tie of kinship seems to absolve such relatives from all restriction in their demands. Here we find the conflict between the desire for individual freedom and the drive for power.

The Working Mother

The changed occupational status of woman brings with it a changed family relationship. If the mother's income is needed in the family, the father often develops a feeling of incompetence. In such instances, the children are likely to defer to the mother as the more stable parent. For a wife to earn more than her husband intensifies this family attitude. Sometimes the mother resents the fact that she must help in the provision of family needs. This fact combined with work fatigue causes her to shift the responsibility of the home care to an older child or to the father.

Tired, resentful parents and overburdened children are unable to develop the spirit of companionable home life. During the mother's absence from home, the children, as a result of their freedom from parental observation, may engage in activities that are socially unacceptable. In the evenings, the various members of the family may tend to drift away from the home for entertainment, since the family atmosphere is not conducive to pleasant relaxation.

If the mother is a career woman, the husband's attitude may be one of pride in his wife's achievements or of discontent because he and their children have not been able to stimulate in her the same interest and enthusiasm as has her outside activity. Here again parental attitude is reflected in the attitudes of the children. There are many homes, however, in which the mother's accomplishments in her profession or business are a source of pride and interest to her children, especially if the latter are old enough to appreciate her work and if she provides for their proper care during her absence. The very fact that she has this outside interest makes of her a *person* as well as a *mother*. Contrariwise, if the mother's interest in her career is so strong that she leaves the care of her family to strangers, her husband and children may experience an attitude of resentfulness toward her work and herself and feel themselves to be neglected and unloved.

Crowded City Living

As has been said earlier, many families of the past enjoyed free country life; cooperative effort in the production of family needs; self-made recreational activities; plenty of space, light, and air; and relatively regular and similar working hours which provided for communal leisure-time activities, and the general self-sufficiency of the family as a social unit. All of this gradually has changed to an almost complete dependence upon outside agencies for the supplying of life necessities as well as of recreational opportunities. We have moved to a mode of life in which the working hours of the various members of the family differ greatly, and to a general dependence of the family upon the community for its survival.

Because of their differing occupational and recreational interests, it is possible for the members of a family not to see one another for several days. A woman of the writer's acquaintance laughingly remarked one day that, during the week, she communicates with her sister by way of notes. Week ends are regarded as times for family reunions. However, the popularity of out-of-town week-end parties may interfere with this opportunity for family unity of activity and interests.

In depressed city areas a real family often does not exist. Parents either may not have been married or they may be divorced. In depressed areas many problems arise from the fact that the family tends to be involved in a continuous series of crises. There may be the problem of unemployment which, at one time or another, is accompanied by illness, arrest, desertion. Soon another crisis arises and another cycle begins. Many undesirable practices occur, including the mother living with a series of men, one at a time, or blatant prostitution. The child who is reared in this atmosphere is deprived of experiences that lead to family stability.

Children in crowded living quarters look upon their homes as prisons, from which they would like to escape. Here a child may be reared by an aunt, another by a friend, and still another by a distant relative. Often the father is absent from the home and many "uncles" become his substitute. By the time children from these homes reach adolescence they are prepared for delinquency.

Slum children often are amoral, aggressive, restless, and loyal to a small circle of friends. Much antisocial behavior evolves from this state of alienation from society caused either by the break-up of the home or the instability of the general society itself. It may be caused by the absence of the parents from the home, which fact leaves the young people to fend for themselves.

From birth onward, deprived individuals have experienced many character-destroying pressures. These people have been stereotyped as "worthless" and labeled as "dumb" or "ignorant." As victims of discrimination and segregation, they are forced to accept the label of "problem people." Children reared in the slums soon come to realize that their world differs from that of many other people. This gives them a "strange" feeling whenever they attempt to enter the mainstream of society.

Apartment-house children are sadly limited in their activity. Frequently the modern child supposedly may be seen, but should never be heard by critical neighbors. Natural energy must be expended in city playgrounds rather than in the home. Parents desire their children to live a normal child's life but they also wish to be proper tenants. Hence they attempt to satisfy their children and their landlord by training their young people to enjoy quiet recreational activities. Many intelligent parents, rebelling against these restrictions, become interested in suburban living that has the advantage of providing for the children more freedom of activity. Such a move penalizes the wage earners of the family by increasing the number of hours consumed in traveling between their job and their home.

Broken Homes

Homes that are broken as a result of the desertion of the family by a parent, or by the separation or divorce of the parents, give rise to one or more of the family maladjustments that have been discussed. To these types of broken homes may be added those which have been disrupted by the death of a parent. In all cases the family unity is interfered with; new adjustments must be made; financial worries may be experienced; and, especially in the homes broken as a result of the separation of the parents, loyalties are divided.

It is difficult to conclude that a broken home has a more serious maladjusting effect upon children than does a home in which there is dissension, nagging, and resentment. It is a fact, however, that a disrupted home, for any reason whatever, has been found to be one of the significant factors of adolescent and adult social maladjustment. Often the remaining parent may attempt through remarriage to re-establish family unity. This may cause greater friction and discord in the family, unless the new member is able to recognize possible difficulties of adjustment and is slow to demand family loyalty from the young members.

EDUCATING FOR MARITAL ADJUSTMENT

Some researchers in the field of social interrelationships and personal and social adjustment tend to regard inadequate home and family life to be a major causative factor of childhood misdemeanors, adolescent delinquency, and adult crime, as well as of serious mental and emotional disorder at any age.

The Need for Education

I have said earlier that much public emphasis has been placed upon the social patterns of home relationships. This trend has led to a minimizing of the fact that in the majority of American homes are developed youthful attitudes of emotional control, constructive behavior, and home and social adaptation. It is important, however, to keep in mind that the exhibition by an increasing minority of young people of maladjusted behavior is a matter of serious social concern.

Undesirable conditions outside the home may become strong motivators of individual maladjustment. Disintegrating factors in the home are significant, even though they do not constitute the prime or only cause of maladaptation. I have discussed some of the maladjusting factors of family life. Vaughan presents a summarized list of family needs and difficulties. He suggests possible means of improving family relationships.

Research in mental hygiene has demonstrated that children need the emotional security provided by a home in which the parents love each other and their offspring. The parents need a sense of stability, too. Our high divorce rate is evidence that people lack the emotional maturity necessary to make a go of marriage and family life. Mates who cannot live together peaceably demonstrate to their youngsters a pattern of conflict that offers little recommendation to them for establishing homes of their own. Many homes were broken by separation or death during the recent war. Housing shortages are fostering friction and chronic worry. Family life is affected adversely by the fact that so many women work in business and industry. Women who have jobs are not inclined to bear children or to care for them properly. Childlessness, promiscuity, and sexual frustration contribute to the instability of marriage. The younger generation is not likely to achieve emotional adulthood under such untoward conditions; later they will get married and perpetuate the same unpropitious kind of home life. It is a vicious circle. We can extricate ourselves only by learning how to become mature persons in spite of the unfavorable social climate. Progress can be made through training in mental hygiene and through education for marriage and family living.[16]

[16] W. F. Vaughan, *Personal and Social Adjustment*, New York: The Odyssey Press, 1953, pp. 170–171.

The Functions of Education

Problems of adjustment associated with marriage and family living can be classified roughly as (1) premarital adjustment, (2) husband-wife adjustment, (3) child care and rearing, and (4) parent-child adjustment. In the past these problem situations were more or less neglected areas of formal education.

Any assistance that young people received in preparation for meeting marriage and family responsibilities was incidental. To the extent that their mentors were mature, well-adjusted married men and women, considerable help was afforded. Preachments, warnings, or prejudiced advice, offered by embittered, frustrated, and maritally unsuccessful relatives or associates, sometimes caused the young people to experience fear of marriage and feelings of insecurity about assuming family responsibility.

One of the outcomes of increased public interest in the preventive aspect of the mental hygiene movement has been greater concern with ways of improving family disintegration and of preserving physically and mentally healthy family units. The principles of good physical and mental hygiene are being applied in a practical fashion through the organization of planned programs of education and of guidance for young people as a preparation for marriage, and for parents as a preparation for child rearing.

The first regular course on the family was taught at Boston University, in 1922, by Ernest E. Groves. Since that time an increasing number of similar courses have come to be offered by high schools and colleges throughout the country. Effort in this direction has been encouraged by national organizations, which recognize the seriousness of the problems that grow out of ignorance concerning our unwholesome attitudes toward matters dealing with the sex life of an individual. Significant progress toward the development of programs of sex education or education for home and family living has been made by these agencies: American Association of Marriage Counselors, American Social Health Association, Family Welfare Association, National Association for Mental Health, and National Conference on Family Relations.

As a result of the efforts of these organizations, especially the ASHA, some form of education for home and family living is required by state law in the schools of Oregon and Michigan. In several other states educational programs in this area are permissive.

There appears to be a rapidly growing interest in acquainting young people with correct factual material concerning their sexual functions and in helping them develop wholesome attitudes and behavior in their relationships with members of the opposite sex. There still are state and city school systems, however, which are reluctant to introduce this area of study into their schools. Moreover, in those schools which do not hesitate to include in their curriculums some preparation for marriage adjustment there is indecision as to whether a well-planned program of study should be presented in the form of a single course or whether the material of study should be divided, with as little overlapping as is possible among various curricular areas: physical education, physiology and hygiene, general science, biology, home economics, English, and the social studies.

Group and individual counseling services are available in many communities. Young people who are contemplating marriage or married couples who are experiencing adjustment difficulties receive information and counsel at a counseling agency that is associated with a local church, a mental or social hygiene agency, or one of the Y's. In addition, various national and state organizations periodically conduct open meetings and group discussions for the purpose of further stimulating public interest in the maintenance of healthful marriage and family conditions.

Scientific research concerning the physical welfare of young adolescents accompanied by education for parents in the rearing of children preceded the present great concern over the basic principles of sexual and marital adjustment. The lowered infant mortality rate is evidence of the success achieved in dealing with the prebirth and postbirth care of mother and child. Progress has not been so satisfactory, however, in attempted education of parents toward providing for their children a home climate in which the latter's mental health is preserved and emotional disturbances prevented.

There are encouraging indications of increasing parental interest in child rearing. Parent and parent-teacher associations are struggling with the problem. Child-study groups, under expert leadership, are thriving. Young mothers and mothers-to-be, as well as some young fathers, are trying to become good parents. They are attending group and individual conferences, and are reading books and magazine and newspaper articles that deal with meeting the home problems of children and adolescents. Because of general interest in the movement, however, the leaders of education in child rearing are encountering several difficulties. Motivated by a strong desire to rear their children properly, some parents read *one* book on the subject. Their enthusiasm is greater than their ability to apply intelligently the precepts presented, however. Hence these parents not only attempt to follow slavishly the book's recommendations but also consider themselves to have become experts in the field as a result of their limited reading. There are other parents who are experiencing serious difficulties that are caused by the willful and tantrum behavior of their preadolescent or adolescent children. These parents take their problems to the "experts" in whom they have so great faith that they expect to be given a quickly working prescription through the application of which can be effected an almost overnight rehabilitation of their wayward children.

Another difficulty that is causing educational leaders considerable concern grows out of the fact that, for the most part, the parents and parents-to-be who seek help in rearing their children are emotionally stable and well-adjusted men and women who are meeting their parental responsibilities with intelligent understanding, but who are eager to improve their approaches. Too often the men and women whose need is great for education in home and family living are completely uninterested. They do not attend parent-teacher meetings, they do not read books and articles on the subject, and they rarely can be persuaded to seek help or counsel.

Finally, special emphasis is being given to the close relationship that exists between an individual's power to achieve satisfactory sexual, martial, and parental adjustment and all the other areas of his personal and social adjustment. Fundamentally, education aimed at the development of sexual control and marital adaptation begins in the cradle. Studies have shown that adolescents and adults who engage in sexual aberrations, delinquency, and crime usually have a history of childhood display of uncontrolled and tantrum behavior, home- and school-experienced frustrations and conflicts that provoked socially disapproved activities even during their early years. For this reason major educational stress is placed upon the development of stable personalities during the early maturing years, although reconditioning of maladjusted home and family attitudes and behavior is not neglected.

QUESTIONS AND PROBLEMS

1. Name and describe adjustment problems that may arise in the family.

2. Discuss differences in adolescent attitudes toward marriage.

3. Discuss the extent to which and ways in which an engaged person should associate with members of the opposite sex.

4. Give advantages and disadvantages of a married couple's having similar interests; in having different interests.

5. Compare the American ideal of personal mate selection with parentally arranged marriage.

6. In what ways can vocational experience prepare a woman for marriage and parenthood?

7. What are the physical, social, and psychological problems associated with promiscuity?

8. Discuss the wisdom of parents' attempting to retain the confidence of their adolescent children.

9. State your attitude toward the desirability of married women engaging in gainful occupational work.

10. List the social agencies in your community that care for family welfare. Visit one of them to discover exactly how it functions.

11. Enumerate factors of family maladjustment that have come to your attention. Report on their basic causes.

12. Discuss various attitudes toward mate selection. Outline some of the problems faced by young people today in mate selection.

13. Report on the relationship between courtship and successful marriage.

14. How can a man or woman be prepared to become an effective parent?

15. Describe Schneiders' concept of an ideal home.

16. What are the chief bases of inadequate family adjustment?

17. How do the dating problems of teen-agers differ from those of their grandparents?

18. Whose responsibility is it to maintain appropriate behavior on a date?

19. Indicate ways in which childhood emotional attachment to family members affects the achievement of successful marital adjustment.

20. Discuss the need for and purpose of marriage counseling.

Selected Readings

Bandura, A., and R. H. Walters, *Adolescent Aggression: A Study of the Influence of Child-Training Practices and Family Interrelationships*. New York: The Ronald Press Company, 1959.

Bell, N. W., and E. F. Vogel (eds.), *A Modern Introduction to the Family*. New York: Free Press of Glencoe, 1960.

Bieber, Irving, M.D., & Associates, *Homosexuality: A Psychoanalytic Study*. New York: Basic Books, Inc., 1962.

Blisten, D., *The Family*. New York: Random House, Inc., 1962.

Bowman, H. A., *Marriage for Moderns*, 4th ed. New York: McGraw-Hill, Inc., 1960.

Christensen, H. T. (ed.), *Handbook of Marriage and the Family*. Chicago, Ill.: Rand McNally & Company, 1964.

Crawley, L. Q., *et al.*, *Reproduction, Sex, and Preparation for Marriage*. Englewood Cliffs, N.J.: Prentice-Hall, Inc., 1965.

Duvall, E. M., *Family Development*, 2nd ed. Philadelphia, Penna.: J. B. Lippincott Company, 1962.

Haas, K., *Understanding Ourselves and Others*. Englewood Cliffs, N.J.: Prentice-Hall, Inc., 1965.

Hereford, C. F., *Changing Parental Attitudes Through Group Discussion*. Austin: The University of Texas Press, 1963.

Hess, R. D., and G. Handel, *Family Worlds: A Psychological Approach to Family Life*. Chicago, Ill.: University of Chicago Press, 1959.

Karlsson, G., *Adaptability and Communication in Marriage*. Totowa, N.J.: The Bedminster Press, 1963.

Kephart, W. M., *The Family, Society, and the Individual*. Boston, Mass.: Houghton Mifflin Company, 1961.

Landis, P. H., *Modern Courtship and Marriage*, 2nd ed. New York: Appleton-Century-Crofts, Inc., 1960.

Levy, J., and R. Monroe, *The Happy Family*. New York: Alfred A. Knopf, Inc., 1938.

Stephens, W. N., *The Family in Cross-Cultural Perspective*. New York: Holt, Rinehart and Winston, Inc., 1963.

Sussman, M. B. (ed.), *Sourcebook in Marriage and the Family,* 2nd ed. Boston, Mass.: Houghton Mifflin Company, 1963.

Whiting, B. B., *Six Cultures: Studies in Child Rearing.* New York: John Wiley & Sons, Inc., 1963.

Winch, R. F., *The Modern Family,* rev. ed. New York: Holt, Rinehart and Winston, Inc., 1963.

❧ 15 ❧

OCCUPATIONAL
ADJUSTMENT

AN AREA OF adjustment that may be a matter of grave concern to an individual is the degree of satisfaction he experiences in his work activities. He is motivated by the same drives and urges that control other phases of his interhuman relations. A normal individual feels the urge to create, to accomplish, to recognize personal or social value in his achievement, and to carry his activity to a successful conclusion. He also is motivated in his work by a desire for personal gain. He desires social benefits to accrue as a result of his labor. Self-interest, self-approval, and the approval of others are essential if he is to appreciate the full value of his accomplishments.

NEED FOR OCCUPATIONAL SELECTION

In general, workers in the United States are engaged in occupational endeavors for which they are well suited and in which they can enjoy successful achievement. Yet, at least one out of five workers is unhappy in his life work. Much still needs to be done to improve vocational life values. Adults whose responsibility it is to help young people adjust successfully to work activities need to give attention to the following aspects of occupational adjustment: wise selection of a career, adequate training for the job, satisfactory ways of obtaining a job, and successful adjustment on the job.

To most boys and girls the selection of a suitable career is a matter for serious consideration. The general school curriculum is not especially helpful to individual pupils as a means of assisting them in their selection of specific vocations. It is true that young people interested in law, medicine, teaching, religious or social work, and other professions can discover through their success in academic studies some degree of their fitness for these professional vocations. However, except for the increasing but still numerically limited special curriculums, few high school students are able to test their aptitude for the many semi-professional or nonprofessional vocations to which the great majority of them will need to turn as a means of earning a living.

Young people give thought to their vocational future. I referred, in the chapter dealing with adjustment and family life, to Christensen's study of young people's plans for the sixty years following their graduation from high school. His study included questions concerning high school students' vocational plans. His findings led to the following conclusions (see also Figure 13) :

Approximately half of the respondents planned for some formal education beyond high school. More females than males intended to start college but fewer of them intended to finish, or to go longer than four years. Most of the males who planned to start college also planned to finish, and many planned to continue beyond the usual four years. Apparently, more females planned to attend college for social reasons and fewer for professional reasons, as compared with males.

Half of the males and slightly over three-fifths of the females saw themselves in either full or part time jobs during their first year out of high school. The male percentage dropped to 39 in the second and third years (probably due to anticipated military service) and then climbed steadily to a peak of 81 in the 20–29 year period, after which it dropped rapidly to 26 in the final period. In contrast, the female

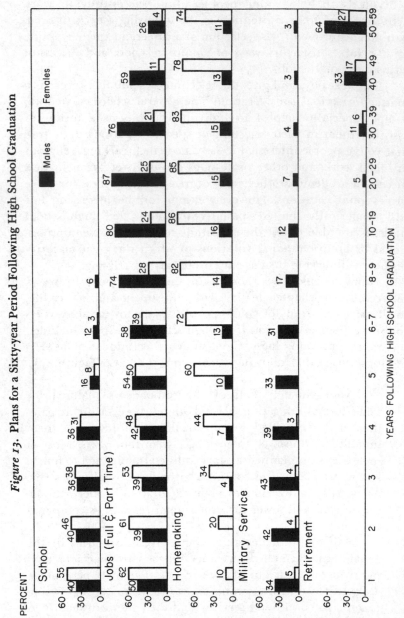

Figure 13. Plans for a Sixty-year Period Following High School Graduation

SOURCE: Harold T. Christensen, "Lifetime Family and Occupational Role Projections of High School Students," *Marriage and Family Living,* May, 1961, p. 182. Reprinted by permission.

percentage declined steadily, starting out ahead of the male and staying ahead during the first four years, but dropping more or less consistently to a mere 4 per cent near the end of life. Desire for part time employment proved to be more characteristic of females than males.[1]

THE INDIVIDUAL AS A WORKER

The worker is not and cannot be looked upon as a mechanical robot. He must understand the purpose and goal of his performance. This impelling curiosity to know and to understand must be satisfied if he is to be a well-adjusted worker. His urge for mastery must find expression in intelligent control of his job and of other phases of the work situation that properly are his responsibility. To the extent that he subordinates his own ideas, interests, or desire for mastery to another person, he recognizes that the authority to which he is subject is just and right and that he will not lose his own self-respect by submitting to the will of another. Hence, in order to be a satisfied worker, he knows and appreciates levels of authority and his own proper place in relation to them.

Human Drives Related to Work

The young child's tendency to refer to objects in his immediate environment as "my dish," "my sunshine," or "my" anything finds its counterpart in the worker's attachment to his work environment. The business or factory is often referred to as "mine." Tools or equipment become so much a part of himself that he may become annoyed if they are used by another person, even when he himself does not need them. A typist may hesitate to give up a typewriter which she has used for a long time even though she is given a better one in its stead. For many years a man had been using an old desk. The drawers stuck, the wood was splintered, and its general appearance was disreputable. When it finally was replaced by a large modern desk, this man remarked that he felt like a stranger in his office and that he

---

[1] Harold T. Christensen, "Lifetime Family and Occupational Role Projections of High School Students," *Marriage and Family Living*, May, 1961, p. 181.

could not concentrate on his work at this desk as he could at his *own* desk.

A few workers are content to be isolated in their work, but many of them need the presence of their kind in order to be satisfied. A newcomer added to the group may break the morale of the workers until they are willing and able to accept him as one of them. Many a man is torn between the satisfaction of promotion to another department and the pull of wanting to remain with his former associates. The greater his loyalty to his old group, the harder it may be for him to adjust to the new workers or to be accepted by them. He is then, for a while, a man without a group, since his former associates no longer consider him to be a member of their group and he feels himself to be unwanted by the new.

These are some of the drives of the worker. Adjustment to his occupational activities depends upon the extent to which he is able to achieve satisfying realization of these motivating urges.

Bases of Vocational Choice

It would seem that a young or older person's reasons for entering any one occupational field would be because of (1) a high degree of interest in work activities, and (2) personal ability to function satisfactorily on the job. This is not always the case, however. Other factors may exercise their influence on the individual's final vocational decision. Powell and Bloom studied adolescent occupational choices through the high school years. Their findings are presented in Table 14.

It can be found by studying Table 14 that many factors enter into adolescent vocational selection. It is worth noting that interest in work has the highest percentage for both boys and girls. Relatively high in importance for boys is *security* and for girls is *service to others* and *interest in people*. Least significant for boys would seem to be *plan to marry,* and for girls *same work as father. Ability to do the work* is not as important to either boys or girls as it probably should be.

Women and Choice of Career

Most girls look forward to marriage and the rearing of a family as their eventual career. They are becoming increasingly interested, however, in preparing themselves for entering a vocational field of activity. In the past, nursing and teaching were considered to be occupations for which women were pre-eminently suited. At present, from early elementary grades through college, women are engaging in educational programs that are the same or similar to those in which men participate. Also, they

TABLE 14

The Percentage of Total Reasons Given as a Basis for the Selection of Certain Vocational Areas

Motivating Factor	Boys	Girls
Interest in work	36.2	27.4
Ability to do the work	6.1	4.3
Interest in people	3.4	15.2
Personal advancement	7.0	3.9
Offers security	11.9	6.0
Service to others	5.3	17.4
Adventure and travel	4.3	5.1
Creative idealism	5.3	4.0
Plan to marry	.1	5.8
Armed services	2.7	.6
Previous experience	3.6	2.6
Variety within the work	1.5	.6
Need education	.4	1.4
Religious	.9	.6
Social prestige	.6	.7
Same work as father	3.3	.5
Parental influence	1.6	1.0
Miscellaneous	2.5	1.9
No reason given	5.2	2.9

Source: Marvin Powell and Viola Bloom, "Development of Reasons for Vocational Choices of Adolescents Through the High School Years," *Journal of Educational Research*, Vol. 56 (1962), p. 132. Reprinted by permission.

are increasingly competing with men in occupational fields that at one time were closed to them. Like men, they are eager to achieve success in their chosen vocation.

Women's high school and college studies usually are pointed at preparing them adequately for entrance into an occupational field of their choice. Some women who marry early either may not have engaged in gainful activity or may leave their job when they marry. Others enter an occupation upon graduation from high school or more usually from college, and continue their work career after marriage except for a period devoted to the birth and early rearing of their children. Some married women remain on the job because of financial necessity; others do so because of their interest in their work.

Married women, especially college graduates, who continue work activities usually have been oriented toward following a career after marriage. Various studies have been undertaken to discover the vocational interests of high school and college students. I shall discuss briefly several of these studies.

Richard and Ida Simpson completed a study [2] dealing with occupational choice among career-oriented college women. The basic hypotheses of the study are as follows:

(1) The career-oriented college women will more often stress, as occupational values, intrinsic features of the work performed, and will less often stress extrinsic occupational rewards not directly related to work tasks. (2) The career-oriented will have been relatively more influenced in their occupational choice by role models who embody values specifically related to occupations, and will have been relatively less influenced by people who embody values of a broader, more generalized, and less occupationally specific kind; concretely, it is hypothesized that the career-oriented will have been influenced relatively more by teachers, professors, and people in the intended occupations, and relatively less by parents, relatives, and peers. These hypotheses are based on the supposition that the attractiveness of specific work tasks, and the encouragement of example of admired persons who embody the virtues of the intended occupations, can help to overcome the ordinary reluctance of women to become strongly committed to work careers.

The report is based on the responses to a questionnaire of 111 college undergraduates in sociology courses in two universities. The procedure used in the study follows:

The female respondents were asked the following question: "Assume that you will marry, and that your husband will make enough so that you will never have to work unless

2 Richard L. Simpson and Ida Harper Simpson, "Occupational Choice Among Career-Oriented College Women," *Marriage and Family Living*, November, 1961.

you want to. Under these conditions, would you prefer (check one) (a) to continue working, even after having children, (b) to quit working if you have children, but definitely go back to work after the children have grown up and left home, (c) to quit working if you have children, and decide later whether to go back to work, (d) not to work at all after you marry, (e) other (explain briefly) ?" Of the 111 women students, 17 checked the first alternative above, 17 checked the second alternative, 58 the third, 11 the fourth and 8 checked "other" and wrote in explanations. All eight of these qualified answers seemed to indicate less career orientation than either of the first two possible answers would have indicated. The 34 women who checked the first or second alternative were designated "career-oriented," and the remaining 77, "non-career-oriented."

Tables 15 and 16 present a summary of the findings. The conclusions of the study are:

All in all, the findings from this survey seem to lend support to the basic idea which guided the specific hypotheses: that women who intend to pursue work careers through all or most of their lives have reached this decision because a rather special constellation of values and influences has been operative. Their occupational values and the sources of influence to whom they listen when making occupational decisions mark them off rather sharply from the more numerous group of women, even college women, whose values are those of middle-class security and conformity and whose personal guides and models lead them into the more common feminine role, that of full-time housewife and mother.[3]

Lee and King conducted a study to investigate the relationship that might exist between the vocational choices of ninth-grade girls and their parents' occupational levels. The subjects of the study were 179 ninth-grade girls at a technical high school in a large Midwestern city. The study attempted to answer the following questions:

1. Do girls prefer occupations at a higher level than the level of their parents' occupations?

[3] *Ibid.*, pp. 378, 379, and 383.

TABLE 15

Reason for Choice of Occupation, Importance of Occupational Features, and Value Rank Among Career and Non-career Women

Response	Career (N = 34) Percent	Non-career (N = 77) Percent	Response	Career (N = 34) Percent	Non-career (N = 77) Percent
Reason for Choice			Helpfulness to others or to society:		
Tasks and self-expression	62	35	Very important	44	55
Occupational Feature			Time to spend with family:		
Kind of tasks involved in work:			Very important	50	46
Very important	74	64	Occupational Value		
Advancement: promotions, growing income, etc.:			Use special abilities	77	53
Very and somewhat important	59	70	Work with people rather than alone or with "things"	56	64
Standards of living:			Freedom from close supervision	3	7
Very and somewhat important	56	77	Prospects of high income	27	21
Prestige of the occupation:			High prestige of occupation	24	16
Very and somewhat important	59	68	Kind of people who are in this occupation	21	14
Esteem among others in the occupation:			Desire to live up to parents' expectations of success	9	18
Very important	44	52	Stable, secure future this occupation provides	9	27
Getting along well with work group:			Help others or make contribution to society	44	48
Very important	59	73	Combine career and good family life	32	21
Parents' pride in success:					
Very important	21	27			

Source: Richard L. Simpson and Ida Harper Simpson, "Occupational Choice Among Career-Oriented College Women," *Marriage and Family Living,* November, 1961, p. 379. Reprinted by permission.

TABLE 16

Influence, Rank, and Strength of Influence Among Career and Non-career Women

Response	Career (N = 34) Percent	Non-career (N = 77) Percent
Source of Influence		
People in the occupation (write-in):		
Most important influence	18	16
Second most important influence	6	1
Teacher or professor:		
Most important influence	35	17
Second most important influence	24	9
Mother:		
Most important influence	12	12
Second most important influence	18	29
Father:		
Most important influence	6	16
Second most important influence	15	21

Response	Career (N = 34) Percent	Non-career (N = 77) Percent
Type of Influence Source Ranked First		
Occupational models (teachers, professors, or people in the occupation)	50	33
Parents or relatives	18	31
Peers	3	13
Others (reading, aptitude tests, counseling)	29	23
Total	100	100
Strength of Influence		
People in the occupation (write-in):		
Strong or some influence	27	20
Teacher or professor:		
Strong influence	56	33

TABLE 16 (continued)

Response	Career (N = 34) Percent	Non-career (N = 77) Percent
Mother:		
Strong influence	38	27
Father:		
Strong influence	38	23
Other relatives (write-in):		
Strong or some influence	0	8
Close friends of same sex at college:		
Strong or some influence	50	47
Other close friends of same sex:		
Strong or some influence	38	34
Close friends of opposite sex:		
Strong or some influence	53	55

Response	Career (N = 34) Percent	Non-career (N = 77) Percent
Other relatives (write-in):		
Most important influence	0	4
Second most important influence	0	1
Close friends of same sex at college:		
Most important influence	0	5
Second most important influence	3	5
Other close friends of same sex:		
Most important influence	0	1
Second most important influence	3	4
Close friends of opposite sex:		
Most important influence	0	7
Second most important influence	12	9

Source: Richard L. Simpson and Ida Harper Simpson, "Occupational Choice Among Career-Oriented College Women," *Marriage and Family Living,* November, 1961, p. 382. Reprinted by permission.

2. Do girls whose mothers are housewives prefer occupations at a higher level than do girls whose mothers are employed outside the home?
3. Do girls have higher occupational preferences than occupational expectancies?
4. Are there differences between the occupational preferences of girls and the occupations suggested for them by their parents?
5. Are there differences between the level of occupational suggestions that fathers and mothers make to their daughters?

[The study] revealed many statistically significant differences. The mean level of the girls' occupational preferences was higher than the mean level of the parents' actual occupations. The parents suggested occupations at a higher level than the girls' occupational preferences and expectancies. The level of the girls' occupational expectancies was lower than the level of their occupational preferences.[4]

Robert Milliken investigated the post-high school plans of senior girls in relation to scholastic aptitude. The study included 5,349 senior high school girls in South Dakota and led to the results shown in Table 17 and the following conclusions:

Students interested in the professional activities, all requiring higher educational training, showed the highest mean AGCT scores. . . . Clerical (combining both stenography and office worker) was the most popular, followed by teaching, nursing, beautician and housewife. It is felt, as other studies have shown, that most young women could have realistically listed "marriage" along with their listed interest areas.

Assuming realism of choice is related to ability, several factors appear. One, those young women selecting scientific professional activities are apparently "realistic" since a college education in the sciences requires high level ability in order to succeed. Second, the girls choosing lower-skill occu-

[4] Billie Louise Lee and Paul King, "Vocational Choices of Ninth Grade Girls and Their Parents' Occupational Levels," *Vocational Guidance Quarterly*, Spring, 1964, pp. 163, 167.

TABLE 17

Converted AGCT Scores for Graduating High School Senior Girls in
South Dakota by Occupation or Proposed College Major

	Mean	Sigma	Number
Scientist	144.5	19.5	14
Pharmacy	130.3	18.0	24
Engineer	129.9	18.3	7
Lawyer	128.4	14.4	5
Behavioral science	125.5	18.5	11
Actor	123.4	18.8	13
Medicine	118.5	17.8	46
Journalism	116.7	19.5	27
Religious activities	114.8	20.9	36
Veterinarian	110.5	22.3	5
Home economics	109.7	21.4	79
Music	107.8	12.1	80
Art	106.6	20.0	110
Business	103.2	20.1	98
Teacher	103.2	19.8	1400
Librarian	102.9	21.7	5
Social welfare	102.8	21.1	62
Nursing	100.5	20.7	1074
Policewoman	98.4	12.9	4
Clerical	97.4	18.5	1620
Housewife	92.8	19.3	160
Military	90.3	18.5	37
Air hostess	89.0	16.0	107
Beautician	87.8	17.8	161
Other skilled activities	84.7	14.8	23
Telephone operator	84.3	16.1	104
Farming	70.4	13.9	13
Practical nurse	68.0	14.6	24
Total	100.0	20.0	5349

Source: Robert Milliken, "Post-High School Plans of Senior Girls in Relation to Scholastic Aptitude," Vocational Guidance Quarterly, Autumn, 1961, p. 51. Reprinted by permission.

pations generally do not require high level academic ability for success on the job. Third, the professions of teaching, nursing, home economics, and social welfare attract many young women whose abilities range from marginal to outstanding.[5]

[5] Robert Milliken, "Post-High School Plans of Senior Girls in Relation to Scholastic Aptitude," Vocational Guidance Quarterly, Autumn, 1961, pp. 51, 52.

The Total Person

The worker does not bring to his job a mere part of himself. There are few, if any, workers who are able to separate their work lives from their other experiences. An individual's health, his ability to evaluate his job in terms of social and personal usefulness, his relations with his family, his social interests—in fact, his whole philosophy of life is reflected in his success and satisfaction or his failure and lack of satisfaction in his occupational life.

Causes of Maladjustment in Work

The maladjusted worker is the fearful worker who has failed in one way or another to find complete satisfaction in his job. The sources of this dissatisfaction may lie within or without the individual. Psychologists and mental hygienists interested in business and industry are attempting to discover the bases of occupational maladjustment and, by amelioration or removal of them, to help individual workers toward better work adjustment.

A worker may become dissatisfied with his job for one or more of a number of reasons. His work may be too fatiguing; he may experience a feeling of personal inadequacy in meeting the demands of his work. Various occupational fears may assail him, such as possible loss of his job, wage cut, incapacity through ill health, unfair supervision, failure to achieve a personal ambition, lack of cooperation among his fellow workers, and old-age dependency. Industrial psychology is aimed at the removal for workers of as many as possible of these sources of discontent or feelings of frustration through the improvement of placement, plant organization, supervision, wage scales, and working conditions.

PROBLEMS OF JOB ADJUSTMENT

Most persons spend the greater part of their waking day in work that is aimed at the meeting of their life needs. Life adjustments are influenced to a great extent by the satisfactions that are experienced on the job as well as by the money that is earned.

Determination of Suitable Work

Some individuals continue in an occupation, earning reasonable success in their work, without ever being certain that they are in the kind of work for which they are best suited. In fact, there are people who do a good job for ten or more years in one kind of work. They then, either by accident or design, prepare themselves for another field in which they believe they will be happier, and more successful economically.

In order to be outstanding in fields such as art, music, and dramatics, a person probably needs certain specific talents that are not possessed by the majority of people. There are tests of musical and artistic aptitude that may give some indication of the degree of talent that a person possesses in one or the other of these two fields. The possession of a special talent usually shows itself early, if the individual is given an opportunity during his school days to exhibit the beginnings of good achievement in the field, if he himself is interested, and if a teacher or parent is quick enough to recognize the special talent and provides further training for the young person. Even though the student shows a definite aptitude in a field, however, everyone concerned needs to be realistic about the extent to which the talented young person shall be encouraged to continue his studies.

Opportunities in the field, financial ability to meet the cost of training, and the person's own willingness to sacrifice time and energy to perfect his skill are important considerations. Too often, young people who possess no more than a fair degree of talent are encouraged to look forward to a vocational career in a field where no more than average or less than average occupational success can be achieved. Such a person had better turn to another vocation for his lifework, and use his special talent as an avocation.

There are parents who regard participation in the arts as an insecure way of earning a living, e.g., a boy who gives evidence of unusual talent in one or another form of art is not permitted to develop his talent but is forced by his parents to prepare instead for a *solid* vocation, such as business, mechanics, or a profession. Many an adult who, as a boy, was denied by his parents the right to follow his own vocational interest, has failed to earn success in the field that was chosen for him. He either dabbles at the same time (on the side) in the field of his own choice or, later in life, gives up the undesired vocation and devotes all of his time and energies to the other, sometimes at great monetary sacrifice.

Barring fields that require special talent, the choice of the vocational course to be followed by an intelligent student may be any one of many. His choice depends upon the opportunities available in one or another of them, if the personal qualities that lead to success in one hold for the others. A young woman, for example, who is interested in and able to work with people may be equally successful as a nurse when the demand for nurses is great, or as a teacher in times of teacher shortage and oversupply of nurses. The specific training for the two vocations differs. Therefore, before her graduation from high school, she decides which vocation she wishes to enter.

Although there are batteries of aptitude and personality tests that can be utilized for the purpose of discovering an individual's fitness for entrance into any one of many vocations, the final choice usually should be made in terms of available openings and the individual's well-considered interest in one field rather than in another. Whatever the choice may be, an important consideration is that, after a person enters a field for which he appears to be qualified and in which he sees opportunities for advancement, he stays in it rather than dissipate his energies by flitting from one field to another.

Individual Potential and Job Analysis

This is a problem that faces all young people and, to a lesser extent, those adults who for one reason or another are forced to change their vocation. In order to choose a vocation intelligently and profitably, an individual needs to familiarize himself with three factors: (1) his own abilities, interests, and personal characteristics, (2) available fields of work and their requirements, and (3) the extent to which his potentialities meet the requirements of the respective occupations.

A complete analysis of any one of these three factors is a serious project and must be undertaken in a businesslike and objective fashion. Opportunities for self-analysis are improving and yielding some reliable data. Many studies are being conducted of the specific and detailed activities of various types of work. It is almost impossible to evolve a complete list of all the minute details of movement and of activity needed for every one of the thousands of specific jobs in which an individual may engage. However, studies made to date have resulted in the compilation of the major requirements of many work fields. Besides a knowledge of the requirements of a vocation and his own fitness for it, the individual needs, while on the job, to gain increased efficiency and to earn advancement. A young man or woman who is really interested in achieving success in his work activities usually is eager to perfect his skills.

The training situation is different for the young person who is planning to enter an occupational field that requires long and intensive training. Concern about immediate study difficulties may cause him to lose interest in his long-range goal. He may become discouraged by an occasional failure in his courses. He may doubt his capacity to prepare adequately for his chosen field.

Granted that the individual is qualified for such training as will make him an efficient worker in a chosen vocation, he still has two factors to consider: (1) possible opportunities for the training needed and (2) financial ability to meet the cost of the training. If either of these two factors is unavailable, the individual is forced into preparation for an allied activity, the training for which is within the realm of possibility.

Public and private agencies are fast meeting the first of these needs. Vocational "scouts" are studying professional, business, and industrial trends. On the basis of their findings, they are predicting the vocational needs of the future, and are aiding in the establishment of proper training facilities and in the encouragement of students for them. Mistakes are made, such as the school that set up an elaborate home-economics program for an expected need five years hence only to discover that not home-economics experts but stenographers and typists represented the new need of their community.

Many vocational-training courses are expensive and therefore prohibitive for some qualified candidates. Scholarships in privately endowed schools and community support of vocational schools are attempting to meet this need. If an individual shows a special ability in a particular field, it is becoming increasingly possible for him to obtain the required training.

The point at which a man or woman may stop his training

and enter into active work on the job varies with the kind of work in which he plans to engage. Usually, for the so-called professions—medicine, law, teaching, engineering or nursing—the worker in the field needs fairly complete pretraining, including supervised practice, before he enters into the field. The young physician spends several years as an intern at a hospital. The teacher goes out into a school and observes an experienced teacher and does some practice teaching under supervision. The lawyer-to-be spends a period of time with a well-established law firm before he hangs out his shingle. This practical experience is needed; most people are hesitant to employ the services of these professional people until they have learned on the job, as well as from books and demonstrations.

In some fields, such as business, it is possible for a person to master the rudiments of his work during his regular schooling and then to engage in the more simple phases of the work. He assumes greater responsibility as he gains greater practical experience in it and continues his studying as he works.

There is a growing educational trend to combine study with work practice. The cooperative study-work plan is used in some colleges such as Antioch, and in an increasing number of high schools. No matter how thorough a person's preliminary preparation for his work life has been, it probably is to his benefit to continue his studying after he has started to work. In most vocational fields, newer methods and improved procedures require that workers in these occupations constantly attempt to become informed about such changes, if they desire to develop greater skill or earn promotion in their work.

In order to meet workers' demands for continued study, evening courses are increasing in number; business and industrial organizations are offering in-service training to their employees, or are allowing their workers to take leaves of absence for continued study. Such continued study is valuable to the employer and to the employees to the extent that through it the efficiency of the worker is increased. If, however, the study is too far removed from the kind of work that is being done on the job, the worker may be distracted from his best job achievement.

The value of training on the job is dependent upon several factors. The workday may need to be lengthened to include both work production and training. As part of the training, the worker may be required to engage in home study. In either case, sufficient time may be denied the worker to engage in relaxing recreational and social activities. If the program of work and study is too strenuous, the worker's health may be affected and the extra study will then interfere with the progress of both the employer and the employee. Study while on the job must be adjusted to the job needs and to the health of the worker. A balanced program, intelligently carried out, motivates interested and successful achievement and results in a high degree of occupational adjustment.

THE ENTRANCE OF AN INDIVIDUAL INTO A FIELD OF WORK

As we have indicated in the foregoing, various factors of adjustment are experienced by the worker. Important among these are the elements that are involved in the experience of entering a vocation, especially securing employment and earning promotion.

The Problem of Securing Employment

Every individual who, upon leaving school, seeks employment should approach this new experience with adequate training in job-getting. Schools have been lax in this respect and until recently, few high school graduates have been aware of desirable techniques for obtaining employment. High school students should be trained in the techniques of written and personal job-seeking, the proper use of reputable agencies, the filling out of application blanks, and the proper behavior during the application interview.

Young people should be taught to recognize the value, in written applications for employment, of neatness, correctness, completeness, legible handwriting, correct spelling, desirable business-letter form, and pertinent content. Success in a personal interview for a position demands that the applicant be appropriately dressed, neatly groomed, well poised, and modest, yet confident in his attitude concerning his own suitability for the position. The applicant should be able to submit for the consideration of the prospective employer the names of responsible persons who will be ready to give an honest statement concerning the applicant's fitness for the particular type of work in which he desires to engage.

Job-seeking is often a painful experience for the sensitive person. However, if a young man or woman has endeavored to prepare himself adequately for the requirements of his chosen work, if he has tried conscientiously, with the help of his advisers, to develop a sincere, pleasing, and cooperative attitude, he need not be unduly disturbed by the fear of failure to achieve his goal. The experiences associated with job-hunting are valuable personality developers even though the first few trials are unsuccessful. Seeking employment is a challenge to the individual; it gives him experience in meeting strangers who later may become important in his life, it tests his own ability to be thoroughly honest with himself, and it enables him to become acquainted with business ideals and techniques.

When he believes that he is ready to engage in a specific field of worker activity, the individual may utilize one or more of the following ways of procuring a job:

Newspaper advertisements
Magazine and occupational periodicals
Relatives or friends
School employment agencies
Government employment agencies
Commercial employment agencies
Various examination techniques, such as civil service,
    licensing, etc.

The least desirable probably are newspaper advertisements, yet they may be helpful. The various agencies may be helpful. Licensing examinations are becoming increasingly popular.

Factors of Job Application

After an individual has located a possible opening in his vocational field, he then has the task of applying for the position. He may submit a letter of application or fill in a more formal application blank provided for his use by the employing agency. In either case, the applicant should provide the possible employer with sufficient information about himself so that the reader can ascertain whether or not the individual is suited to fill the vacancy.

The letter should be businesslike and preferably typewritten, although some employers prefer handwritten letters, especially if the position entails the preparing of materials in longhand. The letter of application should be neatly and carefully prepared and as brief as possible. It should cover the following points:

> Address, age, and sex of the writer
> How knowledge of the vacancy was obtained as related to reason for the application's being submitted
> Substantiating data concerning education and specific training qualifications
> Previous work experience, if any

Personal data having no bearing on the job for which the individual is applying should be omitted.

THE PERSONAL INTERVIEW. Most employers require that the applicant appear for a personal interview with an appropriate member of their staff. The interview can be a difficult experience, especially for a beginner in the world of work. He needs to make a successful adjustment to a stranger who probably has definite ideas concerning the kind of person to be hired.

TABLE 18

Questions Most Frequently Asked by Employers During Interviews

1. What are your future vocational plans?
2. How do you spend your spare time? What are your hobbies?
3. In what type of position are you most interested?
4. Why do you think you might like to work for our company?
5. What courses did you like best? Least? Why?
6. Why did you choose your particular field of work?
7. What percentage of your college expenses did you earn? How?
8. How did you spend your vacations while in school?
9. What do you know about our company?
10. What qualifications do you have that make you feel that you will be successful in your field?
11. What are your ideas of salary?
12. How do you feel about your family?
13. If you were starting college all over again, what courses would you take?
14. Do you have a girl? (or a boy friend?) Is it serious?
15. How much money do you hope to earn at age thirty? thirty-five?
16. Do you think that your extracurricular activities were worth the time you devoted to them? Why?
17. Why do you think you would like this particular type of job?

18. Tell me about your home life during the time you were growing up.
19. Are you looking for a permanent or temporary job?
20. Do you prefer working with others or by yourself?
21. What kind of a boss do you prefer?
22. Are you primarily interested in making money or do you feel that service to your fellow men is a satisfactory accomplishment?
23. Do you live with your parents? Which of your parents has had the most profound influence on you?
24. How did previous employers treat you?
25. What have you learned from some of the jobs you have held?
26. Have you ever changed your major field of interest while in college? Why?
27. Do you feel you have done the best scholastic work of which you are capable?

28. Have you ever had any difficulty getting along with fellow students and faculty?
29. Which of your college years was the most difficult?
30. Do you like routine work?
31. What is your major weakness?
32. Do you demand attention?
33. Are you willing to go where a company sends you?
34. What job in our company would you choose if you were entirely free to do so?
35. Is it an effort for you to be tolerant of persons with a background and interests different from your own?
36. What types of people seem to "rub you the wrong way"?
37. Would you prefer a large or a small company? Why?
38. What are the disadvantages of your chosen field?
39. What have you done that shows initiative and willingness to work?

Source: Robert Calvert, Jr., and J. E. Steele, *Planning Your Career*, New York: McGraw-Hill, Inc., pp. 90–91. Copyright 1963. Used by permission.

The interviewee should be punctual in meeting the appointment. He should be appropriately dressed and carefully groomed. His displayed attitude toward the interview is extremely important. He should avoid displaying either an aggressive, overconfident attitude or one of timidity and/or fear. He needs to speak in a distinct and well-modulated voice, using correct English and avoiding slang expressions. Answers to the interviewer's questions should be stated definitely and briefly. The applicant should not ramble on concerning his abilities, interests, and previous experiences, beyond what is needed to answer questions precisely and accurately. Some of the kinds of questions that an interviewer may ask are suggested by Calvert and Steele in Table 18.

The Problem of Promotion

Yearly increments, occasional bonuses, vacations with pay, and promotions give the employee a goal toward which to aim and a feeling of success in achievement. Promotion and security are ideals that workers desire intensely. Promotion from one kind of service to another, however, should not be based merely on years of service but also on the nature of the advanced work and the ability of the employee to succeed in that kind of work. But, if two individuals seem to possess equal qualifications for the new responsibility, the one with the longer service record should be given the preference. The policy of recognizing consistent faithfulness and achievement tends to develop among workers an appreciation of fair and just treatment.

The Value of Dignifying Work

Pride in workmanship is a very desirable trait but since there are many different kinds of work to be performed, not all persons can hope to perform the same type. Society has tended to dignify mental work and to underestimate the social value of manual labor. Individuals are often deterred from selecting a vocation for which they are qualified and in which they are interested because of the social stigma attached to the activity. Many different types of occupational work are needed if all the various wants of humanity are to be met.

Menial work of any kind is looked upon with disfavor. So simple an activity as the washing of dishes is essential to healthful living; yet some mothers insist that their daughters not perform this service. Other parents do not permit their sons to perform household duties if there are daughters in the family. Thus, wrong attitudes are engendered toward necessary work. Parents and teachers should establish in young people the realization that any work that is worthy of being done should be worthy of the doing by all able-bodied persons.

The foregoing does not mean that everyone should be trained to do many kinds of work well. Specialization usually results in increased efficiency, but the form of specialization to be selected should be based on the possession of the necessary aptitude and a personal interest rather than on unimportant external factors. It is more important to become an efficient typist, ditchdigger, waitress, or charwoman than to persist unsuccessfully in an attempt to obtain employment in a vocational activity chosen mainly because of its social advantages and prestige.

ADJUSTMENT OF THE WORKER
TO THE JOB

The relationships which grow out of his work are certain to influence all of an individual's other relationships. If it is true that as a man is, so will his work be, it is equally true that as his work relationships are, so will he be. A study of occupational adjustment, then, cannot be divorced, except in particulars, from a study of life adjustment in general.

General Personality Adjustment

Individuals differ in their physical structure and vigor, their mental ability, their special aptitudes, and their degree of emotional stability. In like manner, different types of occupational work differ in their physical, mental, aptitudinal, and emotional requirements. There are certain personality traits, however, the possession of which predisposes toward success, no matter what the specific character of the work may be.

Employers are becoming increasingly aware of the value to them of employees who possess such traits as punctuality, industry, honesty, and sincerity, emotional control in difficult situations, loyalty to their employer, neatness and cleanliness, and appreciation of their own position in and relationship to the function and organization of the entire personnel. These qualities are no different from those that affect adjustment in any social relationship. The "spoiled" child, the lazy child, the irresponsible child, the sulky child, or the emotionally uncontrolled child is in danger of becoming the uncooperative, lazy, irritable, and unstable worker.

If the job is unsuitable or if the working conditions are undesirable, the worker's unfavorable characteristics will be intensified; serious job maladjustment may result. The individual who has developed wholesome personality qualities is unlikely to suffer too greatly from job dissatisfaction. If the worker's choice of vocation has not been wise or if working conditions are intolerable, however, even good behavior patterns break down and the worker may become maladjusted.

Personal fitness for entrance into one or another occupational field constitutes a major factor of vocational selection. High school counselors are faced with the problem of helping young people determine the degree to which they possess those personal characteristics that predispose toward successful participation in a desired occupational field. Although the display of industry, conscientiousness, integrity, and cooperation is effective in any occupational field, various areas of vocational activity, by the nature of their demands, set ability limitations.

Physical endurance, strength, and health status are important. For example, a young woman who is intensely interested in teaching is barred from entering the profession because of her diabetic condition. A man who aspires to be a pilot is subjected to rigid examination of his physical and mental status: sight, heart condition, muscular coordination, quickness of response, and physical endurance.

Jobs have intellectual levels. There are forms of work which are peculiarly adapted to superior, average, and subnormal levels of intelligence, respectively. Comparisons of vocational success with mental ability seem to indicate that, on the average, the occupational hierarchy from unskilled labor through semiskilled, skilled, and technical to professional levels of work is accompanied by a corresponding rise in the levels of mental ability.

Workers' Attitudes

Attitudes of workers vary from extreme discontent and bitterness to almost complete happiness, satisfaction, and loyalty. Many factors contribute to this variation in feeling. A worker rarely displays one general attitude toward all phases of his work experiences and environment. Rather it is true that a worker exhibits varying attitudes in his work relationship. He tends to have an accepting or a rejecting attitude toward the job itself. Seldom is he totally indifferent to it.

The individual who is engaged in work of his own choice and for which he is adequately prepared usually evinces interest in it and often is enthusiastic about it, in spite of other undesirable elements in the situation. Contrariwise, the worker whose job represents nothing more to him than his salary or pay check, who has no real aptitude for or interest in it, or who recognizes in himself the lack of proper training, tends, in spite of other favorable conditions, to dislike the work, often finding it so intolerable that he quits it.

In his relations with his immediate superior, an individual is affected by his own ability to adjust to other persons, by the supervisor's attitude toward his workers, or by the worker's degree of skill. A feeling that the supervisor or employer is favoring other workers rather than himself, lack of expressed approval from the supervisor, or the worker's consciousness of his own ineffectiveness (that the supervisor should recognize even though he may not) may develop in the worker an antagonistic attitude that is difficult to overcome.

A worker is seldom neutral in his attitude toward his fellow workers. Appreciation of his own success and of similar effectiveness on the part of his associates develops in the worker a feeling of friendliness and cooperation that usually is reciprocated. Dislike, jealousy, and uncooperativeness grow out of feelings of personal ineffectualness as compared with the other workers and unequal treatment of the workers by the supervisors, or an appreciation by the worker of himself as superior in one way or another to the others.

The worker's attitude toward the organization is closely related to its community status, to the efforts made by the organization to improve working conditions, or to the worker's appreciation of the purpose of the work and his part in it. A respected establishment, providing desirable working conditions and engaging in worth-while production in which the worker has a significant place, tends to develop a feeling of pride, loyalty, and oneness. A worker cannot tolerate being ashamed of his job or of his employer. If economic necessity forces him to remain in his position, his attitude tends to be one of bitterness both toward the organization and toward an unkind fate.

A worker's attitude toward his job, his supervisor, his fellow workers, or the organization itself, affects the success and value of his work. The worker whose attitude toward all phases of his work life is favorable is a contented and effective worker. Any form of antagonism is sure to affect the quality of his work and to decrease his value to his employer.

ADJUSTMENT OF THE JOB
TO THE WORKER

The relationship between supply and demand in the field of employment has an important influence upon the morale of a worker. If an individual is fitted for a type of work in which there is a reasonable demand for well-trained persons, and if then the individual has the opportunities for adequate training with assurance of placement, he views the future with hope and enthusiasm. His attitude toward his training and his subsequent employment favors a desirable adjustment to the job and further study toward advancement.

Adjustment and Employment Conditions

Because of a scarcity of available openings, a person may be barred from entrance into an occupational field for which he is qualified and for which he may have adequate training. A resulting attitude of discouragement and futility will develop. Moreover, if the individual discovers that placement in the coveted field has been made as a result of political or social favoritism, bitterness and social antagonism may result. Economic need may force the individual into another occupational field, but rarely is he able to bring to the new job the enthusiasm and interest that are conducive to happiness and efficiency. If he is intelligent and emotionally stable, he will endeavor honestly to fulfill his obligations in this job but he also will be on the alert to obtain an opportunity in his chosen field. If the latter is too late in coming, he may have lost his original adequacy for the work by the time he reaches his goal, with the result that neither can he gain from it the satisfaction that he had expected nor can he fulfill his early promise of success in it.

In times of business and industrial depression, workers who have jobs are afraid to lose them. They may tolerate undesirable working conditions because they fear that complaints may jeopardize their position. The fear of being "laid off" may interfere with their efficiency. They are unable to bring to the job success in achievement which would be possible if their work were accompanied by a realization of relative security or of advancement. They may be afraid that any sign of decreased efficiency may place them among the first to be discharged. Hence their efficiency is lessened by the worry that they may not be "kept on." They may believe that discharges are made unfairly and that, if they do not have a "drag" with the administration, they may lose out. This attitude may result either in attempts to gain favor or in an attitude of bitterness toward the organization. On the other hand, if job supply is below job demand, the employed worker may feel that the employer is at his mercy, since workers are hard to obtain. Consequently, he may become overbearing, careless in his work, and make demands upon his employer that may be difficult for the latter to meet.

As the worker grows older, unless his work has been such that skilled workmanship and experience have won for him personal recognition, a fear of the loss of his present employment and of his inability to obtain new employment becomes a menace to job adjustment. Unemployment insurance and old-age pension systems are doing much to relieve workers of this worry.

Effect of Wages and Hours upon Adjustment

If the average worker is underpaid and is forced to work for too long hours, he is a dissatisfied worker. Labor organizations, labor-relations boards, and labor-management committees have striven for and are continuing to fight for better wage adjustment. Employers are recognizing the value of rest and relaxation as stimulators of increased and improved production. The eight-hour (and shorter) working day, the five-day working week, and the two-week or longer vacation are helping the worker gain renewed energy for his work hours. Short rest periods during the day are becoming popular. Yet long periods of leisure between work periods distract from concentrated attention to work and may lead to lax or indifferent work habits. Experiments with desirable work and rest ratios help discover, for the different forms of occupational work, the optimum relationship between work and relaxation.

The value of any form of work as represented by the amount of financial reward attached to it has not yet been determined satisfactorily. Such factors as length and amount of training needed for the work, traditional attitudes toward the form of work and years of service, and the demand for the service have been generally accepted as criteria for wage standards. Much worker dissatisfaction is caused by the belief that discriminations in wage scales are based upon factors that are superficial and unworthy. An individual who recognizes himself as a conscientious, able, and hard worker easily may learn to resent his own relatively small wage as compared with that of other persons who with similar training and work experience, less work effort, and shorter hours, receive much higher wages than he does.

Effects of the Physical Conditions of the Job

Certain physiological, psychological, and aesthetic needs of the worker require attention. Improper lighting, insufficient or badly regulated heating and ventilation, unsanitary lavatory facilities, and/or distracting noise in an office or other work room interfere with a worker's health, contentment, and work efficiency. Modern methods of meeting these needs are providing for the worker comfortable furniture and other work equipment, attractive rest-rooms, libraries, company cafeterias, and other healthful conditions. Attractiveness as well as utility in building construction, decoration, furnishings, and landscaping of the grounds satisfy the worker's inherent love for the beautiful, and do much to encourage in him pride of possession and improvement of morale.

Although individual workers vary in their susceptibility to fatigue and the recognition of their work as monotonous, there are factors in the work itself that may arouse fatigue in the worker or cause the work to become uninteresting. A balanced work-and-rest program can reduce materially the fatigue element of a specific kind of work. An arrangement whereby a worker is permitted, within his abilities and training, to vary his work units from one type of activity to another not only reduces the strain of repeating the same operation to the point of complete boredom, but aids also in encouraging the worker's desire to envision his part in the completed product by allowing him to follow the steps of its production.

Work accidents are caused partly by the individual's own carelessness or lack of knowledge or skill and partly by insufficient or inadequate safety devices. The tired worker, the bored worker, and the sick worker tend to have more accidents than do healthy, alert, and interested workers. Anything, then, that the management can do to preserve the health, interest, and alertness of the worker will tend to reduce the incidence of accident. If machinery and equipment are fitted with the best-known safety devices and if precautions are taken by the management to reduce the exposure of their workers to certain occupational diseases, the confidence with which the worker attacks the job increases. The knowledge that his well-being is cared for and that, if an unavoidable accident should occur, he and his family are protected by accident and health insurance will insure the employee's adjustment and his value to his employer.

Supervision and Worker Adjustment

Important to a worker are supervisory recognition of his successful achievement, constructive and unemotional treatment of his mistakes, appreciation of the value of his contribution to the progress of the organization, and available opportunities to take part in group conferences dealing with improved techniques. In fact, any evidence on the part of the supervisor or employer of his realization that the worker is a living, thinking, and feeling human being rather than an inanimate machine will call forth from the average worker a spirit of loyalty, cooperation, and unity of purpose.

The human factor cannot be divorced from occupational work. No matter how humble the worker's position is or how routine his work may be, he still needs to maintain his self-respect in the group. If this is gained as a result of intelligent leadership, other things being equal, an adjusted work life will result. If the leadership takes the form of an attempted domination of an inferior, the worker struggles to maintain his own self respect and the respect of his fellow workers will show itself in bitter denunciation, disloyalty, and rebellion, with consequent reduced and inferior production.

JOB RELATIONS
A Supervisor Gets Results Through People
Foundations for Good Relations
Let each worker know how he is getting along.
Figure out what you expect of him.
Point out ways to improve.

Give credit when due.
   Look for extra or unusual performance.
   Tell him while "it's hot."
Tell people in advance about changes that will affect them.
   Tell them WHY if possible.
   Get them to accept the change.
Make best use of each person's ability.
   Look for ability not now being used.
   Never stand in a man's way.
People must be treated as individuals.

The Unadjusted Worker

Some workers who seem unable to adjust to their job can be found in every form of business and industry. Some persons are definitely unemployable because of their personality lacks and unfortunate habits and attitudes. There are others who, although they can obtain employment, appear to lack the stability and perseverance necessary for efficient job continuance. Examples of such persons are known to all of us.

A young man who had found it difficult to follow high school routine was placed in a routine job. Since he seemed to be a pleasant person he was at first liked by his employer. He soon began to make slight errors, however. When these were brought to his attention, he convinced his employer that if he were given another type of work in the factory, for which he considered himself particularly fitted, there would be no further reason for such errors. This was done, but after a while the same carelessness was evidenced. Because of his likable disposition, his employer was persuaded to try him in still another type of activity; but this young man was unable to continue in any form of work satisfactorily for more than a month or two. He has many good qualities, but his inability to persevere has resulted in constant change of position. He does not recognize this lack in himself and constantly complains about the unfairness of employers. Employment agencies are familiar with the type of worker who seems able to secure a job but unable to hold it.

There are jobs and job conditions that seem to militate against successful achievement on the part of even well-qualified workers. Unhealthful physical environment and unintelligent supervision make it impossible for the average worker long to remain adjusted to his job. Business and industrial research, psychology and mental hygiene, intelligent business and industrial leadership, careful selection of workers, and hygienic working conditions are needed in order to insure desirable job adjustment for workers.

GUIDANCE AND OCCUPATIONAL ADJUSTMENT

Schools and other social agencies are beginning to recognize their function in the preparation of American youth for occupational life. In the schools, especially on the secondary level, attempts are being made to ascertain the individual aptitudes, abilities, and interests of their students. Personality and vocational tests are administered, and a careful study is made of classroom and extra-classroom activities. Further, by means of courses in occupational surveys, reading materials, visits to industry, lectures, and conferences with business and industrial leaders, the schools are acquainting their students with work possibilities. Young people are encouraged to make their vocational choices early enough in high school to insure for themselves adequate and thorough training for their chosen vocation. School systems are enlarging their educational facilities in order to include many of these preparatory training experiences. This is especially true of junior colleges and other post-high school institutions.

When the young people are ready to enter upon their occupational work, school authorities attempt to place their students. This is done either through their own placement departments or in cooperation with local, state, federal, or private employment agencies. Programs of "follow-up" of their working graduates or dropouts are then used for the purpose of helping their former students toward better job adjustment. Follow-up also can serve the purpose of obtaining data concerning working conditions and requirements that will help school counselors in the guidance of their present students toward occupational adjustment.

A comprehensive program of vocational guidance as outlined above is at present an ideal rather than an actual accomplishment. Few communities or school systems are sufficiently well organized, or have the money, building facilities, or trained corps necessary for the complete achievement of these guidance objectives. In an increasing number of communities good beginnings have been made; a greater interest is being exhibited in this direction in all sections of the country.

Guidance on the Job

Apart from major reforms in such matters as wages, hours, supervision, and general working conditions, individual workers need personal help and guidance toward good personal adjustment. A well-organized business or industrial plant includes a personnel department. To preserve the physical and mental health of individual workers, the services of a physician and a nurse, a psychologist, a psychiatrist, and a psychiatric social worker are provided.

Medical assistance and advice are available for the worker who needs it. One insurance company not only provides a large and competent medical staff for its employees but also maintains a completely equipped sanatorium in a healthful and beautiful country environment. To this rest home, employees are sent for recuperation from illness or for rest, either at a very small expense to the employee or without cost to him.

The psychologist's function is to test an applicant for employment and placement, or an employee for promotion or transfer. In a few companies, it is the policy not to discharge an employee if he fails in one department. With the help of the psychologist, he is transferred to other departments until he finds the one in which he is successful. No employee is discharged unless he has shown inability to succeed in any department.

The psychiatrist deals with the individual peculiarities, grievances, emotional disturbances, and personal problems of the workers. He also recommends hygienic improvements in the organization or in general business policies. He is responsible for the individual adjustment of the workers and for the building up of healthy morale and loyalty to the company.

The work of the psychiatric social worker takes him into the home and social life of the maladjusted worker. He gathers data concerning the out-of-work habits and relationships of the worker, for use by the physician, psychologist, or psychiatrist who may be working with an individual's problem of adjustment. He then cooperates in the carrying out of suggestions for the worker's readjustment. His help sometimes continues with an individual after he has been discharged from or has left the company.

It is unfortunate that a guidance program of this type is possible for only large business houses or industrial plants. The small employer cannot afford these services for his workers. There is needed a cooperating agency in each community to which these employers may refer their maladjusted workers. A few such experiments have been started.

Another form of guidance needed by the occupational worker is help toward rehabilitation when and if, through illness, business depression, war experience, or any other cause, he loses the opportunity to continue his present work. The Federal government has been working on this problem, and some private agencies have been meeting the situation more or less adequately.

Adjustment of the Professional Worker

The occupational adjustment of the professional worker differs somewhat from that of other workers. The professions demand from those persons who desire to enter them a general ability level above the average, certain specific aptitudes, long and intense training that usually includes apprenticeship practice during the training. Required also are personal qualities that are basic to the worker's willingness to persevere in his work and to attend punctiliously to details, and ability to work without the direction and supervision of others.

His long and thorough training tends to develop in the professional worker a mastery of, an appreciation of, and an interest in, his work that are not found to so great an extent among other workers. The professional worker views his vocation as a life calling and continues to be a student as well as a worker. Most professions demand that those engaging in them recognize the humane and social functions of their work. Hence the public expects the professional worker to give freely of his time, energy, and skill or knowledge, to the improvement of human welfare, with or without financial reward.

The scientist, the artist, the lawyer, the physician, the nurse, the teacher, and the religious or social worker may be so absorbed in their work, they may be so filled with the urge for creation or service, and their work may have become so much a part of their life interest that the financial returns beyond what they need for simple existence are of minor importance to them. Moreover, since their work is their life, they are willing and eager to devote long hours to it.

Instead of working under the supervision of another person, the professional worker is working more or less in cooperation with others of his kind toward the realization of a common goal. The members of a profession usually are bound by a group code of ethics. A well-known example is the ancient Hippocratic oath which still is administered to those persons who are about to enter upon the practice of medicine. A professional code of ethics, combined with a government licensing of some professional workers, has developed among these workers an attitude of personal responsibility for successful achievement that motivates their entire life pattern.

Because of his absorbing interest in his work and the demands made upon his time, the professional worker often finds it difficult to achieve a hygienic balance between his occupational work and his other responsibilities. As a result, he may experience inadequate adjustment in areas of health, of family relations, and of social and leisure-time relationships.

Since the professions still represent an enviable social status, many individuals, unfitted by general ability, specific aptitude, or emotional constitution, desire to enter them. For these persons there are unsatisfying consequences, either in their attempts to prepare for the profession of their choice, or, if they succeed in passing this hurdle, in their later opportunities of successful achievement. For the well-qualified and well-trained professional man or woman a sane program of efficient and self-sacrificing service, combined with relaxing and enjoyable family and social relationships with his peers, offers a full and complete life of self-realization and social value.

In spite of the difficulties of adjustment in the professional fields of work, professional, administrative and related areas are becoming increasingly popular. More and more young people who can meet entrance requirements are continuing their education on the college level with the purpose of preparing themselves for professional or administrative work activity. Society's growing need for professional and administrative personnel is motivating able boys and girls, as well as those who are intellectually and personally fitted, to select and train for participation in these occupations.

The 1963–64 *Occupational Outlook Handbook* has this to say about professional, administrative, and related occupations:

Professional and administrative occupations have many attractions for young people considering the choice of a career. These occupations offer opportunities for interesting and responsible work and lead to relatively high earnings. As a rule, however, they can be entered only after long periods of specialized education or other preparation, since a broad knowledge of one's field and judgment of a high order are outstanding requirements for success in these types of work.

Approximately one-fourth of all workers in 1962 were in professional, administrative, and related occupations. These occupations—employing about 15½ million people— accounted for about half of all white-collar employment.

Professional occupations are of two main types. The largest group of professions—including those of engineer, architect, physician, lawyer, and teacher—requires formal education in well-organized fields of knowledge. The other group—including occupations such as editor and actor— does not require as much specialized, theoretical knowledge, but demands a great deal of broad background knowledge or creative talent and skill acquired chiefly through experience. Generally, the professions require either college graduation —often with an advanced degree—or experience of such kind and amount as to provide a comparable background. Licenses are required for practice in many professions—medicine, dentistry, and pharmacy, for example—with licensing authorities determining the minimum qualifications which members must have. Professional societies also set up membership standards, which tend to define their respective fields. In many areas of work, however, there is no clear-cut line between professional and other classes of workers.

It is not easy to prepare for and enter professional work. For most professions, one must complete a long period of

Figure 14. Teaching and Engineering Are the Largest Professional Occupations

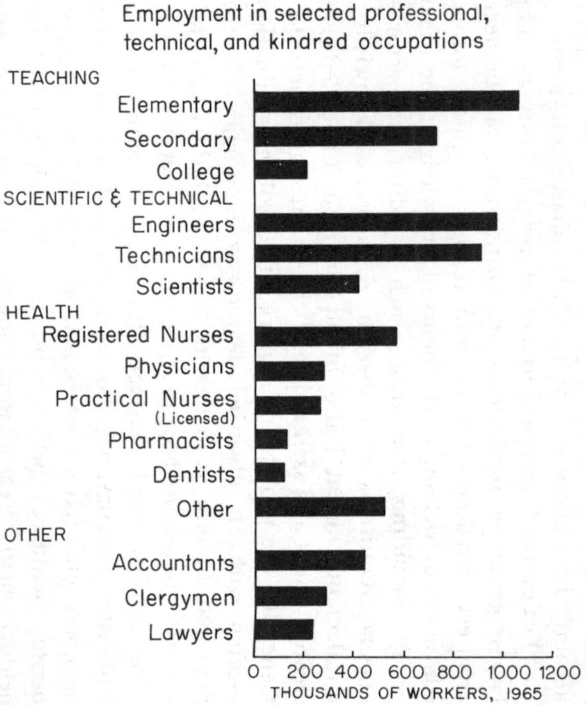

Employment in selected professional, technical, and kindred occupations

TEACHING
Elementary
Secondary
College

SCIENTIFIC & TECHNICAL
Engineers
Technicians
Scientists

HEALTH
Registered Nurses
Physicians
Practical Nurses (Licensed)
Pharmacists
Dentists
Other

OTHER
Accountants
Clergymen
Lawyers

0 200 400 600 800 1000 1200
THOUSANDS OF WORKERS, 1965

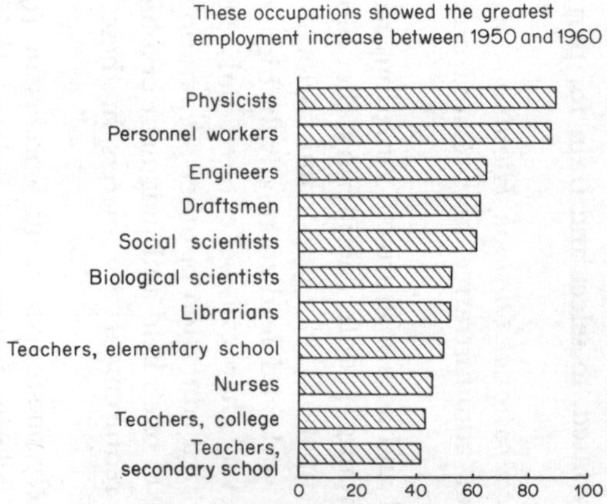

These occupations showed the greatest employment increase between 1950 and 1960

Physicists
Personnel workers
Engineers
Draftsmen
Social scientists
Biological scientists
Librarians
Teachers, elementary school
Nurses
Teachers, college
Teachers, secondary school

0 20 40 60 80 100

SOURCE: U.S. Bureau of the Census.

SOURCE: Arthur M. Ross, Commissioner, Occupational Outlook Brief, *Occupational Outlook Handbook, Occupational Outlook Service*, U.S. Department of Labor, Washington,D.C., 1966–67, pp. 22–25.

education and training. Often, applicants are not accepted for professional training unless their school grades are high, and employers generally give preference in hiring to graduates whose grades in professional school put them high in their class.

Closely related to the professions is a wide variety of technical occupations. People in these occupations work hand-in-hand with engineers, scientists, mathematicians, physicians, and other professional personnel. Their job titles include those of draftsman; engineering aide; programmer; and electronics, laboratory, or X-ray technician. Employment in these technical occupations usually requires a combination of basic scientific knowledge and specialized education or training in some particular aspect of technology or science. Such training may be obtained in technical institutes, junior colleges, and other schools, or through equivalent on-the-job training. Many of the duties of technicians may be performed also by beginning professional workers. However, because of their more limited educational background, technicians generally find it difficult to advance to professional level jobs.

The major professional, technical, and related occupations are shown in [Figure 14].[6]

The Well-adjusted Worker

The well-adjusted worker is the man or woman who is healthy; who is engaged in work that he enjoys, for which he has adequate and progressive training, and in which he is able to utilize to its fullest extent whatever capacity he possesses for creative expression. He is receiving a financial reward commensurate with his work, his needs, and his interests. He has sufficient leisure time to devote to relaxing social and avocational activities. He respects, admires, and is loyal to administrators and supervisors who are tolerant of unavoidable failure and generous with deserved approval, concerned with the general and individual welfare of the worker, and actuated by a belief in the value of

[6] Arthur M. Ross, "Occupational Outlook Brief," *Occupational Outlook Handbook,* Occupational Outlook Service, U.S. Department of Labor, Washington, D.C., 1966–67, pp. 22–25.

cooperation on the part of both the employer and employee in the achievement of worthy products or service for social benefit. A well-adjusted worker is a well-adjusted person in all of his relationships—work, home, and social. He enjoys a pleasant and stimulating home life and relaxing social activities. He is liked

TABLE 19

Vocational Adjustment Test

In the appropriate test below, read each question carefully and encircle the number at the right of the page that most nearly corresponds with your attitudes and behavior.

For Employees:

	No	?	Yes
1. Did you seek vocational guidance before you entered upon your occupational career?	1	2	3
2. Did you, rather than your parents, select your vocation?	1	2	3
3. Do you believe that you are suited for your job?	1	2	3
4. Do you consider your present job to be dignified?	1	2	3
5. Did you prepare for your vocation through part-time work experience while you still were in school?	1	2	3
6. Did you choose your vocation because you like it?	1	2	3
7. Do you have adequate training for your job?	1	2	3
8. Are you well groomed when you apply for a job?	1	2	3
9. Do you dress correctly for your work?	1	2	3
10. Do you fear an interview for a new job?	3	2	1
11. Do you get along well with your coworkers?	1	2	3
12. Can you take criticism from your supervisor?	1	2	3
13. Do you put in an honest day's work?	1	2	3
14. Do you have ample time for recreation?	1	2	3
15. Are your working conditions healthful?	1	2	3
16. Does your job allow for a vacation of at least two weeks each year?	1	2	3
17. Are you working toward advancement in your organization?	1	2	3
18. Do you tend to brag about your job success?	3	2	1
19. Do you receive proper appreciation for work well done?	1	2	3
20. Do you spend much of your time in faultfinding and bickering?	3	2	1
21. Do you arrive at work on time?	1	2	3
22. Do you respect the opinions of others?	1	2	3
23. Do you talk too much on the job?	3	2	1
24. Do family troubles interfere with your work efficiency?	3	2	1
25. Do you fear your boss?	3	2	1
Total Score			————

If your score exceeds 65 you may consider yourself a well-adjusted and successful worker.

For Employers:

	No	?	Yes
1. Are you courteous to all applicants for a position in your organization?	1	2	3
2. Do you expect accurate personal data from all applicants?	1	2	3
3. Do you or a qualified executive interview personally all applicants?	1	2	3
4. Do you try to make an applicant feel at ease during an interview?	1	2	3
5. Are you successful in selecting employees who will fit well into your organization?	1	2	3
6. Do you try to maintain friendly but dignified relations with your employees?	1	2	3
7. Are you equally friendly with male and female employees?	1	2	3
8. Are you certain that your younger employees are of legal age for work?	1	2	3
9. Do you encourage friendliness among your employees?	1	2	3
10. Do you expect your employees to be generally well groomed?	1	2	3
11. Do you help your employees to advance on the job?	1	2	3
12. Do your employees fear you as a supervisor?	3	2	1
13. Do you commend the work of your deserving employees?	1	2	3
14. Do you discourage bickering and faultfinding among your employees?	1	2	3
15. Do you expect your employees to arrive at work on time?	1	2	3
16. Do you give deserving employees who wish to leave your organization a favorable recommendation?	1	2	3
17. Do you give consideration to the opinions of your employees?	1	2	3
18. Do you give proper credit to an employee who offers a valuable suggestion?	1	2	3
19. Do you keep working quarters well lighted and well heated?	1	2	3
20. Do you provide sanitary conditions for your employees?	1	2	3
21. Do you allow adequate time for lunch?	1	2	3
22. Do you provide suitable rest periods during the day?	1	2	3
23. Do you allow your employees to engage in a reasonable amount of conversation on the job?	1	2	3
24. Do you provide sufficient and attractive rest and recreational facilities for your employees?	1	2	3
25. Do your employees have a chance to advance in your organization?	1	2	3

Total Score _____

If your score exceeds 65 you may consider yourself to be meeting employer responsibilities successfully.

Source: Lester D. Crow and A. Crow, *Eighteen to Eighty, Adjustment Problems of Adults*, Boston, The Christopher Publishing House, 1949, pp. 113-114. Used by permission of the authors: the holders of the copyright.

and respected in his community and is as actively engaged in civic projects as his leisure time and income permit. The well-adjusted worker is a well-adjusted citizen. In America, in all types of vocational work, there is an encouragingly large number of such workers.

A period of war and its aftermath tend to create certain worker problems of adjustment that are more severe than those that are experienced during peacetime occupational activity. World War II and the Korean episode were no exceptions to this. During the period of world conflict worker shortage was so extreme that labor conditions deviated sharply from their accustomed pattern. Wages rose rapidly. Hygienic hours of work were disregarded almost completely. Competency on the job was not always possible. Laws governing the employment of women and of minors were relaxed. In spite of some minor tragedies in the work world, a stupendous job of production was accomplished with a minimum of friction between management and labor.

The immediate postwar period was accompanied by occupational difficulties. Sudden cessation of war production and consequent labor layoffs, anticipation of reduced earning power, job competition resulting from the return of war veterans, shortage of materials needed for peacetime production, and an increase in cost of living were among the factors that resulted in a topsy-turvy labor situation. At the time of this writing the work situation appears to be in the process of stabilization. Consumer difficulties engendered by high living costs are being ameliorated somewhat by rising wage scales. Although labor still is seeking a more equitable balance between income and outgo, employment is at an all-time high, and labor-management relations are showing an encouraging trend toward effective cooperation.

OCCUPATIONAL THERAPY FOR THE MALADJUSTED INDIVIDUAL

A satisfactory definition of occupational therapy which can be widely accepted is not easy to formulate. Empirically it involves diversion, education, and expression. Each of these needs to be utilized if desirable results are to be anticipated. When properly applied by a trained therapist, therapeutic results can be anticipated.

A Dynamic Theory of Occupational Therapy

In their discussion of a dynamic theory of occupational therapy, Azima and Azima present ideas that are worthy of study.

Functions of occupational therapy can be envisaged in three distinct areas: diagnostic evaluation, change detection and therapeutic manipulation. In the following pages we shall outline the main points in each of these areas. A detailed discussion of each area will be attempted elsewhere.

A. Diagnostic function. Activities in occupational therapy involving free production can be used for diagnostic purposes on many occasions. Non-directive production of objects can be utilized as materials of a projective test. For this reason the whole theoretical and practical aspects and difficulties of "projective tests" are applicable to "projective material" produced in an occupational therapy setting and necessitate an adequate knowledge of these tests by the occupational therapist. However there are certain differences between the "projective tests" and "projective material" which are of significance in positing the inadequacies as well as the advantages of the latter material in comparison with the former tests. These inadequacies consist of non-systematic mode of application, the nature of created objects and the lack of constancy in form, hence the impossibility of a system of reference to which different creations can be referred and interpretation sought. Projective tests such as Rorschach and TAT offer to the patient either ambiguous figures (Rorschach) or ambiguous situations (TAT) which, however, are always the same. This constancy adds to the formation of a system of "norms" or "usual" responses for different psychopathological states which can be taken as a system of reference for interpretation of associated or perceived content. Such a constancy is not present in free created objects and even though certain repetitive themes and contents or forms can be recognized, no system of reference as yet can be devised.

This is the major insufficiency of "projective material" from the point of view of diagnostic evaluation. However, this very vagueness and inconsistency of created objects can be turned into the main advantage of "projective material" if we consider the mechanisms involving its realization. In projective tests, particularly Rorschach and TAT, the test material is a ready made screen upon which certain ambiguous figures or situations are drawn and which offer the patient a bridge or link for the exposition or projection of his inner world. The patient utilizes certain cues in the external screen to project his phantasies and thus expose them to the observer. This is a guided projection which may limit in many instances the uncovering of the unconscious processes. This occurs because (1) the patient *has* to use the ready made material and (2) he often *knows* that he is being tested and thus because of anxiety may consciously or unconsciously prevent himself from getting engaged or involved in the material. Projective material, on the other hand, in the occupational therapy situation avoids the above mentioned obstacles. The patient is left to choose the object and the technique of manipulation and he is not in a test situation. This is a free projection with little external reference to be molded in its accordance. It is felt that this freedom for projection can be utilized (see "Diagnostic procedure" below) in such a way as to combine the main information usually gained from Rorschach, TAT and figure drawings, concerning psychic events. To the authors the main spheres of psychic life about which these tests give more data are: the ego system (in Rorschach), object-relations (in TAT), body scheme and object-relations (figure drawings).[7] Projective material can be utilized to give data in all these spheres because (1) it is unstructured at the outset (paint, plasticene, clay), like Rorschach; (2) it can be structured into definite form (painting, sculpture) like TAT or figure drawings; (3) it brings into operation tactile and bodily mode of object-relations which are absent in Rorschach and TAT, thus adding to the avenues of projection. To obtain such a diagnostic use out of projective material in occupational therapy, the following tentative procedure and criteria of its application are presented:

[7] Evidently this separation of different spheres by different tests is arbitrary. The contention is that each test gives more emphasis to one sphere than to the others. [Azima and Azima]

Diagnostic procedure can be divided into four steps or phases: preparation, production and completion, association and interpretation.

(a) Preparation phases includes four areas of observation: the mode of approach of the patient to the object, his selection of object, his attitude towards the occupational therapist and towards other patients if he is not tested alone. The close observation and recording of the patient's behavior and reaction in these four areas can give definite diagnostic clues for all psychopathological states.

(b) Production and completion phase begins when the patient starts to manipulate the available objects (paint, plasticene, clay, leather, etc.) in a certain direction, i.e., structuring, construction or destruction. According to the degree of freedom allowed, this phase can be divided into two sub-phases: free (non-directive) creation and directed creation. By free creation is meant a situation where many objects are available but no direction is given to the patient as to what to do, what to choose and how to proceed. It is only suggested to the patient that he "can do what he wants" with them. Directed creation is a situation where a definite object or medium is selected for the patient and then he is left free in his manipulation of it, e g., he is given a piece of plasticene and asked to make whatever comes into his mind. For diagnostic purposes the directed creation is more useful because it limits the extent and the scope of creation to a certain degree and allows a more concentrated field to be explored.

Preparation and production phases correspond to the "administration" phase in projective tests technique.

(c) Association phase begins when the patient has finished his production. At this point the patient is asked to say whatever comes to his mind, to free associate about the object. As in projective tests the patient may be asked to verbalize what the object looks like to him, what it makes him think of, or what it reminds him of. The verbal responses obtained in this way are related to the content of the projected phantasy material indicating, as in projective tests, the way objects are perceived according to the structural balance of the mind.

(d) Interpretation phase begins when the created object and free associations to it are completed. By interpretation is meant the diagnostic not therapeutic interpretation of data, i.e., inferences from the created and verbal material in order to reach an evaluation of the general structural equilibrium of the mind, i.e., the status of drives, ego system and object-relations. Interpretations are not given to the patient when the projected material is used for diagnostic purposes, but are included at the end of the patient's observation record.

B. Change detection. With the rapid growth of research in areas involving alterations of psychodynamic structure, the necessity has arisen for finding certain tools to detect on-going changes with a certain degree of accuracy. Projective tests, except figure drawings, cannot be used in short intervals of time because of the practice and learning effect, e.g., Rorschach cannot be used at weekly intervals to measure the changes in the psychodynamic field during pharmacotherapy. It is felt that the occupational therapy setting, through the use of directed creation, can serve as an adequate indicator of change in studies involving psychodynamic shifts. As was mentioned previously, because of the lack of perceptual clues characteristic of projective tests, projective material does not provide the external reference which, through learning, may distort and prevent the projection of the unconscious events indicative of change. The authors have found that serial created objects can be a useful adjuvant research tool involving long term observation of individual patients where the aim is the detection of change. For created objects to have a research usefulness the same media should be used at regular intervals (usually once a week), with the same occupational therapist present each time and in the same surroundings. Between testing intervals it is preferable that the patient should not visit the occupational therapy situation.

Up to the present time three main areas have been investigated where the detection of change through created objects was of considerable usefulness.

(1) Regression-progression phases of different therapeutic programs involving an initial disorganization leading

to a final reorganization. These therapies include anaclitic therapy with or without prolonged sleep, regressive electric shock with or without sleep and anaclitic therapy. During these treatments it is of crucial importance to chart and to trace the extent and depth of regression, its onset and its evolution. By the assessment of these aspects of regression the somatic and psychotherapeutic part of the program can be regulated. Patients' attitudes towards certain objects and their free production of these are recordable indices of aspects of regression.

Certain tentative criteria have been developed for the general assessment of the regression and disorganization and their evolution which may be noted here. These are a shift in created objects (1) from concrete to abstract in the formal aspects; (2) from abstract to concrete, from elaborate to simple in the content; (3) from more structured to less structured; (4) from comprehensible to incomprehensible; (5) from latent to manifest expression of impulses, particularly to the preponderance of oral elements; (6) from more organized to less organized color forms.

(2) Detection of change in the organization of mood can be made very adequately in the patient's serial projected materials. We have found this to be particularly valuable in the balancing of somatic treatment of difficult manic-depressive patients, where there are rapid shifts in mood and a careful combination and alteration of different tranquillizer and anti-depressant drugs have to be made. Serial projected material can give evidence of shift in the mood from mania to depression or vice versa a few days prior to the overt behavioral alteration, thus allowing an anticipatory change in somatic treatment and stabilization of the patient's state.

(3) Detection of danger signals. These consist mainly of suicidal tendencies and impulsive acts. These may be detected prior to their occurrence by the assessment of the organization of mood, the content of the created object and the changes in the direction of aggressive drives.

C. *Therapeutic function.* There has been a growing controversy about the extent and the role of occupational therapy in the treatment of psychiatric patients, particularly in procedures where the therapeutic aims go beyond diversion and education. The question has been raised concerning the competence of the occupational therapist to do procedures involving psychotherapy and whether he should or should not function as the sole therapist with or without supervision of a psychiatrist. It is felt that the present state of occupational therapy and the psychiatric training which occupational therapists undergo do not give them an adequate knowledge of the dynamics of the mind in order to qualify them as therapists to aim at realizing many of the therapeutic functions (see below) which we consider to be feasible in occupational therapy.

In the following an attempt will be made to formulate the therapeutic functions of occupational therapy according to psychodynamic principles, irrespective of their immediate application by the occupational therapist, or in the occupational therapy setting. What is considered is not what occupational therapy should do or will do, but what it is theoretically possible to accomplish in occupational therapy.

Occupational therapy can be seen to have a therapeutic effect through the realization of functions related to three concepts of: exploration, gratification and defense formation.

(1) *Exploration.* This means the uncovering of unconscious processes through the material available in occupational therapy. This dynamic exploration can be realized through adherence to two fundamental rules of (1) free creations and (2) free associations to and about the created objects. We have used this particular function of occupational therapy up until now in two ways: systematic and sporadic. The systematic use of the created object in uncovering procedure was formerly called "analytic art therapy," either in groups or individually, and later termed "projective group therapy." The details of this procedure have been described elsewhere and we shall not dwell upon them here. The sporadic use of the created object is applied in situations where a short term intensive therapy is intended either in a group or individually. The patients are seen in daily, hourly sessions for a relatively short period of time. The therapeutic technique is identical with projective group or individual therapies.

(2) *Gratification*. This means the offering of certain objects in appropriate situations which will result in a decrease or discharge of dammed up tension due to the frustration and subsequent accumulation of drives in connection with controlling (super-ego) and integrating (ego) systems.

Gratification of needs can be realized in either a relatively direct or an indirect manner.

(a) Direct gratification. This implies that objects identical, similar or symbolically near the primary needed objects (breast-mother, milk, feces) are offered to the patient in a situation effectively similar to the primary mother-child state. This procedure is based upon hypothetical considerations regarding the therapeutic value of planned regression described elsewhere. A therapeutic program based upon these hypotheses has been developed and applied in two different settings: (1) an anaclitic situation [8] involving chronic regressed schizophrenics; (2) an anaclitic situation produced during prolonged sleep treatment with or without concomitant administration of electric shock, or during sensory deprivation. Both of these procedures have been described previously, and have been designated as object-relations therapy. The point of emphasis here is the direct instinctual gratification.

The anticipated result of a satisfactory object-relations therapy is a structural change affecting both the distribution of drives and the severity of the super-ego.

(b) Indirect gratification. This implies essentially social approval through super-ego reinforcement or atonement. This approval can be achieved either actively (by work) or passively (by receiving praise). The point of emphasis here is the decrease in super-ego pressure and for this reason the term "indirect gratification" is used, i.e., indirect release of instinctual needs.

(3) *Defence formation*. This means the utilization of objects in such a way as to strengthen certain ego defences and provide routes for sublimation of aggressive and libid-

[8] The term anaclitic was used by Freud and later by Margolin indicating a situation of "leaning upon" or total dependency on an external object, usually the mother or her substitute. We put particular emphasis on the oral essence of the anaclitic state. [Azima and Azima]

inal impulses. This is an important function which until now has not been systematically investigated in occupational therapy. In many instances sublimation of drives partly occurs indirectly through many non-verbal activities, available in occupational therapy setting. However, to bring a change in the structure of the ego, an attempt should be made to clarify the psychodynamic implications of all activities in occupational therapy which pertain to rehabilitation, education, development of talents and work. It is beyond the scope of the paper to go into this problem, but it should be mentioned that the above activities which form the core of traditional functions of occupational therapy involve principally (1) the defensive functions of the ego, particularly sublimation and reaction formation; (2) the executant function of the ego; and (3) the role of the ego in the dynamics of learning. The ego strengthening function of occupational therapy cannot be adequately understood unless these aspects of the ego functions, particularly dynamics of the learning process, are envisaged in connection with occupational therapy activities. To our knowledge no such attempt has as yet been made in this direction.[9]

Evaluation of Occupational Therapy Activities

An occupational therapist needs objective criteria to evaluate the behavior of individuals as they participate in the therapy provided. To this end the therapist plans activities through which the individual can receive gratifications within a short period of time that are geared within his potential to avoid frustration. For small children this includes the provision of opportunities for satisfaction of the need for love and affection. To illustrate, we cite the problem situations and the therapy provided Douglas and Stephen (both examples of neurotic children) and Christine and Ricky (examples of psychotic children). The story as given by Lela A. Llorens follows:

The neurotic child is hyperactive, restless, fearful, clinging and self-condemning. His hyperactivity and restlessness

[9] H. Azima and Fern I. Azima, "Outline of a Dynamic Theory of Occupational Therapy," *The American Journal of Occupational Therapy*, September-October, 1959, pp. 217–221.

stem from the anxiety produced by a conflict between the need to express emotion and the need to inhibit this expression. He is fearful of people and their attitudes toward him. At the same time, these children seek condemning, punishing attitudes through their clinging, crying and acting-out behavior.

Douglas, nine years old, was an example of the neurotic child. He had difficulty getting along with his peers. He either isolated himself from them or became aggressive and destructive toward them. He was jealous, demanding, impulsive and hyperactive in behavior; he had developed fears of the dark and of being hurt; he had a short attention span and low frustration tolerance.

Douglas was seen for psychological testing and received a full battery of tests. His performance during testing indicated a superior potential intellectually with present functioning at average to bright average levels. His reaction to stress situations markedly interfered with his performance on occasions. Douglas displayed considerable creative ability and originality. He would have liked to be aggressive and assertive but this seemed to connote sexual transgression and carried with it a threat of annihilation.

Douglas' resources for solving his conflicts included intelligence, a rich, fantasy life into which he could retreat for gratification of his impulses without complete loss of control, a real capacity for insight and the strength to oppose a threatening environment. A firm, well established environment was indicated with the opportunity to identify with consistent accepting adults who set limits he could rely on.

The occupational therapist's attitude for Douglas employed warmth, acceptance and an expectation that the environment set limits for ego control. The initial treatment goals provided (1) the opportunity for impulse release through original, creative activities, (2) the opportunity for independence without rejection and with the needed emotional support, (3) an acceptable emotional outlet through aggressive activities, and (4) a secure segment of the total environment.

Another child who demonstrated neurotic symptoms was Stephen, twelve years old. He showed disruptive, explosive, acting-out behavior; he refused to cooperate and resisted all efforts in this direction.

In psychological testing, Stephen was given a full battery of tests. His intellectual functioning was bright-normal with a probable potential of superior to very superior. In the test situation, Stephen was extremely responsive to praise and encouragement, sensitive to environmental stimulation and equally vulnerable to criticism. He tended to be uninterested in prosaic details and to focus on more lofty, ambitious conceptions. When anxieties were acute, impulses tended to break through and interfere with his capacity to organize test material in a logical manner.

His ego appeared mature and well-developed in some areas. He had well internalized controls, the ability to enter empathetically into interpersonal relationships, and was able to utilize various defenses against anxiety. His super-ego was well developed but its relative severity played an important role in intensifying Stephen's anxieties. He was struggling with hostile impulses which he could not express because he feared loss of love and evidenced super-ego anxiety. Stephen had feelings of unworthiness and low self-esteem and was particularly sensitive to criticism and rejection from object relationships. Warmth, understanding, recognition and considerable reassurance were important in any therapeutic relationship with Stephen.

The occupational therapist's attitude for Stephen employed warmth, acceptance and understanding. His treatment plan provided (1) recognition and raising his self-esteem, and (2) opportunity to act independently without loss of love. The fact that he was responsive to praise and encouragement coupled with his high intellectual functioning were valuable assets in fulfilling these needs in the occupational therapy area.

THE PSYCHOTIC CHILD

The psychotic child often demonstrates autistic features in his personality. He may be a withdrawn and unresponsive individual who has extreme difficulty forming relationships with people in the environment. Withdrawal with these children is a learned reaction to frustration from the environment. These children have difficulty in distinguishing themselves from their environment and may have fears concerning separation from objects in the environment. It is altogether possible that an autistic child may be mistaken as feeble-minded because of his markedly retarded ego development. We may also see loss of contact with reality and delusional and hallucinatory trends.

Two children who showed many of these symptoms were Christine and Ricky. Christine, a six-year-old girl, had shown a fear of strangers from the age of three. She screamed and withdrew from them in most instances. At other times, she exhibited much uncontrolled acting-out behavior such as swearing, throwing objects and name-calling. When approached she frequently asked to be let alone.

Christine was seen for psychological evaluation and received a full battery of tests. On projective test responses, Christine showed almost complete indifference to the demands of reality. She showed clear evidence of autistic and perseverative thinking where her initial responses were triggered by inner needs. Interspersed with autistic behavior were periods when Christine was able to show appropriate, reality-oriented responsiveness. At these times her level of anxiety was markedly elevated and was evidenced by verbal confusion.

The occupational therapist's attitude toward Christine incorporated warmth, affection and consistency. Her initial goals provided (1) an opportunity to experience gratification through the use of concrete, structured, reality-oriented activities, and (2) an undemanding, fear-reducing atmosphere.

Ricky, eight years old, seemed to live in a dream world about which he related fantastic stories. He had no sense of responsibility and was demanding and affection-seeking. He resorted to measures of intimidation when demands were not immediately met.

Ricky was tested with a full battery of psychological tests. His level of intellectual functioning was rated high-average with indications of bright-normal to superior potential. During testing Ricky showed frequent loss of reality contact. He seemed preoccupied with threatening, devouring creatures which he would defend against with magical devices. He showed a capacity to relate at a primitive level and appeared to be a schizophrenic child whose potential for improvement depended on consistent, firm, non-stimulating handling with an emphasis on reality structuring.

The occupational therapist's attitude for Ricky incorporated warmth, affection and consistency. His treatment goals, like Christine's, provided (1) the opportunity for impulse release as well as gratification of his needs through the channelization of his fantasy material into reality-oriented activity, and (2) firm, consistent limits for ego control.[10]

The value of using occupational therapy for long-term psychotic patients was studied by Honey and Lindsay. Early in their experiment they found the need to formulate immediate goals in the development of the total program. The objectives as stated by Honey and Lindsay follow:

IMMEDIATE GOALS USED IN DEVELOPING
THE TOTAL PROGRAM

In review, we feel that to try and effect an overall change in the patient's total life pattern, we have had to establish immediate goals. From our experience we feel that the following are important, but each on its own is inadequate.

1. *To use occupation to improve personal skill and satisfactions.*

To improve this, work habits and tolerance must be improved. This can be achieved by striving for better comprehension, execution and retention of directions, better concentration and generally raising the standard of work and productiveness. Satisfaction is achieved by stimulating interest in activity and the accomplishment of it.

2. *To use occupation to improve interpersonal relating and group satisfactions.*

Reduced hostility, aggression or resistiveness gives way to increased accessibility or sociability, and greater independence and co-operation.

[10] Lela A. Llorens, "Psychological Tests in Planning Therapy Goals," *The American Journal of Occupational Therapy*, September-October, 1960, pp. 245, 246.

3. *To run the center as a community center for the
ward.*
A sense of responsibility, or feeling of "belonging"
when developed brings about greater spontaneous attendance and greater initiative in matters of management and maintenance.

4. *To relate the center to the rest of the hospital.*
Accomplished by encouraging patients in the center
to prepare for and participate in other activities in the
hospital, planned by staff or patient organizations.[11]

Evaluating Psychotic Patients Undergoing Occupational Therapy

Various rating scales have been devised for the purpose of
evaluating patients' progress and readiness to leave the hospital.
When occupational therapy is applied, a rating scale is needed to
determine, as objectively as possible, the attitudes of the patient
toward work, people, and self. One such scale, known as the
Minnesota Follow-up Study (MFS Rehab. Evaluation Scale),
was developed to serve occupational therapists and other rehabilitation personnel. The scale's validity and reliability are reported
as meeting satisfactory standards. According to Robert J.
Wolff:

> The MFS Rehab. Rating Scale provides an easy-to-use,
> fairly objective and reliable method of recording the ob-
> served behavior of patients in a rehabilitation therapies
> setting. It has been used successfully with inexperienced
> raters. It appears to be sensitive enough to differentiate
> between patients and describe changes within a patient over
> a period of time. It has been found to be useful in providing
> a quantifiable description of patients in a research study,
> and it is expected to be useful also as an aid in the clinical
> evaluation of patients.[12]

Table 20 presents the scale, along with directions for using it.

[11] P. Honey and J. S. B. Lindsay, "Occupational Therapy for Long-term
Psychotic Patients," *The American Journal of Occupational Therapy*, May-
June, 1960, p. 159.
[12] Robert J. Wolff, "A Behavior Rating Scale," *The American Journal of
Occupational Therapy*, January-February, 1961, p. 14.

TABLE 20

MFS Rehab. Rating Scale

INSTRUCTIONS FOR FILLING OUT THE MFS. REHAB. RATING SCALE

Below you will find fifteen different scales, each one showing one way in which a person can be observed. Each scale runs from one extreme to the other, from "bad" to "good," from "abnormal" to "normal." Please indicate by placing a checkmark (√) in the right place, where you would rate the person you are observing on that particular scale.

Look at each scale separately. Do not try to give an overall impression because, as you well know, people differ not only in the overall impression they create, but especially in how they appear in these different areas: for instance, a patient might be a good worker, but he does not talk at all, or, another example, a patient might get along very well with other patients in a group activity, but he is unable to do work.

It will always be possible to choose *one* spot on the scale that fits a particular person best, do not check more than one place on any one scale.

As you will notice, only the extreme positions on the scales are described. All five positions should be equally considered, however, before you make a rating.

It will help if you read the descriptions. Try to get an idea of the kind of thing you should judge on each scale. If you get a feeling for what the scale as a whole describes, you will be able to fill in for yourself what the other three boxes mean.

If the patient's behavior has changed since you last rated him/her, please rate only as he is now, today—do not try to judge and "average" behavior.

If you feel you do not know enough about a certain bit of behavior (for example, if you have never seen the patient in a group activity, or you have not seen him working, etc.) leave that scale out.

Remember that for X you can, of course, make only one check in either "A" or "B" (or in the box that is shared by "A" and "B")—if a patient talks little or not at all he could not at the same time talk continuously!

Finally, try to be as accurate as you know how. It is more important to have accurate descriptions than to have many descriptions.

Patient's name_____Rater's name_____Date_____

Response to Work, Activity, or Task

    I. *Interest* in work, activity or task:
                little or none / .. / .. / .. / .. / .. / considerable
    II. Ability to *initiate* work or activity:
                little or none / .. / .. / .. / .. / / considerable

III. Ability to *follow through* with a job:
little or none /../../../../../ considerable
IV. Ability to *take direction:*
little or none /../../../../../ considerable
V. Ability to *work with others:*
little or none /../../../../../ considerable
VI. *Quality* of work (how *good* the work is):
poor /../../../../../ good
VII. *Quantity* of work (how *much* work is done):
little or none /../../../../../ considerable

Response to People (socialization)

VIII. *Attitude* toward fellow patients:
indifferent /../../../../../ friendly
IX. Observed *hostility:*
extreme /../../../../../ little or none
X. *Quantity of verbalization* (how much patient talks):
A. not at all /../../../../../
B. talks continuously /../../../../../ talks easily, freely
XI. *Content of verbalization* (how well patient talks):
"gibberish" /../../../../../ normal, sensible
XII. *Participation* in social activities:
little or none /../../../../../ enthusiastic

General Observations

XIII. *Independence* (how well patient seems able to take care of self):
not at all /../../../../../ adequately
XIV. *Dependability:* unpredictable /../../../../../ dependable
XV. *General conduct:* inappropriate /../../../../../ appropriate

Comments

Source: Robert J. Wolff, "A Behavior Rating Scale," *The American Journal of Occupational Therapy*, January-February, 1961, p. 16. Reprinted by permission.

QUESTIONS AND PROBLEMS

1. Why is the selection of a suitable career important to adolescents?

2. Interpret Figure 13. Give as many implications as you can.

3. Outline the personal qualities needed by a worker.

4. Summarize the studies presented in this chapter concerning women's selection of a career.

5. Outline as many causes of maladjustment in the work situation as you can. Indicate what can be done to alleviate them.

6. Prepare a list of the problems associated with job placement.

7. Explain the values to be derived from training on the job.

8. Describe the factors of adjustment of the worker to the job.

9. Describe, in detail, the steps needed by an individual to enter into a field of work.

10. What is meant by dignifying work? How can it be achieved?

11. Administer the vocational adjustment test to yourself. What were the results? Note any improvements needed.

12. What should be the conditions governing a promotion or a raise in salary?

13. Discuss ways and means of orienting or inducting a new employee into his position.

14. Name adjustment problems faced by supervisors. Indicate the extent to which everyone is supervised on the job.

15. What is the value of employees offering suggestions to employers concerning improvements in work procedures?

16. How far should the personal initiative of an employee be permitted?

17. What are among the adjustment problems that arise between employees and employers?

18. Give examples in which the home life of the worker influences his efficiency on the job.

19. Discuss the value of occupational therapy for the mentally ill.

Selected Readings

American Journal of Occupational Therapy. New York: Occupational Association of America. Current Issues.

Blum, M. L., *Industrial Psychology and Its Social Foundations,* rev. ed. New York: Harper & Row, Publishers, 1956.

Deese, J., *Principles of Psychology.* Boston, Mass.: Allyn and Bacon, Inc., 1964. Chapter 16.

Dubin, R., *The World of Work: Industrial Society and Human Relations.* Englewood Cliffs, N.J.: Prentice-Hall, Inc., 1958.

Friedmann, G., *The Anatomy of Work.* New York: Free Press of Glencoe, 1961.

Gross, E., *Work and Society.* New York: The Crowell-Collier Publishing Company, 1958.

Hertzberg, F., B. Mausner, and B. B. Snyderman, *The Motivation to Work,* 2nd ed. New York: John Wiley & Sons, Inc., 1959.

Linn, L., L. A. Weinroth, and R. Shamah, *Occupational Therapy in Dynamic Psychiatry.* Washington, D.C.: The American Psychiatric Association, 1964.

McGregor, D., *The Human Side of Enterprise.* New York: McGraw-Hill, Inc., 1960.

Nosow, S., and W. H. Form (eds.), *Man, Work, and Society.* New York: Basic Books, Inc., 1962.

Nye, F. I., and L. W. Hoffman, *The Employed Mother in America.* Chicago, Ill.: Rand McNally & Company, 1963.

Reiss, A. J., Jr., *Occupations and Social Status.* New York: Free Press of Glencoe, 1961.

Roe, A., *The Psychology of Occupations.* New York: John Wiley & Sons, Inc., 1956.

Scott, T. B., *et. al., A Definition of Work Adjustment.* Minneapolis: University of Minnesota Industrial Relations Center, 1960.

Smith, L. B., *Career Planning.* New York: Harper & Row, Publishers, 1959.

Super, D. E., *The Psychology of Careers.* New York: Harper & Row, Publishers, 1958.

———, and J. Crites, *Appraising Vocational Fitness,* rev. ed. New York: Harper & Row, Publishers, 1962.

Vroom, V. H., *Work and Motivation.* New York: John Wiley & Sons, Inc., 1964.

Webster, E. C., *Decision Making in the Employment Interview.* Montreal, Canada: McGill University Industrial Relations Center, 1964.

Zweig, F., *The Worker in an Affluent Society.* New York: Free Press of Glencoe, 1962.

LEISURE TIME
AND
ADJUSTMENT
PROBLEMS

A WELL-ADJUSTED man or woman gains satisfaction from participation in a reasonable amount of daily activity that is directed
toward the achievement of economic security. The attitude of
self-realization resulting from these efforts continues the adjustment process and provides for the individual the motive power to
become a better citizen. Interesting as his work may be, however,
a normal man or woman does and should desire to engage in
activities that are more or less unrelated to his work. Such activities offer opportunities for relaxation, socialization, or participation in avocational, civic, or educational programs and projects. No matter what his age may be, an individual needs to
experience a balanced program of work and play.

THE RELATIONSHIP BETWEEN
WORK AND PLAY

The extent to which a specific activity is work or play has
been the subject of much discussion. It would seem that in order
to differentiate between the two there is required the use of

certain criteria such as the *goal* or purpose of the activity, the *attitude* or interest of the person at the moment, and the *individual* himself in relation to the activity.

Work Versus Play

When a project is undertaken in order to attain a goal that lies beyond the activity itself or when the attitude is such that the activity is being engaged in for a reason that is external to the doing, the activity falls into the category of *work*. Whether or not monetary compensation is received for the activity is a negligible factor. It is important, however, to know something about the attitude of the person toward the activity. The individual concerned determines what that attitude is. He alone can classify the activity as work or play.

Although it is difficult to formulate an exact definition of play, certain distinctive characteristics can be detected in all activities that are considered to be recreational. The criteria for classifying an activity as play are the same as those for work—the *goal,* the *attitude,* and the *individual.* If the activity is engaged in for the sake of the activity itself and for no other purpose, and if the attitude is one of pleasure that results from a felt interest in the activity at the moment, it can be classified for the individual as `play` or relaxing activity.

In leisure-time activity, relaxation and spontaneous pleasurable expression are the chief concerns of the individual. The relief from muscle and nerve tension derived from such activity results in mental and physical exhilaration. However, if an individual pursues the supposedly recreational activity because of the interest of another person rather than as the result of a genuine interest of his own, the activity which until that time may have been play for him suddenly passes over into the category of work.

Functions of Recreational Activities

Since play is one of the most valuable means of relieving muscle and nerve tension, it is a health-preserving activity for the child, the adolescent, and the adult. To be mentally healthy, an individual needs to learn how to relax during his leisure time.

Recreational activities also provide an opportunity for social development, since the social drives can be satisfied through these media. The great desire to play brings people together; they create opportunities for play and they organize their life so that they have time and a place for it.

The extended leisure time that is available to most workers gives them a chance for relief from the effects of frustration that may be experienced in home and work relationships. Sappenfield has this to say about frustration and recreation.

> Recreations, like fantasy, will provide an escape from the demands of reality; they will function to gratify motives that might otherwise remain frustrated. This will aid in keeping the intensity of such motives sufficiently low for the individual to tolerate their frustration in the course of the everyday adjustments required by routine working and living. . . .
>
> Leisure activities, recreation, and rest will gratify motives that, during the individual's intense preoccupation with reality, must remain in a state of frustration. The gratification achieved by means of such temporary regressions will function to reorganize the motivational pattern, so that the individual can work efficiently when he redirects his attention to his mature responsibilities.[1]

The values gained could be multiplied many times if recreational facilities were made available for individuals within easy reach of their homes. Thereby, they might avoid the exhaustion that accompanies tiring travel after participation in recuperative activities. The automobile affords some relief to the city worker; but holiday jams on the highways introduce annoying factors that offset the health values of wholesome recreational activity.

AGE STATUS AND RECREATIONAL ADJUSTMENT

Throughout his life span an individual needs to experience a balanced program of work and play. His leisure-time activities differ somewhat, of course, from one age level to another. I

[1] Bert R. Sappenfield, *Personality Dynamics: An Integrative Psychology of Adjustment*, New York: Alfred A. Knopf, 1961, pp. 259, 264.

now shall consider briefly the recreational interests during childhood, adolescence, and adulthood.

The Child and Adjustment Through Recreation

The author is not in agreement with any educational philosophy that favors the reduction of all school activity to the play
level. It is true that schoolwork should be so motivated that the
child is interested in its accomplishment and that he recognizes
the value to himself of his study activities. At the same time the
child should be motivated to develop an attitude toward *work* as
activity directed toward a goal, and an attitude toward himself as
a worker possessing purposeful pride in the achievement of a task
that shall be of immediate or delayed benefit to himself and
others. Motivated work—not mere play—is desired.

The individual, however, needs change of activity. He needs
release from the mental strain of purposeful activity, no matter
how satisfying and pleasant that work may be. He needs an
opportunity for participation in forms of activity in which the
interest lies in the activity itself and in the physical and mental
relaxation that can be gained from it. The child must be taught
to play in a healthful fashion. He must learn to develop attitudes
of moderation in his play as well as those of cooperation and
sportsmanship.

It is essential, then, that the school provide adequately for
regular periods of free play and organized games as a relief from
the more serious work of the school day. These recreational
periods should not be so short that they afford insufficient relaxation, nor should they be so long as to tire the child or cause too
long a break and consequent lack of interest in his regular schoolwork.

The child should not be denied participation in play activities as a punishment for failure in his studies, since in that way
an attitude of dislike for and resentment of his regular duties
may be engendered. The school should develop in the child an
understanding of work and play as two important phases of a
person's activities, each having its specific purpose and each
providing for him differing but equally desirable satisfactions
and values.

As a means of furthering a child's physical, emotional, and

social development, adults should provide for him many interesting and health-furthering recreational activities. First the parents, and then the school people, are responsible for seeing to it that the child participates in healthful recreational activities, in both the home and school environments, that are attention-gaining and interesting but not tension-arousing.

Much of a younger child's activity in the home and in nursery school and kindergarten is play-oriented. As the young child plays with other little boys and girls and/or with adults he is activating his physical and mental growth and is developing social consciousness. The child's developing power of sensation and perception, the refinement of his manipulative control and speech habits, the beginning of his mental association and reasoning, his growing recognition of his own emotional states, and the understanding of the emotional behavior of others are some of the means at the disposal of the preschool child in his early adjustment to his social environment. During this period the child gains a gradually developing appreciation of his social world, assisted or retarded by his own gradual physical growth and the kind and amount of stimulation to which he is exposed. Slowness or unevenness of physical growth may inhibit expected learning; insufficient or faulty stimulation may develop social habits that engender present or future maladjustments.

Adults need to watch carefully the child's *rate* and *kind* of physical development and to adjust his environment to his developing needs and abilities. All children are not cut out according to the same pattern, and so they must be treated as individuals and accorded a proper regard for their individual world that comprises many kinds of persons of all ages. They must be led, in so far as their rate and degree of development allow, to make desirable adjustments to a world varied enough to provide for their individual needs.

The Adolescent and Adjustment Through Recreation

Adolescents are gregarious and seek companionship, especially that of persons outside their immediate family group. They yearn for and are exposed to a constantly enlarging social experience as they work and play with adults and with boys or girls of their own age. The adolescent desires opportunities for self-expression in group situations. He enjoys competition with his peers and is eager to win the approval and admiration of fellow adolescents. His interests are wide and often flit from one type of experience to another unless they are guided into channels that are best adapted to his peculiar abilities. The gang spirit is strong during this period and can be utilized by school officials for the formation of educationally valuable club projects. The adolescent is able to develop maturity of judgment, social ease, and efficiency through such group activities.

The adolescent is a combination of self-centered interest and extreme altruism. He thrills to the accomplishment of worthwhile service, which at the same time will afford him an opportunity for self-realization as a member of his group. His maturing body needs exercise, which can be obtained through carefully supervised sports that not only present opportunities for the socializing effects of competition with his peers, cooperation, and good sportsmanship, but become the bases of later adult recreational activities.

The Adult and Adjustment Through Recreation

Adults, as well as children and adolescents, experience the need for relief from work activities through various recreational pursuits. These change somewhat with age. As the individual progresses gradually through his life span, certain definite characteristics seem to be more or less potent at different stages of his adult life. Although the onslaught and decline of these determining behavior patterns are gradual and their progress is conditioned partly by physiological changes and partly by environmental conditions, the adult may be said to pass roughly through three general stages: young adult, middle age, and old age.

Each of these stages exhibits the possession of definite personality characteristics and is marked by specific stimulations both from without and from within the individual that may cause him to encounter problems of adjustment peculiar to his age experience. The satisfactory solution of these problems is dependent on the individual's own powers and his educational background and emotional stability, and on the adequacy of the agencies that are available for his help, education, and guidance.

LEISURE-TIME PROBLEMS OF YOUNG ADULTS. With the shortened work day and work week the individual is attaining an increased amount of leisure time. Mechanical inventions have so lightened his labor that he is ready and sufficiently active to seek added ways to utilize his extra time and energy. Today, swimming pools, both indoor and outdoor, recreation centers, athletic clubs, skating rinks, dancing pavilions, tennis courts, golf links, and parks provide opportunities for the physical development of the individual. The radio, television, motion picture, phonograph, hi-fi, theater, library, and museum offer mental stimulation during leisure hours. There are also many organized and unorganized forms of avocational activity for the individual who wishes to pursue a special hobby.

Community interest in the social and recreational welfare of our citizens and an increasing appreciation among most people of the value of wholesome relaxation and changed activity are evidenced in the balanced programs of work and play that are common in our culture. In the past, the man benefited most from participation in recreational activities, since the care of the home and of children tended to restrict the woman's interest and time. However, mechanical aids to housekeeping, nursery schools, the modern man's willingness to help his wife in household duties, and his increased interest in having her share his recreational interests have combined to give young married adults opportunities for sharing their play as well as their work.

LEISURE-TIME PROBLEMS OF MIDDLE-AGED ADULTS. During middle age the adult is forced by physiological changes in himself to readjust the tempo of his recreational activity. He finds that he cannot, as a rule, compete with younger adults in sports, in dancing, in the keeping of late hours, or in many similar activities. Although some individuals during this age period still exhibit unusual ability in golf, swimming, or other sports, their endurance is not equal to continued physical strain. The recreational interests of the middle-aged man or woman must be limited to quieter and more sedentary forms of leisure-time activities.

This is the period of warm and intimate friendships among persons of similar tastes and activities. Cultural interests such as music, drama, serious literature, art, and hobbies afford the individual enjoyment and stimulation. Social gatherings, card parties, informal and not-too-strenuous dancing, dinner parties, and social and civic community projects give the mature individual opportunities for creative planning and social success.

LEISURE-TIME PROBLEMS OF THE ELDERLY.   With the present increase in the life span, older people tend to continue longer in their vocational activities, often until they are forced to retire at a specified age, such as sixty, sixty-five, or seventy. Even so they are likely to maintain an active interest in community, even world, affairs. Because of physical impairment, however, they find it necessary to reduce the tempo of their activities, especially their leisure-time activities. In spite of the fact that they usually have more time for recreation than they formerly had, the nature of their participation changes. No longer are they able to take part in strenuous physical programs. Rather do they need to limit their recreational activities to quiet projects.

The family and the community have the responsibility of providing for the older citizenry such activities that will not be a strain on their capacities. The elderly rely on association with their peers in group activities that will not exceed their power to perform. Considerable concern is being displayed by the community for the welfare of their senior citizens. Hence it provides opportunities for them to receive instruction in the arts and crafts. Well-equipped meeting places also are provided for them to participate with their fellows in group activities such as quiet games, with appropriate leadership.

THE PROVISION OF RECREATIONAL FACILITIES

Recreational activities may be organized or unorganized. Such leisure-time activities as listening to radio or phonograph recordings, watching television or motion-picture programs, or singing around the piano in the home; gathering with friends in a game room or in the back yard; gardening; fishing; reading light fiction or popular magazines; window shopping (especially in small towns on Saturday night) ; tinkering around the home; and short automobile trips are common experiences in the lives of most Americans. These forms of recreation are relatively unorganized and are engaged in more or less at will, usually with little preparatory planning.

Other forms of recreation are more highly organized and

require the cooperation of outside agencies. Among such leisure-time activities can be included long automobile trips; airplane flights; musical and dramatic presentations, or lectures; participation in organized games or attendance at them; skating, skiing, boating, and similar activities.

These agencies may be either publicly organized and controlled or commercial enterprises. Most communities realize that some of the commercial agencies are socially undesirable. They represent unhygienic physical conditions or unhealthful media of influence. Consequently, there appears to be a concerted drive on the part of community leaders throughout the country not only to provide recreational facilities for their people but also to improve and regulate commercially run projects.

In many cities and towns, schools and other public buildings are thrown open to the public for recreational activities that are suitable for all ages and both sexes. Public lectures, musical programs, motion pictures, plays, and other forms of entertainment are presented in the auditorium. Physical activities, such as basketball, indoor baseball, handball, softball, table tennis, bowling, and dancing are made available in the gymnasium. Individual rooms are given over to small discussion groups, clubs, and chess, checkers, and card games. For outdoor recreation playgrounds, beaches, recreation parks, golf courses, and baseball diamonds are provided.

Semi-private and philanthropic organizations—national, state, and local—have devised well-organized programs of leisure-time activities. The "Y's," the Knights of Columbus, settlement houses, and various socio-civic organizations, such as Rotary, Kiwanis, and Lions clubs as well as community women's clubs, share in this activity.

Many business organizations are providing recreational opportunities for their employees. Religious and other community organizations now offer to teen-agers and to adults of any age many opportunities for participation in interesting activities. No one needs to be without a means of filling his leisure hours.

Publicly supported or semi-private projects are limited, however, by the great financial cost of construction and maintenance, and by the lack of space for adequate facilities. In large cities it often is difficult to find space for recreation in overcrowded areas where the need for it is greatest. Traveling to those areas where space is available may be a long and tiring journey which reduces the benefits that may have been gained from participation in recreational activities. Crowded streetcars, buses, and subways on Sunday nights cause one to question the value of the activity which takes people so far from home and which returns them to their home hot, tired, and generally disgruntled.

If commercially controlled facilities for recreation are organized and regulated by civic-minded owners, they can supplement the work done by public agents. Annual flower shows of community botanical gardens may be supplemented by private showings. Musical organizations and choral societies offer fine entertainment at reasonable price. Youth hostels; organized tours by bus, plane, or train; many excellently run summer camps; swimming pools; golf courses, and tennis courts are some of the recreational facilities that are available in most communities for the average citizen.

In many communities there are certain commercial agencies that are unwholesome. Among these are cellar clubs, some night clubs, poolrooms, gambling establishments, race tracks, unrealistic motion-picture programs, overexciting radio or television programs, trashy or sensational magazines and books, and inartistic comic strips. Even though such media of entertainment may not be definitely harmful to the physical and mental health of those who "enjoy" them, they have little value as adequate and healthful relaxers.

Many communities have attempted legal restrictions of socially disapproved recreation and have appointed officials to carry out their regulations. This is a difficult task. There are people who appear to believe that any regulation or supervision of their leisure-time activities limits their enjoyment. Commercial interests cater to the tastes of their patrons and offer them what they seem to want. Perhaps regulated recreational facilities offer their patrons what the leaders *think* the people should want. Besides regulation and supervision of recreation there is also needed an education of the tastes of the users of such agencies.

EDUCATIONAL OPPORTUNITIES
FOR ADULTS

An increasing number of men and women recognize the value of continuing their education beyond the period of their formal school training. As a result of the desire of adults to devote some part of their leisure time to organized study, many types of educational programs are being made available for their use.

Although there has been a steady growth of adult education, the past twenty-five years have given a decided impetus to its advancement. Today all forms of social and civic organizations and institutions include in their programs certain educational facilities for their members.

Types of Adult Education

Religious organizations have widened their function to include not only religious education but also parent education, health education, forum discussions of public questions, dramatics, training classes for volunteer leaders, radio sermons, and similar projects. Religious organizations for young people, such as the Christian Endeavor Society and the Jewish centers, combine social activities with educational programs. This work is encouraged and extended by organizations such as the International Council of Religious Education, the Federal Council of Churches, the National Conference of Christians and Jews, and the National Catholic Welfare Council.

The United Parents' Association sponsors a comprehensive program of parent education. Men's and women's clubs are not limited in their activities to purely social purposes, but have developed programs of general culture, civic, and practical home education. Universities have established centers to meet the educational needs of persons far removed from the university campus. Correspondence courses sponsored by reliable (and sometimes unreliable) organizations are becoming increasingly popular.

Professional, business, and industrial associations and organizations offer advanced training to their workers. These projects are additions to general and specialized, publicly supported, and privately endowed schools and classes for further education. They are developing a citizenry, the members of which devote their days to gainful occupation and their evenings to further self-improvement.

General cultural education is provided for the masses of the population by programs conducted in libraries, museums, and art galleries; by national parks, public exhibits, expositions, planned tours, and by organizations similar to the New School for Social Research in New York City and the Denver Opportunity School. There is no lack of cultural and educational opportunities for all people.

Education for civic and political responsibility is fostered by such organizations throughout the country as nonpartisan groups, women's political groups, and conferences for first voters. Television forums and round-table discussions are increasingly popular as means of developing an attitude of awareness concerning social and civic institutions and problems. The various occupational groups, as a part of their educational program, are encouraging periodic conventions, conferences, and general meetings, in order to give their members an opportunity to pool experiences and to become acquainted with the current trends and practices of their respective types of work.

Millions of dollars are spent annually by public and private organizations for the education of the American adult population. Who can say what the ultimate benefits may be? A democratically run government cannot succeed unless all of its citizens are alert and intelligent concerning their social institutions, and are developing themselves to the limit of their potentialities. Adjustment implies knowledge and wise use of this knowledge. Any money spent for the achievement of these objectives and any time devoted to it can be repaid many times in terms of the intelligent and constructive behavior of the people who participate in such programs.

Indirect and Subtle Factors of Education

An individual constantly is surrounded by forces that consciously or unconsciously affect him for good or ill. Public opinion shapes the pattern of indirect education and is molded by the varying forces for which it is responsible. The public demands certain types of stimulation. It is only through the more direct influence of educational leadership that any pronounced change can be effected. This general situation applies to the educational influence of newspapers, magazines, radio and television programs, dramatic productions, and motion pictures:

The newspaper is one of the most powerful organs of informal education. The educational value of this medium of education depends upon the leadership potentialities of any particular newspaper and the type of readers for which it is intended. A well-organized, fact-respecting, and liberal but honest newspaper can wield a tremendous educational power. News items; advertising material; editorials; special features; book, musical, and dramatic reviews; the women's page; and sport and financial sections offer daily opportunities for up-to-the-minute education. Moreover, if the newspaper is well written, readers receive daily experience in the correct use of the English language.

The influence of television is similar to that of the newspaper; programs originally were intended as a source of entertainment. Although much of television time still is devoted to entertainment and advertising, it is being used increasingly as an instrument of directed education.

Interested groups are aware of the influencing power of radio and television. They vie with one another in offering stimulating and worth-while programs. Safety, health, history, cooking, buying and general household information, political and social world issues, fine musical and dramatic programs, and town meetings of the air find their place on most radio and television schedules.

Another powerful agency of education is the motion picture. Its influence reaches all ages and all classes of people. Since "screen" life is a relatively inexpensive means of escape from unsatisfying reality, habitual motion-picture "fans" may be persons who have failed to make completely satisfying life adjustments. The busy, well-adjusted individual is likely to choose his pictures carefully so that he is assured of experiencing only the best in the way of motion-picture entertainment. To the extent that the directors or producers of motion pictures aim to present pictures that represent basically sound scripts and that are technically artistic, attendance at motion-picture programs can be educationally valuable.

VALUE OF LEISURE-TIME PROGRAMS

Not only does an individual plan for his working day and the work that he expects to do, but he also attempts to allot time for adequate periods for recreation. His program varies with the type of work in which the individual is engaged, the neighborhood in which he lives, his age, and his physical vigor. Recreational activities cannot be left to chance; they represent the outcomes of careful planning and supervision for adults as well as for young people.

Need for Recreational Activities

No matter how much a person enjoys his regular work he needs an occasional period of relief from it. The arranging of a daily or a weekly program in such way that it will present a healthful balance between productive work and relaxing, interesting social activity, is an art. Not all people can achieve this balance. Too many of us either allow our social interests to interfere with our work life or carry into our supposedly leisure time too much worry about our responsibilities and duties.

The problem of the average adult is not that of finding ways in which to have fun or places to which to go. Rather does an individual's difficulty arise in his inability to choose wisely among the many opportunities that are available. He may wonder how much time he should devote to these activities, or whether he can attract to himself the kind of people with whom he would like to participate in social activities. He may be in doubt as to the amount of time that he should give to one rather than to another kind of recreational interest. He may feel a lack of knowledge concerning the recreational opportunities that are available in his community, in which his participation would be welcomed by the group, and which he could afford.

Recreational programs receive attention when consideration is given to the solution of the delinquency problem. While recreation can be no cure-all for juvenile delinquency it can contribute to both prevention and treatment. In his discussion concerning "The Community and the Delinquents," Kvaraceus outlines ways in which communities fall short in establishing programs for the benefit of youth during their leisure hours. He suggests:

There are a number of ways in which personal and community recreation programs fall far short of attaining the full benefits that can come from the worthy use of leisure time.

1. Many, if not most, recreational activities tend in the direction of monied activity. Unless the child has [money] in his pocket with which to buy a comic book, attend a movie, or pay his dues to a club (for which his parents have already bought a uniform and a camping kit), he is likely to remain idle. In spite of the fact that much money is poured down the recreational funnel by the average family, an adequate base for financing community recreation has not yet been worked out; nor has the public fully accepted the idea of community responsibility for financial support in this area.

2. Recreation tends toward spectator and passive activity for many youths.

3. If the child takes part in a recreational program, this usually means that he is engaged in some sports program that calls for a specialized skill possessed by only a few children.

4. The heavy dependence upon sports as the core recreational activity in many communities leaves seasonal gaps when little or nothing is offered.

5. There is much duplication in membership and participation by a few children, with complete neglect of a large portion of the community's youth. Frequently it is the latter group that is in the greatest need of recreational services.

6. Family recreation is either sporadic or nonexistent.

7. Children and youth are ordinarily given very little real opportunity to participate in the planning or the conduct of their leisure-time activities.

8. Leadership in planning and carrying out public and private recreational programs is largely on an amateur basis.

9. There is exploitation of children and youths in those recreational activities that are chiefly useful to tickle the vanities of fond fathers and mothers.

10. The emphasis in the community's recreational program is too frequently skewed in the direction of boy activities, leaving little opportunity for girl participation.

11. Despite the fact that nearly every educational policies commission set up in recent years has emphasized the "worthy use of leisure time" as one of the major objectives of the schools' program, the systematic development of recreational skills and attitudes has received scant attention in the classroom, gymnasium, or on the playground.

12. There is little or no attempt at evaluation of the recreation program, either within specific organizations or on a community-wide basis.

These are the twelve cardinal defects that must be overcome if the community recreational program is to serve the needs of all boys and girls and thus function as a preventive of delinquency.[2]

Time Devoted to Purely Social Activity

Industry, business, and organized professions recognize the fact that men and women need time off for relaxation. Yearly vacations that range in length from two weeks to several months are granted by most occupational organizations. The five-day working week and shorter daily working hours are becoming increasingly popular. Although during a period of occupational emergency workers may be encouraged to extend their periods of work, most organizations disapprove of their workers' holding dual jobs or of devoting an undue amount of time to purely work activities.

The utilization of mechanical aids in industry, business, and the home is doing much to lighten the burden of production as well as of housekeeping. The American people are enjoying an amount of leisure time that was undreamed of by their forefathers. At the same time, one often hears comments to the effect that we have lost some of the genial friendliness and participation in gracious social living that were characteristic of the past. There may be some truth in this statement. We often waste much of our increased leisure in aimless bustling around and concern with trifling bits of "busyness."

If a person is sincerely interested in meeting his work re-

[2] W. C. Kvaraceus, *The Community and the Delinquent*, Yonkers-on-Hudson: World Book Company, 1954, pp. 320–321.

sponsibilities adequately, he needs sufficient sleep so that he goes to his work the next day refreshed and clearheaded. For the person whose associates live nearby, an informal get-together, a few rubbers of bridge, an evening of canasta, or a few hours of participation in community projects can be a form of relaxation that is engaged in several evenings during the week. Any of these activities benefit rather than harm the individual.

The city dweller may be forced to spend two or three hours in travel if he wishes to engage in social activities at the homes of his special friends. As a result, an evening of social activity may mean that the person does not retire until the wee hours of the morning. Hence he is too tired to do a good day's work. For the city man and woman, social activities usually need to be crowded into week ends, holidays, and vacations. Even then they cannot be too strenuous if they are to be of value to a person. Too often a man or woman who has returned from a vacation needs to rest before he starts to work again.

Recreational Activities as Life Interests

Among recreational interests that are common to all ages are: reading good books; participating in religious and community projects such as leadership in children's and young people's groups, and cooperation in worth-while "special projects"; attending musical and dramatic performances and motion pictures; engaging with one's friends in indoor games such as table tennis, card games, musical programs on the part of those who can play a musical instrument for the fun of it, or just interesting conversation, or engaging in out-of-doors sports such as golf, swimming or boating, and attending professional sports of various types.

There are many recreational activities which a person can begin during his youth and enjoy throughout his life. The difficulties often arise during the middle years. During this period a man or woman may become so engrossed with his business or home responsibilities and duties that he neglects to continue the recreational activities of his earlier years. He gradually drops out of the groups which at one time meant so much to him. As the members of such groups become scattered, he often is too busy to make new friends or to find new activities that are purely social.

Everything he does must have a purpose. He often meets and works with others in commendable projects of one kind or another, but he seldom develops intimate friendships. He acquires a host of acquaintances but gains few friends. He is likely to lose most of those with whom he had been accustomed to engage in social activities unless he spends much of his leisure time with them.

Value of Becoming a Sports Fan

It is better to be an active participant in sports than it is to sit on the bench and cheer the team. Attendance at a big-league or intercollegiate game does have health and social value, however. To watch an outdoor game is to benefit by breathing fresh air. To join a large group of persons in the fun of cheering or "booing" a player, an umpire, or a manager gives one a feeling of belonging. Sometimes a widespread interest in a particular group of players may do much to develop community feeling and cooperation.

Loyalties developed along these lines are good if they are not carried too far. For a game to upset the routines of a large number of persons—especially children—is not good training in emotional control. Moderation in an individual's interests in sports as well as in all his life interests is necessary, if attendance at games is to relax rather than to excite the individual.

Value of Membership in a Club

There is probably no more pathetic individual than the perennial "joiner"—the man or woman who becomes a member of every new club in his community and a follower of every cult. This person's difficulty is either that he has not enough constructive work activity to keep him busy, or that his own personality characteristics are such that he cannot achieve security in any one group. A man (or a woman) who attempts to affiliate himself with too many social or community groups usually does not remain long in any of them. Like the butterfly, he flits from one to another trying to extract from each something that is satisfying. Usually he is disappointed.

The extreme opposite of the joiner is the individual who

refuses to become a member of any organized group. He believes that he has more important things to do. He is likely to assert that all the club wants is a large membership so that a few can benefit from the collected dues. He also may claim that the supposed purposes of an organization do not always present accurately the actual function of the group which may be participating in activities other than those for which it is organized.

Much can be gained by a person of any age from membership in a few well-organized groups, the members of which are bound together by similar and worth-while interests. A group of this kind can become a powerful influence in a community. Furthermore, the individual members experience desirable privileges and responsibilities that are important in any form of group living. A cooperative member of a good club usually can be counted on to be a good citizen.

Every young person can aim to affiliate himself with a club that has a good reputation in the community. It may be a religious, business, political, community, or purely social organization. The individual is given an opportunity to become acquainted with others of his kind. Many men and women maintain their membership throughout their lifetime in an organization of which they had become active members during their adolescence or early adulthood. Also, the attaining of a position of leadership in a club may prepare a person for leadership in other areas—business or industry, community or national.

Unfortunately, there are undesirable clubs that have been organized by groups of malcontents or of inhibited young people. Hence, before a person joins a club, it is his duty to evaluate the ideals of the group and his own ability to make a worth-while contribution to its activities. If the general conduct of club projects appears to be nonconstructive, membership in the group can be avoided and another group sought that is more promising of desirable activities.

RECREATIONAL THERAPY

Good mental health can be fostered through participation in interesting and wholesome recreational activities. In fact, so important is the recreational factor considered that suitable programs of recreation are provided for the mentally ill in the form of recreational therapy. The application of this technique for the treatment of the emotionally disturbed individual has therapeutic value in that it tends (as does occupational therapy) to divert his attention from his worries, fears, or other disturbances that are basic to his mental disorder.

Tension can be reduced through the mentally ill person's participation in programs having to do with books, magazines, music, radio, television, motion pictures, dances, and other social activities. Care must be taken that the kind of recreational therapy utilized is pointed at soothing the troubled person rather than exciting him.

Recreational therapy has a socializing effect as it affords afflicted persons the opportunity to associate with one another in calming situations. As the individual participates with others in play activity, he is helped thereby to forget, temporarily at least, some of his troubles and to lessen his concern about himself. Some recreational activities that have helped the individual during the period of his therapeutic treatment may be continued by him later when he has recovered from his emotional disturbance.

Menninger has this to say about the relationships of recreation to mental health:

> It has been the privilege of many of us practicing medicine in psychiatry to have some very rewarding experiences in the use of recreation as an adjunctive method of treatment. Along with direct psychological help, hydrotherapy, shock and insulin therapy, many of us have, for years, used various forms of education, recreation and occupation in the treatment of our patients. Within the American Psychiatric Association—a national organization of approximately 4,500 psychiatrists—we have a standing committee on leisure time activities. It has planned its work for the coming year on the assumption that professional recreation experience can contribute to psychiatric practice, and psychiatrists can add to the knowledge of professional recreation workers. The intention of this committee is not only to bring the contribution from recreation workers but to present and represent psychiatry to various lay groups concerned with recreation.
>
> Recreation has not only played an important part in the treatment program of many mental illnesses but it has been

a considerable factor in enabling former patients to remain well. Therefore, psychiatrists believe that recreative activity can also be a valuable preventive of mental and emotional ill health.[3]

Present Interest in Recreational Therapy

Most persons think of recreation as comprising those activities in which individuals engage after a busy day for the purpose of amusing themselves and, in certain instances, of diverting attention from routines confronted during the day. Today, recreation is being used to help the psychotic or neurotic person already hospitalized. It not only helps the patient pass the time between his psychotherapeutic sessions with his psychiatrist, but has a curative value as well. In discussing the changing role of recreational therapy in present-day psychiatry, Wahl makes the following salient suggestions:

> With this background in mind we can understand how a psychotic or neurotic person whose illness has been so severe as to result in his hospitalization and isolation from his family and his culture, must feel in the initial phases of psychotherapy. For the most complex types of relationships we have in life are interpersonal relations and though we take them for granted because we engage in them with ease and facility, for the mental patient, these are extremely difficult and painful. These are the areas in which he has had the greatest failures and his most severe punishments and disappointments. Yet this, the most complex act we perform with people, must be reestablished if the patient is to communicate with his therapist and to achieve the insights and share the emotion which his cure will necessarily entail. But it is ironic and illogical to ask him to do the hardest thing first, not the simplest things, viz., to endure the pain and frustration of a tête-à-tête relationship. It is at this point that recreation and occupational therapy have their maximum application. For here we can patiently grade the patient's degree of interaction with others. We can supply him with an area in which he can

[3] William C. Menninger, "Recreation and Mental Health," *Recreation*, Vol. 42 (1948), p. 340.

have unlimited interaction with people or we can give him tasks which have goals which he is much more likely to be able to satisfactorily fulfill and which involve very little contact with others. And these goals in recreation and occupational therapy are symbolic of life's goal which has been too much for him, and which have led him to adopt withdrawal in an attempt to obtain a surcease from his pain.

In other words, one can tailor a program for the patient which will fulfill his needs; one can lose interpersonal contact, the most significant variable involved, according to the patient's capacity. For example, an extremely withdrawn catatonic who cannot be reached in psychotherapy (since this involves an interpersonal relationship which his past memory recalls to him as being frightening and guilt-inducing) can be set to work sometimes on a loom where he has little or no contact with people. He often derives a great comfort from this simple monotonous labor which yet gives him a task outside of himself and for which he can be legitimately rewarded. It restores his sense of accomplishment. There is simple wisdom in the old cliche, "Busy hands make for quiet minds." If we can interest the severely disturbed and pain-racked patient in even the simplest activities, we have accomplished a desirable result. Compare it with the child learning to walk. He must take a first halting step before he can hobble, and hobble before he can run. So such an activity is a first simple step towards the eventual goal of a full-time participant in interpersonal communication and response. We have also given him something creative and definitive which he can do, and with which we can help him. He is initially given a small task which he can achieve and this can be increased to more complex ones. It may be a long time before the patient can graduate from the loom and to do a very simple piece of copper work or weaving a belt. And perhaps at a later time we can advance him to some kind of group project, such as group painting or play or the use of some plastic medium, such as clay or paint. And finally the patient is able to achieve the interrelationship of participating in simple group games. We must constantly bear in mind that these are tasks which are bound to be difficult for the patient in the beginning, and occupational therapy plays an indispensable role in helping patients to again have interrelationships with people which are not of a frightening and defeating character. . . .

We know that the second characteristic of the psychotic patient is that he has lost what we call affect or emotion. He cannot feel empathy or sympathy with others or even for himself. He has lost the capacity to put himself in the place of others, and to experience first hand the closeness to them which this entails. When this is lost there is little capacity to have warm gratifying, human relationships. And for the psychiatric patient this capacity to experience warm emotion is initially difficult, since he has been hurt in just these areas of human relationships. He obeys the ancient proverb, "The burned child shuns the fire." For this reason he tends to shun human interaction and emotion. He withdraws instead into a little cosmos of his own, free from emotion, feeling and dependency upon others.

These affects, too, are things which we can "ration" to the patient by recreation and occupational therapy. Remember the mass of emotion which we felt when we saw our first college football game, when with pounding hearts we would yell ourselves hoarse as we would watch the home team make the touchdown? Something analogous to this can be felt in the simple game of checkers, or identification with a team of fellow croquet players. These situations, simple and unexciting to us as they sound, have an important role to play in the psychiatric rehabilitation of patients. Here again one can give the patient symbolic goals which are nevertheless discreet and which can be graduated according to his ability to solve them.

Through activities such as these, patients can be helped to recover their sense of purpose and self-esteem which, without exception, is damaged in all psychiatric casualties. He may have concealed this damage from himself and others by being a braggart or compensated by a mechanism of reaction formation and formed a delusion of immense power such as thinking of himself as Christ or Napoleon. He may have withdrawn from others and from himself into a deep regressive wounded state. Or he may have protected his damaged sense of adequacy by the use of drugs as does the alcoholic, or the drug addict. The need to feel important, the need to feel that one's work has significance, the need to approve of one's self, and like one's self, even though we appreciate our disadvantages and demerits, is one of the constant goals of life and of psychiatric work. Recreation under a kindly helpful recreation director who lets the patient discover again the sense of personal worth and purpose which can be experienced in the achievement of a small task well and honestly done, performs a great service for his patient; he helps him to regain a very precious thing which he has lost, his self respect. There is also the additional advantage that the patient is at the same time practicing the use of the same kind of skills and attitudes which he will have to apply when he is to return to the real world and to the complex problems of a similar nature which he will encounter there.

The beauty about such use of recreation is that these therapeutic goals are not primarily identified as such. One does not say to the patient when you ask him to be shortstop on the baseball team, "I want you to contribute so that you can increase your skills by dealing with persons," you say instead, "Let's get on the team and we'll beat the other side." One is able to prescribe in effect a highly valuable therapeutic activity without identifying it as such to the patient. Similarly, after a pleasant afternoon on the golf range, or on an evening of bowling we ourselves come back not only with our skill in bowling and golf increased, but having also participated in a meaningful and gratifying human interaction which comprises the real purpose of the meeting; for it becomes silly when we say that we spend the entire afternoon for the purpose of knocking a little pellet from one grass hillock to another, or watching a black ball go down an alley to knock down some wooden pins. Moreover, we have expended in a socially acceptable form the hostility and competitive striving which could take other, and more dangerous, outlets.

The patient, therefore, has less anxiety in facing human beings when it is accomplished in these kinds of contacts. The technical word for this situation is "expectancy set." After a severe and regressive illness the expectancy set is less if you allow a patient to develop his first human contacts in recreation rather than his primary psychotherapeutic setting. And it is for this reason that most psychiatrists in dealing with this type of patient at this particular phase of his illness do not arrange to see him in the office, but instead first have a chat on the ward or on the playground.[4]

EFFECT OF LEISURE ON THE INDIVIDUAL

Available leisure time which is coordinated with successful and pleasant work-filled time does not present serious problems. However, if leisure time results from unemployment in gainful or in satisfying work, the adjustments needed are significant. If during his leisure time the individual is unable to look forward to the challenge of a period of work, leisure time no longer is a period of relaxation but becomes an avenue to boredom and discontent.

The individual who is financially able to refrain from gainful work activity must plan to fill his leisure time with activities that will take on a similitude of work. Welfare or church work, participation in civic projects, playing with inventions, collecting, a planned course in reading, or a program of study in terms of the individual's interest are needed if the individual is to be happy and contented in his extended leisure. For the unemployed individual who needs to work for a living, enforced leisure, instead of being devoted to idle activities or to the nursing of real or imagined worries, might include a program aimed at the improvement of the individual's fitness for work, and directed toward further study and preparation for occupational placement.

Personality Development Through Leisure-time Activities

The play of the growing child contributes fundamentally to his physical, mental, and social development. The child can be given the kind of toys that stimulate him and give him a chance for physical and mental activity through their operation and manipulation. Not only his playthings but also the types of

---

[4] C. W. Wahl, "The Changing Role of Occupational and Recreational Therapy in Present Day Psychiatry," *The American Journal of Occupational Therapy*, September-October, 1957, pp. 280–282.

games in which he engages and the character of his associates are important.

As an individual grows older, an interest outside his work has hygienic value. To be willing to follow this interest in the form of a hobby requires persistence and personal denials, and is a character builder. A hobby may become so absorbing an interest, however, that the individual is forced either to give up his hobby or to leave his present occupational work. Thus an avocational interest may develop into a vocational pursuit and bring financial gain to the person engaging in it. If this hobby becomes too engrossing, the individual may need to turn to other play activities in order to maintain hygienic balance.

Leisure is used to maintain personal integrity. The individual's leisure-time reading and study activities; his attendance at motion-picture houses, theaters, lectures, museums, dances, musical programs; his participation in formal or informal social gatherings, physical sports, or civic projects, and all other activities in which he engages for recreational purposes, not only reflect his personal attitudes but also affect them.

As the individual's recreational activities may be affected by economic or social changes, so is his personality influenced by his changed leisure-time activities. Play is a normal human activity. Healthy individuals are active either mentally or physically during all their waking hours. Therefore, desirable opportunities and equipment for socially approved recreational activities ought to be made available for everyone. Social and individual benefits accrue to the community that is foresighted enough to provide interesting and worth-while recreational opportunities for persons of all ages.

QUESTIONS AND PROBLEMS

1. Differentiate between work and play. Give specific examples of each.

2. Indicate ways in which recreation is health-preserving.

3. List the mental values of play activities.

4. Study changes in recreational activities from early childhood through old age. What differences do you find?

5. Make a survey of your community to determine the space, facilities, and opportunities available for recreation. Report your findings.

6. Discuss the socializing influence of clubs and other forms of group activity.

7. Evaluate the play programs that can be found in the elementary school, in the high school, and in the college.

8. Plan a sound program of leisure-time activities for middle-aged adults.

9. Name some problems that may result from extended leisure time.

10. Describe, in detail, your recreational activities.

11. Name your favorite outdoor sport; your favorite indoor game. Give reasons for your selection. Indicate also the extent to which you participate actively in them.

12. Indicate specific ways in which the *play attitude* can be introduced into or connected with your vocational activity.

13. To what extent should education on the adult level become a public responsibility?

14. Discuss the educational and recreational value of newspapers, radio, television, motion pictures.

15. State benefits that can be achieved by the administration of recreational therapy.

16. Discuss the effect of extended leisure on individuals.

17. Is participation in professional baseball, football, or basketball work or play for the participant?

Selected Readings

Anderson, N., *Work and Leisure*. New York: Free Press of Glencoe, 1962.

Bancroft, J. H., *Games*. New York: The Macmillan Company, 1937.

Brightbill, C. K., *Man and Leisure: A Philosophy of Recreation*. Englewood Cliffs, N.J.: Prentice-Hall, Inc., 1961.

Campbell, R. J., A. R. Martin, W. C. Menninger, and J. Plant, *Recreation and Psychiatry*. New York: National Recreation Association, 1964.

De Grazia, S., *Of Time, Work, and Leisure*. New York: The Twentieth Century Fund, 1962.

Donahue, W., *et al.*, *Free Time: Challenge to Later Maturity*. Ann Arbor: University of Michigan Press, 1958.

Donnelly, R. J., W. G. Helms, and E. D. Mitchell, *Active Games and Contests*, 2nd ed. New York: The Ronald Press Company, 1958.

Galbraith, J. K., *The Affluent Society*. Boston, Mass.: Houghton Mifflin Company, 1959.

Hindman, D. A., *Handbook of Active Games*. Englewood Cliffs, N.J.: Prentice-Hall, Inc., 1951.

Kaplan, M., *Leisure in America: A Social Inquiry*. New York: John Wiley & Sons, Inc., 1960.

Larrabee, E., and R. Meyersohn (eds.), *Mass Leisure*. New York: Free Press of Glencoe, 1958.

Neumeyer, M. H., and E. S. Neumeyer, *Leisure and Recreation*, 3rd ed. New York: The Ronald Press Company, 1958.

Recreation. New York: National Recreation Association. Current Issues.

Sappenfield, B. R., *Personality Dynamics: An Integrative Psychology of Adjustment*. New York: Alfred A. Knopf, Inc., 1961. Chapter 15.

List of Selected Films

MANY TOPICS in this book can receive further clarification through the use of excellent audio-visual aids that are available. It is recommended that the films listed here be previewed by the instructor before class showing in order that attention may be directed to the various phases of adjustment that are presented in them.

All the films included in the list are 16mm. sound films. The running time is given in minutes for each film. The addresses as well as full names of producers and distributors are given in the Directory of Film Sources that follows the List. Some of the films can be obtained from local film libraries.

I. Films Concerned with Personal and Social Adjustment

A Job for Bob (RFA, 30 min.). The story of an ambitious young man who was helped by guidance to find and adjust to a job.

Act Your Age (Emotional Maturity) (C, 14 min.). Presents common types of infantile reactions such as temper tantrums and weeping.

Age of Turmoil (McGraw, 20 min.). Presents sketches of boys and girls in their early teens.

Aptitudes and Occupations (C, 16 min.). Shows the extent to which an individual possesses ability in various fields.

Attitudes and Health (C, 11 min.). Shows how self-confidence and right attitudes are vital to good health.

Better Use of Leisure Time (C, 11 min.). A guide to development of attitudes toward leisure-time activities.

Careers for Girls (MOT, 18 min.) . Presents types of work open to women.

Children's Emotions (McGraw, 22 min.) . The important emotions of childhood are described, and the methods of dealing with them are explained.

Choosing Your Occupation (C, 11 min.) . Includes occupational possibilities and the preparation and guidance needed.

Condition Improved (NFBCan—McGraw—30 min.) . Presents the value of occupational therapy in rehabilitation of the handicapped.

Conflict (McGraw, 18 min.) . Presents four basic types of conflict in problem situations familiar to college students, then illustrates with rats under laboratory conditions.

Date Etiquette (C, 11 min.) . Presents ways of being socially comfortable during the dating experience.

Dating: Do's and Don'ts (C, 13 min.) . Raises questions concerning dating and presents partial answers as guides for discussion.

Developing Friendships (C, 11 min.) . Helps young people understand the meaning of friendships.

Developing Responsibility (C, 11 min.) . Presents the difficulties encountered and the rewards of persistent endeavor.

Developing Self-reliance (C, 11 min.) . Shows how necessary self-reliance is to all successful endeavor and happiness.

Developing Your Character (C, 11 min.) . Portrays what good character is and how it can be achieved.

Early Social Behavior (EBF, 11 min.) . Presents the behavior of young children in various social situations.

Effective Criticism (C, 11 min.) . Concerns the skills involved in taking and in giving criticism.

Emotional Health (McGraw, 20 min.) . Presents problems of emotional disturbance and therapy in severe cases.

Employing Disabled Workers in Industry (Castle, 20 min.) . Shows how handicapped persons have made good adjustment on the job.

Exercise and Health (C, 11 min.) . Shows how physical and mental health depends upon proper physical exercise.

Experimental Studies in Social Climates of Groups (Iowa, 30 min.) . Presents the effects of various forms of group organization upon the behavior of boys.

Family Circles (McGraw, 31 min.) . Shows the extensions of the family circle into other agencies of the community.

Family Life (C, 11 min.) . Shows the happiness that can be gained from a well-managed home.

Family Teamwork (Frith, 18 min.) . Shows family cooperation and adjustment.

Farewell to Childhood (IFB, 20 min.) . Presents a teen-age **girl** who longs for adulthood but fears the privileges associated with it.

Finding the Right Job (C, 11 min.). Emphasizes some of the crucial stages in obtaining a job.

Finding Your Life Work (Mahnke, 22 min.). Shows the thinking and planning of a boy in relation to his vocational choice.

Friendship Begins at Home (C, 16 min.). Presents the value of friendship in the home.

Frustration Play Techniques (NYU, 35 min.). Demonstrates special play techniques for diagnosing personality.

Fun of Making Friends (C, 11 min.). Presents many points about how to make and keep friends.

Gangs Raid the Orchard (NYU, 11 min.). Presents a situation in gang life.

Going Steady (C, 11 min.). Problems of teen-agers when they "go steady."

How to Develop Interest (C, 11 min.). Consideration is given to three fundamental questions concerning interest.

How to Investigate Vocations (C, 11 min.). Concerns the investigation of vocations with the aim of selecting the kind of work best suited to the individual.

How to Keep a Job (C, 11 min.). Shows what should be done to perform successfully on the job.

How to Say No (Moral Maturity) (C, 11 min.). Shows how to say "No" and keep your friends.

Improve Your Personality (C, 11 min.). Presents a frank discussion of personality that is basic to self-analysis.

Make Your Own Decisions (C, 11 min.). Presents a series of five questions and shows how each contributes to the development of self-reliance.

Marriage Films:

> *Are You Ready for Marriage* (C, 16 min.)
> *Choosing for Happiness* (McGraw, 14 min.)
> *Choosing Your Marriage Partner* (C, 13 min.)
> *It Takes all Kinds* (McGraw, 20 min.)
> *Jealousy* (McGraw, 18 min.)
> *Marriage and Divorce* (MOT, 15 min.)
> *Marriage Is a Partnership* (C, 16 min.)
> *Marriage Today* (McGraw, 22 min.)
> *This Charming Couple* (McGraw, 19 min.)
> *Who's Boss* (McGraw, 18 min.)
> *Who's Right* (McGraw, 18 min.)

Meaning of Adolescence (McGraw, 16 min.). Presents present-day adolescent development.

Meaning of Engagement (C, 13 min.). Presents the engagement period as one of preparation for successful marriage.

Mechanical Aptitudes (C, 11 min.). Sound guidance practices are demonstrated in a variety of situations.

Meeting Emotional Needs of Children (NYU, 33 min.). Shows the interdependence of the child and his parents and other adults in his environment.

Meeting the Needs of Adolescents (McGraw, 19 min.). Presents the experiences of a fourteen-year-old boy and his seventeen-year-old sister during their growing up.

Overcoming Fear (C, 13 min.). Shows the value of courage in meeting problems in everyday living.

Overcoming Worry (C, 11 min.). Shows ways to overcome worry.

Personal Qualities for Job Success (C, 11 min.). Shows that personal qualities for job success can be developed in high school.

Personality Conflict (McGraw, 7 min.). Illustrates what happens when two conflicting personalities must work together.

Picture in Your Mind (IFF, 16 min.). Presents causes of prejudice and attempts to indoctrinate the viewer toward a better attitude toward others.

Playtown, USA (AssnFlm, 23 min.). Presents community interest in providing recreational facilities for youth.

Preface to a Life (Castle, 28 min.). Shows the possible impact of several types of environmental influences upon an individual.

Prejudice (AssnFlm, 60 min.). Provides for personal examination of prejudices and stimulates discussion of intercultural relations.

Right or Wrong? (Making Moral Decisions) (C, 11 min.). Presents the problem of what to do when a gang of boys break a warehouse window.

Search for Happiness (MOT, 17 min.). Presents the problems of modern living and suggestions for meeting them.

Self-Conscious Guy (C, 11 min.). Presents Marty who suddenly becomes aware of his feelings of self-consciousness.

Shy Guy (C, 13 min.). Presents the value of friendliness as a means of improving an adolescent's social adjustment.

Shyness (NFBCan, McGraw, 23 min.). Concerns excessive shyness in children and what can be done to help them.

Snap Out of It (C, 13 min.). Shows how emotional balance can be developed once it has been upset.

Social Courtesy (C, 11 min.). Reveals that social effectiveness requires a natural, easy form of behavior that includes the use of courtesy.

Social Development (McGraw, 16 min.). Presents the social behavior patterns of children at various stages of development.

Social-Sex Attitudes in Adolescence (McGraw, 22 min.). Shows the early experiences of a boy and a girl in their dating, falling in love, and marriage.

Toward Emotional Maturity (McGraw, 11 min.). Presents ways in which adolescents can be prepared to understand and control their emotions.

Understanding Your Emotions (C, 13 min.). Shows different emotional responses to the same stimulus.

You and Your Family (AssnFlm, 10 min.). Presents typical family problems illustrating the relationships that should prevail between parents and their children.

You and Your Parents (C, 13 min.). Describes the process of growing away from parents as a normal course of events.

You and Your Work (C, 11 min.). Shows job failure and how rehabilitation helped an individual to succeed.

II. Films Concerned with Maladjustment, Mental Illness, and Therapy

A Criminal Is Born (TFC, 21 min.). Presents the stories of three boys who develop criminal tendencies because of inadequacies of home life.

Activity for Schizophrenia (Castle, 23 min.). Presents behavior characteristic of this psychosis.

Behavior in Hypnotic Regression (Bucknell, 17 min.). Shows extreme regressive behavior.

Boy in Court (NatPro, 12 min.). Presents the procedures used by the juvenile court in dealing with a delinquent.

Breakdown (NFBCan, 41 min.). The story of a young woman's schizophrenic breakdown and her recovery in a mental hospital.

Children of the City (BIS, 30 min.). Shows how a Scottish town handles the adolescent problem.

Children on Trial (IFB, 62 min.). Presents the experiences in approved schools of juvenile delinquents who eventually make satisfactory adjustments.

Frustration Play Techniques (NYU, 35 min.). Demonstrates special techniques for diagnosing personality.

High Wall (McGraw, 32 min.). Presents problems associated with prejudice.

Instructing the Disabled on the Job (Castle, 14 min.). Shows the importance of a supervisor's attitude toward disabled workers.

Mental Mechanisms Series (NFBCan, Distributed by McGraw):
   Feeling of Rejection (23 min.)
   Feeling of Hostility (27 min.)

Overdependency (32 min.)
Feelings of Depression (30 min.)
Mental Symptoms (NFBCan, Distributed by McGraw) :
   Manic State (15 min.)
   Organic Reaction—Senile Type (10 min.)
   Paranoid Conditions (13 min.)
   Schizophrenia: Catatonic Type (12 min.)
   Schizophrenia: Hebephrenic Type (13 min.)

Nurse's Day with the Mentally Ill (PaStaCol, 28 min.) . Presents the work of a psychiatric nurse.

Obesity (Psychosomatic Conditions) (NAMH, 28 min.) . Explains some of emotional factors at the root of overeating and interprets the meaning of the term *psychosomatic conditions*.

Out of Darkness (CBS, Distributed by McGraw, 55 min.) . Report on one woman's step-by-step recovery from mental illness.

Out of True (IFB, 41 min.) . Deals with factors that cause mental illness and therapy that aids in recovery.

People Who Care (NAMH, 25 min.) . Traces Mrs. Dobson's progress from the time of her admission to the hospital to her departure.

Problem Children (NYU, 20 min.) . Suggests ways to handle aggressive and passive child behavior.

Psychiatry in Action (BIS, 62 min.) . Shows the treatment of war-induced neuroses.

Psychoneuroses (NYU, 23 min.) . Presents evidence of psychogenic symptoms as well as of symptoms of organic disease.

Recreational and Occupational Therapy (Castle, 13 min.) . Presents the work done in occupational therapy by hospitals and community agencies.

Return to Action (BIS, 19 min.) . Shows techniques of rehabilitation of the disabled.

The Compulsive Car Thief (NAMH, 28 min.) . Throws light on the emotional origins of certain forms of antisocial behavior and shows the differences between normal pranks and irresponsible acts.

The Quiet One (Athena, 67 min.) . Presents the experiences of a mentally disturbed boy and shows how he is rehabilitated in a school for delinquent boys.

Ways to Settle Disputes (C, 11 min.) . Demonstrates that the settlement of disputes must involve give-and-take and settlement must be desired if it is to be achieved.

What's on Your Mind (NFBCan, 10 min.) . Shows the disadvantages of attempts to use quacks and the advantages of trained psychiatrists in the treatment of mental disturbance.

Who's Delinquent? (McGraw, 16 min.) . Indicates how a newspaper editor attempts to discover the causes of juvenile delinquency and presents a program for improvement of conditions.

Directory of Film Sources

AssnFlm: Association Films, Inc., 35 W. 45th St., New York, N.Y. 10019

Athena: Athena Films, Inc., 165 W. 46th St., New York, N.Y. 10019

BIS: British Information Services, 30 Rockefeller Plaza, New York, N.Y. 10020

Bucknell: Bucknell University, Lewistown, Penna. 17837

C: Coronet Instructional Films, 65 E. South Water St., Chicago, Ill. 60601

Castle: United World Films, 1445 Park Ave., New York, N.Y. 10029

CBS: Columbia Broadcasting System (Films distributed by McGraw-Hill)

EBF: Encyclopaedia Britannica Films, Inc., 1150 Wilmette Ave., Wilmette, Ill. 60091

Frith: Frith Films, 840 Seward St., Hollywood, Calif. 90028

IFB: International Film Bureau, Suite 1500, 6 N. Michigan Ave., Chicago, Ill. 60602

IFF: International Film Foundation, Inc., 1600 Broadway, New York, N.Y. 10019

Iowa: University of Iowa, Bureau of Audio-Visual Instruction, Extension Division, Iowa City, Iowa 52240

Mahnke: Carl F. Mahnke Productions, 215 E. 3rd St., Des Moines, Iowa 50309

McGraw: McGraw-Hill, Inc., Text-Film Department, 330 W. 42nd St., New York, N.Y. 10036

MOT: March of Time Films, 369 Lexington Ave., New York, N.Y. 10016

NAMH: National Association for Mental Health Film Library, 267 W. 25th St., New York, N.Y. 10001

NFBCan: National Film Board of Canada (Films distributed by McGraw-Hill)

NatPro: National Probation and Parole Association, 1790 Broadway, New York, N.Y. 10019

NYU: New York University Film Library, 26 Washington Pl., New York, N.Y. 10003

PaStaCol: Pennsylvania State University, Audio-Visual Services, University Park, Penna. 16802

RFA: Religious Film Association, Inc., 45 Astor Pl., New York, N.Y. 10003

TFC: Teaching Film Custodians, Inc., 25 W. 43rd St., New York, N.Y. 10036

Index